W9-AQR-278

DISCARD

DISCARD

有關本書

About This Dictionary

辭　源

cí　yüán

In 1966, Professor Marco Liang published a book titled "Getting Around In Chinese", (Revised 2003) This popular work was divided into two Sections - a Chinese language primer and a common usage dictionary. After much helpful feedback from both readers of the book and students, Professors William and Marco Liang decided to expand upon the unique aspects of the dictionary section of the work which became the basis of this Dictionary.

In addition to being a completely two-way translation guide "Chinese-English, English-Chinese", the Dictionary breaks from the conventions of a traditional alphabetical English dictionary and a Chinese dictionary that is organized by number of brush-strokes. Instead, a more practical and useful approach is employed of categorizing words, terms, and phrases by situations of everyday usage.

To this end, one hundred eighty nine separate categories were established to encompass a wide variety of situations that occur in normal day-to-day events.

Also, an Appendix section is provided to help English speaking users with Chinese pronunciation and language structure. With the recent emergence of China as a major participant in the global economy, the need for better communication tools between the English and Chinese populous has never been more pressing. This dictionary, with its two-way translation capability and unique layout is an attempt to help filling the void.

NOTE: To English Speaking Readers, to locate an Egnlish word or term for its Chinese translation, please find its Group Number in the alphabetically ordered "INDEX". (P.623)

This book is dedicated to our beloved mother
Mrs. C. A. Liang

謹將此書敬獻給母親梁徐志涵女士

In a very cold winter afternoon in 1945 in Beijing, relaxing and sunshining in the family's courtyard was 52 years old Mrs. C. A. Liang, mother of the authors, William Liang and Marco Liang.

漢英 ⇄ 英漢，雙向分類字典、辭典

也是一本「会话」手册

cí　　　　yüán

Calligraphy in (顏體) Yán Style, by Prof. William Liang.

Chinese ➜ English　　English ➜ Chinese

CATEGORIZED DICTIONARY

Translation of over 20.000
Professional vocabularies, terms,
phrases, & Dialogue In 189 Categories.

It also serves as a
Language Learning Manual

WILLIAM LIANG & MARCO LIANG

© 辭源 Cí Yüán, Chinese–English & English–Chinese CATEGORIZED DICTIONARY·
By William Liang & Marco Liang. First Print: Dec.31st. 2005.
Copyright : The Library Of Congress. TX 6-393-175

Publisher: Marco Liang & Co. Ltd.,
Bardonia, N.Y., U.S.A.

All rights reserved. No part of this book may be reproduced or utilized in any form or by
any means, electronic or mechanical, including photocopying, recording or by any
information, storage or retrieval system without permission in writing from the authors.

辞源
ci yüan
A DIRECTORY 指南

BY GROUPS OF DAILY LIFE USAGE

Group & Page Numbers

A 指南

DIRECTORY

2

A 指南

DIRECTORY

3

APPENDIX
附加资料

Introduction To The Chinese Language
And Its Unique Pronunciation & Structure -595

INDEX
全书索引
623 - 630

A 指南

DIRECTORY

4

CATEGORIZED DICTIONARY
Just A Few Of The Many
Topics Covered Are

- **Hànyǔpīnyīn – A Phonetic System Romanizing Chinese Words** (P.599-611)

- **Only 5 Sounds pronounce Differently from English alphabet letters and you need to learn. They are:**
  j ; q ; x ; c ; zh (See P.612)

A Collection of 854 Useful Chinese Verbs

938 Expressive Terms and Phrases for Everyday Use (P.79-104)

Chinese Grammar Simplified (P.37 & 105-120)

A Collection of 936 Translations Illustrating some of the Subtle Nuances of the Chinese Language (P.133-157)

The English "Eight W's & One H" as used in the Chinese Language (P.121-132)

Table of the 432 Hànyǔ Sounds (P.612-62

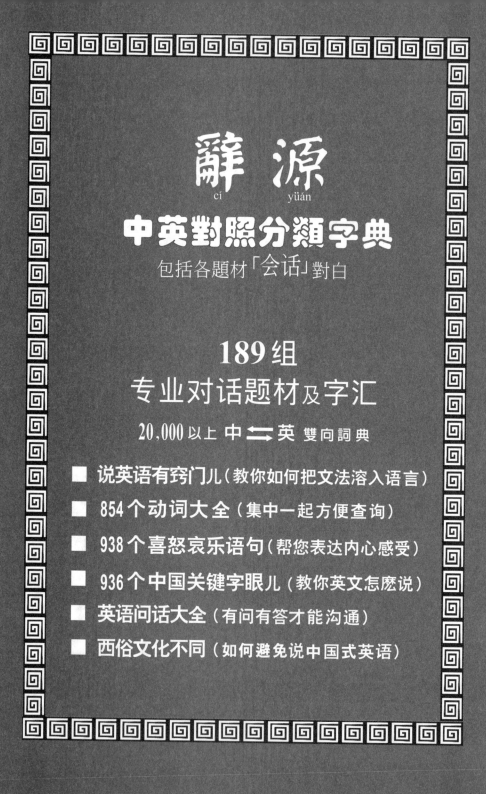

辭源
cí yüán

中英對照分類字典
包括各題材「会话」對白

189 组
专业对话题材及字汇

20,000 以上 中 ⇌ 英 雙向詞典

- 说英语有窍门儿（教你如何把文法溶入语言）
- 854 个动词大全（集中一起方便查询）
- 938 个喜怒哀乐语句（帮您表达内心感受）
- 936 个中国关键字眼儿（教你英文怎麽说）
- 英语问话大全（有问有答才能沟通）
- 西俗文化不同（如何避免说中国式英语）

CATEGORIZED DICTIONARY

辭　源

cí　yüán

Table Of Contents

B 目录

TABLE OF CONTENTS

B 目录

TABLE OF CONTENTS

B 目录

TABLE OF CONTENTS

189 CATEGORIES

B 目录

TABLE OF CONTENTS

13

CATEGORIZED
GLOSSARIES

1 You He
我 你 他

A complete list of Chinese pronouns

The author recommends that you initially take a quick glance at these pronouns which are used by Chinese people in daily conversation. It should be interesting to find traces of Chinese culture which are unique and often very different from the ways Westerners were taught in terminology.

Only 7 words you need to learn

In order to assist the guests of China in learning and speaking "pǔtōnghuà 普通话" quickly and efficiently, the author has numbered **seven** important pronouns and highlighted the less important ones with a blue "★". The words that do not have an asterisk are for Old Timers or for reference uses.

Chinese Is Easy. Take pronouns for instance, with just one single word, "wǒ", one can express two different English words; "I" or "me", because the subject and object of the pronouns are one word in Chinese.

With another word "tā", one can express six different English pronouns: "He, him, She, her, It and it". Since Chinese has differentiation, you need not specify between male and female when speaking.

---

❶ I; me
wǒ

我
我

I; me (humble)
bì-ren; zài xià

敝人；在下
敝人；在下

I (in speech)
běn rén; gè-ren

本人；个人
本人；個人

I (letters to employer)
zhí

职
職

❷ You; you (singular)
nǐ

你；妳
你；妳

❸ You; you (singular)
nín (respectable)

您；您
您；您

---

❹ He; him; She; her; It; it **tā**	他；她；牠；它 他；她；牠；它	you husband and wife **nǐ-men fū qī liǎ**	你们夫妻俩 你們夫妻倆
He; him; She; her **tān** (respectable)	您；她 您；她	you two newly wedded **nǐ-men xiǎo liáng kǒur**	你们小俩口儿 你們小俩口兒
elderly he/she (respectable) **tān; tān lǎo rén jiā** (to aged)	您；您老人家 您；您老人家	★Mr. Doe **Dòe xiān-sheng**	窦先生 竇先生
❺ We; us (to others) **wǒ-men; wǒ-me**	我们 我們	Senior Mr. Doe **Dòe lǎo xiān-sheng**	窦老先生 竇老先生
★We; us (to ourselves) **zán-men; zán-me**	咱们 咱們	★Mrs. Doe **Dòe tài-tai**	窦太太 竇太太
❻ You; you (plural) **nǐ-men; nǐ-me**	你们；妳们 你們；妳們	Senior Mrs. Doe **Dòe lǎo tài-tai**	窦老太太 竇老太太
You all **nín dōu** (plural, polite)	您都 您都	your respectable father **lìng zūn** (See Group 8, 40)	令尊 令尊
❼ They; them **tā-men; tā-me**	他们；她们；牠们；它们 他們；她們；牠們；它們	your respectable mother **lìng tāng** (See Group 8, 40)	令堂 令堂
they; them (respectable) **tān-men; tān-me** (to aged)	您们；您們 您們；您們	★Miss Doe **Dòe xiáo-jie**	窦小姐 竇小姐
★this gentleman **zhè wèi xiān-sheng**	这位先生 這位先生	★Ms. Doe **Dòe nǔ shì**	窦女士 竇女士
★that lady **nà wèi nǔ shì**	那位女仕 那位女仕	your respectable son **lìng láng**	令郎 令郎
★Yes, ma'am! **shì-de xiáo-jie**	是的，小姐！ 是的，小姐！	your respectable daughter **lìng ài**	令嬡 令嬡
★Yes, sir! **shì-de xiān-sheng**	是的，先生！ 是的，先生！	★John Doe **mǒu nán shì**	某男士 某男士
the two of us **zán-me liǎ**	咱们俩 咱們倆	★Mary Doe **móu nǔ shì**	某女士 某女士
the three of you **nǐ-me sā**	你们仨 你們仨	I am; We are **wǒ shì; wǒ mén shì**	我是；我们是 我是；我們是
we father and son **zān-me yé-er liǎ**	咱们爷儿俩 咱們爺兒倆	You are **nǐ shì**	你是；你们是 你是；你們是
you mother and daughter (son) **nǐ-me niáng-er liǎ**	妳们娘儿俩 妳們娘兒倆	He is **tā shì**	他是 他是
you two sisters **nǐ-me jiěr liǎ**	妳们姐儿俩 妳們姐兒倆	She is **tā shì**	她是 她是
you three brothers **nǐ-me gēr sā**	你们哥儿仨 你們哥兒仨	It is **tā shì**	它是；它是 牠是；它是
we brothers **zān-me gēr jǐ-ge**	咱们哥儿几个 咱們哥兒幾個	They are **tā mén shì**	他们是 他們是

Chinese never address their higher generation relatives by their first name. Uncles and aunts are respectfully addressed as "四叔 Sì Shū, Fourth-Uncle", "二婶 Er Shěn, Second-Aunt" or "小舅舅 Xiǎo Jìu-jiu, Little-Uncle" (means the youngest maternal uncle) literarily 小 means small or little.

For an elder brother or sister like "大哥 Dà Gē, Big-Brother" or "三姐 Sān Jǐe, Third-Elder Sister" is called, but for a younger brother, beside calling him by his first name "老四 Lǎo Sì, Old-Four" (means No.4 younger brother) or "小五儿 Xiáo Wǔr, Little-Five" (means No.5 younger brother) is called as a nickname, and their wives are your 弟媳妇 Dì Xí-fu. e.g.: The wife of your number five younger brother is your "五弟媳 Wǔ Dì Xí, Fifth-Younger Sister-In-Law" regardless of her age.

The wife of one's elder brother is 嫂子 sǎo-zi, your No. 3 elder brother's wife is your "三嫂 Sān Sǎo, Third-Sister-In-Law", the husband of your Big-Sister is your "大姐夫 Dà Jǐe-fu, Big-Brother-In-Law" and your younger sisters' husbands are your "妹夫 Mèi-fu, Younger-Brother-In-Law" regardless of their ages.

To address your 2nd younger sister, it is "二妹 Er Mèi" and her husband is your "二妹夫 Er Mèi-fū, 2nd-Younger Brother-In-Law"

relative qīn-qi	亲戚 親戚	**family tree** jiā pǔ	家谱 家譜
direct relative zhí xì qīn shǔ	直系亲属 直系親屬	**ancestor** zǔ xiān; zǔ zōng	祖先;祖宗 祖先;祖宗
blood-relationship xié tǒng	血统 血統	**family member** jiā-ren	家人 家人
kin qīn-qi guān-xi	亲戚关系 親戚關係	**dependent** jiā-jùan	家眷 家眷
paternal fù xì-de	父系的 父系的	**next generation** xià yí dài	下一代 下一代
maternal mǔ xì-de	母系的 母系的	**offsprings** zǐ sūn hòu dài	子孙後代 子孫後代

generation gap	两代间的代沟	concubine	妾；姨太太
liǎng dài jiān-de dài gōu	兩代間的代溝	qiè; yí tài-tai	妾；姨太太
heir; successor	继承人；嗣子	★fiancé	未婚夫
jì chéng rén; sì zǐ	繼承人；嗣子	wèi hūn fū	未婚夫
heiress	女继承人	fiancée	未婚妻
nǚ jì chéng rén	女繼承人	wèi hūn qī	未婚妻
married name	夫家姓	father	父亲
fū jiā xìng	夫家姓	fù-qin	父親
maiden name	娘家姓	mother	母亲
niáng jiā xìng	娘家姓	mǔ-qin	母親
brother (elder)	哥哥	dad; daddy (for kid)	爸爸；爹
gē-ge	哥哥	bà-ba; diē	爸爸；爹
brother (younger)	弟弟	mom; mommy (for kid)	娘；妈
dì-di	弟弟	niáng; mā	娘；媽
sister (elder)	姐姐	parents	父母；双亲
jiě-jie	姐姐	fù mǔ; shuāng qīn	父母；雙親
sister (younger)	妹妹	son	儿子
mèi-mei	妹妹	ér-zi	兒子
siblings	兄弟姐妹	daughter	女儿
xiōng dì jiě mèi	兄弟姐妹	nǚ ér	女兒
half-brothers	异父母兄弟		
yì fù mǔ xiōng dì	異父母兄弟		
half-sisters	异父母姐妹		
yì fù mú jiě mèi	異父母姐妹		

Chinese parents often call their children by their "小名兒 xiǎo míngr, childhood name" or they simply say:
"我們老大 wǒ-men lǎo dà"(our eldest child)
"我們老二 wǒ-men lǎo èr" (our 2nd child)
"我們小老么 wǒ-men xiǎo lǎo yao" (our precious youngest child)

ex-husband	前夫		
qián fū	前夫		
spouse	配偶		
pèi ǒu	配偶		
husband	丈夫；先生	twins	孪生；双胞胎
zhàng-fu; xiān-sheng	丈夫；先生	lüán shēng; shuāng bāo tāi	孿生；雙胞胎
Mr. Doe	外子	adopted son	过继子
wài zǐ	外子	guò jì zǐ	過繼子
wife	妻子；太太；老婆	the only daughter (son)	独生女（子）
qī zǐ; tài-tai; lǎo-po	妻子；太太；老婆	dú shēng nǚ（zǐ）	獨生女（子）
Mrs. Doe	内人	posthumous child	遗腹子；遗腹女
nèi-ren	內人	yí fù zǐ; yí fù nǚ	遺腹子；遺腹女
my better-half	贤内助	great-grandparents	曾祖父母
xián nèi zhù	賢內助	zēng zǔ fù mǔ	曾祖父母
my hubby	老公	great-grandchildren	曾孙辈儿
lǎo gōng	老公	zēng sūn bèir	曾孫輩兒

deceased grandfather **wáng zǔ fù**	亡祖父 亡祖父
late grandmother **xiān zú mǔ**	先祖母 先祖母
paternal grandfather **yé-ye; zǔ fù**	爷爷；祖父 爺爺；祖父
maternal grandfather **wài gōng; wài zǔ fù**	外公；外祖父 外公；外祖父
paternal grandmother **nǎi-nai; zú mǔ**	奶奶；祖母 奶奶；祖母
maternal grandmother **wài pó; lǎo-lao**	外婆；姥姥 外婆；姥姥
senior master **lǎo-ye; lǎo tài yé**	老爷；老太爷 老爺；老太爺
senior mistress **tài-tai; lǎo tài-tai**	太太；老太太 太太；老太太
junior master **shào-ye; gōng zǐ**	少爷；公子 少爺；公子
the No. 4 junior master **sì shào ye; sì gōng zǐ**	四少爷；四公子 四少爺；四公子
junior mistress **xiáo-jie; qiān jīn**	小姐；千金 小姐；千金
the No. 2 junior mistress (married) **èr gū nǎi-nai**	二姑奶奶 二姑奶奶
step-father **jì fù; hòu fù**	继父；後父 繼父；後父
step-mother **jì mǔ; hòu mǔ**	继母；後母 繼母；後母
step-children **jì zí nǚ (tuō yóu-pingr)**	继子女；拖油瓶儿 繼子女；拖油瓶兒
paternal uncle (elder) **dà-ye; bó fù**	大爷；伯父 大爺；伯父
paternal aunt (his wife) **dà mā; bó mǔ**	大妈；伯母 大媽；伯母
paternal uncle (younger) **shū-shu**	叔叔 叔叔
paternal aunt-in-law **shěn-shen**	婶婶 嬸嬸
maternal uncle **jiù-jiu**	舅舅 舅舅

maternal aunt-in-law **jiù mā**	舅妈 舅媽
paternal aunt **gū-gu**	姑姑 姑姑
paternal uncle-in-law **gū fù; gū zhàng**	姑父；姑丈 姑父；姑丈
maternal aunt **yí**	姨 姨
maternal uncle-in-law **yí fù; yí zhàng**	姨父；姨丈 姨父；姨丈
nephew (brother's son) **zhí-zi**	侄子 姪子
nephew (sister's son) **wài-sheng**	外甥 外甥
niece (brother's daughter) **zhí nǔr**	侄女儿 姪女兒
niece (sister's daughter.) **wài shēng nǔr**	外甥女儿 外甥女兒
paternal cousin (male) **táng gē; táng dì**	堂哥；堂弟 堂哥；堂弟
paternal cousin (female) **táng jiě; táng mèi**	堂姐；堂妹 堂姐；堂妹
maternal cousin (male) **biǎo gē; biǎo dì**	表哥；表弟 表哥；表弟
maternal cousin (female) **biáo jiě; biǎo mèi**	表姐；表妹 表姐；表妹
first cousin (same name) **táng xiōng dì jiě mèi**	堂兄弟姐妹 堂兄弟姐妹
first cousin (different name) **biǎo xiōng dì jiě mèi**	表兄弟姐妹 表兄弟姐妹
second cousins **dì èr dài táng biǎo qīn**	第二代堂表亲 第二代堂表親
cousin once removed (aunt) **táng gū; biǎo gū**	堂姑；表姑 堂姑；表姑
cousin once removed (niece) **táng zhí-nü; biǎo zhí-nü**	堂侄女；表侄女 堂姪女；表姪女
cousin once removed (uncle) **táng shū; biǎo shū**	堂叔；表叔 堂叔；表叔
cousin once removed (nephew) **táng zhí; biǎo zhí**	堂侄；表侄 堂姪；表姪

grandson (son's son) **sūn-zi**	孙子 孫子	**wife's** (younger) **brother** **xiǎo jiù-zi; nèi dì**	小舅子；内弟 小舅子；內弟
grandson (dau's son) **wài sūn-zi**	外孙子 外孫子	**wife's** (elder) **sister** **dà yí-zi**	大姨子 大姨子
granddaughter (son's dau.) **sūn nǚr**	孙女儿 孫女兒	**wife's** (younger) **sister** **xiǎo yí-zi**	小姨子 小姨子
granddaughter (dau's dau.) **wài sūn nǚr**	外孙女儿 外孫女兒	**son-in-law** **nǚ-xü**	女婿 女婿
in-laws **yīn qīn**	姻亲 姻親	**daughter-in-law** **ér xí-fur**	儿媳妇儿 兒媳婦兒
brother-in-law (elder sis's) **jiě-fu**	姐夫 姐夫	**father-in-law** (wife's fa.) **yüè fù**	岳父 岳父
brother-in-law (younger sis's) **mèi-fu**	妹夫 妹夫	**father-in-law** (hus's fa.) **gōng-gong**	公公 公公
sister-in-law (elder bro's) **sǎo-zi**	嫂子 嫂子	**mother-in-law** (wife's mo.) **yüè mǔ; zhàng mǔ niáng**	岳母；丈母娘 岳母；丈母娘
sister-in-law (younger bro's) **dì xí-fu**	弟媳妇 弟媳婦	**mother-in-law** (hus's mo.) **pó-po**	婆婆 婆婆
husband's (elder) **brother** **dà bǎi-zi**	大伯子 大伯子	**wife to-be** (a doctor to-be) **zhǔn qī zǐ** (zhǔn yī shēng)	准妻子 準妻子(準醫生)
husband's (younger) **brother** **xiǎo shū-zi**	小叔子 小叔子	**agricultureal society** **nóng yè shè huì**	农业社会 農業社會
husband's (elder) **sister** **dà gū-zi** (dà gū nǎi-nai)	大姑子 大姑子(大姑奶奶)	**great fertility** **duō chǎn**	多产 多產
husband's (younger) **sister** **xiǎo gū-zi** (èr gū nǎi-nai)	小姑子 小姑子(二姑奶奶)	**plentiful offspring** **zǐ sūn chéng qún**	子孙成群 子孫成群
wife's (elder) **brother** **dà jiù-zi; nèi xiōng**	大舅子；内兄 大舅子；內兄		

All Walks Of Life
甚麽樣兒人都有

people **rén wù; rén mín**	人物；人民 人物；人民	guest **kè-ren**	客人 客人（宴客）
citizen **guó mín**	国民 國民	unexpected guest **bú sù zhī kè**	不速之客 不速之客
man (male or female) **rén**	人 人	having company **yǒu kè-ren**	有客人 有客人（洽談事）
population **rén kǒu**	人口 人口	host **nán zhǔ-ren**	男主人 男主人（宴客）
human being; mankind **rén; rén lèi**	人；人类 人；人類	hostess **nǔ zhǔ-ren**	女主人 女主人（宴客）
Your Majesty **bì xià**	陛下 陛下	master **lǎo-ye**	老爷 老爺
Your Highness **diàn xià**	殿下 殿下	mistress **tài-tai**	太太 太太
Your Excellency;Your Honor **gé xià**	阁下 閣下	housewife **jiā tíng zhǔ-fu**	家庭主妇 家庭主婦
landlord **fáng dōng xiān-sheng**	房东先生 房東先生	career woman **zhí yè fù nǔ**	职业妇女 職業婦女
landlady **fáng dōng tài-tai**	房东太太 房東太太	next door neighbor **gé bì lín-jü**	隔壁邻居 隔壁鄰居
tenant **fáng kè**	房客 房客	man; men **nán-ren**	男人 男人
occupant **zhù hù**	住户 住戶	woman; women **nǔ-ren**	女人 女人
traveler **lǔ kè**	旅客 旅客	chick; broad; dame **mǎ-zi; xiǎo niūr**	马子；小妞儿 馬子；小妞兒
tourist **guān guāng kè**	观光客 觀光客	boy **nán háir**	男孩儿 男孩兒
visitor **fǎng kè**	访客 訪客	girl **nǔ háir**	女孩儿 女孩兒

guy; young man; lad **nián qīng-ren**	年轻人 年輕人	fellow; chap **jiā-huo**	家伙 傢伙
child; children **xiǎo háir; xiǎo hái-zi**	小孩儿；小孩子 小孩兒；小孩子	stud **zhuàng dīng**	壮丁 壯丁
baby boy **nán yīng**	男婴 男嬰	adult; grown-up **chéng nián-ren; dà-ren**	成年人；大人 成年人；大人
baby girl **nǚ yīng**	女婴 女嬰	middle aged **zhōng nián-ren**	中年人 中年人
infant **wá-wa; yīng ér**	娃娃；婴儿 娃娃；嬰兒	the old; the aged **lǎo nián-ren**	老年人 老年人
orphan **gū ér; gū nǚ**	孤儿；孤女 孤兒；孤女	friend **péng-you**	朋友 朋友
foster father **yǎng fù**	养父 養父	colleague **tóng shì**	同事 同事
foster mother **yáng mǔ**	养母 養母	buddy **gēr-men**	哥儿们 哥兒們
foster daughter **yáng nǚ**	养女 養女	pal **háo yǒu**	好友 好友
minor; underaged **wèi chéng nián**	未成年 未成年	intimate friend **mì yǒu**	密友 密友
youngster **shào nián**	少年 少年	pen pal **bí yǒu**	笔友 筆友
teenager **shí lá suì-de hái-zi**	十来岁的孩子 十來歲的孩子	internet pal **wáng yǒu**	网友 網友
precocious child **zǎo shú-de xiǎo hái**	早熟的小孩 早熟的小孩	muscleman **yǒu jī ròu-de nán-ren**	有肌肉的男 有肌肉的男人
problem child **wèn tí ér tóng**	问题儿童 問題兒童	fair-weather friend **jiǔ ròu péng-you**	酒肉朋友 酒肉朋友
juvenile delinquent **bù liáng shào nián**	不良少年 不良少年	comrade **tóng zhì**	同志 同志（軍、政、黨）
misbehaved children **huài hái-zi**	坏孩子 壞孩子	homosexual **tóng zhì; tóng xìng liàn**	同志；同性恋 同志；同性戀
spoiled child **guàn huài-de hái-zi**	惯坏的孩子 慣壞的孩子	Lesbian **nǚ tóng zhì** (tóng xìng liàn)	女(同志；同性恋) 女(同志；同性戀)
what a naughty boy **zhèi hái-zi zhěn pí**	这孩子真皮 這孩子真皮	gay **nán tóng zhì** (tóng xìng liàn)	男(同志；同性恋) 男(同志；同性戀)
dude; play cool **qióng rén měi; wánr shuài**	穷人美；玩儿帅 窮兒美；玩兒帥	come-out (admit being gay) **chū guì; zì rèn tóng zhì**	出柜；自认同志 出櫃；自認同志
smart; smart looking **shuài; shuài-qi**	帅；帅气 帥；帥氣	people from all walks of life **shá yàng rén dū yǒu**	啥样儿人都有 啥樣兒人都有

macho; machos nán zǐ qì gài-de rén	男子气概的人 男子氣概的人	sexual perversion xìng biàn tài	性变态 性變態
tomboy nán xìng huà-de nǚ-zi	男性化的女子 男性化的女子	sadism nüè dài kuáng	虐待狂 虐待狂
transvestite yì xìng zhuāng bàn pí zhě	异性装扮癖者 異性裝扮癖者	exhibitionist pù lù kuáng	曝露狂 曝露狂
drag queen nán bàn nǚ zhuāng zhě	男扮女装者 男扮女裝者	flasher (exhibitionist) dà yī pù lù kuáng	大衣曝露狂 大衣曝露狂
sissy niáng niáng qiāng	娘娘腔 娘娘腔	streaker luǒ bēn zhě	裸奔者 裸奔者
bisexual shuāng xìng liàn	双性恋 雙性戀	rapist qiáng jiān fàn	强奸犯 強姦犯
straight; heterosexual yì xìng liàn	异性恋 異性戀	enemy chóu-ren	仇人 仇人
androgyne yī yáng rén	阴阳人 陰陽人	murderer xiōng-shou shā shǒu	凶手；杀手 兇手；殺手
transsexual biàn xìng rén	变性人 變性人	cold-blooded murderer léng xiě shā shǒu	冷血杀手 冷血殺手
rash fellow ér lèng-zi	二愣子 二愣子	prisoner fàn-ren	犯人 犯人
act without thoughts; crude mǎng zhāng fēi (lú mǎng)	莽张飞 (鲁莽) 莽張飛 (魯莽)	terrorist kǒng bù fèn zǐ	恐怖份子 恐怖分子
glared at each other nù shì duì fāng	怒视对方 怒視對方	rioter bào tú	暴徒 暴徒
glared hatred at each other chóu shì duì fāng	仇视对方 仇視對方	reactionaries fǎn dòng fèn zǐ	反动份子 反動份子
kick the bucket; turn up his heels qiào biàn-zi-le	翘辫子了 翹辮子了 (死了)	hostage rén zhì	人质 人質
went rigid & gone (stiff legged) yí chuài tuǐr	一踹腿儿 一踹腿兒 (死了)	skyjack jié jī fàn	劫机犯 劫機犯
dropped dead gěr pì zháo liáng	嗝儿屁著 凉 (升天) 嗝兒屁著涼	kidnap bǎng jià; jié chí	绑架；劫持 綁架；劫持
wolf sè láng	色狼 色狼	bank robber yín háng qiáng fěi	银行抢匪 銀行搶匪
dirty old man lǎo sè guǐ	老色鬼 老色鬼	bandit tú fěi; qiáng fěi	土匪；抢匪 土匪；搶匪
Peeping Tom tōu kuī kuáng	偷窥狂 偷窺狂	robber qiáng dào	强盗 強盜
sex maniac (nymphomaniac) sè qíng kuáng	色情狂 色情狂	rob qiǎng jié	抢劫 搶劫

kidnapper **báng fěi**	绑匪 綁匪	narcotic addict **yǒu dú yǐn-de rén**	有毒瘾的人 有毒癮的人
hostage **rén zhì**	人质 人質	pimp **lā pí-tiao-de**	拉皮条的 拉皮條的
ransom **shú jīn**	赎金 贖金	callgirl **yìng zhāo nǔ láng**	应召女郎 應召女郎
kill a hostage **sī piào**	撕票 撕票	gigolo **chī ruǎn fàn-de**	吃软饭的 吃軟飯的
victim **lí nàn zhě; shòu hài zhě**	罹难者;受害者 罹難者;受害者	male prostitute **nán chāng**	男娼 男娼
survival; survivor **xìng cún; xìng cún zhě**	幸存;幸存者 倖存;倖存者	prostitute; whore **jì-nü**	妓女 妓女
steal **tōu dōng-xi**	偷东西 偷東西	tramp **dàng fù**	荡妇 蕩婦
thief **zéi**	贼 賊	gold digger **tāo jīn nǔ láng**	淘金女郎 淘金女郎
burglar **xiǎo tōur**	小偷儿 小偷兒	stripteaser **tuō yī wǔ niáng**	脱衣舞娘 脫衣舞孃
shoplifter **sān zhī shǒu**	三只手 三隻手	rich people **yǒu qián-ren**	有钱人 有錢人
people of all sorts **sān jiào jiǔ liú**	三教九流 三教九流	mushroom millionaire **bào fā fù hù**	暴发富户 暴發富戶
syndicate **hēi shè huì zǔ zhī**	黑社会组织 黑社會組織	wastrel; prodigal; spendthrift **bài jiā zǐr**	败家子儿 敗家子兒
obnoxious **gǎ zá-zi**	乇杂子 乇雜子	bourgeoisie **zhōng chǎn jiē jí**	中产阶级 中產階級
jerk **hún dàn**	混蛋 混蛋	wage earner **xīn-shui jiē jí**	薪水阶级 薪水階級
con man **jīn guāng dǎng**	金光党 金光黨	poor people **qióng-ren**	穷人 窮人
pickpocket; light-fingered **pá-shou**	扒手 扒手	down and out **pín kùn liáo dǎo**	贫困潦倒 貧困潦倒
snatcher **qiǎng qián bāo dǎi tú**	抢钱包歹徒 搶錢包歹徒	playboy **huā huā gōng zǐ**	花花公子 花花公子
pirate **hǎi dào**	海盗 海盜	glamour girl **mó dēng nǔ láng**	摩登女郎 摩登女郎
rascal **liú máng**	流氓 流氓	millionaire **bǎi wàn fù wēng**	百万富翁 百萬富翁
dope fiend; drug user **xī dú-de rén**	吸毒的人 吸毒的人	multi-millionaire **qiān wàn fù wēng**	千万富翁 千萬富翁

billionaire **yì wàn fù wēng**	亿万富翁 億萬富翁	potter **táo yì jiā**	陶艺家 陶藝家
big shot (tycoon) **dà hēng**	大亨 大亨	expert **zhuān jiā**	专家 專家
celebrity **míng rén; míng líu**	名人；名流 名人；名流	scholar **xüé zhě**	学者 學者
VIP (very important person) **dà rén-wu; yào rén**	大人物；要人 大人物；要人	poet **shī rén**	诗人 詩人
a small potato; nobody **xiǎo rén wù**	小人物 小人物	outstanding person **jié chū rén wù**	杰出人物 傑出人物
enterpriser; industrialist **qì yè jiā**	企业家 企業家	amateur **yè yǘ cóng shì zhě**	业馀从事者 業餘從事者
proprietor **yè zhǔ; shì yè jiā**	业主；事业家 業主；事業家	sponsor **zàn zhù rén**	赞助人 贊助人
chief **shóu lǐng**	首领 首領	hypocrite **wěi jūn zǐ**	伪君子 偽君子
boss **láo bǎn; tóu-zi**	老板；头子 老闆；頭子	double talker **huá tóu; bì zhòng jiù qīng**	滑头；避重就轻 滑頭；避重就輕
shareholder; stockholder **gǔ dōng**	股东 股東	troublemaker **dǎo dàn guǐ; zhǎo má-fan**	捣蛋鬼；找麻烦 搗蛋鬼；找麻煩
partner **hé huǒ rén**	合夥人 合夥人	exaggerator **chuī niú dà wáng**	吹牛大王 吹牛大王（吹牛）
businessman; merchant **shāng-ren; shēng yì rén**	商人；生意人 商人；生意人	bragger **lǎo hàn mài guā**	老汉卖瓜 老漢賣瓜（自誇）
consumer **xiāo fèi zhě**	消费者 消費者	bootlicker; toady **pāi mǎ pì-de; mǎ pì jīng**	拍马的；马屁精 拍馬屁的；馬屁精
old hand **láo shǒur**	老手儿 老手兒	slowpoke **zuò shì màn téng-teng-de**	做事慢腾腾的 做事慢騰騰的
green hand **xīn shǒur**	新手儿 新手兒	curse in rage **nù mà**	怒骂 怒罵
intellectual **zhī shì fèn zǐ**	知识份子 知識份子	furious **dà nù**	大怒 大怒
white-collar job **bái lǐng jiē jí**	白领阶级 白領階級	drop dead! **ní sǐ-le cái hǎo**	你死了才好！ 你死了才好！
illiterate **bù shì zì-de rén**	不识字的人 不識字的人	hillbilly **xiāng xià lǎor**	乡下佬儿 鄉下佬兒
blue-collar job **gōng-ren jiē jí**	工人阶级 工人階級	bumpkin **tǔ bào-zi**	土包子 土包子
craftsman **shǒu-yi-ren**	手艺人 手藝人	matchmaker **yüè xià lǎo rén**	月下老人 月下老人

have been seeing each other **zài jiāo wǎng zhōng**	在交往中 在交往中	introducer **jiè shào rén**	介绍人 介紹人
going steady **gù dìng qíng lǚ**	固定情侣 固定情侣	single; unmarried **dān shēn**	单身 單身
lover; sweetheart **aì-ren; qíng-ren**	爱人；情人 愛人；情人	bachelor **dān shēn hàn; wáng láo wǔ**	单身汉；王老五 單身漢；王老五
mistress **qíng fù**	情妇 情婦	maiden **wèi hūn nǚ zǐ**	未婚女子 未婚女子
in love with him **ài-shang-ta-le**	爱上他了 愛上他了	virgin **chǔ nǚ**	处女 處女
had a crush on him **àn liàn-zhe-ta**	暗恋著他 暗戀著他	divorcee **lí hūn-de nǚ-ren**	离婚的女人 離婚的女人
extramarital relations **wài yù**	外遇 外遇	widower **guān fū**	鳏夫 鰥夫
a two-timer **aì qíng piàn-zi**	爱情骗子 愛情騙子	widow **guǎ-fu**	寡妇 寡婦
bitch; Tom, Dick and Henry **rén jìn kě fū**	人尽可夫 人盡可夫	illegitimate child **sī shēng zǐ**	私生子 私生子
two-timer **zuò xiǎng qí rén zhī fú**	坐想齐人之福 坐想齊人之福	bastard **yé zhǒng**	野种 野種
newlyweds **xīn hūn fū fù**	新婚夫妇 新婚夫婦	half-breed; mixed blood **hùn xiě ér**	混血儿 混血兒
bridegroom **xīn láng**	新郎 新郎	Eurasian **ōu yà hùn xiě ér**	欧亚混血儿 歐亞混血兒
bride **xīn niáng**	新娘 新娘	giant **jù rén; jù dà**	巨人 巨人
best-man **bàn láng**	伴郎 伴郎	dwarf; midget **zhū rú; ǎi-zi**	侏儒；矮子 侏儒；矮子
maid of honor **bàn niáng**	伴娘 伴娘	baldhead **tū-zi**	秃子 秃子
usher **nán bīn xiàng**	男傧相 男儐相	humpback; hunchback **luó guōr; tuó bèi**	罗锅儿；驼背 羅鍋兒；駝背
bridesmaid **nǚ bīn xiàng**	女傧相 女儐相	lame **qüé-zi**	瘸子 瘸子
marriage certificate **jié hūn zhèng shū**	结婚证书 結婚證書	blind **xiā-zi**	瞎子 瞎子
affix chops **gài yìn**	盖印 蓋印	deaf **lóng-zi**	聋子 聾子
witness of wedding **zhèng hūn rén**	证婚人 證婚人	mute; dumb **yǎ-ba**	哑巴 啞巴

stutter; stammer **kē-ba; jiē-ba; kǒu jí**	磕巴；结巴；口吃 磕巴；結巴；口吃	
insane; lunatic **jīng shén bìng; fēng-zi**	精神病；疯子 精神病；瘋子	
clever **cōng-ming**	聪明 聰明	
dumb **bèn**	笨 笨	
fool **shǎ guā**	傻瓜 傻瓜	
stupid; dummy **bèn dàn; chǔn cái**	笨蛋；蠢材 笨蛋；蠢材	
idiot **bái chī**	白痴 白痴	
ignorant **wú zhī**	无知 無知	
naive; simple **tiān zhēn**	天真 天真	
childish **hái-zi qì**	孩子气 孩子氣	
trash **bài lèi**	败类 敗類	
unrighteous **bù sān bú sì**	不三不四 不三不四	
smatterer **bàn diào-zi**	半吊子 半吊子	
lazybones **lǎn gú-tou**	懒骨头 懶骨頭	
unlearned **méi jiào-yang**	没教养 沒教養	
black sheep; a rotten apple **hài qǔn zhī mǎ**	害群之马 害群之馬	
It's outrageous. **tēi bú xiàng huà**	忒不像话 忒不像話	
chicken; craven **dǎn xiáo guǐ**	胆小鬼 膽小鬼	
coward **nāo zhǒng**	孬种 孬種	
(a) worthless wretch **wō-nang fèi**	窝囊废 窩囊廢	

blockhead **hú-tu chóng**		糊涂虫 糊塗蟲
sucker **yuǎn dà tóu**		冤大头 冤大頭
penname **bǐ míng**		笔名 筆名
alias **yòu míng**		又名 又名
nickname **wài hàor**		外号儿 外號兒
bookworm **shū dāi-zi**		书呆子 書呆子
Slim (nickname) **shòu pí hóur**	(外號)	瘦皮猴儿 瘦皮猴兒
Fatso (nickname) **xiǎo pàng**	(外號)	小胖 小胖
little rascal (a pet name) **xiáo-gui**		小鬼 小鬼（暱稱）
shrew **pō fù**		泼妇 潑婦
busybody **ài guǎn xián shì**		爱管闲事 愛管閒事
sharp (glib) tongue **líng yá lì chǐ**		伶牙俐齿 伶牙俐齒
shrewd person **jīng míng néng gàn**		精明能干 精明能幹
grouchy **bào zào**		暴躁 暴躁
quick-tempered **bào pí-qi**		暴脾气 暴脾氣
irascible person **pí-qi dà-de rén**		脾气大的人 脾氣大的人
an impulse **yì shí chōng dòng**		一时冲动 一時衝動
get excited **jī dòng**		激动 激動
villain **xiǎo-ren**		小人 小人
ill-treat **nüè dài**		虐待 虐待

mistreat **cuò dài**	错待 錯待	genius **tiān cái**	天才 天才
snob; snobbish **shì-li yǎn**	势利眼 勢利眼	jack of all trades **wàn shì tōng**	万事通 萬事通
social climber **bā-jie dá guān xiǎn yào**	巴结达官显要 巴結達官顯要	well-taught **yǒu jiào-yang**	有教养 有教養
mordant **jiān suān**	尖酸 尖酸	well-educated **yǒu xüé-wen**	有学问 有學問
sarcastic remarks **lěng yán léng yǔ**	冷言冷语 冷言冷語	well-trained **tiáo jiào chū-de gāo shǒur**	调教出的高手儿 調教出的高手兒
white lies **shàn yì-de huǎng yán**	善意的谎言 善意的謊言	strict; severe **yán gé**	严格 嚴格
acrid; acrimonious **kè bó**	刻薄 刻薄	serious **yán sù**	严肃 嚴肅
stingy; mean **kōu ménr ; lìn sè**	抠门儿；吝啬 摳門兒；吝嗇	stubborn; pigheaded **gù zhí; nìng zhǒng**	固执；拧种 固執；擰種
cunning and fierce **diāo; cán rěn**	刁；残忍 刁；殘忍	tough man **gāng qiāng; yìng hàn-zi**	刚强；硬汉子 剛強；硬漢子
ruthless; relentless; venomous **hěn; hěn dú**	狠；狠毒 狠；狠毒	have guts **yóu zhǒng**	有种 有種
is annoying **tǎo yàn**	讨厌 討厭	gruff; surly **jüè; jüè jiàng**	倔；倔强 倔；倔強
a nuisance; a big bore **tǎo yàn guǐ**	讨厌鬼 討厭鬼	so fed up with you **wǒ shòu gòu-le**	我受够了 我受夠了
he makes me sick **kàn-jian-ta jiù tǎo yàn**	看见他就讨厌 看見他就討厭	I can't put up with you. **wǒ zhēn shòu-bu liáo-nǐ**	我真受不了你 我真受不了妳
a pain in the ass (neck) **zhèi-ge rén hěn nán duì-fu**	这个人很难对付 這個人很難對付	clown **xiáo chǒur**	小丑儿 小丑兒
ferocious **xiōng bā bā-de**	凶巴巴的 凶巴巴的	miser **xiǎo-qi guǐ**	小气鬼 小氣鬼
evildoer **huài-ren**	坏人 壞人	hero **yīng xióng**	英雄 英雄
fierce **xiōng**	凶 凶	heroine **nǚ yīng xióng**	女英雄 女英雄
has a heart of gold **xīn yánr hǎo**	心眼儿好 心眼兒好	patriot **ài guó zhì shì**	爱国志士 愛國志士
filial **xiào-shun**	孝顺 孝順	traitor **mài guó zéi**	卖国贼 賣國賊
well-liked **tǎo rén xǐ huān**	讨人喜欢 討人喜歡	politician **zhèng kè**	政客 政客

English	简体	English	简体
magician biàn xì fǎr-de	变戏法兒的 變戲法兒的	civilian láo bǎi xìng	老百姓 老百姓
fortune teller suàn mìng-de	算命的 算命的	the general public dà zhòng	大众 大眾
face reading kàn miàn xiàng	看面相 看面相	sage shèng-ren	圣人 聖人
geomantic omen; geomancer fēng-shui xiān-sheng	风水先生 風水先生	king guó wáng	国王 國王
scalper huáng niú	黄牛 黃牛（賣入場券）	queen huáng hòu	皇后 皇后
street vendor; peddler xiǎo fàn	小贩 小販	prince wáng zǐ	王子 王子
wino; lush jiú guǐ	酒鬼 酒鬼	princess gōng zhǔ	公主 公主
unemployed shī yè rén kǒu	失业人口 失業人口	nobles guì zú	贵族 貴族
beggar qǐ gài; jiào huā-zi	乞丐；叫化子 乞丐；叫化子	commom people; commoner píng mín	平民 平民
missionary chuán jiào shì	传教士 傳教士	farmer nóng-fu	农夫 農夫
securityman bǎo quán rén yuán	保全人员 保全人員	mere creature kuí lěi	傀儡 傀儡
plain clothes detective xíng jǐng	刑警 刑警	dictator dú cái	独裁 獨裁
traffic policeman jiāo tōng jǐng chá	交通警察 交通警察	savage yě rén	野人 野人
lifeguard jiù shēng yuán	救生员 救生員	barbarian yě mán rén	野蛮人 野蠻人
private detective sī jiā zhēn tàn	私家侦探 私家偵探	pioneer kāi záo zǔ xiān	开凿祖先 開鑿祖先
bodyguard bǎo biāo-de	保镖的 保鏢的	primitive yuán shǐ rén lèi	原始人类 原始人類
hired thug góu tuǐ-zi	狗腿子 狗腿子	aborigine yuán zhù mín	原住民 原住民
officer jūn guān; jǐng guān	军官；警官 軍官；警官	native dāng dì rén	当地人 當地人
veteran tuì wǔ jūn rén	退伍军人 退伍軍人	native inhabitants dāng dì jǔ mín	当地居民 當地居民
retired tuì xiū-de rén	退休的人 退休的人	foreigner; alien wài guó rén	外国人 外國人

occupation **háng yè**	行业 行業	doctor **yī shēng; dài-fu; yī shī**	医生；大夫；医师 醫生；大夫；醫師
employment **zhí yè**	职业 職業	physician **nèi kē yī shī**	内科医师 內科醫師
employer **gù zhǔ**	雇主 雇主	surgeon **wài kē yī shī**	外科医师 外科醫師
employee **gù yuán**	雇员 雇員	pediatrician **xiǎo ér kē yī shī**	小儿科医师 小兒科醫師
self-employed **zì jǐ zuò láo bǎn**	自己做老板 自己做老闆	gynecologist **fù chǎn kē yī shēng**	妇产科医生 婦產科醫生
owner & operator **zì jīng zì yíng zhě**	自经自营者 自經自營者	oculist; ophthalmologist **yǎn kē yī shī**	眼科医师 眼科醫師
unemployment **shī yè**	失业 失業	optician **yàn guāng shī**	验光师 驗光師
job hunting **zhǎo gōng zuò**	找工作 找工作	dentist **yá yī shī**	牙医师 牙醫師
answer the ad **kàn guǎng gào yìng zhēng**	看广告应徵 看廣告應徵	psychiatrist **xīn lǐ yī shēng**	心理医生 心理醫生
part-time job **jiān chāi**	兼差 兼差	dermatologist **pí fū kē yī shēng**	皮肤科医生 皮膚科醫生
handyman **zá xiū gōng**	杂修工 雜修工	venereal disease doctor **xìng bìng yī shēng**	性病医生 性病醫生
temporary job **lín shí gōng**	临时工 臨時工	fracture setter **jiē gǔ shī**	接骨师 接骨師
temporary employee **lín shí gù yuán**	临时雇员 臨時雇員	manipulator massagist **tuī ná shī**	推拿师 推拿師
full-time job **quán zhí**	全职 全職	massagist **àn mó shī**	按摩师 按摩師
permanent job **cháng qí gù dìng gōng zuò**	长期固定工作 長期固定工作	nurse **hù-shi**	护士 護士

professionals **zhuān yè rén shì**	专业人士 專業人士	explorer **tàn xiǎn jiā**	探险家 探險家
pharmacist **yào jì shī**	药剂师 藥劑師	metallurgist **yě jīn xué jiā**	冶金学家 冶金學家
analyst; lab technician **huà yàn shī**	化验师 化驗師	geologist **dì zhí xué jiā**	地质学家 地質學家
veterinarian; vet **shòu yī**	兽医 獸醫	mineralogist **kuàng wù xué jiā**	矿物学家 礦物學家
freelance **zì yóu yè**	自由业 自由業	meteorologist **qì xiàng xué jiā**	气象学家 氣象學家
sculptor **diāo kè jiā**	雕刻家 雕刻家	astronomer **tiān wén xué jiā**	天文学家 天文學家
painter (artist) **huà jiā**	画家 畫家	astrologer **zhān xīng xué jiā**	占星学家 占星學家
artist **yì-shu jiā**	艺术家 藝術家	architect **jiàn zhú shī**	建筑师 建築師
cartoonist **màn huà jiā**	漫画家 漫畫家	designer **shè jì shī**	设计师 設計師
photographer **shè yǐng shī; zhào xiàng shī**	摄影师；照相师 攝影師；照相師	engineer **gōng chéng shī**	工程师 工程師
musician **yīn yuè jiā**	音乐家 音樂家	civil engineer **tǔ mù gōng chéng shī**	土木工程师 土木工程師
composer **zuò qǔ jiā**	作曲家 作曲家	electrical engineer **diàn jī gōng chéng shī**	电机工程师 電機工程師
conductor (band) **zhǐ huī**	指挥 指揮（樂隊）	draftsman; tracer **huì tú yuán**	绘图员 繪圖員
pianist **gāng qín jiā**	钢琴家 鋼琴家	surveyor **cè liáng yuán**	测量员 測量員
chemist **huà xué jiā**	化学家 化學家	publisher **fā xíng rén**	发行人 發行人
physicist **wù lǐ xué jiā**	物理学家 物理學家	editor **zhú bǐ**	主笔 主筆
archaeologists **káo gǔ xué jiā**	考古学家 考古學家	columnist **zhuān lán zuò jiā**	专栏作家 專欄作家
antiquarian **gǔ wù shōu cáng jiā**	古物收藏家 古物收藏家	author; writer **zuò jiā**	作家 作家
scientist **kē xué jiā**	科学家 科學家	reporter **jì-zhe**	记者 記者
astronaut **tài kōng rén; yǔ hāng yuán**	太空人；宇航员 太空人；宇航員	proofreader **jiào duì yuán**	校对员 校對員

program director jié-mu bù zhǔ rèn	节目部主任 節目部主任	ballerina bā léi wǔ xīng	芭蕾舞星 芭蕾舞星
emcee (M.C.) jié-mu zhǔ chí rén	节目主持人 節目主持人	importer jìn kǒu shāng	进口商 進口商
disc jockey (D.J.) yīn yüè bō yīn yüán	音乐播音员 音樂播音員	exporter chū kǒu shāng	出口商 出口商
anchorwoman nǚ xīn wén bō bào yüán	女新闻播报员 女新聞播報員	trader mào yì shāng	贸易商 貿易商
anchorman nán xīn wén bō bào yüán	男新闻播报员 男新聞播報員	agent; broker jīng jì rén	经纪人 經紀人
announcer bō yīn yüán	播音员 播音員	chairman zǒng cái; zhǔ xí	总裁；主席 總裁；主席
demonstrator shì fàn yüán	示范员 示範員	board president dǒng-shi zhǎng	董事长 董事長
producer jiān zhì rén; zhì zuò rén	监制人；制作人 監製人；製作人	vice-president fù dǒng-shi zhǎng	副董事长 副董事長
cameraman yǐng shì shè yǐng shī	影视摄影师 影視攝影師	board trustee (member) dǒng-shi	董事 董事
drama coach xì jù zhí dáo lǎo shī	戏剧指导老师 戲劇指導老師	general manager zǒng jīng lǐ	总经理 總經理
movie director dáo yǎn	导演 導演	manager jīng lǐ	经理 經理
TV director dǎo bō	导播 導播	assistant-manager fù lǐ	副理 副理
actor nán yǎn yüán	男演员 男演員	business manager yíng yè bù jīng lǐ	营业部经理 營業部經理
actress nǚ yǎn yüán	女演员 女演員	sales manager yè-wu jīng lǐ	业务经理 業務經理
leading star zhǔ jüér (zhú jiǎor)	主角儿 主角兒	production manager shēng chǎn bù jīng lǐ	生产部经理 生產部經理
costar pèi jüér (pèi jiǎor)	配角儿 配角兒	staff mù liáo; qüán tǐ zhí yüán	幕僚；全体职员 幕僚；全體職員
comedian xǐ jù yǎn yüán	喜剧演员 喜劇演員	the (man; lady) in charge zhú guǎn	主管 主管
singer gē-shou	歌手 歌手	superintendent zǒng jiān	总监 總監
dancer wú-zhe	舞者 舞者	superior shàng-si; zhǎng-guan	上司；长官 上司；長官
model mó tè ér	模特儿 模特兒	inferiors xià shǔ; bù shǔ	下属；部署 下屬；部署

clerk **zhí yuán**	职员 職員		translator **fān yì yuán**	翻译员 翻譯員（筆譯）
file clerk **dǎng àn guán-li yuán**	档案管理员 檔案管理員		lawyer; attorney **lǜ-shi**	律师 律師
gofer; runner **páo tuǐr-de; xiǎo dì**	跑腿儿的；小弟 跑腿兒的；小弟		notary public **gōng zhèng rén**	公证人 公證人
store clerk **diàn yuán**	店员 店員		public accountant **zhí yè kuài jì shī**	职业会计师 職業會計師
sales clerk **shòu huò yuán**	售货员 售貨員		chief accountant **zǒng kuài jì shī**	总会计师 總會計師
salesman **nán shòu huò yuán**	男售货员 男售貨員		accountant **kuài-ji yuán**	会计员 會計員
saleswoman **nǚ shòu hùo yuán**	女售货员 女售貨員		bookkeeper **guǎn zhàng-de; bù jì yuán**	管帐的；簿记员 管帳的；簿記員
buyer **mǎi-ban**	买办 買辦		cashier **chū nà**	出纳 出納
business representative **yè wù dài biǎo**	业务代表 業務代表		teller **yín háng chū nà**	银行出纳 銀行出納
plant manager **cháng zhǎng**	厂长 廠長		realtor **pǎo hér-de; fáng dì qián kè**	跑合儿的；房地掮客 跑合兒的；房地掮客
superintendent **gōng cháng zǒng jiān**	工厂总监 工廠總監		document broker **dài-shu**	代书 代書
supervisor **jiān dū rén**	监督人 監督人		waiter **pǎo tángr-de; huǒ-ji**	跑堂儿的；夥计 跑堂兒的；夥計
technician **jì shī**	技师 技師		waitress **nǚ pǎo tángr; nǚ shì**	女跑堂儿；女侍 女跑堂兒；女侍
foreman **gōng tóu**	工头 工頭		headwaiter; captain **nán lǐng bān**	男领班 男領班（餐廳）
receptionist **xǔn wèn chù xiáo-jie**	讯问处小姐 訊問處小姐		bartender **jiú bǎo; tiáo jiǔ shī**	酒保；调酒师 酒保；調酒師
computer operator **diàn nǎo shū rù yuán**	电脑输入员 電腦輸入員		bouncer **jiǔ diàn bǎo biāo**	酒店保镖 酒店保鑣
secretary **mì-shu**	秘书 秘書		chef **zhǔ chú; dà shī-fu**	主厨；大师傅 主廚；大師傅
librarian **tú shū guǎn yuán**	图书馆员 圖書館員		cook **chú-zi; chú shī**	厨子；厨师 廚子；廚師
stenographer **sù jì yuán**	速记员 速記員		busboy **xià cài tóng**	下菜童 下菜童
interpreter **kǒu yì yuán**	口译员 口譯員		dishwasher (a person) **xǐ pán-zi-de**	洗盘子的 洗盤子的

cleaning man **qīng jié gōng**	清洁工 清潔工	driver **sī jī; jià shǐ**	司机；驾驶 司機；駕駛
security man **bǎo quán rén yüán**	保全人员 保全人員	chauffeur **zì yòng chē sī jī**	自用车司机 自用車司機
dispatcher **diào dù yüán**	调度员 調度員	butcher **tú fū**	屠夫 屠夫
fireman **jiù huǒ yüán**	救火员 救火員	contractor **bāo gōng-de**	包工的 包工的
conductor (train, bus) **chē zhǎng**	车掌 車掌	cement finisher **shuǐ ní jiàng**	水泥匠 水泥匠
guard; guardsman **jǐng wèi shǒu wèi**	警卫；守卫 警衛；守衛	bricklayer **wǎ-jiang**	瓦匠 瓦匠
doorman **shoǔ mén-de**	守门的 守門的	carpenter **mù-jiang**	木匠 木匠
bellboy **mén tóng**	门僮 門僮（旅館）	painter (laborer) **yóu qī jiàng**	油漆匠 油漆匠
room service **kè fáng fú wù shēng**	客房服务生 客房服務生	electrician **diàn gōng**	电工 電工
maid **nǚ yōng**	女佣 女傭	welder **hàn gōng**	焊工 焊工
helper **yòng-ren**	佣人 傭人	plumber **shuí guǎn gōng**	水管工 水管工
servant **pú-ren**	仆人 僕人	blacksmith **tiě gōng**	铁工 鐵工
butler **nán guǎn jiā**	男管家 男管家	prentice **xüé tú**	学徒 學徒
housekeeper **guǎn jiā**	管家 管家	warden **yù lì**	狱吏 獄吏
nursemaid; nanny **báo mǔ**	保姆 保姆	coroner **yàn shī guān**	验尸官 驗屍官
babysitter **kàn hái-zi-de**	看孩子的 看孩子的	undertaker **bìn zàng yè zhě**	殡葬业者 殯葬業者
maintenance man **wéi xiū gōng-ren**	维修工人 維修工人	trash collecter **shōu lā jī-de**	收垃圾的 收垃圾的
gardener **yüán dīng**	园丁 園丁	garbage man **shōu chú yǘ-de**	收厨馀的 收廚餘的
lawn mower **jián cǎo píng-de**	剪草坪的 剪草坪的	milkman **sòng niú nǎi-de**	送牛奶的 送牛奶的
elevator operator **diàn tī yüán**	电梯员 電梯員	paperboy **sòng bào-de**	送报的 送報的

2B Government Employees 公務員

government employee gōng wù yüán	公务员 公務員	ambassador dà shǐ	大使 大使
title tóu xián	头衔 頭銜	Embassy dà shǐ guán	大使馆 大使館
government official zhèng fǔ guān yüán	政府官员 政府官員	minister (diplomat) gōng shǐ	公使 公使
attaché dà shí guán wǔ guān	大使馆武官 大使館武官	Legation gōng shǐ guán	公使馆 公使館
chief delegate shǒu xí dài biǎo	首席代表 首席代表	special appointment tè rèn	特任 特任
diplomat wài jiāo guān	外交官 外交官	president (China) guó jiā zhǔ xí	国家主席 國家主席
cultural attaché wén huà cān zàn	文化参赞 文化參贊	vice-president (China) fù zhǔ xí	副主席 副主席
commercial attaché shāng wù cān zàn	商务参赞 商務參贊	president (country) zóng tǒng	总统 總統
aide-de-camp shì cóng wǔ guān	侍从武官 侍從武官	vice-president (country) fù zóng tǒng	副总统 副總統
entourage suí yüán	随员 隨員	official residence guān dǐ	官邸 官邸
envoy wài jiāo shǐ jié	外交使节 外交使節	Secretary of State guó wù qīng	国务卿 國務卿
chargé d'affaires dài bàn	代办 代辦	Secretary General zǒng shū-ji; mì shū zhǎng	总书记；秘书长 總書記；秘書長
counselor cān-shi	参事 參事	premier (China) zóng lǐ	总理 總理
consul general zóng lǐng-shi	总领事 總領事	prime minister (England) shǒu xiàng	首相 首相
consul lǐng-shi	领事 領事	governmental spokesman zhèng fǔ fā yán rén	政府发言人 政府發言人

minister (government) bù zhǎng	部长 部長	council speaker yì zhǎng	议长 議長
vice-minister (government) fù bù zhǎng	副部长 副部長	councilman yì yüán	议员 議員
minister of foreign affairs wài jiāo bù zhǎng	外交部长 外交部長	the grand justice dà fǎ guān	大法官 大法官
attorney general (U.S.A.) sī fǎ bù zhǎng	司法部长 司法部長	judge fǎ guān	法官 法官
commissioner jú zhǎng; chù zhǎng	局长；处长 局長；處長	court clerk shū jì guān	书记官 書記官
director sī zhǎng; zhú guǎn	司长；主管 司長；主管	procurator general jiǎn chá zhǎng	检察长 檢察長
protocol director lǐ bīn sī zhǎng	礼宾司长 禮賓司長	prosecutor jiǎn chá guān	检察官 檢察官
deputy director fù sī zhǎng	副司长 副司長	first secretary shí guǎn yī děng mì-shu	使馆一等秘书 使館一等秘書
special assistant zhuān mén wěi yüán	专门委员 專門委員	third secretary shí guǎn sān děng mì-shu	使馆三等秘书 使館三等秘書
favorite candidate zuì jiā hòu xüǎn rén	最佳候选人 最佳候選人	department head kē zhǎng	科长 科長
legislator lì fǎ wěi yüán	立法委员 立法委員	department assistant kē yüán	科员 科員
senator cān yì yüán	参议员 參議員	section chief gú zhǎng	股长 股長
representative zhòng yì yüán	众议员 眾議員	clerk bàn shì yüán	办事员 辦事員
governor zhōu zhǎng	州长 州長	intelligence agent qíng bào yüán	情报员 情報員
state secretary zhōu wù qīng	州务卿 州務卿	police commissioner jǐng zhèng shú zhǎng	警政署长 警政署長
provincial governor shéng zhǔ xí; shéng zhǎng	省主席；省长 省主席；省長	police chief jǐng chá jú zhǎng	警察局长 警察局長
county magistrate xiàn zhǎng; jùn zhǎng	县长；郡长 縣長；郡長	precinct chief jǐng chá fēn jú zhǎng	警察分局长 警察分局長
commissioner chù zhǎng	处长 處長	policeman; policemen jǐng chá	警察 警察（男）
mayor shì zhǎng	市长 市長	policewoman; policewomen nǚ jǐng chá	女警察 女警察
acting mayor dài shì zhǎng	代市长 代市長	police officer; sheriff jǐng guān; jùn jíng zhǎng	警官；郡警长 警官；郡警長

854 Useful Verbs In Chinese Language
854 個動詞精選

Chinese Verb To-Be

Rule One

A Chinese verb "to be" does not change in form while associated with subjects or pronouns. The "am, are and is" in Chinese remains the same word "shì 是".

> wǒ shì = I am
> nǐ shì = You are
> tā shì = He, She, It is
> tā-men shì = They are
>
> I "am" Japanese, you "are" British, he "is" Korean.
> wǒ "shì" Rì Běn Rén, nǐ "shì" Yīng-Guo Rén, tā "shì" Hán-Guo Rén.
> 我 (是) 日本人, 你 (是) 英国人,
> 他 (是) 韩国人

e.g.: ❶ I   "am"   "a"   nurse.
　　　 wǒ   (shì)   ○   hù-shi
　　　 我   (是)   ○   护士

Basically, the indicator "a" is unnecessary in Chinese because the "I" has already denoted "singular".

Not Are

❷ They   "are" not   "students"
　 They   not "are"   student
　 tā-men   bú (-shi)   xué-sheng
　 他们   不 (是)   学生

The plural form "students" is also unnecessary in Chinese as the "They" has already denoted "plural".

❸ It   "is" true,   "isn't"   it?
　○ (shì) zhēn-de,   (bú-shi-ma) ○
　○ (是)   真的,   (不是吗)   ○

The "It and it" are also unnecessary, particularly in replying a sentence. The "It" or "it" is already understood.

❹ John   "is"   my   son-in-law.
　 John   "is"   I   son-in-law.
　 John   (shì)   wó   nǔ xù
　 John   (是)   我   女婿

In some cases, "my" is substituted with "I". (See Group 7, 6 : my; mine)

Rule Two

In Chinese, the verb "to be" is not used when the subject is being described by an adjective, and the adjective is almost always preceded by "very; so; too". e.g.:

"very" ❶ She   "is"   pretty.
　　　　 She   "very"   pretty.
　　　　 tā   hén   měi
　　　　 她   很   美

"so" ❷ It   'is'   delicious!
　　 　○   "so"   delicious!
　　 　○   háo   hǎo chī
　　 　○   好   好吃

"too" ❸ It   "is"   wonderful!
　　 　○   "too"   wonderful!
　　 　○   tài   bàng-le
　　 　○   太   棒了!

Another example may show differently, the "verb to-be" (shì) is used when the subject is being described by a noun.

e.g.: The earth "is" round.
- dì qiú shì yüán-de
- 地球 (是) 圆的

In Chinese, the article "the" many times is not mentioned, (See Group 7, ⓵ and ⓶)

WHAT DOES A BEGINNER DO?

Unfortunately, there is no definite answer. A beginner may only learn these from experience. It is just like the preposition words in English, there is no set rules except by memorizing from the already established format.

Chinese Action Verbs

Many English action verbs are irregular, such as: "do, did, done", "go, went, gone", etc. Others are regular. In English, by attaching an "-ed" to the end of the verb makes it a "past tense" or a "past articiple". e.g. "call, called, called; ask; asked; asked…"

Rule Three

★ Differently in Chinese, verbs never change in form for different tenses. In other words, "all Chinese action verbs" remain the same for all tenses: present, past and future. The tense (time) is indicated by using assistant character(s) in that sentence. e.g. :

> I am at home.
> I was at home.
> I am going home.
> I was going home.
> (See Group 7, ㉝ , ㉞ and ㉟)

After you have read Group Seven's illustrations, you will find spoken Chinese is easy and it will give you enough guidance to form simple sentences using

the verb "to be". As you become more proficient in the Chinese language, using these verbs correctly will come naturally.

For a Past Tense "-ed"

Simply attach a soft "le" sound to the end of any present tense verb, and it becomes a "Past Tense". (了 is not pronounced liǎo)

了° le! "O" means " a soft tone ", it is a very soft expletive sound used in a "statement" in the Chinese language, just like the past tense suffix "-ed" of a verb in English.
(See Group 7 ⑨ PASS TENSE "-的 de")

(eat-le)	" 吃了 "	= ate
(buy-le)	" 买了 "	= bought
(take-le)	" 拿了 "	= took
(see-le)	" 看了 "	= saw

e.g.: ❶ I "asked" him two questionS
I "ask-ed" he two question
wǒ (wèn-le) tā liǎng-ge wèn tí
我 (问了) 他 两个 问题

Chinese never use a plural form. The above mentioned numeral "two" is already plural.* Chinese regard the subject and the object of the same noun or pronoun as equal. Therefore, "He" and "him" are one same word, "tā"* and "I and me" are one word, "wǒ".*

❷ She "bought" half a dozen appleS
her "buy-ed" half dozen apple.
tā (mǎi-le) bàn dá píng-guǒ
她 (买了) 半打 苹果
❸ we "sent" 50 Christmas CardS.
us "mail-ed" 50 (sheet) Christmas Card
wǒ-men (lì-le) wǔ-shi (zhāng) shèng dàn kǎ
我们 (寄了) 五十 (张) 圣诞卡
(See P.73,★ 张 and P.74,★ 封 in Group 5)
❹ I "mailed" my uncle a letter.
me to (I uncle) "mail-ed" a envelope letter
wǒ géi wǒ shú-shu (jì-le) yì (fēng) xìn
我 给 我叔叔 (寄了) 一(封) 信
("géi 给" means give ; for ; to)

For a Past Participle

Just attach a "la" sound to the end of the verb and you'll get it's "past participle".

| 啦! la! | is simply a Chinese suffix sound used in a "statement" in the Chinese language, which indicates that it is a "past participle" verb. e.g.:

(eat-la)	= eaten	"吃 啦!"
(forget-la)	= forgotten	"忘记 啦!"
(take-la)	= taken	"拿 啦!"
(see-la)	= seen	"看 啦!"

Same as English, a "past participle" never appears by itself in a sentence. This set rule also applies to the "啦 la!" sound in making Chinese sentences. It must accompany other character words to form meaningful sentences.

(For Passive Voices, Past Perfect and Future Perfect …See Group 7, 24 26 27)

For a Present Perfect

Insert "yǐ-jing" before the verb, and attach a "la" sound to the end of the verb.

已經°yi-jing is a tone or manner of speaking (语气) in Chinese. It is equivalent to either "have" or "has" in an English present perfect tense.

The pronunciation of the second word in "yǐ-jing" is a soft tone and gives a grammatical implication of "already"; same as "have" or "has" cannot be substituted for "already" (See Group 7, 25).

❶ I   "have"   "mowed"   the lawn .
Lawn   I   "have"   "cut"
<u>cǎo píng</u> <u>wó</u> "yǐ-jing" "jiǎn-la ".
草坪   我   (已经)   (剪啦)

❷ They "have" "decided" to get married.
They   "have"   "decided"   want to   marry
<u>tā-men</u> "yǐ-jing" "jú dìng-la" <u>yào</u> <u>jié hūn</u>
他們   (已经)   (决定啦)   要   结婚

Chinese Passive Voices Are usually presented in initiative forms

❸ He "has" "sold" his automoble.
He's   automoble   "has"   "sold"
<u>tā-de</u>   <u>qì chē</u>   "yǐ-jing"   "mài-la"
他的   汽车   (已经)   (卖啦)

❹ I   "have"   "added"   the salt.
I   salt   "have"   "added"
<u>wǒ</u>   <u>yán</u>   "yǐ-jing"   "jiā-la"
我   鹽   (已经)   (加啦)

For "haven't"

還沒…哪° hai mei…na!

is a tone or manner of speaking (语气) in Chinese, equivalent to " haven't " or "hasn't" in English.
Insert " hái méi " 还没 before the verb and attach a negative "-na 哪!" to the end of the sentence.

e.g. ❶ They "haven't" "come" back.
<u>tā-men</u>   "hái méi"   "huí-lai-na!"
他們   (还没)   (回來哪!)

❷ Little Four "hasn't" "gotten" up.
<u>Xiǎo-sìr</u> "hái méi" "qǐ chuáng-na!"
小四儿   (还没)   (起床哪!)

For a Present Progressive

Insert " zhèng-zai " before the verb. Following this simple method you'll be able to speak "pǔ tōng huà" easily.

正在°zheng-zai this 2-character sound has the same meaning and usage of making progressive tenses as "-ing" in English. e.g.: "work-ing". However, in Chinese the "-ing" is placed before the Verb as a prefix like "ing-work".

❶ She   is   read-ing   a   book.
She   ○   "ing-look"   ○   book
<u>tā</u>   ○   (zhèng-zài)kàn   ○   <u>shū</u>
她   ○   (正在)看   ○   书

Sometimes the 1st sound "zhèng" is omitted, leaving only "zài" before the verb.

e.g.: ❷ He is "take-ing" a bath.

He	○	"ing-bathe.
tā	○	(zài xí zǎo)
他	○	(在)洗澡

❸ Her hubby is "fix-ing" the pipes.

She	old man	"ing-fix"	water	pipe.
tā	lǎo gōng	(zài) xiū lǐ	shuí	guǎn-zi
她	老公	(在) 修理	水	管子

❹ We are leaving.

we	○	"ing-leave"
wǒ-men	○	(zhèng-yào zǒu)
我们	○	(正要走)

854 Useful Chinese Verbs

The Author Has Numbered **185** Most Frequently Used Chinese Verbs for you to memorize, to enable you to interact and deal with Chinese people widely and really "Get Going" in China. The ones with a "blue-★" are the less important ones.

More verbs related to specific fields may be found in their respective glossaries.

A

★abandon
fàng-qi
放弃
放棄

★absent
qūe xí
缺席
缺席

absorb
xī shōu
吸收
吸收

abuse
nüè dài
虐待
虐待

❶accept
jiē shòu
接受
接受

★accompany
péi; péi bàn
陪；陪伴
陪；陪伴

accomplish
chéng-jiu
成就
成就

accuse
zhǐ kòng
指控
指控

★accustom
xí guàn-yü…
习惯于…
習慣於…

acquire
huò dé
获得
獲得

act
jǔ zhǐ
举止
舉止

adapt
shì-ying
适应
適應

❷ add
jiā-shang
加上
加上

address
chēng-hu
称呼
稱呼

★adhere
zhān-shang
粘上
粘上

★adjust
tiáo jié
调节
調節

admire
xiàn-mu
羡慕
羡慕

★admit
chéng rèn
承认
承認

adopt
shōu-yang
收养
收養

adore
chóng bài
崇拜
崇拜

advance
yù zhī; wǎng qián; tí qián
预支;往前;提前
預支;往前;提前

advertise
dēng guǎng gào
登广告
登廣告

★advise
qùàn gào
劝告
勸告

affect
yíng xiǎng
影响
影響

affiliate
fù shǔ
附属
附屬

❸ afford
huā-de qǐ
花得起
花得起

❹ agree
tóng yì
同意
同意

aid
zhī yüán; jiù zhù
支援；救助
支援；救助

❺ allow
yǔn xǔ
允许
允許

amaze
jīng yà
惊讶
驚訝

amend
xiū zhèng
修正
修正

amuse
dòu qù
逗趣
逗趣

analyze
fēn xī
分析
分析

★anger
dà nù
大怒
大怒

❻ answer
huí dá
回答
回答

★apologize
péi-ge bú-shi; dào qiàn
赔个不是;道歉
賠個不是 ;道歉

★appear
chū xiàn
出现
出現

applaud
gú zhǎng
鼓掌
鼓掌

apply (1spread) 1 tú mǒ
(2 job) 2 shēn qǐng
1涂抹 2申请
1塗抹 2申請

appoint
zhǐ pài
指派
指派

appreciate
shǎng shì; gǎn xiè
赏识；感谢
賞識；感謝

approach
zǒu xiàng qián qù
走向前去
走向前去

★approve
zàn tóng
赞同
贊同

★argue
díng zuǐ
顶嘴
頂嘴

arise
shēng qǐ
升起
升起

❼ arrange
ān pái
安排
安排

arrest
dái bǔ
逮捕
逮捕

❽ arrive
dào dá
到达
到達

❾ ask
wèn
问
問

assist
xié zhù
协助
協助

associate
jiāo-wang
交往
交往

★assure you
hǎo zhèng-ni
保证你
保證你

attach
fù jiā
附加
附加

attack
gōng-ji
攻击
攻擊

❿ attend; attend to
cān jiā; zhì lì yú
参加;致力於
參加;致力於

attract
xī-yin
吸引
吸引

⓫ avoid
bì-mian
避免
避免

★awake
jiào xǐng
叫醒
叫醒

B

⓬ bake
kǎo
烤
烤

balance
bǎo chí píng héng
保持平衡
保持平衡

bear
chéng dān
承担
承擔

★beat
dǎ
打
打

⓭ become
biàn chéng
变成
變成

★beg
qǐ qiú
乞求
乞求

WESTCHESTER PUBLIC LIBRARY CHESTERTON, IN

❹ begin | 开始
kāi shǐ | 開始

behave | 行为；举止
xíng wéi; jǔ zhǐ | 行為；舉止

❺ believe | 相信
xiāng xìn | 相信

❻ belong | 属于
shǔ-yü | 屬於

bend | 撅；折弯
jūē; zhé wān | 撅；折彎

bet | 打赌；断言
dá dǔ; duàn yán | 打賭；斷言

betray | 出卖；背叛
chū mài; bèi pàn | 出賣；背叛

★beware | 留神
líu shén | 留神

bid | 出价
chū jià | 出價

bind | 捆；绑
kǔn; bǎng | 捆；綁

★bite | 咬
yǎo | 咬

blame | 指责；怪(某人)
zhǐ zé; guài | 指責；怪(某人)

bleed | 流血
liú xiě | 流血

blend | 混合
hùn hé | 混合

bless | 祝福
zhù fú | 祝福

block | 挡住
dǎng-zhu | 擋住

★blow | 吹
chuī | 吹

bluff | 唬人
hǔ rén | 唬人

blush | 脸红
liǎn hóng | 臉紅

❼ boil | 煮
zhǔ | 煮

❽ borrow | 向别人借
xiàng bié-ren jiè | 向別人借

brag | 吹牛
chuī niú | 吹牛

❾ break (1 in pieces) 1 dǎ pò | 1打破 2弄断
(2 in halves) 2 nòng duàn | 1打破 2弄断

breathe | 呼吸
hū xī | 呼吸

brief | 简报；摘要
jiǎn bào; zhāi yào | 簡報；摘要

❿ bring | 带来
dài-lai | 帶來

broadcast | 广播
guǎng bō | 廣播

brush | 刷
shuā | 刷

build | 建造
jiàn zào | 建造

★burn | 烧
shāo | 燒

burst | 爆炸
bào zhà | 爆炸

⓴ buy | 买；置
mǎi; zhì | 買；置

C

★calculate | 计算
jì suàn | 計算

★call | 叫；打电话
jiào; dǎ (diàn huà) | 叫；打電話

★calm | 平静下来
píng jìng xià-lai | 平靜下來

㉒ can | 能；会
néng; huì | 能；會

㉓ cancel | 取消
qǔ xiāo | 取消

㉔ carry | 用手提著
yòng shǒu tí-zhe | 用手提著

carve | 雕刻
diāo kè | 雕刻

㉕cash
duì xiàn
兑现
兌現

★catch
zhuō; dǎi
捉；逮
捉；逮

cause
qǐ yīn-yú...
起因于...
起因於...

㉖celebrate
qìng zhù
庆祝
慶祝

㉗change
gǎi
改
改

★charge
jì zhàng
记帐
記帳

㉘chat
liáo-tianr
聊天儿
聊天兒

cheat
piàn rén; qī piàn
骗人；欺骗
騙人；欺騙

★check
jiǎn chá
检查
檢查

chew
jiáo
嚼
嚼

choke
zhì xí
窒息
窒息

㉙choose
xüǎn zé
选择
選擇

chop
kǎn; duò
砍；剁
砍；剁

circulate
xún huán
回圈
循環

claim
qǐng qiú
请求
請求

㉚clean
nòng gān-jing
弄干净
弄乾淨

climb
wǎng shàng pá
往上爬
往上爬

㉛close
guān-shang
关上
關上

★collect
shōu-ji
收集
收集

★comb
shū tóu
梳头
梳頭

combine
jié hé
结合
結合

㉜come
lái
来
來

comfort
ān wèi
安慰
安慰

command
mìng lìng
命令
命令

commend
chēng zàn
称赞
稱讚

comment
píng lùn
评论
評論

commit
fàn
犯
犯

★compare
bǐ jiào
比较
比較

★compete
jìng zhēng
竞争
競爭

㉝complain
bào-yüan; mán-yüan
抱怨；埋怨
抱怨；埋怨

★complete
wán chéng
完成
完成

compose
zǔ chéng
组成
組成

comprehend
lí jiě
理解
理解

㉞concern
dān xīn; guà niàn
担心；挂念
擔心；掛念

conclude
duàn dìng
断定
斷定

conduct
xíng wéi
行为
行為

㉟confirm
qüè dìng yí-xiàr
确定一下儿
確定一下兒

confuse
gǎo hú-tu-le
搞糊涂了
搞糊塗了

★congratulate
zhù hè
祝贺
祝賀

conquer
zhēng fú
征服
征服

43

㊱ consider
kǎo lù
考虑
考慮

★consist
qí-zhong bāo kuò
其中包括
其中包括

construct
gòu-cheng
构成
構成

★consult
qǐng-jiao; zī xùn
请教；资讯
請教；資訊

consume
xiāo-hao
消耗
消耗

★contact
jiē-chu
接触
接觸

contain
bāo hán
包含
包含

★continue
jì xù
继续
繼續

contribute
juān zhù
捐助
捐助

control
kòng zhì
控制
控制

㊲ cook
zuò fàn
做饭
做飯

㊳ cool
lěng qùe
冷却
冷卻

cooperate
hé zuò
合作
合作

cope
duì-fu
对付
對付

㊴ copy
chāo xiě; fù zhì
抄写；复制
抄寫；複製

㊵ correct
jiū zhèng
纠正
糾正

㊶ cost
děi yào huā...
得要花...
得要花...

㊷ count
suàn; shǔ-yi shǔ
算；数一数
算；數一數

㊸ cover
gài-shang
盖上
蓋上

crash
xiāng zhuàng
相撞
相撞

crawl
pá
爬
爬

create
chuàng zuò
创作
創作

cross
jiāo chā
交叉
交叉

crush
yā suì; jǐ suì
压碎；挤碎
壓碎；擠碎

★cry
kū; hǎn
哭；喊
哭；喊

★cure
zhì liáo; zhì hǎo
治疗；治好
治療；治好

curl
jüǎn qǚ
卷曲
捲曲

curse
zhòu mà
咒骂
咒罵

㊹ cut 1 with knife   qiē 1 切 (刀) 2 铰 (剪子)
      2 with scissors jioǎ 1 切   2 鉸

D

★damage
sǔn hài
损害
損害

decorate
zhuāng shì
装饰
裝飾

decrease
jiàng dī
降低
降低

deduct
kòu chú
扣除
扣除

defend
bǎo hù
保护
保護

㊺ delay
dān gē
耽搁
耽擱

delete
shān-qü
删去
刪去

㊻ deliver
sòng huò
送货
送貨

★demand
yāo qiú
要求
要求

★deny
fǒu rèn
否认
否認

★depart qǐ chéng	起程 起程	★display zhǎn shì; chén liè	展示；陈列 展示；陳列
depend yī lài	依赖 依賴	dissolve róng jiě	溶解 溶解
47 deposit cún kuǎn	存款 存款	distinguish biàn bié	辨别 辨別
48 design shè jì	设计 設計	disturb dá-rao	打扰 打擾
desire yù wàng	欲望 欲望	divide fēn-kai; chú	分开；除(÷) 分開；除(÷)
detect chá jüé	查觉 查覺	**52** do zuò	做 做
determine jüé dìng	决定 決定	dominate tǒng zhì; zhī pèi	统治；支配 統治；支配
49 develop fā zhǎn	发展 發展	donate jüān zèng	捐赠 捐贈
devote zhuān xīn zhì lì-yü	专心致力于 專心致力於	**53** doubt huái yí	怀疑 懷疑
★die sǐ	死 死	★doze dǎ kē-shui	打瞌睡 打瞌睡
differ from bù tóng-yü...	不同于... 不同於...	drain lòu gān	漏乾 漏乾
dig wā	挖 挖	**54** draw lā; tí kuǎn	拉；提款 拉；提款
digest xiāo-hua	消化 消化	dream zuò mèng	做梦 做夢
dilute chōng dàn	冲淡 沖淡	drill (1hole) 1 **zuān kǒng** (2practice) 2 **cāo liàn**	1 钻孔 2 操练 1 鑽孔 2 操練
★dip zhàn	蘸 蘸	**55** drink hē	喝 喝
★disagree bù tóng yì	不同意 不同意	drip dī gān; dī lòu	滴乾；滴漏 滴乾；滴漏
★disappoint shī wàng	失望 失望	**56** drive kāi chē	开车 開車
50 disapprove bú zàn chéng	不赞成 不贊成	★drop diào luò; diū xià	掉落；丢下 掉落；丟下
51 discuss tǎo lùn	讨论 討論	**57** drown yān-si	淹死 淹死
dispense fēn pèi	分配 分配	**58** dry cā gān; nòng gān	擦干；弄干 擦乾；弄乾

dump	倒掉
dào diào	倒掉
duplicate	复制
fù zhì	複製
(to) dust; dust off	撢（灰尘）
dǎn	撢（灰塵）

E

ease	放松；不费力
fàng sōng; bú fèi lì	放鬆；不費力
⑤⑨eat	吃
chī	吃
edit	编辑
biān jí	編輯
educate	教育
jiào yù	教育
⑥⓪elect	选举
xüán jǔ	選舉
embrace	拥抱
yǒng bào	擁抱
employ	雇用
gù yòng	雇用
⑥①empty	倒干净
dào gān-jing	倒乾淨
enable	才能够；達成
cái néng gòu; dá chéng	才能夠；達成
★enclose	内附
nèi fù	內附
encounter	遭遇
zāo yù	遭遇
⑥②end	结束
jié shù	結束
endanger	波及
pō jí	波及
endure	忍受
rěn shòu	忍受
engage	从事
cóng shì	從事
⑥③enjoy	享受；欣赏
xiǎng shòu; xīn shǎng	享受；欣賞

★enquire	打听
dǎ-ting	打聽
enroll	入学
rù xüé	入學
ensure	保证
bǎo zhèng	保證
⑥④enter	进入
jìn rù	進入
entrap; lead into a trap	坑人
kēng rén	坑人
equal	等于
děng-yü	等於
equip	配备
pèi bèi	配備
erase	擦掉
cā diào	擦掉
err	出差错
chū chà-cuo	出差錯
escape	逃跑
táo pǎo	逃跑
establish	创办
chuàng bàn	創辦
exaggerate	夸张
kuā zhāng	誇張
examine	检查
jiǎn chá	檢查
excel	胜过
shèng guò	勝過
⑥⑤exchange	交换
jiāo huàn	交換
excite	激动；兴奋
jī dòng; xīng fèn	激動；興奮
⑥⑥excuse	原谅
yüán liàng	原諒
exercise	操练
cāo liàn	操練
exert	尽力
jìn lì	盡力
exhaust	排气
pái qì	排氣

| exhibit | 展览作品 |
| zhán lǎn zuò pǐn | 展覽作品 |

| exist | 存在 |
| cún zài | 存在 |

| expand | 扩充；发展 |
| kuò chōng; fā zhǎn | 擴充；發展 |

| expect | 期待 |
| qí dài | 期待 |

| ★expel (1student) 1 kāi chú | 1 开除 2 排散出 |
| (2air) 2 pái sàn-chu | 1 開除 2 排散出 |

| ★expend | 花费 |
| huā fèi | 花費 |

| ★explain | 解释 |
| jiě shì | 解釋 |

| explore | 探索 |
| tàn suǒ | 探索 |

| ⑥⑦export | 出口 |
| chū kǒu | 出口 |

| expose | 暴露；暴光 |
| pù lù; pù guāng | 暴露；曝光 |

| ★express | 表达 |
| biǎo dá | 表達 |

| extend | 伸出 |
| shēn chū | 伸出 |

F

| face | 面对 |
| miàn duì | 面對 |

| fade | 褪色 |
| tùn sè | 褪色 |

| fail | 忘记；未能 |
| wàng-ji; wèi néng | 忘記；未能 |

| fall | 掉下来 |
| diào-xia-lai | 掉下來 |

| ★fasten (1 rope) 1 jì-shang | 1 繫上 2 扣上 |
| (2 button) 2 kòu-shang | 1 繫上 2 扣上 |

| fear | 恐惧 |
| kǒng jù | 恐懼 |

| ★feed | 喂 |
| wèi | 餵 |

| ⑥⑧feel | 感觉 |
| gǎn jüé | 感覺 |

| fetch | 去拿 |
| qù ná | 去拿 |

| fight | 打架 |
| dǎ jià | 打架 |

| file | 归档 |
| guī dǎng | 歸檔 |

| fill | 填满 |
| tián mǎn | 填滿 |

| ⑥⑨find | 发现 |
| fā xiàn | 發現 |

| ⑦⓪finish | 结束；做完 |
| jié shù; zuò wán | 結束；做完 |

| fire (1gun) 1 kāi qiāng 2 开除 | 1 开枪 2 开除 |
| (2job) 2 kāi chú | 1 開槍 2 開除 |

| ⑦①fit | 合适；适合 |
| hé shì; shì hé | 合適；適合 |

| ⑦②fix | 弄好；安装 |
| nòng hǎo; ān zhuāng | 弄好；安裝 |

| flatter | 过奖 |
| guò jiǎng | 過獎 |

| flunk | 不及格 |
| bù jí gé | 不及格 |

| ★flush | 冲水 |
| chōng shuǐ | 沖水 |

| ★fly | 飞 |
| fēi | 飛 |

| fold | 折叠 |
| zhé dié | 折疊 |

| ⑦③follow | 跟随 |
| gēn suí | 跟隨 |

| force | 强迫 |
| qiáng pò | 強迫 |

| forecast | 预测 |
| yù cè | 預測 |

| ⑦④forget | 忘记 |
| wàng jì | 忘記 |

| ⑦⑤forgive | 原谅 |
| yüán liàng | 原諒 |

forward (1 letter) **1zhuǎn jì** 1转寄 2往前
(2 straight) **2wǎng qián** 1轉寄 2往前

freeze
lěng dòng　　　冷冻
　　　　　　　　　冷凍

★① fry **zhá** (2nd tone)　炸 (第二音)
★② bumb **zhà** (4th tone)　炸 (第四音)

G

76 gain　　　　　增加
zēng jiā　　　　增加

gamble　　　　　赌
dǔ　　　　　　賭

77 gather　　　　集合；归纳
jí hé; guī nà　集合；歸納

78 get　　　　　得到
dé-dao　　　　得到

get lost　　　　　滚蛋
gǔn dàn　　　　滾蛋

★ get rid of　　　除掉；斩草除根
chú diào; zhán cǎo chú gēn 除掉；斬草除根

giggle　　　　　傻笑
shǎ xiào　　　傻笑

79 give (1 turn over possession) **1 gěi** 1 给 2 送
(2 gift) **2 sòng** 1 給 2 送

★ glance　　　　大概看一下儿
dà gài kàn yí xiàr　大概看一下兒

glare furiously; gnash　怒视；咬牙切齿
nù shì; yǎo yá qiè chǐ　怒視；咬牙切齒

★glue　　　　　贴
tiē　　　　　貼

80 go　　　　　去
qù　　　　　去

81 go back　　　回去
huí-qù　　　　回去

82 go home　　　回家
huí jiā　　　　回家

83 go out　　　出去
chū-qù　　　　出去

84 go to bed　　去睡觉
qù shuì jiào　去睡覺

85 grab　　　　抓住
zhuā-zhu　　　抓住

graduate　　　　毕业
bì yè　　　　畢業

★grant　　　　批准；允准
pī zhǔn; yǔn zhǔn　批准；允准

86 greet　　　　致意；问候
zhì yì; wèn hòu　致意；問候

grieve　　　　　悲伤
bēi shāng　　　悲傷

grind　　　　　磨碎
mó suì　　　　磨碎

grow　　　　　长大
zhǎng dà　　　長大

★guarantee　　　保证
bǎo zhèng　　　保證

87 guess　　　　猜
cāi　　　　　猜

★guide　　　　引导
yín dǎo　　　引導

H

88 handle　　　处理
chù-li　　　　處理

★happen　　　　发生
fā shēng　　　發生

★hate　　　　　恨；讨厌
hèn; tǎo yàn　恨；討厭

haul　　　　　拖拉
tuō lā　　　　拖拉

89 have; has　　有
yǒu　　　　　有

heal　　　　　治愈；治好
zhì yù; zhì hǎo　治癒；治好

90 hear　　　　听见
tīng-jian　　　聽見

91 help　　　　帮助；救命
bāng-zhu; jiù mìng　幫助；救命

★hide　　　　　藏
cáng　　　　　藏

hijack 劫持
jié chí 劫持

★hint 暗示
àn shì 暗示

★hire 雇用
gù yòng 雇用

★hit 一拳；击中
yì qüán; jí zhòng 一拳；擊中

92 hold 握住；抱住
wò zhù; bào zhù 握住；抱住

hook 钩住
gōu-zhu 鉤住

93 hope 希望
xī wàng 希望

★hug 拥抱一下儿
yōng bào yí xiàr 擁抱一下兒

humiliate 羞辱
xīu rǔ 羞辱

94 hurry 匆忙；赶紧
cōng máng; gán jǐn 匆忙；趕緊

95 hurt 伤害
shāng hài 傷害

I

★identify 识别
shì bié 識別

★ignore 忽略
hū lüè 忽略

illustrate 画图说明
huà tú shuō míng 畫圖說明

impress 深刻印象
shēn kè yìn xiàng 深刻印象

96 improve 改进
gǎi jìn 改進

97 include 包括
bāo kuò 包括

increase 增加
zēng jiā 增加

indicate 显示；表示
xiǎn shì; biǎo shì 顯示；表示

induce 引诱
yǐn yòu 引誘

indulge 沈迷
chén mí 沈迷

infect 传染
chuán rǎn 傳染

★influence 影响
yíng xiǎng 影響

★inform 告知
gào zhī 告知

infuse 注入；灌输
zhù rù; guàn shū 注入；灌輸

inherit 继承
jì chéng 繼承

inject 注射
zhù shè 注射

★injure 损害；受伤
sǔn hài; shòu shāng 損害；受傷

★inquire 打听
dǎ-tīng 打聽

★insert 插入
chā rù 插入

★insist 坚持
jiān chí 堅持

inspect 检查；审查
jiǎn chá; shěn chá 檢查；審查

insult 污辱
wū rǔ 污辱

insure 保证
bǎo zhèng 保證

intend 打算；存心
dǎ suàn; cún xīn 打算；存心

★interest 有兴趣
yǒu xìng-qü 有興趣

interfere 干涉
gān-she 干涉

★interpret 解释；口译
jiě shì; kǒu yì 解釋；口譯

interrupt 打断谈话
dǎ duàn tán huà 打斷談話

| interview | 会见；采访 |
| huì jiàn; cái fǎng | 會見；採訪 |

| intrigue | 阴谋；策划 |
| yīn móu; cè huà | 陰謀；策劃 |

| ★introduce | 介绍 |
| jiè shào | 介紹 |

| intrude | 闯入 |
| chuǎng rù | 闖入 |

| invade | 侵犯 |
| qīn fàn | 侵犯 |

| invent | 发明 |
| fā míng | 發明 |

| invest | 投资 |
| tóu zī | 投資 |

| 98 invite | 邀请 |
| yāo qǐng | 邀請 |

| involve | 牵扯进去 |
| qiān chě jìn-qù | 牽扯進去 |

| 99 iron | 熨烫 |
| yùn tàng | 熨燙 |

| isolate | 隔离 |
| gé lí | 隔離 |

| issue | 发行 |
| fā xíng | 發行 |

J

| 100 join | 参加；连接 |
| cān jiā; lián jiē | 參加；連接 |

| jump | 跳 |
| tiào | 跳 |

K

| 101 keep | 保存；保持 |
| bǎo cún; bǎo chí | 保存；保持 |

| kick | 踢 |
| tī | 踢 |

| kidnap | 绑架 |
| bǎng jià | 綁架 |

| ★kill | 杀死 |
| shā-si | 殺死 |

| 102 kiss | 接吻 |
| jiē wěn | 接吻 |

| ★knock | 敲 |
| qiāo | 敲 |

| 103 know (1 aware) 1 **zhī-dao** | 1 知道 2 认识 |
| (2 recognize) 2 **rèn-shi** | 1 知道 2 認識 |

L

| 104 lack | 缺乏 |
| qūē fá | 缺乏 |

| landing | 着陆 |
| zhuó lù | 著陸 |

| last | 持续 |
| chí xù | 持續 |

| laugh at | 嘲笑 |
| cháo xiào | 嘲笑 |

| ★lay | 放置 |
| fàng zhì | 放置 |

| lead | 领导 |
| líng dǎo | 領導 |

| leak | 漏；漏水 |
| lòu; lòu shuǐ | 漏；漏水 |

| lean | 倾斜；靠 |
| qīng xié; kào | 傾斜；靠 |

| 105 learn | 学 |
| xüé | 學 |

| lease | 契租 |
| qì zū | 契租 |

| 106 leave | 离开；走；动身 |
| lí-kai; zǒu; dòng shēn | 離開；走；動身 |

| lecture | 演讲 |
| yán jiǎng | 演講 |

| legislate | 立法 |
| lì fǎ | 立法 |

| 107 lend | 借给 |
| jiè-gei | 借給 |

| 108 let | 出让；出租 |
| chū ràng; chū zū | 出讓；出租 |

| level | 弄平 |
| nòng píng | 弄平 |

lick tiǎn	舔 舔
★lie tǎng; shuō huǎng	躺；说谎 躺；說謊
lift jǔ-qi; tái-qi	举起；抬起 舉起；擡起
★light dián huǒ; dián dēng	点火；点灯 點火；點燈
⑩ like xǐ-huan	喜欢 喜歡
★limit xiàn dìng; xiàn zhì	限定；限制 限定；限制
link lián jié	连结 連結
list liè biǎo	列表 列表
⑩ listen tīng	听 聽
⑪ live zhù	住 住
load zhuāng zǎi	装载 裝載
locate wèi yú	位于 位於
⑫ lock suǒ-shang	锁上 鎖上
look kàn	看 看
⑬ (let me take a) look ràng-wo qiáo-qiao	讓我瞧瞧 讓我瞧瞧
⑭ lose diū; sàng shī	丢；丧失 丢；喪失
★loosen fàng sōng	放松 放鬆
⑮ love ài	爱 愛
lower jiàng dī	降低 降低

M

⑯ mail jì	寄 寄
maintain wéi chí	维持 維持
⑰ make zhì zào	制造 製造
★making excuses zhǎo jìe kǒu	找藉口 找藉口
★manage chú-li	处理 處理
★marry (for female) jià	嫁 嫁
★marry (for male) qǔ	娶 娶
master jīng tōng yú	精通于 精通於
match xiāng pèi	相配 相配
mate jiāo pèi	交配 交配
⑱ measure liáng	量 量
⑲ meet jiàn miàn; jié shì	见面；结识 見面；結識
melt róng huà	溶化 溶化
memorize jì láo	记牢 記牢
mention tí jí	提及 提及
minus jiǎn qù; jiǎn	减去；减（－） 減去；減（－）
miss méi pèng-dao; cuò guò-le	没碰到；错过了 沒碰到；錯過了
★mistake gǎo cuò-le; nòng cuò-le	搞错了；弄错了 搞錯了；弄錯了
misunderstand wù huì	误会 誤會

★mix
hùn hé
混合
混合

★mop
tuō dì bǎn; cā
拖地板；擦
拖地板；擦

★move
bān jiā; yí dòng
搬家；移动
搬家；移動

multiply
xiāng chéng; chéng
相乘；乘（×）
相乘；乘（×）

murder
móu shā
谋杀
謀殺

mourn
āi dào ; diào sāng
哀悼；吊丧
哀悼；弔喪

N

nag
láo-dao
唠叨
嘮叨

nail
dīng-zhu
钉住
釘住

★near
kào jìn
靠近
靠近

⑫⓪ need
xū yào
需要
需要

★neglect
hū lüè
忽略
忽略

negotiate
xié shāng
协商
協商

nod
diǎn tóu
点头
點頭

note
jì lù
纪录
紀錄

★notice
zhù yì
注意
注意

★notify
tōng zhī
通知
通知

nourish
zī yǎng
滋养
滋養

O

★object
fǎn duì
反对
反對

obliged to you
gǎn jī nín
感激您
感激您

obligated
chī rén zuí ruǎn
吃人嘴软
吃人嘴軟

observe
guān chá
观察
觀察

★occupy
zhàn jǔ; shǐ yòng zhōng
占据；使用中
佔據；使用中

occur
fā shēng
发生
發生

★offend
chù nù
触怒
觸怒

★offer
lǐ ràng; géi yǔ
礼让；给予
禮讓；給予

omit
shěng diào
省掉
省掉

⑫① open
dǎ-kai
打开
打開

★operate
cāo zuò
操作
操作

★oppose
fǎn duì
反对
反對

⑫② order (1 food) diǎn (cài)   1 点（菜）2 订（货）
        (2 goods) dìng (huò)   1 點（菜）2 訂（貨）

⑫③ organize
zǔ-zhi
组织
組織

outrage
jī nù
激怒
激怒

overcome
kè fú
克服
克服

overdo
guò fèn
过分
過分

overturn
diān fù
颠覆
顛覆

★overweigh
guò zhòng
过重
過重

⑫④ owe
qiàn
欠
欠

★own
yōng yǒu
拥有
擁有

P

⑫ pack
dǎ bāo
打包
打包

★paint (1 painting) **huà huà**
(2 furniture) **yóu qī**
1画画 2油漆
1畫畫 2油漆

part
fēn lí
分离
分離

participate
cān yǔ
参与
參與

★pass
guò; chāo guò
过；超过
過；超過

patch
bǔ
补
補

pawn; hock
diǎn; dòng
典；当
典；當

⑫ pay
fù kuǎn
付款
付款

★peel
xiāo pí
削皮
削皮

peep
tōu kuī
偷窥
偷窺

★permit
zhún xǔ
准许
准許

★pick
pá; tiāo xuǎn
扒(扒手)；挑选
扒(扒手)；挑選

⑫ pick up (1 with a car) **jiē**
(2 from ground) **shí qǐ**
1接 2拾起
1接 2拾起

★pile
luò qǐ-lai
摞起来
摞起來

pin
yòng zhēn bié-zhu
用针别住
用針別住

★plan
jì-hua
计画
計畫

plant
zhòng huā
种花
種花

⑫ play
wánr; bàn yǎn
玩儿；扮演
玩兒；扮演

pluck
bá máo
拔毛
拔毛

plug
sāi-zhu; chā chā tóu
塞住；插插头
塞住；插插頭

plus
jiā-shang; jiā
加上；加（+）
加上；加（+）

point
zhǐ-chu
指出
指出

poke
chuō; bō nòng
戳；拨弄
戳；撥弄

★polish
cā liàng
擦亮
擦亮

pop
bào-kai
爆开
爆開

pose
bǎi zī-shi
摆姿势
擺姿勢

⑫ postpone
yán qí
延期
延期

pour
dào; qīng pén
倒；倾盆
倒；傾盆

practice
liàn xí
练习
練習

praise
zàn měi
赞美
讚美

pray
qí dǎo
祈祷
祈禱

precede
lǐng xiān
领先
領先

predict
yù yán
预言
預言

★prefer
bǐ jiào xǐ huān
比较喜欢
比較喜歡

★prepare
zhǔn bèi
准备
準備

prescribe
kāi yào-fang
开药方
開藥方

present
chéng xiàn
呈献
呈獻

preserve
fáng fǔ
防腐
防腐

★press
yā; àn
压；按
壓；按

presume **tuī cè; shè xiǎng**	推测；设想 推測；設想
prevent **fáng zhǐ**	防止 防止
print **yìn shuā**	印刷 印刷
proceed **jiē-zhe shuō**	接著说 接著說
produce **shēng chǎn**	生产 生產
prohibit **jìn zhǐ**	禁止 禁止
⑫⑨ promise **dā yìng; chéng nuò**	答应；承诺 答應；承諾
promote **shēng qiān**	升迁 升遷
★pronounce **fā yīn; xūān chēng**	发音；宣称 發音；宣稱
propose **tí chū jiàn yì**	提出建议 提出建議
prosper **wàng shèng**	旺盛 旺盛
protect **bǎo hù**	保护 保護
★prove **zhèng shí**	证实 證實
provide **tí gōng**	提供 提供
publish **chū bǎn**	出版 出版
⑬⓪ pull **lā**	拉 拉
pull off **tuō diào**	脱掉 脫掉
⑬① punish **chǔ fá**	处罚 處罰
purify **jìng huà**	净化 淨化
⑬② push **tuī**	推 推

| ⑬③ put
fàng | 放
放 |
| ★puzzle
mí huò bù jiě | 迷惑不解
迷惑不解 |

Q

★qualify **hé gé; shèng rèn**	合格；胜任 合格；勝任
quarrel **chǎo jià**	吵架 吵架
quench **píng xí xià-lai**	平息下来 平息下來
★question **zhí wèn**	质问 質問
★quit **bú gàn-le; jiè-le**	不干了；戒了 不幹了；戒了
★quote **yǐn yòng**	引用 引用

R

★raise **shēng; zhàn qǐ-lai**	升；站起来 升；站起來
ramble; stroll **liū-da**	溜达 溜達
rape **qiáng jiān**	强奸 強姦
★reach **dǐ dá**	抵达 抵達
★react **fǎn yìng**	反应 反應
⑬④ read **kàn shū; kàn bào**	看书；看报 看書；看報
realize **tǐ-hui dào**	体会到 體會到
⑬⑤ receive **shōu dào**	收到 收到
recognize **rèn chū-lai**	认出来 認出來
recommend **tuī jiàn**	推荐 推薦

★record jì lù	纪录 紀錄	replace dài tì	代替 代替
recover huī fù	恢复 恢復	reply dá-fu	答复 答復
★reduce jián shǎo	减少 减少	⑭report bào gào	报告 報告
★refer lùn jí; tán dào	论及；谈到 論及；談到	★request qǐng qiú	请求 請求
reflect fǎn yìng	反映 反映	★require děi yào yǒu…	得要有… 得要有…
⑯refuse jù jué	拒绝 拒絕	reserve bǎo liú	保留 保留
regard rèn wéi; dāng zuò	认为；当作 認為；當作	reset chóng xīn pái liè	重新排列 重新排列
★register dēng jì; zhù cè	登记；注册 登記 註冊	resist kàng jù	抗拒 抗拒
★regret hòu huǐ	后悔 後悔	respond zuò chū fǎn yìng	做出反应 做出反應
relate yǒu guān	有关 有關	⑭rest xiū-xi	休息 休息
★relax fàng sōng	放松 放鬆	restore xiū fù; fù zhí	修复；复职 修復；複職
release shì fàng	释放 釋放	result jié-guo; chéng-guo	结果；成果 結果；成果
relieve jiǎn qīng	减轻 减輕	retire tuì xiū	退休 退休
rely yī lài	依赖 依賴	retreat chè tuì	撤退 撤退
⑰remember jì-zhu	记住 記住	★return huí lái	回来 回來
⑱remind tí-xing	提醒 提醒	review fù xí; fù shěn	复习；复审 復習；復審
remove nuó-kai; tuō; zhāi	挪开；脱；摘 挪開；脫；摘	reward chóu bào	酬报 酬報
⑲rent zū	租 租	★ride chéng chē	乘车 乘車
⑭repair xiū-li	修理 修理	★ring (1 door) àn líng (2 telephone) dǎ diàn huà	1按铃 2打电话 1按鈴 2打電話
★repeat chóng-fu	重复 重復	★rise shēng; qǐ lì	升；起立 升；起立

rob qiǎng jié	抢劫 搶劫	search sōu xún	搜寻 搜尋
roll juǎn; gǔn	卷；滚 捲；滾	seduce yǐn yòu	引诱 引誘
rot fǔ làn	腐烂 腐爛	**145** see kàn-jian	看见 看見
rub mó; róu	磨；揉 磨；揉	★seem sì-hu shì…	似乎是… 似乎是…
rule tǒng zhì	统治 統治	seize zhuā-zhu	抓住 抓住
run pǎo	跑 跑	select xuǎn zé	选择 選擇
rush chōng jìn; chōng chuǎng	冲进；冲闯 衝進；衝闖	**146** sell mài	卖 賣
rust shēng xiù	生锈 生銹	send pài qiǎn; sòng	派遣；送 派遣；送

S

		sense yì shì-dao…	意识到… 意識到…
sacrifice xī shēng	牺牲 犧牲	sentence pàn xíng	判刑 判刑
★satisfy mǎn yì; mǎn zú	满意；满足 滿意；滿足	separate fēn lí	分离 分離
143 save (1 life) jiù (2 money) shěng; chú xù	1 救 2 省；储蓄 1 救 2 省；儲蓄	**147** serve fú wù	服务 服務
saw jù-kai	锯开 鋸開	★set shè dìng	设定 設定
144 say shuō	说 說	★settle ān dùn xià-lai	安顿下来 安頓下來
scan sǎo miáo	扫描 掃描	shade zhē bì	遮蔽 遮蔽
scare jīng xià; pà	惊吓；怕 驚嚇；怕	**148** shake yáo	摇 搖
scatter sàn bù	散布 散佈	shame xiū kuì	羞愧 羞愧
scold chì zé; zé mà	斥责；责骂 斥責；責罵	share fēn xiǎng	分享 分享
scratch zhuā; sāo	抓；搔 抓；搔	sharpen mó kuài; mó lì	磨快；磨利 磨快；磨利
screw (see wrench and twist) nǐng-jin-qù	拧进去（螺丝钉） 擰進去（螺絲釘）	**149** shave guā hú-zi	刮胡子 刮鬍子

shed liú chū	流出 流出	⑭ speak shuō	说 說	
shelter bì hù	庇护 庇護	speed jiā sù	加速 加速	
shift zhuǎn huàn; zhuǎn biàn	转换;转变 轉換;轉變	⑮ spell pīn zì	拼字 拼字	
shine shǎn liàng	闪亮 閃亮	⑯ spend huā fèi	花费 花費	
shiver chàn dǒu	颤抖 顫抖	spit tǔ tán; tú kóu shuǐ	吐痰;吐口水 吐痰;吐口水	

spoil (1child) **guàn huài-le** 1 惯坏了 2 变质了
(2food) **biàn zhí-le** 1 慣壞了 2 變質了

shock diàn jí; xiū kè	电击;休克 電擊;休克	sponsor zàn zhù	赞助 贊助
shoot shè	射 射	sprain niǔ shāng	扭伤 扭傷
shorten jián duǎn	剪短 剪短	spray pēn	喷 噴
shout dà hǎn; dà jiào	大喊;大叫 大喊;大叫	spread mǒ-kai	抹开 抹開
⑮⓪ show gěi-ren kàn	给人看 給人看	sprinkle (1salt) (2 water) sǎ	1 撒 2 洒 1 撒 2 灑
show off xüàn yào	炫耀 炫耀	squat dūn	蹲 蹲
★shrink suō; suō shuǐ	缩;缩水 縮;縮水	squeeze jǐ	挤 擠
shut guān; bì	关;闭 關;閉	stab cì	刺 刺
⑮① sleep shuì	睡 睡	stain wū rǎn	污染 污染
slip huá dǎo	滑倒 滑倒	⑮⑦ stand zhàn-zhe	站著 站著
smell (verb) wén; xiù	闻;嗅 聞;嗅	stare at dèng-zhe yǎn-jing kàn	瞪著眼睛看 瞪著眼睛看
⑮② smile wéi xiào	微笑 微笑	⑮⑧ start kāi shǐ	开始 開始
⑮③ smoke xī yān	吸烟 吸菸	starve è biǎn-le	饿扁了 餓扁了
smuggle zǒu sī	走私 走私	state chén shù	陈述 陳述
sort (sort out) fēn lèi (tiāo chū)	分类(挑出) 分類(挑出)		

57

⑮⑨ stay **tíng liú**	停留 停留	
★ steal **tōu**	偷 偷	
sting **cì** (by pin); **zhē** (by bee); **dīng** (by musq.)	刺;螫;叮 刺;螫;叮	
★ stink **fā chòu**	发臭 發臭	
★ stir **jiǎo-huo**	搅和 攪和	
⑯⓪ stop **tíng zhǐ**	停止 停止	
★ store **chú cáng**	储藏 儲藏	
straighten **lā zhí**	拉直 拉直	
strain **lā jǐn**	拉紧 拉緊	
strand **gē qiǎn**	搁浅 擱淺	
strenghten **jiā qiáng**	加强 加強	
★ stretch **shēn cháng; shēn zhí**	伸长;伸直 伸長;伸直	
strike **yòng mù gùn dǎ; jí**	用木棍打;击 用木棍打;擊	
strike (a match) **huá huǒ chái**	划(火柴) 划(火柴)	
on strike **bà gōng**	罢工 罷工	
strip **tuō guāng**	脱光 脱光	
study **niàn shū; dú shū**	念书;读书 念書;讀書	
submit **tí chú**	提出 提出	
subscribe **dìng yüè**	订阅 訂閱	
substract **jiǎn-qù**	减去 減去	

suck **xī**	吸 吸	
sue **kòng gào**	控告 控告	
suffer **dé bìng; méng shòu**	得病;蒙受 得病;蒙受	
suggest **jiàn yì**	建议 建議	
★ suit **shì hé**	适合 適合	
summarize **zhāi yào**	摘要 摘要	
supervise **jiān dū**	监督 監督	
supply **gōng yìng**	供应 供應	
support **zhī yüán**	支援 支援	
★ surprise **jīng xǐ**	惊喜 驚喜	
surrender **tóu xiáng**	投降 投降	
surround **huán rào**	环绕 環繞	
survey **cè liáng ; fǔ kàn**	测量;俯瞰 測量;俯瞰	
survive **cún huó**	存活 存活	
suspect **huái yí**	怀疑 懷疑	
swallow **tūn**	吞 吞	
swear **fā shì**	发誓 發誓	
★ sweat **chū hàn**	出汗 出汗	
★ sweep **sǎo dì**	扫地 掃地	
★ swim **yóu yǒng**	游泳 游泳	

swing **yáo bǎi**	摇摆 搖擺	throw **rēng; pāo**	扔；抛 扔；抛
switch **zhuǎn huàn**	转换 轉換	★tie (1 big articles 大件) **kǔn** 1 捆 2 绑 (2 small articles 小件) **bǎng** 1 捆 2 綁	
symbolize **xiàng zhēng**	象徵 象徵	tolerate **róng rěn**	容忍 容忍
sympathize **tóng qíng**	同情 同情	torture **zhé mó**	折磨 折磨

T

⑯take **ná; chèng**	拿；乘（车） 拿；乘（車）	total **zǒng gòng**	总共 總共
		★touch **mō; pèng**	摸；碰 摸；碰
take 20 efforts **fèi jìn**	费劲 費勁	★tour **lǚ yóu**	旅游 旅遊
⑯talk **tán huà**	谈话 談話	track **zhuī zōng**	追踪 追蹤
⑯teach **jiào**	教 教	trade **jiāo yì**	交易 交易
★tear **sī**	撕 撕	train **shòu xùn**	受训 受訓
tease **dòu**	逗 逗	transfer **zhuǎn xué; zhuǎn chē**	转学；转车 轉學；轉車
⑯tell **gào sù**	告诉 告訴	⑯translate **fān-yi**	翻译 翻譯
tense **jǐn bēng; jǐn zhāng**	紧绷；紧张 緊繃；緊張	transmit **chuán sòng**	传送 傳送
terminate **zhōng zhǐ**	终止 終止	transport **yùn shū**	运输 運輸
terrify **kǒng bù**	恐怖 恐怖	⑯travel **lǚ xíng**	旅行 旅行
test **shì yàn**	试验 試驗	treasure **zhēn xí**	珍惜 珍惜
testify **zuò zhèng**	作证 作證	treat **duì dài**	对待 對待
⑯thank **xiè**	谢谢 謝謝	trick **hǒng piàn**	哄骗 哄騙
★think **xiǎng**	想 想	trip **bàn dǎo**	绊倒 絆倒
threaten **kǒng hè**	恐吓 恐嚇	trouble **má-fan; dá rǎo**	麻烦；打扰 麻煩；打擾

★trust
xìn rèn
信任
信任

⓰ try
shì
试
試

⓱ turn
zhuǎn
转
轉

⓲ turn off
guān dēng
关灯
關燈

⓳ turn on
kāi dēng
开灯
開燈

twist (see screw and wrench)
nǐng wān; nǐng-zai yì qǐ
拧弯；拧在一起
擰彎；擰在一起

type
dǎ zì
打字
打字

U

unbind
sōng-kai
松开
鬆開

★understand
dǒng
懂
懂

unite
lián hé
联合
聯合

unload
xiè huò
卸货
卸貨

★unlock
kāi suǒ
开锁
開鎖

★unzip (see zip up)
lā-kai lā liàn
拉开拉炼
拉開拉煉

urge
cuī cù
催促
催促

⓲ use
yòng
用
用

V

vacuum
zhēn kōng xī fǎ
真空吸法
真空吸法

value
jià zhí
价值
價值

view
guān kàn
观看
觀看

★visit
bài huì; cān guān
拜会；参观
拜會；參觀

volunteer
dāng yì gōng
当义工
當義工

vote
tóu piào
投票
投票

W

⓭ ★wait; wait for
děng; děng hòu
等 ；等候
等 ；等候

★wait on
cì-hou
伺候
伺候

★wake
xǐng lái
醒来
醒來

⓮ walk
zǒu lù
走路
走路

⓯ want (money, pen...)
yào (noun) (qián, bǐ...)
要... （名词）
要... （筆；錢...）

⓰ want to (cry, buy...)
xiǎng yào (verb) (kū, mǎi...)
想要... （动词）
想要...(買；哭...)

warn
jǐng gào
警告
警告

⓱ wash
xǐ
洗
洗

⓲ waste
làng fèi
浪费
浪費

★watch
kān-shǒu;; níng shì
看守；凝视
看守；凝視

wave
huī shǒu
挥手
揮手

weaken
xūē ruò; jiǎn ruò
削弱；减弱
削弱；減弱

⓳ wear
chuān (clothes) ; 2 dài (attachments)
1穿2戴
1穿2戴

★weigh
chēng zhòng-liang
称重量
稱重量

⓰ welcome
huān yíng
欢迎
歡迎

⓱ wet
nòng shī
弄湿
弄濕

widen **jiā kuān**	加宽 加寬	
⑱ win **yíng dé**	赢得 贏得	
wipe **cā; mǒ**	擦；抹 擦；抹	
⑱ wish **dàn yüàn; gāi-you dūo hǎo**	但愿；该有多好 但願；該有多好	
withdraw **chè huí**	撤回 撤回	
witness **mù jí**	目击 目擊	
⑱ work **gōng-zuo**	工作 工作	
★worry **dān xīn**	担心 擔心	
worship **chóng bài**	崇拜 崇拜	
wrap **bāo-qi-lai**	包起来 包起來	

wrinch (see screw and twist) **bān**	扳（用手与臂） 扳	
wrinkle **qǐ zhòu wén**	起皱纹 起皺紋	
⑱ write **xiě**	写 寫	

Y

yawn **dǎ hē-qian**	打呵欠 打呵欠	
yearn **kě-wang**	渴望 渴望	
yell **hū hǎn**	呼喊 呼喊	
yield **shōu yì; xiào guǒ**	收益；效果 收益；效果	

Z

★zip up (see unzip) **lā-shang lā liànr**	拉上拉炼儿 拉上拉煉兒	

One Two Three Units, Weights & Measures

一二三 與 度量衡（天天用）

The Chinese numbers, numerals, units, weights and measures use the same units of measurements as English. e.g.: 5 pounds (of) meat; two bottles (of) wine; or five feet (of) rope. Even the word order in which we speak English is the same as in Chinese, except that the Chinese drop out the "of", e.g.: "two can beer" instead of "two cans of beer"; "four pack chewing gum" instead of "four packs of chewing gum".

Furthermore, Chinese do not use plural forms of objects, because the numeral is meant to specify that.   A complete list of units follows

★ In Chinese, the numbers "1,2,3..." are purely digits which can only be used in telephone numbers. This is unlike English, in which numerals are also adjectives and can indicate "**quantity**" or "**amount**".

Therefore, the phrase "**3,2 egg**" sounds strange to the Chinese just like "**two bacon**" to the westerners.

In order to make a Chinese numeral into an adjective, a special word called a "**numeric adjective**" must be placed between the numeral and the noun.

ex.: two "个ge" egg

The "**个ge**" is a commonly used numeric adjective for general nouns. (See P. 71 ★ ; P. 76 ★, Group 5)

★**two** (as a digital number) **èr** (never say 两 liǎng)	二(2) 二 (see P. 67★)
three (as a digital number) **sān**	三(3) 三
four (as a digital number) **sì**	四(4) 四
five (as a digital number) **wǔ**	五(5) 五
six (as a digital number) **liù**	六(6) 六
seven (as a digital number) **qī**	七(7) 七
eight (as a digital number) **bā**	八(8) 八
nine (as a digital number) **jiǔ**	九(9) 九
ten (as a digital number) **shí**	十(10) 十
number (No.) **dì; hòu mǎr; hòu**	第;号码儿;号 第;號碼兒;號
dial **bō**	拨 撥

zero; nought; and **líng** (as a digital number)	零(0) 零
★**one** (as a digital number) **yī** (always pronunces 1st tone)	一(1) 一 (not yí or yì)

電話號碼
Phone number

09 - 8765 - 4321
líng jiǔ - bā qī liù wǔ - sì sān èr yī
零九 - 八七六五 - 四三二一

❶ May I have your telephone number?
Beg ask you's phone no. what number
qǐng wèn nín-de diàn huà hào mǎr jǐ hào
请问 您的 电话 号码儿 几号?

❷ What is your mobile phone number?
You's mobile phone no. what number?
nín-de xíng dòng diàn huà jǐ hào
您的 行动 电话 几号?

❸ My cellular phone no. is 0935-312-344
I's hand phone number is 0935-312-344
wǒ-de shǒu jī hào mǎr shì …
我的 手机 号码儿 是 ….

❹ What is the local area code number?
Local area code number what number?
běn dì-de qū yù biān hào jǐ hào
本地的 区域 编号 几号

❺ Our area code number is 201.
We's area code no. is 201
wǒ-men-de qū yù biān hào shì èr líng yī
我們的 区域 编号 是 二零一

❻ My office telephone number is 2001-3444
I company telephone number is
wǒ gōng sī diàn huà hào mǎ shì
我 公司 电话 号码 是
èr líng líng yī - sān sì sì sì
二 零 零 二，三 四 四 四

❼ What is your extension number?
You's extension number what number
nín-de fēn jī hào mǎr jǐ hào
您的 分机 号码儿 几号?

❽ Dial "zero" for operator.
Switchboard please dial "0"
zǒng jī qǐng bō líng
总机 请 拨 「零」

❾ This is my home telephone number.
This is I home's telephone number
zhè-shi wǒ jiā-de diàn huà hào mǎr
这是 我家的 电话 号码儿。

❿ I'll give you my private telephone No.
I have I's private tele. number give you
wó bǎ wǒ-de sī rén diàn huà hào mǎr géi-ni
我 把 我的 私人 电话 号码儿 给你。

⓫ You can always find me thru this number.
You beat this telephone definitely
ní dǎ zhè-zhi diàn huà yí dìng
你 打 这只 电话 一定
able find I
zhǎo-de dào -wo
找得到 我。

⓬ You can always leave a message.
Find not I, you can leave message
zhǎo bú dào-wo, ní ké yǐ liú yán
找不到 我，你 可以 留言。

⓭ Would you find Mr. D's phone no. for me?
Please substitute I check Mr. Doe's
qǐng tì-wo zhá-yi xiàr Doe xiān-sheng-de
请 替我 查一下儿 竇先生的
phone no. , would you
diàn huà hào mǎr, hǎo-ma?
电话 号码儿， 好吗?

⓮ What is Mr. Doe's room no. please?
Beg ask Mr. Doe live what no. room
qǐng wèn D. xiān-sheng zhù jǐ hào fáng jiān
请问 竇先生 住 几号 房间

⓯ Please connect me with Room 811.
Please for I connect 811 no. room
qǐng gěi wǒ jiē bā yī yī hào fáng jiān
请 给我接 八一一号 房间

⓰ My zip code is N.Y. 10954
I's post area code is NY 10954
wǒ-de yóu dì qū yù shì NY 10954
我的 邮递区域 是 NY 一零九五四

See Telephone Dialogue, Group 41C.

eleven (ten-one)	十一(11)
shí yī	十一
twelve (ten-two)	十二(12)
shí èr	十二

★The above 12 numerals are very useful. For example, just attach one single sound like "**yüè** 月 month" to the end of any of the 12 numerals, you'll get the English words of the 12 months. e.g.:

two "**yüè**" is February. (èr yüè 二月)
five "**yüè**" is May. (wǔ yüè 五月)
six "**yüè**" is June. (liù yüè 六月)
ten "**yüè**" is October. (shí yüè 十月)
(See Chap. 30, month, day 年月日)

numeral; numerical	数字；数字的
shù zì; shù zì-de	數字；數字的
thirteen (ten three)	十三(13)
shí sān	十三
fourteen (ten four)	十四(14)
shí sì	十四
fifteen (ten five)	十五(15)
shí wǔ	十五
sixteen (ten six)	十六(16)
shí liù	十六
nineteen (ten nine)	十九(19)
shí jiǔ	十九
twenty (two-ten)	二十(20)
èr shí	二十
twenty-one (two-ten one)	二十一(21)
èr-shi yī	二十一
twenty-six (two-ten six)	二十六(26)
èr-shi liù	二十六
thirty (three-ten)	三十(30)
sān shí	三十
thirty-five (three-ten five)	三十五(35)
sān-shi wǔ	三十五

forty (four-ten)	四十(40)
sì shí	四十
fifty (five-ten)	五十(50)
wǔ shí	五十
point; dot (o'clock)	点；点钟
diǎn; diǎn zhōng	點；點鐘
how many point (what time)	幾點？
jí diǎn	幾點？
hour	小时；鐘頭
xiǎo shí; zhōng tóu	小時；鐘頭
★ half = half an hour; half a dollar 半
bàn   (see P. 68★ a half) 半
minute (′)	分；分钟
fēn; fēn zhōng	分；分鐘
second (″)	秒；秒钟
miǎo; miǎo zhōng	秒；秒鐘

幾點 What time

❶ What time is it?
Now   how many point?
<u>xiàn zài</u>   <u>jí diǎn</u>
现在   几点？

❷ What time do you have?
<u>You's</u> <u>watch</u> <u>how many point?</u>
<u>nǐ-de</u>   <u>biǎo</u>   <u>jí diǎn</u>
你的   表   几点？

❸ It is ten-thirty in the morning.
<u>Now</u> is <u>morning</u> 10 point <u>half.</u>
<u>xiàn zài</u> <u>shì</u> <u>zǎo-shang</u> <u>shí diǎn bàn</u>
现在   是   早上   十点半。

❹ It is ten p.m. in New York.
<u>Now</u> <u>New York</u> <u>is</u> <u>evening</u> ten <u>o'clock</u>
<u>xiàn zài</u> <u>niǔ yüè</u> <u>shì</u> <u>wǎn-shang</u> <u>shí diǎn</u>
现在   紐約   是   晚上   十点。

❺ It is 40 seconds till midnight.
<u>Now</u> is <u>night</u> <u>lack</u> 40 <u>second</u> to 12 <u>point</u>
<u>xiàn zài</u> <u>shì</u> <u>yè-li</u> <u>chà</u> <u>sì-shi miǎo</u> <u>shí èr diǎn</u>
现在 是 夜里 差   四十秒   十二点。

❻ It's two-ten in the afternoon.
<u>Now</u> <u>is</u> <u>afternoon</u> 2 <u>point</u> 10 <u>minute</u>

xiàn zài shì xià-wu liáng diǎn shí fēn
现在 是 下午 两点 十分。

⑦ I'll call you at midnight sharp.

me   midnight   sharp   give you
wó   wǔ yè shí èr dián zhěng   géi-ni
我   午夜十二点   整   給妳

beat telephone.
dǎ   diàn huà
打   電話。

⑧ It's noon.

Now   is   noon   12 point
xiàn zài   shì   zhōng-wu   shí èr   diǎn
现在   是   中午   十二   点。

⑨ It's six o'clock sharp.

Now   is   six point   exactly
xiàn zài   shì   liù diǎn   zhěng
现是   是   六点   整。

⑩ What time is your flight?

You's   flight   how many point   up fly?
nǐ-de   bān jī   jí diǎn   qǐ fēi
你的   班机   几点   起飞？

⑪ The bus leaves every hour on the hour.

Bus every hour one trip, exact point leave
gōng chē   méi xiǎo shí   yì bān,
公车   每 小时   一班,
méi   zháng diǎn   kāi chē
每   整点   开车。

⑫ The train is leaving in one minute.

Train   still have   1   minute   then drive
huǒ chē   hái yǒu   yī   fēn zhōng   jiù   kāi-le
火车   还有   二   分钟   就   开了

⑬ Is this standard time?

This is   standard   time   (ma?)
zhè shì   biāo zhǔn   shí jiān   mā
这 是   标准   时间   吗

⑭ What is the local time?

Local   time   now   how many point
běn dì   shí jiān   xiàn zài   jí diǎn?
本地   时间   现在   几点？

⑮ We use the Day light Saving Time here.

We   here   is   use   summer time
wǒ-men   zhè-li   shì   yòng   xià lìng shí jiān
我们   这里   是   用   夏令 时间。

⑯ She will be five minutes late.

he/she   will   late   five   minute   arrive
tā   yào   wǎn   wǔ   fēn zhōng   dào
他/她   要   晚   五   分钟   到

⑰ One-oh-seven in the morning.

Daybreak   1 point   petty   7 minute
líng chén   yì diǎn   líng   qī fēn
凌晨   一点   零   七分

⑱ I'm sorry, I'm in a hurry.

Sorry,   I   am   chase   time
bào qiàn,   wǒ   zài   gǎn   shí jiān
抱歉,   我   在   赶   时间。

⑲ I'm pressed for time.

me   time   not enough
wǒ   shí jiān   bú gòu-le
我   时间   不 够了。

⑳ I've got to go.

I   'v got to   walk   no other way
wǒ   fēi   zǒu   bù kě
我   非   走   不可

㉑ I'm already late.

I   now   already   late
wǒ   xiàn zài   yǐ jīng   wǎn-le
我   现在   已经   晚了

㉒ Or I'll miss the train.

Otherwise   train   then   drove
bù rán   huǒ chē   jiù   kāi-le
不然   火车   就   开了

㉓ You still have one hour and 10 minutes.

You   still have   one   hour   petty   10 minute
nǐ   hái yǒu   yì xǎo shí   líng   shí fēn
你   还有   一小时   零   十分。

(See Group 30B Clocks & Watches and
Group 44B Times & Appointments.)

See Group **44A; B; C, Year, Day, Times, & Appointments, Holidays, Occasions.**

eighty-one (**eight-ten one**) 八十一(81)
bā-shí yī 八十一

ninety-six (**nine-ten six**) 九十六(96)
jiǔ-shí liù 九十六

hundred 百(單位)
bǎi (unit) 百

thousand 千(單位)
qiān (unit) 千

10-thousand 万(單位)
wàn (unit) 萬

16 (10-thousand); (16 wàn)十六万
shí liù (wàn) (16, 0000) 十六萬

million (hundred-**wàn**) 百万(單位)
bǎi wàn (unit) 百萬

10 million (thousand-**wàn**)千万
qiān wàn 千萬

100 million 亿(單位)
yì (unit) 億

billion (ten-**yì**) 十亿
shí yí 十億

trillion (one-**zhào**) 兆(單位)
zhào (unit) 兆

one dollar (one piece silver) 一元；一块錢
yì yuán; yí kuài qián 一元；一塊錢

ten cents (like a dime) 一毛錢；一角
yì máo qián; yì jiáo 一毛錢；一角

seven cents 七分錢
qī fēn qián 七分錢

petty cash 零钱
líng qián 零錢

discount 打折
dǎ zhé 打折

15% discount (price×0.85)打八五折
dǎ bā wǔ zhé 打八五折

10% discount (price×0.90) 打九折
dá jiǔ zhé 打九折

How much

In Chinese, it is "How much money?"

See Group **38A, Banking**

❶ How much is it in Renminbi?
<u>Altogether</u> <u>how much money</u> <u>Renminbi</u>
yí gòng **duō-shao qián** **Rén Mín Bì**
一共 多少钱 人民币

❷ Twelve dollars and a half
<u>Twelve</u> <u>piece</u> <u>half</u>
shí èr **kuài** **bàn**
十二 块 半 (see P.64★half)

❸ It's 60 dollars and 95 cents.
<u>Altogether</u> <u>sixty</u> <u>piece</u> <u>nine</u> <u>10-cent</u> <u>five</u>
yí gong **liù shí** **kuài** **jiǔ** **máo** **wǔ**
一共 六十 块 九 毛 五

❹ Plus 13 percent tax.
<u>Plus</u> <u>percent</u> <u>13's</u> <u>tax</u>
wài jiā **bǎi fēn zhī** **shí sān-de** **shuì**
外加 百分之 十三的 税。

❺ Plus 10 percent service charge.
<u>Plus</u> <u>percent 10</u> <u>service</u> <u>fee</u>
wài jiā **yì chéngr** **fú wù** **fèi**
外加 一成儿 服务 费。

❻ There's a 20 percent handling charge.
<u>Inside</u> <u>include</u> <u>percent 20</u> <u>formality</u> <u>fee</u>
lǐ-mian **bāo kuò** **liǎng chéngr** **shǒu xǔ fèi**
里面 包括 两成儿 手续费。

❼ It's 5 thousand 2 hundred 73 dollars.
<u>shì</u> <u>wǔ qiān</u> <u>liáng bǎi</u> <u>qī-shi sān</u> <u>kuài qián</u>
是 五千 两百 七十三 块錢

❽ How about a discount?
<u>Knock down a</u> <u>discount</u> <u>!?</u>
dǎ-ge **zhé kòu** **-ba**
打個 折扣 吧

❾ Fifty percent off. (knock off 50%)
<u>dǎ</u> <u>duì zhé</u> (price multiplys 0.5)
打 對折 (fold it in two halves)

⑩ figured it wrong; miscalculated
suàn　　cuò-le
算　　　错了

⑪ It is almost　50 billian　Yen
chà-bu duō　wú bǎi yì　Rì Bì
差不多　　　五百亿　　　日幣

English	Simplified / Traditional
unit dān wèi	单位 單位
weight zhòng liàng	重量 重量
weights and measures dù liàng héng	度量衡 度量衡
length cháng duǎn; qí jiān	长短；期间 長短；期間
width kuān zhǎi	宽窄 寬窄
lineal (linear) measure cháng dù	长度 長度
broad measure kuò dù	阔度 闊度
height gāo dù	高度 高度
thickness hòu dù	厚度 厚度
depth shēn dù	深度 深度
size chǐ cùn	尺寸 尺寸
square measure miàn jī	面积 面積
cubic measure tǐ jī; róng jī	体积：容积 體積：容積
liquid measure yè liàng	液量 液量
dry measure gān liàng	乾量 乾量
measure of capacity róng liàng	容量 容量
circular measure hú dù	弧度 弧度

English	Simplified / Traditional
angular measure jiǎo dù	角度 角度
temperature wēn dù	温度 溫度
degree dù shù	度数 度數
below zero líng dù yǐ xià	零度以下 零度以下
freezing point bīng diǎn	冰点 冰點
boiling point fèi diǎn	沸点 沸點
melting point róng diǎn	融点 融點
point diǎn-zi	点子 點子
dot xiǎo yuán diǎnr	小圆点儿 小圓點兒
bale dà bāo	大包 大包
circle yüán qüān	圆圈 圓圈
diameter zhí jìng	直径 直徑
radius bàn jìng	半径 半徑

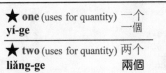

★ **one** (uses for quantity) yí-ge	一个 一個
★ **two** (uses for quantity) liǎng-ge	两个 兩個

English	Simplified / Traditional
a ; an ge; yí-ge (never say yī-ge)	个；一个 個；一個
several háo jǐ gè	好几个 好幾個
some yì xiē; sháo xǔ	一些；少许 一些；少許
very little yì diǎn diǎn	一点点 一點點

a few **jǐ-ge; sì wǔ-ge**	幾個; 四五个 幾個; 四五個	even number **shuāng shùr**	双数儿 雙數兒
a couple of **liǎng sān-ge**	兩個; 兩三个 兩個; 兩三個	category **lèi bié**	类别 類別
★ a half; half a (see P.64★half) **yí bàn; bàn-ge**	一半; 半个 一半; 半個	kind **zhǒng lèi**	种类 種類
a part of it **yí bù-fen**	一部分 一部分	individual **gè tǐ; gè rén**	个体; 个人 個體; 個人
the whole **zhěng gèr-de**	整个儿的 整個兒的		

altogether
yí gòng 一共
一共

a trip
yí tàng 一趟
一趟

once
yí cì; yì huí 一次; 一回
一次; 一回

twice
liǎng cì 两次
兩次

three times
sān cì 三次
三次

four times
sì cì 四次
四次

again
zài cì 再次
再次

repeat
chóng fù 重复
重復

each time
měi cì 每次
每次

always
lǎo-shi 老是
老是

often
cháng cháng 常常
常常

double
shuāng bèi; jiā bèi 双倍; 加倍
雙倍; 加倍

five-fold
wǔ bèi 五倍
五倍

six times
liù bèi 六倍
六倍

odd number
dān shùr 单数儿
單數兒

When ⟶ is used for measurements
or units it's pronounced with 2nd or 4th tone

➤ **For Easy Detection, the following**
(yí)s in blue indicate 2nd tone
(yì)s in black indicate 4th tone

a pound (lb.) of beef (454 gms.) 一磅
yí bàng (niú ròu) 一磅（牛肉）

a catty (Chinese) of flour (1.33 lbs.) 一斤
yì jīn (miàn fěn) 一斤（麵粉）

an ounce (oz.) of ginseng 一兩（人参）
yì liǎng (rén shēn) 一兩（人參）

a metric ton (M.T.) of salt 一公噸（盐）
yì gōng-dùn (yén) 一公噸（鹽）

a kilogram (kg.) of rice 一公斤（米）
yì gōng jīn (mǐ) 一公斤（米）

a gram (gm.) of essence 一公克（香精）
yì gōng kè (xiāng jīng) 一公克（香精）

a milligram (mg.) of MSG 一公絲（味精）
yì gōng sī (wèi jīng) 一公絲（味精）

a foot (same feet) of brocade 一呎（锦缎）
yì chǐ (jǐn duàn) 一呎（錦緞）

five feet (same foot) of satin 五呎（缎子）
wú chǐ (duàn-zi) 五呎（緞子）

an inch of gold chain 一吋（金链子）
yí cùn (jīn liàn-zi) 一吋（金鏈子）

a meter (m.) of lace 一公尺（花边儿）
yì gōng chǐ (huā biānr) 一公尺（花邊兒）

a yard (yd.) **of material** **yì mǎ (yī liào)**	一码（衣料） 一碼（衣料）	**a piece of strawberry pie** **yí kuài (cǎo méi pài)**	一块（草莓派） 一塊（草莓派）
a centimeter (cm.) **of** **yì gōng fēn**	一公分 一公分	**a slice of steak** (thick & large) **yí piàn (niú pái)**	一片（牛排） 一片（牛排）
a mile of mountain road **yì lǐ (shān lù)**	一哩（山路） 一哩（山路）	**a slice of bacon** (thin & small) **yí piànr (xián ròu)**	一片儿（咸肉） 一片兒（鹹肉）
a kilometer (km.) **of wire** **yì gōng lǐ (diàn xiàn)**	一公里（电线） 一公里（電線）	**a bouquet of roses** **yí shù (méi guì huā)**	一束（玫瑰花） 一束（玫瑰花）
a square meter (m2) **yì píng fāng gōng chǐ**	一平方公尺 一平方公尺	**a pile of newspapers** **yí luò (bào zhǐ)**	一摞（报纸） 一摞（報紙）
a sq. mile **yì píng fāng lǐ**	一平方哩 一平方哩	**a coat of paint** **yì céng (yóu qī)**	一层（油漆） 一層（油漆）
a cubic (cu.) **yí lì fāng**	一立方 一立方	**a 3-layer ice cream** (密叠) **sān céng-de (bīng qí lín)**	三层的（冰淇淋） 三層的（冰淇淋）
a cubic inch (cu.in.) **yí lì fāng cùn**	一立方寸 一立方寸	**a 3-tier cake** **sān céng-de (dàn gāo)**	三层的蛋糕（高架式） 三層的蛋糕（高架式）
a cubic centimeter (c.c) **yí lì fāng gōng fēn**	一立方公分 一立方公分	**a package of gifts** **yì bāo guǒ (lǐ wù)**	一包裹（礼物） 一包裹（禮物）
a liter (l.) **of milk** **yì gōng shēng (niú nǎi)**	一公升（牛奶） 一公升（牛奶）	**a pack of toothpick** **yì xiǎo bāor (yá qiānr)**	一小包儿（牙签儿） 一小包兒（牙籤兒）
a ton of coal **yí dùn (méi)**	一噸（煤） 一噸（煤）	**a handful of soil** **yì bǎ (ti)**	一把（土） 一把（土）
an acre of land **yì mǔ (dì)**	一亩（地） 一畝（地）	★ **a box of chocolate** **yì hér (qiǎo kè lì)**	一盒儿（巧克力） 一盒兒（巧克力）
a set of tools **yì zǔ (gōng jù)**	一组（工具） 一組（工具）	**a carton of cigarettes** **yì tiáor (xiāng yān)**	一条儿（香烟） 一條兒（香煙）
a page (P.) **yí yè**	一頁 一頁	**a loaf of bread** **yì tiáo (miàn bāo)**	一条（面包） 一條（麵包）
a sheet of stationery **yì zhāng (xìn zhǐ)**	一张（信纸） 一張（信紙）	**a case of wine** **yì xiāng (pú-tao jiǔ)**	一箱（葡萄酒） 一箱（葡萄酒）
a ream of paper **yì lǐng (zhǐ)**	一令（纸） 一令（紙）	**a jar of jam** **yí guànr (guǒ jiàng)**	一罐儿（果酱） 一罐兒（果醬）
a line of words **yì háng (zì)**	一行（字） 一行（字）	**a bottle of vinegar** **yì píngr (cù)**	一瓶儿（醋） 一瓶兒（醋）
a roll of wallpaper (large) **yì juǎn (bì zhǐ)**	一卷（壁纸） 一卷（壁紙）	**a bowl of noodles** **yì wǎn (miàn)**	一碗（面） 一碗（面）
a roll of film (small) **yì juǎnr (jiāo piàn)**	一卷儿（胶片） 一卷兒（膠片）	**a side dish of peas** **yì xiǎo diér (wān dòu)**	一小碟儿（豌豆） 一小碟兒（豌豆）
a bar of soap **yí kuàir (féi zào)**	一块儿（肥皂） 一塊兒（肥皂）	**a dish of cookies** **yì dié (xiǎó xī diǎn)**	一碟（小西点） 一碟（小西點）

单位

4

Units

69

| a plate of fried rice | 一盘 (炒饭) |
| yì pán (chǎo fàn) | 一盤 (炒飯) |

| a platter of roast chicken | 一大盘 (烤鸡) |
| yí dà pán (kǎo jī) | 一大盤 (烤雞) |

| a trayful of food | 一托盘 (吃的) |
| yì tūo pán (chī-de) | 一託盤 (吃的) |

| a kettle of boiling water | 一壶 (开水) |
| yì hú (kāi shuǐ) | 一壺 (開水) |

| a pot of millet gruel | 一锅 (小米儿粥) |
| yì guō (xiáo mǐr zhōu) | 一鍋 (小米兒粥) |

| a cup of coffee (带把手) | 一杯 (咖啡) |
| yì bēi (kā fēi) | 一杯 (咖啡) |

| a glass of milk (玻璃杯) | 一杯 (牛奶) |
| yì bēi (niú nǎi) | 一杯 (牛奶) |

| a spoonful of olive oil | 一匙 (橄榄油) |
| yì chí (gán lǎn yóu) | 一匙 (橄欖油) |

| a course of food | 一道 (菜) |
| yí dào (cài) | 一道 (菜) |

| a section of pipe | 一段 (管子) |
| yí duàn (guǎn-zi) | 一段 (管子) |

| a section of sugar cane | 一节 (甘蔗) |
| yì jié (gān-zhe) | 一節 (甘蔗) |

| a drop of eyedrop | 一滴 (眼药) |
| yì dī (yǎn yào) | 一滴 (眼藥) |

| a round of mahjong game | 一圈儿麻將 |
| yì qüānr (má jiàng) | 一圈兒麻將 |

| a can of beer | 一罐头 (啤酒) |
| yí guàn-tou (pí jiǔ) | 一罐頭 (啤酒) |

| a string of rosary | 一串 (念珠) |
| yí chuàn (niàn zhū) | 一串 (念珠) |

| a cluster of grapes | 一串 (葡萄) |
| yí chuàn (pú-tao) | 一串 (葡萄) |

| a bunch of keys | 一串 (鑰匙) |
| yí chuàn (yào-shi) | 一串 (鑰匙) |

| a bunch of kids; dogs | 一群 (小孩子；狗) |
| yì qǘn (xiǎo hái-zi; gǒu) | 一群 (小孩子；狗) |

| a school of fish | 一群 (鱼) |
| yì qǘn (yú) | 一群 (魚) |

| a crowd of people | 一群 (人) |
| yì qǘn (rén) | 一群 (人) |

| a stick of butter | 一小条 (牛油) |
| yì xiǎo tiáo (niú yóu) | 一小條 (牛油) |

| a bundle of old clothes | 一捆 (旧衣服) |
| yì kǔn (jiù yī-fu) | 一捆 (舊衣服) |

| a web (bolt) of cloth | 一匹 (布) |
| yì pǐ (bù) | 一匹 (布) |

| a pint (pt.) of milk | 一品脱 (牛奶) |
| yì pǐn tuō (niú nǎi) | 一品脫 (牛奶) |

| a quart (qt.) of cream | 一夸脱 (奶油) |
| yì kuǎ tuō (nǎi yóu) | 一誇脫 (奶油) |

| a gallon of gas | 一加仑 (汽油) |
| yì jiā lún (qì yóu) | 一加侖 (汽油) |

| a team of players | 一队 (球员) |
| yí duì (qiú yüán) | 一隊 (球員) |

| ten rounds of fights | 十个 (回合) |
| shí-ge (huí hé) | 十個 (回合) |

| a row of seats | 一排 (座位) |
| yì pái (zuò wèi) | 一排 (座位) |

| a dozen (dz.) eggs | 一打 (鸡蛋) |
| yì dá (jī dàn) | 一打 (雞蛋) |

| a gross ash trays (12 打) | 一箩 (烟灰缸) |
| yì luó (yān huī gāng) | 一籮 (煙灰缸) |

| a bag of tomatoes | 一袋子 (西红柿) |
| yí dài-zi (xī hóng shì) | 一袋子 (蕃茄) |

| a basket of fruit | 一篮子 (水果) |
| yì lán-zi (shuí gǔo) | 一籃子 (水果) |

| a basket of bananas | 一筐子 (香蕉) |
| yì kuāng-zi (xiāng jiāo) | 一筐子 (香蕉) |

| a bucket of hot water | 一木桶 (热水) |
| yí mù tǒng (rè shuǐ) | 一木桶 (熱水) |

| a barrel of liquor | 一橡木桶 (陈酒) |
| yí xiàng mù tǒng (chén jiǔ) | 一橡木桶 (陳酒) |

| a pail of paint | 一小桶 (油漆) |
| yì xiáo tǒng (yóu qī) | 一小桶 (油漆) |

| a cask of draft beer | 一桶 (生啤酒) |
| yì tǒng (shēng pí jiǔ) | 一桶 (生啤酒) |

'One' What?
「一」甚麼？

There are some English nouns, which do not have quite the same numerical values that Chinese have. For instance, a tie, a table, or a cow…are all words that have clear numerical values in English. But for Chinese, a unique numeric adjective must be inserted.

> For example: "a tie" -- must be said as -- "a (条 tiáo) tie",
> "a table"-- must be said as -- "a (张 zhāng) table",
> "a cow" -- must be said as -- "a (头 tóu) cow",
> Why? There is no definitive reason.
> That's just the way the Chinese language is constructed.
> Are these numerical adjectives interchangeable? No.
> Is there a rule as to how they are to be spoken? The answer is Yes, and No.
> Do the Chinese people have to memorize all these countless numerical adjectives. No.
> Chinese know these things intuitively, they can absent-mindedly say "a (朵 duǒ) flower"
> just like you say "John F. Kennedy" or "Clark Gable",
> rather than saying: "John F. Gable" or "Clark Kennedy".

NUMERIC ADJECTIVES

★ **ge 个**
a soft sound

is a most commonly used "numeric adjective" for most nouns, like general objects, things, people, months…etc.
i.e.: one tangerine: yí-ge jú-zi (一个橘子)
two months: liǎng-ge yüè (两个月)
Never say "二个èr-ge" See P. 62★Two, Group 4.

Examples

e.g. : ❶ I want three hot dogs, one with chili sauce and two plain, please.

Me want	three	hot dog,	one add		chili sauce,		two	anything	all	not add
wǒ yào	sān-ge	rè gǒu,	yí-ge	jiā	Mò Xī Gē jiàng,		liǎng-ge	shén-me	dū	bù jiā
我 要	三个	热狗,	一个	加	墨西哥酱,		两个	甚幺	都	不加

❷

Two	are	mine	and		the rest		are	hers.
Two	is	I's	○		remain's		is	she's
liǎng-ge	shì	wǒ-de,	○		shèng xià-de		shì	tā-de.
两个	是	我的,	○		剩下的		是	她的。

The following is a list of
Special Numeric Adjectives
that the author has summed up for your Reference Uses

★ When One is used as a Numeral Number it pronunces the **1st tone (yī)**
i.e.: **yī**; èr; sān; sì…… **one**; two; three; four…,
① When 「一」 is used for quantity or amount as "a" or "an"
「一」 pronunces the **4th tone (yì)** all the time.
e.g.: a pack 一包"yì" bāo: a bottle 一瓶"yì" píng: a group 一组"yì" zǔ.
② Unless 「一」 appears before another "4th tone",
then 「一」 changes to **2nd tone (yí)**
e.g.: a set 一套 "yí" tào;   altogether 一共 "yí" gòng

2nd tone (yí) & 4th tone (yì)
For your immediate recognation, the author has highlighted the **2nd** tone "yí"'s in blue color in the following phreses.

yí wèi   (a respective person) gentleman
一位   先生 xiān-sheng; teacher 老师
lǎo shī; guest 客人 kè-ren
(see ⑰ P.78)

yí dùn   (a meal) 饭 fàn; a (spell) beaten up
一顿   毒打 dú dǎ; bad scold 臭骂 chòu mà

yì nǎo-zi (a brainful) bad ideas 坏主意 huài
一脑子   zhú-yi; greenbacks 黄金梦 huáng
jīn mèng

yí pì gǔ (a buttocks) obligations 人情债
一屁股   rén qíng zhài; debt 债 zhài.

pèng yì bí-zi (a nose tip) ashes 灰 huī (em-
碰一鼻子   barresment when being refused)

yì kǒu   (a mouthful) Beijing accent 北京
一口   腔儿 běi jīng qiāngr

wú kǒu five (family members) 人 rén；
五口   coffin 棺材 guān-cai ; well 井 jǐng

mán zuǐ-de (a mouthful) dirty talk 脏话 zāng
满嘴的   huà; morality justice and virtue
仁义道德 rēn yì dào dé

★ **yí dù-zi** (a bellyful) moralless 男盗女娼 nán dào
一肚子   nǚ chāng; have a bellyful of repressed
grievance 慪一肚子氣 òu yí dù-zi qì; anger
怨气 yüàn qì; knowledge 学问 xüé-wen

yì shǒu (a hand) good cooking 好菜 hǎo
一手   cài

yì shēn (a body) know-how skill 功夫 gōng
一身   -fu ; sweat smell 臭汗 chòu hàn

yì fú   (cloth width) oil painting 油画 yóu
一幅   huà (see ❸ P.77)   ; map 地图 dì tú

yí duàn (a spell) marriage 姻缘 yīn yüán
一段

yí dàng-zi (a case) business; event 事 shì
一当子

yì mén   (a course) marriage 亲事 qīn shì
一门   knowledge 学问 xüé-wen

yì zhuō (a table) wedding banquet 喜酒
一桌   xí jiǔ ; mahjong 麻将 má jiàng
(see ❿ P.77)

yì méi
一枚
(a buttonlike) coin 硬币 yìng bì; badge 徽章 hūi zhāng; button 钮扣 niǔ kòu; bomb 炸弹 zhà dàn (see ⑯ P.78)

★**yì zhāng**
一张
(a zhāng) table 桌子 zhuō-zi; (a sheet) paper 纸 zhǐ; photo 照片 zhào piàn; map 地图 dì tú; stamp 邮票 yóu piào

yì gān
一干
(a related) convict 人犯 rén fàn

yì chuáng
一床
(a bed) quilt 棉被 mián bèi

yì qí
一期
(an installment) payment 帐款 zhàng kuǎn

yì liǎn
一脸
(a face) helplessly 茫然 máng rán; doubts 疑惑 yí huò

yì pāo
一泡
(a release) urine 尿 niào

★**yì bǎ**
一把
(a handful) snot 鼻涕 bí tì; tears 眼泪 yǎn lèi; rice 米 mǐ (a thing with handle) chair 椅子 yǐ-zi; umbrella 雨伞 yǔ sǎn; toothbrush 牙刷 yá shuā; knife 刀 dāo

yì zhī
一只(隻)
(an ornament) ring 戒指 jiè-zhi; bracelet 手镯 shǒu zhuó; watch 手表 shóu biǎo

yì zhī
一只(隻)
(one of things found in pairs) shoe 鞋 xié; stocking 袜子 wà-zi; hand 手 shǒu; eye 眼睛 yǎn-jing

yì zhī
一隻
(animal) cat 猫 māo; fox 狐狸 hú-li; chicken 鸡 jī

yì tiáo
一条
(strip, length and long or narrow winding things.) dog 狗 gǒu tie 领带 lǐng dài; trousers 裤子 kù-zi; road 马路 mǎ lù; snake 蛇 shé; river 河 hé; fish 鱼 yú (see ❶ P.77)

yì dǐng
一顶
(top) a hat 帽子 mào-zi; sedan chair 轿子 jiào-zi

yí zuò
一座
(straight /stable) bridge 桥 qiáo; brass statue 铜像 tóng xiàng; mountain 山 shān; temple 庙 miào; clock 钟 zhōng

yì fān
一番
(a sort of) good wishes 好意 hǎo yì; filial obedience 孝心 xiào xīn

yì xí
一席
(time) conversation 谈话 tán huà

yì zhuāng
一桩
(event) hidden secret 心事 xīn shì; scandal 丑闻 chǒu wén; big event 大事 dà shì

yì piān
一篇
(write up) composition 文章 wén zhāng

yì zé
一则
(article) news release 新闻 xīn wén; tiding 消息 xiāo xì

yì tōng
一通
(complete) telephone conversation 电话 diàn huà

yì zhǐ
一纸
(paper) certificate 证书 zhèng shū

yí pài
一派
(made up) nonsense 胡言 hú yán

yì tóu
一头
(head) cow 牛 niú; (confusion) mist 雾水 wù-shui

yì pī
一匹
horse 马 mǎ; wolf 狼 láng (web; bolt) 锦缎 brocade jǐn duàn

yì běn
一本
(little investment) thousandfold profits 萬利 wàn lì. very profitable

yì běnr
一本儿
(a volume) book 书 shū; magazine 杂志 zá zhì; passport 护照 hù zhào

yì běn
一本
(an act) seriousness 正经 zhèng jīng; bible 圣经 shèng jīng

yì pán
一盘
(a game) chess 棋 qí; loose sand 散沙 sǎn shā (not united)

yì zhǎn
一盏
(a denoting lamps) lamp/ light 灯 dēng

yì jiān
一间
(a room) room 屋子 wū-zi; study 书房 shū fáng; bedroom 卧房 wò fáng

yì suǒ
一所
(a location) house 房子 fáng-zi; school 学校 xué xiào; hospital 医院 yī yuàn

yì jiā
一家
(a family engaged in a certain trade) barbershop 理发厅 lí fà tīng; shop; store 店铺 diàn pù

yí dòng
一栋
(a building, more than one story）apartment 公寓 gōng yù；building 楼房 lóu fáng；high rises 大高楼 dà gāo lóu (see ⑭ P.78)

yì tiē
一帖
(a prescriptiom) herbal medicine 草药 cǎo yào；medical plaster 膏药 gāo-yao

yí jiàn
一件
(an article, event) garment 衣服 yī-fu；matter 事情 shì-qing (see ⑱ P.78)

yì zhī
一枝
(a branch, slender, straight, stiff) flower 花 huā；pencil 铅笔 qiān bǐ；

yì zhī
一支
(a stick, branch) brush 毛笔 máo bǐ；walking cane 拐杖 guǎi zhàng；troops 队伍 duì-wu

yì gēn
一根
(a very long thing) string 绳子 shéng-zi；bamboo pole 竹竿 zhú gān；hair 头发 tóu-fa

yì gēnr
一根儿
(a small stick)cigarette 香烟 xiāng yān；toothpick 牙签儿 yá qiānr；match 火柴 huǒ chái

yì zōng
一宗
(a transaction) business 买卖 mǎi mài

yì míng
一名
(a member) sailor 水手 shuí shǒu；ballgame player 球员 qiú yuán

yì yuán
一员
(an organization member) know-how 大将 dà jiàng；politician 政要 zhèng yào

yí shàn
一扇
(a panel) door 门 mén；window 窗户 chuāng-hu (see ⑥ P.77)

yì zūn
一尊
(a statue) Buddha 佛像 fó xiàng (see ⑫ P.78)

yí jiè
一介
(ordinary) civilian 平民 píng mín

yí kè
一客
(a quick lunch/meal) pork chops 猪排 zhū pái；fried rice 炒饭 chǎo fàn

yì bāng-zi
一帮子
(a gang) hoodlums 流氓 liú máng；hired thugs 打手 dá-shou

yì chén
一尘
(a dust) spick-and-span 不染 bù rǎn

yì fā
一发
(a shot) bullet 子弹 zǐ dàn

yì fān
一帆
(sail) with the wind 风顺 fēng shùn Bon Voyage

yí fèn
一份
(issue; portion) newspaper 报纸 bào zhǐ；gift 礼物 lǐ wù；meal 定食 dìng shí；job 工作 gōng zuò

★ **yì fēng**
一封
(seal) letter 信 xìn；love letter 情书 qíng shū (see ⑱ P.78)

yí ge
一个
(general individual measure) person 人 rén；room 房间 fáng jiān；ball 球 qiū；cake 蛋糕 dàn gāo

yì xí
一袭
(an outfit) casual clothes 便装 biàn zhuāng；long gown 长袍 cháng páo

yí zhèn
一阵
(a spell of time) argument 吵闹 chǎo nào；breeze 微风 wéi fēng；shower 雨 yǔ；wind 风 fēng

yì shuāng
一双
(a pair: come in pairs) shoes 鞋 xié；socks 袜子 wà-zi；chopsticks 筷子 kuài-zi

yí duì
一对
(a pair; face each other/stand together) stone lions 石狮子 shí shī-zi；flower vases 花瓶 huā píng；couple 夫妻 fū qī；candle 蜡烛 là zhú；peculiar persons 活宝 huó bǎo (see ⑧ P.77)

yí fù
一副
(a pair)spectacles 眼镜 yǎn jìng；(pair) gloves 手套 shǒu tào；scroll 对联 duì lián；shoe-laces 鞋带 xié dài

yí fù
一副
(a face, carry out) bad attitude 德行 dé-xing；naive looking 天真的样子 tiān zhēn-de yàng-zi

yì wěi
一尾
(a tail) fish 鱼 yú

yì tái
一台
(a set) television 电视 diàn shì；air conditioner 冷气 lěng qì

yí bù
一部
(a series) novel 小说 xiǎo shuō；sedan 轿车 jiào chē (see ⑲ P.78)

★ **yí liàng**
一辆
(a vehicle) sports car 跑车 pǎo chē；truck 卡车 kǎ chē; bicycle 自行车 zì xīng chē；pedicab 三轮车 sān lún chē (see ④ P.77)

yì dǔ
一堵
(a block) wall 墙 qiáng

yì shǒu 一首	(a denoting songs & poems) song 歌 gē; poem 诗 shī (see ❾ P.77)
yì kē 一颗	(small round) pearl 珍珠 zhēn zhū ; diamond 钻石 zuàn shí (see ❷ P.77)
yì kē 一棵	(head) cabbage 白菜 bái cài ; tree 树 shù ; plant 植物 zhí wù
yì wán 一丸	(round pill) Chinese medicine 牛黄清心丸 niú huáng qīng xīn wán
yí lì 一粒	(small and round) rice 米 mǐ; grain 谷子 gǔ-zi; bead 珠子 zhū-zi; sand 沙 shā
yí zhù 一注	(bet) gambling money 赌金 dǔ jīn
yì gǔ 一股	(flutter) fragrancevu 香味 xiāng wèi
yì duǒ 一朵	(bud) flower 花 huā; cloud 浮云 fú yǔn; cauliflower 菜花 cài huā
yì bān 一班	(scheduled) bus 公车 gōng chē ; train 火车 huǒ chē ; flight 飞机 fēi jī
yì chū 一齣	(a performance) Beijing Opera 京戏 jīng xì
yì sāo 一艘	(a vessel) ocean-going ship 船 chuán
yí jià 一架	(a structure) airplane 飞机 fēi jī; (a stand) piano 钢琴 gāng qín (see ⓯ P.78)
yì fēn 一分	(a notch) effort of work 努力 nǔ lì ; rewarded 收获 shōu huò
yì chǎng 一场	(an inning or intertaining event) rain 雨 yǔ; movie 电影 diàn yǐng; nonsense argument 闹剧 nào jù; ball game 球赛 qiú sài ; war 战争 zhàn zhēng (see ❺)
yì chéngr 一成儿	(a ten percent) tip 小费 xiǎo fèi ; commission 佣金 yòng jīn (see ❼)
yí zhù 一炷	(a joss stick) 香 xiāng;烧香拜佛 shāo xiāng bài fó; burn a joss stick to worship God 上炷香 shàng zhù xiāng; pay respect to the dead by burning him a joss stick
yì pī 一批	(a shipment, batch, in lots) ammunition 军火 jūn huǒ; (in lots) merchandise 货物 huò wù
yì sī 一丝	(a trace; slim) hope 希望 xī wàng; smile 笑容 xiào róng; nude 不挂 bú guà
yì bǐ 一笔	(a sum; deal) money 钱 qián; business 买卖 mǎi mài; chaotic account 胡涂帐 hú-tu zhàng
yì qǐ 一起	(a happening) murder case 谋杀案 móu shā àn; car accident 车祸 chē huò
yí miàn 一面	(face) mirror 镜子 jìng-zi; national flag 国旗 gúo qí (see ⓫ P.78)
yì fēi 一飞	(fly) a sudden success 冲天 chōng tiān
yí shì 一事	(an event) nothing accomplished 无成 wú chéng
yì zhī 一知	(scanty) and 半解 bàn jiě a smattering of knowledge
yì zhēn 一针	(a niddle) see the blood 见血 jiàn xiě. hit the nail on the head
yì láo 一劳	(an effort) get things done once and for all 永逸 yǒng yì
yì shì 一视	(look at) treat equally without discrimination(colleague)同仁 tóng rén
yì wú 一无	(own nothing) belongings 所有 suǒ yǒu; not own a thing in the world
yí bì 一臂	(an arm) strength 之力 zhī lì; lend me a hand
yì tōng 一通	(grasp a thing) hundred things 百通 bǎi tōng; Knowing one knowing all.
yí jiàn 一箭	(an arrow) two hawks 双鵰 shuāng diāo; kill two birds with one stone
yí qiào 一窍	(the slightest) blocked 不通 bù tōng utterly ignorant of something
yí bù 一步	(a step) reach sky 登天 dēng tiān attain the highest level in one step
yì míng 一鸣	(a whistle) surprise 惊人 jīng rén; set the world on fire

yí xiào (a laugh) treat 置之 zhì zhī; treat it
一笑 with a laugh (see ⑳ P.78)

yì yán (using one sentence) 以蔽之 yì yán
一言 yǐ bì zhī. (to put it in a nutshell)
难尽 yì yán nán jìn (can hardly
complete the story) (It's a long story)

yì yán (one sentence) 爲定 wéi dìng
一言 (both agreed) (It's a deal.
（九鼎 jiú dǐng; the nine ancient
tripod of sacrificial vessel from
Xià Dynasty)
yì yán jiú dǐng (I give you my word)

yì máo (a hair) not be pulled 不拔 bù bá
一毛 never spend a penny on friends

yí bèi-zi (a lifetime) with you 跟你 gēn nǐ
一辈子 跟你一辈子 gēn-ni yí bèi-zi (want to
grow old with you)

a or an

**The most commonly used
numeric adjective**

★ | "a" or "an" |

"**a**", "**an**" and "**one**" have the same
written characters (一个)

When (一个) is used for "**a**" or "**an**"
it pronounces the 2nd tone "**yí ge**"
Sometimes the "**yí**" sound is dropped in
conversation and leaves only the
"**ge**" sound. (See Examples Below)

e.g.:

A | I want "a" hamburger.
wǒ yào "**ge**" hàn bǎo bāo
我 要 "个" 汉堡包

B | I'm going to find "a" screw.
I go find "a" screw
wǒ qù zhǎo "**ge**" luō-si dīngr
我 去 找 "个" 螺丝钉儿

C | I want to buy "a" camera.
wǎ yào mǎi "**tái**" xiàng jī
我 要 買 "台" 相機

"a" or "an" is often omitted and just use the
"numeric adjective" followed. Because "a"
and "an" are neither important in the
sentence. Same applies to other numerical
adjectives, like "bottle, stick, pack…etc." the "**yi**" sound
is often dropped.

D | Give me "a" bottle of soy sauce.
To (I; me) " bottle " soy sauce
géi - wo "píngr" jiàng yóu
给 我 "瓶儿" 酱油

E | He wants "a" cigarette
tā yào "gēnr" xiāng yān
他 要 "根儿" 香烟

F | Go get a chair somewhere and sit down.
Go find "a" chair bring sit down
qù zhǎo -ba yǐ-zi -lai zuò-xia
去 找 "把" 椅子 来 坐下

★ The "-ba;把" on No.F, is the numeric
adjective for "chair"
See Page **73** ★ yì bǎ 一把

G | He is "a" jerk
He is "jerk"
tā shì "hún qiúr"
他 是 浑球儿

Because: "I am **three** men" is impossible, as
well as "They are **man**" is also not true to the
fact. Thus the Chinese thought that neither
the singular "**a**" nor the **plural form** "**s**" is
necessary.

★

The beginners may just use "个 ge" for substitutions of all numeral adjectives even though they may not be totally correct. As you become more proficient in the Chinese language, using these numeral adjectives will come naturally.

❶ He birthday. I want give he a "○" alligator belt
他 生日 我 要 送 他 一 (条) 鳄鱼 皮带
tā shēng-rì wǒ yào sòng-ta yì (tiáo) è yú pí dài

❷ This "○" pearl so big
这 (颗) 珍珠 好 大
zhèi (kē) zhēn zhū hǎo dà

❸ This "○" oil painting is reproduction.
这 (幅) 油画 是 复制品
zhèi (fú) yóu huà shì fù zhì pǐn

❹ He newly bought a "○" sports car.
他 新 买了 一 (辆) 跑车
tā xīn mǎi-le yí (liàng) pǎo chē

❺ we go see a "○" movie good no good ?
咱们 去 看 "○" (场) 电影儿 好不好
zán-men qù kàn "○" (chǎng) diàn yǐng hǎo-bu hǎo

❻ This "○" door has stuck.
这 (扇) 门 打不开了
zhèi (shàn) mén dǎ bù kāi-le

❼ They want two "10 percent" commission.
他们 要 两 (成儿) 佣金
tā-men yào liǎng (chéngr) yòng jīn

❽ I want order a "pair" ivory chops (seal).
我 要 订 一 (对) 象牙 图章
wǒ yào dìng yí (duì) xiàng yá tú zhāng

❾ I for you sing a "○" song
我 给 妳 唱 一 (首) 歌
wǒ géi nǐ chàng yì (shǒu) gēr

❿ There's a mahjong game after dinner
dinner after have a "table" mahjong
饭后 有 "○" (桌) 麻将
fàn hòu yǒu "○" (zhuō) má jiàng

⑪ Each one   holds   **a**   "○"   national flag.

一人   拿   一   (面)   国旗

yì rén   ná   yí   (miàn)   gúo qí

⑫ This   "zūn"   Buddha statue   is   Tang Dynasty's

这   (尊)   佛像   是   唐朝的

zhèi   zūn)   fó xiàng   shì   táng cháo-de

⑬ Women   always   short of   **one**   "○"   dress.

女人   永远   少   一   (件)   洋装

nǔ rén   yóng yüán   shǎo   yí   (jiàn)   yáng zhuāng

⑭ He   owns   **a**   "dòng"   ten-story   building

他   有   一   (株)   十层   大楼

tā   yǒu   yí   (dòng)   shí céng   dà lóu

⑮ This   "○"   piano   is   Germany goods

这   (架)   钢琴   是   德国货

zhèi   (jià)   gāng qín   shì   Dé Guó huò

⑯ I   need   a   coin   for   the   telephone call.

I   need   a   "○"   coin   beat   telephone

我   需要   一   (枚)   硬幣   打   電話

wǒ   xǖ yào   yì   (méi)   yìng bì   dǎ   diàn huà

⑰ A   gentleman   is   here   to   see   you.

Have   a   "○"   gentleman   come   see   you

有   "○"   (位)   先生   來   看   您

yǒu   "○"   (wèi)   xiān-sheng   lái   kàn   nín

⑱ ○   You   have   a   "○"   registered   letter,   sir.

先生，   您   有   "○"   (封)   掛號   信   ○

xiān-sheng,   nín   yǒu   "○"   (fēng)   guà hào   xìn   ○

⑲ The Red Chamber   is   a   worth   reading   monumental work.

Red Chamber Dream   is   a "volune"   worth   a look's   tremendous   writing

红樓夢   是   一   (部)   值得   一看的   巨作

hóng lóu mèng   shì   yí   (bù)   zhí-de   yí kàn-de   jǜ zuò

⑳ Just   ignore   his   rude   remarks.

This   kind   thing   only   a   "laugh"   treat it

這   種   事情   只有   一   (笑)   置之

zhè zhong   shì-qing   zhí yǒu   yí   (xiào)   zhì zhī

What's The Matter?
怎麼了？(有話直說)

Now You tell me what's the matter!

叫人纳闷儿 jiào rén nà mènr
I was wondering. (It puzzles me.)

难道......? nán dào....?
Can you have forgotten?

❶ **The baggage is "overweight".**

Baggage	"overweight"
xíng-li	**(guò zhòng-le)**
行李	（過重了）

❷ **The fireworks were "fantastic"**

Fired	firework	real	fantastic
fàng-de	**yān-huo**	**zhēn-shi**	**(yì jué)**
放的	煙火	真是	（一絕）

❸ **My ex-boyfrind was "tricky".**

I	previous	boyfriend	(really slicky)
wó	**yǐ qián-de**	**nán péng-you**	**(zhēn huá-tou)**
我	以前的	男朋友	（真滑頭）

❹ **The rent is "high", but the food is "inexpensive".**

Rent	"expensive"	but	food	"not expensive"
fáng zū	**(guì)**	**kě-shi**	**chī-de**	**(bú guì)**
房租	（貴）	可是	吃的	（不貴）

❺ **The color of the drapery is too "bright".**

Drapery's	color	too	"bright"
chuāng lián-de	**yán-se**	**tài**	**(liàng lì-le)**
窗簾的	顏色	太	（亮麗了）

❻ **We had a very "pleasant" evening.**

That day	evening	play-ed	very	"pleasant"
nèi tiān	**wǎn-shang**	**wánr-de**	**fēi cháng**	**(yú kuài)**
那天	晚上	玩兒得	非常	（愉快）

1051

The author has collected some **1051** adjectives encompassing every aspect of daily life capable of satisfying the reader with its thoroughness and sense of completeness. They will guide you to successfully speak Chinese without the help of a teacher.

别人來瘋儿 **bié rén lái fēngr**
Don't get carried away!

A

a bit (salt) **sháo xǔ**	少许	少許（鹽巴）
a good alibi **piàn-de tiān yī wú fèng**	骗得天衣无缝	騙得天衣無縫
a lot **hěn duō**	很多	很多
absent **qüē xí**	缺席	缺席
abusive language **kǒu chū è yán**	口出恶言	口出惡言
accurate **zhǔn qüè**	准确	準確
active **huó yüè**	活跃	活躍
actual **shí jì**	实际	實際
acid **suān xìng-de**	酸性的	酸性的
addicted **shàng-le yǐn-le**	上了瘾了	上了癮了
(take) advantage of you **zhàn nǐ pián-yi**	占你便宜	佔你便宜
afraid **hài pà**	害怕	害怕
aggressive **jī jí**	积极	積極
ahead of time **tí zǎo; tí qián**	提早；提前	提早；提前
alone **dān dú yí-ge-ren**	单独一个人	單獨一個人

English	Simplified	Traditional
amazing **dà chī yì jīng**	大吃一惊	大吃一驚
ambiguous **hán hú bù qīng**	含糊不清	含糊不清
ancient **gǔ dài-de**	古代的	古代的
angry with **nù; fā huǒr**	怒；发火儿	怒；發火兒
(trying to) annoy her **qì-ta yí xiàr**	气她一下儿	氣她一下兒
(stop) annoying him **bié rě-ta**	别惹他	別惹他
anxious **jiāo lù**	焦虑	焦慮
appropriate **shì dàng-de**	适当的	適當的
aroused; hot **xìng chōng dòng**	性冲动	性衝動
artificial **rén zào-de**	人造的	人造的
asleep; fell asleep **shuì zháo-le**	睡著了	睡著了
assail women with obscenities **tiáo xì**	调戏	調戲
attractive **yǒu xī yǐn lì**	有吸引力	有吸引力
automatic **zì dòng-de**	自动的	自動的
available **xiàn chéngr-de**	现成儿的	現成兒的
average **píng jün**	平均	平均

aware **jǐng jüé**	警觉 警覺	blank **kòng bái-de**	空白的 空白的
awful **xià rén; kě pà**	吓人；可怕 嚇人；可怕	blind **máng mù; xiā-le yǎn**	盲目；瞎了眼 盲目；瞎了眼
awkward **bèn zhòng**	笨重 笨重	blow up **fā pí-qi**	发脾气 發脾氣
B		blow one's top **dà fā léi tíng**	大发雷霆 大發雷霆
back **hòu miàn; hòu tuì**	後面；後退 後面；後退	bluffer (bluffing) **hǔ rén**	唬人 唬人
backward **dào xíng nì shī**	倒行逆施 倒行逆施	(is) blushing **liǎn hóng-le**	脸红了 臉紅了
bad **huài; dǎi**	坏；歹 壞；歹	bold **yīng yǒng-de**	英勇的 英勇的
bald **tū tóu**	秃头 秃頭	bony **gǔ shòu rú chái**	骨瘦如柴 骨瘦如柴
bare **chì luǒ; guāng-zhe**	赤裸；光著 赤裸；光著	(give me a) boost **tái-wo yì-ba**	抬我一把 抬我一把
basic **jī běn-dę guāng-zhe**	基本的 基本的	boost the morale **dǎ qì**	打气 打氣
Beat it, and get to work! **nǐ hái mó-ceng shén-me**	你还磨蹭甚麼 你還磨蹭什麼	bossy **guǎn dōng guǎn xī-de**	管东管西的 管東管西的
beautiful **měi lì**	美丽 美麗	bottom **zuì dī-de; dǐ bù**	最低的；底部 最低的；底部
becoming **shì hé; dé tǐ**	适合；得体 適合；得體	boast; brag **chuī niú**	吹牛 吹牛
before **zhī qián; wèi…yǐ qián**	之前;未…以前 之前;未…以前	brave **yóng gǎn**	勇敢 勇敢
behind **luò hòu; -de hòu miàn**	落後；的後面 落後；的後面	brief **duǎn zhàn**	短暂 短暫
beloved **xīn ài-de**	心爱的 心愛的	bright **liàng**	亮 亮
best **zuì hǎo-de**	最好的 最好的	broad **kuān**	宽 寬
betray a friend **chū mài péng-you**	出卖朋友 出賣朋友	broken **duàn-le; pò-le; suì-le**	断了；破了；碎了 斷了；破了；碎了
better **bǐ jiào hǎo**	比较好 比較好	bull; bullshit **hú shuī bā dào**	胡说八道 胡說八道
★big (相反 little) (见 large) **dà; hǎo dà; hěn dà**	大;好大；很大 大;好大；很大	busy **máng**	忙 忙

but dàn shì	但是 但是	Cheer up!; Cheers! kāi xīn yì diǎnr	开心一点儿 開心一點兒
but also ér qiě	而且 而且	childish hái-zi qì; yòu zhì	孩子气；幼稚 孩子氣；幼稚
(let) bygones be bygones jì wǎng bú jiù	既往不咎 既往不咎	chilly liáng sōu sōu-de	凉飕飕的 涼颼颼的
C		chubby pàng hū hū-de	胖呼呼的 胖呼呼的
(he) calls me names tā mà-wo sān zì jīngr	他骂我三字经儿 他罵我三字經兒	circle yuán qüān	圆圈 圓圈
calm zhèn jìng	镇静 鎮靜	circular huán xíng-de	环形的 環形的
canned guàn toú-de	罐头的 罐頭的	classic gú diǎn-de	古典的 古典的
capable yǒu néng lì	有能力 有能力	clean qīng jié	清洁 清潔
(improve) career opportunities gǎi shì yè yùn	改事业运 改事業運	clear qīng chè	清澈 清澈
carefree wú yōu wú lǜ	无忧无虑 無憂無慮	clever cōng-ming	聪明 聰明
casual bù jǔ lǐ jié	不拘礼节 不拘禮節	close jiē jìn	接近 接近
cellular xì bāo zǔ chéng-de	细胞组成的 細胞組成的	clumsy bèn shǒu bèn jiǎo-de	笨手笨脚的 笨手笨腳的
center zhōng xīn; zhōng yāng	中心；中央 中心；中央	coherent yí shì	一致 一致
central zhèng zhōng jiān; zhōng yāng	正中间；中央 正中間；中央	cold liáng-de; liáng-le	凉的；凉了 涼的；涼了
ceremonial yí shì	仪式 儀式	collective jù jí ér chéng-de	聚集而成的 聚集而成的
certain yóu bǎ-wo	有把握 有把握	come-on! shǎo lái! (zhèi tào)	少来！（这套） 少來！（這套）
charming yǒu mèi lì	有魅力 有魅力	comfortable shū-fu	舒服 舒服
chatting xián liáo; liáo tiānr	闲聊；聊天儿 閒聊；聊天兒	commercial shāng-ye-de	商业的 商業的
cheap pián-yi	便宜 便宜	common pǔ tōng; cháng jiàn-de	普通；常见的 普通；常見的
cheerful xìng gāo cǎi liè	兴高采烈 興高采烈	common sense yì-bān cháng shì	一般常识 一般常識

complain bào-yüan	抱怨 抱怨	creative chuàng zaò	创造 創造
complete wán zhěng	完整 完整	crook huài dàn	坏蛋 壞蛋
complex fù zá	复杂 複雜	(sit) crossed-legged (relaxed) qiào-zhe èr láng tuǐr	跷著二郎腿儿 蹺著二郎腿兒
compliment gōng wéi huà	恭维话 恭維話	cruel cán rěn	残忍 殘忍
comprehensive guǎng fàn	广泛 廣泛	cube lì fāng kuàir	立方块儿 立方塊兒
conception gài niàn; guān niàn	概念；观念 概念；觀念	(have a) crush on him mí liàn-zhe-ta	迷恋著他 迷戀著他
concise jiǎn ér míng	简而明 簡而明	curious hào qí	好奇 好奇
concrete yǒu xíng	有形 有形	cute xiáo qiǎo líng lóng	小巧玲珑 小巧玲瓏

D

(increase) self-confident zēng jiā zì xìn xīn	增加自信心 增加自信心		
connected yǒu guān lián	有关联 有關聯	dangerous wéi xiǎn	危险 危險
conscious yǒu zhī-jüe	有知觉 有知覺	dark hēi àn	黑暗 黑暗
consistent qián hoù yí zhì	前后一致 前後一致	dead sǐ-le	死了 死了
constant gù dìng-de	固定的 固定的	deep shēn	深 深
continuous lián xǜ-de	连续的 連續的	definite míng què	明确 明確
contrary xiāng fǎn-de	相反的 相反的	deliberately gù yì-de	故意的 故意 的
cool; Play cool liáng kuài; wánr shuài	凉快；玩儿帅 涼快；玩兒帥	dense mì jí	密集 密集
corner jiǎo luò; jiē jiǎo	角落；街角 角落；街角	dependable kě kào	可靠 可靠
correct zhèng qüè	正确 正確	dependent yī kào	依靠 依靠
crazy fēng kuáng-le	疯狂了 瘋狂了	depressed jǔ sàng; yōu yù	沮丧；忧郁 沮喪；憂鬱
credible kě xìn-de	可信的 可信的	desperate qióng tú mò lù	穷途末路 窮途末路

diagonal **duì jiǎor xiàn**	对角儿线 對角兒線	double **jiā bèi**	加倍 加倍
diagonally across the street **mǎ lù xié duì miàn**	马路斜对面 馬路斜對面	down **xià; xiàng xià**	下；向下 下；向下
diameter **zhí jìng**	直径 直徑	doze off **dǎ kē shuì**	打瞌睡 打瞌睡
different **bù tóng**	不同 不同	dry **gān-de**	干的 乾的
difficult **kùn nán**	困难 困難	drunk **zuì-le**	醉了 醉了
dim **àn dàn**	暗淡 暗淡	due **dào qí**	到期 到期
direct **zhí jiē**	直接 直接	dull **dùn**	钝 鈍
(give him a) dirty look **dèng-ta yì yǎn**	瞪他一眼 瞪他一眼	(act) dumb **dá mǎ-hu yǎn**	打马虎眼 打馬虎眼
disappointed **shī wàng**	失望 失望		
discrimination against **qí shì**	歧视 歧視	**E**	
diseased **yǒu bìng**	有病 有病	each **měi gè; měi yí gè**	每个；每一个 每個；每一個
disgusting; feel nauseated **zhēn tǎo yàn**	真讨厌 真討厭	eager **kě wàng**	渴望 渴望
divorced **lí hūn-le**	离婚了 離婚了	easy jiā wù shì-de **róng-yi**	容易 容易
dizzy **tóu yūn mù xüàn**	头晕目眩 頭暈目眩	efficient **xiào lǜ gāo**	效率高 效率高
Do you or don't you? **nǐ shī…, shī bù …**	你是…，是不…？ 你是…，是不…？	electrical **diàn-de**	电的 電的
domestic **jiā wù shì-de**	家务事的 **家務事的**	elementary **jī běn-de**	基本的 基本的
dominant **zhī pèi**	支配 支配	emergent **jǐn jí-de**	紧急的 緊急的
don't argue with **bié dǐng zuǐ**	别顶嘴 別頂嘴	emotional **gǎn qíng-de**	感情的 感情的
don't make a big fuss of it **bié xiǎo tí dà zuò**	别小题大作 別小題大作	empty **kōng-de**	空的 空的
dote on her son **nì ài ér-zi**	溺爱儿子 溺愛兒子	energetic **jīng lí wàng shèng**	精力旺盛 精力旺盛
		engaged **yǐ dìng hūn**	已订婚 已訂婚

English	Pinyin	Simplified/Traditional

enjoyable
yǒu qù-de
有趣的
有趣的

enjoyed it very much; had a good time
chē chuáng
開心 开心

enough
zú gòu
足够
足夠

ensure
bǎo zhèng; qüè bǎo
保证；确保
保證；確保

entire
zhěng gèr-de
整个儿的
整個兒的

essential
bù kě qüē shǎo-de
不可缺少的
不可缺少的

every
gè gè
个个
個個

evil
xié è
邪恶
邪惡

exact
qüè qiè; zhèng hǎo
确切；正好
確切；正好

exhausted; dog-tired; beat 精疲力尽
jīng pí lì jìn
精疲力盡

expensive
guì
贵
貴

extra large
tè dà hàor
特大号儿
特大號兒

extrovert
wài xiàng
外向
外向

extreme
jí duān-de
极端的
極端的

eye-catching
qiáng yǎn
抢眼
搶眼

F

facial
liǎn bù-de
脸部的
臉部的

(in) fact; as a matter of fact 其实
qí shí
其實

fair
gōng píng
公平
公平

false
jiǎ-de
假的
假的

familiar
shóu xī
熟悉
熟悉

famous
yǒu míng
有名
有名

fantastic
hǎo-de bù dé liǎo
好得不得了
好得不得了

far
yüǎn
远
遠

fashionable
liú xíng
流行
流行

fast
kuài
快
快

fat
pàng; féi
胖；肥
胖；肥

fatigued; tired out
pí jüàn
疲倦
疲倦

fell head foremost
nǎo dài xiàng qián zāi
脑袋向前栽
腦袋向前栽

female
nǚ xìng
女性
女性

feminine
yóu nǚ rén wèir
有女人味儿
有女人味兒

final; finals
zuì hòu-de; jüé sài
最后的；决赛
最後的；決賽

financially embarrassed (strapped)手头紧
shǒu tóu jǐn
手頭緊

fine
zhè yàng jiù hǎo
这样就好
這樣就好

firm
wěn gù
稳固
穩固

fixed
gù dìng-de
固定的
固定的

flat
biǎn; píng
扁；平
扁；平

flashy
shǎn guāng
闪光
閃光

flatter
chǎn mèi; fèng chéng
谄媚；奉承
諂媚；奉承

★ (make my) flesh crawl
ròu má (See P.86 ★)
肉麻
肉麻

foolish	傻	generous	慷慨
shǎ	傻	kāng kǎi	慷慨

(Oh, before I) forget.	我先插 个嘴	giant	巨大；超大
wǒ xiān chā-ge zuǐ	我先插個嘴 (不然就忘了)	jù dà ; chāo dà	巨大；超大

Forget it!	拉倒；算了	gibberish	语无伦次
lā dǎo; suàn-la!	拉倒；算了	yǔ wú lún cì	語無倫次

forgetful	健忘	★ gives me goose pimples	起鸡皮疙瘩
jiàn wàng	健忘	qǐ jī pí gē-da (See P.85★)	起雞皮疙瘩

formal	正式的	glad to; willing to	乐意；高兴
zhèng shì-de	正式的	lè yì; gāo xìng	樂意；高興

(have made) a fortune	发大财了	gogetter	积极能干
fā dà cái-le	發大財了	jī jí néng gàn	積極能幹

fragile	易碎	good	好
yì suì	易碎	hǎo	好

frank	直率	good looking	好看
zhí shuài	直率	hǎo kàn	好看

free	自由	goof	混日子；摸鱼
zì yóu	自由	hùn rì-zi; mō yú	混日子；摸魚

fresh	新鲜	gorgeous	高贵华丽
xīn xiān	新鮮	gāo guì huá lì	高貴華麗

friendly	友好	gossip; jaw	嚼舌根子
yóu hǎo	友好	jiáo shé gēn-zi	嚼舌根子

frozen	冰冻的	(You've) got it all made.	不愁吃不愁穿
bīng dòng-de	冰凍的	bú chóu chī bù chóu chuān	不愁吃不愁穿

frustrated; down and out	潦倒 (See P.142)	got off with	就了了；没事儿了
liáo dǎo	潦倒	jiù liǎo-le; méi shìr-le	就了了；沒事兒了

frustrated with life	挫折感 (See P.142)	grateful	感谢
cuò zhé gǎn	挫折感	gǎn xiè	感謝

full	满了	great	好棒；伟大
mǎn-le	滿了	hǎo bàng; wěi dà	好棒；偉大

fun	好玩儿	grievance; repressed	委屈
hǎo wánr	好玩兒	wě qǔ	委屈

funny	滑稽；可笑	guessing	瞎蒙
huá-ji; kě xiào	滑稽；可笑	xiā mēng	瞎矇

(in a) fury	狂怒
kuáng nù	狂怒

H

had one too many	他喝多了
tā hē duō-le	他喝多了

G

(in) general; generally	通常；一般来说	he had to have…	他一定是…
tōng cháng; yì bān lái shuō	通常；一般來說	tā yí dìng-shi	他一定是…

handsome **jùn; yīng jùn**	俊；英俊 **俊；英俊**	hollow **zhōng jiān shì kōng-de**	中间是空的 中間是空的
handy **ná qǚ fāng bìan**	拿取方便 **拿取方便**	homesick **xiǎng jiā; sī xiāng**	想家；思乡 想家；思鄉
happy **kuài lè; xìng fú**	快乐；幸福 **快樂；幸福**	honest **chéng shí; lǎo-shi**	诚实；老实 誠實；老實
hard **yìng**	硬 **硬**	hopeful **chōng mǎn xī wàng**	充满希望 充滿希望
harmful **yǒu hài-de**	有害的 **有害的**	horny **zhěng tīan sè mī mī-de**	整天色咪咪的 整天色咪咪的
harsh **cū cāo**	粗糙 **粗糙**	horrible **háo kě pà**	好可怕 好可怕
harvest **shōu gé zhuāng-jia**	收割庄稼 **收割莊稼**	hot-tempered **huǒ bào pí-qi**	火爆脾气 火爆脾氣
hate to part with (throw away) 舍不得 **shě-bu-de** **捨不得(丟掉)**		huge **háo dà**	好大 好大
hateful; loathsome **kě wù**	可恶 **可惡**	humble **qiān gōng-de**	谦恭的 謙恭的
healthy **jiàn kāng**	健康 **健康**	humid **kōng qì cháo shī**	空气潮湿 空氣潮濕
heavy **zhòng**	重 **重**	humorous **yōu mò**	幽默 幽默
heavy set lady **fēng mǎn**	丰满 **豐滿 (體態)**	husky **kuí-wu**	魁武 魁武
Hell with it! **guǎn-ta!**	管它！ **管它！**		

I

heptagon **qī jiǎo xíng**	七角形 **七角形**	ice-cold **bīng liáng-de**	冰凉的 冰涼的
hexagon **liù jiǎo xíng**	六角形 **六角形**	iced **bīng guò-de**	冰过的 冰過的
helpful **yǒu yì-de**	有益的 **有益的**	ideal **lí xiǎng-de**	理想的 理想的
hide the truth **mán-zhe**	瞒着 **瞞著**	idle lives **guǐ hùn; wú suǒ shì shì**	鬼混；无所事事 鬼混；無所事事
high (position) **gāo**	高 (位置；职位) **高**	ignorant **bù xué wú shù**	不学无术 不學無術
hit the sack; turn in **qù shuì jiào**	去睡觉 **去睡覺**	ignore him **bù shuǎi-ta; bù lǐ-ta**	不甩他；不理他 不甩他；不理他
(get) high (intoxicated) **piāo piāo rán**	飘飘然 **飄飄然 (酒毒品)**	ill; sick **bìng-le; shēng bìng-le**	病了；生病了 病了；生病了

illegal **fēi fǎ**	非法 非法	
image **xíng xiàng**	形像 形像	
imitation **fǎng zhì-de**	仿制的 仿製的	
immediate **lì kè**	立刻 立刻	
impatient **jí xìng-zi; méi nài xīn**	急性子；没耐心 急性子；沒耐心	
immuture **bù chéng shóu**	不成熟 不成熟	
important **zhòng yào**	重要 重要	
impossible **bù kě néng**	不可能 不可能	
in a second; in a minute **mǎ shàng lái**	马上来 馬上來	
in front of **zài…-de qián miàn**	在…的前面 在…的前面	
in her late 50's **tā wǔ-shi bā jiǔ suì**	她五十八、九岁 她五十八、九歲	
in his middle 20's **tā èr-shi wǔ liù suì**	他二十五、六岁 他二十五、六歲	
in their early 30's **tā-men sān shí chū tóu**	他们三十出头 他們三十出頭	
in his/her teens **qīng shào nián shí qí**	青少年时期 青少年時期	
incoming (calls; letters) **jìn lái-de** (diàn huà; xìn)	进来的（电话；信） 進來的（電話；信）	
incorrect **cuò wù; bú zhèng qüè**	错误；不正确 錯誤；不正確	
incredible **bù kě sī yì; lí qí**	不可思议；离奇 不可思議；離奇	
independent **dú lì-de**	独立的 獨立的	
independable **bù kě kào**	不可靠 不可靠	
individual **gè rén-de**	个人的 個人的	

inner **nèi bù-de**	内部的 內部的	
innocent **tiān zhēn; bù dǒng shì gù**	天真;不懂事故 天真;不懂事故	
inside **lǐ miàn**	里面 裏面	
inside out **fǎn-le; lǐ cháo wèi**	反了；里朝外 反了；裡朝外	
integrity **lián jié**	廉洁 廉潔	
intellectual **yǒu xüé-wen**	有学问 有學問	
intelligent **yǒu zhì-hui**	有智慧 有智慧	
international **guó jì xìng-de**	国际性的 國際性的	
interrupt **dǎ chà**	打岔 打岔	
intimate **qīn mì-de**	亲密的 親密的	
introvert **nèi xiàng-de rén**	内向的人 內向的人	
irregular **bù guī zé**	不规则 不規則	
irrelevant **niú tóu bú duì má zuǐ**	牛头不对马嘴 牛頭不對馬嘴	
irritates me **rě-wo yí dù-zi qì**	惹我一肚子气 惹我一肚子氣	

J

jealousy; jealous of **chī cù; dù-ji**	吃醋；妒忌 吃醋；妒忌	
joyful **chōng mán xǐ yüè**	充满喜悦 充滿喜悅	
just **zhèng hǎo; qià hǎo; jiù**	正好;恰好;就 正好;恰好;就	

K

(a) kick back **ná huí kòu**	拿回扣 拿回扣	

kidding; joking kāi wán xiào	开玩笑 開玩笑	lewd conduct wěi xiè	猥亵 猥褻
kind hé-qi; yǒu ài xīn	和气；有爱心 和氣；有愛心	liberal kāi míng	开明 開明

L

★large (相反 small)（见 big） dà hàor-de	大号儿的 大號兒的	lifetime yì shēng-de	一生的 一生的
lame bó; qüé	跛；瘸 跛；瘸	light (1 weight) qīng (2 brightness) liàng	1 轻 2 亮 輕 亮
last zuì hòu yí-gè	最后一个 最後一個	likely hén kě néng	很可能 很可能
lasting chí jiǔ	持久 持久	likelihood kě néng xìng	可能性 可能性
late wǎn	晚 晚	★little (相反 big)（见 small） xiǎo; hǎo xiǎo	小；好小 小；好小
latest zuì xīn-de	最新的 最新的	lively huó pō	活泼 活潑
lazy lǎn	懒 懶	live huó-de	活的 活的
lean (1 against) yǐ; kào (2 meat) shòu ròu	1 倚；靠 2 瘦肉	local dāng dì-de	当地的 當地的
least zuì shǎo-de	最少的 最少的	lonely gū dú	孤独 孤獨
left zuǒ	左 左	long (1 lengthwise) cháng (2 timewise) jiǔ	1 长 2 久
left-hand zuǒ cè-de	左侧的 左側的	longing kě wàng	渴望 渴望
left-handed zuó piě-zi	左撇子 左撇子	(act the) lord; put on airs bǎi-zhe-ge chòu jià-zi	摆著个臭架子 擺著個臭架子
legal hé fǎ-de	合法的 合法的	lost diū-le	丢了 丟了
(take) legal action tí chū sù sòng	提出诉讼 提出訴訟	lost hold méi zhuā zhù	没抓住 沒抓住
legitimate zhèng dàng hé fǎ	正当合法 正當合法	loud dà shēng	大声 大聲
less bǐ jiào shǎo	比较少 比較少	lovely kě ài-de	可爱的 可愛的
level shuǐ pīng	水平 水平	low dī	低（位置；职位） 低
		lucky xìng yùn	幸运 幸運

lunar	阴；阴历		meaningful	有意义地
yīn; yīn lì	陰；陰曆		yǒu yì yì-de	有意義地
lustful	欲火焚身		mentally disturbed	忐忑不安
yù huǒ fén shēn	慾火焚身		tǎn tè bù ān	忐忑不安
			merry	快乐
M			kuài lè	快樂
mad at me	跟我生气		middle	中间
gēn wǒ shēng qì	跟我生氣		zhōng jiān	中間
magic	魔术般的		(I) might as well	索性
mó shù bān-de	魔術般的		suó-xing	索性
main	干线；主要		mighty	强大
gàn xiàn; zhǔ yào	幹線；主要		qiáng dà	強大
major	较多的；主要的		mild	温和
jiǎo duō-de; zhǔ yào-de	較多的；主要的		wēn hé	溫和
male	男性		mineral	矿物质的
nán xìng	男性		kuàng wù zhí-de	礦物質的
(a) man of integrity	有骨气		minor	较少的；次要的
yóu gǔ qì	有骨氣		jiáo shǎo-de; cì yào-de	較少的；次要的
manly	男人气		mischief	恶作剧
nán rén qì	男人氣		è zuò jù	惡作劇
masculine; viriles	阳刚气		miserable	痛苦；苦恼
yáng gāng qì	陽剛氣		tòng kǔ; kú nǎo	痛苦；苦惱
many	好几个		mixed	混合的
háo jǐ gè	好幾個		hùn hé-de	混合的
marital status	婚姻状况		mobile	自由流动
hūn yīn zhuàng kuàng	婚姻狀況		zì yóu liú dòng	自由流動
marked	做了记号儿的		modern	新式的
zuò-le jì hàor-de	做了記號兒的		xīn shì-de	新式的
(getting) married	要结婚		modest	谦虚
yào jié hūn	要結婚		qiān xǔ	謙虛
(is) married	已结婚		moist	潮湿
yǐ jié hūn	已結婚		cháo shī	潮濕
(was) married	以前结过婚		molest	毛手毛脚
yǐ qián jié-guo hūn	以前結過婚		máo shǒu máo jiǎo	毛手毛腳
material	物质的		moody	心情不好
wù zhí-de	物質的		xīn qíng bù-hao	心情不好
maternal	母系的		more	再多一点儿
mǔ xì-de	母系的		zài duō yì diǎnr	再多一點兒
mature	成熟		most	最
chéng shóu	成熟		zuì	最

most probobly **bā chéngr**	八成儿 八成兒	necessary **bì yào-de**	必要的 必要的
much **xǔ duō; dà liàng**	许多；大量 許多；大量	neglected **hū lüè-le**	忽略了 忽略了
muddy **ní nìng**	泥泞 泥濘	neither is **liǎng-ge dōu bù**	两个都不 兩個都不
multiple **bèi shù; duō chóng-de**	倍数；多重的 倍數；多重的	(you have the) nerve **ní liǎn pī dào hěn hòu**	你脸皮倒很厚 你臉皮倒很厚
musical **yīn yüè-de**	音乐的 音樂的	nervous **shén jīng; jǐn zhāng**	神经；紧张 神經；緊張
muscular **yǒu jī ròu-de**	有肌肉的 有肌肉的	new **xīn**	新 新
mutual **xiāng hù-de**	相互的 相互的	next **xià yí-ge**	下一个 下一個
N		next-door **gé bì**	隔壁 隔壁
nagged my ears off **láo-dao sǐ rén**	唠叨死人 嘮叨死人	nice **tǐng hǎo-de**	挺好的 挺好的
naive **tīan zhēn; wú zhī**	天真；无知 天真；無知	nice-looking **hǎo kàn**	好看 好看
naive remarks **shuō huà yòu-zhi**	说话幼稚 說話幼稚	no (See 28 ; 29 ; 30 , Group 7) **bù; bú duì**	不；不對
nagging **dié dié bù xiū**	喋喋不休 喋喋不休	noble **gāo guì**	高贵 高貴
narrow **zhǎi**	窄 窄	noisy **chǎo; zào yīn**	吵；噪音 吵；噪音
narrow-minded **xiǎo xīn yǎnr**	小心眼儿 小心眼兒	non-stop **zhí dá**	直达 直達
national **guó jiā-de**	国家的 國家的	none **méi yǒu yí-ge shì**	没有一个是… 沒有一個是 …
native **bén tǔ; dāng dì**	本土；当地 本土；當地	none the less **yī rán**	依然 依然
nauseous smell **fǔ chòu**	腐臭 **腐臭**	nonsense **guí chě dàn**	鬼扯淡 鬼扯淡
near **jìn**	近 近	nor **yě bú shì**	也不是 也不是
nearby **fù jìn**	附近 附近	normal **zhèng cháng**	正常 正常
neat **zhěng jié**	整洁 整潔	nosy **hào guǎn xián shì**	好管闲事 好管閒事

notable **xiǎn zhù**	显著 顯著	ordinary **pǔ tōng-de**	普通的 普通的
now **xiàn zài; zhèi huǐr**	这会儿；现在 這會兒；现在	original **yuán lái-de**	原来的 原來的
nutrious **yǒu yíng yǎng**	有营养 有營養	other **bié-de**	别的 别的

O

		out **wài biān**	外边 外邊
oblong **cháng fāng**	长方 長方	outdoor **hù wài**	户外 戶外
obscure **bù qīng-chu**	不清楚 不清楚	outgoing **wài chū-de** (lǚ kè; xìn)	外出的（旅客；信） **外出的（旅客；信）**
obvious **míng xiǎn**	明显 明顯	out-of-date **guò shí-le**	过时了 過時了
occasional **óu ěr**	偶尔 偶爾	out-of-town **chū yuǎn ménr-le**	出远门儿了 出遠門兒了
octagon **bā jiǎo xíng**	八角形 八角形	outside **wài biānr**	外边儿 外邊兒
odd **qí yì; jī shù**	奇异；奇数 奇異；奇數	outstanding **chū sè**	出色 出色
of **zhī; -de**	…之；…的 …之；…的	oval **tuǒ yuán xíng**	椭圆形 橢圓形
offensive **mào fàn**	冒犯 冒犯	over **jié shù**	结束 結束
official **gōng wù shàng-de**	公务上的 公務上的	overseas **hǎi wài**	海外 海外
old **lǎo**	老 老	overtime **jiā bān**	加班 加班
on **-de shàng miàn**	的上面 的上面	overweight **guò zhòng**	过重 過重
one night affair **yí yè qíng**	一夜情 一夜情	own **yōng yǒu; zì jǐ-de**	拥有；自己的 擁有；自己的
only **zhǐ**	只 只		

P

opposite **duì miàn**	对面 對面	paid **yǐ fù**	已付 已付
or **huò zhě**	或者 或者	painful **téng tòng**	疼痛 疼痛
orderly **yǒu zhì-xü**	有秩序 有秩序	painted **yóu qī guò-le**	油漆过了 油漆過了

pale cāng bái	苍白 蒼白	pick-up gals diào mǎ-zi	吊马子 吊馬子
panic kǒng huāng	恐慌 恐慌	pick-up guys diào kǎi-zi	吊凯子 吊凱子
parallelogram píng xíng sì biān xíng	平行四边形 平行四邊形	pitiful kě lián	可怜 可憐
partial yí bù fèn	一部份 一部份	plain qīng chǔ-de	清楚的 清楚的
particular tè bié-de	特别的 特別的	plastic sù jiāo-de	塑胶的 塑膠的
pare-time jiān zhí	兼职 兼職	play a trick on one zhuō nòng rén	捉弄人 捉弄人
passing jīng guò	经过 經過	pleasant yǔ kuài-de	愉快的 愉快的
passionate rè qíng	热情 熱情	pleased mǎn zú-le	满足了 滿足了
passive xiāo jí; bèi dòng	消极;被动 消極;被動	plenty hǎo duō hǎo duō	好多好多 好多好多
past guò qù-de	过去的 過去的	plump pàng dū dū-de	胖嘟嘟的 胖嘟嘟的
paternal fù xì-de	父系的 父系的	polite yóu lǐ mào	有礼貌 有禮貌
patient rěn nài	忍耐 忍耐	polygon duō jiǎo xíng	多角形 多角形
peaceful hé píng	和平 和平	poor qióng; kě lián	穷;可怜 窮;可憐
peak diān fēng	颠峰 顛峰	popular rén rén xǐ ài	人人喜爱 人人喜愛
peculiar guài pì	怪癖 怪癖	positive zhèng miàn-de	正面的 正面的
pentangle wú jiǎo xíng	五角形 五角形	possible kě néng	可能 可能
perfect wán zhěng wú qūē	完整无缺 完整無缺	powerful qiáng yǒu lì	强有力 強有力
persistent jiān chí	坚持 堅持	practical shí yòng	实用 實用
(that's too) personal nǐ wèn-de tài duō-le-ba	你问的太多了吧! 你問的太多了吧!	precious bǎo guì	宝贵 寶貴
pick on tiāo tì; zhǎo chár	挑剔;找碴儿 挑剔;找碴兒	prejudiced zhǒng zú piān jiàn	种族偏见 種族偏見

precise **jīng qüè**	精确 精確
pregnant **yóu xǐ-le**	有喜了！ **有喜了！**
pretty **piào liàng**	漂亮 漂亮
present **lái-le; chū xí**	来了；出席 來了；出席
primary **chū jí-de**	初级的 初級的
principal **shǒu yào-de**	首要的 首要的
(higher) priority **yōu xiān kǎo lǜ**	优先考虑 優先考慮
private **sī rén shǐ yòng-de**	私人使用的 私人使用的
professional **zhuān yè-de**	专业的 專業的
propose **qiú hūn**	求婚 求婚
public **gōng gòng-de**	公共的 公共的
pull a long face **lā-zhe-ge lú liǎn**	拉著个驴脸 拉著個驢臉
pull yourself together **zhèn zuò qǐ-lai**	振作起来 振作起來
(take a) pull at the cigarette **chōu kǒu yān**	抽口菸 抽口菸
(has a lot of) pull **yǒu shì-li**	有势力 有勢力
pulling my leg **qǔ xiào-wo**	取笑我 取笑我
pure **chún**	纯 純
(Don't) push me! **bié bī-wo**	别逼我！ 別逼我！
(You've) pushed him too far! **nǐ qī rén tài shèn**	你欺人太甚 你欺人太甚

Q

quadrangle **sì jiǎo xíng**	四角形 四角形
qualified **hé gé**	合格 合格
quarreling **chǎo jià**	吵架 吵架
quick **xǜn sù**	迅速 迅速
quiet **ān jìng**	安静 安靜
quite **shí fēn**	十分 十分
queer **gǔ guài**	古怪 古怪

R

radius **bàn jìng**	半径 半徑
radical **jī jìn**	激进 激進
rapid **kuài sù**	快速 快速
rare **hǎn jiàn**	罕见 罕見
ready **zhǔn bèi hǎo-le**	准备好了 準備好了
ready-made **xiàn chéngr-de**	现成儿的 現成兒的
real **zhēn-de**	真的 真的
(the) real McCoy **rú jiǎ bāo huàn-de zhēn huò**	如假包换的真货 如假包換的真貨
rear **hòu bù; hòu biān**	後部；後边 後部；後邊
reasonable **hé lǐ-de**	合理的 合理的
recent **zuì jìn-de**	最近的 最近的

reckless lú mǎng	鲁莽 魯莽	repairative huī fù	恢复 恢復
rectangle cháng fāng xíng	长方形 長方形	repeated fǎn fù	反复 反覆
regular yì bān guī gé-de	一般规格的 一般規格的	repellent pái chì	排斥 排斥
related yǒu guān lián-de	有关联的 有關聯的	repercussive fǎn yìng	反应 反應
relative xiāng duì-de	相对的 相對的	replete chōng mǎn	充满 充滿
relaxed qīng sōng yú kuài	轻松愉快 輕鬆愉快	reposeful zhèn jìng	镇静 鎮靜
releasable kě ràng dù-de	可让渡的 可讓渡的	reprehensive qiǎn zé	谴责 譴責
relevant yǒu guān-xi	有关系 有關係	representational dài biǎo	代表 代表
reliable kě kào	可靠 可靠	repressed grievance òu qì (See P.72 ★, "One" what?)	怄气 慪氣
religious qián chéng	虔诚 虔誠	repressive yì zhì	抑制 抑制
(was) reluctant to (use; eat; give up) shě-bu-de (yòng; chī…)	舍不得 捨不得(用；吃…)	reprobate duò luò	堕落 墮落
remanent cán liú	残留 殘留	repulsive shǐ rén yàn wù	使人厌恶 使人厭惡
remarkable jié chū-de	杰出的 傑出的	reputable míng yù hǎo	名誉好 名譽好
remedial bǔ jiù	补救 補救	resemblant xiāng sì	相似 相似
remunerative yǒu bào chóu-de	有报酬的 有報酬的	resistless wú fǎ kàng jù-de	无法抗拒的 無法抗拒的
renascent zài shēng	再生 再生	resolute jiān jué	坚决 堅決
renewable kě gēng xīn-de	可更新的 可更新的	resounding hóng liàng	宏亮 宏亮
renitent kàng yā	抗压 抗壓	respectable shòu rén zūn jìng-de	受人尊敬的 受人尊敬的
renowned zhù míng-de	著名的 著名的	respective gè bié-de	个别的 個別的
repairable néng xiū lǐ	能修理 能修理	responsible dān dāng zé rèn	担当责任 擔當責任

responsive yóu fǎn yīng	有反应 有反應	right away; right off mǎ shàng	马上 馬上
restful píng jìng-de	平静的 平靜的	rigid wěn gù-de; yán gé	稳固的；严格 穩固的；嚴格
restive hào dòng	好动 好動	righteous zhèng zhí	正直 正直
resultant jié guǒ	结果 結果	riotous bào luàn	暴乱 暴亂
retail líng shòu	零售 零售	risible ài xiào; kě xiào	爱笑；可笑 愛笑；可笑
retentive bǎo liú	保留 保留	risky wéi xiǎn	危险 危險
retired tuì xiū-le	退休了 退休了	rival jìng zhēng	竞争 競爭
retrograde dào tuì-de	倒退的 倒退的	robust qiáng zhuàng	强壮 強壯
reversible zhèng fǎn miàn liǎng yòng	正反面两用 正反面两用	rocking yáo gǔn	摇滚 搖滾
revocatory jiě chú	解除 解除	roily hún zhúo	混浊 混濁
revolting bèi pàn	背叛 背叛	rolling gǔn dòng	滚动 滾動
rewarding yǒu yì	有益；有利 有益；有利	romantic làng màn	浪漫 浪漫
rewardless; yǒu lì tú láo wú gōng	徒劳无功 徒勞無功	rompish wán pí	顽皮 頑皮
rhombus; diamond líng xíng; xié fāng xíng	菱形；斜方形 菱形；斜方形	roomy kuān chǎng	宽敞 寬敞
rhomboid cháng líng tǐ	长菱体 長菱體	rotating xuán zhuǎn	旋转 旋轉
rhythmic yǒu yùn lǜ-de	有韵律的 有韻律的	rough cū cāo	粗糙 粗糙
rich fù yǒu	富有 富有	round yüán xíng	圆形 圓形
ridden shòu zhé mó	受折磨 受折磨	rousing xīng fèn	兴奋 興奮
ridiculous huāng miù; mò míng qí miào	荒谬;莫名其妙 荒謬;莫名其妙	routine lì xíng-de	例行的 例行的
right duì; yòu	对；右 對；右	royal huáng jiā-de	皇家的 皇家的

rubbishy **yì wén bù zhí**	一文不值 一文不值	scientific **kē xüé-de**	科学的 科學的
rude **méi lǐ mào**	没礼貌 沒禮貌	screaming **jiān jiào**	尖叫 尖叫
rueful **bēi cǎn**	悲惨 悲慘	seagoing **hái-li háng xíng-de**	海里航行的 海裡航行的
rugged **gāo dī bù píng**	高低不平 高低不平	searching **zǐ xì-de**	仔细的 仔細的
ruinous **huǐ miè xìng-de**	毁灭性的 毀滅性的	seasonable **jì jié xìng-de**	季节性的 季節性的
rumors **yáo yán; chuán shuō**	谣言;传说 謠言;傳說	seated **jiù zuò**	就座 就座
runty **fā yǜ bù liáng-de**	发育不良的 發育不良的	secondary **cì yào-de**	次要的 次要的
rural **xiāng cūn-de**	乡村的 鄉村的	secret **yǐn mì**	隐密 隱密
(Don't)rush me! **bié cuī-wo**	别催我! 別催我!	secular **shì sú-de**	世俗的 世俗的
		sectional **qǜ yǜ-de**	区域的 區域的

S

sad **bēi āi**	悲哀 悲哀	sedate **ān xiáng**	安详 安詳
safe **ān qüán**	安全 安全	sedulous **qín miǎn**	勤勉 勤勉
same **tóng yàng; yí yàng**	同样;一样 同樣;一樣	segregated **zhǒng zú gé lí**	种族隔离 種族隔離
satisfactory **lìng rén mǎn yì**	令人满意 令人滿意	selected **jīng guò tiāo xüǎn-de**	经过挑选的 經過挑選的
satisfied **mǎn zú**	满足 滿足	self-abased **zì bēi**	自卑 自卑
saving **chǔ xǜ**	储蓄 儲蓄	self-centered **wéi wǒ dú zūn-de rén**	唯我独尊的人 唯我獨尊的人
scarce **qüē fá**	缺乏 缺乏	self-important; arrogant **zì dà**	自大 自大
scared **dǎn xiǎo; bù gǎn**	胆小;不敢 膽小;不敢	self-respect; self-esteem **zì zūn; zì zūn xīn**	自尊;自尊心 自尊;自尊心
schedular **àn zhào shí jiān biǎo**	按照时间表 按照時間表	selfish **zì sī**	自私 自私
scheming **guǐ zhà**	诡诈 詭詐	senior **nián zhǎng-de**	年长的 年長的

sensible **hé qíng-li**	合情理 合情理	shocking **hài rén tīng wén-de**	骇人听闻的 駭人聽聞的
sensitive **mín gǎn**	敏感 敏感	short (A article) **duǎn** (B people) **ǎi**	短 (A 东西) 矮 (B 人)
sentimental **gǎn qíng-de**	感情的 感情的	shartcoming **qūe diǎn; duǎn chù**	缺点；短处 缺點；短處
separated **fēn jǔ-le**	分居了 分居了	short-handed **rén shǒu bù zú**	人手不足 人手不足
seprable **néng fēn kāi-de**	能分开的 能分開的	shook-up **chī bù xiāo**	吃不消 吃不消
sequent **jì xù**	继续 繼續	shrew **jīng míng**	精明 精明
serious **yán sù**	严肃 嚴肅	shut **guān bì**	关闭 關閉
serviceable **shì yòng**	适用 適用	shy **hài xiū; mián tǎn**	害羞；腼腆 害羞；靦腆
set me up **xiàn hài-wo**	陷害我 陷害我	sick **yǒu bìng**	有病 有病
settled **ān dìng xià-lai**	安定下来 安定下來	silent **wú shēng; chén mò**	无声；沈默 無聲；沈默
severe **yán lì**	严厉 嚴厲	silly **yǔ chǔn-de**	愚蠢的 愚蠢的
sex **xìng ; xìng bié**	性；性别 性；性別	silver **yín-de**	银的 銀的
sexual harassment **xìng sāo rǎo**	性骚扰 性騷擾	similar **lèi sì**	类似 類似
shaky **zhàn lì**	战栗 戰慄	simple **jiǎn dān**	简单 簡單
shallow **qiǎn**	浅 淺	simulated **jiǎ zhuāng**	假装 假裝
(no) shame; brazen it out **hòu-zhe liǎn pí …**	厚着脸皮… 厚著臉皮…	sincere **zhēn chéng**	真诚 真誠
shameful **ké chǐ; wú chǐ**	可耻；无耻 可恥；無恥	single **dān yī**	单一 單一
shameless **bú hài sào; bú yào liǎn**	不害臊；不要脸 不害臊；不要臉	situated **zuò luò**	座落 座落
shaped **chéng xíng-de**	成形的 成形的	skilled **qiǎo miào**	巧妙 巧妙
sharp **xī zhuāng bí tǐng; ruì lì**	西装笔挺；锐利 西裝筆挺；銳利	slack **lán-san; kuān sōng**	懒散；宽松 懶散；寬鬆

(didn't) sleep a wink all night zhěng yè méi hé yǎn	整夜没阖眼	整夜沒闔眼
sleepy kùn	困	睏
(I'm so) sleepy. wǒ kùn-de yào mìng	我困得要命	我睏得要命
slender xì cháng; miáo tiáo	细长；苗条	細長；苗條
slicky huá tóu	滑头	滑頭
slight qīng wéi	轻微	輕微
(always does a) sloppy job zuò shì tuō ní dài shuǐ	做事拖泥带水	做事拖泥帶水
slow huǎn màn	缓慢	緩慢
slow-footed màn téng-teng-de	慢腾腾的	慢騰騰的
★small (相反 large) (见 little) xiǎo hàor-de	小号儿的	小號兒的
smart jī-ling	机灵	機靈
smart looking shuài; xiāo sǎ	帅；潇洒	帥；瀟灑
smashed jiǔ zuì; pò suì-de	酒醉；破碎的	酒醉；破碎的
smoky mào yān	冒烟	冒煙
smooth guāng huá	光滑	光滑
sober méi zuì; qīng xǐng	没醉；清醒	沒醉；清醒
(enhance) social lives gǎi shàn shè jiāo shēng huó	改善社交生活	改善社交生活
so-called jiù-shi suǒ wèi-de	就是所谓的	就是所謂的
soft róu ruǎn	柔软	柔軟
soggy pào-de ruǎn pā pā-de	泡得软趴趴的	泡得軟趴趴的
solar tài yáng; yáng lì	太阳；阳历	太陽；陽曆
solid gù tǐ	固体	固體
(you are) something else nǐ zhēn rén bú lù xiàng	你真人不露相	你真人不露相
sorry bào qiàn	抱歉	抱歉
sore téng tòng	疼痛	疼痛
sorrowful shāng xīn-de	伤心的	傷心的
so-so hái hǎo; pǔ tōng	还好；普通	還好；普通
sound shēng-yin; tīng qǐ-lai	声音；听起来	聲音；聽起來
sounds quite convincing tīng-zhe mán yǒu dào-li	听着蛮有道理	聽著蠻有道理
sounds inviting tīng qǐ-lai mán hǎo-de	听起来蛮好的	聽起來蠻好的
(I had a) sound sleep wǒ shuì-de hǎo xiāng	我睡得好香	我睡得好香
speakable kě yǐ shuō-de	可以说的	可以說的
special tè bié-de	特别的	特別的
spectacled dài yǎn jìngr-de	戴眼镜儿的	戴眼鏡兒的
spectacular zhuàng lì	壮丽	壯麗
speedy xùn sù	迅速	迅速
spiteful pō là	泼辣	潑辣
(I'm) splitting. wǒ xiān zǒu-yi bù	我先走一步	我先走一步
squabble kóu jiǎo	口角	口角
square zhèng fāng xíng	正方型	正方型

stable **láo gù**	牢固 牢固	substantial **shí zài-de dōng-xi**	实在的东西 實在的東西
stark **jiāng yìng**	僵硬 僵硬	successful **chéng gōng-de**	成功的 成功的
startle; scared me **xià yí tiào**	吓一跳 嚇一跳	sudden **tú rán**	突然 突然
steady **wěn dìng**	稳定 穩定	suddenly **hū rán; lěng-bu fáng**	忽然；冷不防 忽然；冷不防
sticky **nián**	黏 黏	suitable **shì hé**	适合 適合
stiff **yìng**	硬 硬	sure **bì dìng**	必定 必定
still **jìng zhǐ; réng rán**	静止；仍然 靜止；仍然	sweet talk **tián yán mì yǔ**	甜言蜜语 甜言蜜語
stay still **bié dòng**	别动 別動		

T

stingy **xiǎo-qi**	小气 小氣	talented **yǒu cái néng**	有才能 有才能
straight **zhí-de**	直的 直的	(talk) rubbish **xiā bāi**	瞎掰 瞎掰
strange **qí guài**	奇怪 奇怪	talkative **duō zuǐ**	多嘴 多嘴
stretchy **kě shēn zhǎn-de**	可伸展的 可伸展的	tall **gāo; shòu gāo**	高；瘦高 高；瘦高
strict **yán gé**	严格 嚴格	tamed **tīng huà; xǔn fú guò-de**	听话；驯服過的 聽話；馴服過的
strong (tea) **qiáng zhuàng; nóng**	强壮；浓 強壯；濃（茶）	tarnished **shī qù sè zé**	失去色泽 失去色澤
stout; solidly built **jiē-shi**	结实 結實	tasteful **yǒu shén méi gǎn**	有审美感 有審美感
struggling **zhēng zhá**	挣扎 掙紮	technical **zhuān mén xué shù-de**	专门学术的 專門學術的
studious **yòng gōng**	用功 用功	tedious **rǒng cháng fá wèi**	冗长乏味 冗長乏味
stumbled **diē-le yì jiāo**	跌了一跤 跌了一跤	telling **yǒu lì; yǒu xiào**	有力；有效 有力；有效
stupid **yú chǔn**	愚蠢 愚蠢	temperate **shì dù**	适度 適度
stylish **shí máo**	时髦 時髦	temporary **lín shí-de**	临时的 臨時的

tender róu ruǎn	柔软 柔軟	tolerate; endure róng rěn	容忍 容忍
tense jǐn zhāng	紧张 緊張	top dǐng; zuì shàng fāng	顶；最上方 頂；最上方
tetrahedron sì miàn tǐ	四面体 四面體	topical yǒu huà tí	有话题 有話題
terminal zuì zhōng	最终 最終	torturous zhé-mo rén	折磨人 折磨人
terrible kě pà-de	可怕的 可怕的	total zǒng gòng	总共 總共
terrific liǎo-bu qǐ	了不起 了不起	touchable mō-de dào	摸得到 摸得到
thankful gǎn xiè	感谢 感謝	tough qiáng rèn	强韧 強韌
there you are shuō-de duì	说得对 說得對	tradable kě jiāo yì-de	可交易的 可交易的
there you go again. nǐ kàn, yòu lái-le	你看，又来了！ 你看，又來了！	traditional chuán tǒng-de	传统的 傳統的
thick (1 liquid) chóu; nóng (2 board) hòu	1 稠；浓 2 厚	tragic bēi cǎn-de	悲惨的 悲慘的
thin; skinny shòu	瘦 瘦	transferable kě ràng dù-de	可让渡的 可讓渡的
triangle sān jiǎo xíng	三角形 三角型	trapezium sì biān bù guī ze	四边不规则 四邊不規則
thin (1 liquid) xī (2 board) báo; bó	1 稀 2 薄	treasurable zhēn guì	珍贵 珍貴
thinkable ké xiǎng xiàng-de	可想象的 可想像的	trembleing zhèn chàn	震颤 震顫
thorough wán quán	完全 完全	trickish jiǎo huá	狡猾 狡猾
thoughtful xì xīn	细心 細心	trustful xìn rèn	信任 信任
tidy zhěng qí	整齐 整齊	trust me xiāng xìn-wo	相信我 相信我
tight jǐn	紧 緊	truthful shuō shí huà	说实话 說實話
tired lèi	累 累	tutorial jiā jiào-de	家教的 家教的
together yì qǐ	一起 一起	typical diǎn xíng	典型 典型

U

unconscious **bù xǐng rén shì**	不省人事 不省人事	
ugly **nán kàn**	难看 難看	
ultimate **zuì zhōng**	最终 最終	
unappreciative **bù zhī háo dǎi**	不知好歹 不知好歹	
unbelievable **bù kě xìn**	不可信 不可信	
under a lucky star **zào-hua; fú fèn**	造化；福份 造化；福份	
uneducated **méi shòu guò jiào yù-de**	没受过教育的 沒受過教育的	
unhappy **bú kuài lè**	不快乐 不快樂	
untrustworthy **bù kě kào**	不可靠 不可靠	
up **xiàng shàng; wǎng shàng**	向上；往上 向上；往上	
(it) upsets me; it paints me **bǎ-wo rě máo-le**	把我惹毛了 把我惹毛了	
upside down **dào-zhe fàng; fàng dào-le**	倒着放；放倒了 倒著放；放倒了	
usable **kě yòng**	可用 可用	
used **yòng guò-de**	用过的 用過的	
used to **yǐ qián**	以前 以前	
used to be... **yǐ qián shì...**	以前是… 以前是…	
useful **yǒu yòng**	有用 有用	
usually **tōng cháng lái shuō**	通常来说 通常來說	
utile **shí yòng**	实用 實用	

V

vacant **kōng**	空 空	
vain **wú xiào**	无效 無效	
valid **zhèng qüè**	正确 正確	
valuable **yǒu jià zhí**	有价值 有價值	
variable **biàn huà**	变化 變化	
various **bù tóng yàng shì-de**	不同样式的 不同樣式的	
very **tēī; hěn; fēi cháng**	忒；很；非常 忒；很；非常	
vibrational **zhèn dòng-de**	振动的 振動的	
(has all kinds of) vices **chī hē piáo dǔ dōu lái**	吃喝嫖睹都来 吃喝嫖睹都來	
viewable **zhí dé yí kàn**	值得一看 值得一看	
vigorous **jīng lì chōng pèi**	精力充沛 精力充沛	
violent **měng liè**	猛烈 猛烈	
visit with **chuàn mén-zi**	串門子 串門子	
vivid **xiān míng**	鲜明 鮮明	
vocal **fā shēng yīn-de**	发声音的 發聲音的	
visional **shì lì-de**	视力的 視力的	
voguey **liú xíng-de; shí máo-de**	流行的；时髦的 流行的；時髦的	
voluntary **zì yüàn-de**	自愿的 自願的	
vomitous **xiáng tù**	想吐 想吐	

W

English	Pinyin	Simplified	Traditional

wandering
pái huái; liú làng
徘徊；流浪
徘徊；流浪

warm
nuǎn-he
暖和
暖和

warm-hearted
rè xīn
热心
熱心

watchful
zhù yì
注意
注意

water-proof
fáng shuǐ-de
防水的
防水的

watery
shuǐ wāng wāng-de
水汪汪的
水汪汪的

weak (tea)
ruǎn ruò; dàn
软弱；淡
軟弱；淡(茶)

wealthy
yǒu qiǎn
有钱
有錢

wearing
chuān-de; dài-de
穿的；戴的
穿的；戴的

weird
guài guài-de
怪怪的
怪怪的

weekly
měi zhōu yí cì-de
每周一次的
每週一次的

well
ān hǎo; bìng hǎo-le
安好；病好了
安好；病好了

welcome
shòu huān yíng
受欢迎
受歡迎

well-developed
fā zhǎn liáng hǎo
发展良好
發展良好

well-done
zuò-de hǎo
做得好
做得好

well-informed
xiāo xí líng tōng
消息灵通
消息靈通

well-known
yǒu míng
有名
有名

well-off
hùn-de bú cuò; fù-yü
混得不错；富裕
混得不錯；富裕

well-read
bó xué
博学
博學

wet
shī
湿
濕

What's in it for me?
yóu wǒ shén-me hǎo-chu
有我甚麼好处
有我甚麼好處

What lousy luck!
dǎo méi
倒楣
倒楣

white-haired
bái fǎ-de
白发的
白髮的

whitening
piǎo bái-de
漂白的
漂白的

wholehearted
rè chéng-de
热诚的
熱誠的

wholesale
pī fā
批发
批發

wicked
xié è
邪恶
邪惡

wide
kuān
宽
寬

wide-open
gōng rán-de; dà kāi-de
公然的；大开的
公然的；大開的

(a) wide variety
wǔ huā bā mén
五花八门
五花八門

widespread
pǔ jí
普及
普及

wild
yě xìng
野性
野性

willful; wilful
rèn xìng
任性
任性

willing
qíng yüàn
情愿
情願

willless
miǎn qiáng
勉强
勉強

winding
wān qǔ-de
弯曲的
彎曲的

windy
fēng sōu sōu-de
风飕飕的
風颼颼的

winning
yíng-le
赢了
贏了

wintry
dōng tiān sì-de
冬天似的
冬天似的

English	Pinyin	Chinese (Simplified)	Chinese (Traditional)
wireless	wú xiàn-de	无线的	無線的
wise	yǒu zhì huì	有智慧	有智慧
wishful	kě wàng	渴望	渴望
with	dài	带	帶
without	bú dài	不带	不帶
wooden	mù zhì-de	木制的	木製的
woolen	yáng maó zhì pǐn	羊毛制品	羊毛製品
wordless	wú huà kě shuō	无话可说	無話可說
working	gōng zuò	工作	工作
worn-out	chuān pò-le; yòng huài-le	穿破了；用坏了	穿破了；用壞了
worrisome	fán rén	烦人	煩人
worse	gèng zāo gāo	更糟糕	更糟糕
worst	zuì zāo-de	最糟的	最糟的
worth	zhí	值	值
worth it	zhí dé	值得	值得
(not) worth it	bù zhí dé; huá bù lái	不值得；划不来	不值得；劃不來
worthless	yì wén bù zhí	一文不值	一文不值
worthwhile	huá-de lái	划得来	劃得來
wounded	shòu shāng	受伤	受傷
wrong	cuò; cuò-le	错；错了	錯；錯了

Y

English	Pinyin	Chinese (Simplified)	Chinese (Traditional)
yakety yak	díe díe bù xīu	喋喋不休	喋喋不休
yawned out a good night	dǎ hā qiàn dào wǎn ān	打哈欠道晚安	打哈欠道晚安
year-end	nián zhōng	年终	年終
yearly	nián nián-de	年年的	年年的
year-round	zhěng nián-de	整年的	整年的
yellowish	huáng bù jīr-de	黄不唧儿的	黃不唧兒的
yes	shì-de; duì	是的；对	是的；對
young	nián qīng	年轻	年輕
yummy	měi wèi ké kǒu	美味可口	美味可口

Z

English	Pinyin	Chinese (Simplified)	Chinese (Traditional)
zealous	rè xīn; rè chéng	热心；热诚	熱心；熱誠
zero	líng dù	零度	零度
zigzag	qǔ zhé	曲折	曲折

Particularities Of The Chinese Language

窍门儿（文法融入语言）

The author was born in a Sino-American bilingual family in Beijing. As the age of four, Marco started to receive a classic Chinese upbringing from his father, his old-fashioned but well-taught and scrupulous grandmother and his "ancient" family tutors. He started with The Three-Character Primer (三字经Sān Zì Jīng), The Analects of Confucius (論語Lún Yǔ) and The Teaching of Mencius (孟子Mèng Zǐ). His education also included practicing Chinese calligraphy and painting. He had lessons in English conversation with Emily Curran, chief dietitian at Rockefeller's Beijing Xié Hé Hospital 协和医院 and the daughter of Charley Curran, famous American portrait artist. Emily was also the daughter-in-law of the Liang family.

This well-balanced Eastern and Western background, plus the advanced postgraduate education in chemistry that he received in America enabled Marco to devise "The particularities of 普通话 pǔtōnghuà" in a scientific way.

Here, he presented a list of essential Chinese terminology and grammar. By simply applying these concepts to vocabulary found in the subsequent glossaries, the user can form logical Chinese sentences very fast.

1. nèi

那（音 "内"）
The (I)

那 **nèi** refers to something afar that you're pointing at, looking at, thinking of, or even something not in sight. It is similar to the English article "The".

In Chinese, the "The" is omitted or not necessarily mentioned, especially when it concerns a unique object: "sun, moon, earth, names, places…". e.g.:

❶ "The" Himalayas have the highest peak.
- ○ Himalayas peak most high
- ○ Xí Mǎ Lā Yǎ shān fēng zuì gāo
- ○ 喜玛拉雅 山峰 最 高

In making this sentence, all you need to know are the four key words.

1 "peak" is to be found in Group 76B, Geography
2 "have" is in Group 3, Verbs
3 "highest" is in Group 7, 57 最

❷ "The" file is missing
- ○ File ○ not in sight
- ○ dǎng àn ○ bú jiàn-le
- ○ 档案 ○ 不见了。

❸ "The" elevator is out of order
- ○ Elevator ○ broken down
- ○ diàn tī ○ huài-le
- ○ 电梯 ○ 坏了

105

2. zhèi

这 (音 "J")
The (II)

这 zhèi refers to an object or person within reach or sight. It is also similar to the English article "The". This "The" is pronounced "zhèi" and is seldomly omitted from conversation.

e.g.: ❶ "The" chair is made of paper.
The "bá" chair is paper made
zhèi (bá) yǐ-zi shì zhǐ zuò-de
这(把) 椅子 是 纸 做的

❷ "The" rascal will never get anywhere.
"The" little rascal really unpromising.
(zhèi hái-zi) zhēn méi chū-xi
(这孩子) 真 没出息。

❸ "The" tie is made of pure silk.
The "tiáo" tie is pure silk's
zhèi (tiáo) lǐng dài shì chún sī-de
这(条) 领带 是 纯 丝的

3. nà-ge; nà xiē

那个；那些
That & Those

那个 nà-ge refers to a particular person or object that is not within close proximity but within eye-sight which you are pointing out. It is similar to "that" in English.. The pronunciation is "nà-ge" or "nài-ge"

e.g.: ❶ "That" woman is my landlady.
"That" woman is I's landlord wife.
(nà-ge) nǚ-ren shì wǒ-de fáng dōng tài-tai
(那个) 女人 是 我的 房东太太
In a plural form, it is "nà xiē or nài xiē 那些", which is equal to "Those" in English.
e.g.: ❷ "Those" glasses are soiled.
"Those" glass is dirty's
(nà xiē) bēi-zi shì zāng-de
(那些) 杯子 是 脏的

4. zhè-ge; zhè xiē

这个；这些
This & These

这个 zhè-ge refers to a particular person or object that is in close proximity within reach. It is similar to "this" in English. It also pronounces "zhèi-ge"

e.g.: ❶ "This" peach is extra large.
"This" peach special big.
(zhè-ge) táo-zi tè bié dà
(这个) 桃子 特别 大

In a plural form, it is "zhè-xiē or zhèi-xiē 这些" which is equal to "These" in English.

e.g.: ❷ "These" people are my colleagues.
"These" people is I's colleague
(zhè-xie) rén shì wǒ-de tóng shì
(这些) 人 是 我的 同事
In a plural form, it is "nà xiē or "nài xiē 那些", which is equal to "Those" in English.

5. tā

牠;它 (他;她:見 Group 1A)
It (for He and She see Group 1A)

牠;它 tā Actually the tā includes all English subjects of "He, She and It", plus their object forms: "him, her and it", because Chinese language has no "gender" distinction, and again, the "He or She" is already a mutually understood person. Most of the times the "It" is omitted because it is understood without words.

e.g.: ❶ Who ? is it
Who yā? ○ ○
shuí ya? ○ ○
谁 呀? ○ ○

❷ It smells sweet.
○ ○ so fragrant.
○ ○ hǎo xiāng.
牠 香!

❸
┌─────────────────────────────────┐
│ " it" is not omited as an object │
└─────────────────────────────────┘

Would you put it away?
Make "it" put away would you?
bǎ "tā" ná zǒu hǎo-ma?
把 "它" 拿走 好吗?

┌──────────────────────┐
│ 6. -de (soft tone) │
└──────────────────────┘

(你,我,他…) -的（I）
my & mine (possession)

┌──────┐
│ 的 de │ is a bound subordinate particle
└──────┘
which is attached to a noun or a pronoun to
make it a possessive noun or possessive
pronoun. It has the same meaning as adding
apostrophe "s" ('s).

┌───┐
│   │
│   # Apostrophe "s"   │
│   │
│   add the suffix **-de** (的)   │
│   │
│ ┌───────────────────────────────────┐ │
│ │ "my ; mine"……………… "wǒ- de"   │ │
│ │ "your ; yours"…………… "nǐ- de"   │ │
│ │ "his ; her ; hers ; its "…… "tā- de"│ │
│ │ "our ; ours" …………"wǒ-men- de"   │ │
│ │ "your ; yours" …….. "nǐ-men- de"   │ │
│ │ "their ; theirs " ……..."tā-men- de" │ │
│ └───────────────────────────────────┘ │
│   │
│ When referring to one's own family   │
│ members, close relatives or personal   │
│ belongings, the "-de" is often dropped.│
│   │
│   **e.g.:** "I uncle"   for "**my** uncle" │
│   "I wife"   for "**my** wife"   │
│   "you key" for "**your** key" │
│   "he home" for "**his** home" │
│   │
│   **For non-related persons:**   │
│   **e.g.:** "my landlady" the "-ed" is kept. │
│   │
└───┘

❶ This is not my cousin's money
This not is "I" cousin ('s) money
zhè bú shì (wǒ) biǎo gē -de qián
这 不是 （我） 表哥(的) 钱

★This cousin is maternal and a male. For a
female or a paternal cousin; see Group
1B, Relatives.

---

❷ This (dog's) tail is short.
This (dog's) tail very short.
zhèi (zhǐ) (gǒu- de) yǐ-ba hén duǎn
这(只) 狗(的) 尾巴 很 短。

┌──────────────────────┐
│ 7. -de (soft tone) │
└──────────────────────┘

(大,小,长,短,颜色…) -的（II）
the…one; the…ones

┌──────┐
│ 的 de │ is a light tone which serves
└──────┘
several purposes. Here, it is used to
make a noun into an adjective.

e.g.: ❶ It is "red".
○ shì "hóng -de"
○ 是 "红 的"
❷ It is "sour".
○ shì "suān- de"
○ 是 "酸 的"

Paired with a preposition or a relative
clause to form a sentence, "- de" means "the
(adjective) one".

e.g.: ❶ She wants the "white one"
She want that "white's"
tā yào nà-ge (bái-de).
她 要 那个 （白 的）

❷ Give him the "short one"
Give him that "short's"
gěi tā nà-ge (duǎn -de).
给 他 那个 （短 的）

❸ Put the "good ones" away.
Have those "good's" removed.
bǎ nà xiē (hǎo -de) ná-kai.
把 那些 （好 的） 拿开

┌──────────────────────┐
│ 8. -de (soft tone) │
└──────────────────────┘

(物品或机關…) 之 ; -的（III）
of

┌────────┐
│ 的- de │ can also be used to express the
└────────┘
term " of" in a similar fashion.

e.g.: ❶ The color " of" the wall is too dark.
The wall "s" color too dark.
zhèi-ge qiáng (-de) yán-se tài shēn
这个 墙(的) 颜色 太 深

❷ I am the president "of " Bank of China.

I	is	China Bank	"s"	president
wǒ	shì	zhōng gúo yín háng (-de)		jīng lǐ
我	是	中国银行(的)		经理

9. -de (soft tone)

(过去式) -的！; 的？ (IV)
past tense

> On page **38**, Group **3** you have learned Chinese **Past Tense**.
> The following is another type of past tense verb used in a different situation.

的**-de** is another type of past tense verb like English suffix "**-ed**" ending. It is used in an interrogative question "**?**" or an affirmative answer "**!**". The suffix sound is "**-de** 的", not "**-le** 了".

e.g.: ❶ It was I who "stole the watch.

watch	is	I	"steal-**ed**"
biǎo	shì	wǒ	(tōu-**de**)!
錶	是	我	(偷的)!

❷ Who "broke" the crystal glass?

crystal glass	is	who	"break-**ed**"
shuǐ jīng bēi	shì	shuí	(dǎ pò-**de**)?
水晶杯	是	谁	(打破的)?

"It was" in the following examples is not necessarrily mentioned, because it is understood in Chinese language.

❸ I was the one who "killed" the man.

man	is	I	"kill-**ed**"
rēn	shì	wó	(shā-**de**)!
人	是	我	(杀的)!

❶ It was he who "did" it.

It	was	he	who	"did"	it.
○	Is	he	○	"do-**ed**"	○
○	shì	tā	○	(nòng-**de**)!	○
○	是	他	○	(弄的)!	○

❷ It was Lee who "bought" it.

It	was	Lee	who	"bought"	it.
○	Is	Lee	○	"buy-**ed**"	○
○	shì	lǐ	○	(mǎi-**de**)!	○
○	是	李	○	(买的)!	○

10. -er (soft tone)

-儿(I)
things that are little

儿**-er** is a light joining sound used as a suffix. When "**-er**" is attached to a noun it indicates that the mentioned object is "considerably small".

> **e.g.:** bird (鸟儿 niǎor)
> toothpick (牙签儿 yá qiānr)

But tigar (老虎 láo-hu) is not small, therefore láo-hu"r" is not logical unless it refers to tigar earings, ornaments, toys, etc.

So, a "pack" of chewing gum is

yì bāor	kǒu xiāng táng
一包儿	口香糖

while a "bag" of brown sugar is

yì bāo	hóng táng
一包	红糖

11. -er (soft tone)

-儿(II)
on time-close words

When 儿**-er** is attached to a time-related word, it had to be a time-close word.

❶ yesterday (昨儿个 zúor-ge)
❷ today (今儿个 jīnr-ge)
❸ tomorrow (明儿个 míngr-ge)
❹ in a while (一会儿 yì huìr)
❺ take a break (休息一下儿 xiū-xi yì xiàr)

e.g.: ❶ You come "a little later".

you	"late a little"	again	come
nín	(wǎn yì diǎnr)	zài	lái
您	(晚一点儿)	再	来

❷ Dinner will be ready "in a minute"

"wait a while"	will	start dinner
(děng yì huǐr)	jiù	kāi fàn
(等一会儿)	就	开饭

❸ He'll be with you in a minute
You "sit a while" he immediately come

nín	(zuò yì xiz)	tā	mǎ shàng lái
您	(坐一下儿)	他	馬上 来

12. -ne? (soft tone)

(缓和语气) - 呢？；呀？（I）

do and does

呢 **-ne?** is an interrogative or emphatic particle placed at the end of sentence to mitigate the effect. There is no English equivalent to this form of "-ne?" just like the lower cased "do" or "does" placed in the middle of an English question. It is used in polite situations to convey a gentle or humble demeanor.

e.g.: ❶ What "do?" you want

You	want	what	"do?"
nín	yào	shén-me	(ne?)
您	要	甚幺	（呢？）

❷ Where "does?" he want to go

He	want	go	where	"do?"
tā	yào	qù	nǎr	(ya?)
他	要	去	哪儿	（呀？）

❸ Which one "do?" you like

You	like	which	"do?"
ní	xǐ huān	něi-ge	(ne?)
你	喜欢	哪个	（呢？）

13. na...-ne?

-哪 ...-呢？（II）

What about...?

When 呢... **ne?** is placed after a person, it means "What about..." or "How about..." "怎办呢？"

e.g.: ❶ I'll take a nap. What about you?

I	go	sleep a while	"what"	you	"about"
wǒ	qù	shuì yí xiàr	(na)	nǐ	(-ne?)
我	去	睡一下儿	（哪...）	你	(-呢？)

❷ I'm going to the pub. "how about" Ted?

I	think	to pub go,	"how"	Ted	"about"
wó xiǎng	dào jiǔ bà qù	(na)	Ted	(-ne?)
我	想	到 酒吧去	（哪...）	Ted	(-呢？)

14. -ne? (soft tone)

...-呢？（III）

Where is...

When 呢 **-ne?** is placed after a person, it means "Where is?" or "Where are? "

e.g.: "Where are" my pants?
(see ⑥ my) I pants "where is "

wǒ	kù-zi	(ne?)
我	裤子	（呢？）

15. -ya?!

呀？！

expressing surpise

呀 **yā!** is a particle used after a phrase for emphasis or expressing surprise.

e.g.: ❶ Who is she? (unexpected person)

She	is	who	"yā?"
tā	shì	shuí	(yā?)
她	是	谁	（呀？）

❷ How come you are still here?

You	how come	still	not left	"yā!"
ní	zě-me	hái	méi zǒu	(yā!)
你	怎幺	还	没走	（呀！）

❸ You are something else!

You	really	have	talent	
nǐ	hái zhēn	yóu	liǎng xià-zi	(yā!)
你	还 真	有	两下子	（呀！）

❹ "It's you" who makes me furious!
"You yā! You yā!" You make me furious!

(nǐ yā, nǐ yā,)	zhēn	qì-sǐ wǒ-le!
(你呀!你呀!)	真	气死我了！

❺ Who is it ringing at this late hour?

Who "yā?"	this late	still	bite phone	come
shuí-yā?	zhè-me wǎn-le	hái	dǎ diàn-huà	lái
谁(呀?)	这幺 晚了	还	打电话	来

16. -de (soft tone)

-得 (轻尾音)（I）

the result

得 **dé** is a very soft suffix sound, attached to a verb or an adjective, and an adverbial

adverbial expletive to express the effort or degree of one's actions. When attached to an object's adjective it expresses that the adjective is a property of the noun, like "it is (so)…", "he did it (so)…"…, but English has no similar word.

e.g.: ❶ She's "extremely" beautiful.
She   "beautiful-**de**"   not like true
tā   (měi-**de**)   bù xiàng huà
她   （美得）   不像话。

❷ I   "trembled"   with cold.
I   "cold-**de**"   tremble
wó   (lěng-**de**)   dǎ dūo-suo
我   （冷得）   打哆嗦

❸ I "laughed" till my sides split.
I   "laugh-**de**"   abdomen   become   ache
wó   (xiào-**de**)   dù-zi   dū   tòng-le
我   （笑得）   肚子   都   痛了

❹ The smell of this cheese is "killing me".
This   cheese   "stink-**de**"   want   life
zhèi ge   rǔ luò   (chòu-**de**)   yào   mìng
这个   乳酪   （臭得）   要   命

17.dé; dé dào (2nd tone)
得；得到 (II)
gain; get; obtain

得 **dé**   has the same written character like the (No,1) "得-de" in **16.** , however this is a second tone and the meaning is different too. It means "gain", "obtain", "get" or "become" in English.

e.g. ❶ I "got" straight A's in my class.
I   school   courses   all   "get" A.
wǒ   xúé xiào   gōng kè   quán   (dé) A
我   学校   功课   全   （得）A

❷ He's "got" pneumonia.
tā   (dé-le)   fèi yán
他   （得了）   肺炎

❸ You have "gained" a lot of weight.
You   "fat-become"   very   much
nǐ   (pang-le)   hěn duō
你   （胖了）   很   多

18. děi (3nd tone)
得；得要 (III)
have to

得 **děi** or （**děi yào**）   has the same Chinese written character, but the pronunciation of this "得" is again different. It pronounces "děi" and is a 3rd tone.
    It is equal to "have to" in English.

"děi" is a time flexible word, most times the time "drags a little bit" without hurting things. It is quite different from "must" which means "urgent" or "time pressed".

e.g.: ❶ I "have to" go now, but I'll accept a short one before I hit the road.
wó   (děi)   zǒu-le,   bú guò   ké-yi   hē
我   （得）   走了，   不过   可以   喝
      yì xiǎo bēi   zài zǒu
      一小杯   再走

❷ Sorry, I "have to" pick up my wife.
Sorry,   I   "have to"   go pick up   I wife.
bào qiàn   wó(děi yào)   qù jiē   wó lǎo-po
抱歉，   我 （得要）   去接   我 老婆

19. bì xù (yào)
必须(要)
must

必须 **bì xǖ**   has the same meaning as like "must" in English. (time not flexible)

e.g.: ❶ I have an emergency case, I "must"go.
I have emergency patient "must" leave.
wó   yǒu-ge jí zhěn bìng rén, (bì xǖ) zǒu
我   有个   急诊   病人 .（必须） 走

❷ I "must" go to the court on Monday.
I   Monday   must   appear court.
wó   lǐ bài yī   (bì xǖ)   chū tíng
我   礼拜一   （必须）   出庭

❸ You "must"   pay   the   fine.
You   must   pay   ○   fine.
wó   (bì xǖ yào)   fù   ○   fá kuǎn
你   （必须要）   付   ○   罚款

20. bù dé bù

不得不
had to

不得不 **bù dé bù** is refering to something which was done by force, similar to English "had to". **e.g.:**

❶ I "had to" do what he said, he had a gun.
I "had to" listen he's, he have gun
wǒ (bù dé bù) tīng tā-de, tā yǒu qiāng
我 (不得不) 听 他的，他 有 枪.

❷ I "had to" marry him, I was pregnant.
I "had to" marry him, I pregnant-le
wǒ (bù dé bù) jià-gei tā wǒ huái yùn-le
我 (不得不) 嫁给 他 我 怀孕了。

21. fēi dĕi…bù kĕ

非得……不可
will have to

非得…不可 **fēi dĕi… bù kĕ**

has a futurity meaning as the English word "will have to". (See 45B 非…不可)

e.g.: You "will have to" do something about it, after all he is your son.

You "must" think a way "no choice"
nǐ (fēi dĕi) xiǎng-ge fǎ-zi (bù kĕ)
你 （非得） 想个 法子 （不可），

he after all is you son.
tā bì jìng shì nǐ ér-zi
他 毕竟 是 你 儿子

22. ba?

(否定试探) 吧？（Ⅰ）
won't; isn't (negative)

吧 **ba?** is a particle used after a doubtful sentence, it is an explorative voice

ex.: ❶ You "won't" quit me, will you?
You "won't" have me drop-ba?
nǐ bú huì bá wǎ shuǎi diào (ba?)
你 不会 把我 甩掉 （吧?）

❷ Today "is not" Sunday, is it?
Today "is not" Sunday -ba?
jīn tiān bú-shì xīng qí rì (ba?)
今天 不是 星期日 （吧?）

23. ba!

(肯定试探) 吧！（Ⅱ）
will; is (positive)

吧 **ba!** is a particle used after an imperative sentence, it is a suggestive soft sound.

Ex.: ❶ You are the intern, aren't you?
you "are" intern-ba?
nǐ shì shí xí yī shēng (ba?)
你 是 实习医生 （吧?）

❷ He will come back, won't he?
He "will" come back-ba?
tā huì huí lái (ba?)
他 会 回来 （吧?）

24. bèi

被
passive voice

被 **bèi** Any "past participle" after a verb "to be" and makes a meaningful sentence, that sentence is a "passive voice" and means "by".

e.g.: ❶ He was beaten up.
He "was beaten up" a spell.
tā (bèi rén zòu-la) yí dùn
他 （被人 揍啦） 一顿

❷ Houses were demolished by a tornado.
Houses "by" tornado "destroied"
fáng-zi dū (bèi) Lóng Jüàn Fēng (huǐ-la)
房子都 （被） 龙卷风 （毁啦）

❸ He is well-liked in school.
He in school very (by people like)
tā zài xué xiào hĕn (tǎo rén xǐ-huan)
他 在 学校 很 （讨人喜欢）
(讨= by 被 bèi)

25. yǐ jīng

已经
already

A grammatical translation of 已经 **yǐ jīng** which is equal to English "has or have" in a perfect tense was clearly explained on P.39 ★s, Group 3 . This particular **yǐ jīng** has nothing to do with grammatical tenses. It is "already" in English and both characters are heavy tones. Furthermore, it is an adverb, and you may use it as you do "already" in English.

e.g.: ❶ He "already" ate. (a past tense)
tā (yǐ jīng) chī-le (not la)
他 (已经) 吃了 (not 啦)

❷ I told him "already". (a past tense)
I "already" told him. (a past tense)
wó (yǐ jīng) gào sù tā-le (not la)
我 (已经) 告诉 他了 (not 啦)

26. záo yǐ-jing
早已经
past perfect tense

早已经 **záo yǐ-jing**

The pronunciation of the third character are light sounds, and are equivalent to the "had" occured before a past participle verb. Both mean that the event "had already occurred" before the complain.

e.g.: ❶ I "had" had my supper. (meal)
I "had" had (eaten)
wǒ zǎo yǐ-jing (chī–la)
我 早已經 (吃啦)

❷ What "had" happened?
prior (mostly omitted) what happened?
(gāng cái) (zěn-me-la)
（剛才） (怎麼啦？)

27. nà shí zǎo-jiu
那时早就
Future perfect

那时早就 **nà shí zǎo-jiu** these characters are equivalent to "will have", the pronunciation of the fourth character is a light tone. It's a "forecast that something may happen in the future" like an English future perfect tense.**e.g.:**

"By the time" the doctor gets here,
❶ he "will have" bled to death already.
Wait until doctor arrive he"will have" bled to death
(děng yī-sheng dào-le)tā (zǎo-jiu) liú xiě liú sǐ-le
等医生 到了 他 (早就) 流血 流死啦

❷ I suppose he "will have" started the journey.
Figured he today "will have" start journey

suàn-le suàn tā jīn tiān gāi dòng shēn-le
算了算 他 今天 該 動身了

28. bú or bù
不
don't (in lower case)

bú (before a 4th tone word)
bù (before 1st, 2nd, 3rd tones)

不 **bù** This expression is the same as the the lower case letters "don't or doesn't". It's a declaration to reveal a fact.

e.g.: ❶ He "doesn't" speak English.
tā (bú) huì shuō yīng yǔ
他 (不) 会 说 英语

❷ I "don't" smoke or drink.
wǒ (bù) chōu yān (bú) hē jiǔ
我 (不) 抽烟 (不) 喝酒

29. bié
别
Don't (capitalized)

别 **bié** is like a "future tense", the expression is the same as the capitalized "Don't". It is an instruction, a command or telling others what not to do.

e.g. "Don't" stay up too late.
(bié) áo-de tài wǎn
(别) 熬得 太 晚

30. béng
甭
need not to

甭 **béng** this expression has the same meaning as "no need to" in English.

e.g.: ❶ It's late. You "need not to" go home. Stay overnight!
This late hour you need not leave. Stay.
zhè-me wǎn-le, nín (béng)zǒu-le zhù xià-ba
这么 晚了, 您 (甭) 走了，住下吧！

❷ Forget it! He is hopeless
"Need not" mention，he no hope

(béng)　　　tí-le!　　tā méi zhǐ-wang-le
(甭)　　　提了!　　他　没指望了

31.méi

没
didn't

没 **méi** is a "past tense", refering to something did not do in the past. The expression is the same as the lower cased verb "didn't ".

e.g.: He "didn't" pay the bill and left.
he "didn't" pay money yet left.

tā　(méi)　fù　qián　jiù　zǒu-le
他　(没)　付　钱　就　走了

32. zhe

著
while

著 **zhe** is a very light suffix sound.
It means " while " in English.

e.g : A father shouted:
"While I'm supporting you with board and room , and you're returning me with hatret ."

You "eat" me, "drink" me and "hate" me!

nǐ (chī-zhe) wǒ, (hē-zhe) wǒ, (hèn-zhe) wǒ
你 (吃著) 我、(喝著) 我、(恨著) 我 !

33. zài

在
in; on; at; am; is; are

在 **zài** This one single sound has a multiple meanings in Chinese.
It means: " in; on; at; am; is; are…"

e.g.: ❶ Marco was born "in" Beijing.
Má Er Kòu chū shēng (zài) Běi Jīng
玛尔蔻 出生 (在 in) 北京

❷ His father's house was "on" dàfósì E. St.
tā bà-ba-de fáng-zi (zài) Dà Fó Sì dōng jiē
他 爸爸的 房子 (在 on) 大佛寺 东街

❸ He used to live "at" House No. 3.
tā yǐ qián zhù (zài) mén pái sān hào
他 以前 住 (在 at) 门牌 三号

❹ That big mansion "is" still there.
nà suǒ dà zhái dì xiàn zài hái (zài) nàr
那所 大 宅第 现在 还 (在 is) 那儿

❺ His family members "are" all in America.
tā-de jiā rén quán (zài) Měi Guó
他的 家人 全 (在 are) 美国。

❻ I "am" home.
wǒ (zài) jiā-li
我 (在 am) 家里。

❼ The five brothers "are" all abroad.
tā-men gēr wǔ-ge dōu (zài) guó wài
他们 哥儿五个 都 (在 are) 国外。

34. dāng shí

当时
was; were

当时 **dāng shí** has the same meaning as: " was or were ".

e.g.: ❶ I "was" in Italy.
wǒ (dāng shí) zài Yì Dà Lì
我 (当时) 在 义大利

❷ We "were" just kids.
wǒ-men (dāng shí) zhǐ shì ge xiǎo hái-zi
我们 (当时) 只 是 个 小孩子

35. dāng shí zhèng-zai

当时正 or 当时正在
was x-ing

当时正 **dāng shí zhèng-zai** has the same meaning as: "was or were" plus –ing except the "ing" is placed before the verb.

e.g.: ❶ I was sleep-ing.
I "was" "ing-sleep"
wǒ (dāng shí) (zhèng-zai-shuì jiào)
我 (当时) (正在 睡觉)

❷ We were talk-ing on the phone.
We "were" "ing-talk" phone.
wǒ-men (dāng shí) (zhèng-zai-dǎ) diàn huà
我们 (当时) (正在打) 电话

36. yǐ qián

以前
used to

以前 **yǐ qián** has the same meaning as the English " used to ".

e.g. : ❶ I "used to" have a lot of vices.

I	"used to"	vices	all all	do
wó	(yǐ qián)	chī hē piáo dǔ	yàng yàng	lái
我	（以前）	吃喝嫖赌	样样	来

e.g. ❷ I "used to" live in Denver.

wó	(yǐ qián)	zhù zài	Dān Fó Shì
我	（以前）	住在	丹佛市

37. yǐ qián shì

以前是
used to be

以前是 **yǐ qián shì** has the same meaning as the English " used to be ".

e.g.: ❶ She "used to be" a policewoman.

tā	(yǐ qián shì)	○	nǚ jǐng chá
她	（以前是）	○	女警察

e.g.: ❷ They "used to be" very skinny.

They	"used to be"	bone thin as branch
tā-men	(yǐ qián shí)	gǔ shòu	rú chái
他们	（以前是）	骨瘦	如柴

38. dài

带
with

带 **dài** This sound has the same meaning as the English word "with".

e.g.: ❶ I want a hamburger "with" onion in it

I	want	a	hamburger "with"	onion
wǒ	yào	yí-ge	hàn bǎo bāo	(dài)	yáng cōng
我	要	一个	汉堡包	（带）	洋葱。

❷I want this table "with" four chairs.

I want	this	table "with"	four	chair.
wǒ yào	zhè zhāng	zhuō-zi	(dài)	sì bá	yǐ-zi
我 要	这张	桌子	（带）	四把	椅子

39. bù dài

不带
without

不带 **bú dài** This sound has the same meaning as the English word " without ".

I want a bowl of beef noodles "without" garlic.

wǒ	yào	yì wǎn	niú ròu miàn	(bú dài)	dà suàn
我	要	一碗	牛肉面	（不带）	大蒜

40. tì-ni (soft tone)

替妳（替我）
for (you; me) (I)

替你 **tì-ni** has the same meaning as "for" in English in terms of: "I'll do it for you".

e.g.: You are tired, let me do it "for" you.

You are tired,	I	"for"	you	to	do
nǐ	lèi-le,	wǒ	(tì)	-ni	lái	zuò
你	累了，	我	（替）	妳	来	做

41. géi-ni (soft tone)

给你（给我）
for (you; me) (II)

给你 **gèi-ni** is interchangeable with 为妳"wèi-nǐ", both means "for you".

e.g.: I've fried two eggs "for" you.

I	"to you"	fried	two	egg.
wǒ	(géi-ni)	zuò-le	liǎng-ge	jī dàn
我	（给妳）	煎了	两个	蛋

Literally "给你 géi nǐ" is "give you", and it should follow with a "numeral" and a "noun" e.g.:

I	"give you"	five	dollars.
wǒ	(géi-ni)	wǔ	kuài qián
我	（给你）	五	块钱。

In conversational Chinese "给你 géi-nǐ" means do things for you "为妳 wèi-nǐ". It's placed after the "action verb", but in Chinese, it's before the "verb".

e.g.: I knited a sweater "for you".
       I "for you" knited a sweater.
       wǒ (géi-ni) zhī-le jiàn máo yī
       我 (给你)   织了件   毛衣

42. nǐ géi-wo

你给我
(an order) **do as I say**

你給我 **nǐ géi-wo** literally it means "give me" when it is followed with a noun. However when a verb is followed it means "It's an order" or "Do as I say."

e.g.: Get lost! (Beat it!)
       You   (my order) roll egg
       nǐ   (géi-wo)   gǔn dàn
       你   (给我)   滚蛋!

When "please" is attached to "géi-wo", it is a statement of "request" which has the meaning of "doing something for me"

❶ Would you toast 2 slices of bread for me?
Please you "do me" toast 2 slice   bread
qíng-ni (géi-wo) káo liǎng piàn miàn bāo
请 你   (给我)   烤   两片   面包
❷ Please, vacuum the rug.
Please you "do me" make rug   suck a suck
qíng-ni (géi-wo) bǎ dì tǎn   xī-yi xì
请你   (给我)   把 地毯   吸一吸

43. wǒ hùi; wǒ hùi-de

(尊命) 我会…; 我会的!
(Yes! sir.) **I shall**

我会的 **wǒ hùi-de** is an affirmative answer to comply with someone's request, the same as "I shall " in English.

e.g.: I "shall" give him your message.
       wǒ   (hùi) zhuǎn gào   tā (de)
       我   (会)   转告   他(的)!

44. lǐ bài wǔ

(說了算) 礼拜五 (獨斷獨行)
will (See 46 Will be)

礼拜五 **lǐ bài wǔ** in English is "Friday….". The author uses this word to represent the idea of any "time, hour, day, month or year…" words that express simple futurity with implications of intention, determination, obligation, or necessity. The English speaking people symbol it future tense…"I will ".

Because there is no equivalent word in Chinese for "I will ", even though it could mean " 将要 jiāng yào" in someway, but " 将要 " is hardly used in the Chinese language.

The Chinese simply use a "a time word" or "a date word" to substitute and eliminate the use of "I will " to make it a future tense.

e.g.: ❶ "I'll" pay you back Friday.
       Money I   "Friday" return you
       qián   wǒ (lǐ bài wǔ) huán-ni
       钱   我   (礼拜五)   还你。

In Chinese "in, on, at" are often omitted

❷ "He'll" pick you up at two o'clock.
He "two o'clock" come pick up you
tā (liáng diǎn) lái jiē   -ni
他 (两点)   来   接   你

❸ The election "will be" on May 1st.
"five month one No."   ○   election
(wǔ yuè   yí hào)   ○   xuán jǔ
(五月   一号)   ○   选举

45. jiù

就
otherwise I will

A 就 **jiù** "就"is another word symbols the "future tense" and it's a conditional word as "if not, I will" in English.

       e.g.: "I'll" sue you in court.
              wǒ   (jiù)   gào   nǐ
              我   (就)   告   你!

B 非…不可 **fēi…bù kě** is also "I will" it is to show ones desire. (See 21 非得…不可)

Particularities Of Chinese Language

e.g.: "I'll" teach him a good lesson.

"I'll" beat him a spell "must"
wǒ (fēi) zòu-ta yí dùn (bù kě)
我 （非） 揍 他 一 顿 （不可）

Very often, Chinese use a "present tense" sentence for a "future tense".

e.g.: "I'll" kill you! I "dare" you!
I "kill" you! You! "dare"
wó (zǎi-le) nǐ! ní (gǎn)!
我 （宰了） 你! 你 （敢）!

46. jiāng yú...

将於...（将在）
will be (past participle)

将於 **jiāng yú** is used in passive voices similar to the English "future perfect tense". "将於" is seldom used in spoken Chinese except in announcements, statements or reports. **e.g.:**

❶ The meeting "will be" held on Monday.
Meeting "will be" Week One hold
hùi yì (jiāng yǔ) zhōu yī jǔ xíng
会议 （将於） 周一 举行

❷ Wedding "will be" taken place in Paris.
Wedding "will be" Paris take place.
hūn lǐ (jiāng zài) bā lí jǔ xíng
婚礼 （将在） 巴黎 举行
(Please see 44 WILL "礼拜五")

47. dǎ-suan; xiǎng

打算；想
going to

打算 **dǎ-suan** is a word to express simple futurity with determination, equivalent to "going to" in English.

e.g. I'm "going to" take in a flick.

I "going to" go see a movie.
wó (dǎ-suan) qù kàn chǎng diàn yǐngr
我 （打算） 去看 场 电影儿

48. níng kě

宁可
would rather

宁可 **níng kě** is an auxiliary verb used to express a condition; it has the same meaning as the lower cased "would rather" in English.

e.g.: "I'd rather" stay home and watch TV.
I "rather" stay home see TV.
wǒ (níng kě) zài jiā kàn diàn shì
我 （宁可） 在 家 看 电视

49. jiù huì

就会
would

就会 **jiù huì** an auxiliary verb used to express a condition; it has the same meaning as the lower case letters "would" in English.

e.g.: I wife "would" get mad.
wǒ tài-tai (jiù huì) shēng qì-de
我 太太 （就会） 生气的

50. bù rán...zǎo-jiu

不然....早就
would have

不然早就 **bù rán...zǎo-jiu**

is equivalent to the English lower case letters "would have".
e.g.: Your brother "would have" helped you.
(bù rán) nǐ gē-ge (zǎo-jiu) bāng-ni jiě jué-la
（不然） 你 哥哥 （早就） 帮你 解决啦!

51. yīng gāi

应该
should

应该 **yīng gāi** is an auxiliary verb used to express duty, propriety or obligation, same as the English lower case letters "should".

e.g.: You "should" buy her a gift.
nǐ (yīng gāi) sòng   tā-ge   lǐ wù
你 (应该)   送"give" 她个   礼物

52. zǎo jiù yīng gāi

早就应该
should have

早就应该 **zǎo jiù yīng gāi**

is equivalent to "should have" in English.
e.g.: You "should have" told me.
ní (zǎo-jiu yīng gāi) gào-su-wo
你 (早就应该)   告诉我

53. shuō-bu dìng huì

说不定会
might

说不定会 **shuō-bu dìng huì**

An auxiliary expression with future sense
equivalent to"may" in meaning; expressing a
shade of doubt or some hope of possibility
(a likelihood) like "might" in English.
e.g.: ❶ The president "might" come.
president   "might"   come.
zóng tǒng   (shuō-bu dìng huì)   lái
总统   (说不定会)   来

❷ He "might" hit the jackpot, you'll never know.
He "might"   hit first prize hard say
tā (shuō-bu dìng) zhòng tóu jiǎng hěn nán shuō
他 (说不定)   中头奖   很难说

54. shuō-bu dìng zǎ-jiu

说不定早就
might have

说不定早就 **shuō bú ding zǎo-jiu**

The same as " might have " in English. **e.g.:**
❶ My wife "might have" known it all along.
I old lady   "might have"   know.
wó lǎo-po (shuō-bu dìng zǎo-jiu) zhī-dao
我 老婆   (说不定早就)   知道

❷ If it hadn't been for you, I "might have"
been dead.
If not is you, I   "might have"   died.
yào bú-shi nǐ wó (shuō-bu dìng zǎo-jiu) sǐ-le
要不是 你 我   (说不定早就)   死了

55. wǒ xiǎng yào

我想要
I'd like

我想要 **wó xiǎng yào** has the same
meaning as " I'd like ". It is a nicer word
than "I want", it's more polite.
e.g.: ❶ "I'd like" a whisky on the rocks.
"I wish want" cup whisky add ice cube.
(wó xiǎng yào) bēi wēi shì jì jiā bīng kuàir
(我想要)   杯 威士忌 加 冰块儿

❷ "I'd like" a table for two, please.
"I wish want" a small table two person
(wó xiǎng yào) ge xiǎo zhuō liǎng wèi
(我想要)   个   小桌   俩 位

56. "bǐ jiáo"

比较...
comparative (See 72)

比较... **bǐ jiáo** is a special word to be
added before any adjective to make it a
"comparative", because Chinese language
does not have a special word for
comparatives like " cheaper, better,
worse or more …".

e.g.: ❶ English is "more" complicated.
English   "comparatively complicate"
yīng wén   (bí jiāo)   fù zá
英文   (比较)   复杂

❷ Coffee is   cheap(er) in Brazil
Coffee in Brazil "comparatively cheap"
kā fēi zài Bā Xī (bí jiāo) pián-yi
咖啡 在 巴西   (比较)   便宜

Particularities Of Chinese Language

❸Learning the Chinese language is easi(er)

Chinese lanugage "comparatively easy" learn

Zhōng Guó Huà　(bí jiǎo)　róng-yi　　xué
中国话　　　（比较）　容易　　学

---

57. zuì

最
superlative

最...**zuì** is the sound of a word to be added before any adjective to make it a "superlative" as "the -est or the most" in English. **e.g.**:

❶She is "the prettiest" girl in the school.

She is　all school "most"　pretty's　　girl
tā-shi　quán　jiào　（zuì）piào liàng-de　nǚ háir
她是　全　校　（最）　漂亮的　　女孩儿

❷This is the "lowest" price I can offer you.

This is I　give you's "most" low　price
zhè-shi　wó　gěi　nín-de　（zuì）　dī　jià qián
这 是 我　给　您的　（最）　低　价钱

---

58. hǎo yí-ge

好一个！
What a!

好一个 **hǎo yí-ge** is equivalent to "What a…!" in English.

e.g.: ❶ "What a" house you have!

(Great! a place)　beautiful　　house
(hǎo yì-suǒ)　piào-liang-de　fáng-zi
（好一所）　漂亮的　　房子！

❷ "What an"　　alibi!
(hǎo yí-ge)　jiè kǒu
（好一个）　藉口

---

59. cái

才
not…until

才 **cái** equal to "not…until" in English.

e.g.: ❶ We're "not" eating "until" 8:30

wǒ-men　bā diǎn bàn（cái）chī fàn
我们　　八点半　（才）吃饭

---

❷He "won't" come home "until" Monday

tā　lǐ bài yī　(cái)　huí　jiā ne
他　礼拜一　（才）　回　家呢！

---

60. gān cuì

乾脆
may as well

乾脆 **gān cuì** has the equal English meaning of "**may as well**", in someway similar to "straightforward".

e.g.: I "may as well" stay overnight too.

wǒ（gān cuì）yě zài　zhèr　guò yè　suàn-le
我　（乾脆）也 在 这儿 过夜　算了

---

61. méi bàn-fa

没办法；没法子
couldn't

没办法 **méi bàn-fa; méi fǎ-zi**

Similar to "couldn't" in English. For example:

❶ I "couldn't" help you, the car wasn't mine.

I "couldn't" help you,　car　not is　I's.
wǒ (méi bàn-fà) bāng nǐ máng, chē-zi　bú-shi　wǒ-de
我 （没办法）帮你忙　车子　不是　我的

❷I'm sorry. We "couldn't" come to your party

Really sorry. We "couldn't" join you's party.
zhēn bào qiàn,　wǒ-men　(méi bàn-fà)　cān jiā
真抱歉　　我们　（没办法）　参加
　　　　nín-de　yàn huì
　　　　您的　宴会

---

62. ké néng zǎo-jiu

可能早就
could have

可能早就 **ké néng zǎo-jiu** This has the same meaning as "could have" in English.

e.g.: Otherwise, we "could have" been married.

fǒu zé-de huà,　zān-men　(ké néng zǎo-jiu)
否则的话，　咱们　（可能早就）
jié hūn-la
结婚啦

63. yào bú shì

要不是
If it hadn't been

要不是你 **yào bú shì nǐ** This has the same meaning as "If it hadn't been…" in English.

e.g.: "If it hadn't been" for you, I would have been drowned.

(yào bú shì) nǐ, wó zǎo-jiu yān-si-le
(要不是) 你 我 早就 淹死了

64. zuì jìn yì zhí

最近一直
have been

最近一直 **zuì jìn yì zhí** A "present perfect tense". It has the same meaning as "have been" or "has been" in English. And they follow with an **"adjective"**

e.g.: ❶ He "has been" sick in the hospital.
tā (zuì jìn yì zhí) shēng bìng zhù yuàn
他 (最近一直) 生病 住院

❷ I "have been" extremely busy.
I "have been" busy to death
wǒ (zuì jìn yì zhí) máng-de yào sǐ
我 (最近一直) 忙得 要死

❸ My wife "has been" depressed.
I wife "has been" depressed
wǒ nèi-ren (zuì jìn yì zhí) mèn mèn bú lè
我内人 (最近一直) 闷闷不乐

65. yì zhí

一直
present perfect progressive

一直 **yì zhí** A present perfect progressive tense. It has the same meaning as " have been" or "has been" in English and they follow with an **"progressive tense"**

e.g.: ❶ I "have been" think-ing of you.
I "have been" "ing-think" you.

wǒ (yì zhí) (zài xiǎng niàn) nǐ
我 (一直) (在想念) 你

❷ I "have been" "teach-ing" at Fu Jen U.
I "have been" at Fu Jen U. "ing-teach"
wǒ (yì zhí) zài Fǔ Rén Dà Xǘ jiāo shū
我 (一直) 在 辅仁大学 教书

66. běn lái yì zhí

本来一直
had been

本来一直 **běn lái yì zhí**

A "past perfect progressive tense" It has the same meaning as "had been" in English. **e.g.:**

I "had been" thinking of getting married.

I "had been" "ing-think" get married
wó (běn lái yì zhí) xiǎng yào jié hūn
我 (本来一直) 想要 结婚

67. díng hǎo

顶好
had better

顶好 **díng hǎo** The same as "had better".

e.g.: ❶ You "had better" quit smoking.
You "had better" make smoking lay off.
nǐ (díng hǎo) bǎ yān jiè diào
你 (顶好) 把 烟 戒掉

❷ You "had better" give yourself up to the police
You "had better" go surrender to police.
nǐ (díng hǎo) qù tóu àn
你 (顶好) 去 投案

68. xī wàng

希望
I hope

希望 **xī wàng** is equivalent to "hope".

e.g.: ❶ I "hope" you'll get the job.

I "hope" you can get this job.
wǒ (xì wàng) nǐ néng dé dào zhè fènr gōng zuò
我 (希望) 你 能 得到 这份儿 工作

❷ I "hope" she'll change her mind.
I　"hope"　she can back heart turn idea
wǒ (xì wàng)　nǐ néng　　huí xīn　zhuǎn yì
我　(希望)　她 能　　回心　转意

69. gāi yǒu duō hǎo
...该有多好
I wish (No.1)

该有多好 **gāi yǒu duō hǎo** It's a word to have a longing desire or crave, similar to "wish" in English, "dàn yuàn 但愿" in Chinese. But it never complied with the desire

e.g.: ❶ I "wish" you were a man.
You　"if is"　man　how good will it be
nǐ　(yào-shì)　nán-ren　(gāi yǒu duō hǎo)
你　(要是)　男人　　(该有多好)

❷ I "wish" that he could get over with it.
　"wish"　he big trouble turn small
(dàn yuàn)　tā　dà shì huà xiǎo
(但愿)　他　大事化小

70. zhù ; dàn yuàn ; ciá hǎo
祝 ; 但愿 ; 才好
I wish (No.2)

祝 **zhù** It's a word to give a specified greeting to someone, similar to "wish you"
e.g : ❶ I "wish" you a happy marriage.
　"Wish"　you　newly wed happiness
(zhù)　nǐ　　xīn hūn kuài lè
(祝)　你　　新婚快乐

❷ "Wish"　heaven　protect　he
(dàn yuàn) cāng tiān　bǎo yòu　tā
(但愿) 苍天　保佑　他

❸　I "wish" him drop dead.
He　drop dead in streets "considered right".
tā　héng sǐ jiē tóu　　ciá hǎo
他　横死街头　　才好 wish

71. yì diānr
一點儿
a little bit

or 一點 **yì diǎn** is very little or a little bit. You just attach "yì diǎn" (which is 一點) to the end of any adjective, and it becomes a "comparative".
e.g.:　I'd like my slacks a little bit….

shorter… "短 duǎn yì diǎn"
tighter… "緊 jǐn yì diǎn"

72. bǐ
...比...
than (See 56)

比...**bǐ** is equivalent to "than" in English
❶ You are younger "than" she is.
You　"than"　she　younger
ní　(bǐ)　tā　nián qīng
你　(比)　她　年轻
❷ Tangerines are cheaper "than" apples.
Tangerine　"than"　apple　cheep
jú-zi　(bǐ)　píng-guo　pián-yi
橘子　(比)　苹果　便宜

73. méi (tā)......
没(他)......
not as…as…

没 **méi** (tā;wǒ…) … This single sound has the same meaning as "not as" in English.
e.g.: ❶You're "not as" good-looking "as" I.
　You　"not as"　I　good-look
has　nǐ　(méi)　wá　hǎo kàn
　你　(没)　我　好看

❷This papaya is "not as" sweet "as" the one we bought yesterday.
This　papaya "not as" yesterday　sweet.
zhèi-ge　mù-gua　(méi)　zuó tiān　tián
这个　木瓜　(没)　昨天　甜

❸Your　house is "not as"　big as "**his**".
　You's　house　"not as"　**him**　big
nǐ-de　fáng-zi　(méi)　**tā**　dà
你的　房子　(没)　他　大

★Most times possessive words (his,your…) are substituted with objects (him,you…)

The English Eight W's & One H

問個夠!（問句大全）

The English word-order for a question is quite different from Chinese. English interrogatives such as "Am, Are, Is, What, Where…" are prefixes and are placed at the beginning of a question. Conversely, Chinese interrogatives are suffixes and are placed at the end. **e.g.:** "He is Who?"; "Your name is What?"; "Mark goes Where?"; "She like this color Does?"… With study and practice, the adjustment to asking questions in Chinese should be natural and intuitive..

How To Ask A Question

1. Do? or Does?

…ma? **(enquiry)**
…吗？(打聽、好奇)

吗？ma? is a Chinese suffix used in asking a question or making an enquiry, equivalent to the capitalized "**Do**?" or "**Does**?" as a prefix in English phrases.

e.g.: ❶ "Do" you know Marco?

You	know	Marco	"Do?"
nǐ	rèn-shi	Má Er Kòu	(-ma?)
你	认识	玛尔蔻	(吗?)

❷ "Does" he speak German?

He	can speak	German	"Does?"
tā	huì shuō	Dé Guó Huà	(-ma?)
他	会 说	德国话	(吗?)

2. Are? Is? Am?

shì…ma? **(seeking idendity)**
是…吗？(確認無誤)

是…吗？shì…ma? is a phrase-final particle used in questions seeking for identity, equivalent to the three English capitalized verbs "Are?"; "Am?" and "Is?".

★ In Chinese, they are all "**shì…ma?**"

e.g.: ❶ "Is" she the manager?

She	"is"	here's	manager	"ma?"
tā	(shi)	zhèr-de	jīng lǐ	(-ma?)
她	(是)	这儿的	经理	(吗?)

❷ "Are" these genuine jade?

These	all	"are"	real	jade's	"ma?"
zhè xiē	doū	(shi)	zhēn	fěi cuì-de	(-ma?)
这些	都	(是)	真	翡翠的	(吗?)

❸ Doctor, "Am" I pregnant?

Doctor,	I	"am"	conceived	"ma?"
dài-fu,	wǒ	(shì)	huái yùn-le	(-ma?)
大夫，	我	(是)	怀孕了	(吗?)

3 Did ?

yǒu-mei yǒu…? **(checking)**
你有没有…？(查詢)

有没有…? yǒu-mei yǒu…?

Followed by a present tense verb like:

"see", "give", "tell"…, it is equivalent to the English capitalized "Did?".

e.g.: ❶ "Did" you ask them?

You	"did?"		ask	they
ní	(yǒu-mei yǒu?)		wèn	tā-men
你	(有没有?)		问	他们

❷ "Did" he invite she?

He	"did?"		invite	her
tā	(yǒu-mei yǒu?)		qíng	-ta
他	(有没有?)		请	她

If "有没有 yǒu-mei yǒu?" is followed by a noun like "money", "children", "time"…, it means "Do you have?".

你（有没有）钱?
nǐ "yǒu-mei yǒu" qián?
You "have no have" money?

4. Have? or Has?
…la-ma? (reminding)
…啦吗? (提醒、监控)

…啦吗?…la-ma? is only half of a "present perfect" tense question. It is incomplete as just a word "Have" or "Has" in English. (只是半句问话)

In order to make the English "present perfect" sentence complete, a "past participle verb" must be attached to it. But differently the Chinese, "-la" is already "past partciple", another "past partciple" is unnecessary. Therefore a "present" verb is all that it needs in a "-la-ma?" question.

e.g.: ❶ "Have you" fed the baby?

You	"feed"	baby	"Have?"
nǐ	(wèi)	hái-zi	(-la-ma?)
你	(喂)	孩子	(-啦吗?)

❷ " Has she" called you?

She	to you	call telephone	"Has?"
tā	géi-ni	(dǎ diàn huà)	(-la-ma?)
她	给你	(打电话)	(-啦吗?)

❸ "Have you" made the reservation?

You	"make"	reservation	"Have?"
nǐ	(dìng)	wèi-zi	(-la-ma?)
你	(订)	位子	(-啦吗?)

5. Shall? (offering services)
…hǎo-bu háo? No.1
我…好不好? (主动服務)

…好不好?…hǎo-bu hǎo? is a polite phrase with the same meaning as "Shall I (we)?" in English. It is used in a question in offering services and is expecting "shall" in the answer.

★The subject is always "I" or "we".

e.g.: ❶ "Shall I" bring you a blanket?

I	for you	bring a	blanket	come	"Shall?"
wó	gěi nín	ná tiáo	máo tǎn-lai		(hǎo-bu hǎo?)
我	给您	拿条	毛毯	来	(好不好?)

❷ "Shall we" have a drink before dinner?

We	drink	glass	wine	then	eat	dinner	"Shall?"
zán-men	hē	bēi	jiǔ	zài	chī	fàn	(hǎo-bu hǎo?)
咱们	喝	杯	酒	再	吃饭		(好不好?)

6. Will? (request or demanding)
…hǎo-bu háo? No.2
你…好不好? (要求)

…好不好?…hǎo-bu hǎo?

hǎo-bu hǎo? has the same meaning as "Will you?" in English. It's a polite question of proposition and is expecting "will" in the answer.

e.g.: ❶ "Will you" turn down the TV a bit?

Have	TV	turn	small	a bit	"Will?"
bǎ	diàn shì	níng	xiǎo	yì diǎnr	(hǎo-bu hǎo?)
把	电视	拧	小	一点儿	(好不好?)

❷ "Will you" please shut your mouth?

Please	you	shut up!	"Will?"
qíng	nǐ	bì zuǐ!	(hǎo-bu hǎo?)
请	你	闭嘴!	(好不好?)

❸ "Will you" come to my office please?

To	I	office	come	a spell	"Will?"
dào	wǒ	bàn gōng shì	lái	yí xiàr	(hǎo-bu hǎo)
到	我	办公室	来	一下儿	(好不好?)

7. Would you?(consideration)
(nín)…hǎo-bu háo? No.3
(您)……好不好？(體貼、關心)

您…好不好? nín…**hǎo-bu hǎo?**

This expression softens the tone of speech and the force of a statement or request. It's equivalent to "Would you like" in English. Sometimes, it is even a nice word of consideration or flattery.

e.g.: ❶ "Would" you like some hot tea?

You	drink	cup	hot tea	"Would?"
nín	hē	bēi	rè chá	(hǎo-bu hǎo?
您	喝	杯	热茶	(好不好?)

★**"Would"** also means "Are you willing to?"
您 愿意…吗? (nín yuàn-yi…ma?)

❷ "Would you" like to come to my luncheon?

You	"willing?"	attend	I's	luncheon	"ma?"
nín	"yuàn-yi"	cān jiā	wǒ-de	wǔ yàn	(ma?)
您	(愿意)	参加	我的	午宴	(吗?)

" Would " also means

会不会…? **huì-bu huì…?**

❶ "Would you" give up your business?

You	"would?"	give up	you's	business
nǐ	(huì-bu huì)	fàng qì	nǐ-de	shēng-yi
你	(会不会)	放弃	你的	生意

❷ "Would you" rather die for her?

You	"would"	for her	die	(ma?)
nǐ	(níng yüàn)	wèi tā ér	sǐ	(ma?)
你	(宁愿)	为 她而	死	(吗?)

8. May …?
ké-yi … ma?
可以…吗? (See 12)

我可以…吗? wǒ **ké-yi…ma?**

This is a phrase used for permission, equivalent to the English capitalized question verb "May I (we)?"

e.g.: ❶ "May I" borrow your pen?

"May"	borrow	you's	pen	use	a spell	"ma?"
(ké-yi)	jiè	nín-de	bǐ	yòng	yí-xiàr	(ma?)
(可以)	借	您的	笔	用	一下儿	(吗?)

❷ "May I" have one of these brochures?

"May"	take	aO	propaganda	manual	"ma?"
(ké-yi)	ná	yí-fen	xüān chuán	shǒu cè	(ma?)
(可以)	拿	一份	宣传	手册	(吗?)

❸ "May I" leave now?

I	"may"	take off	"ma?"
wǒ	(ké-yi)	zǒu-le	(ma?)
我	(可以)	走了	(吗?)

9. Don't or Doesn't
bù…ma?
不…吗?

不…吗? **bù…ma?** has the same meaning as the capitalized English verbs "Don't?" or "Doesn't?".

e.g.: ❶ "Don't" you like me?

You	"don't"	like	me	"ma?"
nǐ	(bù)	xǐ-huan	wǒ	(ma?)
你	(不)	喜欢	我	(吗?)

❷ "Don't" we wear uniform?

We	"don't"	wear	uniform	"ma?"
zán-men	(bù)	chuān	zhì fú	(ma?)
咱们	(不)	穿	制服	(吗?)

❸ "Doesn't" he speak English?

He	"no can"	speak	English	"ma?"
tā	(bú huì)	shuō	yīng yǔ	(ma?)
他	(不会)	说	英语	(吗?)

10. Didn't …?
méi…ma?
没…吗?

没…吗? **méi…mā?** has the same meaning as the capitalized "Didn't…? "

e.g.: ❶ "Didn't" he propose to you?

He	"Didn't"	to you	propose	"ma?"
tā	(méi)	xiàng nǐ	qiú hūn	(ma?)
他	(没)	向你	求婚	(吗?)

❷ " Didn't " he buy you a ring?

He	"Didn't"	for you	buy a	ring	"ma?"
tā	(méi)	géi-ni	mǎi-ge	jiè-zhi	(ma?)
他	(没)	给你	买个	戒指	(吗?)

❸ " Didn't " they notify you ?

They	"Didn't"	notify	you	"ma?"
tā-men	(méi)	tōng zhī	-ni	(ma?)
他们	(没)	通知	你	(吗?)

11. Can? (technically)
huì…ma? (NO.1)
会…吗?

会…吗? **hùi…ma?** has the same meaning as "Can…?" in the sense of technically or being know-how.

e.g.: ❶ "Can" you fix the computer?

You "Can" fix computer "ma?"
nǐ (huì) xiū diàn nǎo (ma?)
你 (会) 修 电脑 (吗?)

❷ "Can" you swim?

You "Can" swim "ma?
nǐ (huì) yóu yǒng (-ma?)
你 (会) 游泳 (吗?)

12. Can? (permission)
néng…ma? (NO.2)
能…吗? (允许) (See 8)

能…吗? **néng…ma?** is equivalent to "Can?" in the sense of "to be permitted to", like "ay". **e.g.:**

❶ Doc, "Can" he get up and walk a bit?

Doc, he "Can" get up walk a walk "ma?"
dài-fu, tā (néng) qǐ-lai zǒu-yi zǒu (ma?)
大夫, 他 (能) 起来 走一走 (吗?)

❷ "Can" we smoke in classroom?

We "Can" at classroom smoke "ma?"
wǒ-men (néng) zài jiào shì chōu yān (ma?)
我们 (能) 在 教室 抽烟 (吗?)

13. Can? (physically)
néng…ma? (NO.3)
能…吗? (体能)

能…吗? **néng…ma?** is equivalent to "Can?" in the sense of "to be able to", "physically capable" or "time permitting".

e.g.: ❶ "Can" you help me move the cabinet?

You "can" help me move a bit cabinet "ma?"
nǐ (néng) bāng-wo bān-yi-xia guì-zi (ma?)
你 (能) 帮我 搬一下 柜子 (吗?)

❷ "Can" you teach me Chinese tomorrow?

You tomorrow "can" teach I Chinese "ma?"
nǐ míng-tian (néng) jiāo-wo Hàn yǔ (ma?)
你 明天 (能) 教我 汉语 (吗?)

14. Could? (polite)
néng-gou…ma? (NO.1)
能够…吗?

能够…吗? **néng-gou…ma?** is equivalent to the capitalized "Could?" in the sense of "capability" or "willingly".

e.g.: "Could" you do me a favor?

You "could" help me a busy "ma?"
nín (néng-gou) bāng wǒ -ge mángr (-ma?)
您 (能够) 帮 我 个 忙儿 (吗?)

15. Could? (available)
yǒu kòngr…ma? (NO.2)
有空儿…吗?

有空儿…吗? **yǒu kòngr…ma?** This "Could" means "have spare time" **e.g.:** "Could" he pick me up at the airport?

He "has time" to airport come pick I "ma?"
tā (yǒu kòng) dào jī chǎng lái jiē-wo (-ma?)
他 (有空) 到 机场 来 接我 (吗?)

16. Could? (possibility)
kě néng…ma? (NO.3)
可能…吗?

可能…吗? **kě néng…ma?** has the same meaning as "Could?" in the sense of "possibility" or "the chances of…"

e.g.: ❶ "Could" he be elected?

He "could" elected "ma?"
tā (kě néng) xuǎn-de shàng (ma?)
他 (可能) 选得上 (吗?)

❷ "Could" he lend me his sports car?

He "could" lend I he's run car "ma?"
tā (kě néng) jiè wǒ tā-de pǎo chē (ma?)
他 (可能) 借 我 他的 跑车 (吗?)

> The word "possible" which means "the chances" has nothing to do to do with the grammatical question "Could…?".

17. Should …?
yīng gāi … ma?
应该…吗?

应该…吗? **yīng gǎi…ma?** is a question that implies duty, propriety or obligation, similar to the capitalized verb "Should …?" in English.

e.g.: ❶ "Should" I tell him the truth?
I "Should" to she speak truth "ma?"
wǒ (yīng gāi) gēn-ta shūo shí huà(-ma?)
我 (应该) 跟他 说 实话 (吗?)

❷ "Should" aliens file an income tax return?
Foreigner "should" report income tax "ma?"
wài-guo rén (yīng gāi) bào suǒ dé shuì(ma?)
外国人 (应该) 报 所得税 (吗?)

18. Where …?
nǎr?
哪儿?

哪儿? **nǎr?** is a suffix used to indicate a question meaning "Where?" as a prefix in English.

e.g.: ❶ "Where" are you staying?
You now live "where?"
nǐ mù qián zhù (nǎr?)
你 目前 住 (哪儿?)

❷ "Where" do you live?
You home live "where?"
nǐ jiā zhù (nǎr?)
你 家 住 (哪儿?)

❸ "Where" are my trousers?
Me's trouser at "where?"
wǒ-de kù-zi zài (nǎr?)
我的 裤子 在 (哪儿?)

19. What …?
shén-me? or shé-me?
甚么? or 什么?

甚么? **shén-me?** also pronounced "shé-me?什么?" and has the equivalent meaning of "What…?" in English.

e.g. ❶ "What" do you want to eat?
You want ○ eat (some) "what?"
nín yào ○ chī diǎnr (shén-me?)
您 要 ○ 吃 点儿 (甚么?)

❷ "What" kind of deal can you give me?
You can give me "What" kind discount
nǐ ké-yi géi-wo (shé-me?) yàng-de yōu huì
你 可以 给我 (什么?) 样的 優惠

❸ "What" make is your refrigerator ?
You's air-condition is "what?" trade mark's
nǐ-de lěng qì shi (shé-me?) pái-zi-de
你的 冷气 是 (什么?) 牌子的

20. What Numeral?
jǐ?
几?

几? **jǐ?** is a Chinese question indicator which literally means "What Numeral?". The answer to a "jǐ" question could never be a large quantity or amount .(See Group 4: Units)
ex.: How many bottles? "jǐ píng?" 几瓶
How many pounds? "jǐ bàng?" 几磅
The "jǐ" question has already limited the answer to no more than "several". That's why when "How old" is used upon children

it is :

"How old are you?"		
You	"what numeral?"	age
你	"几?"	岁
ní	"jǐ?"	suì

When "How old are you?" is used upon adults. (See P.129 40)

❶ "What?" grade is your daughter in
You daughter in "What Numeral?" grade
ní nǔ ér shàng (jǐ?) nián jí
你 女儿 上 (几?) 年级

For a contemporary house:
❷ This house has "What Numeral?" year
zhèi-suǒ fáng-zi yǒu (jǐ) nián-le?
这所 房子 有 (几?) 年了

(See 37 : "How Many 几个")

21. What time?

jí diǎn?
几点？

几点？**jí diǎn?** means : the hour hand and the minute hand are pointing at number what "dot" or "point" (点子 diǎn-zi) on the watch.

❶ "What time" (how many o'clock) is it?

Now	"what numeral"	(dot or point)
xiàn zài	(jí?)	(diǎn)
现在	几？	点

❷ "What time" is your flight taking–off?

You	airplane	"No. what point?"	up-fly
nǐ	fēi jī	(jí diǎn?)	qǐ fēi
你	飞机	（几点？）	起飞

❸ "What time" are you leaving?

You	"No. what dot?"	walk
nǐ	(jí diǎn?)	zǒu
你	（几点？）	走

22. What Numeral date

jí hào?
几号？

e.g.: ❶ "What date" is her birthday on?

She is	"What Numeral date?"	birthday
tā-shi	(jí hào?)	shēng-ri
她是	（几号？）	生日

❷ What month and date is it ?

Today is	"what Numeral month Numeral date?"
jīn tiān　shì	(jí yüè jǐ hào?)
今天　是	"几月几号？"

23 What Numeral month

jí yüè?
几月？

There is no special word for each of the 12 months as in English.

"月 **yüè**" literally means "moon". Chinese simply name January "1- **yüè**"; February "2- **yüè**"... and November "11- **yüè**".

几月？**jǐ-yüè?** is " Number what **yüè**?"

(For "Month, Week, Day" see 44A)

❶In "What month" is she expecting? (baby)

He (she)	"what Numeral month"	expecting
tā	(jí yüè?)	dài chǎn
他	（几月?）	待产

★ How many "months?" in Chinese is:
"几个jǐ ge" "月yüè"
(See P. 71 "**ge** 个", Group 5)

❷ "Which month" is a leap month?

"What Numeral month?"	is	leap year
(jí yüè?)	shì	rùn yüè
（几月?）	是	闰月

24. Which day?

nǎ tiān?
哪天？

哪天？**nǎ tiān?** is "Which day" or "What day" in English. It's only used in a situation in which something is expected to occur within the near days. (See 28 When)

e.g.: ❶ On "What day" are you leaving?

You	"which day?"	walk
ní	(nǎ tiān?)	zǒu
你	（哪天？）	走

❷ On "Which day" will your school begin?

school	"which day?"	open class
xué xiào	(nǎ tiān?)	kāi-xué (kè)
学校	（哪天？）	开学(课)

25. What year?

nǎ tiǎn? or nǎ-yi tiǎn?
哪年？ or 哪一年？

e.g.: "Which year" was he born in?

(He) She is	"which year?"	bore
tā-shi	(nǎ nián?)	chū shēng-de
他是	（哪年？）	出生的

★The "是 shì" refers to a "past event".
★Without "shì" it refers to a "future event".

e.g.: In "Which year" will you graduate?

You	"which year?"	graduate
nǐ	(nǎ nián?)	bì yè
你	（哪年？）	毕业

26. What if ?

yào-shi bù xíng-ne?
要是不行呢？

e.g.: ❶ "What if?" he says "no"

He	"if"	say	no	"then what?"
tā	(yào-shi)	shuō	bù xíng	(ne?)
他	(要是)	说	不行	(呢?)

❷ "What if" he changes his mind?

"If"	he	change	idea	"then what?"
(yào-shi)	tā	gǎi biàn	zhí-yi	(ne?)
(要是)	他	改变	主意	(呢?)

27. Which...?

něi-ge?
哪个?

哪个? **něi-ge?** also pronounces "**nǎ -ge?**" both have the equivalent meaning of "Which" or "Which one" in English.

e.g.: ❶ " Which one " do you prefer ?

You	compare	like	"Which ?"
nǐ	bí jiáo	xǐ huān	(něi-ge?)
你	比较	喜欢	(哪个?)

❷ I don't know "Which is which" now

I	don't know	"which is which"
wǒ	bù zhī dào	(něi-ge shì něi-ge-le)
我	不知道	哪个? 是 哪个了

28 . When?

jǐ shí? or hé shí?
几时? or 何时?

几时 **jǐ shí?**; 何时 **hé shí?** both mean "When" in English, usually "jǐ-shí" infers the length of time is shorter than "hé-shí".

e.g.: ❶ "When" do you return to Japan

You	"when?"	return	Japan
ní	(jǐ shí?)	huí	Rì Běn
你	(几时?)	回	日本

❷ "When" was the last time you saw her?

You	last	one time	see	she	is	"when?"
nǐ	zuì hòu	yí cì	kàn-jian-ta	shi	(hé shí?)
你	最后	一次	看见她	是	(何时?)

29. Why?

wèi shé-me? or wèi shén-me?
为什么? or 为甚么?

为甚么 ... ? **wèi shén-me...?** is a suffix used as a question, just as "Why" is used in English.

e.g.: ❶ "Why" do you dislike her?

You	"why?"	detest	she
nǐ	(wèi shén-me?)	bú dài-jian-ta
你	(为甚么?)	不待见她

❷ "Why" do you want to learn Chinese?

You	"why?"	want	learn	China talk
nǐ	(wèi shén-me)	yào	xüé	Zhōng Guó huà
你	(为甚么?)	要	学	中国话

❸ "Why" do you always come late?

You	"why?"	always	late arrive
nǐ	(wèi shé-me)	lǎo-shi	chí dào
你	(为什么?)	老是	迟到

❹ "Why" do you want to quit your job?

You	"why?"	want to	resign
nǐ	(wèi shén-me)	yào	cí zhí
你	(为甚么?)	要	辞职

30. How Come?

zěn-me...
怎么 ... (much milder than "Why"?)

怎么...呢? **zén-me...ne?** is a question milder then "Why?". Usually this question requires no answer It's rather like a statement or a light complaint, similar to "How come?" in English.

e.g.: ❶ "How come" he didn't show up?

He	"how come?"	didn't	show face
tā	(zěn-me?)	méi	lòu miànr-ne?
他	(怎么?)	没	露面儿呢?

❷ "How come" you've stopped drinking?

You	"how come?"	quit	drinking
ní	(zěn-me?)	jiè	jiǔ-le-ne?
你	(怎么?)	戒	酒了呢?

★ "-ne" is often omitted.

31.Why don't ...?

hé bù? or...bù hǎo mā?
何不? or ...不好吗?

可不? **hé bù?** or 不好吗? **bù hǎo-ma?**

is a suggestive prefix used in a question, similar to "Why not" or "Why don't you?".

e.g.: ❶ "Why don't" you take a break?

You	"why not?"	rest	a while
nǐ	(hé bù?)	xiū-xi	yí xiàr
你	(何不？)	休息	一下儿

❷ "Why don't" we dine out today?

We	today	go	restaurant	"why not?"
zán-men	jīn tiān	xià	guǎn-zi	(bù hǎo-ma)
咱们	今天	下	馆子	（不好吗？）

32. Why didn't…?
zě-me méi …?
怎么没…?

| 怎么没…? **zěn-me méi…?** |

is a light complaint about something that should have been done or an inquisitory question to find out the reasons. It's like English "Why didn't...?"

"怎么" also pronounces "zě-me?"

e.g.: ❶ "Why didn't" she drive her car?

Her	"why didn't"	drive car	come
tā	(zě-me méi?)	kāi chē	lái
她	(怎么没？)	开车	来

❷ "Why didn't" you wear your raincoat?

You	"why didn't?"	wear	raincoat
ní	(zěn-me méi?)	chuān	yǔ yī
你	(怎么没？)	穿	雨衣

33. Who or Whom
shéi? or shuí?
谁?

In Chinese, "Who" and "Whom" are one word just like "her and she" or "him and he" are. The pronunciations are the same.

e.g.: "who like I?" ; "me like Who?"
"whom like he?" ; "her like Whom"

❶ "Who" are those people?

Those crowd	people	is	"who?"
nà qún	rén	shì	(shéi ?)
那群	人	是	（谁？）

❷ I don't know "whom" to believe?

I	don't know	should	believe	"who?"

wǒ	bù	zhī	dào	gāi	xiāng xìn (shéi ?)
我	不	知	道	该	相信 （谁？）

❸ "Who" do you think you are?

You	think	you is	"Number what?"
ní	yǐ-wei	nǐ-shi	(láo jǐ?)
你	以为	你是	（老几？）

★ "**láo dà** 老大" is the "No.1" Boss

34. Whose…?
shéi-de? or shuí-de?
谁的?

| 谁的? **shéi-de? or shuí-de?** |

Either way you prefer to pronounce, they both mean the English "Whose….?".

e.g.: ❶ "Whose" turtleneck sweater is this?

This	high collar	sweater	is	"who's" ?
zhèi-ge	gāo lǐngr	máo yī	shì	(shéi-de?)
这个	高领儿	毛衣	是	（谁的？）

❷ "Whose" wig looks more natual?

"who's?"	wig	look	like real
(shéi-de?)	jiǎ fǎ	kàn qǐ-lai	bī zhēn
（谁的？）	假发	看起来	逼真

35. How about? (NO.1)
na…zěn-me bàn?
哪…怎么办?

| 哪怎么办?…**zěn-me bàn?** |

is equivalent to "How about?" or "What to do with…?"

❶ "How about" your house?

If so,	you	house	"what do?"
nā,	ní	fang-zi	(zěn-me bàn?)
哪，	你	房子	（怎么办？）

❷ "How about" your debt?

You's	debt	"how about?"
nǐ-de	zhài wù	(zěn-me bàn?)
你的	债务	（怎么办？）

36. How about? (NO.2)
nǐ kàn zěn yàng?
你看怎样?

| 你看怎样? **nǐ kàn zěn yàng** |

is equivalent to "What do you think of…" or "How about this way…" in English.

e.g.: ❶ "How about" tomorrow morning?
You look tomorrow morning "How about?"
nǐ kàn míng-tiān zǎo-chen (zěn yàng?)
你 看 明天 早晨 （怎样？）

❷ "How about" some homemade sherbet?
Have some homemake juice ice cream "H.A"
lái diǎnr jiā zuò guǒ zhī bīng-qí lín (z.y.?)
来点儿 家做 果汁 冰淇淋 （怎样）

37. How many?
jǐ-ge?
几个？

几个？**jǐ-ge?** is equivalent to "How many?" in English.

(See 20 : "What Numeral 几")

e.g.: ❶ "How many" sisters do you have?
You have "how many?" sister
ní yǒu (jǐ-ge?) jiè mèi
你 有 （几个?） 姐妹

❷ "How many" hot dogs can you eat?
You can eat "how many?" hot dog
nǐ néng chī (jǐ-ge?) rè gǒu
你 能 吃 （几个?） 热狗

❷ "How many" cars does John have?
John have "what numeral?" car
John yǒu (jǐ?) liàng qì chē
John 有 （几?）辆 汽车
("liàng" is the numeric adjective for vehicles, see P. 74 ★, Group 5.)

38. How much? (not money)
duō-shao?
多少？

多少？**duō-shao?** is equivalent to "How much?", but it isn't referring to "money" unless money is specially mentioned.

e.g.: ❶ "How much" sugar do I put in?
I need put "how much?" sugar
wǒ yào fàng (duō-shao?) táng
我 要 放 （多少?） 糖

❷ "How much" are two and two?
two plus two is "how much?"
èr jiā èr shì (jǐ?) or (duō-shao?)
二 加 二 是 （几？） （多少？）

★If the total comes to a large amount, instead of "jǐ?", "duō-shao?" is used.

❸ "How old" is this mansion?
This mansion has "How much?" age
zhèi-suǒ dà shà yǒu (duō-shao?) nián-le
这所 大厦 有 （多少?） 年了

39. How much money?
duō-shao qián?
多少钱？

多少钱？**duō-shao qián?**

Actually "How much" already implies "money" in English. But in Chinese, it has to be said as "How much money?" instead of "How much".

❶ "How much" are the eggs?
Egg "How much money?" one unit
jī dàn (duō-shao qián?) yí gè
鸡蛋 （多少钱？） 一个

❷ "How much" will it cost
cost "How much money?"
děi yào huā (duō-shao qián?)
得要花 （多少钱？）

❸ "How much" is it worth
It worth "How much money?"
tā zhí (duō-shao qián?)
它 值 （多少钱?）

40. How old? (for adult)
duō shǎo suì? (guì gēng)
多少岁？（贵庚）

多少岁？ **duō shǎo suì?**

is "How much age", it's equivalent to "How old" in English, however this Chinese term is used upon adults. For even older or aged persons Chinese would respectfully use the word "貴庚 guì gēng" or "高壽 gāo shòu" for how old.

(Age for youngsters, see P. 125, 20)

e.g.: ❶ "How old" is your (aged) father?

<u>Your respectable father</u> <u>this year</u> "How old?"
lìng zūn jīn nián (guì gēng or gāo shòu)?
令尊　今年　（贵庚）　（高寿)?

❷ "How old" is Dr. Lee?

<u>Dr. Li</u> <u>this year</u> "How much age?"
lǐ dài-fu jīn nián (duō-shao suì?)
<u>李大夫</u>　<u>今年</u>　（多少岁?)

❸ "How old" is this mansion?

<u>This○</u> <u>mansion</u> <u>estimate</u> "How much age?"
zhèi-suǒ dà shà yǒu (duō-shao nián-le?)
<u>这所</u>　<u>大厦</u>　<u>有</u>　（多少年了?)

41. Excuse me!
qǐng wèn!
请问!

请问! **qǐng wèn!** is "Please instruct me" (请教您 qǐng jiào nín) which is equal to "May I ask…?" or "How do you…?". Usually a polite opening phrase like "抱歉 bào qiàn" (Sorry) or "打扰您 dá rǎo nín" (Bothering you!) is said prior to 请问 qǐng-wèn. Then followed by actual questions. **e.g.:**

❶ Excuse me, "How do you" go to the P.O.?

<u>Sorry</u> <u>allow ask</u> go <u>post office</u> "How" <u>walk</u>
<u>bào qiàn</u>, qǐng-wèn qù yóu jú (zě-me) <u>zǒu</u>
<u>抱歉</u>　请问　去　邮局　（怎幺）　<u>走</u>

❷ "How do you" make a pizza?

<u>allow ask</u> <u>pizza</u> "How" <u>make</u>
qǐng wèn pī sà (zě-me) zuò
<u>请问</u>　<u>披萨</u>　（怎幺）　做

42. How far?
duō-yuǎn?
多远?

多远? **duō yuǎn?** is equivalent to "How far" in English.

e.g.: ❶ "How far" is it from here to L.A.?

<u>From</u> <u>here</u> <u>reach</u> <u>L.A.</u> estimate "How far?"
cóng zhè-lǐ dào Luò Shān Jī yǎo (duō yuǎn?)
<u>从</u>　<u>这里</u>　<u>到</u>　<u>洛杉矶</u>　<u>有</u>　（多远?)

❷ "How far" can you swim?

You <u>swim</u> <u>can</u> <u>swim</u> "How far?"

nǐ yóu yǒng ké-yi yóu (duō yuǎn?)
你　游泳　可以　游　（多远?)

43. How often?
duō jiǔ yí cì?
多久一次?

多久一次? **duō jiǔ yí cì?** is equivalent to "How often" in English.
e.g.: "How often" do you see her?

<u>You</u> "How long?" <u>see</u> she "once" <u>face</u>
nǐ （duō jiǔ?) jiàn tā (yí cì) miàn
你　（多久?)　<u>见</u>　她　（一次）　<u>面</u>

44. How fast?
duō kuài?
多快?

多快? **duō kuài?** is a Chinese suffix referring to "speed" as "How fast can it be?".

e.g.: ❶ "How fast?" can this car run?

<u>This○</u> <u>car</u> <u>can</u> <u>run</u> "how fast?"
zhei bu che neng pao (duō kuài?)
<u>這部</u>　<u>車</u>　<u>能</u>　<u>跑</u>　（多快?)

❷ "How fast" is my heart beating?

<u>I's</u> <u>heart</u> <u>jump</u> estimate "how fast?"
wǒ-di xīn tiào-de yǒu (duō kuài?)
<u>我的</u>　<u>心</u>　<u>跳得</u>　<u>有</u>　（多快?)

多慢? **duō màn?** is "How slow? the opposite word of "How fast".

45. How soon…?
duó kuài néng…?
多快能…? (盡速做好)

多快能…? **duō kuài néng…?.**

Literally it is "How fast enable you" which means "What is the shortest time needed". It is equivalent to "How soon" in English.

e.g.: ❶ "How soon?" will it be done?

"How fast enable" done
(duó kuài néng?) <u>hǎo</u>
（多快能?)　<u>好</u>

❷ "How soon?" can you get here?
You   "How fast enable"   arrive
<u>nǐ</u>   (duó kuài néng?)   <u>dào</u>
你   (多快能?)   到

46. How long? (timewise)
duō jiǔ?
多久?

多久? **duō jiǔ?** is a Chinese suffix used in questions, equivalent to "How long" timewise in English..

e.g.: ❶ "How long" do I have to wait?
<u>I</u> <u>have to</u> <u>wait</u> "How long?"
○ <u>yào</u> <u>děng</u> (duō jiǔ?)
○ 要 等 (多久?)
("要 yào" is short for "得要 děi yào")

❷ "How long" will it take to finish the job
  <u>estimate</u> "How long?" <u>done</u>
  <u>yào</u> (duō jiǔ?) <u>zuò hǎo</u>
  要 (多久?) 做好
(★ "要 yào" is short for "約莫要 yūe-mo yào")

47. How long? (lengthwise)
duō cháng?
多长?

多长? **duō zháng?** is a Chinese suffix used in questions, equivalent to "How long", lengthwise.

e.g.: ❶ "How long" is the swimming pool?
  <u>This</u> <u>swimming pool</u> "How long?"
  <u>zhèi-ge</u> <u>yóu yǒng chí</u> (duō zháng?)
  这个 游泳池 (多长?)
❷ "How long" a bamboo pole do you want?
  <u>You</u> <u>bamboo pole</u> <u>want</u> "How long?"
  <u>nǐ</u> <u>zhú gān</u> <u>yào</u> (duō zháng?)
  你 竹竿 要 (多长?)

多短? **duō duǎn?** is "How short? No.1" It is "only" used as an opposite word for "How long, lengthwise".

48. How wide?
duō kuān?
多宽?

多宽? **duō kuān?** is equivalent to "How wide" in English.
e.g.: ❶ "How wide" is the refrigerator?
  <u>This</u> <u>refrigerator</u> <u>estimate</u> "How wide?"
  <u>zhèi-ge</u> <u>bīng xiāng</u> <u>yǒu</u> (duō kuān?)
  这个 冰箱 有 (多宽?)
❷ "How wide" is it across your shoulders?
  <u>You's</u> <u>shoulder</u> <u>estimate</u> "How wide?"
  <u>nǐ-de</u> <u>jiān báng</u> <u>yǒu</u> (duō kuān?)
  你的 肩膀 有 (多宽?)

多窄? **duō zhǎi?** is the opposite word of "How wide". It's "How narrow?".

49. How tall?
duō-gāo? (N0.1)
多高? (本体)

多高? **duō gāo?** This Chinese term has two different meanings in English. It could mean "How tall" or "How high". However, at this point we take this "duō gāo" as the English "How tall", which means the mentioned object itself is slender and tall like a "high-rise" or a "9 feet tall man".

e.g.: ❶ "How tall" are you?
  <u>You</u> "how tall?"
  <u>nǐ</u> (duō gāo?)
  你 (多高?)
❷ She is "tall" for her age.
<u>She</u> <u>only</u> <u>few</u> <u>age year,</u> <u>such</u> "tall!?"
<u>tā</u> <u>cái</u> <u>jǐ</u> <u>suì</u> , <u>zhè-me</u> (gāo!)
她 才 几 岁, 这么 (高!)
❸ "How tall" is this skyscraper?
<u>This</u> <u>skyscraper</u> <u>estimate</u> "How tall?"
<u>zhèi-ge</u> <u>mó tiān dà lóu</u> <u>yǒu</u> (duō gāo?)
这个 摩天大楼 有 (多高?)

多矮? **duō ǎi?** is "How short? No.2" in English. It is "only" used as an opposite word for "How tall?", not "How high?".

50. How high?
duō-gāo? (N0.2)
多高? (位置)

The English Eight W's & One H

duō gāo? This "duō gāo" is different, it is equivalent to "How high?" in English. It means that the things are placed in a high place as a painting is hanging high on the wall or "how high?" a person's position is.

e.g.: ❶ "How high" can a kite fly?

Kite	can	let go	"how high?"
fēng-zheng	kě-yi	fàng	(duō gāo?)
风筝	可以	放	（多高？）

❷ "How high" are we flying?

We's	plane	now	fly's	estimate	"How high?"
zán-men-de	fēi jī	xiàn zài	fēi-de	yǒu	(duō gāo?)
咱们的	飞机	现在	飞得	有	（多高?）

❸ I'm not sober and he's "high".

I	not drunk.	He had	"one too many"
wǒ	méi zuì,	tā	(hē duō-le)
我	没醉，	他	（喝多了) (飘飘欲仙)

❹ Hang it up as "high" as you can reach.

Have it	hung	exceed	"high"	exceed	good.
bǎ-ta	guà-de	yuè	(gāo)	yuè	hǎo
把它	挂得	越	（高）	越	好

多低? duō dī? is "How low?" in English. It is "only" used as an opposite word of "How high, not "How tall?'.

51. How heavy?

duō zhòng?
多重？

This	thing	"how heavy?"
zhèi-ge	dōng-xi	(duō zhòng?)
这个	东西	（多重？）

多轻? duō qīng? is the opposite word of "How heavy", it is "How light?".

52. How thick? (No.1) (board)

duō hòu?
多厚？

❶"How thick?" is this plywood?

This piece	plywood	estimate	"How thick?"
zhèi-kuài	sān jiá bǎn	yǒu	(duō hòu?)
這塊	三夾板	有	（多厚?)

❷ You surely are shameless!

You's	face skin	estimate	"How thick?"
nǐ-di	liǎn pí	yǒu	(dū hòu?)
你的	臉皮	有	（多厚?)

多薄? duō báo? is "How thin", the opposite word of"How thick?". It is referring to the sheet or board mentioned.

53. How thick? (No.2) (soup)

duō nóng? or duō chóu?
多浓？or 多稠？

Referring to the thickness of the liquid：
❶"How thick" do you want your mush?

You's	mush	want	"How thick?"
nǐ-di	yù-mi zhōu	yào	duō (nóng/chóu)
你的	玉米粥	要	多 （浓or稠）?

As referring to the taste of the drink:
❷ Is your coffee "strong enough?"

You's	coffee	enough	"strong"	(ma?)
nǐ-di	kā fēi	gòu	(nóng)	ma?
你的	咖啡	夠	（浓)	嗎?

多稀? duō xī? is "How thin?" as the soup or paint is being diluted.

多淡? duō dàn? is "How weak?" as the tea or coffee is being diluted.

54. good no good?

hǎo-bu hǎo?
好不好？

❶ Good no good eat?hǎo bù hǎo chī (tasty)
❷ You drink no drink? nǐ hē bù hē (beer)
❸ He love no love? tā ài-ni bú-ài-ni (you)
❹ You go no go? nǐ qù bú qù (Hawaii)
❺ She come no come? tā lái bù lái (my party)
❻ You want no want? nǐ yào bú yào (ice cream)
❼ You like no like? ní xǐ bù xǐ huān (play cards)
❽ He know no know?tā rèn bú rèn-shi (my son)
❾ He can no can? tā huì bù huì (swimming)

Substitutional verbs See Group 3

Treasury of Hard To Translate Chinese Proverbs

關鍵字眼兒936

Because of the differences in the structural nature between English and Chinese, many day-to-day words or phrases can not be translated with a dictionary while still retaining the original meaning. e.g.: "on the other hand 但話说回來 dàn huà shuō huí-lai", but the direct translation is "在另一只手上".

It is because of these types of difficulties that the learner would face, that the author has collected a few hundred day-to-day proverbs, and provides the equivalent meaning in Chinese. This collection is a valuable tool for beginners as well as advanced students who wish to learn Chinese.

Marco Liang will teach you to think in a new way, avoiding tedious drills, translations, and monotonous grammar. All you need to do is blend the following words or phrases into your everyday Chinese dialogue.

This saves time, provides fluency and allows for enjoyable and meaningful conversation in Chinese. You should then feel confident while communicating with native speakers.

A

a bad turn out for it
jié guǒ bù lí xiǎng
结果不理想
結果不理想

(in) a larger sense
guǎng yì-de shuō
广义的说
廣義的說

a slip of tongue
shuō liū-le zuǐ
说溜了嘴
說溜了嘴

a tall order
kē qiú
苛求
苛求

a very difficult task
jiān nán-de gōng zuò
艰难的工作
艱難的工作

about
guān yú; chà bù duō
关于；差不多
關於；差不多

above
gāo yú; shàng shù-de
高于；上述的
高於；上述的

above all
zhì zhòng yào-de
最重要的
最重要的

absent minded
xīn bú zài yān
心不在焉
心不在焉

(in) accordance with the rules
yī jù guī dìng
依据规定
依據規定

according to
yī jù
依据
依據

across
chuān yüè; duì miàn
穿越；对面
穿越；對面

act upon (on)
yóu suǒ xíng dòng
有所行动
有所行動

add up
lěi jiā
累加
累加

addition of
wài jiā
外加
外加

English	Pinyin	简体	繁体
(in) addition to	cǐ wài	此外	此外
(in) advance	shì xiān; yù xiān	事先；预先	事先；預先
advance the time of meeting	tí qián kāi huì	提前开会	提前開會
afraid of	pà-de shì	怕的是	怕的是
after	zhī hòu	之后	之後
after all	bì jìng	毕竟	畢竟
and again	zài zhě	再者	再者
against	fǎn duì	反对	反對
against one's will	miǎn qiáng	勉强	勉強
all (are)	quán dōu	全都	全都
all at once	yí xià-zi	一下子	一下子
all in all	zuì zhòng yào-de	最重要地	最重要地
all my lifetime	wǒ yì shēng	我一生	我一生
all of a sudden	tú rán jīan	突然间	突然間
all the same	quán duō yí yàng	全都一样	全都一樣
all thumbs	bèn shǒu bèn jiǎo	笨手笨脚	笨手笨腳
all walks of life	gè háng gè yè	各行各业	各行各業
along	yán-zhe	沿着	沿著
also	yě	也	也
amazing	líng rén chī jīng	令人吃惊	令人吃驚
and	hé; hái yǒu	和；还有	和；還有
and so forth	zhū rú cǐ lèi	诸如此类	諸如此類
and so on; et cetera (etc.)	déng děng	等等	等等
and yet	rán ér	然而	然而
angry beyond measure	zhèn nù	震怒	震怒
(in) answer to	jìng fù zhě	敬覆者	敬覆者
anyone	rèn hé yí-ge rén	任何一个人	任何一個人
anyway	fǎn zhèng	反正	反正
(construct an) appealing offer	shì chū shàn yì	释出善意	釋出善意
appeals to his taste	hé tā-de wèi kǒu	合他的胃口	合他的胃口
appear defenseless	ruǎn ruò wú néng	软弱无能	軟弱無能
apt to	shàn cháng	擅长	擅長
argumentative and angry	hào díng zuǐ ài shēng qì	好顶嘴爱生气	好頂嘴愛生氣
around	wéi rào-zhe; sì wéi	围绕着；四围	圍繞著；四圍
arrogance; stump	xiāo zhāng; tiǎo xìn	嚣张；挑衅	囂張；挑釁
arrogant	ào màn	傲慢	傲慢
as	yí yàng; yī zhào	一样；依照	一樣；依照
as a matter of fact	shì shí shàng	事实上	事實上
as a token of	xiàng zhēng	象征	象徵
(in) a sense	móu zhǒng céng miàn lái shuō	某种层面来说	某種層面來說

as for; as to; as regards zhì yǔ	至于 至於	at length zhōng jiù	终究 終究
aside from the facts piē kāi shì shí bù tán	撇开事实不谈 撇開事實不談	at one's service rèn píng chāi qiǎn	任凭差遣 任憑差遣
as if hǎo xiàng shì	好像是 好像是	at random suí yì-de	随意地 隨意地
as though yǎn ruò	俨若 儼若	attempt to qì tú	企图 企圖
as is the case yīn wèi rú cǐ	因为如此 因為如此	at the sight of yí kàn jiàn	一看见… 一看見…
as is the custom yī zhào wǎng lì	依照往例 依照往例	at the beginning dāng chū	当初 當初
as it is rú mù qián xiàn kuàng	如目前现况 如目前現況	at the end mò wěi; zuì hòu	末尾; 最后 末尾; 最後
as long as zhǐ yào	只要 只要	at the expense of xī shēng	牺牲 犧牲
as soon as yùe kuài yùe	越快越… 越快越…	at the point of dào –de dì bù	到…的地步 到…的地步
as the saying goes sú huà shuō-de hǎo	俗话说得好 俗話說得好	at the risk of mào-zhe fāng xiǎn	冒着风险 冒著風險
as well as yě shì yí yàng	也是一样 也是一樣	at the thought of; the mere thought of yì xiǎng dào	一想到…
ask for yāo qíu	要求 要求	at this rate yí cǐ lái kàn	依此来看 依此來看
(you) asked for it shì nǐ zì zhǎo	是你自找 是你自找	at times yǒu shí-hou	有时候 有時候
astonished; shocked kàn shá yǎn-le	看傻眼了 看傻眼了	atmosphere get unpleasant qì fēn biàn chà	气氛变差 氣氛變差
at zài	在 在	attend to zhào gù	照顾 照顧
at any cost bú jì dài jià	不计代价 不計代價	attend to superficials neglect essentials běn mò dào zhì	本末倒置
at any rate bù guǎn zěn yàng	不管怎样 不管怎樣	autonomous zì jǐ zuò zhǔ	自己做主 自己做主
at command súi shí dài mìng	随时待命 隨時待命	available in a moment mǎ shàng jiù lái	马上就来 馬上就來
at intervals měi gé yí duàn shí jiān	每隔一段时间 每隔一段時間	avoid arousing suspicions guā tián lǐ xià	瓜田李下 瓜田李下
at leisure yōu xián	悠闲 悠閒	awkward bèn zhòng	笨重 笨重

awkward situation jìn tuì liǎng nán	進退兩難 進退兩難	before long bù jiǔ	不久 不久
		beforehand shì xiān	事先 事先

B

back and forth lái huí	来回 來回	(to) begin with yà gēnr; gēn běn	压根儿;根本 壓根兒;根本
back to back bèi duì bèi	背对背 背對背	behind de hòu miàn; lùo hòu	的后面;落后 的後面;落後
back up zhī yǜan	支持 支援	below zhi xià	之下 之下
(in) bad circumstances zài bù liáng huán jìng xià	在不良环境下 在不良環境下	beneath de xià miàn	的下面 的下面
balance with yǔ píng héng	与..平衡 與..平衡	beneficial hǎo chù duō duō	好处多多 好處多多
bargain for yù liào ;qí wàng	预料;期望 預料;期望	beneficial and rewarding míng lì shuāng shōu	名利雙收 名利雙收
bargain over tǎo jià huán jià	讨价还价 討價還價	beside de páng biān	的旁边 的旁邊
baloney yí pài hú yán	一派胡言 一派胡言	besides chú cǐ zhī wài	除此之外 除此之外
be aware jǐng jüé	警觉 警覺	beside the point lí tí tài yüǎn	离题太远 離題太遠
be careful xiǎo-xin	小心 小心	beyond chāo chū	超出 超出
bear (keep) in mind láo jì	牢记 牢記	beyond description nán yǐ yán yù	难以言喻 難以言喻
bear the loss chéng dān sǔn shī	承担损失 承擔損失	beyond doubt bù róng zhì yí	不容置疑 不容置疑
bear fruit yǒu chéng jiù	有成就 有成就	beyond one's reach nán yǐ dá chéng	难以达成 難以達成
bear with it rěn shòu xià qù	忍受下去 忍受下去	(put it)black on white zán-men bái zhǐ hēi zì	咱们白纸黑字 咱們白紙黑字
beat a bargain yì jià	议价 議價	blame yourself guài nǐ zì gěr	怪你自个儿 怪你自個兒
because yīn-wei	因为 因為	(full of) boasts mán zuǐ dà huà	满嘴大话 滿嘴大話
become personal qīn fàn yǐn sī	侵犯隐私 侵犯隱私	boil down dǎo zhì	导致 導致
before zhī qián	之前 之前	★ boil a frog in cold water léng shuǐ zhǔ qīng wā	冷水煮青蛙 冷水煮青蛙 (see p.151★)

bored; boring fá wèi; yèn fán	乏味；厌烦 乏味；厭煩	by means of yǐ ...-de fāng fǎ	以…的方法 以…的方法
both (are) liǎng-ge dōu	两个都 兩個都	by no means jüé bù	绝不 絕不
bow and shake one's own hands (up/down)作揖 zuō yī (salutation, both hands holding together) 作揖		By the way… Ou, duì-le	喔，对了！ 喔，對了！
break even dǎ píng; méi péi qián	打平；没赔钱 打平；沒賠錢	by then dào shí-hou; dào nà shí	到时候；到那时 到時候；到那時
break lose táo tuō	逃脱 逃脫	by way of jīng yóu	经由 經由

C

break off with fēn shǒu	分手 分手	call attention to jiào tā-men zhù yì	叫他们注意 叫他們注意
break one's heart shāng xīn	伤心 傷心	call it a day shōu gōng-ba	收工吧！ 收工吧！
break out bào fā	爆发 爆發	call off; cancel qǔ xiāo	取消 取消
break the peace pò huài hé píng	破坏和平 破壞和平	calm down lěng jìng xià-lai	冷静下来 冷靜下來
break through tū pò	突破 突破	can't stand for wú fá rěn shòu	无法忍受 無法忍受
breathe one's last qù shì; sǐ-diao	去世；死掉 去世；死掉	carry on ;continue jì xù	继续 繼續
bring back dài huí-lai	带回来 帶回來	carry out complete; accomplish 执行 zhí xíng	执行 執行
bring down jiàng dī	降低 降低	(fail to) carry through yóu shǐ wú zhōng	有始无终 有始無終
bring it up to date hé hū cháo liú	合乎潮流 合乎潮流	careless cǎo shuài; xīn bú zài	草率；心不在 草率；心不在
but dàn shì	但是 但是	(in) case wàn yī	萬一 萬一
but also ér qiě	而且 而且	cast away pāo kāi	抛开 抛開
but to zhǐ néng	只能 只能	cause to fall jié guó kuǎ tāi	結果垮台 結果垮台
by bèi; yǐ; yóu	被；以；由 被；以；由	caused him to experience ràng-ta chī jìn kǔ-tou	讓他吃盡苦头 讓他吃盡苦頭
by any chance qià qiǎo; zhèng hǎo	恰巧；正好 恰巧；正好	change my mind gǎi biàn zhǔ yì	改变主意 改變主意
by hook or by clook fù tāng dáo huǒ	赴汤蹈火 赴湯蹈火		

(in) charge of fù zhú guǎn zhī zé	负主管之责 負主管之責	come up with xiǎng chū-ge diǎn-zi	想出个点子 想出個點子
cheated me out of one grand piàn-le-wo yī qiān kuài	骗了我一千块 騙了我一千塊	(I) commend you (knee down!) nǐ géi-wo...(a verb, guì-xia)	你给我⋯ 你給我（跪下）
clear out qīng chú	清除 清除	commit oneself to zhì lì yú	致力于 致力於
closely abide by instruction s qüè shí zūn shǒu zhǐ lìng	确实遵守指令 確實遵守指令	common sense pù tōng cháng shì	普通常识 普通常識
clue you into bá ní lǐng rù	把你领入 把你領入	(in) comparison with bǐ jiào qǐ-lai	比较起来 比較起來
clumsy bèn zhuó	笨拙 笨拙	completed thoroughly chè dǐ-de wán chéng	彻底的完成 徹底的完成
coax her into huā yán qiǎo yǔ	花言巧语 花言巧語	comply with pèi hé	配合 配合
(a) cold comfort fū yǎn xìng-de ān wèi	敷衍性的安慰 敷衍性的安慰	conceited zì mìng bù fán; zì fù	自命不凡；自负 自命不凡；自負
come across qiǎo yù	巧遇 巧遇	(to) concern about kǎo lǜ dào	考虑到 考慮到
come and go lái lái qǜ qǜ	来来去去 來來去去	(all) concerned yǒu guān rén yüán	有关人员 有關人員
come across one's mind tú rán xiǎng dào	突然想到 突然想到	concerned about the future tiào wàng wèi lái	眺望未来 眺望未來
come along with yì qǐ	一起 一起	concentrate on zhuān zhù yǘ	专注于 專注於
come in contact with yóu suǒ jiē chù	有所接触 有所接觸	(in) conclusion (lastly) sǒng zhī	总之 總之
come (step) forward zǒu shàng qián lái	走上前来 走上前來	conflict chōng tú	冲突 衝突
(didn't) come out of the blue bìng fēi píng kōng ér lái	并非凭空而来 並非憑空而來	(regardless of the) consequence bú jì hòu guǒ	不计後果 不計後果
come to a conclusion dá chéng jié lùn	达成结论 達成結論	(take) the consequences zì chéng hòu guǒ	自承後果 自承後果
come to a halt bèi pò tíng zhǐ	被迫停止 被迫停止	(in) consideration of kǎo lǜ dào	考虑到 考慮到
come to an understanding hù xiāng lí jiě	互相理解 互相理解	consist (made up) of suó zǔ chéng	⋯所组成 ⋯所組成
come to the conclusion jié lùn shì	结论是 結論是	constantly jīng cháng	经常 經常
come to the rescue jiā rù jìu yüán háng liè	加入救援行列 加入救援行列	continue with the plan yī jì huà jìn xíng	依计画进行 依計畫進行

continuously **chí xǔ-de**	持续地	持續地
(in) contrast with each other **bí cǐ xíng chéng duì bǐ**	彼此形成对比	彼此形成對比
controversial **zhēng lùn xìng shì jiàn**	争论性事件	爭論性事件
cool head **lěng jìng-de tóu nǎo**	冷静的头脑	冷靜的頭腦
cooperate with **hé zuò**	合作	合作
(being) cooperative **gēn rén hé zuò**	跟人合作	跟人合作
cope (deal) with **duì-fu; chú lǐ**	对付；处理	對付；處理
got away with it **xiāo yáo fǎ wài**	消遥法外	消遙法外
Count me in. **suàn wǒ yí fènr**	算我一份儿	算我一份兒
court for resolution **sù zhū fǎ lǜ**	诉诸法律	訴諸法律
crack a joke **kāi-ge wán xiào**	开个玩笑	開個玩笑
crafty scoundrel; wily old fox **lǎo jiān jù huá**	老奸巨猾	老奸巨猾
creates resentment **yǔ rén jié yüàn**	與人結怨	與人結怨
criticize **pī-ping**	批评	批評
(I) cross my fingers for you. **zhù nǐ xīn xiǎng shì chéng**	祝你心想事成	祝你心想事成
cross (occur to) my mind **hū rán xiǎng dào**	忽然想到	忽然想到
cross off (out) **huà diào**	划掉	劃掉
crucial interests **zhǔ yàu lì yì**	主要利益	主要利益
cry wolf **"láng lái-le!"**	「狼來了」	「狼來了」
cunning **diāo; jiǎo huá**	刁；狡猾	刁；狡猾

cut out the sweet talks **shǎo lái zhèi tào**	少来这套	少來這套

D

dangerous situations **wéi xiǎn qíng kuàng**	危险情况	危險情況
day by day (gradually) **yì tiān yì tiān-de**	一天一天的	一天一天的
day in and day out **zhěng tiān-de**	整天的	整天的
deal; a deal **yì yán wéi dìng**	一言为定	一言為定
(a) debate **bèi fèn dǎng**	辩论会	辯論會
decided **jüé dìng**	决定	決定
deeply implanted hatred **shēn chóu dà hèn**	深仇大恨	深仇大恨
defeat is to be avoided **bì miǎn shī bài**	避免失败	避免失敗
deliberately create difficulties **gù yì diāo nàn**	故意刁難	故意刁難
(in) demand of **xü qiú liàng dà**	需求量大	需求量大
demonstrate your passion for **zhōng xīn biǎo dá**	衷心表达	衷心表達
dependable **kě kào**	可靠	可靠
(you) deserve it **huó gāi**	活该	活該
despite **jǐn guǎn**	尽管	儘管
difficult situation **kùn jìng**	困境	困境
disgraceful; lose face **diū liǎn**	丢脸	丟臉
disheartened **xiè qì**	泄氣	洩氣
dispassionately **píng xīn jìng qì**	平心静气	平心靜氣

dispose of; get rid of chú lǐ diào	处理掉 處理掉

E

do oneself justice fā huī yì jǐ zhī cháng	发挥一己之长 發揮一己之長	(to) each his own gè yóu suǒ hào	各有所好 各有所好
do your upmost jìn xīn jìn lì	尽心尽力 盡心盡力	(a lot) easier qīng sōng-de duō	轻松得多 輕鬆得多
doing things unprecisely zuò shì mǎ-hu	做事马虎 做事馬虎	easygoing suí hé	随和 隨和
Does it ring a bell? xiáng-qi lái-le-ma	想起来了吗? 想起來了嗎?	(in) effect (actually) shí jì-shang	实际上 實際上
doesn't make sense gǒu pì bù tōng	狗屁不通 狗屁不通	either you or him nǐ yě xíng, tā yě xíng	你也行;他也行 你也行;他也行
doesn't work xíng bù tōng	行不通 行不通	either one suí biàn nǎ-ge	(两个中) 随便哪个 (兩個中) 隨便哪個
(It's) done zuò wán-le	做完了 做完了	elimination of pái chú	排除 排除
don't beat around the bush bié guǎi wānr mò jiǎor	别拐弯儿抹角儿 別拐彎兒抹角兒	embarrassing nán wéi qíng; nán kān	难为情;难堪 難為情;難堪
don't get me wrong bié wù huì wǒ yì-si	别误会我意思 別誤會我意思	end up -de xià chǎng; -de jié jú	的下场;的结局 的下場;的結局
don't let me down bié ràng wǒ shī wàng	别让我失望 別讓我失望	endured a crushing defeat cǎn bài	惨败 慘敗
don't stand a chance méi jī huì	没机会 沒機會	engaged in cóng shì yú	从事于 從事於
don't stir up bié zhāo rě shì fēi	别招惹是非 別招惹是非	(take an) equivocal attitute mó léng liáng kě	模棱两可 模稜兩可
don't take it personally jiù shì lùn shì	就事论事 就事論事	especially yóu qí	尤其 尤其
(you guys)don't stir up trouble bié qǐ hòng	别起哄 別起哄	enthusiastic rè xīn	热心 熱心
double talk hǔn yáo shì tīng	混淆视听 混淆視聽	entire life yí bèi-zi	一辈子 一輩子
drag on rǒng cháng	冗长 冗長	(on an)equal footing píng qǐ píng zuò	平起平座 平起平座
draw the conclusion xià jié lùn	下结论 下結論	even if; even though jí shǐ; jí huò	即使;即或 即使;即或
(in) due time shí jiān yí dào	时间一到 時間一到	eventually zhōng yú	终于 終於
during zài cǐ qí jiān	在此期间 在此期間	ever since zì cóng	自从 自從

every so often ǒu rán	偶然	偶然
everything's under way yí qiè jiù xù	一切就绪	一切就緒
exact zhèng zhèng qüè qüè-de	正正确确的	正正確確的
except chú cǐ zhī wài	除此之外	除此之外
expectation yǔ qí-de xiào guǒ	预期的效果	預期的效果
Excuse me, sir! jìe guāng!	借光!	借光！
(make an) excuse jiè kǒu	借口	藉口
(as was) expected bù chū suǒ liào	不出所料	不出所料
expertise zhuān yè zhī shì	专业知识	專業知識
(to) express biǎo shì	表示	表示

F

face to face dāng miàn	当面	當面
fail to appreciate favors bù shí tái-jü	不识抬举	不識抬舉
fail to live up to expectation bù zhēng qì	不争气	不爭氣
fair and square chéng shí gōng zhèng	诚实公正	誠實公正
false bù zhēn shí	不真实	不真實
(in) favor of zàn tóng; yōng hù	赞同;拥护	贊同;擁護
fed up with you shòu gòu-le	受够了	受夠了
feel refreshed and recharged jīng shén wéi zhī yí zhèn	精神为之一振	精神為之一振
(not) feel like to respond him lǎn-de dā-li-ta	懒得理睬他	懶得理睬他

(on your own) feet zhàn wěn-le jiǎo	站稳了脚	站穩了腳(自立)
fellow delegates gè wèi dài biǎo	各位代表	各位代表
figure out zhuó-mo; xiǎng chū	琢磨；想出	琢磨；想出
(you've got it all) figured out xiōng yǒu chéng zhú	胸有成竹	胸有成竹
first and foremost shǒu xiān yào shì	首先要事	首先要事
firsthand dì yì shǒu-de	第一手的	第一手的
firsthand experience qīn shén jīng yàn	亲身经验	親身經驗
first of all shǒu xiān yīng gāi	首先应该	首先應該
flash on the mind líng jī yí dòng	灵机一动	靈機一動
flat out zhí jié liǎo dàng	直截了当	直截了當
follow the footsteps of gēn suí jiǎo bù	跟随脚步	跟隨腳步
follow up procedure hòu xù chéng xù	后续程序	後續程序
fool around guǐ hùn	鬼混	鬼混
for wèi-le	为了	為了
for a change gǎi-ge fāng shì	改个方式	改個方式
for all I know jǜ wó suǒ zhī	据我所知	據我所知
for better, for worse bù guán hǎo huài	不管好坏	不管好壞
for certain (sure) qüè dìng	确定	確定
for ever yóng yüǎn	永远	永遠
for example jǚ lì lái shōu	举例来说	舉例來說

for fear of **dān yōu**	担忧 擔憂	
for instance **pì rú**	譬如 譬如	
for one thing **qí yī**	其一 其一	
for the benefit of **wèi-le lì yì**	为了利益 為了利益	
for the better **gǎi shàn**	改善 改善	
for the present foremost **mù qián**	目前 目前	
for the purpose of **wèi-de shì**	为的是 為的是	
for the sake of **wèi-le;-de yuán gù**	为了;的缘故 為了;的緣故	
for the time being **mù qián; lín shí**	目前;临时 目前；臨時	
for want of **yīn-wei qūe fá**	因为缺乏 因為缺乏	
(a) friend in need **xūe zhōng sòng tàn zhī yǒu**	雪中送炭之友 雪中送炭之友	
free oneself of debt **miǎn yǘ fù zhài**	免于负债 免於負債	
from **cóng**	从 從	
(look) from a different angle **huàn-ge jiǎo dù lái kàn**	换个角度来看 換個角度來看	
from my heart **fā zì nèi xīn**	发自内心 發自內心	
from now on **cóng xiàn zài kāi shǐ**	从现在开始 從現在開始	
from time to time **bù shí**	不时 不時	
(in) front of **de miàn qiān**	的面前 的面前	
frugal with expenses **shěng chī jiǎn yòng**	省吃俭用 省吃儉用	
frustrated; have no effect (See P.86) **xiè qì**	泄气 洩氣	

G

gain the upper hand **qǔ dé xiān jī**	取得先机 取得先機	
generous at other people's expense **kāng tā rén zhī kǎi**	慷他人之慨	
get ahold of **zhuā-zhu**	抓住 抓住	
get along **xiāng chù**	相处 相處	
get back at him **xiàng tā bào fù**	向他报复 向他報復	
get down to business **tán zhèng jīng shì**	谈正经事 談正經事	
get good or get out **zuò-bu hǎo jiù gǔn dàn**	做不好就滚蛋 做不好就滾蛋	
get hold of him **zhǎ-de dào tā**	找得到他 找得到他	
get into a mess **gǎo-de yì tuán zāo**	搞得一团糟 搞得一團糟	
gets on my nerves **zhēn tǎo yàn**	真讨厌 真討厭	
get one down **lìng rén jǔ sàng**	令人沮丧 令人沮喪	
get over; overcome **kè fú**	克服 克服	
get the hang of **dé xīn yìng shǒu**	得心应手 得心應手	
get the better of you **bèi rén jiā qī fù**	被人家欺负 被人家欺負	
get the work done **wán chéng rèn wù**	完成任务 完成任務	
get to the bottom of **zhuī gēn jiù dǐ**	追根究底 追根究底	
get to the point **yán guī zhèng zhuàn**	言归正传 言歸正傳	
(it was a) gift **shì rén sòng-de**	是人送的 是人送的	
give full measure **jìn qüán lì**	尽全力 盡全力	

give short measure tōu gōng jiǎn liào	偷工减料 偷工減料
great common measure zuì dà gōng yüē shù	最大公约数 最大公約數
go nuts fā fēng	发疯 發瘋
go on jì xǜ shuō	继续说 繼續說
go to (excess) extremes zǒu jí duān	走极端 走極端
(You've) gone too far! nǐ tài guò fèn-le	你太过份了！ 你太過份了！
(in) good circumstances chǔ yǘ hǎo-de huán jìng	处于好的环境 處於好的環境
good for nothing bù chéng cái	不成材 不成材
good idea háo zhǔ yì	好主意 好主意
Good afternoon! nín hǎo!	您好！(下午用) 您好！
Good evening! nín hǎo!	您好！(晚上用) 您好！
Good morning! zǎo ; nín zǎo!	早！；您早！ 早！；您早！
Good night! wǎn ān!	晚安！ 晚安！
Good noon(Chinese:Have you had your lunch?) -nin chī fàn-le-ma?	您吃飯了嗎？
Good-bye! Good day! huí jiàn! zài jiàn!	回见！再见！ 回見！再見！
got it wrong gǎo cuò-le!	搞错了 搞錯了
gracious goodness tiān-a!	天啊！ 天啊！
(lose) ground jié jié bài tuì	节节败退 節節敗退
grumble fā láo-sao	发牢骚 發牢騷
(I) guarantee you wó bǎo zhèng-ni	我保证你 我保證你

H

(I) had to bù dé bù	不得不 不得不
handle situation yìng duì zhuàng kuàng	应对状况 應對狀況
harassing calls sāo rǎo diàn huà	骚扰电话 騷擾電話
harbour evil designs bù huái hǒu yì	不怀好意 不懷好意
(at) hard edge pīn mìng; bó dòu	拼命；搏斗 拼命；搏鬥
(a) hard nut to crack nán jiě-de wèn tí	难解的问题 難解的問題
hard up xǖ qián kǒng jí	需钱孔急 需錢孔急
hardly jī hū bù	几乎不 幾乎不
hardly any jī hū méi yǒu	几乎没有 幾乎沒有
hardly ever hén shǎo; jī hū bù céng	很少；几乎不曾 很少；幾乎不曾
hard to deal with nán chán	难缠 難纏
harmonious hé xié	和谐 和諧
have a word with you gēn nǐ jiǎng jù huà	跟你讲句话 跟你講句話
have confidence in yǒu xìn xīn	有信心 有信心
have no idea of yì wú suǒ zhī	一无所知 一無所知
have nothing to do with yǘ...wú guān	与…无关 與…無關
have the worst of it zāo dào shī bài	遭到失败 遭到失敗
have sympathy for tóng qíng	同情 同情
(I) havn't got all day. méi gōng-fu gēn nǐ pào mó-gu	没工夫跟你泡蘑菇 沒工夫跟你泡蘑菇

held in secret bì xǔ bǎo mì	必须保密 必須保密
Hell with it! huō chū qù-le	豁出去了! 豁出去了!
hence yīn cǐ; cóng cǐ	因此；从此 因此；從此
here and there (hither and thither) dào chù	到处 到處
hesitate to; hate to bù hǎo yì-si (to bother people)	不好意思 不好意思 (打擾)
hint at it; give a hint àn shì	暗示 暗示
hit the nail on the head yì zhēn jiàn xiě	一针见血 一針見血
hold off on the work yán hòu gōng zuò	延后工作 延後工作
hold one's ground jiān chí xià qù	坚持下去 堅持下去
(in) honor of zhì jìng	致敬 致敬
a hopeless case bù kě jiù yào	不可救药 不可救藥
however bú guò	不过 不過
humble; modest qiān xū	谦虚 謙虚
humorous yōu mò	幽默 幽默
(suffer from) hunger hē xī běi fēngr	喝西北风儿 喝西北風兒
hush money zhē xiū fèi; fēng kǒu fèi	遮羞费；封口费 遮羞費；封口費

I

identify zhǐ rèn; qùe dìng	指认；确定 指認；確定
if jiǎ rú; rú guǒ; yào-shi	假如；如果；要是 假如；如果；要是
if I were you wǒ yào-shi nǐ-de huà	我要是你的话 我要是你的話

if you were in my shoes nǐ yào shì wǒ-de huà	你要是我的话 你要是我的話
ignore whatever you say zhuāng zuò méi tīng jiàn	装作没听见 裝作沒聽見
I have not the least idea yì diǎnr yě bù zhī dào	一点儿也不知道 一點兒也不知道
ill at ease; feel small bù-hǎo yì-si (embarrassing)	不好意思 不好意思 (難爲情)
ill-tempered pí-qi bù-hǎo	脾气不好 脾氣不好
I mean business bié xī pí ziào liǎn-de	别嘻皮笑脸的 别嘻皮笑臉的
imagination xiǎng xiàng lì	想像力 想像力
immature bù chéng shú	不成熟 不成熟
immediate respond lì jí fǎn yìng	立即反应 立即反應
immediately; right away lì kè; mǎ shàng	立刻；馬上 立刻；馬上
(the) importance of zhòng yào xìng	重要性 重要性
impossible bù kě nēng	不可能 不可能
inadvertently yí-bù líu shén	一不留神 一不留神
in a manner of speaking jiù móu zhǒng chéng dù ér yán	就某种程度而言 就某種程度而言
incidentally shùn biàn yì tí	顺便一提 順便一提
inconsiderate bú gù bié rén	不顾别人 不顧別人
incredible xié-hur; xié ménr	邪乎儿；邪门儿 邪乎兒；邪門兒
inferiority complex zì bēi gǎn	自卑感 自卑感
inhuman bù rén dào	不人道 不人道
insist jīan chí	坚持 堅持

| instead of | 用以代替 |
| yòng yǐ dài tì | 用以代替 |

| instructions not clear | 指示不够明确 |
| zhǐ shì bú gòu míng què | 指示不夠明確 |

| in terms of | 就…而论 |
| jiù… ér lùn | 就…而論 |

| in the first place | 当初；根本 |
| dāng chū; gēn běn | 當初；根本 |

| in the hope of | 希望成功 |
| xī wàng chéng gōng | 希望成功 |

| in the meantime (meanwhile) | 同时 |
| tóng shí | 同時 |

| in the presence of | 在…的面前 |
| zài –de miàn qián | 在…的面前 |

| in the right direction | 正确的方向 |
| zhèng què-de fāng xiàng | 正確的方向 |

| in the years to come | 未来的几年 |
| wèi lái-de jǐ nián | 未來的幾年 |

| in very simple terms | 以最简单方式 |
| yǐ zuì jiǎn dān fāng shì | 以最簡單方式 |

| intentionally | 刻意 |
| kè yì | 刻意 |

| into | 放入 |
| fàng rù | 放入 |

| intuitive | 凭直觉 |
| píng zhí jué | 憑直覺 |

| (stay) issue-oriented | 锁住议题 |
| suǒ zhù yì tí | 鎖住議題 |

| It won't do. | 不行 |
| bù xíng | 不行 |

| It'll do. | 行 |
| xíng | 行 |

J

| just | 就 |
| jiù | 就 |

| just the other way around | 恰恰相反 |
| qià qià xiāng fǎn | 恰恰相反 |

| (cannot be) justified | 站不住脚 |
| zhàn-bu zhù jiǎo | 站不住腳 |

k

| keep a close check on | 密切注意 |
| mì qiè zhù yì | 密切注意 |

| keep an eye on it | 特别注意一下 |
| tè bié zhù yì yí xià | 特別注意一下 |

| keep cool (keep calm) | 保持镇静 |
| bǎo chí zhèn jìng | 保持鎮靜 |

| keep me advised | 随时向我通报 |
| suí shí xiàng wǒ tōng bào | 隨時向我通報 |

| keep my finger crossed | 祈祷你成功 |
| qí dáo nǐ chéng gōng | 祈禱你成功 |

| keep the ball rolling | 继续努力 |
| jì xǔ nǔ lì | 繼續努力 |

| keep your word | 遵守诺言 |
| zūn shǒu nuò yán | 遵守諾言 |

| kill two birds with one stone | 一箭双雕 |
| yí jiàn shuāng diāo | 一箭雙雕 |

| knee down and bow | 磕头 |
| kē tóu (pay one's respect to an elder) | 磕頭 |

| (is) knowledgeable | 有学问 |
| yǒu xǔe-wen | 有學問 |

| known for certain | 确信 |
| què xìn | 確信 |

L

| (at) long last | 总算；终于 |
| zǒng suàn; zhōng yú | 總算；終於 |

| (a) last resort | 最后的手段 |
| zuì hòu-de shǒu duàn | 最後的手段 |

| laugh it off | 一笑置之 |
| yí xiào zhì zhī | 一笑置之 |

| lavish in his riches | 大肆挥霍 |
| dà sì huī huò | 大肆揮霍 |

| lazy bones | 懒骨头 |
| lǎn gú-tou | 懶骨頭 |

| (at) least | 起码；最少 |
| qǐ mǎ; zùi shǎo | 起碼；最少 |

| (don't) let us down | 别让我们失望 |
| bié ràng wǒ-men shī wàng | 別讓我們失望 |

like father, like son yǒu qí fù bì yǒu qí zǐ	有其父必有其子 有其父必有其子	make a fortune fā dà cái	发大财 發大財
listen not to naysayers ěr páng fēng	耳旁风 耳旁風	make both ends meet shōu zhī píng héng	收支平衡 收支平衡
loan me jiè-gei wǒ	借给我 借給我	make clear nòng qīng chǔ	弄清楚 弄清楚
look after zhào gù	照顾 照顧	make good on promises shí xiàn chéng nuò	实现承诺 實現承諾
look back on huí gù	回顾 回顧	make important decisions zuò zhòng dà jué dìng	做重大决定 做重大決定
look closely zǐ xì-de kàn	仔细的看 仔細的看	make month ends meet liàng rù wéi chū	量入为出 量入為出
look down on (see think highly of) qiáo bù qǐ; kàn bù qǐ	看不起 瞧不起；看不起	makes my mouth water chuí xián sān chǐ	垂涎三尺 垂涎三尺
look forward to qí dài	期待 期待	make no difference wú suǒ wèi	无所谓 無所謂
Look here! ('cuse me!) wǒ shuō!	我说！ 我說！	make no secret of háo bù yǐn mán	毫不隐瞒 毫不隱瞞
look high and low for dào chù xún zhǎo	到处寻找 到處尋找	make one's way huò dé chéng gōng	获得成功 獲得成功
look into it (investigate) diào chá	调查 調查	make peace with hé hǎo	和好 和好
look like kàn qǐ lái xiàng	看起来像 看起來像	make progress to jiā jín jiǎo bù	加紧脚步 加緊腳步
look out for(watch out) xiǎo xīn	小心 小心	make room for téng chū kōng jiān	腾出空间 騰出空間
look up to jíng yǎng	景仰 景仰	(it) makes sense yǒu dào-li	有道理 有道理
lose ground jié jié bài tuì	节节败退 節節敗退	make the most of it shàn jiā lì yòng	善加利用 善加利用

M

		make time téng chū shí jiān	腾出时间 騰出時間
made from camphor wood cóng zhāng mù tí liàn-de	从樟木提炼的 從樟木提煉的	make up for it bǔ cháng	补偿 補償
made of camphor wood yòng zhēng mù zuò-de	用樟木做的 用樟木做的	make up stories niē zào shì shí	捏造事实 捏造事實
majority dà duō shù	大多数 大多數	make up with hé hǎo rú chū	和好如初 和好如初
make a fool of me ràng wǒ chū yáng xiàng	让我出洋相 讓我出洋相	make up your mind nǐ dào dí yào zěn yàng	你到底要怎样 你到底要怎樣

make use of lì yòng	利用 利用
man of the world jiàn guò shì miàn-de rén	见过世面的人 見過世面的人
man to man talk haǒ hāor-de tán-yi tán	好好的談一談 好好的談一談
many a time hěn duō cì	很多次 很多次
(in) many ways zài hěn duō fāng miàn	在很多方面 在很多方面
(or that) matter guān yǔ nà jiàn shì	关于那件事 關於那件事
mature chéng shú	成熟 成熟
may not bear it kě néng chéng shòu bù liǎo	可能承受不了 可能承受不了
meet with miàn tán	面谈 面談
meet you half way bí cǐ gè ràng yí bù	比此各讓一步 比此各讓一步
(in) memory of jì niàn mǒu rén	纪念某人 紀念某人
mess up gǎo dé yì tuán zāo	搞得一团糟 搞得一團糟
minority shǎo shù	少数 少數
minute differences wéi xiǎo-de chā bié	微小的差别 微小的差別
(in the) middle of zhèng zuò dào yí bàn	正做到一半 正做到一半
mind your own business sháu guǎn xián shì	少管闲事 少管閒事
misleading wù dǎo rén	误导人 誤導人
monkey around dǎo dàn	捣蛋 搗蛋
monotonous and boring dān diào fá wèi	单调乏味 單調乏味
most important tasks zuì zhòng yào-de shì qíng	最重要的事情 最重要的事情

moral integrity gǔ qì	骨气 骨氣
(a) moral sense dào dé jī zhǔn	道德基准 道德基準
more or less (somewhat) duō duō sháo shǎo	多多少少 多多少少
(not) motivated by money bú-shi wèi-le qián	不是为了钱 不是為了錢
move on to jì xù qián wǎng	继续前往 繼續前往
moved too slowly dòng zuò màn	动作慢 動作慢
much the same jī hū yí yàng	几乎一样 幾乎一樣
mutter dí-gu	嘀咕 嘀咕
mutually beneficial results hù huì chéng guǒ	互惠成果 互惠成果
mutual understanding yǒu gòng shì	有共识 有共識
(it's) my bread and butter zhè shì wǒ-de fàn wǎn	这是我的饭碗 這是我的飯碗
(to) my knowledge jù wó suǒ zhī	据我所知 據我所知
(in) my judgment zài wǒ kàn lái	在我看来 在我看來
(in) my opinion wǒ rèn wéi	我认为 我認為
my word is good wǒ shuō huà suàn huà	我說話算話 我說話算話

N

(in) name but not in reality yǒu míng wú shí	有名无实 有名無實
(in the) name of her yǐ tā-de míng yì	以她的名义 以她的名義
nasty wò chuò	龌龊 龌龊
(in) need of zhèng xū yào	正需要 正需要

negotiating tán pàn; xié shāng	谈判；协商 談判；協商	no way out sǐ lù yì tiáo	死路一条 死路一條
neither (one) ; neither liǎng-ge dōu bù	两个都不 兩個都不	no wonder nán guài	难怪 難怪
(You have the) nerve. ní hǎo yì-si	你好意思 你好意思	none (are) qüán dōu bù	全都不 全都不
never cóng lái bù	从来不 從來不	none the less yī rán	依然 依然
never cut one short bù xǔ chā zuǐ	不许插嘴 不許插嘴	non-productive endeavors wú suǒ shì shì	无所事事 無所事事
never mind bú bì guà-zai xīn-shang	不必挂在心上 不必掛在心上	not a bit yī diánr yě bù	一点儿也不 一點兒也不
nevertheless suī rán rú cǐ; bú guò	虽然如此；不过 雖然如此；不過	not at all méi zhèi huí shì	没这回事 沒這回事
no longer bú zài	不再 不再	not hesitate to háo bù yóu yǔ-de	毫不犹豫的 毫不猶豫的
no matter how wú lùn rú hé	无论如何 無論如何	not my cup of tea háo wú xìng qù	毫无性趣 毫無性趣
no matter what bù guán zěn yàng	不管怎样 不管怎樣	not only bú dàn	不但 不但
no matter who bù guǎn shì shuí	不管是谁 不管是誰	not reconciled bù gān xīn	不甘心 不甘心
no more than skin deep fū qiǎn	肤浅 膚淺	not socially polite bú tài lǐ mào	不太礼貌 不太禮貌
(stand) no nonsense bù háo rě	不好惹 不好惹	not the least idea yī diánr yě bù zhī dào	一点儿也不知道 一點兒也不知道
no other alternatives méi yǒu qí tā bàn-fa	没有其它办法 沒有其他辦法	not to mention jiù gèng bié tí	就更别提 就更別提
no one méi rén	没人 沒人	not worth while bù zhí dé	不值得 不值得
no problem méi wèn tí	没问题 沒問題	not yet hái méi	还没 還沒
no return bù guī lù	不归路 不歸路	nothing better to do xián-de wú liáo	闲得无聊 閒得無聊
no such thing méi yǒu zhè huí shì	没有这回事 沒有這回事	nothing but zhǐ bú guò shì	只不过是 只不過是
(in) no time yí xià-zi	一下子 一下子	nothing in common xìng qù bù tóng	兴趣不同 興趣不同
no way jüé duì bù xíng	绝对不行 絕對不行	nothing in particular suái biàn ná zhǒng	随便那种 隨便那種

nothing will gain from it yì dián hǎo chù méi yǒu	一點好處沒有 一點好處沒有
(wasn't) noticing méi liú shén	没留神 沒留神
nowadays dāng jīn; shí xià	当今；时下 當今；時下
now and then óu ěr	偶尔 偶爾
now or never bù xíng lā dǎo	不行拉倒 不行拉倒
(You're) nuts. nǐ shén jīng bìng	你神经病 你神經病

O

objective solution kè guān-de fāng fǎ	客观的方法 客觀的方法
(be) obvious to all yǒu mù gòng dǔ	有目共赌 有目共賭
occupy oneself with máng yú	忙于 忙於
odds are against shèng suàn bú dà	胜算不大 勝算不大
off lí kāi; gé lí	离开；隔离 離開；隔離
off and on; on and off duàn duàn xù xù	断断续续 斷斷續續
on account of yóu yú	由于 由於
on all sides sì miàn bā fāng	四面八方 四面八方
on an average (the whole) yì bān lái shuō	一般来说 一般來說
on and on jì xù bú duàn-de	继续不断的 繼續不斷的
on behalf of dài biǎo	代表 代表
on-going misfortunes zhóng zhǒng zāo yù	种种遭遇 種種遭遇
on purpose (intentionally) gù yì-de	故意的 故意的
on second thought(s) wǒ zài yì xiǎng	我再一想 我再一想
on the condition that -de tiáo jiàn xià	的条件下 的條件下
on the contrary xiāng fǎn-de	相反的 相反的
on the decline yüè lái yüè chā	越来越差 越來越差
on the decrease jiàng dē zhōng	降低中 降低中
on the increase shēng gāo; shàng zhǎng	升高；上涨 升高；上漲
on the one hand yì fān miàn lái shuō	一方面来说 一方面來說
On the other hand dàn, huà yòu shuō huí lai-liao	但话又说回来了 但話又說回來了
on (to) the reverse xiāng fǎn-de	相反的 相反的
on the safe side bǐ jiào ān quán	比较安全 比較安全
on time zhǔn shí	准时 準時
once yí dàn	一旦 一旦
once and again yí zài-de	一再地 一再地
once and for all yì láo yǒng yì	一劳永逸 一勞永逸
once in a blue moon nán dé yí cì	难得一次 難得一次
once in a while óu ěr	偶尔 偶爾
one after another jiē zhǒng ér lái	接踵而来 接踵而來
(the) one and only way bú èr fǎ mén	不二法门 不二法門
one by one yí gè yí gè-de	一个一个地 一個一個地
one on one yī duì yī	一对一 一對一

one of a kind
shì tóng yí lèi-de
是同一类的
是同一類的

oral proposal
kǒu tóu jiàn yì
口头建议
口頭建議

(in) order to
wèi-le dá chéng
为了达成
為了達成

open-minded
xīn xiōng kuān; wú piān jiàn
心胸宽;无偏见
心胸寬;無偏見

open the session
xiān fā yán
先发言
先發言

opposite sex
yì xìng
异性
異性

(in) opposition to
fǎn duì
反对
反對

other than
chú cǐ zhī wài
除此之外
除此之外

otherwise
bù rán-de huà
不然的话
不然的話

(in) other words
huàn jù huà shuō
换句话说
換句話說

out of
yòng guāng-le
用光了
用光了

out of the blue
tú rú qí lái
突如其来
突如其來

(all) out of breath
shàng qì bù jiē xià qì
上气不接下气
上氣不接下氣

out of the ordinary
bù xún cháng
不寻常
不尋常

(it's) out of the world
bù tóng fán xiǎng
不同凡响
不同凡響

(you are) out of your mind
nǐ fēng-le!
你疯了!
你瘋了!

over for good
jié jú
结局
結局

overwhelming
zhuàng lì
壮丽
壯麗

owing to
yóu yú
由于
由於

owing to the fact
shì shí shàng lái shuō
事实上来说
事實上來說

P

pass the buck to
bǎ zé rèn tuī xiè gěi ...
把责任推卸给...
把責任推卸給...

pay your own way
zì shí qí lì
自食其力
自食其力

pause for a moment
zhàn shí tíng xià jiǎo bù
暂时停下脚步
暫時停下腳步

peaceful settlement
hé píng jiě jüé
和平解决
和平解决

take a perfunctory attitude
yìng-fu; fū-yan
应付;敷衍
應付;敷衍

perhaps
shuō bú ding; huò xǔ
说不定;或许
說不定;或許

perplexed; at a loss what to do
máng rán bù zhī
茫然不知
茫然不知

personal interests
gè rén lì yì
个人利益
個人利益

(good) personality
yǒu rén yüán
有人缘
有人緣

(to) pick holes; captious
zhǎo chár
找碴儿
找碴兒

picky
jī dàn lǐ tiāo gú-tou
鸡蛋里挑骨头
雞蛋裡挑骨頭

Please!
qǐng!; yǒu wán méi wán!
请!;有完没完!
請!;有完沒完!

pocket money
líng yòng qián
零用钱
零用錢

pointless
háo wú yì yì
毫无意义
毫無意義

poll and marked a ballot
bǎ piào tóu-gei ...
把票投给...
把票投給...

popular
rén rén xǐ-huan
人人喜欢
人人喜歡

(the other party's) position
duì fāng-de lì chǎng
对方的立场
對方的立場

potentially dangerous situation
qiǎn zài-de wéi jī
潜在的危机
潛在的危機

practice makes perfect
shú néng shēng qiǎo
熟能生巧
熟能生巧

premise of evolution nían dù zhǎn wàng	年度展望 年度展望	put it in a nutshell jiǎn ér yán zhī	简而言之 簡而言之
presented with difficult problems yù dào kùn nán shí	遇到困难时 遇到困難時	put it into practice fù zhū xíng dòng	付诸行动 付諸行動
presumptuous fàng-si; mào mèi	放肆；冒昧 放肆；冒昧	put off; hold over yán qí	延期 延期
previous to now zài cǐ zhī qián	在此之前 在此之前	**Q**	
pride yáng yáng dé yì; zì zūn	扬扬得意；自尊 揚揚得意；自尊	★quit you anytime. (see p.136★) suí shí liū	随时溜 隨時溜
priority yōu xiān kǎo lù	优先考虑 優先考慮	quiet down bié chǎo-le	别吵了 別吵了
(in) processing zhèng zài zhí xíng zhōng	正在执行中 正在執行中	quite a lot of bù shǎo-de	不少的 不少的
professional interests gōng zuò shàng-de lì yì	工作上的利益 工作上的利益	(sound) quite convincing tīng-zhe mán yǒu bí-zi yóu yǎnr-de	听著蛮有鼻子有眼儿的
(I) promise you wǒ dā-ying-ni	我答应你 我答應你	Quite so! méi cuòr	没错儿！ 沒錯兒！
promising yǒu wéi	有为 有為	quite the contrary zhèng hǎo xiāng fǎn	正好相反 正好相反
proud jiāo ào; zì háo	骄傲；自豪 驕傲；自豪	**R**	
proud of you yí nǐ wéi róng	以你为荣 以你為榮	rack one's brains jiǎo jìn nǎo zhī	绞尽脑汁 絞盡腦汁
provocative and controversial tiǎo xìn zhēng lùn	挑衅争论 挑釁爭論	rather hái suàn; pǒ wéi	还算；颇为 還算；頗為
(in) public dāng zhòng	当众 當眾	(I'd) rather níng kě	宁可 寧可
(has a lot of) pull hén yǒu shì lì	很有势力 很有勢力	(can't) reach any consensus méi yǒu gòng shì	没有共识 沒有共識
pull yourself together zhèn zuò qǐ lái	振作起来 振作起來	reacted in response to lì jí huí yìng	立即回应 立即回應
(it's a) pun shuāng guān yǔ	双关语 雙關語	reassess our plan chóng xīn tiáo zhěng jì huà	重新调整计划 重新調整計劃
put aside our differences bìng qì bí cǐ-de chā yì	摒弃彼此的差异 摒棄彼此的差異	reckon gū-mo-zhe	估摸著 估摸著
put heads together shāng tán; huì shāng	商谈；会商 商談；會商	(to) refer the matter … bá cǐ shì …	把此事… 把此事…
put in black on white bái zhǐ hēi zì	白纸黑字 白紙黑字	(in) regard to yǒu guān yú	有关于 有關於

English	Chinese (Simplified)	Pinyin
(feel) relaxed	舒坦	舒坦
shū-tan		
relevant for present	活在当下	活在當下
huó zài dāng xià		
reluctant ; (not) reconciled to	不甘心	不甘心
bù gān xīn		
remain in command of	继续统领	繼續統領
jì xù tóng lǐng		
remain profitable	有盈余	有盈餘
yǒu yíng yú		
revenge	报复	報復
bào fù		
righteous	正直	正直
zhèng zhí		

S

safety concern　安全考量　安全考量
kán qüán kǎo liáng

satisfied with conditions　尚称满意　尚稱滿意
shàng chēng mǎn yì

Say, Mr.! ('cuse me!)　嘿，我说！　嘿，我說！
hèi, wǒ shuō!

scared out of my wits　吓破了胆　嚇破了膽
xià pò-le dǎn

schedule is demanding　时间排得满满　時間排得滿滿
shí jiān pái-de mán mǎn

schedule priorities　安排优先处理　安排優先處理
ān pái yōu xiān chú lǐ

(in) search of　寻求　尋求
xún qiú

(on) second thought(s)　我再一想　我再一想
wǒ zài yì xiǎng

see eye to eye　看法一致　看法一致
kàn fǎ yí zhì

see the changes　看它的变化　看它的變化
kàn tā-de biàn huà

see the point　领会到　領會到
lǐng huì dào

seems unprofitable　无利可图　無利可圖
wú lì kě tú

self-contradictory　自相矛盾　自相矛盾
zì xiāng máo dùn

self-explanatory　不解自明　不解自明
bù jiě zì míng

send for you　把您接来住　把您接來住
bǎ nín jiē lái zhù

sense hostility　感到敌意　感到敵意
gǎn dào dí yì

sense of humor　幽默感　幽默感
yōu mò gǎn

settle on ; agree on　先决定好　先決定好
xiān jué dìng hǎo

settle down　安定下来　安定下來
ān dìng xià lái

(a) sense of determination　有判断力　有判斷力
yǒu pàn duàn lì

(it) serves his purpose　得逞　得逞
dé chěng

(it) serves you right　活该　活該
huó gāi

(man of) shady character　不三不四的人　不三不四的人
bù sān bú sì-de rén

(make me) sick　倒胃口　倒胃口
dǎo wèi-kou

hopelessly stupid (make you sick in the stomach)　真窝囊；真窝囊
zhēn wō-nang

since ; now that　自从；既然　自從　既然
zì cóng ; jì rán

sincere　真诚　真誠
zhēn chéng

skill　技术；技能　技術；技能
jì shù ; jì néng

sluggish without my noticing　蔫不唧儿的；偷偷儿的
niān bù jīr-de ; tōu tōur-de　蔫不唧兒的；偷偷兒的

so　所以；如此　所以；如此
suó yǐ ; rú cǐ

so am I ; so are you　我也是；你也是　我也是；你也是
wó yě shì ; ní yě shì

so do I ; so do they　我也；他们也　我也；他們也
wó yě ; tā-men yě

so far	到目前为止 / 到目前為止	dào mù qián wéi zhǐ
so far as I know	就我所知 / 就我所知	jiù wó suǒ zhī
so so	还好 / 還好	hái hǎo
So what?	那又怎样？/ 那又怎樣？	nà yòu zěn yàng
social behavior	社交场合 / 社交場合	shè jiāo chǎng hé
(to) some degree …	多少有点儿… / 多少有點兒…	duō shǎo yóu diǎnr …
someone	有人 / 有人	yǒu-ren
sometimes …	有时候… / 有時候…	yǒu shí-hou …
somewhere safe	安全地带 / 安全地带	ān qüán dì dài
soon	不久 / 不久	bù jiǔ
sooner or later …	迟早会… / 遲早會…	chí zǎo huì …
Sorry!	抱歉 / 抱歉	bào qiàn
specially	专门地 / 專門地	zhuān mén-di
speed up	加速 / 加速	jiā sù
(in) spite of	虽然；尽管 / 雖然；儘管	suī rán; jín guǎn
split hairs; get into a dead end	躜牛角尖儿 / 躜牛角尖兒	zuān niú jiǎo jiānr
standard of living	生活水准 / 生活水準	shēng huó shuǐ zhǔn
stand by	待命 / 待命	dài mìng
still	仍然 / 仍然	réng rán
stiff competition	劲敌 / 勁敵	jìng dí

stand the loss	承担损失 / 承擔損失	chéng dān sǔn shī
stick to your word	坚守承诺 / 堅守承諾	jiān shǒu chéng nuò
strong point	优点 / 優點	yōu diǎn
strike a balance	取得平衡 / 取得平衡	qǔ dé píng héng
(by) striking first	先发制人 / 先發制人	xiān fā zhì rén
stingy	小气 / 小氣	xiǎo-qi
subconscious	下意识 / 下意識	xià yì shì
successfully	成功 / 成功	chéng gōng
such as	诸如 / 諸如	zhū rú
such being the case	依现在情形来看 / 依現在情形來看	yī xiàn zài qíng xíng lái kàn
suddenly occurred	忽然想到 / 忽然想到	hū rán xiǎng dào
sum up (summerize)	总结 / 總結	zǒng jié
(to) sum up the subject	总结论 / 總結論	zǒng jié lùn
surely enough	无疑的 / 無疑的	wú yí-de
survival of the fittest	适者生存 / 適者生存	shì zhě shēng cún
superiority complex	优越感；傲慢 / 優越感；傲慢	yōu yüè gǎn; aò màn
superior to	比别人优越 / 比別人優越	bǐ bié rén yōu yüè

T

take a break	休息一下儿 / 休息一下兒	xiū xí yí xiàr
take a chance	试试运气 / 試試運氣	shì-shi yǜ-qi

English	简体	繁体
take a step cái qǔ bù zòu	采取步骤	採取步驟
take a turn for the better háo zhuǎn	好转	好轉
take advice from others cái qǔ bié rén jiàn yì	采取别人建议	採取別人建議
take hold of zhuā-zhu	抓住	抓住
take into account kǎo lù	考虑	考慮
take into consideration jiā yí kǎo lù	加以考虑	加以考慮
(Don't) take it for granted bié rèn-wei lí suǒ yīng gāi	别認為理所应该	別認為理所應該
take it or leave it yào bú yào, yí jù huà	要不要？一句话	要不要？一句話
take a matter philosophically xiǎng-de kāi	想得开	想得開
take a matter too hard; no way out xiǎng-bu kāi	想不开	想不開
take orders fú cóng	服从	服從
take one by surprise gǎn dào fēi cháng jīng yà	感到非常惊讶	感到非常驚訝
take the risk mào zhè-ge xiǎn	冒这个险	冒這個險
take your time màn mānr lái	慢慢儿来	慢慢兒來
talk it over with gēn rén tǎo lùn yí xiàr	跟人讨论一下儿	跟人討論一下兒
talk one into shuì fú	说服	說服
talk to him in person gēn běn rén tán	跟本人谈	跟本人談
talk too much duō zuǐ	多嘴	多嘴
tell him to his face dāng miàn gào-su-ta	当面告訴他	當面告訴他
(to) tell the truth shuō shí huà	说实话	說實話

English	简体	繁体
(to) temporize yíng hé cháo liú	迎合潮流	迎合潮流
terribly frightened xià huài-le	吓坏了	嚇壞了
than bǐ	比	比
Thank you xiè-xie nín	谢谢您	謝謝您
that will be the day (没指望) tài-yang dǎ xī-bianr chū-lai	太阳打西边儿出来	太陽打西邊兒出來
the best life has to offer shēng mìng-de jīng huá	生命的精华	生命的精華
the dispute zhéng zhí	争执	爭執
(in) the face of miàn duì shì shí	面对事实	面對事實
(in) the middle of zhèng zuò-dào yí bàn	正做到一半	正做到一半
then bǐ shí; yǔ shì	彼时；于是	彼時；於是
therefore yīn cǐ	因此	因此
think highly of kàn-de qǐ (see look down on)	看得起	看得起
think over all aspects of it qüán fāng wèi-de kǎo liáng	全方位的考量	全方位的考量
though; although suī rán	虽然	雖然
thought yǐ wéi	以为	以為
through (thru) chuān yüè; wán bì	穿越；完毕	穿越；完畢
through out history yóu shí yǐ lái	有史以来	有史以來
throw himself into rè xīn cóng shì yú	热心从事于	熱心從事於
till zhí dào	直到	直到
(in) time léi-de zhèng qiǎo	来得正巧	來得正巧

tired out lèi huài-le	累坏了 累壞了	
to do away with fèi chú	废除 廢除	
to do justice to it zhǔ chí gōng dào	主持公道 主持公道	
(a) token of my appreciation yì diánr xiǎo yì-si	一点儿小意思 一點兒小意思	
too tài; tēi; yě	太;忒;也 太;忒;也	
too good to believe hǎo-de méi huà shuō	好得没话说 好得沒話說	
toward cháo xiàng	朝向 朝向	
(using dirty) tricks niānr huài; shǐ huài	蔫儿坏;使坏 蔫兒壞;使壞	
trouble maker dǎo dàn guǐ	捣蛋鬼 搗蛋鬼	
(It's) true shì zhēn-de	是真的 是真的	
trumped up; unwarranted mò xǔ yǒu	莫须有 莫須有	
trustworthy kě kào	可靠 可靠	
turn against him kāi shǐ duì tā fǎn gǎn	开始对他反感 開始對他反感	
turn in (1 submit) jiǎo rù 1 (2 go to bed) qù shuì jiào 2	缴入 去睡覺	
take turns lún líu	轮流 輪流	
turns my stomach háo ě-xin	好恶心 好惡心	
turn over to… yí jiāo-gei…	移交给… 移交給…	

U

uncertain; not sure méi bǎ-wo	没把握 沒把握	
unambitious méi zhì-qi; méi yě xīn	没志气;没野心 沒志氣;沒野心	

unclear and deceptive mó léng liáng kě	磨棱两可 磨稜兩可	
under de xià miàn	的下面 的下面	
under control yí qiè jiù xù	一切就绪 一切就緒	
under no circumstances jué bù	决不 決不	
under the command of -de zhǐ huī zhī xià	的指挥之下 的指揮之下	
under way jiù xù	就绪 就緒	
(I) understand that.. jù wó suǒ zhī	据我所知 據我所知	
(It's) understood. bù yán ér yù	不言而喻 不言而喻	
undertaken yǐ-jing zhuó shǒu zài zuò	已经著手在做 已經	
unexpectedly bú liào	不料 不料	
unexpected misfortune(death) sān cháng liáng duǎn	三长两短 三長兩短	
unimportant and irrelevant wú guān jǐn yào	无关紧要 無關緊要	
unless chú fēi	除非 除非	
unpresentable hán-chen; ná-bu chū shǒu	寒碜;拿不出手 寒碜;拿不出手	
until yì zhí děng dào	一直等到 一直等到	
(return it) until payday fā xīn-shui nèi tiān huán-ni	发薪水那天还你 發薪水那天還你	
untrustworthy bù kě kào	不可靠 不可靠	
up against zāo yù	遭遇 遭遇	
up to you nǐ kàn-zhe bàn	你看著办 你看著辦	
ups and downs rén shēng qǐ fú	人生起伏 人生起伏	

used up yòng guāng-le	用光了 用光了	what to do with rú hé chǔ zhì	如何处置 如何處置
usually tōng cháng	通常 通常	when; When dāng; hé shí	当；何时 當；何時

V

very demanding yāo qíu hěn gāo	要求很高 要求很高	when it comes to yì tán dào	一谈到 一談到
very successful in life yì shēng hěn chéng gōng	一生很成功 一生很成功	whether shì fǒu	是否 是否
virtual shí jì shàng	实际上 實際上	which ones? nǎ xiē	哪些？ 哪些？
vital shēng mìng	生命 生命	whisper about qiè qiè sī yǔ	窃窃私语 竊竊私語
vowed fā shì	发誓 發誓	whosoever understands the times shì shí wù zhě	識時務者

W

		Why not? hé lè ér bù wéi	何乐而不为？ 何樂而不為？
warlike hào zhàn-de	好战的 好戰的	(create a) win-win situation chuàng zào shuāng yíng	创造双赢 創造雙贏
was very heated yüè yǎn yüè liè	越演越烈 越演越烈	waffle bì zhòng jiù qīng	避重就轻 避重就輕
wear out nòng-de jīng pí lì jìn	弄得精疲力尽 弄得精疲力盡	while tóng shí yě; dāng	同时也；当 同時也；當
(You're) welcome bú kè-chi	不客气 不客氣	wicked qüē dé	缺德 缺德
welcomed with open arms rè qíng huān yíng	热情欢迎 熱情歡迎	(a) wide variety wǔ huā bā mén	五花八门 五花八門
well done biǎo xiàn hén hǎo	表现很好 表現很好	will not have been finished jüé duì gǎn-bu wán	绝对赶不完 絕對趕不完
What do you say? nǐ yì jiàn rú hé	你意见如何？ 你意見如何？	(a) will of my own yǒu zì jǐ-de xiáng fǎ	有自己的想法 有自己的想法
What happened? gāng cái zěn-me-le	刚才怎么了？ 剛才怎麼了？	wit and wisdom zhì náng	智囊 智囊
What if …? yào shì bù xíng-ne	要是不行呢？ 要是不行呢？	with gēn; dài	跟；带 跟；帶
what not … shén-me-de (déng děng)	… 甚么的 … 甚麼的 (等等)	with a solution jiě jüé zhī dào	解决之道 解決之道
What shall we do then? dào shí-hou zěn-me bàn	到时候怎么办？ 到時候怎麼辦？	with all my heart qüán xīn qüán lì	全心全力 全心全力
		with my heart and soul qüán xīn qüán yì-de	全心全意地 全心全意地

with the exception of **chú-le…yǐ wài**	除了…以外 除了…以外			

Y

You are crazy! **nǎo-dai guǎr shǎo gēn jīn**	脑袋瓜儿少根筋 腦袋瓜兒少根筋

withdraw from **tuì chū**	退出 退出

You are mad! **nǐ fā fēng-le**	你发疯了 你發瘋了！

within one's reach **ké-yi dá chéng**	可以达成 可以達成

You are insane! **shāng tiān hài lǐ**	伤天害理！ 傷天害理！

without **bú dài**	不带 不帶

You are nuts! **nǐ shén jīng bìng**	你神经病！ 你神經病！

witty **jī zhì; huī xié**	机智；诙谐 機智；詼諧

You are the one to blame **guài nǐ**	怪你 怪你

words in everyone's mout **sān jiān qí kǒu**	三缄其口 三緘其口

You asked for it! **nǐ zì zhǎo**	你自找！ 你自找！

work hand in hand **gòng tóng xié shǒu**	共同协手 共同協手

You be good! (Take care) **nǐ duō bǎo zhòng**	你多保重！ 你多保重！

work independently **dú lì zuò yè**	独立作业 獨立作業

You blew it. **ràng ní gǎo zá-le**	讓你搞砸了 讓你搞砸了

work out (solve) **jiě jué**	解决 解決

You can take my word **wǒ jüé bù shí yán**	我绝不食言 我絕不食言

wonder what has become of **bú zhī xià chǎng rú hé**	不知下场如何 不知下場如何

You deserve it! **nǐ huó gāi**	你活该！ 你活該！

won't take it from you **bù chī nǐ zhè tào**	不吃你这套 不吃你這套

You've fallen on your feet. **nǐ yùn-qi dào bú cuò**	你运气倒不错 你運氣倒不錯

(go from bad to) worse **yüè lái yüè zāo**	越来越糟 越來越糟

You go to hell! **qù nǐ mā-de**	去你妈的！ 去你媽的！

worth one's while **zhí dé yí shì**	值得一试 值得一試

worth the money **zhí huí piào jià**	值回票价 值回票價

(That) would be strange. **nà cái guài-ne**	那才怪呢！ 那才怪呢！

We Are Family
閒話家常
10A

English	简体	繁體
read the electricity meter kàn diàn biǎo	看电表	看電錶
read the water meter kàn shuí biǎo	看水表	看水錶
light bill (water; gas) diàn fèi (shuǐ; méi qì)	电费 (水;煤气)	電費(水;煤氣)
telephone bill diàn huà fèi	电话费	電話費
doctor's bill yī yào fèi	医药费	醫藥費
paying taxes fù shuì	付税	付税
file income tax return bào suǒ dé shuì	报所得税	報所得税
rent is due fáng-qian dào-le	房钱到了	房錢到了
the rent fáng-qian	房钱	房錢
remodelling house xiū-li fáng-zi	修理房子	修理房子
garden (see Group 75B,Plants) huā yuánr	花园儿	花園兒
garden table/ umbrella hù wài yáng sǎn zhuō	户外阳伞桌	戶外陽傘桌
porch mén láng; yáng tāi	门廊；阳台	門廊；陽臺
patio nèi yuànr	内院儿	內院兒
backyard hòu yuànr	后院儿	後院兒
courtyard tíng yüàn	庭院	庭院
fence lí-ba	篱笆	籬笆
greenhouse huā fáng	花房	花房
plant flowers; grow flowers zhòng huār (see Group 75A,Flours)	种花儿	種花兒
water the plants jiāo huār	浇花儿	澆花兒
lawn cǎo píng	草坪	草坪
mow the lawn jián cǎo	剪草	剪草
lawn mower jián cǎo jī	剪草机	剪草機
lawn sprinkler cǎo dì sá shuǐ qì	草地洒水器	草地灑水器
baby-sitting kān hái-zi	看孩子	看孩子
crib xiǎo háir chuáng	小孩儿床	小孩兒床
cradle yáo lán	摇篮	搖籃
baby carriage yīng ér tuī chē	婴儿推车	嬰兒推車
she's obedient hǎo guāi; tīng huà	好乖；听话	好乖；聽話
she's good at whining tā hǎo huì sā jiāor	她好会撒娇儿	她好會撒嬌兒

Stop teasing her! **bié dòu-ta**	别逗她 別逗她
What a naughty boy! **zhèi hái-zi zhēn pí**	这孩子真皮 這孩子真皮
keep a dog **yǎng yì tiáo gǒu**	养一条狗 養一條狗
The cat's stretching (limbs) **māo shēn lǎn-yao**	猫伸懒腰 貓伸懶腰
pet **chǒng wù**	宠物 寵物
feed the dog **wèi gǒu**	喂狗 喂狗
dog food **gǒu shí**	狗食 狗食
is housebroken (宠物) **bú luàn dà xiǎo biàn**	不乱大小便 不亂大小便
have an aquarium; keep fish 养鱼 **yǎng yǘ** (see 74C.Aquatic) 	養魚
keep pet bird **yáng niǎor**	养鸟儿 養鳥兒
someone's at the door **yǒu rén jiào mén**	有人叫门 有人叫門
answer the door **kāi mén-qù**	开门去 開門去（叫門）
open the door **kāi-kai mén**	开开门 開開門（通風）
Keep the door shut **suí shǒu guān mén**	随手关门 隨手關門
unlock the door **bǎ mén suó dǎ-kai**	把门锁打开 把門鎖打開
lock the desk **suǒ-shang zhuō-zi**	锁上桌子 鎖上桌子
draw the curtain **lā-shang chuāng-lianr**	拉上窗帘儿 拉上窗簾兒
get a splinter in my hand **zha-le-ge cì**	扎了个刺 扎了個刺
clean up **dá-sao**	打扫 打掃
broom **sào-zhou**	扫帚 掃帚

dust pan **bò jī**	簸箕 簸箕
sweep the floor **sǎo dì**	扫地 掃地
wall corners **qiáng jī jiǎor**	墙犄角儿 牆犄角兒
all places including corners 旮里旯儿 **jī-li gā lár**	旯里旮旯兒
★**a thorough cleaning job** 好好的打扫打扫 **hǎo hāor-de dá-sao dá-sao** 好好的打掃打掃	
feather duster **jī máo dǎn-zi**	鸡毛掸子 雞毛撢子
dust the table **dǎn zhuō-zi**	掸桌子 撢桌子
to wipe window panes **cā bō-li**	擦玻璃 擦玻璃
swab it hard **shǐ jìn cā**	使劲擦 使勁擦
use a greater force **shí bǎ jìn**	使把劲 使把勁
mop **tuō-ba**	拖把 拖把
mop the floor **tuō dì bǎn**	拖地板 拖地板
wax **là**	腊 臘
wax the floor **dì bán dǎ là**	地板打腊 地板打臘
vacuum the rug **xī dì tǎn**	吸地毯 吸地毯
plump the cushions **bǎ kào diàn pāi sōng-le**	把靠垫拍松了 把靠墊拍鬆了
patio party **hòu yüànr cān jù**	后院儿餐聚 後院兒餐聚
barbeque; Bar-B-Q **kǎo ròu**	烤肉 烤肉
barbeque rack **kǎo ròu jià-ze**	烤肉架子 烤肉架子
sharpen the knife **mó dāo**	磨刀 磨刀

knife sharpener; whrtstone **mó dāo shí**	磨刀石 磨刀石	lay tablecloth **pū zhuō bù**	铺桌布 鋪桌布
mitten **lián zhí shǒu tào**	连指手套 連指手套	set the table **bǎi zhuō**	摆桌 擺桌
tongs **huǒ qián-zi**	火钳子 火鉗子	I blew it! **ràng-wo gǎo zá-le**	让我搞砸了 讓我搞砸了
charcoal **mù tàn**	木炭 木炭	punch bowl's broken **jī wéi jiǔ gāng pò-le**	鸡尾酒缸破了 鷄尾酒缸破了
coal **méi**	煤 煤	Don't worry. **bú bì fàng-zai xīn-shang**	不必放在心上 不必放在心上
odds and ends **zá qī zá bā-de dōng-xi**	杂七杂八的东西 雜七雜八的東西	Get down to business ! **gàn diǎnr zhèng shì**	干点儿正事！ 幹點兒正事！
miscellaneous **gè-shi gè-yàng-de dōng-xi**	个式各样的东西 個式各樣的東西	petty; trifling things **jī máo suàn pí-de shì**	鸡毛蒜皮的事 鷄毛蒜皮的事
tinder; kindling **huó zhǒng**	火种 火種	Stop jabbering ! **bié jī jī zhā zhā-de**	别叽叽喳喳地 別嘰嘰喳喳地
build a fire **shēng huǒ**	生火 生火	tray **tuō pán**	托盘 托盤
it's smoky **yān hǎo dà**	烟好大 煙好大	paper cup **zhǐ bēi**	纸杯 紙杯
I'm shedding over the smoke **qiàng-de wǒ liú yǎn lèi**	呛得我流眼泪 嗆得我流眼淚	paper plate **zhǐ pán-zi**	纸盘子 紙盤子
go get the fan **qǔ ná-ba shàn-zi**	去拿把扇子 去拿把扇子	paper napkin **zhǐ cān jīn**	纸餐巾 紙餐巾
your nose's running **nǐ zài liú bí-ti**	你在流鼻涕 你在流鼻涕	disposable bottle **yòng wán jí diū píng**	用完即丢瓶 用完即丢瓶
blow your nose **xǐng bí-ti**	擤鼻涕 擤鼻涕	ice bucket **bīng jiǔ tǒng**	冰酒桶 冰酒桶
use greater force **shǐ jìn**	使劲 使勁	pull-tab can **yì kāi guàn**	易开罐 易開罐
blow it hard **shǐ jìn xǐng**	使劲擤 使勁擤	going to a shower **sòng chǎn qián (jià qián) lǐ**	送产前(嫁前)礼 送產前(嫁前)禮
get me a tissue **géi-wo ná-zhang miàn zhǐ**	给我拿张面纸 給我拿張面紙	I graduated ! **wǒ bì yè-le**	我毕业了！ 我畢業了！
wipe your mouth **cā zuǐ**	擦嘴 擦嘴	Congratulations! **gōng xǐ**	恭喜！ 恭喜！
wash your hands **xí shǒu**	洗手 洗手	drink to **jǔ bēi zhù hè**	举杯祝贺 舉杯祝賀
comb your hair **bǎ tóu-fa shū-yi-shu**	把头发梳一梳 把頭髮梳一梳	Bottoms Up! **gān bēi**	干杯 乾杯

English	简体	pinyin	繁體

Don't interrupt them! 别打岔！
bié dǎ chà 别打岔！

Let's send for mom. 把娘接來住
bǎ niáng jiē-lai zhù 把娘接來住

Happy birthday to you 祝你生日快乐
zhù nǐ shēng rì kuài lè 祝你生日快樂

take a pull at the cigarette 抽口烟
chōu kǒu yān 抽口煙

bum a light 借个火儿
jiè-ge huǒr 借個火兒

Cheers! 来，喝一口！随意！
lái，hē yì kǒu；súi yì 來，喝一口！随意！

gabbled away for a long time 叽里咕噜地
Jī-li gū lū-de shuō-le bàn tiān 说了半天

rude to one's elder 没大没小
méi dà méi xiǎo 沒大沒小

dinner's ready 开饭了
kāi fàn-le 開飯了

delicious 真好吃
zhēn hǎo chī 真好吃

it's tasty 味道好
wèi dào hǎo 味道好

that really hit the spot 吃得真过瘾
chī-de zhēn guò yǐn 吃得真過癮

What a crowd! 真热闹
zhēn rè-nao 真熱鬧

pass me the pepper 递我胡椒粉
dì-wo hú jiāo fěn 遞我胡椒粉

get yourself a plate 去拿个盘子
qù ná-ge pán-zi 去拿個盤子

help yourself 自各儿动手
zì gěr dòng shǒu 自各兒動手

bring me the salt 去把盐拿来
qù bǎ yán ná-lai 去把鹽拿來

clear the table 捡桌
jiǎn zhuō 撿桌

bus the dishes 收盘碗
shōu pán wǎn 收盤碗

you don't have to do that 您甭客气
nín béng kè-qi 您甭客氣

I'd be glad to! 应该的！
yìng gāi-de! 應該的！

make myself useful 闲著也是闲著
xián-zhe yě-shi xián-zhe 閒著也是閒著

Don't bother! 不用麻烦
bú yòng má-fan 不用麻煩

There's no bother. 不麻烦
bù má-fan 不麻煩

be sensible; be tactful 别没眼里见儿
bié méi yǎn-le jiànr 別沒眼裡見兒

don't wear out your welcome 别不识相
bié bù shí xiàng 別不識相

I can't read your mind 不是你肚子里的蛔虫
bú-shi nǐ dù-zi lǐ-de huí-chóng 不是你肚子裡的蛔蟲

here's the rag 抹布在这儿
mǒ bù zài zhèr 抹布在這兒

I'll do the dishes 我洗盘子
wó xǐ pán-zi 我洗盤子

you dry them 你来擦
nǐ lái cā 你來擦

water pipe 水管子
shuí guǎn-zi 水管子

waterhose 水龙带
shuǐ lóng dài 水龍帶

leaking 漏水
lòu shuǐ 漏水

laundry 该洗的衣服
gāi xǐ-de yī-fu 該洗的衣服

dirty 脏
zāng 髒

spot; smudge 污点
wū diǎn 汙點

smear 油渍
yóu zì 油漬

dry cleaning 干洗
gān xǐ 乾洗

wash 湿洗
shī xǐ 濕洗

clean 干净
gān-jing 乾淨

washing machine **xǐ yī jī**	洗衣机 洗衣機	clothes hanger **guà yī jiàr**	挂衣架儿 掛衣架兒
detergent **xǐ yī fěn**	洗衣粉 洗衣粉	crumpled up **nòng zhòu-le**	弄皱了 弄皺了
bleach **piǎo bái**	漂白 漂白	it wrinkles **qǐ zhòu wén**	起皱纹 起皺紋
bleaching powder **piǎo bái fěn**	漂白粉 漂白粉	ironing **yùn tàng**	熨烫 熨燙
knead & rub **róu cuō**	揉搓 揉搓	electric iron **diàn yùn-dou**	电熨斗 電熨斗
scrub **cā xǐ**	擦洗 擦洗	steam iron **zhēng qì yùn-dou**	蒸气熨斗 蒸氣熨斗
rinse **chōng xǐ**	冲洗 沖洗	scalded by boiling water **gěi kāi shuǐ tàng-la**	给开水烫了 給開水燙了
spin **tuō shuǐ**	脱水 脫水	atomizer **pēn wù qì**	喷雾器 噴霧器
wring it dry **nǐng gān**	拧干 擰乾	ironing board **tàng yī bǎnr**	烫衣板儿 燙衣板兒
shrink **suō shuǐ**	缩水 縮水	no-ironing; drip dry **mǐan tang; mǐan yùn**	免烫；免熨 免燙；免熨
shrink resistant **bù suō shuǐ**	不缩水 不縮水	fold up the clothes **bǎ yī-fu dié hǎo**	把衣服叠好 把衣服疊好
colorfast **bú tùi sè**	不褪色 不褪色	brush the clothes **shuā yī-fu**	刷衣服 刷衣服
fade **tùi sè**	褪色 褪色	pile up; stack **luò qǐ-lai**	摞起来 摞起來
clothes dryer **hōng gān jī**	烘干机 烘乾機	moth eaten **chóng yǎo-le**	虫咬了 蟲咬了
to sun garment **shài yī-fu**	晒衣服 曬衣服	cockroach bitten **zhāng-lang yǎo-le**	蟑螂咬了 蟑螂咬了
clothes-tine **shài yī shéngr**	晒衣绳儿 曬衣繩兒	mouse bitten **hào-zi yǎo-le**	耗子咬了 耗子咬了（小）
air dry **liàng gān; fēng gān**	晾干；风干 晾乾；風乾	gnawed by rats **láo-shu kěn-le**	老鼠啃了 老鼠啃了（大）
sun dry **shài gān**	晒干 曬乾	moldy **fā méi-de**	发霉的 發黴的
clip **jiá-zi**	夹子 夾子	wasp stung **géi mǎ fēng zhē-le**	给蚂蜂蜇了 給螞蜂蜇了
bamboo pole **zhú gānr**	竹竿儿 竹竿兒	mosquito bitten **géi wén-zi dīng-le**	给蚊子虰了 給蚊子叮了

living room **kè tīng**	客厅 客廳	**ring the doorbell** **àn língr**	按铃儿 按鈴兒
food, clothing & shelter **nǔ rén nèi yī**	衣食住 衣食住	**buzzer** **diàn língr**	电铃儿 電鈴兒
creature comforts **jǐn shēn zhēn zhī yī**	物质享受 物質享受	**the doorbell is ringing** **mén líng zài xiǎng**	门铃在响 門鈴在響
peephole **dà mén kuī yán kǒng**	大门窥眼孔 大門窺眼孔	**burglar alarm** **fáng dào diàn língr**	防盗电铃儿 防盗電鈴兒
door keys **fáng mén yào-shi**	房门钥匙 房門鑰匙	**intercom** **duì jiǎng jī**	对讲机 對講機
keyhole **yào-shi dòng**	钥匙洞 鑰匙洞	**video-intercom** **yǐng xiàng duì jiǎng jī**	影像对讲机 影像對講機
key ring **yào-shi qüānr**	钥匙圈儿 鑰匙圈兒	**pin-hole lens camera** **zhēn kǒng shè yǐng jī**	针孔摄影机 針孔攝影機
door lock **mén suǒ**	门锁 門鎖	**surveillance camera** **jiān shì shè yǐng jī**	监视摄影机 監視攝影機
combination lock **duì hàor mì má suǒ**	对号儿密码锁 對號兒密碼鎖	**monitor** **jiān shì qì**	监视器 監視器
lock **suǒ; suǒ-shang**	锁；锁上 鎖；鎖上	**wallpaper** **bì zhǐ**	壁纸 壁紙
unlock **kāi suǒ**	开锁 開鎖	**drapery** **chuāng liánr**	窗帘儿 窗簾兒
door bolt **chā xiāo**	插销 插銷	**wall-to-wall carpeting** **zhěng jiān pū-zhe dì tǎn**	整间铺著地毯 整間鋪著地毯
door knocker **qiāo mén-de mén huán**	敲门的门环 敲門的門環	**carpet** **dì tǎn**	地毯 地毯
doormat **cā jiǎo diànr**	擦脚垫儿 擦腳墊兒	**rug** **xiǎo kuàir dì tǎn**	小块儿地毯 小塊兒地毯
umbrella stand **yǔ sǎn jiàr**	雨伞架儿 雨傘架兒	**fireplace** **bì lú**	壁炉 壁爐

mantelpiece **lú jià**	炉架 爐架	unplug it **bá diào chā tóur**	拔掉插头儿 拔掉插頭兒
poker **bō huǒ bàng**	拨火棒 撥火棒	coffee table **kā fēi zhuōr**	咖啡桌儿 咖啡桌兒
fire screen **huǒ lú píng fēng**	火炉屏风 火爐屏風	aquarium **jīn yú gāng**	金鱼缸 金魚缸
fire-place fender **huǒ lú wéi-zi**	火炉围子 火爐圍子	bird cage **niǎor lóng-zi**	鸟儿笼子 鳥兒籠子
log **dà mù tóu kài**	大木头块 大木頭塊	ceiling lamp **dǐng dēng**	顶灯 頂燈
furniture **jiā-jü**	家俱 家俱	chandelier **duō tóu háo huá diào dēng**	多头豪华吊灯 多頭豪華吊燈
folding screen **zhé dié shì píng fēng**	折叠式屏风 折叠式屏風	elaborate **jīng qiǎo-de**	精巧的 精巧的
sofa **shā fā**	沙发 沙發	floor lamp **luò dì dēng**	落地灯 落地燈
loveseat **S xíng qín rén yǐ**	S 形情人椅 S 形情人椅	table lamp **tái dēng**	台灯 臺燈
throw pillow **kào zhěn**	靠枕 靠枕	lamp shade **dēng zhàor**	灯罩儿 燈罩兒
cushion **kào diànr**	靠垫儿 靠墊兒	footlight **xiǎo yè dēng**	小夜灯 小夜燈
upholstery easy chair **xiǎo shā fā**	小沙发 小沙發	switch **diàn mén; kāi guān**	电门；开关 電門；開關
table **zhuō-zi**	桌子 桌子	turn on the light **kāi-kai dēng (diàn mén)**	开开灯（电门） 開開燈（電門）
end table **shā fā wěi zhuōr**	沙发尾桌儿 沙發尾桌兒	turn off the switch **guān-shang diàn mén (yüán)**	关上电门（源） 關上電門（源）
telephone **diàn huà**	电话 電話	dimmer switch **míng àn tiáo jiá diàn mén**	明暗调节电门 明暗調節電門
square table **bā xiān zhuō**	八仙桌 八仙桌	outlet **chā zuòr**	插座儿 插座兒
mahjong table **má jiàng zhuō**	麻将桌 麻將桌	plug **chā tóur**	插头儿 插頭兒
rectangle table **cháng fāng zhuō**	长方桌 長方桌	plug in; plug it up **chā shàng chā tóur**	插上插头儿 插上插頭兒
folding table **zhé dié zhuō**	折叠桌 折叠桌	extension cord **yán cháng xiàn**	延长线 延長線
corner table **qiáng jiǎor zhuō**	墙角儿桌 牆角兒桌	corner shelves **qiáng jiǎor jià**	墙角儿架 牆角兒架

nest of tables **tào jīr**	套几儿 套幾兒
wire's hot **yǒu diàn**	有电 有電
no juice; no electricity **méi diàn**	没电 沒電
flash light **shǒu diàn tǒng**	手电筒 手電筒
battery; cell **diàn chí**	电池 電池
battery is flat **diàn chí méi diàn-le**	电池没电了 電池沒電了
electric charger **chōng diàn qì**	充电器 充電器
vacuum **xī chén qì**	吸尘器 吸塵器
space heater **diàn nuǎn lú**	电暖炉 電暖爐
air-conditioner **lěng qì jī**	冷气机 冷氣機
BTU **lěng qì dù dān wèi**	冷气度单位 冷氣度單位
freon **lěng méi**	冷媒 冷媒
floor fan **luò dì shì diàn shà**	落地式电扇 落地式電扇
ceiling fan **diào shàn**	吊扇 吊扇
television (TV) **diàn shì**	电视 電視
radio **shōu yīn jī**	收音机 收音機
DVD player **fàng yǐng jī**	放影机 放影機
piano **gāng qín**	钢琴 鋼琴
piano bench **gāng qín dèng**	钢琴凳 鋼琴凳

potted plant **pén zāi** (see 59B plants)	盆栽 盆栽
miniature garden **pén jǐng**	盆景 盆景
hanging planter **xüán diào pén jǐng**	悬吊盆景 懸吊盆景
flower vase **huā píngr** (see 59A flowers)	花瓶儿 花瓶兒
photo album **xiàng piàn bù**	相片簿 相片簿
shelf **shū jià**	书架 書架
things **dōng-xi**	东西 東西
bric-a-brac **xiǎo gú-dong**	小古董 小古董
whatnot **fàng xiáo bǎi-she-de gé jià**	放小摆饰的格架 放小擺飾的格架
table lighter **zhūo xíng dá huǒ jī**	桌型打火机 桌型打火機
ashtray **yān huī gāng**	烟灰缸 煙灰缸
magazine **zá zhì**	杂志 雜誌
periodical **zhōu kān**	周刊 週刊
newspaper, paper **bào zhǐ**	报纸 報紙
novel **xiǎo shūir**	小说儿 小說兒
half-a-bath **kè yòng xí shǒu jiān**	客用洗手间 客用洗手間

(See Group 10H, 家庭电器用品
Household Electric Appliances)

Bedroom
卧房

bedroom **wò fáng**	卧房 臥房	headboard **chuáng tóu bǎnr**	床头板儿 床頭板兒
closet **yī chú**	衣橱 衣櫥	bed stand **chuáng jià**	床架 床架
cabinet **chú guì**	橱柜 櫥櫃	box spring **tán huáng chuáng zùo**	弹簧床座 彈簧床座
bed **chuáng**	床 床	spring mattress **tán huáng diàn**	弹簧垫 彈簧墊
single bed **dān rén chuáng**	单人床 單人床	mattress **chuáng diàn**	床垫 床墊
double bed **shuāng rén chuáng**	双人床 雙人床	foam rubber; foam **pào mò xiàng jiáo**	泡沫橡胶 泡沫橡膠
twin beds **duì chuáng**	对床 對床	make the bed **pū chuáng**	铺床 鋪床
bunk bed **shuāng céng chuáng**	双层床 雙層床	bedding **pù-gai**	铺盖 鋪蓋
upper bunk **shàng pù**	上铺 上鋪	bed pad **rù-zi**	褥子 褥子
lower bunk **xià pù**	下铺 下鋪	quilt; comforter **mián bèi**	棉被 棉被
inflatable bed **kōng qì chuáng**	空气床 空氣床	spun silk filled quilt **sī mián bèi**	丝棉被 絲棉被
waterbed **shuǐ chuáng**	水床 水床	blanket **máo tǎn**	毛毯 毛毯
platform bed **dì pù chuáng**	地铺床 地鋪床	electric blanket **diàn tǎn**	电毯 電毯
sleep on floor **dǎ dì pù**	打地铺 打地鋪	sheet; linen **bái chuáng dān**	白床单 白床單
cot **fán bù chuáng**	帆布床 帆布床	pillow **zhěn-tou**	枕头 枕頭

pillow case **zhěn-tou tàor**	枕头套儿	枕頭套兒
bedcover; bedspread **chuáng zhàor**	床罩儿	床罩兒
nightstand **chuáng tóu jī**	床头几	床頭几
bed lamp **chuáng tóu dēng**	床头灯	床頭燈
luminous clock **yè míng zhōng**	夜明锺	夜明鐘
radio alarm clock **wú xiàn diàn nào zhōng**	无线电闹钟	無線電鬧鐘
go to bed; hit the sack **shàng chuáng shuì jiào**	上床睡觉	上床睡覺
sleep **shuì jiào**	睡觉	睡覺
take a nap **xiǎo shuì; wǔ jiào**	小睡；午觉	小睡；午覺
take forty winks **dǎ-ge dǔnr**	打个盹儿	打個盹兒
relax your muscles **fàng sōng jī ròu**	放松肌肉	放鬆肌肉
folding fan **zhé shàn**	摺扇	摺扇
sandalwood fan **tán xiāng shàn**	檀香扇	檀香扇
sleeping bag **shuì dài**	睡袋	睡袋
dresser **shū zhuāng tái**	梳妆台	梳妝檯
vanity bench **shū zhuāng dèng**	梳妆凳	梳妝凳
looking glass **chuān yī jìng**	穿衣镜	穿衣鏡
closet **yī chú**	衣橱	衣櫥

walk-in closet **bù rù shì yī chú**	步入式衣橱	步入式衣櫥
clothes hanger **gùa yī jiàr**	挂衣架儿	掛衣架兒
hook **yī mào gōur**	衣帽钩儿	衣帽鉤兒
mosquito net **wén zhàng**	蚊帐	蚊帳
mosquito incense **wén xiāng**	蚊香	蚊香
bamboo back scratcher **zhú bèi zhuā-zi**	竹背抓子	竹背抓子
chest of drawers **wú dǒu guì**	五斗柜	五斗櫃
wallet **pí jiá-zi**	皮夹子	皮夾子
trunk **dà mù xiāng**	大木箱	大木箱
slippers **tuō xié**	拖鞋	拖鞋
shoe rack **xié jià-zi**	鞋架子	鞋架子
shoetree **xié chēng-zi**	鞋撑子	鞋撐子
shoehorn **xié bá-zi**	鞋拔子	鞋拔子
shoelaces **xié dài-zi**	鞋带子	鞋帶子
tie your shoe laces **jì xié dài**	系鞋带	繫鞋帶
untie your shoe laces **jiě xié dài**	解鞋带	解鞋帶
shoe polish **pí xié yóur**	皮鞋油儿	皮鞋油兒
shoeshine **cā pí xié**	擦皮鞋	擦皮鞋

10 D Bathroom 澡房

bathroom zǎo fáng	澡房 澡房	
scales bàng chèng	磅秤 磅秤	
tip the scales at… liáng tǐ zhòng	量体重 量體重	
water heater rè shuǐ qì	热水器 熱水器	
full-bath qüán tào yù shì	全套浴室 全套浴室	
bathtub xí zǎo pén	洗澡盆 洗澡盆	
basin xí liǎn pén	洗脸盆 洗臉盆	
tap water; tap zì lái shuǐ	自来水 自來水	
faucet shuǐ lóng tóu	水龙头 水龍頭	
medicine cabinet zǎo fáng jìng guì	澡房镜柜 澡房鏡櫃	
mirror jìng-zi	镜子 鏡子	
take a bath xí-ge zǎo	洗个澡 洗個澡	
bubble bath pào mò yǜ	泡沫浴 泡沫浴	
shower spray lián-peng tóu	莲蓬头 蓮蓬頭	
lukewarm water wēn shuǐ	温水 溫水	

shower lín yǜ	淋浴 淋浴	
take a shower chōng-ge zǎo	冲个澡 沖個澡	
hand shower huó dòng shǒu chōng tóu	活动手冲头 活動手冲頭	
shower curtain lín yǜ lián-ze	淋浴帘子 淋浴簾子	
shower cap lín yǜ mào	淋浴帽 淋浴帽	
back brush xǐ bèi shuā	洗背刷 洗背刷	
sponge hǎi mián	海绵 海綿	
wooden clogs mù jī	木屐 木屐	
toiletries guàn xǐ yòng-pin	盥洗用品 盥洗用品	
a bar of soap yí kuài féi zào	一块肥皂 一塊肥皂（新的）	
a piece of soap yí kuài féi zào	一块肥皂 一塊肥皂（用過）	
toilet soap xiāng zào	香皂 香皂	
medicated soap yào zào	药皂 藥皂	
soap dish féi zào dié	肥皂碟 肥皂碟	
to lather qǐ pào mò	起泡沫 起泡沫	

English	Chinese	Pinyin		English	Chinese	Pinyin

wash your hands
xí shǒu
洗手
洗手

wash your face
xí liǎn
洗脸
洗臉

hand dryer
hōng shǒu jī
烘手机
烘手機

automatic hand dryer
zì dòng hōng shǒu jī
自动烘手机
自動烘手機

dry your face
cā liǎn
擦脸
擦臉

washcloth
miàn jīn
面巾
面巾

towel
máo jīn
毛巾
毛巾

face towel
xiǎo fāng kuài xí liǎn jīn
小方块洗脸巾
小方塊洗臉巾

terrycloth towel
bù cā shǒu jīn
布擦手巾
布擦手巾

bath towel
xí zǎo jīn
洗澡巾
洗澡巾

towel rack
máo jīn jià
毛巾架
毛巾架

towel ring
máo jīn huán
毛巾环
毛巾環

talcum powder
shuǎng shēn fěn
爽身粉
爽身粉

comb
shū-ze
梳子
梳子

hairbrush
fǎ shuā
发刷
髮刷

a tube of toothpaste
yī tiáo yá gāo
一条牙膏
一條牙膏

with fluoride
jiā fú
加氟
加氟

toothbrush
yá shuā
牙刷
牙刷

tooth powder
yá fěn
牙粉
牙粉

dental floss
yá xiàn
牙线
牙線

bad breath antiseptic
shù kóu xiāo dú shuǐ
漱口消毒水
漱口消毒水

tongue stripper (Chinese)
guā shé-ze
刮舌子
刮舌子

tumbler (bathroom)
shù kǒu bēi
漱口杯
漱口杯

dentures
jiǎ yá
假牙
假牙

shave
guā hú-ze
刮胡子
刮鬍子

shaving brush
guā hú shuā
刮胡刷
刮鬍刷

shaving mug
guā hú zhōng
刮胡盅
刮鬍盅

shaving cream
guā hú gāo
刮胡膏
刮鬍膏

razor
guā hú dāo
刮胡刀
刮鬍刀

razor blade
dāo piàn
刀片
刀片

single-edge blade
dān miàn daō piàn
单面刀片
單面刀片

double-edge blade
shuāng miàn daō piàn
双面刀片
雙面刀片

electric shaver
diàn guā hú dāo
电刮胡刀
電刮鬍刀

after shaving lotion
guā hú xiāng shuǐ
刮胡香水
刮鬍香水

earpick
ěr wā sháor
耳挖勺儿
耳挖勺兒

earwax
ér shǐ
耳屎
耳屎

swab
mián huā bàng
棉花棒
棉花棒

tissue
miàn zhǐ
面纸
面紙

toilet paper
wèi shēng zhǐ
卫生纸
衛生紙

tissue holder
wèi shēng zhǐ jià
卫生纸架
衛生紙架

sanitary napkin **yüè jīng dài**	月经带 月經帶	plunge it a couple of times **chuō jǐ xiàr**	戳几下儿 戳幾下兒
tampon **yüè jīng bàng**	月经棒 月經棒	push it; work **yòng lì chuō; yòng lì**	用力戳；用力 用力戳；用力
on my period **yüè jīng lái-le**	月经来了 月經來了	punch it hard **shǐ jìng chuō**	使劲戳 使勁戳
toilet **má tǒng**	马桶 馬桶	it worked **xíng-le**	行了 行了
flush toilet **chōng má tǒng**	冲马桶 沖馬桶	it's unblocked **tōng-le**	通了 通了
flush level **má tǒng bán-shou**	马桶板手 馬桶板手	wipe it clean **bǎ-ta cā gān jìng**	把它擦乾净 把它擦乾淨
toilet brush **má tǒng shuā-zi**	马桶刷子 馬桶刷子	use the toilet brush **yòng má tǒng shuā-zi**	用马桶刷子 用馬桶刷子
toilet blocked **má tǒng bù tōng**	马桶不通 馬桶不通	use hydrochloric acid **yòng yán suān**	用盐酸 用鹽酸
plunger **má tǒng chuō-zi**	马桶戳子 馬桶戳子	use carbolic acid **yòng shí tàn suān**	用石炭酸 用石炭酸
unblock the toilet **bǎ má tǒng nòng tōng**	把马桶弄通 把馬桶弄通		

the study **shū fáng**	书房 書房	chair **yǐ-zi**	椅子 椅子
book **shū**	书 書	swivel chair **xüán zhuán yǐ**	旋转椅 旋轉椅
bookmark **shū qiān**	书签 書籤	rocking chair **yáo yǐ**	摇椅 搖椅
dog-ear **shū yè zhé jiǎo**	书页折角 書頁折角	studio couch **zuò wò liǎng yòng chuáng**	坐卧两用床 坐臥兩用床
bookcase **shū guì**	书柜 書櫃	couch **wò tà**	卧榻 臥榻
caster **jiǎo lún**	脚轮 腳輪	backscratcher **sāo yǎng bèi zhuā-zi**	搔痒背抓子 搔癢背抓子
bookshelf **shū jià-zi**	书架子 書架子	scattered rugs **fēn sàn-de xiǎo dì tǎn**	分散的小地毯 分散的小地毯
bookends **shū dǎng**	书挡 書擋	safe **báo xiǎn guì**	保险柜 保險櫃
desk **shū zhuōr**	书桌儿 書桌兒	combination of the safe **báo xiǎn guì mì mǎr**	保险柜密码儿 保險櫃密碼兒
drawer **chōu tì**	抽屉 抽屜	dictionary **zì diǎn**	字典 字典
drawer knob **chōu tì niǔ**	抽屉钮 抽屜鈕	handbook **shǒu cè**	手册 手冊
odds and ends **zá qī zá bā-de**	杂七杂八的 雜七雜八的	diary **rì jì**	日记 日記
desk lamp **shū zhuō dēng**	书桌灯 書桌燈	envelope **xìn fēngr**	信封儿 信封兒
clamp light **jiá-zi dēng**	夹子灯 夾子燈	letter opener **chāi xìn dāor**	拆信刀儿 拆信刀兒
arm lamp **shēn bì dēng**	伸臂灯 伸臂燈	magnifying glass **fàng dà jìng**	放大镜 放大鏡

scrap book **jiǎn tiē bù**	剪貼簿 剪貼簿	card **kǎ piàn**	卡片 卡片
address book **dì zhǐ bù**	地址簿 地址簿	abacus **suàn-pan**	算盘 算盤
telephone index card **diàn huà suó yín kǎ**	电话索引卡 電話索引卡	waste paper basket **zì zhí lǒur**	字纸篓儿 字紙簍兒
paper **zhǐ**	纸 紙	walking cane **shǒu zhàng**	手杖 手杖
odds and ends **líng xīng zá wù**	零星杂物 零星雜物		

More Stationery Goods 文具用品 **in Group 40**B.

dining room **fàn tīng**	饭厅 飯廳	candle **là zhú**	腊烛 蠟燭
chandelier **shuǐ jīng diào dēng**	水晶吊灯 水晶吊燈	lazy Susan **zhuàn pán**	转盘 轉盤
dining table **cān zhuō**	餐桌 餐桌	buffet (cabinet) **jiǔ guì**	酒柜 酒櫃
round table **yüán zhuō**	圆桌 圓桌	table runner **shòu cháng zhuō bù**	瘦长桌布 瘦長桌布
oval table **tuǒ yüán zhuō**	椭圆桌 橢圓桌	punch bowl **bō-li shuí guǒ jiǔ gāng**	玻璃水果酒缸 玻璃水果酒缸
extension table **néng shēn suō-de zhuō-zi**	能伸缩的桌子 能伸縮的桌子	silver platter **shuāng ěr chún yín tūo pán**	双耳纯银拖盘 雙耳純銀拖盤
dropleaf table **dài huó bǎnr-de zhuō-zi**	带活板儿的桌子 帶活板兒的桌子	dining chair **cān yǐ**	餐椅 餐椅
extension leaves **shēn suō zhuō-de húo bǎnr**	伸缩桌的活板儿 伸縮桌的活板兒	armchair **fú-shou yǐ**	扶手椅 扶手椅
tablecloth **zhuō bù**	桌布 桌布	side chair **zhí bèi kè-ren cān yǐ**	直背客人餐椅 直背客人餐椅
a frog (for flowers) **chā huā tiě zhēn zuòr**	插花铁针座儿 插花鐵針座兒	nursery chair **xiǎo hái yǐ**	小孩椅 小孩椅
centerpiece **cān zhuō zhōng-jian huā-shi**	餐桌中间花饰 餐桌中間花飾	children's high chair **ér tóng gāo yǐ**	儿童高椅 兒童高椅
unique **dú tè; tè bié**	独特；特别的 獨特；特別的	dinnerware **zhěng tào cān jù**	整套餐具 整套餐具
exotic **wài guó fēng wèi**	外国风味 外國風味	bone china; fine china **gāo jí bái cí qì**	高级白瓷器 高級白瓷器
candle stick **là zhú tái**	腊烛台 蠟燭台	tableware **cān jù**	餐具 餐具
candelabra **wú zhuǎ là zhú tái**	五爪腊烛台 五爪蠟燭台	porcelain; chinaware **cí qì**	瓷器 瓷器

plate	餐盘	chafing dish	西式火锅
cān pán	餐盤（大）	xī shì huǒ guō	西式火鍋
dish	碟子	finger bowl	洗手指尖的碗
dié-zi	碟子（小）	xǐ shóu zhǐ jiān-de wǎn	洗手指尖的碗
soup dish	浅汤碗	tea set	茶具
qiǎn tāng wǎn	淺湯碗	chá jù	茶具
salad bowl	沙拉碗	tea pot	茶壶
shā lā wǎn	沙拉碗	chá hú	茶壺
bread basket	面包篮	cup 'n saucer	茶杯和茶碟
miàn bāo lán	麵包籃	chá bēi hé chá dié	茶杯和茶碟
butter dish	面包碟儿	teaspoon	茶匙
miàn bāo diér （个人）	麵包碟兒	chá chí	茶匙
silverware	刀叉银器	doily	钩针织杯垫儿
dāo chā yín qì	刀叉銀器	gōu zhēn zhī bēi diànr	鉤針織杯墊兒
knife	刀子	coffee bean	咖啡豆
dāo-zi	刀子	kā fēi dòu	咖啡豆
fork	叉子	coffee grinder	磨咖啡器
chā-zi	叉子	mó kā fēi qì	磨咖啡器
tablespoon	汤匙	coffee brewer	咖啡壶
tāng chí	湯匙	kā fēi hú	咖啡壺
chopsticks	筷子	demitasse	饭后小咖啡杯
kuài-zi	筷子	fàn hòu xiǎo kā fēi bēi	飯後小咖啡杯
chopstick-rest	筷子架儿	napkin	餐巾
kuài-zi jiàr	筷子架兒	cān jīn	餐巾
serving cart	手推餐车	napkin ring	餐巾圈
shǒu tuī cān chē	手推餐車	cān jīn jüàn	餐巾圈
platter	椭圆形上菜盘	paper napkin	纸餐巾
tuǒ yüán xíng shàng cài pán	橢圓形上菜盤	zhǐ cān jīn	紙餐巾
serving fork	上菜叉	paper napkin holder	纸餐巾架
shàng cài chā	上菜叉	zhǐ cān jīn jià	紙餐巾架
serving knife	上菜刀	hot hanky	热毛巾
shàng cài dāo	上菜刀	rè máo jīn	熱毛巾
serving spoon	上菜匙	pitcher; ewer	冰水水壶
shàng cài chí	上菜匙	bīn shuí shuǐ hú	冰水水壺
soup tureen	西式双耳汤罐	wine bucket	冰酒桶
xī-shi shuāng ěr tāng guàn	西式雙耳湯罐	bīn jiú tǒng	冰酒桶
dipper; ladle	上汤勺	cork	软木塞
shàng tāng sháo	上湯勺	ruǎn mù sāi	軟木塞
casserole	瓷锅；玻璃锅	corkscrew	软木塞瓶启子
cí guō; bō-li guō	瓷鍋；玻璃鍋	ruǎn mù sāi píng qǐ-zi	軟木塞瓶啟子

crystal glass **shuǐ jīng bēi**	水晶杯 水晶杯	vinegar bottle **cù píngr**	醋瓶 醋瓶
wine glass **jiǔ bēi**	酒杯 酒杯	oil bottle **yóu píngr**	油瓶儿 油瓶兒
goblet **gāo jiǎo bēi**	高脚杯 高腳杯	soy sauce bottle **jiàng yóu píngr**	酱油瓶儿 醬油瓶兒
brandy balloon **bái lán dì jiǔ bēi**	白兰地酒杯 白蘭地酒杯	thermos; thermos flask **rè shuǐ píng**	热水瓶 熱水瓶
tumbler **wēi shì jì jiǔ bēi**	威士忌酒杯 威士忌酒杯	toaster **kǎo miàn bāo jī**	烤面包机 烤麵包機
beer mug **pí jiǔ mǎ kè bēi**	啤酒马克杯 啤酒馬克杯	egg cup (3-minute egg) **zhǔ nèn dàn bēi-jia**	煮嫩蛋杯架 煮嫩蛋杯架
creamer **nǎi yóu guànr**	奶油罐儿 奶油罐兒	toothpick **yá-qianr**	牙签儿 牙籤兒
sugar bowl **táng gùanr**	糖罐儿 糖罐兒	toothpick holder **yá qiān píng**	牙签瓶 牙籤瓶
salt shaker **yán píngr**	盐瓶儿 鹽瓶兒	nut crackers **hé táo jiá-zi**	核桃夹子 核桃夾子
pepper shaker **hú jiāo fěn píngr**	胡椒粉瓶儿 胡椒粉瓶兒		

kitchen utensils **chú fáng yòng jù**	厨房用具 廚房用具	scrubber **xǐ shuā tuán**	洗刷团 洗刷團
cupboard **chú fáng chú guì**	厨房橱柜 廚房櫥櫃	scouring pad **cā guō bù**	擦锅布 擦鍋布
refrigerator **diàn bīng xiāng**	电冰箱 電冰箱	metallic scrubber **gāng sī cā guō tuán**	钢丝擦锅团 鋼絲擦鍋團
freezing compartment **bīng dòng céng**	冰冻层 冰凍層	paper towel **zhí shǒu jīn**	纸手巾 紙手巾
ice cube tray **jié bīng hér**	结冰盒儿 結冰盒兒	water purifier **lǜ shuǐ qì**	滤水器 濾水器
defrost **jiě dòng**	解冻 解凍	garbage disposer **cán yáo yán suì jī**	残肴研碎机 殘餚研碎機
deodorizer; air freshener **bīng xiāng chú chòu jì**	冰箱除臭剂 冰箱除臭劑	dishwasher (machine) **xí wǎn jī**	洗碗机 洗碗機
deep freezer **bīng guì**	冰柜 冰櫃	dish drier (dryer) **hōng wǎn jī**	烘碗机 烘碗機
kitchen counter **liú lǐ tái**	流理台 流理台	electric mixer; blender **dá guǒ zhī jī**	打果汁机 打果汁機
kitchen sink **shuǐ cáo pén**	水槽盆 水槽盆	electric juicer **yā guǒ zhī jī**	压果汁机 壓果汁機
dish detergent **xí wǎn jīng**	洗碗精 洗碗精	kitchen stove **lú zào**	炉竈 爐竈
dishcloth **cā wǎn bù**	擦碗布 擦碗布	gas stove **méi qì lú zào**	煤气炉竈 煤氣爐竈
rag **mǒ bù**	抹布 抹布	electric range **diàn lú zào**	电炉竈 電爐竈
mop **tuō-ba**	拖把 拖把	oven **kǎo xiāng**	烤箱 烤箱
mop the floor **tuō dì**	拖地 拖地	baking pan **kǎo pán**	烤盘 烤盤
loofah sponge **sī guā jīn**	丝瓜筋 絲瓜筋	microwave oven **wéi bō lú**	微波炉 微波爐

English	Simplified	Traditional
induction cooker diàn cí lú	电磁炉	電磁爐
hot plate diàn lú	电炉	電爐
exhauster chōu fēng jī	抽风机	抽風機
ventilator tōng fēng jī	通风机	通風機
shelf jià-zi	架子	架子
kitchen ladder chú fang xiǎo tī-zi	厨房小梯子	廚房小梯子
stool dèng-zi	凳子	凳子
use this apron yòng zhè-ge wéi-qún	用这个围裙	用這個圍裙
aluminum foil lǔ bó zhǐ	铝箔纸	鋁箔紙
plastic wrap bǎo xiān mó	保鲜膜	保鮮膜
pot guō	锅	鍋
wok zhōng guó chǎo cài guō	中国炒菜锅	中國炒菜鍋
spatula chǎo cài chǎnr	炒菜铲儿	炒菜鏟兒
stewing pot dùn guō	炖锅	燉鍋
double boiler shuāng céng guō	双层锅	雙層鍋
pressure cooker yā lì guō	压力锅	壓力鍋
kettle zhú shuǐ hú	煮水壶	煮水壺
pan píng dǐ guō	平底锅	平底鍋
skillet cháng bǐng biǎn guō	长柄扁锅	長柄扁鍋
non-sticky skillet bù zhān guō	不粘锅	不粘鍋

English	Simplified	Traditional
casserole dài gài-zi cí kǎo guō	带盖子瓷烤锅	帶蓋子瓷烤鍋
sand pot shā guō	沙锅	沙鍋
steamer zhēng guō	蒸锅	蒸鍋
Chinese bamboo steamer zhēng lóng	蒸笼	蒸籠
pot lid guō gài	锅盖	鍋蓋
automatic rice cooker diàn fàn guō	电饭锅	電飯鍋
potato peeler xiāo pí dāor	削皮刀儿	削皮刀兒
jar guàn-zi	罐子	罐子
jar opener nǐng gài qì	拧盖器	擰蓋器
bottle píng-zi	瓶子	瓶子
bottle opener kāi píng qì	开瓶器	開瓶器
cap píng gài-zi	瓶盖子	瓶蓋子
can opener kāi guàn tóu dāor	开罐头刀儿	開罐頭刀兒
coffee grinder mó kā fēi qì	磨咖啡器	磨咖啡器
coffee brewer kā fēi hú	咖啡壶	咖啡壺
knife sharpener mó dāo qì	磨刀器	磨刀器
whetstone mó dāo shí	磨刀石	磨刀石
chopper duò ròu dāo	剁肉刀	剁肉刀
cleaver qiē cài dāo	切菜刀	切菜刀
bread knife qiē miàn bāo dāo	切面包刀	切麵包刀

English	Pinyin	Simplified	Traditional
cutting board	qiē cài bǎnr	切菜板儿	切菜板兒
rolling pin	gǎn miàn zhàng	杆面杖	桿麵杖
potato masher	dǎo mǎ líng shǔ qì	捣马铃薯器	搗馬鈴薯器
pie dish	kǎo pài pán	烤派盘	烤派盤
cake mold	dàn gāo kǎo pán	蛋糕烤盘	蛋糕烤盤
minute glass	zhǔ dàn jì shí qì	煮蛋计时器	煮蛋計時器
egg beater	dǎ dàn qì	打蛋器	打蛋器
shredder (for carrot)	cǎ-ceng; cā sī bǎnr	礤蹭;擦丝板儿	礤蹭;擦絲板兒
grater (for garlic or cheese)	cā suàn bǎnr	擦蒜板儿	擦蒜板兒
meat grinder	jiǎo ròu qì	绞肉器	絞肉器
perforated spoon	lòu dòng chí	漏洞匙	漏洞匙
sieve	shāi-zi	筛子	篩子
sift	shāi sǎ	筛撒	篩撒
strainer	lòu sháo	漏勺	漏勺
funnel	lòu dǒur	漏斗儿	漏斗兒
ladle	háng bǐng sháo	长柄勺	長柄勺
dipper	dǎ yóu sháo	打油勺	打油勺
rope	cū shéng	粗绳	粗繩
cord	xì shéngr	细绳儿	細繩兒
string	xiǎo xì shéngr	小细绳儿	小細繩兒

English	Pinyin	Simplified	Traditional
brush	shuā-zi	刷子	刷子
fire extinguisher	miè huǒ qì	灭火器	滅火器
mouse trap	bú shǔ qì	捕鼠器	捕鼠器
insecticide spray	shā wén shuǐ	杀蚊水	殺蚊水
cockroach killer	zhāng láng yào	蟑螂药	蟑螂藥
sticky flypaper	bǔ yíng zhǐ	补蝇纸	捕蠅紙
a variety of bottles and jars	gè zhóng ping guàn	各种瓶罐	各種瓶罐
tin cans	má kóu tiě	马口铁罐	馬口鐵罐
beverage containers	yǐn liào róng qì	饮料容器	飲料容器
aluminum foil packs	lǜ bó bāo zhuāng	铝箔包装	鋁箔包裝
a variety of waste papers	gè zhóng zhǐ lèi	各种纸类	各種紙類
styrofome ware	bǎo lì lóng qì pǐn	保丽龙器品	保麗龍器品
styrofome buffer materials	bǎo lì long bāo zhuāng diàn	保丽龙包装垫	保麗龍包裝墊
plastic bags	sù jiāo dài	塑胶袋	塑膠袋
garbage bag	lā jī dài	垃圾袋	垃圾袋
trash can	lā jī tǒng	垃圾桶	垃圾桶
dump the trash	dào lā jī	倒垃圾	倒垃圾
In the garbage can!	diū-dao shèng cài tóng-li	丢到剩菜桶	丟到剩菜桶裡
kitchen waste for compost	duī féi chú yú	堆肥厨馀	堆肥廚餘
general recyclable goods	yì bān huí shōu lā jī	一般回收垃圾	一般回收垃圾

Household Electric Appliances
家庭電器用品

household	家庭；家用的
jiā tíng; jiā yòng-de	家庭；家用的
appliances	器具；设备
qì jù; shè bèi	器具；設備
electric appliances	电器用品
diàn qì yòng pǐn	電器用品
maintenance	维修
wéi xiū	維修
main switch	总开关
zǒng kāi guān	總開關
electric heater	电暖炉
diàn nuǎn lú	電暖爐
electric radiator	烝气式暖炉
zhēng qì shì nuǎn lú	蒸氣式暖爐
sewing machine	缝纫机
féng rèn jī	縫紉機
skeleton key	万能钥匙
wàn néng yào-shi	萬能鑰匙
master-key	通用钥匙
tōng yòng yào-shi	通用鑰匙
emergency light	紧急照明灯
jǐn jí zhào míng dēng	緊急照明燈
round-pin plug	圆脚插头
yuán jiǎo chā tóu	圓腳插頭
flat-pin plug	扁脚插头
biǎn jiǎo chā tóu	扁腳插頭
adapter	分接插头
fēn jiē chā tóu	分接插頭
socket	电灯头
diàn dēng tóu	電燈頭

light bulb	电灯泡儿
diàn dēng pàor	電燈泡兒
opal light bulb	乳白灯泡儿
rǔ bái dēng pàor	乳白燈泡兒
yellow light bulb	黄色灯泡儿
huáng-se dēng pàor	黃色燈泡兒
semi-frosted light bulb	磨砂灯泡儿
mó shā dēng pàor	磨砂燈泡兒
candle-shaped bulb	烛形灯泡儿
zhú-xing dēng pàor	燭形燈泡兒
fluorescent light	日光灯
rì guāng dēng	日光燈
fluorescent tube	日光灯管
rì guāng dēng guǎn	日光燈管
fluorescent light fixture	日光灯架
rì guāng dēng jià	日光燈架
light went off	灯不亮了
dēng bú liàng-le	燈不亮了
I'll fix it.	我来修
wǒ-lai xiū	我來修
bulb is burned out	灯泡儿坏了
dēng pàor huài-le	燈泡兒壞了
replace the light bulb	换个灯泡儿
huàn-ge dēng pàor	換個燈泡兒
not bright enough	不够亮
bú gòu liàng	不夠亮
change a brighter one	换个大一点儿的
huàn-ge dà-yi diǎnr-de	換個大一點兒的
electric fan	电扇
diàn shàn	電扇

English	Pinyin	Simplified	Traditional
current leakage	lòu diàn	漏电	漏電
circuit	diàn lù	电路	電路
three –prong outlet	sān jiǎo chā tóu	三角插头	三角插頭
fuse	báo xiǎn sī	保险丝	保險絲
fuse is burned out	báo xiǎn sī duàn-le	保险丝断了	保險絲斷了
starter	qǐ rán qì	起燃器	起燃器
starter is not working	qǐ rán qì huài-le	起燃器坏了	起燃器壞了
transformer	biàn yā qì	变压器	變壓器
vacuum	xī chén qì	吸尘器	吸塵器
floor polisher	dǎ là jī	打腊机	打蠟機
hygrometer	shī dù jì	湿度计	濕度計
dehumidifier	chú shī jī	除湿机	除濕機
central air system	zhōng yāng lěng qì xì-tong	中央冷气系统	中央冷氣系統
heating system	nuǎn qì xì-tong	暖气系统	暖氣系統
water pipe connector	shuí guǎn jiē tóu	水管接头	水管接頭
elbow	shuí guǎn wān tóu	水管弯头	水管彎頭

English	Pinyin	Simplified	Traditional
T-joint	dīng xíng jiē tóu	丁型接头	丁型接頭
public utility	gōng gòng shì yè	公共事业 (水電煤氣)	公共事業
consumer	yòng hù	用户	用戶
water meter	shuí biǎo	水表	水錶
gas meter	méi qì biǎo	煤气表	煤氣表
ammeter; electric meter	diàn biǎo	电表	電錶
cable	diàn lǎn	电缆	電纜
electric wire/cord	diàn xiàn	电线	電線
volt	fú tè; diàn yā	伏特；电压	伏特；電壓(單位)
ampere	ān péi	安培	安培
watt	wǎ tè	瓦特	瓦特
wattage	wǎ tè shù	瓦特数	瓦特數
per kilowatt hour	měi dù	每度	每度
electric current	diàn liú	电流	電流
disconnect	duàn diàn	断电	斷電
power failure	tíng diàn	停电	停電

Related Terms: Group 33C, 音响 Audio;
Group 49C, 自己动手 Do It Yourself.

School Talk
學校用語

bulletin board **gōng gào bǎn**	公告板 公告板		chalk **fén bǐ**	粉笔 粉筆
catalogue **dà xué jiǎn zhāng**	大学简章 大學簡章		world map **shì jiè dì tú**	世界地图 世界地圖
brochure **xüé xiào jiǎn zhāng**	学校简章 學校簡章		back pack **bēi bāo**	背包 背包
registration fee **bào míng fèi**	报名费 報名費		schedule **kè chéng biǎo**	课程表 課程表
enroll **bào míng; rù xüé**	报名；入学 報名；入學		entrance examination **rù xüé kǎo shì**	入学考试 入學考試
sign in **bào dào**	报到 報到		oral examination **kǒ shì**	口试 口試
tuition **xüé fèi**	学费 學費		written examination **bǐ shì**	笔试 筆試
sundry expenses **zá fèi**	杂费 雜費		disqualify **wèi lù qǔ**	未录取 未錄取
register **zhù cè**	注册 註冊		intelligence quotient test **zhì lì cè yàn** (I.Q. test)	智力测验 智力測驗
registrar **zhù cè zhǔ rèn**	注册主任 註冊主任		orientation **xīn shēng xùn liàn**	新生训练 新生訓練
classroom **jiào shì**	教室 教室		roll call **diǎn míng**	点名 點名
platform **jiǎng tái**	讲台 講臺		period (class) **yì jié kè**	一节课 一節課
blackboard **hēi bǎn**	黑板 黑板		time for class **shàng kè**	上课 上課
eraser (for blackboard) **bǎn cā**	板擦 板擦		class dismiss **xià kè**	下课 下課
eraser (for paper) **xiàng pí**	橡皮 橡皮		homework **jiā tíng zuò yè**	家庭作业 家庭作業

dictation **mò shū; tīng xiě**	默书；听写 默書；聽寫	mark **fēn shùr; jì hàor**	分数儿；记号儿 分數兒；記號兒
quiz **xiáo kǎo**	小考 小考	pass **jí gé; gùo guān**	及格；过关 及格；過關
examination; exam **kǎo shì**	考试 考試	full mark **yì bǎi fēn**	一百分 一百分
midterm exam **qí zhōng kǎo**	期中考 期中考	top ten **qián shí míng**	前十名 前十名
final exam **dà kǎo**	大考 大考	cheating (exam.) **zuò bì**	作弊 作弊
test **cè yàn**	测验 測驗	conduct **cāo xìng**	操行 操行
oral test **kǒu shì**	口试 口試	unruly at school **bù shǒu guī-jü**	不守规矩 不守規矩
question-answer test **wèn dá tí**	问答题 問答題	bad test score **kǎo shì chéng jī bù-hao**	考试成绩不好 考試成績不好
true-false test **shì fē tí**	是非题 是非題	flunk; fail **bù jí gé**	不及格 不及格
completion test **tián zì tí**	填字题 填字題	make-up test **bú kǎo**	补考 補考
multiple choice test **xüǎn zé tí**	选择题 選擇題	repeat (course) **chóng xiū**	重修 重修
cancellation test **shān tú cè yàn**	删涂测验 刪塗測驗	present **dào**	到 到
identification test **jiě shì cè yàn**	解释测验 解釋測驗	tardy; late **chí dào**	迟到 遲到
correction test **gǎi cuò cè yàn**	改错测验 改錯測驗	absent **kuàng kè**	旷课 曠課
comprehension **lí jiě lì**	理解力 理解力	skip class **qiáo kè**	跷课 蹺課
apprehension **lǐng huì**	领会 領會	ask for leave **qǐng jià**	请假 請假
absent-minded **xīn bú zài yān**	心不在焉 心不在焉	private affair leave **shì jià**	事假 事假
cramming **lín shí bào fó jiǎo**	临时抱佛脚 臨時抱佛腳	sick leave **bìng jià**	病假 病假
transcript **chéng jī dān**	成绩单 成績單	leave of absence **zhǔn jià**	准假 准假
average **píng jǔn**	平均 平均	on leave **xiū jià zhōng**	休假中 休假中

home visiting **jiā tíng fǎng wèn**	家庭访问 家庭訪問	athletic meet **yùn dòng huì**	运动会 運動會
dropout **zhōng tú chuò xüé**	中途辍学 中途輟學	Homecoming Day **fǎn xiào jié**	返校节 返校節
withdrawal **zì dòng tuì xüé**	自动退学 自動退學	lecture **shòu kè; yán jiǎng**	授课；演讲 授課；演講
transfer **zhuǎn xüé**	转学 轉學	topic **jiǎng tí**	讲题 講題
intermediate class **chā bān**	插班 插班	alma mater **mǔ xiào**	母校 母校
suspension **xiū xüé**	休学 休學	alumni association **xiào yǒu huì**	校友会 校友會
dismissal **kāi chú**	开除 開除	alumnus **xiào yǒu**	校友 校友
corporal punishment **tǐ fá**	体罚 體罰	school bulletin **xiào kān**	校刊 校刊
dormitory; dorm **sù shè**	宿舍 宿舍	alumnus **nán xiào yǒu**	男校友 男校友
room & board **gōng shàn sù**	供膳宿 供膳宿	alumna **nǚ xiào yǒu**	女校友 女校友
cafeteria **zì zhù cān tīng**	自助餐厅 自助餐廳	schoolmate **tóng xiào tóng xüé**	同校同学 同校同學
campus **xiào yüán**	校园 校園	roommate **shì yǒu**	室友 室友
physical education **tǐ yǜ**	体育 體育	classmate **tóng bān tóng xüé**	同班同学 同班同學
gym; gymnasium **tǐ yǜ güǎn**	体育馆 體育館	boy scout **nán tóng zǐ jǜn**	男童子军 男童子軍
playground **cāo chǎng**	操场 操場	girl scout **nǚ tóng zǐ jǜn**	女童子军 女童子軍
auditorium **lǐ táng**	礼堂 禮堂	student government **xüé shēng zì zhù huì**	学生自助会 學生自助會
recreation center **kāng lè zhōng xīn**	康乐中心 康樂中心	student council **xüé shēng huì**	学生会 學生會
summer vacation **shǔ jià**	暑假 暑假	fraternity **xiōng dì huì**	兄弟会 兄弟會
winter vacation **hán jià**	寒假 寒假	sorority **jiě mèi huì**	姐妹会 姐妹會
summer camp **xià lìng yíng**	夏令营 夏令營	extracurricular activities **kè wài huó dòng**	课外活动 課外活動

English	Pinyin	Simplified	Traditional
reception; welcome party	huān yíng huì	欢迎会	歡迎會
farewell party	xí bié huì	惜别会	惜別會
parent-teacher association	jiā zhǎng huì	家长会	家長會
graduate	bì yè shēng	毕业生	畢業生
well-educated	shòu-guo liáng hǎo jiào yù	受过良好教育	受過良好教育
library	tú shū guǎn	图书馆	圖書館
library card	jiè shū kǎ	借书卡	借書卡
borrow	jiè	借	借
due	dào qí	到期	到期
pass due	guò qí	过期	過期
overdue fine	guò qí fá kuǎn	过期罚款	過期罰款
returned book	huán shū	还书	還書
cataloguing	biān mù lù	编目录	編目錄
classification	fēn lèi	分类	分類
paperback	píng zhuāng shū	平装书	平裝書
hardback	jīng zhuāng shū	精装书	精裝書
alphabetical	yī zì mǔ cì xù	依字母次序	依字母次序
contents	mù lù nèi róng	目录内容	目錄內容
index	suó yǐn	索引	索引
title	shū míng	书名	書名

English	Pinyin	Simplified	Traditional
author	zuò zhě	作者	作者
preface	qián yán	前言	前言
foreword	xù	序	序
footnote	zhù jiǎo	注脚	註腳
chart	tú biǎo	图表	圖表
volume (book)	cè	册（书）	冊
textbook	jiào kē shū	教科书	教科書
literature	wén xüé	文学	文學
novel	xiǎo shuō	小说	小說
poetry	shī	诗	詩
prose	sǎn wén	散文	散文
drama	xì jù	戏剧	戲劇
biography	zhuàn jì	传记	傳記
digit	ā lā bó shù zì	阿拉伯数字	阿拉伯數字
even number	ǒu shùr	偶数儿	偶數兒
odd number	qī shùr	奇数儿	奇數兒
evenly odd number	shuāng qī shùr	双奇数儿	雙奇數兒
positive number	zhèng shùr; zhèng hàor	正数儿；正号儿	正數兒；正號兒
negative number	fù shùr; fù hàor	负数儿；负号儿	負數兒；負號兒
ordinal number	xù shùr	序数儿	序數兒

plus **jiā hàor**	加号儿 加號兒	one-half **èr fēn zhī yī**	二分之一 二分之一
addition **jiā fǎ**	加法 加法	one-third **sān fēn zhī yī**	三分之一 三分之一
minus **jiǎn hàor**	减号儿 減號兒	two-thirds **sān fēn zhī èr**	三分之二 三分之二
subtraction **jián fǎ**	减法 減法	one-quarter **sì fēn zhī yī**	四分之一 四分之一
times sign **chéng hàor**	乘号儿 乘號兒	double **liǎng bèi**	两倍 兩倍
multiplication **chéng fǎ**	乘法 乘法	triple **sān bèi**	三倍 三倍
division sign **chú hàor**	除号儿 除號兒	quadruple **sì bèi**	四倍 四倍
division **chú fǎ**	除法 除法	quintuple **wǔ bèi**	五倍 五倍
percent; percentage **bǎi fēn bǐ**	百分比 百分比	sextuple **liù bèi**	六倍 六倍
integral number **zhěng shù**	整数 整數	sevenfold **qī bèi**	七倍 七倍
unit **yí wèi shù**	一位数 一位數	horizontal line **shuǐ píng xiàn**	水平线 水平線
three figures **sān wèi shù**	三位数 三位數	vertical line **chuí zhí xiàn**	垂直线 垂直線
decimal point **xiǎo shù diǎnr**	小数点儿 小數點兒	oblique line **xié xiàn**	斜线 斜線
forward; carry **xiàng qián; jìn wèi**	向前；进位 向前；進位	curve **qū xiàn**	曲线 曲線

Schools & Departments
學校與科系

school **xüé xiào**	学校	學校
kindergarten **yòu zhì yüán**	幼稚园	幼稚園
nursery school **tuō ér sǒ**	托儿所	託兒所
orphanage **gū ér yüàn**	孤儿院	孤兒院
grade school; primary school **xiǎo xüé**	小学	小學
junior high school **chū zhōng**	初中	初中
senior high school **gāo zhōng**	高中	高中
vocational school **zhí yè xüé xiào**	职业学校	職業學校
technical school **jì shù xüé yüàn**	技术学院	技術學院
commercial school **shāng yè xüé xiào**	商业学校	商業學校
industrial school **gōng yè xüé xiào**	工业学校	工業學校
agricultural school **nóng yè xüé xiào**	农业学校	農業學校
boarding school **jì shàn sù xüé xiào**	寄膳宿学校	寄膳宿學校
correspondence school **hán shòu xüé xiào**	函授学校	函授學校
school for deaf-mute **lóng yǎ xüé xiào**	聋哑学校	聾啞學校
school for the blind **máng rén xüé xiào**	盲人学校	盲人學校
handicapped school **cán zhàng xüé xiào**	残障学校	殘障學校
mental retarded school **ruò zhì xüé xiào**	弱智学校	弱智學校
public school **gōng lì xüé xiào**	公立学校	公立學校
private school **sī lì xüé xiào**	私立学校	私立學校
day school **rì xiào**	日校	日校
evening school **yè xiào**	夜校	夜校
branch school **fēn xiào**	分校	分校
institute **zhuān kē; xüé shè**	专科；学社	專科；學社
academy **zhuān xiào**	专校	專校
military academy **jūn xiào**	军校	軍校
college **xüé yüàn**	学院	學院
university **dà xüé**	大学	大學
graduate school **yán jiù yüàn**	研究院	研究院
college of liberal arts **wén xüé yüàn**	文学院	文學院

college of science lǐ xué yüàn	理学院 理學院		philology; linguistics yǔ yán xüé	语言学 語言學
college of arts and sciences wén lǐ xué yüàn	文理学院 文理學院		education jiào yù	教育 教育
college of engineering lǐ gōng xué yüàn	理工学院 理工學院		pedagogics jiào yù xüé	教育学 教育學
college of law fǎ xué yüàn	法学院 法學院		sinology hàn xüé	汉学 漢學
college of commerce shāng xué yüàn	商学院 商學院		journalism xīn wén xüé	新闻学 新聞學
college of sociology shè huì xué yüàn	社会学院 社會學院		library science tú shū guǎn xüé	图书馆学 圖書館學
college of agriculture nóng xué yüàn	农学院 農學院		archeology káo gǔ xüé	考古学 考古學
theological seminary shén xüé yüàn	神学院 神學院		philosophy zhé xüé	哲学 哲學
medical college yī xüé yüàn	医学院 醫學院		mass communications dà zhòng chuán bō	大众传播 大眾傳播
music conservatory yīn yüè xüé yüàn	音乐学院 音樂學院		music yīn yüè	音乐 音樂
department xì	系 系		arts yì shù	艺术 藝術
scholarship jiǎng xüé jīn	奖学金 獎學金		industrial engineering gōng yè gōng chéng	工业工程 工業工程
fellowship yán jiù yüàn jiǎng xüé jīn	研究院奖学金 研究院獎學金		chemistry huà xüé	化学 化學
geography dì lǐ	地理 地理		lab; laboratory shí yàn shì	实验室 實驗室
history lì shǐ	历史 歷史		geology dì zhí xüé	地质学 地質學
mathematics shù xüé	数学 數學		seismology dì zhèn xüé	地震学 地震學
algebra dài shù	代数 代數		astronomy tiān wén xüé	天文学 天文學
geometry jǐ hé	几何 幾何		meteorology qì xiàng xüé	气象学 氣象學
calculus wéi jī fēn	微积分 微積分		physics wù lǐ	物理 物理
differential equations wéi fēn fāng chéng	微分方程 微分方程		metallurgy yě jīn	冶金 冶金

mining engineering kuàng yè gōng chéng	矿业工程 礦業工程	statistics tǒng jì xüé	统计学 統計學
architectural engineering jiàn zhú gōng chéng	建筑工程 建築工程	accounting kuài jì xüé	会计学 會計學
electrical engineering diàn jī gōng chéng	电机工程 電機工程	navigation háng hǎi xüé	航海学 航海學
mechanical engineering jī xiè gōng chéng	机械工程 機械工程	naval architecture zào chuán xüé	造船学 造船學
atomic energy yüán zǐ néng	原子能 原子能	political science zhèng zhì	政治 政治
nuclear engineering hé zǐ gōng chéng	核子工程 核子工程	diplomacy wài jiāo	外交 外交
chemical engineering huà xüé gōng chéng	化学工程 化學工程	sociology shè huì xüé	社会学 社會學
computer & information diàn nǎo zī xùn	电脑信息 電腦資訊	physiology shēng lǐ xüé	生理学 生理學
aeronautical engineering háng kōng gōng chéng	航空工程 航空工程	psychology xīn lǐ xüé	心理学 心理學
civil engineering tǔ mù gōng chéng	土木工程 土木工程	logic luó jí xüé	逻辑学 邏輯學
water conservancy shuǐ lì	水利 水利	biology shēng wù xüé	生物学 生物學
environmental engineering huán jìng gōng chéng	环境工程 環境工程	the study of ecology shēng tài xué	生态学 生態學
food & nutrition shí pǐn yíng yǎng	食品营养 食品營養	botany zhí wù xüé	植物学 植物學
food science shí pǐn kē xüé	食品科学 食品科學	forestry sēn lín xüé	森林学 森林學
fishery technology shuí chǎn xüé	水产学 水產學	zoology dòng wù xüé	动物学 動物學
international trade guó jì mào yì	国际贸易 國際貿易	clinical practice nèi kē yī xüé	内科医学 內科醫學
business administration shāng yè guǎn lǐ	商业管理 商業管理	surgery wài kē yī xüé	外科医学 外科醫學
management science guǎn lǐ kē xüé	管理科学 管理科學	plastic surgery zhěng xíng wài kē	整型外科 整型外科
hotel & restaurant manag. cān lǚ guǎn lǐ	餐旅管理 餐旅管理	ophthalmology yǎn kē xüé	眼科学 眼科學
economics jīng jì xué	经济学 經濟學	deontology chǐ kē xüé	齿科学 齒科學

dermatology pí fū bìng xüé	皮肤病学 皮膚病學	intensive course mì jí kè chéng	密集课程 密集課程
hematology xiě yè xüé	血液学 血液學	master program shuò shì kè chéng	硕士课程 碩士課程
pharmacology yào jì xüé	药剂学 藥劑學	doctor program bó shì kè chéng	博士课程 博士課程
nursing hù lǐ xüé	护理学 護理學	seminar zhuān tí yán tǎo	专题研讨 專題研討
gynecology fù kē xüé	妇科学 婦科學	conduct study and research overseas chū guó jìn xiū yán jiù	出国进修研究 出國進修研究
obstetrics chǎn kē xüé	产科学 產科學	quarter system xüé qí zhì	学期制 學期制
anatomy jié pōu xüé	解剖学 解剖學	semester; term xüé qí	学期 學期
neurology shén jīng xüé	神经学 神經學	academic year xüé nián	学年 學年
genetics yí chuán xüé	遗传学 遺傳學	term paper qí mò bào gào	期末报告 期末報告
gene mutation jī yīn tú biàn	基因突变 基因突變	rector zhuān xiào xiào zhǎng	专校校长 專校校長
veterinary science shòu yī xüé	兽医学 獸醫學	president dà xüé xiào zhǎng	大学校长 大學校長
major in zhǔ xiū	主修 主修	chancellor dà xüé míng yù xiào zhǎng	大学名誉校长 大學名譽校長
minor in fù xiū	副修 副修	commandant jūn xiào xiào zhǎng	军校校长 軍校校長
selective subject (optional) xüǎn xiū kē mù	选修科目 選修科目	dean yüàn zhǎng	院长 院長
credit xüé fēn	学分 學分	department head xì zhǔ rèn	系主任 系主任
required subject bì xiū kè chéng	必修课程 必修課程	professor (prof.) jiào shòu	教授 教授
major subject zhǔ xiū kē mù	主修科目 主修科目	associate prof. fù jiào shòu	副教授 副教授
minor subject fù xiū kē mù	副修科目 副修科目	counselor; adviser zhí dǎo jiào shòu	指导教授 指導教授
course of study xüé kē	学科 學科	emeritus professor míng yù jiào shòu	名誉教授 名譽教授
basic studies jī běn xüé kē	基本学科 基本學科	instructor jiào shī	教师 教師

lecturer jiǎng shī	讲师 講師	freshman dà yī shēng; chū sān shēng	大一生；初三生 大一生；初三生
visiting lecturer tè yūē jiǎng zuò	特约讲座 特約講座	sophomore dà èr shēng; gāo yī shēng	大二生；高一生 大二生；高一生
teaching assistant zhù jiào	助教 助教	junior dà sān shēng; gāo èr shēng	大三生；高二生 大三生；高二生
principal; headmaster zhōng xué xiào zhǎng	中学校长 中學校長	senior dà sī shēng; gāo sān shēng	大四生；高三生 大四生；高三生
master xiǎo xué xiào zhǎng	小学校长 小學校長	postgraduate yán jiù suǒ xué shēng	研究所学生 研究所學生
teacher lǎo shī	老师 老師	foreign student wài-guo xué-sheng	外国学生 外國學生
school teacher zhōng xiǎo xué lǎo shī	中小学老师 中小學老師	auditor páng tīng shēng	旁听生 旁聽生
substitute teacher dài kè lǎo shī	代课老师 代課老師	evening student yiè xiào shēng	夜校生 夜校生
tutor jiā tíng jiào shī	家庭教师 家庭教師	under-graduate dà xué xué-sheng	大学学生 大學學生
faculty quán tǐ jiào yuán	全体教员 全體教員	degree xué wèi	学位 學位
faculty & staff jiào zhí yuán	教职员 教職員	honorary degree míng yù xué wèi	名誉学位 名譽學位
academic dean jiào wù zhǎng	教务长 教務長	bachelor (B.A.) xué shì	学士 學士
dean of students xùn dáo zhǎng	训导长 訓導長	master (M.A.) shuò shì	硕士 碩士
registrar zhù cè zhǔ rèn	注册主任 註冊主任	doctorate (Ph.D.) bó shì xué wèi	博士学位 博士學位
school physician xiào yī	校医 校醫	commencement bì yè dián lǐ	毕业典礼 畢業典禮
janitor xiào yòu; xiào gōng	工友；校工 工友；校工	thesis bì yè lùn wén	毕业论文 畢業論文
student xüé-sheng	学生 學生	dissertation bó shì lùn wén	博士论文 博士論文
pupil xiǎo xué shēng	小学生 小學生	diploma wén-ping	文凭 文憑
high school student zhōng xüé shēng	中学生 中學生	yearbook nián jiàn	年鉴 年鑒
undergraduate dà xüé shēng	大学生 大學生		

12

God & Buddha

神與佛

religion zōng jiào	宗教 宗教	internuncio Jiào Tíng Gōng Shǐ	教廷公使 教廷公使
belief xìn yǎng	信仰 信仰	cardinal hóng yī zhǔ jiào	枢机（红衣）主教 樞機（紅衣）主教
Catholicism tiān zhǔ jiào	天主教 天主教	archbishop zóng zhǔ jiào	总主教 總主教
God; Lord The Divinity shàng dì; zhǔ; shén	上帝；主；神 上帝；主；神	bishop zhǔ jiào	主教 主教
Holly See uó Mǎ Jiào Tíng	罗马教廷 羅馬教廷	priest; father shén fù	神父 神父
Madonna shèng mǔ xiàng	圣母像 聖母像	nun; sister xiū nǚ	修女 修女
Virgin Mary Shèng Mú Mǎ Lì	圣母玛丽 聖母瑪麗	wimple xiū nǚ tóu jīn	修女头巾 修女頭巾
Holy Father shèng fù	圣父 聖父	brother xiū shì	修士 修士
Holy Son shèng zǐ	圣子 聖子	Catholic church tiān zhǔ jiào táng	天主教堂 天主教堂
Holy Spirit shèng líng	圣灵 聖靈	cathedral dà zhǔ jiào zǒng táng	大主教总堂 大主教總堂
Trinity sān wèi yì tǐ	三位一体 三位一體	monastery xiū dào yuàn	修道院 修道院
Holy Water shèng shuǐ	圣水 聖水	chapel xiáo lǐ bài táng	小礼拜堂 小禮拜堂
sprinkle holy water sǎ shèng shuǐ	洒圣水 灑聖水	Bible Society chá jīng bān	查经班 查經班
soul xīn líng	心灵 心靈	faith xìn	信 信
Pope; the Supreme jiào huáng	教皇 教皇	hope wàng	望 望
nuncio Jiào Tíng Dà Shǐ	教廷大使 教廷大使	charity ài	爱 愛

Bible	圣经	Old Testament	旧约
shèng jīng	聖經	jiù yūē	舊約
Rosary	玫瑰经	New Testament	新约
méi guī jīng	玫瑰經	xīn yūē	新約
hear Mass	望弥撒	Ten Commandments	十诫
wàng mí sā	望彌撒	shí jiè	十誡
cross	十字架	church	教堂
shí zì jià	十字架	jiào táng	教堂
make the sign of the cross	划十字	Baptist church	浸信会
huà shí zì	劃十字	jìn xìn huì	浸信會
Catholic	天主教徒	Episcopalian	圣公会教徒
tiān zhǔ jiào tú	天主教徒	shèng gōng huì jiào tú	聖公會教徒
baptized	领洗了	Jesus Christ	耶稣基督
líng xǐ-le	領洗了	Yē Sū Jī Dū	耶穌基督
communion	领圣体	Methodist church	美以美会
lǐng shèng tǐ	領聖體	měi yí měi huì	美以美會
the Host	圣体	Protestant Episcopal	圣公会
shèng tǐ	聖體	shèng gōng huì	聖公會
confession	告解	Assemblies of God	神召会
gào jiě	告解	shén zhào huì	神召會
offertory; offering	奉献金	Presbyterian church	长老会
fèng xiàn jīn	奉獻金	zháng lǎo huì	長老會
Christianity	基督教	Lutheran Church	路德教会
jī dū jiào	基督教	lù dé jiào huì	路德教會
Christian	基督徒	Protestantism	新教教会
jī dū tú	基督徒	xīn jiào jiào huì	新教教會
gentiles	异教徒	Protestant	新教教徒
yì jiào tú	異教徒	xīn jiào jiào tú	新教教徒
Mormonism	摩门教	pastor	本堂牧师
mó mén jiào	摩門教	běn táng mù-shi	本堂牧師
Mormon	摩门教徒	missionary	传教士
mó mén jiào tú	摩門教徒	chuán jiào shì	傳教士
homilist; preacher	讲道师	preach	传道
jiǎng dào shī	講道師	chuán dào	傳道
apologetics	护教学	evangelical meeting	布道大会
hù jiào xüé	護教學	bù dào dà huì	佈道大會
Judaism	犹太教	gospel	福音
yóu tài jiào	猶太教	fú yīn	福音
Jewish Synagogue	犹太教会	pray	祷告
yóu tài jiào huì	猶太教會	dǎo gào	禱告

devout **qián chéng-de**	虔诚的 虔誠的	**Buddhist robe** **jiā shā**	袈裟 袈裟
prayer **dǎo gào wén**	祷告文 禱告文	**nunnery** **ní gū ān**	尼姑庵 尼姑庵
choir **chàng shī bān**	唱诗班 唱詩班	**nun** **ní gū**	尼姑 尼姑
Sunday school **zhǔ rì xué xiào**	主日学校 主日學校	to become a monk or nun **chū jiā**	出家 出家
salvation **dé jiù**	得救 得救	ascetic **chū jiā rén**	出家人 出家人
eternal life **yǒng shēng**	永生 永生	**wandering monk** **yǔn yóu (xíng-jiao) sēng**	云游（行脚）僧 雲遊（行脚）僧
enter heaven **jìn tiān táng**	进天堂 進天堂	**Sakyamuni** **Shì Jiā Móu Ní**	释迦牟尼 釋迦牟尼
paradise **lè yüán**	乐园 樂園	**god; a divinity** **shén**	神 神
Hell **dì yù**	地狱 地獄	**ghost** **guǐ**	鬼 鬼
judgment day **shěn pàn rì**	审判日 審判日	**Buddha** **Fó; Rú Lái Fó**	佛；如来佛 佛；如來佛
doomsday **shì jiè mò rì**	世界末日 世界末日	**image of Buddha** **fó xiàng**	佛像 佛像
devil **mó guǐ**	魔鬼 魔鬼	**Goddess of Mercy** **Guān Shì Yīn Pú-sà**	观世音菩萨 觀世音菩薩
Satan **Sā Dàn**	撒旦 撒旦	**Reclining Buddha** **Wò Fó**	卧佛 卧佛
phantom; soul; spirit **yōu líng**	幽灵 幽靈	**Goddess Mazu** **Mǎ Zǔ**	妈祖 媽祖
Buddhism **fó jiào**	佛教 佛教	**God of Wealth** **Cái Shén Yé**	财神爷 財神爺
devotion **guī yī**	皈依 皈依	**Gate God** **Mén Shén**	门神 門神
Buddhist **fó mén; fó jiào tú**	佛门；佛教徒 佛門；佛教徒	**Kitchen God** **Zào Wáng Yé**	灶王爷 竈王爺
temple **miào**	庙 廟	**Buddhist Sutra** **fó jīng**	佛经 佛經
monk **hé-shang**	和尚 和尚	**fingering beads** **niàn zhū**	念珠 念珠
neophyte **xiǎo shā mí**	小沙弥 小沙彌	**Chanting Sutra** **niàn fó; niàn jīng**	念佛；念经 念佛；念經

those who have the cause yǒu yuán	有缘	香炉 incense burner xiāng lú	香爐
cause and condition yīn yuán	因缘 因緣	burn joss sticks shāo xiāng	烧香 燒香
form cause jié yuán	结缘 結緣	consecration kāi guāng	开光 開光
causation; cause and effect yīn guǒ	因果 因果	baptism guàn dǐng	灌顶 灌頂
Namo Amitabha Nán Wú E Mí Tuó Fó	南无阿弥陀佛 南無阿彌陀佛	Rosary niàn zhū	念珠 念珠
make a vow fā shì	发誓 發誓	seven emotions qī qíng	七情 七情
make a wish xǔ yuàn	许愿 許願	six carnal desires liù yù	六欲 六慾
epiphany xiǎn líng	显灵 顯靈	six indriyas; sense-organs liù gēn	六根 六根
action and vow xíng yuàn	行愿 行願	six gunas; objects ofthr sense liù chén	六尘 六塵
release soul from suffering chāo dù	超渡 超渡	no lewd conducts bù yín yù	不淫欲 不淫慾
manes yīn hún	阴魂 陰魂	mundance world Hóng chén	红尘 紅塵
mortal body ròu shēn	肉身 肉身	sunyata; emptiness kōng	空 空
reincarnation zài tóu tāi	再投胎 再投胎	unreal/real; negative/positive kōng yǒu	空有 空有
wheel of propagation fā lún	法轮 法輪	immaterial is the material sè jí shì kōng	色即是空 色即是空
this life jīn shì	今世 今世	Fast zhāi jiè	斋戒 齋戒
pre-existence qián shì	前世 前世	abstinence xiǎo zhāi	小斋 小齋
after life lái shì	来世 來世	benefactor; doner shī zhǔ	施主 施主
follower xìn tú	信徒 信徒	clasp hands shuāng shǒu hé shí	双手合十 雙手合十
kneel guì	跪 跪	vegetarian chī sù rén	吃素人 吃素人
incense xiāng	香 香	virati; no killing bù shā shēng	不杀生 不殺生

English	Chinese (Simplified)	Chinese (Traditional)
adoration chóng bài	崇拜	崇拜
worship bài shén	拜神	拜神
ancestor worship bài zǔ xiān	拜祖先	拜祖先
Taoism dào jiào	道教	道教
God of Warriors Guān Dì	关帝	關帝
Lamaism Lǎ-ma jiào	喇嘛教	喇嘛教
Lama lǎ-ma	喇嘛	喇嘛
Dalai Lama Dá Lài Lǎ Mā	达赖喇嘛	達賴喇嘛
Banchan Lama Bān Chán Lǎ Mā	班禅喇嘛	班禪喇嘛
hassock pú tuán	蒲团	蒲團
sit cross-legged in meditation dǎ zuò	打坐	打坐
sitting contemplation zuò chán	坐禅	坐禪
benevolence; merit gōng dé	功德	功德
Wisdom Eyes huì yǎn	慧眼	慧眼
Dharma Eyes fá yǎn	法眼	法眼
Flesh Eyes ròu yǎn	肉眼	肉眼
Relic Shè Lì Zǐ	舍利子	舍利子
holy ashes líng gǔ	灵骨	靈骨
Moslemism huí jiào	回教	回教
Moslem huí jiào tú	回教徒	回教徒
Mosque qīng zhēn sì	清真寺	清真寺
Mohammed Mò Hǎn Mò Dé	默罕默德	默罕默德
Allah Zhēn Zhǔ	真主	真主
solate lǐ bài	礼拜	禮拜
Juma prayer service wǔ yüè lǐ bài	五月礼拜	五月禮拜
hadj cháo shèng	朝圣	朝聖
pilgrim cháo shèng zhě	朝圣者	朝聖者
ablution zhāi jiè mù yù	斋戒沐浴	齋戒沐浴
Collation zhāi rì yè diǎn-xin	斋日夜点心	齋日夜點心
Koran Alkoran Kě Lán Jīng	可兰经	可蘭經
Confucius Kóng Zǐ; Kóng Fū Zǐ	孔子；孔夫子	孔子；孔夫子
Mencius Mèng Zǐ; Mèng Fū Zǐ	孟子；孟夫子	孟子；孟夫子
Confucianism rú jiào	儒教	儒教
atheism wú shén lùn	无神论	無神論
atheist wú shén lùn zhě	无神论者	無神論者
superstition mí xìn	迷信	迷信
spell zhòu yǔ	咒语	咒語
curse zǔ zhòu	诅咒	詛咒
heresy xié jiào	邪教	邪教

13A

Fruits

水果

fruit **shuí-guo**	水果 水果	tangerine **jǘ-zi**	橘子 橘子
a large variety of **gè shì gè yàngr -de**	各式各样儿的 各式各樣兒的	Mandarin orange **mì gān jú**	蜜柑橘 蜜柑橘
seasonal fruit **jì jié xìng shuí-guo**	季节性水果 季節性水果	orange **chéng-zi**	橙子 橙子
kiwi **mí hóu táo**	獼猴桃 彌猴桃	persimmon **shì-zi**	柿子 柿子
banana **xiāng jiāo**	香蕉 香蕉	cantaloupe **hā mì guā**	哈蜜瓜 哈蜜瓜
cherry **yīng-tao**	樱桃 櫻桃	honeydew melon **tián-gua**	甜瓜 甜瓜
starfruit; carambola **yáng táo**	杨桃 楊桃	watermelon **xī-gua**	西瓜 西瓜
wax apple **lián wù**	莲雾 蓮霧	papaya **mù guā**	木瓜 木瓜
peach **táo-zi**	桃子 桃子	musk melon **xiāng guā**	香瓜 香瓜
apricot **xìngr**	杏儿 杏兒	mango **máng guǒ**	芒果 芒果
flat peach **biǎn táo**	扁桃 扁桃	apple **píng guǒ**	苹果 蘋果
plum **lǐ-zi**	李子 李子	fig **wú huā guǒ**	无花果 無花果
jujube; date **zaǒr**	枣儿 棗兒	citron **xiāng yuán**	香橼 香櫞
pear **lí**	梨 梨	Sakyamuni (fruit) **shì jiā; fān lì zhī**	释迦；番荔枝 釋迦；番荔枝
lemon **níng méng**	柠檬 檸檬	pineapple Sakyamuni **bō luó shì jiā**	菠萝释迦 菠蘿釋迦

coconut **yé-zi**	椰子 椰子		shaddock pomelo **wén dàn ; yòu-zi**	文旦;柚子 文旦;柚子
sugar cane **gān-zhe**	甘蔗 甘蔗		durian **liú lián**	榴槤 榴槤
lichee nut **lì zhī**	荔枝 荔枝		rambutan **hóng máo dān**	红毛丹 紅毛丹
Dragon Eye (lichee family) **lóng yǎn**	龙眼 龍眼		mangosteen **shān zhú guǒ**	山竹果 山竹果
pineapple **bō luó; fèng lí**	菠萝;凤梨 菠蘿;鳳梨		haw **shān-zha**	山楂 山楂
pomegranate **shí-liu**	石榴 石榴		olive **gán lǎn**	橄榄 橄欖
guava **fān shí-liu**	蕃石榴 蕃石榴		gage **qīng méi**	青梅 青梅
red guava **hóng fān shí-liu**	红蕃石榴 紅蕃石榴		water chestnut **bí-qi**	荸荠 荸薺
cumquat **jīn júr**	金橘儿 金橘兒		Beijing Sweet Turnip **Xīnr-li Měi**	心儿里美 心兒裡美
cranberry **màn yüè jú**	蔓越橘 蔓越橘		fresh **xīn xiān**	新鲜 新鮮
mulberry **sāng rènr**	桑葚儿 桑葚兒		juicy **zhī duō**	汁多 汁多
strawberry **cǎo méi**	草莓 草莓		ripe fruit **shú-le**	熟了 熟了
Buddah's Hand (fruit) **fó shǒu**	佛手 佛手		unripe **méi shú**	没熟 沒熟
loquat **pí pá**	枇杷 枇杷		peel **bō pí**	剥皮 剝皮
seedless grape **wú zǐ pú-tao**	无子葡萄 無子葡萄		rotten **làn-le**	烂了 爛了
grapefruit **pú táo yòu**	葡萄柚 葡萄柚		verminated **zhǎng chóng-le**	长虫了 長蟲了

水果

13 A

Fruits

A good example was the Chinese food term "yáng-táu" （楊桃） which literally could not be translated into English and, moreover, it was a fruit not to be found in the Western world. Marco Liang thought that in shape it had the appearance of a star, the translation given within was "starfruit". And a Taiwan fruit with the appearance of the head of a Buddha, the author named it "釋迦摩尼 Sakyamuni".

Ho Ching-hsien

President, Taipei Language Institute
October, 1963

197

13B

beverage **yǐn liào**	饮料 飲料	Pepsi Cola; Pepsi **bǎi shì kě lè**	百事可乐 百事可樂
cold drink **léng yǐn**	冷饮 冷飲	7-up **qī xi qì shuǐ**	七喜汽水 七喜汽水
hot drink **rè yǐn**	热饮 熱飲	apple cider **píng guǒ xī dá**	苹果西打 蘋果西打
soft drink **wú jiǔ jīng yǐn liào**	无酒精饮料 無酒精飲料	orange pop (soda) **liǔ chéng qì shuǐ**	柳橙汽水 柳橙汽水
iced tea **bīng hóng chá**	冰红茶 冰紅茶	grape pop (soda) **pú táo qì shuǐ**	葡萄汽水 葡萄汽水
iced coffee **bīng kā fēi**	冰咖啡 冰咖啡	strawberry soda **cǎo méi qì shuǐ**	草莓汽水 草莓汽水
lemon squash **xiǎo lǜ níng méng yǐn liào**	小绿柠檬饮料 小綠檸檬飲料	sarsaparilla **shā shì qì shuǐ**	沙士汽水 沙士汽水
lemonade **níng méng shuǐ**	柠檬水 檸檬水	root beer **mài gēn shā shì**	麦根沙士 麥根沙士
orangeade **liǔ chéng yǐn liào**	柳橙饮料 柳橙飲料	ginger ale **jiāng zhī qì shuǐ**	姜汁汽水 薑汁汽水
orange juice **liǔ chéng zhī**	柳橙汁 柳橙汁	cream soda **nǎi yóu qì shuǐ**	奶油汽水 奶油汽水
juice **guǒ zhī**	果汁 果汁	ice cream soda **bīng qí lín jiā qì shuǐ**	冰淇淋加汽水 冰淇淋加汽水
soda; pop **qì shuǐ**	汽水 汽水	yoghurt; yogurt **xiào mǔ nǎi**	酵母奶 酵母奶
★Coca Cola; Coke **ké kóu kě lè**	可口可乐 可口可樂	buttermilk **suān niú nǎi**	酸牛奶 酸牛奶
Cherry Coke **yīng táo kě lè**	樱桃可乐 櫻桃可樂	fresh milk **xiān nǎi**	鲜奶 鮮奶
Lemon Coke **níng méng kě lè**	柠檬可乐 檸檬可樂	skim milk **tuō zhī niú nǎi**	脱脂牛奶 脱脂牛奶

★straw **xī guǎn**	吸管 吸管	**Café Au Lait** **ròu guì niú nǎi kā fēi**	肉桂牛奶咖啡 肉桂牛奶咖啡	饮 料
coaster **bēi diàn**	杯垫 杯墊	**black coffee** **wú tang wú nǎi kā fēi**	无糖无奶咖啡 無糖無奶咖啡	
ice cube **bīng kuài**	冰块 冰塊	**decaf coffee** **wú kā fēi yīn kā fēi**	无咖啡因咖啡 無咖啡因咖啡	13 B
crushed ice **suì bīng**	碎冰 碎冰	**hot chocolate; cocoa** **rè qiǎo kè lì; ké kě**	热巧克力；可可 熱巧克力；可可	
coffee **kā fēi**	咖啡 咖啡	More Chinese Teas And Beverages in Group 25A, "Tea & Chitchatting" Also 25B, "Long Time No See"		Beverages
cream **nǎi yóu**	奶油 奶油			
instant coffee **jí róng kā fēi**	即溶咖啡 即溶咖啡	**tea** **chá**	茶 茶	
freshly brewed **xiàn zhǔ-de**	现煮的 現煮的（咖啡）	**tea** **chá yè**	茶叶 茶葉	
Espresso **yì shì nóng yā kā fēi**	义式浓压咖啡 義式濃壓咖啡	**tea bag** **chá yè bāo**	茶叶包 茶葉包	
Cappuccino **yì shì rè nǎi kā fēi**	义式热奶咖啡 義式熱奶咖啡	**ice water** **bīng shuǐ**	冰水 冰水	
Irish Coffee **Aì Er Lán kā fēi**	爱尔兰咖啡 愛爾蘭咖啡	**mineral water** **kuàng quán shuǐ**	矿泉水 礦泉水	
Persian Mocha **qiǎo kè lì kā fēi**	巧克力咖啡 巧克力咖啡	**distilled water** **zhēng liù shuǐ**	蒸馏水 蒸餾水	

tidbits líng shí	零食 零食	prune gān lǐ-zi; lǐ-zi fǔ	干李子；李子脯 乾李子；李子脯
finger food líng zuǐ	零嘴 零嘴	raisins pú-tao gānr	葡萄乾儿 葡萄乾兒
goodies hǎo chī-de diǎn xīn	好吃的点心 好吃的點心	confectionary táng guǒ	糖果 糖果
mixed nuts zá yangr-de jiān guǒr	杂样儿的坚果儿 雜樣兒的堅果兒	fruit drops yìng shuí guǒ táng	硬水果糖 硬水果糖
walnut hé-tao	核桃 核桃	lemon drops níng méng shuí guǒ táng	柠檬水果糖 檸檬水果糖
walnut kernel hé-tao rénr	核桃仁儿 核桃仁兒	orange drops jú-zi shuí guǒ táng	橘子水果糖 橘子水果糖
pecan Měi Guó cháng hé-tao	美国长核桃 美國長核桃	strawberry drops cǎo méi shuí guǒ táng	草莓水果糖 草莓水果糖
salted roast almond xián sū xìng rénr	咸酥杏仁儿 鹹酥杏仁兒	caramel niú nǎi táng	牛奶糖 牛奶糖
salted cashew xián yāo guǒr	咸腰果儿 鹹腰果兒	peanut brittle huā shēng táng	花生糖 花生糖
pistachio kāi xīn gǔor	开心果儿 開心果兒	black sesame seed candy hēi zhī-ma táng	黑芝麻糖 黑芝麻糖
Roasted Hazelnut zhēn zǐr	榛子儿 榛子兒	white sesame seed candy bái zhī-ma táng	白芝麻糖 白芝麻糖
dried persimmon shì bǐngr	柿饼儿 柿餅兒	mint drops bò-he táng	薄荷糖 薄荷糖
betel nut bīn láng	槟榔 檳榔	ginger drops jiāng táng	姜糖 薑糖
crackers xián bǐng gān	咸饼乾 鹹餅乾	ginseng drops rén shēn táng	人参糖 人參糖
potato chips mǎ líng shǔ piànr	马铃薯片儿 馬鈴薯片兒	cinnamon drops ròu guì táng	肉桂糖 肉桂糖

crunchy candy sū táng	酥糖 **酥糖**
peanut tart huā shēng duī	花生堆 **花生堆**
cotton candy mián huā táng	棉花糖 棉花糖
marshmallow mián huā qiúr ruǎn táng	棉花球儿软糖 棉花球兒軟糖
chocolate qiǎo kè lì táng	巧克力糖 巧克力糖
malt sugar; maltose mài yá táng	麦芽糖 麥芽糖
fudge ruǎn qiǎo kè lì táng	软巧克力糖 **軟巧克力糖**
candy bar guǒ rén qiǎo kè lì tiáo	果仁巧克力条 果仁巧克力條
chocolate /whisky filling jiǔ xīn qiǎo kè lì táng	酒心巧克力糖 酒心巧克力糖
nougat niú gá táng	牛轧糖 牛軋糖
soft candy; jelly drops shuí guó ruǎn táng	水果软糖 水果軟糖
walnut soft candy hé-tao ruǎn táng	核桃软糖 核桃軟糖
wintermeloncandy dōng guā táng	冬瓜糖 冬瓜糖
durian props liú lián táng	榴槤糖 榴槤糖
bubble gum pào pào táng	泡泡糖 泡泡糖
chewing gum kǒu xiāng táng	口香糖 口香糖

refreshment chá diǎn	茶点 茶點
snacks xiǎo chí; diǎn-xin	小吃；点心 小吃；點心
tea party chá diǎn huì	茶点会 茶點會
gingersnap xiǎo jiāng bǐng	小姜饼 **小薑餅**
chocolate brownies qiǎo kè lì bǐng gān	巧克力饼干 **巧克力餅乾**
milkshake nǎi xí	奶昔 奶昔
malt (milkshake + malt) mài yá fěn nǎi xí	麦芽粉奶昔 麥芽粉奶昔
popsicle bīng bàng	冰棒 冰棒
Smoothies bīng shā	冰沙 冰沙
popcorn yǔ-mi huār	玉米花儿 玉米花兒
roasted soy bean liáng chǎo dòur	凉炒豆儿 涼炒豆兒
Dried Jujube Lei guà-le zǎor	挂了枣儿 掛了棗兒
Cow Marrow Sweet Tea niú suí miàn chá	牛髓面茶 牛髓麵茶
Lotus Root Tea óu fěn	藕粉 藕粉
Fried Meatless Sausage guàn-chang	灌肠 灌腸
Dragon Boat Rice Pudding zòng-zi	粽子 粽子

Liquor, Wine & Beer
酒類

cocktail party **jī wéi jiǔ huì**	鸡尾酒会 雞尾酒會	Bourbon (whisky) **Měi Guó wēi shì jì**	美国威士忌 美國威士忌
alcohol **jiǔ jīng**	酒精 酒精	Scotch (whisky) **Sū Gé Lán wēi shì jì**	苏格兰威士忌 蘇格蘭威士忌
alcoholic drink **hán jiǔ jīng yǐn liào**	含酒精饮料 含酒精飲料	champagne **xiāng bīn**	香槟 香檳
bottoms up **gān bēi**	干杯 乾杯	sparkling wine **qǐ pào jiǔ**	起泡酒 起泡酒
It's powerful. **zhèi-ge jiú hǎo chòng**	这个酒好冲 這個酒好衝	uncork **bá sāi-zi**	拔塞子 拔塞子
cheers **suí yì**	随意 隨意	sherry **yáng huáng jiǔ**	洋黄酒 洋黃酒
a drink **yì bēi jiǔ**	一杯酒 一杯酒	Rum **lán mú jiǔ**	兰姆酒 蘭姆酒
liquor; spirit **liè jiǔ**	烈酒 烈酒	liqueur **tián jiǔ**	甜酒（饭後） 甜酒（極小高腳杯）
wine; port wine **pú táo jiǔ**	葡萄酒 葡萄酒	crème de cacao **tián ké ké jiǔ**	甜可可酒 甜可可酒
beer **pí jiǔ**	啤酒 啤酒	crème de menthe **tián bò-he jiǔ**	甜薄荷酒 甜薄荷酒
draft (draught) beer **shēng pí jiú**	生啤酒 生啤酒	anisette **tián huí xiāng jiǔ**	甜茴香酒 甜茴香酒
Claret wine **hóng pú táo jiǔ**	红葡萄酒 紅葡萄酒	brandy; Cognac **bái lán dì**	白兰地 白蘭地
Hock wine **bái pú táo jiǔ**	白葡萄酒 白葡萄酒	V.O. (very old 10-12 yrs.) **bái lán dì**	白兰地 白蘭地（10-12年）
Dubonnet（品牌） **Fà Guó tián pú táo jiǔ**	法国甜葡萄酒 法國甜葡萄酒	V.S.O. (very special old) **bái lán dì**	白兰地 白蘭地（12-17年）
whisky **wēi shì jì**	威士忌 威士忌	V.S.O.P. (old pale 20-25 yrs.) **bái lán dì**	白兰地 白蘭地（20-25年）

X.O. (extra old 40↑yrs.) **bái lán dì**	白兰地 白蘭地（40年以上）	dry **bù tián-de jiǔ**	不甜的酒 不甜的酒
vodka **É Guó fú tè jiā jiǔ**	俄国伏特加酒 俄國伏特加酒	a shot (1 fl.oz.) **yì xiǎo zhōng**	一小盅 一小盅（30C.C.）
gin **qín jiǔ; dù sōng zí jiǔ**	琴酒；杜松子酒 琴酒；杜松子酒	double shot (2 fl.ozs.) **yí dà zhōng**	一大盅 一大盅（60C.C.）
vermouth **kǔ ài jiǔ**	苦艾酒 苦艾酒	On the Rocks **wēi shì jì jiā bīng kuài**	威士忌加冰块 威士忌加冰塊
aperitif **kāi wèi jiǔ**	开胃酒 開胃酒	soda water **sū dá shuǐ**	苏打水 蘇打水
cocktail **jī wéi jiǔ**	鸡尾酒 雞尾酒	highball **liè jiǔ chān qì shuǐ**	烈酒搀汽水 烈酒攙汽水
Alexander (drink) **Yǎ Lì Shān Dà**	亚历山大 亞歷山大	yellow wine (Chinese) **huáng jiǔ**	黄酒 黃酒
Bloody Mary (drink) **Xiě Xīng Mǎ Lì**	血腥玛丽 血腥瑪麗	rice wine (Chinese) **mí jiǔ**	米酒 米酒
Eggnog **niú nǎi dàn huáng jiǔ**	牛奶蛋黄酒 牛奶蛋黃酒	kaoliang spirit (Chinese) **gāo-liang jiǔ**	高粱酒 高粱酒
Gin Fizz **bīng zhèn dù sōng-zi jiǔ**	冰镇杜松子酒 冰鎮杜松子酒	mao tai liquor (Chinese) **máo tái**	茅台 茅臺
Gin Tonic **dù sōng zǐ jī wéi jiǔ**	杜松子鸡尾酒 杜松子雞尾酒	moonshine; bootleg **sī jiǔ**	私酒 私酒
Manhattan (a cherry 一粒樱桃) **wēi shì jì jī wéi jiǔ**	威士忌鸡尾酒 威士忌雞尾酒	beer cask **shēng pí jiú tǒng**	生啤酒筒 生啤酒筒
Martini (an olive 一粒橄榄) **níng méng qín jī wéi jiǔ**	柠檬琴鸡尾酒 檸檬琴雞尾酒	beer mug **dài bàr-de pí jiǔ bēi**	带把儿的啤酒杯 帶把兒的啤酒杯
Pink Lady (cocktail) **Hóng Fěn Jiā Rén**	红粉佳人 紅粉佳人（雞尾酒）	liqueur glass **jí xiǎo-de gāo jiǎo bēi**	极小的高脚杯 極小的高腳杯
Screwdriver **fú tè jiā jú zhī jiǔ**	伏特加橘汁酒 伏特加橘汁酒	champagne glass **xiāng bīn jiǔ bēi**	香槟酒杯 香檳酒杯
punch bowl **guǒ zhī jī wéi jiǔ**	果汁鸡尾酒 果汁雞尾酒	Collins glass **shòu gāo-de jiǔ bēi**	瘦高的酒杯 瘦高的酒杯
Hawaii punch **Xià Wēi Yí guǒ zhī jiǔ**	夏威夷果汁酒 夏威夷果汁酒	cocktail glass **jī wéi jiǔ bēi**	鸡尾酒杯 雞尾酒杯
soft drink **wú jiǔ jīng yǐn liào**	无酒精饮料 無酒精飲料	muddler **jiǎo bàng**	搅棒 攪棒
chaser **xià jiǔ-de bīng shuǐ**	下酒的冰水 下酒的冰水	shaker **yáo jiǔ bēi**	摇酒杯 搖酒杯
straight **hē chún liè jiǔ**	喝纯烈酒 喝純烈酒		

Grocery Shopping
15 A
買菜

groceries **zá huò**	杂货 雜貨	broad bean **cán dòu**	蚕豆 蠶豆
canned food **guàn-tou shí pǐn**	罐头食品 罐頭食品	pinto bean **hēi bān dòu**	黑斑豆 黑斑豆
frozen food **lěng dòng shí pǐn**	冷冻食品 冷凍食品	sour cabbage **suān cài**	酸菜 酸菜
dehydrated food **tuō shuǐ shí pǐn**	脱水食品 脫水食品	bean curd **dòu-fu**	豆腐 豆腐
salad oil ; vegetable oil **shā lā yóu**	沙拉油 沙拉油	frozened bean curd **dòng dòu-fu**	冻豆腐 凍豆腐
peanut oil **huā shēng yóu**	花生油 花生油	soymilk skin **dòu-fu pí**	豆腐皮 豆腐皮
sunflower seed oil **kuí huā yóu**	葵花油 葵花油	pressed bean curd **dòu-fu gānr**	豆腐干儿 豆腐乾兒
olive oil **gán lǎn yóu**	橄榄油 橄欖油	shredded pressed bean curd **dòu-fu sī**	豆腐丝 豆腐絲
lard **zhū yóu**	猪油 豬油	fermented bean curd **dòu-fu rǔ**	豆腐乳 豆腐乳
shortening **yóu sū**	油酥 油酥	stinky fermented bean curd **chòu dòu-fu rǔ**	臭豆腐乳 臭豆腐乳
sesame seed oil **má yóu; xiāng yóu**	麻油；香油 麻油；香油	barley **dà mài**	大麦 大麥
mung bean **lǜ dòu**	绿豆 綠豆	wheat **xiǎo mài**	小麦 小麥
small red bean **hóng dòu**	红豆 紅豆	flour **miàn fěn**	面粉 麵粉
kidney bean **dà hóng dòu**	大红豆 大紅豆	wholewheat flour **qüán mài miàn fěn**	全麦面粉 全麥麵粉
black bean **hěi dòu**	黑豆 黑豆	buckwheat flour **qiáo mài miàn**	荞麦面 蕎麥麵
soybean **huáng dòu**	黄豆 黃豆	wheat gluten **miàn-jin**	面筋 麵筋

rice **mǐ**	米 米	mullet egg **wū yú zǐ**	乌鱼子 烏魚子
coarse rice **cāo mǐ**	糙米 糙米	bird's nest **yàn wō**	燕窝 燕窩
millet **xiáo mǐr**	小米儿 小米兒	shark's fin **yú chì**	鱼翅 魚翅
glutinous rice **nuò mǐ**	糯米 糯米	dried mushroom **xiāng gū**	香菇 香菇
starch; corn starch **qiàn fěn; tuán fěn**	芡粉；团粉 芡粉；團粉	egg **jī dàn**	鸡蛋 雞蛋
cornmeal **yǜ-mǐ(bàng-zi)miànr**	玉米面儿；棒子面儿 玉米麵兒；棒子麵兒	Salted Duck Egg **xián yā dàn**	咸鸭蛋 鹹鴨蛋
crushed corn meal **yǜ-mi shēnr**	玉米籸儿；棒子籸儿 玉米籸兒；棒子籸兒	Thousand-year-old Egg **pí dàn**	皮蛋 皮蛋
Job's-tear seeds **yì rén mǐ**	薏仁米 薏仁米	Salted Fish **xián yú**	咸鱼 鹹魚
dehydrated noodles **gān miàn tiáor**	干面条儿 乾麵條兒	★ Crispy Porkfluffy **ròu sōng** (See P.245 & P.246★肉乾jerky)	肉松 肉鬆
instant noodles **fāng bìan miàn**	方便面 方便麵	★ Tasty Porkflossy **ròu róng**	肉绒 肉絨
macaroni **tōng xīn fěn**	通心粉 通心粉	Chinese pickles **pào cài**	泡菜 泡菜
pea-starch vermicelli **dōng fěn**	冬粉 冬粉	Korean Pickles **Hán Guó pào cài**	韩国泡菜 韓國泡菜
rice noodles **mí fěn**	米粉 米粉	pickles (cucumber) **suān huáng-gua**	酸黄瓜 酸黄瓜
agar-agar **zǐ cài**	紫菜 紫菜	hot sauce **là jiāo jiàng**	辣椒酱 辣椒醬
hair-like seaweed **fǎ cài**	发菜 髮菜	mayonnaise; mayo **shā lā jiàng**	沙拉酱 沙拉醬
seaweed **hǎi dài**	海带 海帶	ketchup; catchup **xī hóng shì jiàng**	西红柿酱 西紅柿醬
kelp **dà hǎi dài**	大海带 大海帶	powdered milk **nái fěn**	奶粉 奶粉
dried jellyfish **hǎi zhé pí**	海哲皮 海哲皮	condensed milk **liàn rǔ**	炼乳 煉乳
dried tiny shrimps **gān xiā-mi**	干虾米 乾蝦米	headcheese **zhū tóu ròu dòng piàn**	猪头肉冻片 豬頭肉凍片
dried scallop **gān bèi**	干贝 乾貝	sandwich meat **sān míng zhì ròu**	三明治肉 三明治肉

15B

Meats 肉類

meat	肉	pork liver	猪肝
ròu	肉	zhū gān	豬肝
suckling pig	乳猪	pig's heart	猪心
rǔ zhū	乳豬	zhū xīn	豬心
pork	猪肉	pig's tongue	猪舌头
zhū ròu	豬肉	zhū shé-tou	豬舌頭
sliced pork	猪肉片儿	pig's stomach; tripe	猪肚儿
zhū ròu piànr	豬肉片兒	zhū dǔr	豬肚兒
shredded pork	猪肉丝儿	large intestine	大肠
zhū ròu sir	豬肉絲兒	dà cháng	大腸
diced pork	猪肉丁儿	chitterlings	小肠儿
zhū ròu dingr	豬肉丁兒	xiǎo cháng	小腸兒
finely chopped pork	猪肉末儿	pig's brain	猪脑子
zhū ròu mòr	豬肉末兒	zhū nǎo-zi	豬腦子
ground pork	绞猪肉	pigskin	猪皮
jiǎo zhū ròu	絞豬肉	zhū pí	豬皮
pork chop	猪排	pig's head	猪头
zhū pái	豬排	zhū tóu	豬頭
spareribs	猪排骨	hog mask	猪头皮
zhū pái-gu	豬排骨	zhū tóu pí	豬頭皮
short ribs	小排骨	pig's ear	猪耳朵
xiǎo pái-gǔ	小排骨	zhū ěr-duo	豬耳朵
pork shoulder	肘子	fat (meat)	肥肉
zhǒu-zi	肘子	féi ròu	肥肉
pig's hock 'n feet	蹄膀	lean meat	瘦肉
tí páng	蹄膀	shòu ròu	瘦肉
pork sinew	猪蹄筋	pig's belly (streaky pork)	五花肉
zhū tí jīn	豬蹄筋	wǔ huā ròu	五花肉
pig's kidney	猪腰子	Chinese sausage	香肠儿
zhū yāo-zi	豬腰子	xiāng chángr	香腸兒

beef niú ròu	牛肉 牛肉	beef tongue niú shé-tou	牛舌头 牛舌頭
sliced beef niú ròu piànr	牛肉片儿 牛肉片兒	mutton yáng ròu	羊肉 羊肉
ground beef jiǎo suì-de niú ròu	绞碎的牛肉 絞碎的牛肉	sliced mutton yáng ròu piànr	羊肉片儿 羊肉片兒
hamburger meat hàn bǎo ròu	汉堡肉 漢堡肉	lamb gāo yáng	羔羊 羔羊
beef brisket niú nán	牛腩 牛腩	lamb chop yáng pái	羊排 羊排
beef sinew niú jīn	牛筋 牛筋	deer meat lù ròu	鹿肉 鹿肉
beef tendon niú jiàn-zi	牛腱子 牛腱子	venison xiǎo lù ròu	小鹿肉 小鹿肉
ox tail niú wěi	牛尾 牛尾	rabbit meat tù ròu	兔肉 兔肉
beef stomach; beef tripe niú dǔ	牛肚 牛肚		
tenderloin yāo ròu	腰肉 腰肉		

poultry **jīa qín**	家禽 家禽	chicken feet **jī jiǎo**	鸡脚 雞腳
fowl **yě qín**	野禽 野禽	chicken gizzard **jī zhēn**	鸡胗 雞胗
chicken **jī**	鸡 雞	chicken liver **jī gān**	鸡肝 雞肝
stewing chicken **dùn tāng jī**	炖汤鸡 燉湯雞	chicken heart **jī xīn**	鸡心 雞心
silkie chicken **wū gǔ jī**	乌骨鸡 烏骨雞	goose **é**	鹅 鵝
spring chicken **zǐ jī**	子鸡 子雞	duck **yā-zi**	鸭子 鴨子
chicken leg **jī tuǐ**	鸡腿 雞腿	duckling **xiǎo yā**	小鸭 小鴨
chicken thigh **jī shàng tuǐ; tuǐ kuài**	鸡上腿；腿块 雞上腿；腿塊	pigeon **gē-zi**	鸽子 鴿子
drumstick **jī xià tuǐ; bàng bàng tuǐ**	鸡下腿；棒棒腿 雞下腿；棒棒腿	wild duck **yě yā**	野鸭 野鴨
chicken wing **jī chì bǎng**	鸡翅膀 雞翅膀	turkey **huǒ jī**	火鸡 火雞
chicken breast **jī xiōng**	鸡胸 雞胸	ostrich meat **tuó niǎo ròu**	驼鸟肉 鴕鳥肉
chicken neck **jī bó-zi**	鸡脖子 雞脖子		

seafood **hǎi xiān**	海鲜 海鮮	**cuttlefish; inkfish** **mò yǘ**	墨鱼 墨魚
fish **yǘ**	鱼 魚	**sardine** **shā dīng yǘ**	沙丁鱼 沙丁魚
shrimp **xiā**	虾 蝦	**pomfret** **chāng yǘ**	鲳鱼 鯧魚
prawn **míng xiā**	明虾 明蝦	**halibut** **dà bǐ mù yǘ**	大比目鱼 大比目魚
lobster **lóng xiā**	龙虾 龍蝦	**sole** **dié yǘ; bǐ mù yǘ**	鲽鱼；比目鱼 鰈魚；比目魚
crab **páng-xie**	螃蟹 螃蟹	**mackerel** **qīng yǘ**	鲭鱼 鯖魚
king crab **hòu**	鲎 鱟	**herring** **fēi yǘ**	鲱鱼 鯡魚
oyster **mǔ lì; shēng háo**	牡蛎；生蚝 牡蠣；生蠔	**trout** **zūn yǘ**	鳟鱼 鱒魚
clam **gé lì**	蛤蜊 蛤蜊	**bream** **jì yǘ**	鲫鱼 鯽魚
frog leg **tián jī tuǐ**	田鸡腿 田雞腿	**tuna fish** **wěi yǘ**	鲔鱼 鮪魚
snail **guā niú**	蜗牛 蝸牛	**eel** **shàn yǘ**	鳝鱼 鱔魚
scallop **hǎi shàn; xiān bèi**	海扇；鲜贝 海扇；鮮貝	**carp** **lǐ yǘ**	鲤鱼 鯉魚
sea slug; sea cucumber **hǎi shēn**	海参 海參	**cod** **xüě yǘ**	鳕鱼 鱈魚
abalone **bāo yǘ**	鲍鱼 鮑魚	**salmon** **guī yǘ**	鲑鱼 鮭魚
octopus **zhāng yǘ**	章鱼 章魚	**sea perch** **lú yǘ**	鲈鱼 鱸魚
squid **wū zéi**	乌贼 烏賊	**mouth breeder** **wú guō yǘ**	吴郭鱼 吳郭魚

the spinach is shrivelled　菠菜蔫儿了！bō cài niānr-le

vegetables qīng cài	青菜 青菜	soybean sprouts huáng dòu yár	黄豆芽儿 黃豆芽兒
lettuce shēng cài	生菜 生菜	green soybean máo dòu	毛豆 毛豆
spinach bō cài	菠菜 菠菜	string bean biǎn dòu	扁豆 扁豆
rape yóu cài	油菜 油菜	green peas wān dòu	豌豆 豌豆
amaranth xiàn cài	苋菜 莧菜	snow pea pod wān dòu jiár	豌豆夹儿 豌豆夾兒
water convolvulus kōng xīn cài	空心菜 空心菜	cowpea jiāng dòu	豇豆 豇豆
mustard greens jiè cài	芥菜 芥菜	corn yù-mi	玉米 玉米
tarragon wō jǔ	莴苣 萵苣	corn on the cob yù mi bàng-zi	玉米棒子 玉米棒子
cabbage bái cài; bāo xīn cài	白菜；包心菜 白菜；包心菜	taro yù-tou	芋头 芋頭
celery (Chinese) cabbage shān dōng dà bái cài	山东大白菜 山東大白菜	arrow-head cí-gu	慈菇 慈菇
kale gān lán cài	甘蓝菜 甘藍菜	Chinese yam shān-yao	山药 山藥
broccoli lǜ huā yé cài	绿花椰菜 綠花椰菜	burdock niú bàng	牛蒡 牛蒡
cauliflower cài huā; huā yé cài	菜花；花椰菜 菜花；花椰菜	potato mǎ líng shǔ; tǔ dòu	马铃薯；土豆 馬鈴薯；土豆
sugar pea sprouts wān dòu miáor	豌豆苗儿 豌豆苗兒	sweet potato fān shǔ; bái shǔ	蕃薯；白薯 蕃薯；白薯
bean sprouts dòu yár cài	豆芽儿菜 豆芽兒菜	lotus root lián ǒu	莲藕 蓮藕

water caltrop **líng-jiao**	菱角 菱角	edible grass-stem **jiāo bái**	茭白 茭白
carrot **hú luó-bo**	胡萝卜 胡蘿蔔	mushroom **xiāng gū**	香菇 香菇
radish **xiǎo hóng luó-bo**	小红萝卜 小紅蘿蔔	golden mushroom **jīn gū**	金菇 金菇
turnip **luó-bo**	萝卜 蘿蔔	button mushroom **yáng gū**	洋菇 洋菇
kohlrabi **piě-lan (piě-la)**	苤兰 苤蘭	grey mushroom **bào yǔ gū**	鲍鱼菇 鮑魚菇
cucumber **huáng-gua**	黄瓜 黃瓜	straw mushroom **cǎo gū**	草菇 草菇
wintermelon **dōng-gua**	冬瓜 冬瓜	woody ear (tree fungus) **mù ěr**	木耳 木耳
pumpkin **nán-gua**	南瓜 南瓜	lily flower **huáng huā; jīn zhēn cài**	黄花；金针菜 黃花；金針菜
squash **xiǎo nán guā**	小南瓜 小南瓜	leek **jiǔ-cai**	韭菜 韭菜
loofah **sī-gua**	丝瓜 絲瓜	chive **jiǔ huáng**	韭黄 韭黃
zucchini **hù guā**	瓠瓜 瓠瓜	celery **qín cài**	芹菜 芹菜
bitter gourd **kǔ guā**	苦瓜 苦瓜	watercress **shuǐ qín cài**	水芹菜 水芹菜
gourd **hú-lu**	葫芦 葫蘆	parsley **hé lán qín yè**	荷兰芹叶 荷蘭芹葉
eggplant **qié-zi**	茄子 茄子	cilantro; coriander leaves **xiāng cài**	香菜 香菜
tomato **xī hóng shì**	西红柿 西紅柿	fennel stalks and leaves **huí xiāng cài**	茴香菜 茴香菜
bell pepper **qīng jiāo**	青椒 青椒	garlic stem **suàn miáo**	蒜苗 蒜苗
beet **zǐ luó-bo tóu**	紫萝卜头 紫蘿蔔頭	onion **yáng cōng tóu**	洋葱头 洋蔥頭
cedar shoot **xiāng-chun tóu**	香椿头 香椿頭	scallion; green onion **xiǎo cōngr; qīng cōng**	小葱儿；青葱 小蔥兒；青蔥
bamboo shoot **zhú sǔn**	竹笋 竹筍	okra **qīu kuí jiá**	秋葵荚 秋葵莢
avocado **è lí**	鳄梨 鱷梨	asparagus **lú sǔn**	芦笋 蘆筍

Ingredients & Spices
作料與香料

ingredients zuó-liao	作料	作料
condiments; relishs zuǒ liào	佐料	佐料
seasoning tiáo wèi pǐn	调味品	調味品
spice xiāng liào	香料	香料
essence xiāng jíng; jīng yóu	香精；精油	香精；精油
flavor wèi-dao	味道	味道
pine mushroom sōng róng; sōng lù	松茸；松露	松茸；松露
white truffle bái sōng lù	白松露	白松露
black truffle hēi sōng lù	黑松露	黑松露
broth gāo tāng	高汤	高湯
cooking wine liào jiǔ	料酒	料酒
MSG (monosodium glutamate) wèi jīng	味精	味精
ginger jiāng	姜	薑
garlic suàn	蒜	蒜
salt yán	盐	鹽
low sodium salt dī nà yán	低钠盐	低鈉鹽
vinegar cù	醋	醋
sugar bái táng	白糖	白糖
maltose; malt sugar mài yá táng	麦芽糖	麥芽糖
brown sugar hóng táng	红糖	紅糖
crystal sugar; rock candy bīng táng	冰糖	冰糖
frosted sugar táng shuāng	糖霜	糖霜
artificial sweetener dài táng	代糖	代糖
Equal (a brand name) yī-kou	伊蔻	伊蔻（代糖品牌）
artificial color rén gōng sè sù	人工色素	人工色素
jello guǒ dòng jiāo fěn	果冻胶粉	果凍膠粉
soy sauce jiàng yóu	酱油	醬油
low-salt soy sauce dī yán jiàng yóu	低盐酱油	低鹽醬油
shrimp sauce xiā yóu	虾油	蝦油
shrimp paste xiā jiàng	虾酱	蝦醬

fish sauce **yú lù**	鱼露 **魚露**		numb seeds; xanthoxylum **huā jiāo**	花椒 花椒
oyster sauce **háo yóu**	蚝油 蠔油		curry **gā-li; jiā-li**	咖哩 咖哩
broad bean paste **dòu bàn jiàng**	豆瓣酱 豆瓣醬		dill **shí luó**	莳萝 蒔蘿
sweet bean paste **tián miàn jiàng**	甜面酱 甜麵醬		cinnamon **ròu guì**	肉桂 肉桂
honey **fēng mì**	蜂蜜 蜂蜜		vanilla **xiāng cǎo**	香草 **香草**
sesame seed paste **zhī-ma jiàng**	芝麻酱 芝麻醬		mint; peppermint **bò-he**	薄荷 薄荷
red distillers' grains **hóng zāo**	红糟 紅糟		orange peel **chén pí**	陈皮 陳皮
distillers'sweet rice **jiǔ niáng**	酒酿 酒釀		nutmeg **dòu kòu**	荳蔻 荳蔻
fermented black soya **dòu chǐ**	豆豉 豆豉		sage **shú wéi cǎo**	鼠尾草 鼠尾草
egg white **dàn bái; dàn qīng**	蛋白；蛋清 蛋白；蛋清		bay leave **yüè guì yè**	月桂叶 月桂葉
yolk **dàn huáng**	蛋黄 蛋黃		mustard **jiè-mo**	芥末 芥末
baking powder **sū dá fěn**	苏打粉 蘇打粉		five-spice powder **wǔ xiāng fěn**	五香粉 五香粉
yeast **fā xiào fěn**	发酵粉 發酵粉		clove **dīng xiāng**	丁香 丁香
horseradish **chòng cài**	冲菜 衝菜（辣根菜）		star anise **bā jiǎo; dà liào**	八角；大料 八角；大料
hot pepper; red pepper **là jiāo**	辣椒 辣椒		aniseed; anise **dà huí xiāng**	大茴香 大茴香
chili powder **mò xī gē là jiāo fěn**	墨西哥辣椒粉 墨西哥辣椒粉		cumin **xiǎo huí xiāng**	小茴香 小茴香
cayenne pepper **hóng là jiāo fěn**	红辣椒粉 紅辣椒粉		fennel **huí xiāng**	茴香 茴香
peppercorn **hú jiāo lì**	胡椒粒 胡椒粒		meat tenderizer **nèn jīng**	嫩精 嫩精
black pepper **hēi hú jiāo**	黑胡椒 黑胡椒		crumb **miàn bāo zhār**	面包渣儿 麵包渣兒
white pepper **bái hú jiāo**	白胡椒 白胡椒		crust **gān miàn bāo pí**	干面包皮 乾麵包皮

Using Chopsticks
(The Only Way)
拿筷子（唯一方法）

Chopsticks are regarded as genteel extensions of the fingers.   This concept evolved from the days when man indeed ate with his fingers. In a Chinese scholarly family, one of the most important lessons in childhood was to learn how to use the chopsticks properly.

As in the West, table manners, like improper chopstick movements, give away one's family upbringing. Bad chopstick movements make diamond rings and jade bracelets ugly at the table. It's important to learn how to use the chopsticks.

	Place the first chopstick in the hollow between thumb and index finger and let the middle part of the chopstick rest on the "tip" of the half-curled 4th finger with the upper part held firmly at "the thumbpit" by the thumbpit. From now on, The three fingers (1st, 4th and 5th) and the stick remain stationary and do not move.
	Hold the other chopstick between the tips of the 2nd and the 3rd fingers (index finger & middle finger) as you would hold a cigarette, and steady the upper part of this stick against the base of the 2nd finger by utilizing the thumb's tip joint to press and keep it in place. Now the sticks are parallel and even at the ends.
	When using the chopsticks, you move only the 2nd and the 3rd fingers "up and down" together. With the help of the thumb's tip holding the 2nd chopstick steadily, this simple balancing action will bring the points of the chopsticks closer together or separate them apart like you would use a pair of tongs.

restaurant **fàn guǎnr**	饭馆儿 飯館兒	Baozi Jiaozi Shop **bāo-zi jiǎo-zi guǎnr**	包子饺子馆儿 包子餃子館兒
4-settings please **qíng bǎi sì wèi**	请摆四位 請擺四位	Noodle Shop **miàn guǎnr**	面馆儿 麵館兒
menu **cài dān**	菜单 菜單	Guangdong Tea House **guǎng dūng chá lóu**	广东茶楼 廣東茶樓
catering service **wài huì**	外烩 外燴	quick lunch **kuài cān**	快餐 快餐
buffet **xī shì zì zhù cān yàn**	西式自助餐宴 西式自助餐宴	midnight snack **xiāo yè**	宵夜 宵夜
smorgasbord **Ruì Diǎn shì zì zhù cān**	瑞典式自助餐 瑞典式自助餐	beer joint; tavern **xiǎo jiú guǎnr**	小酒馆儿 小酒館兒
cafeteria **dān diǎn zì zhù cān tīng**	单点自助餐厅 單點自助餐廳	pub; bar **jiǔ bà**	酒吧 酒吧
café **kā fēi guǎnr**	咖啡馆儿 咖啡館兒	gay bar **tóng xìng liàn jiǔ bà**	同性恋酒吧 同性戀酒吧
hamburger shop **hàn bǎo diàn**	汉堡店 漢堡店	Lesbian bar **nǚ tóng xìng liàn jiǔ bà**	女同性恋酒吧 女同性戀酒吧
noodle stand **miàn tān-zi**	面摊子 麵攤子	supper **wǎn fàn**	晚饭 晚飯
meal **cān; dùn**	餐；顿 餐；頓（飯）	dinner **wǎn cān; wǎn yàn**	晚餐；晚宴 晚餐；晚宴
breakfast **zǎo cān**	早餐 早餐	banquet **jiǔ xí**	酒席 酒席
brunch **zhōu mo-de záo wǔ cān**	周末的早午餐 週末的早午餐	feast **jié qìng yàn**	节庆宴 節慶宴
lunch **wǔ fàn**	午饭 午飯	to serve **shàng cài**	上菜 上菜
luncheon **wǔ yàn**	午宴 午宴	to bus dishes **xià cài**	下菜 下菜

17B

Gourmet

美食人生

gourmet lǎo tāo; měi shí jiā	老饕;美食家 老饕;美食家
choosy eater tiāo zuǐ	挑嘴 挑嘴
fussy about food tiāo shí	挑食 挑食
particular about food chī dōng-xi jiǎng-jiu	吃东西讲究 吃東西講究
invitation qíng tiě	请帖 請帖
reserve a table dìng wèi-zi	订位子 訂位子
invite you yāo qǐng-nin	邀请您 邀請您
buy you a dinner qǐng-ni chī dùn biàn fàn	请你吃顿便饭 請你吃頓便飯
take a rain check gǎi-tian yí dìng qù	改天一定去 改天一定去
take you to dinner dài-ni qù chī fàn	带你去吃饭 帶你去吃飯
some other time gǎi-tian	改天 改天
come and join us guò lái yí kuàir zuò	过来一块儿坐 過來一塊兒坐
I'll treat you.. wǒ qǐng-ni	我请你 我請你
go Dutch gè fù gè-de	各付各的 各付各的
bill; check zhàng dān	帐单 帳單

Check, please! jié zhàng; suàn zhàng	结帐；算帐 結帳；算帳
I'll take care of it! wǒ fù	我付！ 我付！
Let me! (pay the bill) wǒ lái	我来！ 我來！
Next time! (treat) xià cì ní qǐng	下次你请！ 下次你請！
Well, if you insist! nà wǒ-jiu bú kè-qi-le	哪我就不客气了！ 哪我就不客氣了！
keep the change! béng zhǎo-la	甭找啦！ 甭找啦！
I'd like a toothpick. qǐng géi wǒ-ge yá qiānr	请给我个牙签儿 請給我個牙籤兒
Charge it to my account. jì wǒ zhàng	记我账！ 記我賬！
good service fú wù zhōu dào	服务周到 服務周到
service charge fú wù fèi	服务费 服務費
ten percent (10%) tip yì chéngr xiǎo fèi	一成儿 小费 一成兒 小費
tax included hán shuì	含税 含税
tax excluded bù hán shuì	不含税 不含税
appetite wèi-kou	胃口 胃口
no appetite méi wèi-kou	没胃口 沒胃口

English	Chinese		English	Chinese

| appetizing | 有胃口 | | to suck | 吸 |
| yǒu wèi-kou | 有胃口 | | xī | 吸（吸管） |

| stimulate appetite | 开胃 | | to drink | 喝 |
| kāi wèi | 開胃 | | hē | 喝 |

| digest | 消化 | | thirsty | 渴 |
| xiāo huà | 消化 | | kě | 渴 |

| vegetarian | 吃斋；吃素者 | | quench thirst | 解渴 |
| chī zhāi; chī sù zhě | 吃齋；吃素者 | | jié kě | 解渴 |

| refresh | 吃点心喝饮料 | | to feed | 喂 |
| jī diǎn-xin hē yǐn liào | 吃點心喝飲料 | | wèi | 餵 |

| meat eater | 无肉不饱 | | to eat | 吃 |
| wú ròu bù bǎo | 無肉不飽 | | chī | 吃 |

| tough (meat) | 老（肉）；韧 | | hungry | 饿 |
| lǎo; rèn | 老（肉）；韌 | | è | 餓 |

| tender | 嫩 | | starving | 饿死了 |
| nèn | 嫩（肉） | | è-si-le | 餓死了 |

| rare (steak) | 偏生 | | stomach rumbles | 饿得慌 |
| piān shēng | 偏生（牛排） | | è-de-huang | 餓得慌 |

| medium rare (steak) | 三分熟 | | table manner | 吃相 |
| sān fēn shú | 三分熟（牛排） | | chī xiàng | 吃相 |

| medium (steak) | 五分熟 | | to gulp | 狼吞虎咽 |
| wǔ fēn shú | 五分熟（牛排） | | láng tūn hǔ yàn | 狼吞虎嚥 |

| medium well (steak) | 七分熟 | | to gnaw (bone) | 啃 |
| qī fēn shú | 七分熟（牛排） | | kěn | 啃（骨頭） |

| well done | 全熟的；老的 | | to swallow | 咽 |
| quán shú; lǎo-de | 全熟的；老的 | | yàn | 嚥 |

| crisp; crispy; short | 脆 | | nibble | 一小口；细嚼 |
| cuì | 脆 | | yī xiáo kǒu; xì jiáo | 一小口；細嚼 |

| brittle | 酥；易碎 | | have enough (food) | 够了 |
| sū; yì suì | 酥；易碎 | | gòu-le | 夠了 |

| to chew | 嚼 | | I'm full; satisfied | 吃饱了 |
| jiáo | 嚼（口香糖） | | chī bǎo-le | 吃飽了 |

| gritty | 牙碜 | | overstuffed (food) | 吃多了 |
| yá-chen | 牙碜 | | chī duō-le | 吃多了 |

| to bite | 咬 | | hiccup | 打嗝儿 |
| yǎo | 咬 | | dǎ gér | 打嗝兒 |

| to lick | 舔 | | delicious | 好吃 |
| tiǎn | 舔（甜筒霜淇淋） | | hǎo chī | 好吃 |

| to sip | 啜 | | unpalatable | 难吃 |
| chuò | 啜（美酒） | | nán chī | 難吃 |

English	Pinyin	Chinese
edible	能吃的	能吃的
néng chī-de		
inedible	不能吃的	不能吃的
bù néng chī-de		
greedy	嘴馋	嘴饞
zuǐ chán		
taste it	尝尝	嚐嚐
cháng-chang		
very tasty	味美可口	味美可口
wèi měi ké kǒu		
break open with teeth	嗑	嗑（瓜子）
kē		
dissolve in mouth	含著	含著（糖果）
hán-zhe		
please pass me	请递给我	請遞給我
qǐng dì géi-wo		
junk food	垃圾食物	垃圾食物
lā jī shí wù		
nourishment	补品	補品
bú pǐn		
on a diet	节食	節食
jié shí		
low calorie	低卡路里	低卡路里
dī kǎ lù lǐ		
oily	油分分的	油兮兮的
yóu xī xī-de		
greasy	油腻	油膩
yóu nì		
spicy	口味重	口味重
kǒu wèi zhòng		
too salty	太咸	太鹹
tài xián		
not salty enough	不够咸	不夠鹹
bú gòu xián		
dip	蘸	蘸
zhàn		
sour	酸	酸
suān		
tart flavour; acidity	酸味	酸味
suān wèi		

English	Pinyin	Chinese
sweet	甜	甜
tián		
smells sweet	闻著很香	聞著很香
wén-zhe hěn xiāng		
aroma; fragrant	芳香；香味	芳香；香味
fāng xiāng; xiāng wèi		
stink; stinky	恶臭；臭气	惡臭；臭氣
è chòu; chòu qì		
bitter	苦	苦
kǔ		
astringent (unripe persimmon)	涩	澀
sè		
peppery hot	非常辣	非常辣
fēi cháng là		
pungent (hot)	辛辣的	辛辣的
xīn là-de		
hot	烫；热的；辣的	燙；熱的；辣的
tàng; rè-de; là-de		
lukewarm	温的；不烫	溫的；不燙
wēn-de; bú tàng		
cold	冷的；凉了	冷的；涼了
lěng-de; liáng-le		
chilled	冰镇的	冰鎮的 (用冰塊)
bīng zhèn-de		
fishy (smell)	腥味	腥味（魚）
xīng wèi		
hircine smell (mutton)	膻味	膻味（羊肉）
shān wèi		
urine smell (kidney)	尿臊味	尿臊味（腰子）
niào sāo wèi		
rotten	腐烂了	腐爛了
fǔ làn-le		
musty; moldy; mildew	发霉了	發黴了
fā méi-le		
stale/ soft up (potato chips)	皮了	皮了 (不脆)
pí-le		
soggy	泡得软趴趴的	泡得軟趴趴的
pào-de ruǎn pā pā-de		

Chinese cuisine **zhōng guó pēng rèn**	中国烹饪 中國烹飪	**boiled; boil tender** **zhǔ-de; zhǔ làn**	煮的；煮烂 煮的；**煮爛**
recipe **shí pǔ**	食谱 食譜	**1-minute boiling** **cuān**	氽 氽
trimmings **pèi liào; shì liào**	配料；饰料 配料；飾料	**warm it up** **tàng-yi xiàr; rè-yi xiàr**	烫一下儿；热一下儿 燙一下兒；熱一下兒
presentation **sè xiāng wèi jù quán**	色香味俱全 色香味俱全	**steamed** **zhēng-de**	蒸的 蒸的
cooking **pēng rèn; zùo fàn**	烹饪；做饭 烹飪；做飯	**paste** **hú**	糊 糊
Beijing cuisine **Běi Jīng cài**	北京菜 北京菜	**batter** **miàn hú**	面糊 麵糊（焦炸用）
Cantonese cuisine **Guǎng Dōng cài**	广东菜 廣東菜	**browned** **biān guōr**	煸锅儿 煸鍋兒（煎黃）
Shanghai cuisine **Shàng Hǎi cài**	上海菜 上海菜	**stewed; smothered** **zhōng huǒ dùn**	中火炖 中火燉
Hunan cuisine **Hú Nán cài**	湖南菜 湖南菜	**simmer; coddle** **xiáo huǒ wēi**	小火煨 小火煨
Szechwan cuisine **Sì Chuān cài**	四川菜 四川菜	**fricasseè** **liū**	溜 溜（快炒勾芡）
Jiangzhe cuisine **Jiāng Zhè cài**	江浙菜 江浙菜	**big fire stir** **bào**	爆 爆（大火快炒）
Japanese cuisine **Rì Běn cài**	日本菜 日本菜	**served: simmer on table** **bào**	煲 煲（小火慢爛）
French cuisine **Fà Guó cài**	法国菜 法國菜	**sauté** **xī shì mèn chǎo**	西式焖炒 西式燜炒
Italian cuisine **Yì Dà Lì cài**	义大利菜 義大利菜	**stir-fry** **zhōng cān chǎo cài fǎ**	中餐炒菜法 中餐炒菜法
German cuisine **Dé Guó cài**	德国菜 德國菜	**scramble** **chǎo suì**	炒碎 炒碎（蛋）

to thicken by means of starch 勾芡		
gōu qiàn	勾芡	
to thicken a soup	打卤	
dá lǔ	打滷	
fried	煎的	
jiān-de	煎的	
deep fried	炸的	
zhà-de	炸的	
soy sauce braised	红烧	
hóng shāo	紅燒	
roasted	焖烤的	
mēn kǎo-de	燜烤的	
pot roasted with soy sauce 卤的		
lǔ- de	鹵的	
charcoal broiled	炭烤	
tàn kǎo	炭烤	
barbecued	户外烧烤的	
hù wài shāo kǎo-de	戶外燒烤的	
foods resimmered together (on rice…) 烩		
huì	燴	
grilled; sear	烙的	
lào-de	烙的	
smoked	熏的	
xūn-de	燻的	
toasted	烘的	
hōng-de	烘的	
baked	烤箱烤的	
kǎo xiāng kǎo-de	烤箱烤的	
pot roasted	加盖焖烤	
jiā gài mèn kǎo	加蓋燜烤	
steeped (tea)	沏；闷泡	
qī; mēn pào	沏；悶泡（茶）	
pickled	腌的	
yān-de	醃的	
to sift	筛	
shāi	篩	
to dust	撒粉	
sá fěn	撒粉	
stir	搅拌	
jiǎo bàn	攪拌	

to grind	磨碎	
mó suì	磨碎	
spread	抹散开	
mǒ sàn kāi	抹散開	
coat (a cake)	（蛋糕）外面涂抹糖衣	
wài miàn tú mǒ táng yī	外面塗抹糖衣	
freeze	结冰；冻	
jié bīng	結冰；凍	
defrost	退冰；解冻	
tuì bīng; jié dòng	退冰；解凍	
melt	溶化	
róng huà	溶化	
dissolve	溶解	
róng jiě	溶解	
cut	切	
qiē	切	
chop	剁；砍	
duò; kǎn	剁；砍	
chunk (meat)	大块肉	
dà kuài ròu	大塊肉	
dice (meat)	肉丁儿；切丁	
ròu dīngr; qiē dīng	肉丁兒；切丁	
slice (meat)	片儿；切片	
piànr; qiē piàn	片兒；切片	
shred (meat)	细丝；切丝	
xì sī; qiē sī	細絲；切絲	
meat dust (finely chopped)	肉末儿	
ròu mòr (see p.239 ★北海肉末兒燒餅)		
hold the garlic (MSG)	免加大蒜（味精）	
miǎn jiā dà suàn (wèi jīng)	免加大蒜（味精）	
fishbone	鱼刺；鱼骨	
yú cì; yú gǔ	魚刺；魚骨	
bone the fish first	先剔掉鱼刺	
xiān tī diào yú cì	先剔掉魚刺	
fish scale	鱼鳞	
yú lín	魚鱗	
scrape the scales off; scale 括掉鱼鳞		
guā diào yú lín	括掉魚鱗	

（请参看 10G, Kitchen 厨房）
(See P.176-178)

Romance Of Chinese Cooking 中國廚藝

*N*one of the following Chinese dishes were selected from restaurant menus nor copied from Chinese cook books. All of the dishes in this chapter were actually sampled and tasted by the author, Marco at his parents' home in Beijing before he was 20 years old when he left Beijing for further studies in the United States.

*E*ighty percent of the dishes in this chapter were everyday cuisine and came from the family's chef. The author's gourmet parents had their menu changed every meal in order not to dull their appetite, the rest came from the hands of the caterers and or were sampled in restaurants with senior family members.

*T*he author's old fashioned grandmother took the Confucian saying: "聞其聲不忍食其肉，是以君子遠庖廚也" ; "After Hearing The Crying Out Of The Birds And Fish, Man Cannot Bear To Eat Their Meat, thus Gentlemen Stay Away From The Kitchen" literally. That meant that the kitchen was off-limits for men in the Liang family.

*H*owever, either because the author was "hungry all times" or was just plain curious, or perhaps because he was really interested in cooking, Marco often sneaked into the kitchen and watched the chef cooking.

*A*t age 24, while the author was a postgraduate at the University of Denver, in Colorado, he wrote his first Chinese recipe book purely from memory and went on a T.V. show teaching American housewives how to blend Lubby Pineapple into their daily meals. The President of the Board of Trustees of Denver U., Dr. Bob Silig was so impressed that he invited him to open a cooking class at the university."Romance Of Chinese Cooking" thus became the talk of the town.

Mongolian Bar-B-Q	蒙古烤肉	**Mongolian Pot**	涮羊肉
Méng Gú kǎo ròu	蒙古烤肉	**shuàn yáng ròu**	涮羊肉

Roast Suckling Pig **káo rǔ zhū**	烤乳猪 烤乳豬	**Sandpot Giant Fish Head** **shā guō yǔ tóu**	砂锅鱼头 砂鍋魚頭
Chrysanthemum Pot **jǔ huā guō**	菊花锅 菊花鍋	**Sandpot Bean Curd** **shā guō dòu-fu**	砂锅豆腐 砂鍋豆腐
Charcoal Pot Combination **shí jín huǒ guō**	什锦火锅 什錦火鍋	**Sandpot Combination** **shā guō shí jǐn**	砂锅什锦 砂鍋什錦
Sour-cabbage Pot **suān cài bái ròu huǒ guō**	酸菜白肉火锅 酸菜白肉火鍋	**Honeyed Ham** **mì zhī huó tuǐ**	蜜汁火腿 蜜汁火腿
All In One (a chafing dish) **qüán jiā fú**	全家福 全家福	**Braised Pork Shoulder** **pá zhǒu-zi**	扒肘子 扒肘子
The Monk's Dish **luó hàn zhāi** (vegetarian)	罗汉斋 羅漢齋	**The Lion's Head** **hóng shāo shī-zi tóu**	红烧狮子头 紅燒獅子頭

紅燒獅子頭 hóng shāo shī-zi tóu
The Lion's Head

Chinese celebrate their special occasions by performing a Lion Dance, because lions symbolize happiness. The following dish of giant meatballs resembles the heads of lions, especially when meatballs are set on a platter with brown colored cabbage leaves draped over them as their mane.

One pound of hand-chopped pork with some fat left in the meat. The meat is not ground, thus to prevent it from sticking together and become tough.

Mix the meat with 2 soaked and chopped black mushrooms, 6 coarsely chopped water chestnuts, 1/8 cup of pine seeds, 3 sticks chopped green onion (white part), some finely chopped fresh ginger, 3 tablespoons of cornstarch, 1 egg, lightly beaten, 1 teaspoon of sugar, 2 tablespoons of soy sauce, 2 tablespoons of cooking wine, MSG, and salt. Shape mixture into six giant meatballs. Toss each ball from one hand to another for six or seven times to make the ingredients stick tightly together. Heat one cup of oil in the wok over high heat, bring oil to 350 degrees F., fry meatballs till all sides lightly brown (be careful, so they don't fall apart). Set balls aside in a dish for further use.

Cut one head of Chinese cabbage lengthwise into twelve long pieces and fry cabbage in the remaining oil to a light brown color. Drain oil from wok and place the meatballs on top of the cabbage. Add a few sections of scallion (3-inch sections), 8 cloves of garlic, a few slices of fresh ginger, 1/8 cup of soy sauce, a pinch of white pepper and MSG, 1 teaspoon of sugar, cooking wine and two cups of chicken broth or water. Bring to a boil, cover with lid, and simmer over low heat for 30 minutes. Serve with rice.

Fried Crispy Meat-Balls **jiāo zhá xiǎo wán-zi**	焦炸小丸子 焦炸小丸子	**Meat-Ball Fricasseé** **liū zhá wán-zi**	溜炸丸子 溜炸丸子

Shredded Pork Sìchuān Sauté	鱼香肉丝	Sweet and Sour Pork	咕咾肉	
yǔ xiāng ròu sī	魚香肉絲	gú lǎo ròu (Cantonese)	咕咾肉	

Shredded Pork Sìchuān Sauté 鱼香肉丝
yǔ xiāng ròu sī 魚香肉絲

Sìchuān Pork & Eggs 鱼香肉丝炒蛋
yǔ xiāng ròu sī chǎo dàn 魚香肉絲炒蛋

3-MinuteLamb/Scallion 葱爆羊肉
cōng bào yáng ròu 葱爆羊肉

3-Minute Beef/Scallion 葱爆牛肉
cōng bào niú ròu 葱爆牛肉

3-Min. Lamb Stomach 爆羊肚儿
bào yáng dǔr 爆羊肚兒

3-Min. Lamb Lower Stomach 爆毛肚儿
bào máo dǔr 爆毛肚兒

3-Min. Inner lamb Stomach 爆肚仁儿
bào dǔ rénr 爆肚仁兒

Soy Sauce Braised-Mutton 红烧羊肉
hóng shāo yáng ròu 紅燒羊肉

Fried & Braised-Mutton 烧羊肉
shāo yáng ròu 燒羊肉

Soy Sauce Braised Beef 红烧牛肉
hóng shāo niú ròu 紅燒牛肉

Soy Sauce Braised Beef Brisket 红烧牛腩
hóng shāo niú nán 紅燒牛腩

Soy Sauce Braised Beef Sinew 红烧牛筋
hóng shāo niú jīn 紅燒牛筋

Soy Sauce Braised Pork 红烧肉
hóng shāo ròu 紅燒肉

Braised Pig's Hock 'n Feet 红烧蹄膀
hóng shāo tí páng 紅燒蹄膀

Braised Pig's Sinew 红烧蹄筋
hóng shāo tí jīn 紅燒蹄筋

Sliced Beef /Oyster Sauce 蚝油牛肉
háo yóu niú ròu 蠔油牛肉

Sliced Beef in Curry Sauce 炒咖哩牛肉片
chǎo gā-li niú ròu piàn 炒咖哩牛肉片

Shredded Beef Sìchuān Way 干煸牛肉丝
gān biǎn niú ròu sī 乾煸牛肉絲

Diced Pork Fried in Soy Paste 酱爆肉丁儿
jiàng bào ròu dīngr 醬爆肉丁兒

Double Cooked Pork 回锅肉
huí guō ròu 回鍋肉

Sweet and Sour Pork 咕咾肉
gú lǎo ròu (Cantonese) 咕咾肉

Sweet and Sour Pork 糖醋里肌
táng cù lǐ-ji (Pekingese) 糖醋裹肌

Sweet and Sour Spareribs 糖醋排骨
táng cù pái-gu 糖醋排骨

Steamed Pork in Rice-Flour 粉蒸肉
fěn zhēng ròu 粉蒸肉

Spareribs in Rice-Flour 粉蒸排骨
fěn zhēng pái-gu 粉蒸排骨

Braised Pork Intestines 九转大肠
jiú zhuǎn dà cháng 九轉大腸

Chitterlings / Ginger 姜丝肠旺
jiāng sī cháng wàng 薑絲腸旺

和尚跳牆
hé-shang tiào qiáng

Monks Jump Over The Wall

This is a clever, descriptive, and even humorous name. It's a stew made with chopped pork and small hard-boiled eggs. The eggs look like the shaved heads of Monks and they give the appearance of Monks breaking their vegetarian fast, jumping over the wall of the Monastery, and falling into a chopped pork stew.

Break Fast Combination Jar 佛跳墙
fó tiào qiáng 佛跳牆

Stir Fried Pig's Kidney 炒腰花儿
chǎo yāo huār 炒腰花兒

Stir Fried Pork Liver 炒猪肝
chǎo zhū gān 炒豬肝

Pork Liver /Tartar Sauce 醋溜猪肝
cù liū zhū gān 醋溜豬肝

Stir Fried Pig's Heart 炒猪心
chǎo zhū xīn 炒豬心

Boiled Pork/Crushed Garlic 蒜泥白肉
suàn ní bái ròu 蒜泥白肉

Chinese Poultry Dishes
19B
中餐家禽類

poultry dishes **jī yā qín lèi**	鸡鸭禽类 雞鴨禽類
Savoury and Crisp Duck **xiāng sū yā-zi**	香酥鸭子 香酥鴨子
Crispy Whole Chicken **cuì pí jī**	脆皮鸡 脆皮雞
Chicken à la Paper **zhǐ bāo jī**	纸包鸡 紙包雞
3-Cup Chicken **sān bēi jī**	三杯鸡 三杯雞

三杯雞 sān bēi jī
3-Cup Chicken

One cut-up spring chicken simmered in a mixture of: 1 cup of soy sauce, 1 cup of sesame seed oil and 1 cup of cooking wine. Cook for twenty minutes, serve with rice.

Eight-piece Chicken **jiāo zhá bā kuài**	焦炸八块 焦炸八塊
Crispy Baby Pigeon **cuì pí rǔ gē**	脆皮乳鸽 脆皮乳鴿
Mashed Chicken Bird's Nest **jī róng yàn wō**	鸡茸燕窝 雞茸燕窩
Soy Sauce Braised Chicken **hóng shāo jī**	红烧鸡 紅燒雞
Duck's Tongue Fricassee **huì yā tiáo**	烩鸭条 燴鴨條

Sliced Chicken/Bamboo Shoot **dōng sǔn jī piàn**	冬笋鸡片 冬筍雞片
Sliced-Chicken in Egg White **fú róng jī piàn**	芙蓉鸡片 芙蓉雞片
Curry Chicken **gā lǐ jī**	咖哩鸡 咖哩雞
Chicken Rice-flour Dressing **fěn zhēng jī**	粉蒸鸡 粉蒸雞
Chestnut Chicken **lì-zi jī**	栗子鸡 栗子雞
Spicy Chicken **guài wèi jī**	怪味鸡 怪味雞
Beggar's Chicken **jiào huā jī**	叫化鸡 叫化雞

叫化雞 jiào huā jī
Beggar's Chicken

This recipe originated from a beggar, who combined together the chopped chicken gizzards, heart and liver, mushrooms, scallops, chestnuts, lotus seeds, dried shrimps, seasoning and half a cup of presoaked glutinous rice and used this mixture as a stuffing for the bird. He then wrapped the bird in lotus leaves, tied it securely, coated it with yellow clay and roasted it in a logwood fire for several hours. He then shattered this roast and enjoyed it with a bottle of cheap wine.

8-Jewel Diced Chicken **bā bǎo jī dīngr**	八宝鸡丁儿 八寶雞丁兒	**Black Mushroom Wings** **xiāng gū jī chì**	香菇鸡翅 香菇雞翅
Diced Chicken in Bean Sauce **jiàng bǎo jī dīngr**	酱爆鸡丁儿 醬爆雞丁兒	**Chicken in Lotus Leaf** **hé yè jī**	荷叶鸡 荷葉雞
Diced Chicken/ Sìchuān Pepper **gōng bǎo jī dīngr**	宫保鸡丁儿 宮保雞丁兒	**Chicken In Winter Mellon** **dōng guā zhēng jī**	冬瓜蒸鸡 冬瓜蒸雞
Sliced Pigeon Fricassee **shēng chǎo gē piàn**	生炒鸽片 生炒鴿片	**Sesame Oil Chicken** **má yóu jī**	麻油鸡 麻油雞
Fried Pigeon Flakes/Lettuce **chǎo gē sōng**	炒鸽松 炒鴿鬆	**Tear-up Chicken** **shǒu pá jī**	手扒鸡 手扒雞
Onion Oiled Chicken **cōng yóu féi jī**	葱油肥鸡 蔥油肥雞	**Salted Chicken** **yán shuǐ jī**	盐水鸡 鹽水雞
8-Jewel Ducking **bā bǎor yā**	八宝儿鸭 八寶兒鴨	**Fried Chicken Steak** **xiāng jī pái**	香鸡排 香雞排
Salted Duck **yán shuǐ yā**	盐水鸭 鹽水鴨	**Charcoal broiled Chicken** **tàn kǎo jī**	碳烤鸡 碳烤雞
Chicken-shred Peas **jī sī wān dòu**	鸡丝豌豆 雞絲豌豆	**Garlic Chicken** **suàn tóu jī**	蒜头鸡 蒜頭雞
Princess's Chicken **Guì Fēi jī**	贵妃鸡 貴妃雞	**Pot Stewed Chicken Feet** **lǔ fèng zhuǎ**	卤凤爪 鹵鳳爪
Soft Fried Chicken Gizzard **ruǎn zhá zhēn gān**	软炸胗肝 軟炸胗肝	**Angelica Chicken** **dāng guī jī**	当归鸭 當歸雞
Ginseng Chicken **shēn xū hóng zǎo dùn jī**	参须红枣炖鸡 參鬚紅棗燉雞	**Roast Chicken Beijing Way** **guà lú kǎo jī**	挂炉烤鸡 掛爐烤雞

Chinese Seafood Dishes
中餐海鮮類
19C

爐螃蟹 lú páng xiè
Wok Roast Crabs

When eating river crabs as a meal, allow four crabs per person. Thoroughly brush and clean 1 dozen live river crabs. Place them in an extra large wok with a rice bowl placed upside-down in the center. Add 2 cups of water and cover with lid. Use high heat and make sure that the crabs are not escaping. In ten minutes, the wok will be dried out and the crabs will turn flaming red. Serve.

***D**ipping Sauce: 2 cups quality vinegar, 1 cup finely chopped fresh ginger, 4 tablespoons of sugar. Crabs are considered poikilothermal animals. Therefore, the Chinese use a lot of fresh ginger in the dipping sauce to counterbalance and neutralize the chills emanating from the crabmeat. Besides, ginger provides with you an unforgettable exotic taste.*

During a traditional crab meal, no other stir-fry dishes are served, except for a good pot of 花雕 Huā Diāo wine or 绍兴 Shào Xīng wine (sherry will also do) previously heated by immerging the wine pot in very hot water.

After the meal, while westerners may use a finger bowl to clean their finger tips, the Chinese use a dish of steeped tealeaves to remove the fishy smell and follow this by wiping their fingers with individual perfumed hot towels.

The dinner ends with a large bowl of very hot soupy noodles and nothing else. No sweets, especially fruits are served, except a pot of high quality and very hot strong jasmine tea. (Chinese use no sugar in their tea)

Sliced Fish in Vinegar Sauce **cù liū yú piànr**	醋溜鱼片儿 醋溜魚片兒	Sweet and Sour Carp **táng cù lǐ yú**	糖醋鲤鱼 糖醋鯉魚
Sliced-Fish in Wine Sauce **zāo liū yú piànr**	糟溜鱼片儿 糟溜魚片兒	Soy Sauce Braised Fish **hóng shāo yú**	红烧鱼 紅燒魚
Fried-Fish in Hot Bean-Sauce **dòu bàn yú**	豆瓣鱼 豆瓣魚	Soy Sauce Braised Eel **hóng shāo mán yú**	红烧鳗鱼 紅燒鰻魚

Red wine-grained Eel **hóng zāo mán**	红糟鳗 紅糟鰻	**Shrimp/ Bean Curd Sauté** **xiā rén dòu-fu**	虾仁豆腐 蝦仁豆腐
Shreded Eel Fricassee **chǎo shàn yú sī**	炒鳝鱼丝 炒鱔魚絲	**Shrimp Sauté/Crispy-Rice** **guō bā xiā rén**	锅巴虾仁 鍋巴蝦仁
Eel Of Coral **chǎo shàn hú**	炒鳝瑚 炒鱔瑚	**Shrimp Scrambled Eggs** **xiā rén chǎo dàn**	虾仁炒蛋 蝦仁炒蛋
Fried Frog Legs **zhá tián-ji tǔi**	炸鸡腿 炸田雞腿	**Crab Leg Scrambled Eggs** **xiè tuí chǎo dàn**	蟹腿炒蛋 蟹腿炒蛋
Sea Slug Fricassee **hóng shāo hǎi shēn**	红烧海参 紅燒海參	**Oyster Scrambled Eggs** **mǔ lì chǎo dàn**	牡蛎炒蛋 牡蠣炒蛋
Turtle Fricassee **hóng shāo jiǎ yú**	红烧甲鱼 紅燒甲魚	**Plain Stir-fried Shrimp** **qīng chǎo xiā rénr**	青炒虾仁儿 青炒蝦仁兒
Braised Sea Slug & Pork Shank **hǎi shēn tí páng**	海参蹄膀 海參蹄膀	**Soy Sauce Braised Fishtail** **hóng shāo huá-shui**	红烧划水 紅燒劃水
Braised Shark's Fin **hóng shāo yú chì**	红烧鱼翅 紅燒魚翅	**Braised Giant Fish Head** **hóng shāo yú táo**	红烧鱼头 紅燒魚頭
Shark's Fin/Crab Meat Fricassee **xiè huáng yú chì**	蟹黄鱼翅 蟹黃魚翅	**Braised Chucks of Carp** **hóng shāo wǎ kuài**	红烧瓦块 紅燒瓦塊
Crab Sautéed in Soy Paste **jiàng bào qīng xiè**	酱爆青蟹 醬爆青蟹	**Braised Giant Fish Lips** **hóng shāo yú chún**	红烧鱼唇 紅燒魚唇
Abalone/Asparagus Fricassee **lú sǔn bào yú**	芦笋鲍鱼 蘆筍鮑魚	**3-Way Carp** **lǐ yú sān chī**	鲤鱼三吃 鯉魚三吃
Shark's Fin Fricassee **pá yú chì**	扒鱼翅 扒魚翅	**Deep Fried Fish in Slices** **jiāo zhá yú piàn**	焦炸鱼片 焦炸魚片
Crab In Egg Sauce **huá dàn páng xiè**	滑蛋螃蟹 滑蛋螃蟹	**Smoked Yellow Fish** **xǔn huáng yú**	熏黄鱼 燻黃魚
Tea-smoked Chunks Of Fish **chá xǔn wǎ kuài**	茶熏瓦块 茶燻瓦塊	**Bone-eatable Eel** **sū yú**	酥鱼 酥魚
Smoked Prawns in pairs **xǔn dùi xiā**	熏对虾 燻對蝦	**Scallion Braised bream** **gān shāo jì yú**	干烧鲫鱼 乾燒鯽魚
Fried Prawns in Brown Sauce **gān shāo míng xiā**	干烧明虾 乾燒明蝦	**Steamed Grouper** **qīng zhēng shí bān**	清蒸石斑 清蒸石斑
Shrimp in Tomato Sauce **xī hóng shì chǎo xiā rén**	西红柿炒虾仁 西紅柿炒蝦仁	**Steamed Conger Eel** **qīng zhēng hǎ mán**	清蒸海鳗 清蒸海鰻
3-Minute Shrimp Tomato Paste **zhuā chǎo xiā rénr**	抓炒虾仁儿 抓炒蝦仁兒		
Minute Shrimp /Sugar Pea Sprouts **dòu miáo xiā rén**	豆苗虾仁 豆苗蝦仁		
Minute Shrimp /Fresh Baby Soybeans **qīng dòu xiā rén**	青豆蝦仁		

中餐海鲜类

Chinese Seafood Dishes

Chinese Vegetable Dishes

19D

中餐青菜類

Very few Chinese vegetable dishes consist only pure vegetables like regular American vegetable dishes. Because Chinese vegetable dishes are designed and cooked more salty, spicy and tasty so that they can be eaten with plain rice smoothly as a chaser. Therefore ground, diced, sliced or shredded meat or seafood are blended into them for flavoring.

vegetable dishes **qīng cài lèi**	青菜类 青菜類	**Leek Fried Bean Curd** **Jiǔ cài chǎo**	韭菜炒豆腐 韭菜炒豆腐
Gourmet's V-8 Sauté **sù shí jǐn**	素什锦 素什錦	**Stir-fried soybean sprouts** **chǎo huáng dòu yár**	炒黄豆芽儿 炒黃豆芽兒
Celery Cabbage Vinegar Sauce **cù liú bái cài**	醋溜白菜 醋溜白菜	**3-Minute Bean Sprouts** **chǎo dòu yá cài**	炒豆芽菜 炒豆芽菜
Shrimp-egg /Celery Cabbage **xiā zǐ qiàng bái cài**	虾子熗白菜 蝦子熗白菜	**Stir-fried Tomato & Egg** **xī hóng shì chǎo dàn**	西红柿炒蛋 西紅柿炒蛋
Stir-fried Cabbage/ Dried Shrimps **kāi yáng bái cài**	开阳白菜 開陽白菜	**Shredded Beef Bell Pepper Sauté** **qīng jiāo niú ròu sī**	青椒牛肉丝 青椒牛肉絲
Hot 'n Numb Bean Curd **má pó dòu-fu**	麻婆豆腐 麻婆豆腐	**Pressed Bean Curd/Shreded Beef** **dòu gān chǎo nú ròu sī**	豆干炒牛肉丝 豆乾炒牛肉絲
Ground pork Bean Curd **shào-zi dòu-fu**	绍子豆腐 紹子婆豆腐	**Stuffed Bell Pepper** **ràng qīng jiāo**	瓤青椒 瓤青椒
Red-cooked Bean Curd **hóng shāo dòu-fu**	红烧豆腐 紅燒豆腐	**Stuffed Eggplant** **ràng qié-zi**	瓤茄子 瓤茄子
Bean Curd Family Style **jiā cháng dòu-fu**	家常豆腐 家常豆腐	**Braised Eggplant** **hóng shāo qié-zi**	红烧茄子 紅燒茄子
Grilled Bean Curd **guō tiē dòu-fu**	锅贴豆腐 鍋貼豆腐	**Braised Red Radish** **hóng shāo xiǎo hóng luó-bo**	红烧小红萝卜 紅燒小紅蘿蔔

Batter Deep-fried Vegetables
(Dipping Sauce: much sugar, vinegar, fruits)

焦炸鲜青/糖醋鲜果

(sticks of eggplant, bell pepper, cucumber, string bean, sweet potato, cabbage, onion…)

Eggplant Vinegar Sauce **cù liū qié-zi**	醋溜茄子 醋溜茄子
Soy Bean/Eggplant Sauté **huáng dòu mèn qié-zi**	黄豆焖茄子 黃豆燜茄子

Eggplant in Meat Sauce **shào-zi qié-zi**	绍子茄子 紹子茄子
French Fried Bean Curd **jiāo zhá dòu-fu**	焦炸豆腐 焦炸豆腐
French Fried Meatless Balls **zhá sù wán-zi**	炸素丸子 炸素丸子
Stuffed Bean Curd **ràng dòu-fu**	瓤豆腐 瓤豆腐
Stuffed Winter Melon **ràng dōng guā**	瓤冬瓜 瓤冬瓜
Stuffed Bitter Melon **ràng kǔ guā**	瓤苦瓜 瓤苦瓜
Bitter Melon/Fermented Beans **dòu chǐ cháo kǔ guā**	豆豉炒苦瓜 豆豉炒苦瓜
Chopped Mustard Bamboo Shoot **chǎo xué-li hóng**	炒雪里红 炒雪裏紅
Chopped Mustard Soymilk Skin **bǎi yè xüé-li hóng**	百叶雪里红 百葉雪裏紅
Ants On Tree **má yǐ shàng shù**	蚂蚁上树 螞蟻上樹

螞蟻上樹 má yǐ shàng shù
Ants On Tree

Seasoned ground pork sautéed with 冬粉 *pea-starch vermicelli, also known as* 細粉 *cellophane noodles (this gives the appearance of ants crawling all over the tree branches). This dish is not a meal of noodles; it is an entree and goes well with rice.*

Stir-fried Fresh Soy Beans **qīng chǎo máo dòu**	清炒毛豆 清炒毛豆
Stir-fried Fresh Broad Bean **chǎo cán dòu**	炒蚕豆 炒蠶豆
Stir-fried Snow Pea Pods **chǎo wān dòu jiá**	炒豌豆夹 炒豌豆夾
Stir-fried Sugar Pea Stalks **chǎo wān dòu miáor**	炒豌豆苗儿 炒豌豆苗兒

Stir-fried Yellow Leek **chǎo jiǔ huáng**	炒韭黄 炒韭黃
Oil Simmered Bamboo Shoot **yóu mèn sǔn**	油闷笋 油悶筍
String Bean/Pork Sauté **mèn biǎn dòu**	闷扁豆 悶扁豆
Stir-fried Cauliflower **chǎo cài huār**	炒菜花儿 炒菜花兒
Sìchuān Pan Broiled String Beans **gān biān sì jì dòu**	干煸四季豆 乾煸四季豆
Garlic Omelet **dà suàn tān jī dàn**	大蒜摊鸡蛋 大蒜攤雞蛋
Scallion Omelet **xiǎo cōngr tān jī dàn**	小葱儿摊鸡蛋 小蔥兒攤雞蛋
Leek Omelet **Jiǔ cài tān jī dàn**	韭菜摊鸡蛋 韭菜攤雞蛋
Steamed Shrimp Custard **xiā rén zhēng dàn**	虾仁蒸蛋 蝦仁蒸蛋
Crab Meat & Cabbage Saute **xiè fěn bái cài**	蟹粉白菜 蟹粉白菜
Soy Paste Vegetables **Chǎo Dòur Jiàng**	炒豆儿酱 炒豆兒醬
Eggplant Sìchuān Way **yǔ xiāng qié-zi**	鱼香茄子 魚香茄子

瓠塌子 Hù Tā-zi
Hu gourd Pancake

Shread one Hu gourd in a bowl, mix it with one egg, 1/4 cup chopped green onion, MSG and pepper. Add 4 tsb. high gluten flour (no water) and mix it into a batter. Pancake the mixture with 2 tbs. oil till both side lightly brown. (tiny dried shrimps "蝦皮 xiā pí" *are optional).*

Dipping Sauce: Minced garlic and Soy sauce. (hot sauce)

Other juicy vegetables and gourds such as turnip, Shān Dōng cabbage, eggplant, are good substitutes.

Combination Cold Cuts **shí jǐn pīn pánr**	什锦拼盘儿 什錦拼盤兒	Wine Pickled Pig's Feet **zùi zhū jiǎo**	醉猪脚 醉豬脚
Minute Chicken Cold Cut **bái zhǎn jī**	白斩鸡 白斬雞	Shredded Wine Pickled Pig's Ear **zùi zhū ěr-duo**	醉猪耳朵 醉豬耳朵
Smoked Chicken **xǔn jī**	熏鸡 燻雞	Wine Pickled Duck Feet **zùi yā zhǎng**	醉鸭掌 醉鴨掌
Wine Pickled Chicken **zùi jī**	醉鸡 醉雞	Wine Pickled Raw Shrimps **jiǔ zùi shēng xiā**	酒醉生虾 酒醉生蝦
		Wine Pickled Raw Crabs **jiǔ zùi huó xiè**	酒醉活蟹 酒醉活蟹

醉雞 zùi jī
Wine Pickled Chicken

Marco's Recommendation: Cut up one spring chicken into four pieces, place them in a casserole of water, and bring it to a boil. After it boils, continue cooking at high heat for only ONE minute, then turn off the heat. Cover the casserole with a lid and wait for it to cool. Remove the chicken and place it in a container, adding one cup of Chinese yellow wine (or Sherry) mixed with 1/2 teaspoon of salt and (1 tablespoon of sugar) Soak overnight in refrigerator and it will begin to gel.
Remove the chicken and chop it up (do not remove the bones), arranging the pieces attractively on a platter. Serve cold as an appetizer.

Tea Leaf Smoked Chicken **tǒng-zi jī**	桶子鸡 桶子雞
Smoked Liver **xǔn gān**	熏肝 燻肝
Freshly fried Liver Sausage **zhá lù yǐnr**	炸鹿隐儿 炸鹿隱兒
Cantonese barbecue pork **guǎng shì chā shāo**	广式叉烧 廣式叉燒
Cantonese barbecue duck **guǎng shì kǎo yā**	广式烤鸭 廣式烤鴨
Cantonese Sausage **Guǎng Dōng Là Chángr**	广东腊肠儿 廣東臘腸
Cantonese Liver Sausage **Guǎng Dōng Gān Chángr**	广东肝肠儿 廣東肝腸
Hunan Bacon **Hú Nan Là Ròu**	湖南腊肉 湖南臘肉
Jinhua Ham **Jīn Huá HuóTuǐ**	金华火腿 金華火腿

Toasted Mullet Roe kǎo wū yú zǐ	烤乌鱼子 烤烏魚子	Smoked Chicken/Cucumber xūn jī sī bàn huáng-gua	熏鸡丝拌黄瓜 燻雞絲拌黃瓜
Thousand-Year-Old-Egg sōng huā lěng pānr	松花冷盘儿 松花冷盤兒	Jellyfish/Vinegar Dressing bàn hǎi zhé pí	拌海蜇皮 拌海蜇皮
1000-Year Egg/Bean Curd pí dàn dòu-fu	皮蛋豆腐 皮蛋豆腐	Pot Stewed Beef Tendon lǔ niú jiàn-zi (cold)	卤牛腱子 鹵牛腱子
Braised Pork Shoulder jiàng zhǒu-zi (cold cut)	酱肘子 醬肘子	Pot Stewed Beef Tongue lǔ niú shé (cold)	卤牛舌 鹵牛舌
a side dish of… yī xiǎo pánr	一小盘儿 一小盤兒	shreded seaweed hǎi dài cài sī	海带菜丝 海帶菜絲
Chicken Breast/Cucumber Salad jī sī bàn huáng-gua	鸡丝拌黄瓜 雞絲拌黃瓜	Pickled Kohlrabi yān piě-la; yān piě-lan	腌苤兰 醃苤蘭
Scallian Bean Curd Salad liáng bàn dòu-fu	凉拌豆腐 涼拌豆腐	Mutton-Jello yáng gēng	羊羹 羊羹
Mustard Spinach Salad Jiè-mo liáng bàn bó cài	芥末凉拌菠菜 芥末涼拌菠菜	Meat-Jello ròu dòng	肉冻 肉凍
Celery Cabbage Salad liáng bàn bái cài xīnr	凉拌白菜心儿 涼拌白菜心兒	Bitter Melon Salad liáng bàn kǔ guā	凉拌苦瓜 涼拌苦瓜
Turnip Salad liáng bàn luó-bo sīr	凉拌萝卜丝儿 涼拌蘿蔔絲兒	Glazed Walnuts táng mì hé táo rénr	糖蜜核桃仁儿 糖蜜核桃仁兒
Celery/Bean curd Noodles qín cài bàn dòu gān sī	芹菜拌豆乾丝 芹菜拌豆乾絲	Glazed Cashews táng mì yāo guǒr	糖蜜腰果儿 糖蜜腰果兒
Garlic Eggplant / Olive Oil dà suàn qié nír	大蒜茄泥儿 大蒜茄泥兒	Chicken à la Jell-Ribbon jī sī lā pí	鸡丝拉皮 雞絲拉皮
Smashed Cucumber Salad pāi xiǎo huáng-guar	拍小黄瓜儿 拍小黃瓜兒	Chicken à la Jell-Ribbon ròu sī lā pí	肉丝拉皮 肉絲拉皮
Smashed Radish Salad pāi xiǎo hóng luó-bór	拍小红萝卜儿 拍小紅蘿蔔兒	Shreded pig's tripe /Cucumber dǔ sī huáng-gua	肚丝黄瓜 肚絲黃瓜

Ham & Winter Melon Soup 火腿冬瓜汤		**Egg Drop Soup**	蛋花汤
huó tuǐ dōng guā tāng 火腿冬瓜湯		**dàn huā tāng**	蛋花湯
Chicken Mushroom Soup 香菇炖鸡汤		**Soup Mutton Stew**	红烧羊肉汤
xiāng gū dùn jī tāng 香菇燉雞湯		**hóng shāo yáng ròu tāng** 紅燒羊肉湯
Beef-Ball Soup 牛肉丸子汤		**Soup Beef Stew**	红烧牛肉汤
niú ròu wán-zi tāng 牛肉丸子湯		**hóng shāo niú ròu tāng** 紅燒牛肉湯
Beef Stomach Soup 牛肚儿汤		**Beef Tomato Soup**	西红柿牛肉汤
niú dǔr tāng 牛肚兒湯		**xī hóng shì niú ròu tāng** 西紅柿牛肉湯
Beef Internal Organ Soup 牛杂汤		**Spinach/ Bean Curd Soup** 菠菜豆腐汤
niú zá tāng 牛雜湯		**bō cài dòu-fu tāng** 菠菜豆腐湯
Lamb Internal Organ Soup 羊杂汤		**Tomato / Bean Curd Soup** 西红柿豆腐汤
yáng zá tāng 羊雜湯		**xī hóng shì dòu-fu tāng** 西紅柿豆腐湯
Minute Mutton-Ball Soup 氽丸子		**Dried Shrimp Cabbage Soup** 干虾白菜汤
cuān wán-zi 氽丸子		**gān xiā bái cài tāng** 乾蝦白菜湯
Fish-Ball Soup 鱼丸汤		**Zhàcài / Pork Shred Soup** 榨菜肉丝汤
yú wán tāng 魚丸湯		**zhà cài ròu sī tāngs** 榨菜肉絲湯
Turnip Ball/Sliced Fish Soup 萝卜球儿鱼片汤		**Clam /Fresh Ginger Clear Soup** 蛤砺清汤
Luó-bo qiúr yú piàn tāng 蘿蔔球兒魚片湯		**gé lì qīng tāng** 蛤礪清湯
Pork-Ball Soup 肉丸汤		**Bird's Nest Soup**	燕窝汤
ròu wán tāng 肉丸湯		**yàn wō tāng**	燕窩湯
Shrimp-Ball Soup 虾丸汤		**Shark's Fin Soup**	鱼翅汤
xiā wán tāng 蝦丸湯		**yú chì tāng**	魚翅湯
Egg Dumpling Soup 蛋饺儿冬粉汤		**Turtle Soup**	甲鱼汤
dàn jiǎor dōng fěn tāng 蛋餃兒冬粉湯		**Jiǎ yú tāng**	甲魚湯
Three-Shred Soup 三丝汤		**Sparerib And Turnip Soup** 萝卜炖排骨
sān sī tāng 三絲湯		**Luó-bo dùn pái-gu** 蘿蔔燉排骨
Sea-Food Soup 三鲜汤		**Seaweed Soup**	海藻汤
sān xiān tāng 三鮮湯		**hǎi zǎo tāng**	海藻湯
Sour & Hot Soup 酸辣汤		**Chicken Custard Soup**	鸡蛋羹
suān là tāng 酸辣湯		**Jī Dàn Gēng**	雞蛋羹

Chinese Staple Food, Rice

20 A

中國飯食

| staple food | 主食 | Omelet Wrapped Rice | 蛋包饭 |
| zhǔ shí | 主食 | Dàn Bāo Fàn | 蛋包飯 |

| Steamed Rice | 白饭 | Pork-liver Fried Rice | 猪肝炒饭 |
| bái fàn | 白飯 | zhū gān chǎo fàn | 豬肝炒飯 |

| Fried Rice | 炒饭 | Leftovers and Rice Gruel | 烩饭 |
| chǎo fàn | 炒飯 | huì fàn | 燴飯 |

| Cantonese Roast Duck/Rice | 广东烤鸭饭 | Cantonese Sautéd Rice | 广东烩饭 |
| Guǎng Dōng kǎo yā fàn | 廣東烤鴨飯 | Guǎng Dōng huì fàn | 廣東燴飯 |

| Barbecued Pork and Rice | 叉烧饭 | Seafood/Meat Sautéd Rice | 什锦烩饭 |
| chā shāo fàn | 叉燒飯 | shí jǐn huì fàn | 什錦燴飯 |

| Roast Suckling pig/Rice | 烤乳猪饭 | Sliced beef Sauté with Rice | 牛肉烩饭 |
| káo rǔ zhū fàn | 烤乳豬飯 | niú ròu huì fàn | 牛肉燴飯 |

| Cantonese Sausage/Rice | 广东腊肠饭 | Sliced Beef/Egg with Rice | 滑蛋牛肉饭 |
| Guǎng Dōng là cháng fàn | 廣東臘腸飯 | huá dàn niú ròu fàn | 滑蛋牛肉飯 |

| Canton. Liver Sausage/Rice | 广东肝肠饭 | Sliced Beef/Egg Porridge | 滑蛋牛肉粥 |
| Guǎng Dōng gān cháng fàn | 廣東肝腸飯 | huá dàn niú ròu zhōu | 滑蛋牛肉粥 |

| Canton. Roast Chicken/Rice | 广东肥鸡饭 | Thousand-Year Egg Porridge | 皮蛋瘦肉粥 |
| Guǎng Dōng féi jī fàn | 廣東肥雞飯 | pí dàn shòu ròu zhōu | 皮蛋瘦肉粥 |

| Roast-Specials and Rice | 三宝饭 | Rice Porridge; Congee | 稀饭；清粥 |
| sān bǎo fàn | 三寶飯 | xī fàn; qīng zhōu | 稀飯；清粥 |

| Combination Fried Rice | 什锦炒饭 | Sweet Potato/Rice Congee | 白薯稀饭 |
| shí jín chǎo fàn | 什錦炒飯 | bái shǔ xī fàn | 白薯稀飯 |

| Egg Fried Rice | 蛋炒饭 | Mung Bean Gruel | 绿豆稀饭 |
| dàn chǎo fàn | 蛋炒飯 | lǜ dòu xī fàn | 綠豆稀飯 |

| Shrimp Fried Rice | 虾仁炒饭 | Millet Gruel | 小米儿粥 |
| xiā rén chǎo fàn | 蝦仁炒飯 | xiáo mǐr zhōu | 小米兒粥 |

| Ham and Egg Fried Rice | 火腿蛋炒饭 | Crushed Corn Gruel | 玉米籸儿粥 |
| huó tuǐ dàn chǎo fàn | 火腿蛋炒飯 | yù-mi shēnr zhōu | 玉米籸兒粥 |

| Pork and Egg Fried Rice | 肉丝蛋炒饭 | Cornmeal Gruel | 棒子面儿粥 |
| ròu sī dàn chǎo fàn | 肉絲蛋炒飯 | bàng-zi miànr zhōu | 棒子麵兒粥 |

| Salted Fish Fried Rice | 咸鱼炒饭 | | |
| xián yǔ chǎo fàn | 鹹魚炒飯 | | |

Chinese Wheaten Food
中國麵食
20B

The main staple of the Southern Chinese is rice, whereas the Northern Chinese eat mainly wheat, corn and coarse grains. The following leavened dough breads and grain foods are most popular with the Northerners.

leavened dough	发面
fā miàn	發麵
Birthday Peach Bun	寿桃
shòu táo	壽桃
Steamed Bun	馒头
mán-tou	饅頭
Steamed Roll (bread)	花卷儿
huā jüǎnr	花捲兒
Thousand-thread Bun	银丝卷儿
yín sī jüǎnr	銀絲捲兒
Steamed Bun/Pork Filling	肉包子
ròu bāo-zi	肉包子
Steamed Bun with Leek Filling	韭菜包子
jiǔ cài bāo-zi	韭菜包子
Steamed Bun / Vegetable Filling	菜包子
cài bāo-zi	菜包子
Non-meat Filling Bāo-zi	素包子
sù bāo-zi	素包子
Steamed Bun with 3-K Filling	三鲜包子
sān xiān bāo-zi	三鮮包子
Miniature Soupy Tang Bāo	小笼汤包儿
xiǎo lóng tāng bāor	小籠湯包兒
Miniature Crab Roe Bāor	蟹黄小笼包儿
xiè huáng xiǎo lóng bāor	蟹黃小籠包兒
Dog-won't-care Bāo-zi	狗不理的包子
gǒu-bu lǐ-de bāo-zi	狗不理的包子

狗不理的包子
Dog-won't-care Bāo-zi

These dumplings are made of leavened dough, and are steamed and served in a bamboo steamer basket called 蒸笼 *zhēng lóng. This Bāo-zi was originated in* 天津 *Tiānjīn and was made under a secret recipe. The pork filling was so tender, so loose and soupy, the taste was so "BAD" that dogs won't even bother to stop and look at it.*

The author, here. tips you off the secret of making this bāo-zi bad: There is a ten percent specially made jello broth mixed into the ground pork filling along with minced fresh ginger roots and salt (avoid color from soy sauce) The mixed filling is at all times kept under refrigeration.

That's why **gǒu bù lǐ-de bāo-zis** *are made to order, the jello filling melts in the sealed dumplings while steaming and are served piping hot. You'll have to eat them with chopsticks and with the help of a soupspoon, the soupy taste is really something else.*

The Jello Broth: *Simmer chicken or bird bones, pig's feet or pig's head skin for hours to make the broth gel, chill and remove the floating fat with a fork.*

Grill & Steamed Meat Pie 煎包儿
jiān bāor 　　　　　　煎包兒

Steamed Roast Pork Bun 叉烧包
chā shāo bāo 　　　　　叉燒包

Giant Grilled Round-bread 锅饼
gūo-bing 　　　　　　　鍋餅

Grilled Bun (like rye bread)馍；杠子头
mó; gàng-zi tóu 　　　　馍；槓子頭

Steamed Cornmeal (millet) Bread 窝头
wō-wo tóu 　　　　　　　窩頭

Steamed Cornbread 丝糕
Sī gāo 　　　　　　　　絲糕

Steamed Cornmeal Leek pie 韭菜团子
jiǔ cài túan-zi 　　　　韭菜團子

Pot Grilled Millet Meal Bread 贴饽饽(饼子)
tiē bō-bo; tiē bǐng-zi 　贴餑餑；贴餅子

Fish /Millet Meal Bread 贴饽饽熬鱼
tiē bō-bo áo yǔ 　　　　貼餑餑熬魚

to knead dough

*T*he dough used for making various kinds of Chinese pancakes (tortillas) is entirely different from that used for making American pancakes.

*C*hinese pancakes are elastic and chewy. The dough is unleavened and made with medium-gluten flour and cold water. It is made very soft and then covers with a damp cloth and set it aside and let it rest 10 minutes for "*xǐng miàn* 醒面 dough awakening"

noodles

3-Minute Mutton Noodles 羊肉煨汆儿面
yáng ròu wèi chūnr miàn 羊肉煨汆兒麵

Knife-cut Noodles 切面
qiē miàn 　　　　切麵

Hand-pared Noodles 刀削面
dāo xiāo miàn 　　刀削麵

Hand-pulled Noodles 手拉面
shǒu lā miàn 　　　手拉麵

Chopstick-pared Noodles 拨鱼儿
bō yǔr 　　　　　　撥魚兒

Stir-fried Cat Ears 炒猫耳朵
chǎo māo ěr-duo 　炒貓耳朵

Dough-lump Soup 麸答汤
gē-da tāng 　　　麸答湯

Cornmeal-lump Soup 棒子面儿麸答汤
bàng-zi miànr gē-da tāng 棒子麵兒麸答湯

Flat Piece of Dough Soup 片儿汤
piànr tāng 　　　　　片兒湯

Big Pot Noodles 呛面
qiàng miàn 　　呛麵

Beef stew Noodles 红烧牛肉面
hóng shāo niú ròu miàn 紅燒牛肉麵

芝麻酱面 (a cold meal)
Sesame Paste Noodles
zhī má jiàng miàn

Do not overboil the noodels, rinse with cold water (chewy and loose).Top with shredded cucumber, turnip and lettuce.

Dressing: *4 tbs. each of Sesame Paste olive oil and soy sauce, MSG and 1/2 cup of water.*

Your choice of either minced garlic or Hot Mustard (★ a green or yellow hot paste, comes in tubes, not the hot dog mustard).Your choice of vinegar.

Birthday Thread Noodles 寿面
shòu miàn 　　　　　　壽麵

Pork Chop / Soupy Noodles 排骨面
Pái-gu miàn 　　　　　排骨麵

Plain Soupy Noodles 阳春面
yáng chūn miàn 　　陽春麵

Soupy Noodles Shreded Chicken 鸡丝面
jī sī miàn 雞絲麵

Chicken Leg / Soupy Noodles 鸡腿面
jī tuǐ miàn 雞腿麵

炸酱面 zhá jiàng miàn
Beijing Soy-Paste Noodles

Meat Sauce: Mix well 1/5 cup each Soybean Paste, Sweet Flour Paste and 2 tbs. water (if too dry). Fry the mixture with 1/2 cup of oil in a skillet under low heat. Scratching back and forth constantly with a spatula to prevent the sauce from sticking or burning on the bottom. After water's evaporated (changing boiling to frying) it starts to bubble, add one cup diced pork, 1/2 cup chopped green onion, 2 tbs. soy sauce, 1 tbs. sugar and MSG. Turn to high heat and stir until it bubbles, dilute with 1/5 cup of water.

(Diced brown bean curd and dried shrimps and catsup are optional.)

SERVE: Top the boiled noodles with Zhá Jiàng Sauce, garnish with finely shredded cucumber, minute-boiled fresh bean sprouts (not canned), crushed garlic or vinegar.

Soupy Noodles/ Hot Pickle 榨菜肉丝面
zhà cài ròu sī miàn 榨菜肉絲麵

Combination Fried Noodle 什锦炒面
shí jín chǎo miàn 什錦炒麵

Shreded Pork Fried Noodle 肉丝炒面
ròu sī chǎo miàn 肉絲炒麵

Cantonese Stir-fried Noodles 广东炒面
Guǎng Dōng chǎo miàn 廣東炒麵

Thread Noodles/ poached egg 挂面加卧果儿
gùa miàn jiā wò guǒr 掛麵加臥果兒

Stir-fried Flat Noodles 炒河粉
chǎo hé fěn 炒河粉

打卤面 dá lǔ miàn
Thick Soupy Noodles

Pre-soak dried black mushrooms, tiny shrimps, wood-ears, and lily flowers (or use the fresh ones) boil them in Chicken broth (or water with Bouillon Cubes). Add salt, pepper, 2 tbs. soy sauce for coloring, half a pound of paper-thin sliced pork (or cooked meat or seafood). When it boils add corn starch water for thickening and pour 2 beaten eggs into the soup drop by drop while stirring with a ladle to give it a chrysanthemum look. Drop evenly into the soup one cup of tiny fresh oysters which are coated with dry corn starch (to prevent oysters from shrinking and getting tough.)

Stir-fried Rice Noodles 炒米粉
chǎo mí fěn 炒米粉

Soupy Rice-noodles 米粉汤
mí fěn tāng 米粉湯

Pork Fried glutinous-cake 肉丝炒年糕
ròu sī chǎo nián gāo 肉絲炒年糕

Oyster Thread Noodles 蚵仔面线
kē zǐ miàn xiàn 蚵仔麵線

Fried Bean Curd Vermicelli 油豆腐细粉
yóu dòu-fu xì fěn 油豆腐細粉

Dumpling Soup; Won Ton 馄饨
hún-tun 餛飩

Sesame Seed Biscuit 烧饼
shāo-bing(Chinese breakfast) 燒餅

Fried Fluffy Crispy Stick 油条
yóu tiáo (Chinese breakfast) 油條

Soy Bean Milk; Soy Milk 豆浆
dòu jiāng (Chinese breakfast) 豆漿

Sour Bean Milk 豆汁儿
dòu zhīr 豆汁兒

Cold Pea jello Bowl 凉粉儿
liáng fěnr 涼粉兒

Chinese Dumplings
中國帶餡兒麵食

饺子 jiǎo-zi
Boiled Dumplings
A Typical Meal For Northern Chinese

Cut dough into grape sized segments. Flatten them by hand, sprinkle flour and roll them out into discs of approximately 2.5-inch in diameter. Make a filling consisting of ground pork, mutton or beef with salad oil, soy sauce, minced fresh ginger, chopped scallion and MSG, mix with finely chopped vegetable at your choice: cabbage, celery (water squeezed out), leek 韭菜 or pre-fried grated carrots. Hold one dough-disc up in your left palm and place one teaspoon of the filling in the center, fold it to a moon-shape and seal edges tightly with your right hand fingers right in your palm (not on the table). Be sure to sprinkle flour on the tray before placing the dumplings on it (to prevent from sticking).

Ten minutes before serving time, put no more than 20 dumplings at one time in a pot of boiling water, stir gently just preventing them from sticking together or on the bottom (be careful not to break them). Use high heat and cover with lid, when water boils add 1/2 cup of cold water to bring down the temperature and wait till water boils again. Thus, both the skin and stuffing will be cooked. Drain and serve. (Vegetarian filling: ❶ scrambled eggs, pre-boiled spinach, soaked vermicelli and mushrooms plus a handful of potato chips, all chopped. (Vegetarian filling: ❷ Stir-fry in 5 tbs. oil one grated carrot and 1/4 onion till soft, add finely chopped string beans or smashed peas, scramble egg, coriander leaves and crushed potato chips (substitution for 油條 yóu tiáo)
❸ scrambled eggs, leek 韭菜 and dried tiny shrimps or shrimp *sauce*.

(Special filling : Ground pork and 茴香菜 fennel stalks.)
*D*ipping sauce: soy sauce, vinegar, minced garlic and hotsauce.

rolled out flat dough ★ **pí-zi** (See P.254★ **pizza** 披萨)	皮子 皮子	**Fried Spring Roll** **zhá chūn jüǎnr**	炸春卷儿 炸春捲兒
Grilled Leek Pie ★ **jiǔ-cai hé-zi**	韭菜合子 韭菜合子	**Fried triumpling** **zhá sān jiǎor**	炸三角儿 炸三角兒
Grilled Spinach & egg Pie ★ **pó cài jī dàn hé-zi**	菠菜鸡蛋合子 菠菜雞蛋合子	**Horseshoe Dumpling** **huí-tou**	回头 回頭
Shreded Turnip Cake **luó-bo sīr bǐng**	萝卜丝儿饼 蘿蔔絲兒餅	**Ends-meet Dumpling** **dā liánr huǒ-shao**	褡裢儿火烧 褡褳兒火燒

锅贴儿 guō tiēr
Pan-Fried Dumplings

Cut dough into large grape sized segments, follow previous instructions for making boiled dumplings except they're made on the table and only the top part of the dumplings are sealed while both ends are left unsealed. Heat 1 tablespoon of oil in a non-sticky skillet over medium heat, place these dumplings side-by-side in it like sardines (not too close), add 1/4 cup of water with 1 tablespoon of cornstarch in it. Cover with lid and turn the fire low, cook them till water has evaporated and the bottom of the dumplings is lightly brown. (the starch makes the dumplings crispy at the bottom and the steam makes the top part soft). Serve them bottomside up in a platter. Dipping sauce: soy sauce, vinegar, minced garlic and hot sauce.

Suggested Fillings: Add oil to Ground Beef: A. mix with chopped onion. B. with hand smashed frozen peas and some onion. C. with grated carrot (more oil) and some onion. D. with chopped celery including the leaves. E. with chopped Korean Pickles or German Sauerkraut. F. onion and curry. With Ground Pork: A. leek, B. scallion/shrimp, C. string beans, D. cabbage.

牛肉馅儿饼 niú ròu xiànr bǐng
Beijing Beefburger

Make a filling consisting of ground beef with some fat in it, mix well with salad oil, MSG and wine to make it juicy. Add black soy paste 豆瓣酱 (or substitute: soy sauce). Cut dough into segments as large as a small lime, Flatten them by hand and use a rolling pin to roll out into a disk of approximately 4 inches in diameter. Hold the disk up in your palm and place 2 tablespoonfuls of this filling in the center, pull edges up together and seal them tightly on the top to form a ball. Now press the balls flat and place them in a frying pan with 1 tablespoonfuls of oil. Use medium heat and fry both sides until light brown. Serve piping hot.

Method Of Eating: Hold a pair of chopsticks in your right hand and a spoon in your left hand. Pick up the burger with your chopsticks and let it rest straight-up on the spoon as if the spoon were a stand. This will enable you to bite a tiny hole on the burger skin for you to suck the beef juice or letting the exotic tasting juice dumping out into the spoon for you to enjoy.

This way, one can avoid an accident from occurring by inadvertently biting into the burger and making the juice splash onto the other guests.

Attention: Try not to serve them with American ketchup.
Dipping sauce: Soy sauce, vinegar, minced garlic and hotsauce.

烙饼 lào bǐng
Chinese Grilled Flatcake

This is a main staple wheat food for the Northern Chinese. Cut dough into orange sized segments. Flatten each segment by hand. Use the rolling pin and roll it out into a disk of about 9 inches in diameter. Apply lard, shortening or salad oil on top of the dough-disk, sprinkle salt and roll the disk into a long tube and stretch the tube by pulling it out to one foot long, pouring 1 tbs. oil on it, curl it around to form a round disk with the appearance of a curled up snake. Set it aside 5 minutes and roll it out to 9 inches. Grill with 2 tbs. oil till light brown. (Setting dough aside is called "醒面 dough awakening", this action is to stop the dough from shrinking back after each rolling out. This procedure infuses the 烙饼 Lào Bǐng layers with good taste) Wrap the piping hot Flatcake in a paper towel and crush it with force before serving it in a basket. Tastes best with scrambled eggs, cold cuts or any other stir-fried vegetable dishes.

Loosened Crisp Flatcake	抓饼	
zhuā bǐng	抓餅	
Flatcake By catty	斤饼	
jīn bǐng	斤餅	
Striped Flatcake Sauté	肉丝烩饼	
ròu sī huì bǐng	肉絲燴餅	
Egg Flatcake	蛋饼	
dàn bǐng	蛋餅	
Egg Fried Striped Flatcake	蛋炒饼	
dàn chǎo bǐng	蛋炒餅	
Pork Fried Striped Flatcake	肉丝炒饼	
ròu sī chǎo bǐng	肉絲炒餅	
Mung bean pancake/yóu tiáo	煎饼卷油条	
jiān-bing jüǎn yóu tiáo	煎餅捲油條	
Sesame Cake / cold cut meat	烧饼夹肉	
shāo-bing jiá ròu	燒餅夾肉	
★**Beihai Sesame Cake Burger**	北海肉末烧饼	
Bé-Hǎi Ròu Mòr Shāo-bing	北海肉末燒餅	

葱花儿饼 Cōng Huār Bǐng
Scallion Flatcake

Put 3 tbsp. medium gluten flour in a bowl, add 1/4 cup of water and stir with chopsticks very fast, add more flour to make it a very soft piece of dough (for 2 cakes). Add 1 tbs . oil and stir well, cover it with lid and let it rest 5 minutes.

Roll one out with rolling pin to an 8-inch disk, apply 1 1/2 tbs. lard, shortening or oil on the surface, sprinkle 1/3 cup each finely chopped green onion and raw bacon, add salt and roll it up to a long tube. Then curl it up to a disk, apply 1 tbs. oil on it, roll it out again (or hand-flatten it in a plastic bag) Grill it in 1 tbs. lard.

★*Regular Cōng Huār Bǐng uses "網油 wǎng yóu" (a net formed sheet-fat from pork intestines). which is hardly found in supermarket. Using Bacon for substitution is Marco's Invention.*

Chinese Hot-dough Food
中國燙麵食品

烫面 Tàng Miàn
Precooked Hot-dough

When unleavened-dough dumplings are cooked in a steamer instead of in boiling water, the steam cannot supply enough moisture to penetrate the dough to make it soft, elastic and chewy like if they were boiled in water. The ancient Chinese discovered a method to precook the dough by pouring 2/3 cup of boiling water all at once onto 1/2 lb. all-purpose flour in a bowl. Then mixing it vigorously and add more flour to make it a piece of half-cooked soft dough. Then, shape the dough to a ball and cover it with a damp cloth , set aside and let it cool off.

The following dumplings are steamed and served in a "蒸笼 steaming bamboo basket" and are made with this kind of unleavened Hot-dough.

Hot-dough Dumpling	烫面饺儿	
Tàng Mèn Jiǎor	燙麵餃兒	
Hot-dough Shrimp Dumpling	虾仁蒸饺儿	
Xiā Rén Zhēng jiǎor	蝦仁蒸餃兒	
Hot-dough Yellow Croaker Dp.	黄鱼蒸饺儿	
Huáng Yǔ Zhēng Jiǎor	黃魚蒸餃兒	
Hot-dough Sea Slug Dumpling	三鲜蒸饺儿	
Sān Xiān Zhēng Jiǎor	三鮮蒸餃兒	
Hot-dough Pork Dumpling	猪肉蒸饺儿	
Zhū Ròu Zhēng Jiǎor	豬肉蒸餃兒	
Hot-dough Beef Dumpling	牛肉蒸饺儿	
Niú Ròu Zhēng Jiǎor	牛肉蒸餃兒	
Hot-dough Vegetarian Dumpling	素蒸饺儿	
Sù Zhēng Jiǎor	素蒸餃兒	
Steamed Shāo-mai	烧卖	
Shāo-mai	燒賣	

薄饼 bó bǐng
Extra-thin Doilycakes

Shape **Hot-dough** into a long sausage of about 1 ½ inch in diameter. Cut dough into 1-inch size segments. Flatten each segment by hand, brush one side of each segment with oil and place one segment on top of another with oiled sides facing each other (to prevent the two pieces of dough from sticking together when cooking)

Flatten each pair of segments by hand. Using a rolling pin and roll it out into a disk of about 5 to 9 inches in diameter. *(for different type of meals)*

Grill Doilycakes over medium low heat one minute on each side oil free.

春餅

(Stack Doilycakes in a napkin lined bowl with cover. Separate each cake into two extra-thin cakes when Serving).

春饼 Chūn Bǐng
Spring Festival Rolls

This is a special meal served during the Spring Festival Days which marks the change of seasons. Use the 9-inch extra thin Doilycakes as a wrapper to fix your own Spring Rolls at a family luncheon.

At least ten different kinds of cold cuts including pot-roast pork, liver, pig heart, smoked chicken, large intestines, pig ear, stewed pork shoulder & fancy sausages are finely shredded and rotating on the lazy Susan, plus many stir-fried vegetable (all in shreads) dishes.

The following are some recommended stir-fry dishes that can be wrapped into the wrapper other then scrambled eggs.

leftovers **shèng cài**	剩菜 剩菜
Shreded Pork in Soy Paste **jīng jiàng ròu sī**	京酱肉丝 京醬肉絲
Stir-fried Spinach **chǎo bō cài**	炒菠菜 炒菠菜
Fried shredded Chinese cabbage **sù chǎo bái cài sīr**	素炒白菜丝儿 素炒白菜絲兒
Shredded Pork and Celery **ròu sī chǎo qín cài**	肉丝炒芹菜 肉絲炒芹菜
Stir-fried Pork Shreads/Chives **jiǔ huáng ròu sī**	韭黄肉丝 韭黄肉絲
Pork and Fongus Omelet **chǎo mù xū ròu**	炒木须肉 炒木須肉
Stir-fried Vegetables **chǎo hé cài**	炒合菜 炒合菜
Hé Cài Wearing A Hat **hé cài dài màor**	合菜带帽兒 合菜带帽兒

炒合菜 chǎo hé cài
Stir Fried Assorted Vegetables

Under high heat, in 3 tbs. oil, quick stir-fry the mixture of (1/2 cup finely shredded pork tenderloin, 1 tbs. Soy sauce, 1 tbs. wine and 1/2 tsp. corn starch). Stir one minute, add ½ cup of finely shredded green onion and remove it into a bowl for further use. *(The corn starch seals the meat juice under sudden high heat for tenderness)*

Use same wok, high heat with 3 tbs. oil, stir fry minced garlic, fresh ginger, shredded mushroom and mixed leafy vegetables (such as: spinach, celery cabbage, fresh bean sprouts, leek…etc.) add salt, MSG, pepper *(only one or two minutes, never overcook the vegetables)* Then pour back the cooked meat plus 1/2 cup of pre-boiled vermicelli "細粉 xì fěn" and mix well with chopsticks

合菜带帽儿 Hé Cài Dài Màor
Fried Vegetables Wearing a Hat

Chinese usually serve the above dish topped with a large scallio omelet, and call it "dài màor" which means "wearing a hat". This addition of "the hat" really enhances the taste of this dish.

The Wrapper for Beijing Duck

The usages of the hot-dough to make various kinds of wheat food are many. One of the popular usages of the extra-thin double-layer flatcakes is the 5-inch Doilycake with which to wrap the world famous Beijing Duck. They are well-suited for the purpose, because of their softness, elasticity and chewiness.

北京烤鸭 Běi Jīng Kǎo Yā
Beijing Duck

The proper way of eating Beijing Duck: *Put one or two slices of crispy Beijing Duck's "Skin" on a 5-inch extra thin Doilycake, dip one or two sticks of 3-inch sections of the white part of "山東 Shān Dōng scallion" into the Duck Sauce, and wrap them all together. With just one single bite, you'll be floating out of this world.*
The Duck Sauce consists of sweet bean paste, honey and sesame oil.

What is the reason the Chinese gourmets eat only the duck's skin and are not particularly interested in the meat? and why does the skin have to have a litte fat attached to it when wrapped in the Doilycake? Please ask the Russian gourmets why oily caviar is served on a cracker?

What's the damage?

When ordering a Beijing Ducks in a restaurant, even though the ducks have been already air-blown, sewed and sealed, and are hanging there air-drying, a 30 to 35-minute roasting time is still required prior to each order.

Beijing Ducks are not cooked in an oven, they are hung on hooks and charcoal broiled in a closed chamber with countless times of honey and oil brushings.

While the bird is piping hot, an experienced chef slices off its skin (no lean meat attached) in front of you and your guests in less than three minutes.

A whole duck gives you only two or three plates of the "skin" with one duck head in a separate plate. As the dinner goes on, duck heads are kept adding and gathered on to the same plate placed on the side table. They are not for you to eat, they are simply to figure out your bill.

Beijing Duck 3-way	烤鸭三吃	**Duck Meat /Bean Sprouts**	鸭油炒掐菜
kǎo yā sān chī	烤鴨三吃	**yā yóu chǎo qiā cài**	鴨油炒掐菜
Duck-fat Scrambled Eggs	鸭油溜黄菜	**Scallion-white/Duck Sauce**	葱白蘸甜面酱
yā yóu liū huáng cài	鴨油溜黃菜	**cōng bái zhàn tián miàn jiàng**	蔥白蘸甜麵醬

鸭架子熬白菜 Yā Jià-zi Ao Bái Cài
Duck-bone & Cabbage Stew

Usually the remains of the duck are wrapped for you to take home. To eat it cold. But most people cut it up and stew it with a large head of cabbage to make a tasty stew, or cook it with rice into a congee.

Chinese Sweet Dishes
中國甜點

Chinese only use assorted fruits and green tea for dessert. The following sweet dishes are served between meat dishes as one of the main courses.

In a 12 or 14 course banquet, usually there are two courses of sweet dishes, and the purpose of doing so is to have the sweet courses provide a break, giving the guests a sparkle of fresh taste, and helping them to continue to enjoy the remaining dishes that follow.

Even though the dishes are sweet, they are never served at the end of a meal as the Westerners do with their desserts.

Mashed Jujube Birth-cake **zǎo nír shòu táo**	枣泥儿寿桃 棗泥兒壽桃	
Steamed Red Bean Bun **dòu shā bāor**	豆沙包儿 豆沙包兒	
Hot Banana Candy **bá sī xiāng jiāo**	拔丝香蕉 拔絲香蕉	
Lotus Seed Soup **lián zǐ tāng**	莲子汤 蓮子湯	
Silver Fungus Soup **bīng táng yín ěr tāng**	冰糖银耳汤 冰糖銀耳湯	
Bird's Nest Soup **yàn wō tāng**	燕窝汤 燕窩湯	
Almond Jello Soup **xìng rénr dòu-fu**	杏仁儿豆腐 杏仁兒豆腐	
Lichee and Jujube Soup **guì yuán hóng zǎor tāng**	桂圆红枣儿汤 桂圓紅棗兒湯	
8-Jewel Pudding **bā bǎor fàn**	八宝儿饭 八寶兒飯	
All-Grain and Bean Congee **là bār zhōu**	腊八儿粥 臘八兒粥	

八宝儿饭
Bā Bǎor Fàn

8-Jewel Pudding

Line and arrange nicely the bottom and sides of a large bowl, with 8 kinds of preserved fruits, such as preserved cherry, green plum, yellow colored dehydrated pineapple, black dried lichee, maroon colored Chinese date, white lotus seed and raisins for decoration. First put half the amount of the presoaked (one hour) glutinous rice, then add 1/2 cup of Sweet Red Bean Paste *(豆沙 Dòu Shā)* as a filling in the center and cover with remaining rice. Add one cup of water, 1/8 cup each of shortening and sugar, and steam the pudding for 1/2 hour.
Unmold it upside down onto a platter.

Rice Stuffed Lotus Root jiāng mí ǒu	江米藕 江米藕	Fried Full-moon Dumpling zhá yuán xiāo	炸元宵 炸元宵
Thousand-layer rice cake yǔn piàn gāo	云片糕 雲片糕	Jujube Puree Flowery Cake zǎo nír hūa gāo	枣泥儿花糕 棗泥兒花糕
Altar Honey-bar Pagoda mì gòng	蜜供 蜜供	Honeyed Fritter sà qí mǎ	萨其马 薩其馬
Osmanthus Rice-ball Soup guì huā tāng yüán	桂花汤圆 桂花湯圓	Almond Cookie xìng rénr sū	杏仁儿酥 杏仁兒酥
Fermented Rice-ball Soup jiǔ niàng tāng yüán	酒酿汤圆 酒釀湯圓	Moon Cake yüè bǐng	月饼 月餅
New Year Cake nián gāo	年糕 年糕	Beijing Moon Cake fān māor yüè-bing	翻毛儿月饼 翻毛兒月餅
Fried New Year Cake zhá nián gāo	炸年糕 炸年糕	Guǎng Dōng Moon Cake Guǎng Dōng yüè-bing	广东月饼 廣東月餅
Full-moon Dumpling yüán xiāo	元宵 元宵	Hot Yam Candy bá sī shān-yao	拔丝山药 拔絲山藥

拔丝山药
Hot Yam Candy

Cut yam into 1-inch irregular chunks and deep fry them till golden brown (just like French Fries). Drain and set aside for further use. Place 1 cup of sugar and 4 tablespoons of water in a wok and heat over low heat till sugar is melted. Add 1/2 cup salad oil and stir till water evaporates and mixture becomes the consistency of liquid candy. Put the deep fried yam back in the wok, mix well, and then pour the entire content of the wok into a large bowl. Serve immediately with a side bowl of ice water.

EATING METHOD:One guest uses his chopsticks to take a piece of the candy-coated yam out of the liquid candy bowl (the hot oil will keep the candy in a liquid state). While he is lifting the yam, a thread-like trail is forming, the guest sitting next to him is supposed to hit the trail with his chopsticks and break it. The first guest puts his piece of yam right into the ice water and let it harden and eat.

Mung Bean Cake lǜ dòu gāo	绿豆糕 綠豆糕	Donkey Rolling lú dá gǔnr	驴打滚儿 驢打滾兒
Yellow Pea-flour Cake wān dòu huángr	豌豆黄儿 豌豆黃兒	Chilled Glutinous Balls ài wō-wo	艾窝窝 艾窩窩
Egg Roll dàn jüǎnr	蛋卷儿 蛋捲兒	Haw Jelly shān-zha gāo	山楂糕 山楂糕

Tea & Chitchatting
飲茶與聊天兒

Most of the times Chinese sweet dishes are served with a pot of hot tea as a 24-hour conversational snack, and sometimes even salty dishes such as dumplings of all kinds and noodles are also served, especially for midnight snacks.

having tea **yǐn chá**	饮茶 飲茶	**weak tea** **dàn chá**	淡茶 淡茶
chat **liáo tiānr**	聊天儿 聊天兒	**plumade** **suān méi tāng**	酸梅汤 酸梅湯
brew tea **qī chá**	沏茶 沏茶	**Sweetmeats; Preserved Fruit** 蜜饯 **mì jiàn**　　　蜜餞	
green tea leaves **lù chá**	绿茶 綠茶	**Dehydrated Peach** **táo fǔ**	桃脯 桃脯
black tea **hóng chá**	红茶 紅茶	**Dehydrated Apricot** **xìng fǔ**	杏脯 杏脯
jasmine tea **xiāng piàn** (mò-li huā chá)	香片 香片（茉莉花茶）	**Candied jujube** **jīn sī mì zǎor**	金丝蜜枣儿 金絲蜜棗兒
ginseng tea **rén shēn chá**	人参茶 人參茶	**Fried Sweet Cashew** **mì zhī yāo guǒr**	蜜汁腰果儿 蜜汁腰果兒
chrysanthemum tea **jú huā chá**	菊花茶 菊花茶	**Mongolian Milk Jello** **nǎi làor**	奶酪儿 奶酪兒
oolong tea **wū lóng chá**	乌龙茶 烏龍茶	**Sugarcoated Haw on stick** 冰糖葫芦儿 **bīng táng hú-lur**　冰糖葫蘆兒	
milk tea with pearls **zhēn zhū nǎi chá**	珍珠奶茶 珍珠奶茶	**Guān Dōng Malt Candy** **guān dōng táng**	关东糖 關東糖
More Beverages (飲料) **in 13B**		**Glutinous Rice Sweet Sticks**江米条儿 **jīang mí tiáor**　江米條兒	
strong tea **nóng chá**	浓茶 濃茶	**Barbecued Porkpaper** 炭烤薄肉干儿 **tàn kǎo bó ròu gānr** 炭烤薄肉乾兒	
dilute **chōng dàn**	冲淡 沖淡	★**Dehydrated Porkstrips** 肉脯 **ròu fǔ** (see p.205 ★ 肉鬆;肉絨) 肉脯	

★ **Pork Jerky** 猪肉干儿
  zhū ròu gānr 豬肉乾兒

★ **Beef Jerky** (see p.205 ★ 肉鬆;肉絨) 牛肉干儿
  niú ròu gānr 牛肉乾兒

Sugar Roasted Chestnuts **táng chǎo lì-zi**	糖炒栗子 糖炒栗子
Chestnut flour Cake **Lì-zi Miànr Wō Tóu**	栗子面儿窝头 栗子麵兒窩頭
Peanuts With Shell **dài kér huā shēng**	带壳儿花生 帶殼兒花生
Five-spice Peanuts **wǔ xiāng huā shēng rénr**	五香花生仁儿 五香花生仁兒
Five-spice Watermelon Seeds **wǔ xiāng guā zǐr**	五香瓜子儿 五香瓜子兒
Pumpkin Seeds **nán guā zǐ**	南瓜子 南瓜子
Sunflower Seeds **kuí huā zǐ**	葵花子 葵花子
Bamboo Shoot Soybean **sǔn dòur**	笋豆儿 筍豆兒
Rocklike Broad Bean **tiě cán dòu; bèng dòur**	铁蚕豆;蹦豆儿 鐵蠶豆;蹦豆兒
Fried crispy Broad Bean **sū zhá cán dòu**	酥炸蚕豆 酥炸蠶豆
Five-spice Dry Bean Curd **wǔ xiāng dòu gān**	五香豆干 五香豆干
Preserved Pine Seed **táng sōng zǐr**	糖松子儿 糖松子兒
Preserved Lotus Seed **táng lián zǐ**	糖莲子 糖蓮子
Fortune Cookie **xìng ùn qiān-bing**	幸运签饼 幸運籤餅

Dear Mr. Liang:

Thank you very much for your letter of April the 1ˢᵗ. I am sorry that I did not receive your kind gift of beef jerky. Perhaps someone else is now enjoying it, I'm sorry to say.

I would like very much to come to Taiwan and indeed planned to do so until other pressing affairs kept me in this country for some time.

As to opinion about my book, favorable or not, they do not concern me one-way or the other. I write freely, and as I wish.

Again thanking you, I am

Sincerely yours,

Pearl S. Buck

Pearl S. Buck
賽珍珠

★ **I 've just brewed some jasmine tea.**
我刚泡了一壶香片。
wǒ gāng pào-le yì hú xiāng piàn

★ **What kind of tea is it? It's delicous.**
这是什么茶？好好喝！
zhè shì shé-me chá? háo hǎo hē!

★ **This tea is a little too strong for me.**
这个茶有点儿太浓。
zhèi-ge chá yóu diǎnr tài nóng

★ **The fragrance of the tea is really nice.**
这个茶好香！
zhèi-ge chá hǎo xiāng

★ **I won't spoil good Chinese tea with sugar.**
昂贵的好茶我才不会加糖呢。
áng guì-de hǎo chá wǒ cái bú huì jiā táng-ne

★ **Never use lemon and sugar in jesmin tea.**
香片从来不加柠檬和糖的！
xiāng piàn cóng lái bù jiā níng méng hé tang-de

★ **We'll use the demitasse.**
咱们今儿个用小茶杯喝茶。
zán-me jīnr-ge yòng xiǎo chá bēi hē chá

★ **What a beautiful set of bone china.**
这套江西瓷真是没话说。*(白骨瓷 bái gǔ cí)*
zhèi tào Jiāng Xī cí zhēn-shi méi huà shuō

Long Time No See

25B

老没見了

1. **Long time no see.**
   老没见了！
   lǎo méi jiàn-le

2. **What a surprise!**
   真没想到！
   zhēn méi xiǎng dào

3. **Look! Which wind blew you in?**
   你看！哪阵风把你吹来了？
   nǐ kàn! nǎ-zhen fēngr bá nǐ chuī-lai-le?

4. **Right. It's been seven years.**
   是呀！一晃儿七年了。
   shì-ya! yí huàngr qī nián-le.

5. **You haven't changed a bit.**
   你一点儿都没变。
   nǐ yì diǎnr dōu méi biàn

6. **You've lost some weight.**
   妳瘦了！
   nǐ shòu-le.

7. **I've gained a lot of weight.**
   我胖了一圈儿。
   wǒ pàng-le yì qüānr

8. **You look just fine. How's Jack?**
   你气色好好。 Jack 好吗？
   nǐ qì-se háo hǎo. Jack hǎo-ma?

9. **We're divorced.**
   我们离婚了！
   wǒ-men lí hūn-le!

10. **What a pity!**
    好可怜！
    háo kě lián

11. **We have nothing in common.**
    我们没有共同嗜好。
    wǒ-men méi yǒu gòng tóng shì hào

12. **What are you up to?**
    你在忙甚麼？
    nǐ zài máng shén-me

13. **We just got married last year in May.**
    我们去年五月才结婚。
    wǒ-men qù-nian wǔ yüè cái jié hūn.

14. **How's married life?**
    婚後生活如何？
    hūn hòu shēng huó rú hé？

15. **Nothing to complain.**
    毫无怨言。
    háo wú yüàn yán.

16. **I wished I hadn't.**
    後悔莫及。
    hòu huǐ mò jí

17. **My wife is pregnant.**
    我太太有喜了！
    wǒ tài-tai yóu xǐ-le!

18. **She is 4-month pregnant.**
    她怀了四个月的孕了！
    tā huái-le sì-ge yüè-de yùn-le!

19. **She is due to delivery this week.**
    她这个星期就要生了！
    tā zhè-ge xīng qí jiù-yao shēng-le!

20. **Her daughter is pretty!**
    她女儿蛮漂亮的！
    tā nǚ-er mán piào-liang-de!

21. **She is cute.**
    她好秀气。
    tā hǎo xiù-qi.

22. **She is adorable!**
    她好可愛！
    tā háo kě ài

23. He will be four in May.
他今年五月就满四岁了。
tā jīn-nian wǔ yuè jiù mǎn sì suì-le.

24. She has just turned six.
她才刚满六岁。
tā cái gāng mǎn liù suì.

25. My twin boys are 18 months old.
我的双胞胎儿子一岁半
wǒ-de shuāng bāo tāi ér-zi yí suì bàn.

26. He's handsome.
他长得很俊！
tā zhǎng-de hěn jùn!

27. He's tall for his age.
他长得好高！
tā zhǎng-de hǎo gāo.

28. He has his mother's eyes.
他眼睛像他妈！
tā yǎn-jing xiàng tā mā!

29. His quick-temper takes after his father.
他的爆脾气随他爸爸！
tā-de bào pí-chi suí-ta bà-ba!

30. He is in the seventh grade.
他今年国中一年级。
tā jīn nián guó zhōng yì nián jí

31. She'll graduate in June.
（他她它）六月就毕业了。
tā liù yuè jiù bì yè-le

32. He's always in the top threes.
他在班上老是前三名。
tā zài bān-shang lǎo shì qián sān míng.

33. He's extremely smart.
他是聪明绝顶！
tā-shi cōng míng jüé dǐng!

34. Like father like son.
有其父必有其子
yǒu qí fù bì yǒu qí zǐ

35. He's husky.
他长得很结实！
tā zhǎng-de hěn jiē-shi!

36. Hi, there, can I join you guys?
嘿！我可以跟你们一块儿坐吗？
wǒ ké-yi gēn nǐ-men yì kuàir zuò-ma?

37. Of course, we were just chatting.
当然！我们只在聊天儿。
dāng rán! wǒ-men zhǐ-zai liáo tiānr

38. Sure, pull up a chair and sit down.
当然可以！拉把椅子坐下。
dāng rán ké yǐ!   lā-ba yǐ-zi zuò xià.

39. What's new?
有什么新鲜事儿吗？
yǒu shé-me xīn xiān shìr-ma?

40. Guess what? Marie is in town!
你猜怎样？ Marie 回来了！
nǐ cāi zěn yàng? Marie lái-le!

41. I was supposed to meet her here.
我们讲好了在这儿碰面。
wǒ-men jiáng hǎo-le zài zhèr pèng miàn

42. Speak of the devil
说曹操，曹操就到。
shuī cáo-cao, cáo-cao jiù dào.

43. I'm sorry for being late.
抱歉我来晚了。
bào qiàn wǒ lái wǎn-le

44. It was crowded on the bus.
公车里好挤。
gōng chē-li háo jǐ

45. It was jam packed in the streets.
街上塞车。
jiē-shang sāi chē

46. My car broke down.
我车抛锚了。
wǒ chē pāo máo-le

47. You are right on time.
你很准时。
ní hén zhǔn shí

48. You are in time for watermelon.
来得真巧我们正在切西瓜。
lái-de zhēn qiǎo wǒ-men zhèng-zai qiē xī guā

49. How have you been?
你近来可好？
nǐ jìn lái ké hǎo?

50. I've been fine, and you?
托福，托福！您呢?
tuō fú, tuō fú!   nín-ne?

51. **Where have you been?**
你跑到哪儿去了？
ní pǎo-dao nǎr qù-le?

52. **I have been in Japan for fifteen years.**
我一直在日本待了十五年。
wǒ yì zhí zài Rì Běn dāi-le shí wǔ nián.

53. **No wonder!**
难怪！
nán guài.

54. **Is this a business trip or for pleasure?**
你这次是出差，还是来玩儿的？
nǐ zhè cì shì chū chā, hái-shi lái wánr-de

55. **It's a combination of both.**
两样儿都有。
liǎng yàngr dōu yǒu

56. **I want you to meet my colleague, Joe.**
我给你介绍一下我的同事，Joe。
wǒ géi-ni jiè shào yí xià wǒ-de tóng shì, Joe

57. **Hi, there!**
你好！
ní hǎo！

68. **I've heard so much about you.**
久闻大名！
jiǔ wén dà míng!

59. **Nice meeting you.**
幸会！
xìng huì!

60. **I've been away for twelve years now.**
我离开这儿已经十二年了。
wǒ lí-kai zhèr yǐ-jing shí èr nián-le.

61. **I'm dying for a bowl of beef noodles.**
我巴不得想吃碗牛肉面。
wǒ bā-bu dé xiǎng chī-wan niú ròu miàn.

62. **Let's get together sometime next week.**
咱们下礼拜哪一天聚一聚。
zán-me xià lǐ bài nǎ-yi tiān jù-yi jù.

63. **Lunch at my house, Sunday.**
星期日中午在我家吃饭。
xíng qí rì zhōng-wu zài wǒ jiā chī fàn

64. **How are the Liangs?**
梁家一家人都还好吧？
Liáng-jia yì jiā rén dōu hái hǎo-ba?

65. **I haven't seen Bill for years.**
我好几年没看见 Bill 了。
wǒ háo-ji nián méi kàn-jian Bill-le.

66. **He has been abroad.**
他一直都在国外。
tā yì zhí dōu zài guó wài.

67. **My two kids have kept me busy enough.**
我两个孩子就够我忙的了。
wó liǎng-ge hái-zi jiù gòu wǒ máng-de-le

68. **It's so hot out there.**
外边儿好热。
wài biānr hǎo rè

69. **That plumade really hit the spot.**
这杯酸梅汤可真解渴。
zhè bēi suān méi tāng kě zhēn jié kě

70. **Would you like a piece of cheesecake?**
你要来块儿乳酪蛋糕吗？
nǐ yào lái kuàir rǔ luò dàn gāo-ma?

71. **I'm on a diet.**
我在减肥。
wǒ zài jiǎn féi.

72. **I'd like a diet Coke, please.**
我想来杯无糖可乐。
wó xiǎng lái-bei wú táng kě lè.

73. **I'd like a cup of decaf coffee.**
我要一杯不含咖啡因的咖啡。
wǒ yào yì bēi bù hán kā fēi yīn-de kā fēi

74. **Would you like a refill?**
再给您续加一点儿咖啡吧？
zài gěi nín xù jiā yì diǎnr kā fēi-ba?

75. **Coffee keeps me awake at night.**
我喝咖啡睡不著觉？
wǒ hē kā-fei shuì-bu zháo jiào

76. **Coffee doesn't bother me at all.**
我喝咖啡照睡不误。
wǒ hē kā fēi zhào shuì bú wù.

77. **Time flies!**
时间过得好快！
shí jiān guò-de hǎo kuài!

78. **It's getting dark. I've got to go.**
天快黑了。我得要走了。
tiān kuài hēi-le. wó děi-yao zǒu-le.

Western Entrees
西餐主菜

western dishes **xī cài**	西菜 西菜	**Hamburger Steak** **jiǎo niú ròu cān pái**	绞牛肉餐排 絞牛肉餐排
French cuisine **Fà Guó pēng rèn**	法国烹饪 法國烹飪	**Round Steak** **xiǎo niú tuǐ pái**	小牛腿排 小牛腿排
entrée; main course **zhǔ cài**	主菜 主菜	**rump steak** **tún ròu niú pái**	臀肉牛排 臀肉牛排
à la carte **líng diǎn cài dān**	零点菜单 零點菜單	**Chateaubriand** **Fà Guó shì hòu niú pái**	法国式厚牛排 法國式厚牛排
Broiled Lobster **jú kǎo lóng xiā**	焗烤龙虾 焗烤龍蝦	**Surf and Turf** **hǎi xiān niú pái dà cān**	海鲜牛排大餐 海鮮牛排大餐
Broiled Prawn **jú míng xiā**	焗明虾 焗明蝦	**Roast Prime Ribs** **kǎo shàng xuǎn lè gǔ ròu**	烤上选肋骨肉 烤上選肋骨肉
Deep Fried Shrimp **zhá dà xiā**	炸大虾 炸大蝦	**Chicken-fried Steak** **jiāo zhá zhū pái**	焦炸猪排 焦炸豬排
French Fried Sole **jiāo zhá yǔ pái**	焦炸鱼排 焦炸魚排	**Tenderloin Pork Steak** **dà zhū pái**	大猪排 大豬排
beef steak **niú pái**	牛排 牛排	**Pork Chops/ apple sauce** **zhū pái/ píng guǒ jiàng**	猪排/苹果酱 豬排/蘋果醬
Veal Cutlet **xiǎo niú nèn pái**	小牛嫩排 小牛嫩排	**Sauerkraut** (与德国猪脚共食) **Dé Guó suān cài**	德国酸菜 德國酸菜
Fillet Mignon **fēi lì niú pái**	菲力牛排 菲力牛排	**German Hocks** **Dé Guó zhū jiǎo**	德国猪脚 德國豬腳
New York Steak **Niǔ Yuē niú pái**	纽约牛排 紐約牛排	**Broiled Lamb Chop** **shāo kǎo yáng pái**	烧烤羊排 燒烤羊排
Sirloin Steak **shàng yāo niú pái**	上腰牛排 上腰牛排	**Shish Kebab** **kǎo yáng ròu chuàn**	烤羊肉串 烤羊肉串
T-bone Steak **dīng gǔ niú pái**	丁骨牛排 丁骨牛排	**Roast Chicken** **kǎo jī**	烤鸡 烤雞
Tenderloin Steak **yāo ròu pái**	腰肉排 腰肉排	**Roast Turkey/cranberry sauce** **káo huǒ jī/ hóng méi jiàng**	烤火鸡/红莓酱 烤火雞/紅莓醬

Turkey Gizzard Dressing **huǒ jī zhēn gān tián xiàn**	火鸡胗肝填馅 火雞胗肝填餡	**Barbequed Beef** **huó kǎo niú ròu**	火烤牛肉 火烤牛肉
Pot Roast Pork/gravy **mèn kǎo zhū ròu /lǔ-zi**	闷烤猪肉/卤子 悶烤豬肉/鹵子	**Barbequed Pork** **huó kǎo zhū ròu**	火烤猪肉 火烤豬肉
Pot Roast Beef/gravy **mèn kǎo niú ròu/lǔ-zi**	闷烤牛肉/卤子 悶烤牛肉/鹵子	**Bar-B-Q Spareribs** **huó kǎo zhū pái-gu**	火烤猪排骨 火烤豬排骨
Grilled Ham Steak **huó tuǐ pái**	火腿排 火腿排	**Spaghetti & Meat Balls** **Yì shì wán-zi miàn**	义式丸子面 義式丸子麵
Calf Liver Steak **xiǎo niú gān pái**	小牛肝排 小牛肝排	**Spaghetti & Meat Sauce** **Yì shì ròu jiàng miàn**	义式肉酱面 義式肉醬麵
Southern Fried Chicken **Měi shì zhá jī**	美式炸鸡 美式炸雞	**Spaghetti Seafood** **Yì Dà Lì hǎi xiān miàn**	义大利海鲜面 義大利海鮮麵
Chicken Stew **xī shì dùn jī**	西式炖鸡 西式燉雞	**Black Spaghetti Inkfish** **Yì Dà Lì mò yǔ miàn**	义大利墨鱼面 義大利墨魚麵
Chicken Curry **gā-li jī**	咖哩鸡 咖哩雞	**Baked Cheese Macaroni** **rǔ luò kǎo tōng xī fǎn**	乳酪烤通心粉 乳酪烤通心粉
Beef Curry **gā-li niú ròu**	咖哩牛肉 咖哩牛肉	**Lasagna** **Yì Dà Lì qiān céng miàn**	义大利千层面 義大利千層麵
Portuguese Chicken **Pú shì pá jī**	葡式扒鸡 葡式扒雞	**Tortilini** **yì dà lì hún-tun**	义大利馄饨 義大利餛飩
Deep Fried Fish Steak **jiāo zhá yǔ pái**	焦炸鱼排 焦炸魚排	**Calzone** **yì dà lì hé-zi**	义大利合子 義大利合子
Smoked Pomfret **yān xǔn chāng yú**	烟熏鲳鱼 煙燻鯧魚	**Pepperoni/olive Pizza** **xiāng-chang gán lǎn pī sà**	香肠橄榄披萨 香腸橄欖披薩
Halibut Steak **bǐ mù yǔ pái**	比目鱼排 比目魚排	**Shrimp/mushroom Pizza** **xiā rén xiāng-gu pī sà**	虾仁香菇披萨 蝦仁香菇披薩
Breaded Filet of Sole **jiāo zhá dié yǔ pái**	焦炸鲽鱼排 焦炸鰈魚排	**Anchovy and Olive Pizza** **yín yǔ gán lǎn pī sà**	银鱼橄榄披萨 銀魚橄欖披薩
Filet of Cod **xüě yǔ pái**	鳕鱼排 鱈魚排	**Pineapple/Ham Pizza** **bō luó huó tuǐ pī sà**	菠萝火腿披萨 菠蘿火腿披薩
Seafood Volauvent **sū pí hǎi xiān**	酥皮海鲜 酥皮海鮮	**Salami Pizza** **xǔn niú ròu piàn pī sà**	熏牛肉片披萨 燻牛肉片披薩
Hungarian Goulash **Xiōng Yá Lì dùn niú ròu**	匈牙利炖牛肉 匈牙利燉牛肉	**Smoked Oyster Pizza** **xǔn mǔ lì pī sà**	熏牡蛎披萨 燻牡蠣披薩
Beef Stew **dùn niú ròu**	炖牛肉 燉牛肉	**Beef and Onion Pizza** **niú ròu yáng cōng pī sà**	牛肉洋葱披萨 牛肉洋蔥披薩
Smothered Chicken **Měi shí dùn jī**	美式炖鸡 美式燉雞	**Beef /Bell pepper Pizza** **niú ròu qīng jiāo pī sà**	牛肉青椒披萨 牛肉青椒披薩
Lamb Stew **dùn yáng ròu**	炖羊肉 燉羊肉	**Vegetarian Pizza** **sù pī sà**	素披萨 素披薩

Hors D'oeuvres & Appetizers
酒菜與開胃小吃

hors d'oeuvre jī wéi jiǔ xiǎo chī	鸡尾酒小吃 雞尾酒小吃	
caviar yǔ zǐ jiàng	鱼子酱 魚子醬	
Stuffed Celery/Cream Cheese rǔ luò ràng qín cài	乳酪瓢芹菜 乳酪瓢芹菜	
Chilled Sticks of Carrot bīng zhèn hú luó-bo tiáo	冰镇胡萝卜条 冰鎮胡蘿蔔條	
Chicken Salad Spread jī róng xiáo diǎn-xin	鸡蓉小点心 雞蓉小點心	
Potato Chip/Avocado Dip yáng yù piàn è lí jiàng	洋芋片鳄梨酱 洋芋片鱷梨醬	
Smoked Salmon Rolls xǔn guī yǔ jüǎnr	熏鲑鱼卷儿 燻鮭魚捲兒	
Deviled Eggs dàn huāng ràng yüán dàn	蛋黄瓢原蛋 蛋黃瓢原蛋	
Herring in Sour Cream suān nǎi yóu qīng yǔ	酸奶油鲭鱼 酸奶油鯖魚	
Goose Liver Canapés é gān jiàng xiǎo xián diǎn	鹅肝酱小咸点 鵝肝醬小鹹點	
Anchovy & Cheese Canapés tí yǔ xiǎo xián diǎn	鳀鱼小咸点 鯷魚小鹹點	
Cocktail Canapés Fà Guó shí jǐn xiǎo xián diǎn	法国什锦小咸点 法國什錦小鹹點	
Finger Sandwich mí nǐ sān míng zhì	迷你三明治 迷你三明治	
Raw Oysters shàng xǔǎn shēng háo	上选生蚝 上選生蠔	

Appetizers

appetizer kāi wèi xiǎo chī	开胃小吃 開胃小吃	
cold cuts lěng pānr	冷盘儿 冷盤兒	
Assorted Cold Cuts shí jín lěng pánr	什锦冷盘儿 什錦冷盤兒	
Sea-food Cocktail hǎi xiān zhōng	海鲜盅 海鮮盅	
Crab Meat Cocktail xiè ròu zhōng	蟹肉盅 蟹肉盅	
Shrimp Cocktail xiā rén zhōng	虾仁盅 蝦仁盅	
Chilled Fruit Cup shí jǐn shuí guǒ zhōng	什锦水果盅 什錦水果盅	
choice of fruit juices gè zhóng guǒ zhī	各种果汁 各種果汁	
Baby Tomato /Crab Meat xiè ròu ràng xī hóng shì	蟹肉瓢西红柿 蟹肉瓢西紅柿	
Smoked Oyster xǔn mǔ lì	熏牡蛎 燻牡蠣	
Chilled Vegetable Juice bīn zhèn xiān cài zhī	冰镇鲜菜汁 冰鎮鮮菜汁	
Escargot Fà Guó kǎo tián luó	法国烤田螺 法國烤田螺	
Asparagus Tip Cocktail lú sǔn jiān zhōng	芦笋尖盅 蘆筍尖盅	

Soups & Salads
湯與沙拉

Clam Chowder Soup 蛤蜊浓汤
gé-li nóng tāng 蛤蠣濃湯

Chili Con Carne 墨西哥牛肉红豆
Mò Xī Gē niú ròu hóng dòu 墨西哥牛肉紅豆

French Onion Soup 法国洋葱汤
Fà-Guo yáng cōng tāng 法國洋蔥湯

Chicken Noodle Soup 美式清鸡汤
Měi shì qīng jī tāng 美式清雞湯

Beef & Vegetable Soup 美式牛肉菜汤
Měi shì niú ròu cài tāng 美式牛肉菜湯

Minestrone Vegetable Soup 义式杂菜汤
Yì shì zá cài tāng 義式雜菜湯

Oxtail Soup 牛尾浓汤
niú wěi nóng tāng 牛尾濃湯

Chicken Mushroom Soup 香菇清鸡汤
xiāng gū qīng jī tāng 香菇清雞湯

Cream Mushroom Soup 奶油香菇汤
nǎi yóu xiāng gū tāng 奶油香菇湯

Cream Tomato Soup 奶油西红柿汤
nǎi yóu xī hóng shì tāng 奶油西紅柿湯

Cream of Corn Soup 奶油玉米浓汤
nǎi yóu yù-mi nóng tāng 奶油玉米濃湯

Russian Borsch 罗宋汤
lúo sòng tāng 羅宋湯

Bouillon 清炖肉汤
qīng dùn ròu tāng 清燉肉湯

Clear Turtle Soup 甲鱼清汤
jiǎ yǔ qīng tāng 甲魚清湯

Cold Consommé 冷牛肉清汤
lěng niú ròu qīng tāng 冷牛肉清湯

Jelled Consommé 结冻牛肉清汤
jié dòng niú ròu qīng tāng 結凍牛肉清湯

salads

Salad 沙拉
shā là 沙拉

Waldorf Salad 苹果生菜沙拉
píng-guo shēng cài shā là 蘋果生菜沙拉

Lettuce /Tomato Salad 生菜西红柿沙拉
shēng cài xī hóng shì shā là 生菜西紅柿

Fresh Fruit Salad 什锦水果沙拉
shí jǐn shuí-guo shā là 什錦水果沙拉

Cole Slaw 凉拌白菜丝
liáng bàn bái cài sī 涼拌白菜絲

Caesar Salad 凯撒沙拉
Kǎi Sā shā là 凱撒沙拉

Chef Salad 招牌沙拉
zhāo pái shā là 招牌沙拉

Italian Chef Salad 义式什锦沙拉
Yì shì shí jǐn shā là 義式什錦沙拉

Tossed Salad 清淡油醋沙拉
qīng dàn yóu cù shā là 清淡油醋 沙拉

Apple 'n White Meat Salad 苹果鸡肉沙拉
píng-guo jī ròu shā là 蘋果雞肉沙拉

Cottage cheese/ Pineapple 奶渣菠萝沙拉
nǎi zhā bō luó shā là 奶渣菠蘿沙拉

Chicken Salad 鸡肉沙拉
jī ròu shā là 雞肉沙拉

Macaroni & Cheese Salad 通心粉乳酪沙拉	Italian Dressing	义大利沙拉酱
tōng xīn fěn rǔ luò shā là 通心粉乳酪沙拉	Yì Dà Lì shā lā jiàng	義大利沙拉醬
Macaroni & Ham Salad 通心粉火腿沙拉	French Dressing	法国沙拉酱
tōng xīn fěn huó tuǐ shā là 通心粉火腿沙拉	Fà Guó shā lā jiàng	法國沙拉醬
Shrimp Salad 虾仁沙拉	Russian Dressing	俄国沙拉酱
xiā rén shā là 蝦仁沙拉	È Guó shā lā jiàng	俄國沙拉醬
Lobster Salad 龙虾沙拉	Thousand Island Dressing 千岛沙拉酱	
lóng xiā shā là 龍蝦沙拉	Qiān Dǎo shā lā jiàng	千島沙拉醬
Crabmeat Salad 蟹肉沙拉	Blue Cheese Dressing	篮纹乳酪酱
xiè ròu shā là 蟹肉沙拉	Lán Wén shā lā jiàng	籃紋乳酪醬
Tomato and Egg Salad 西红柿蛋沙拉	Roquefort Dressing	羊乳酪沙拉酱
xī hóng shì dàn shā là 西紅柿蛋沙拉	Yáng Rǔ Luò shā lā jiàng 羊乳酪沙拉醬	

Chinese Pí-ze and Italian Pizza
中国「皮子」和义大利「披萨」

The Chinese proudly assert that the worldly acclaimed Italian pizza had its humble origins in China, and was then brought to Italy through the silk road by Marco Polo.

Folklore has it that Marco Polo discovered the Beijing "合子 Hé-zi" which looks exactly like the Italian pizza, except that it consists of two layers of the flat dough, called "皮子 Pí-zi" (skin), filled in the middle with a meaty paste, sealed around the edges, and pan grilled. (See P.237★pí-zi 皮子)

Marco Polo used only one "皮子 Pí-zi" instead of two, artistically substituted the meaty paste with the favorite local tomatoes, cheeses (which were then unknown in China), and colorful meats, heated it up, and the Italian "Pizza" was born!

jǐu cài Hé-zi 韭菜合子 **Grilled Leek Pie** are about four inches in diameter, not oil fried. They are simply medium heat grilled, oil free .(see P 237★)

bó cài Hé-zi 菠菜合子 **Grilled Spinach Pie** are also grilled without oil in a skillet. Oven has never been a Chinese cooking utensil (see Group 21)

MARCO'S INVENTION–CURRY BEEF HE-ZI
Roll out tw 6-inch Pí-zi for each HE-ZI and grill.
THE FILLING: Stir fry one cup grated carrots till the oil changed to red color, add 1/2 cup finely chopped onion, one cup ground beef, 1/2 tsp. salt, 1 tbs. sugar, one large spoon carry powder and MSG. Stir 5 minutes. Seal between two Pí-zi and grill with 1 spoon oil.

Vegetable & Potato Dishes

青菜與馬鈴薯

Buttered Carrots niú yóu hú luó-bo	牛油胡萝卜 牛油胡蘿蔔	
Buttered Sweet Peas niú yóu wān dòu	牛油豌豆 牛油豌豆	
Buttered Broccoli niú yóu lǜ huā yé cài	牛油绿花椰菜 牛油綠花椰菜	
Honeyed Yam mì zhī fān shǔ	蜜汁蕃薯 蜜汁蕃薯	
Buttered Sweet Potatoes niú yóu fān shǔ	牛油蕃薯 牛油蕃薯	
Buttered String Beans niú yóu biǎn dòu	牛油扁豆 牛油扁豆	
Buttered Cauliflower niú yóu cài huā	牛油菜花 牛油菜花	
French Fried Onion Rings zhá yáng cōng qūānr	炸洋葱圈儿 炸洋蔥圈兒	
Creamed Spinach nǎi yóu bō cài	奶油菠菜 奶油菠菜	
Baked Cream Cabbage nǎi yóu jú bái cài	奶油焗白菜 奶油焗白菜	
Baked Cream Spinach nǎi yóu jú bō cài	奶油焗菠菜 奶油焗菠菜	
Baked Cream Cauliflower nǎi yóu jú cài huā	奶油焗菜花 奶油焗菜花	
Buttered Okra nǎi yóu qiū kuí jiá	奶油秋葵荚 奶油秋葵莢	
Eggplant Italian Style Yì shì rǔ luò káo qié-zi	义式乳酪烤茄子 義式乳酪烤茄子	
Stewed Tomatoes dùn xī hóng shì	炖西红柿 燉西紅柿	

Creamed Corn nǎi yóu yù-mi	奶油玉米 奶油玉米	
Corn On The Cob dài gǔ yù-mi	带骨玉米 帶骨玉米	
Baked Squash káo xiǎo nán-gua	烤小南瓜 烤小南瓜	
Baked pumpkin káo nán-gua	烤南瓜 烤南瓜	
Baked Eggplant/Cheese rǔ luò kǎo qié-zi	乳酪烤茄子 乳酪烤茄子	
Asparagus Tips/Mayo dàn jiàng lú sǔn jiānr	蛋酱芦笋尖儿 蛋醬蘆筍尖兒	

Potatoes

Baked Potato káo mǎ líng shǔ	烤马铃薯 烤馬鈴薯	
Mashed Potato mǎ líng shǔ ní	马铃薯泥 馬鈴薯泥	
French Fried Potatoes zhá mǎ líng shǔ tiáo	炸马铃薯条 炸馬鈴薯條	
Mashed Potato jiān mǎ líng shǔ qiúr	煎马铃薯球儿 煎馬鈴薯球兒	
Fried Potato Patties zhá mǎ líng shǔ ní	炸马铃薯泥 炸馬鈴薯泥	
Fried Sweet Potatoes zhá bái shǔ	炸白薯 炸白薯	
Honeyed Yam Mì Zhī Shān Yào	蜜汁山药 蜜汁山藥	

Dessert

西式甜點

Lemon Custard Pie **níng méng pài**	柠檬派 檸檬派	**Fruit Tart** **shuǐ-guo dàn tǎ**	水果蛋塔 水果蛋塔
Chocolate Custard Pie **qiǎo kè lì dàn gēng paì**	巧克力蛋羹派 巧克力蛋羹派	**Portuguese Custard** **pú táo yá dàn tǎ**	葡萄牙蛋塔 葡萄牙蛋塔
Lemon Chiffon Pie **níng méng xǘé fǎng pài**	柠檬雪纺派 檸檬雪紡派	**Lemon Tart** **níng méng dàn tǎ**	柠檬蛋塔 檸檬蛋塔
Cherry Pie **yīng táo pài**	樱桃派 櫻桃派	**Peach Melba** **shuǐ mì táo nǎi sū**	水蜜桃奶酥 水蜜桃奶酥
Apple Pie **píng guǒ pài**	苹果派 蘋果派	**Meringue Ice Cream** **dàn bái bīng qí lín**	蛋白冰淇淋 蛋白冰淇淋
Apple Pie á la Mode **píng guǒ paì jiā bīng qí lín**	苹果派加冰淇淋 蘋果派加冰淇淋	**vanilla ice cream** **xiāng cǎo bīng qí lín**	香草冰淇淋 香草冰淇淋
Sponge Cake **hǎi mián dàn gāo**	海绵蛋糕 海綿蛋糕	**strawberry ice cream** **cǎo méi bīng qí lín**	草莓冰淇淋 草莓冰淇淋
a 3-tier birthday cake **sān céng shēng-ri dàn gāo**	三层生日蛋糕 三層生日蛋糕	**strawberry sundae** **cǎo méi shèng dài**	草莓圣代 草莓聖代
a 3-layer ice cream **sān sè dàn gāo**	三色蛋糕(一层) 三色蛋糕	**chocolate sundae** **qiǎo kè lì shèng dài**	巧克力圣代 巧克力聖代
Vanilla Cheese Cake **xiāng cáo rǔ luò dàn gāo**	香草乳酪蛋糕 香草乳酪蛋糕	**Banana Split** **xiāng jiāo chuān**	香蕉船 香蕉船
Cake with sugar icing **táng yī dàn gāo**	糖衣蛋糕 糖衣蛋糕	**Baked Alaska** **huó kǎo bīng qí lín**	火烤冰淇淋 火烤冰淇淋
Chocolate Cake **qiǎo kè lì dàn gāo**	巧克力蛋糕 巧克力蛋糕	**ice cream cone** **tián tǒng bīng qí lín**	甜筒冰淇淋 甜筒冰淇淋
Fruitcake **shuǐ-guo dàn gāo**	水果蛋糕 水果蛋糕	**sherbet** **guǒ zhī bīng qí lín**	果汁冰淇淋 果汁冰淇淋
Assorted Fancy Cookies **jīng zhì xiǎo xī diǎn**	精致小西点 精致小西點	**pudding** **bù dīng**	布丁 布丁
Cream Puff **nǎi yóu pào fú**	奶油泡芙 奶油泡芙	**jelly** **guǒ dòng**	果冻 果凍
shartcake **jiāng guǒ sū**	浆果酥 漿果酥	**fruit cup** **shí jín shuí guǒ**	什锦水果 什錦水果

26F Western Breakfast 西式早餐

breakfast **zǎo cān**	早餐 早餐
first course **dì yī dào cài**	第一道菜 第一道菜
fruit **shuí-guo**	水果 水果
juices **guǒ zhī**	果汁 果汁
stewed dehydrated fruit **dùn shuǐ-guo gān**	炖水果乾 燉水果乾
canned fruit **guàn tóu shuǐ-guo**	罐头水果 罐頭水果
fresh orange juice **xiān liǔ chéng zhī**	鲜柳橙汁 鮮柳橙汁
tomato juice **xī hóng shì zhī**	西红柿汁 西紅柿汁
grapefruit juice **pú táo yòu zhī**	葡萄柚汁 葡萄柚汁
apple juice **píng-guo zhī**	苹果汁 蘋果汁
stewed prunes **dùn lǐ-zi**	炖李子 燉李子
sliced peaches in syrup **guàn-tou shuǐ mì táo**	罐头水蜜桃 罐頭水蜜桃
fresh pineapple **xīn xiān bō luó**	新鲜菠萝 新鮮菠蘿
half grapefruit **bàn-ge pú táo yòu**	半个葡萄柚 半個葡萄柚
half cantaloupe **bàn-ge hā mì guā**	半个哈密瓜 半個哈密瓜

主食 main course

main course **zhǔ cān**	主餐 主餐
Grilled Ham **guō tiē huó tuǐ**	锅贴火腿 鍋貼火腿
Bacon **xián ròu**	咸肉 鹹肉
Link Sausage **xiāng cháng**	香肠 香腸
Beef Kidney Stew **dùn niú yāo**	炖牛腰 燉牛腰
Creamed Chipped Beef **nǎi yóu niú ròu piàn**	奶油牛肉片 奶油牛肉片
Minute Steak (breakfast) **xiǎo niú pái**	小牛排 小牛排
Fried Eggs **jiān dàn**	煎蛋 煎蛋
sunny side up **dān miàn-de**	单面的 單面的 (煎蛋)
over-easy (egg) (tender) **nèn-de**	嫩的 嫩的 (煎蛋)
well; well done (egg) (old) **lǎo-de**	老的 老的 (煎蛋)
Soft Boiled Eggs **nèn zhǔ dàn**	嫩煮蛋 嫩煮蛋
Three-minute Eggs **sān fēn zhōng zhǔ dàn**	三分钟煮蛋 三分鐘煮蛋

Poached Eggs wò jī dàn; wò guǒr	沃鸡蛋;沃果儿 沃雞蛋;沃果兒	jam guǒ jiàng	果酱 果醬
scrambled eggs niú nǎi chǎo dàn	牛奶炒蛋 牛奶炒蛋	marmalade jú pí guǒ jiàng	橘皮果酱 橘皮果醬
Ham Omelet huó tuǐ tān dàn	火腿摊蛋 火腿攤蛋	strawberry jam cǎo méi guǒ jiàng	草莓果酱 草莓果醬
Cheese Omelet rǔ luò tān dàn	乳酪摊蛋 乳酪攤蛋	French Toast Fà shì jiān miàn bāo piàn	法式煎面包片 法式煎麵包片
Spanish Omelet Xī Bān Yá jiān dàn juǎn	西班牙煎蛋卷 西班牙煎蛋捲	Waffles yā huā jiān-bing	压花煎饼 壓花煎餅
Jelly Omelet guǒ jiàng jiān dàn juǎn	果酱煎蛋卷 果醬煎蛋捲	Hot Cake / Maple Syrup xī shì jiān bǐng	西式煎饼 西式煎餅
Souffléd Sweet Berry Omelet tián méi dàn juǎn	甜莓蛋卷 甜莓蛋捲	Buckwheat Pancakes qiáo mài jiān bǐng	荞麦煎饼 蕎麥煎餅
Savoury Omelet cài xīn tān dàn	菜心摊蛋 菜心攤蛋	maple syrup fēng táng jiāng	枫糖浆 楓糖漿
Plain Omelet sù jiān dàn juǎn	素煎蛋卷 素煎蛋捲	Miniature Danish Rolls xiǎo tián miàn bāo juǎn	小甜面包卷 小甜麵包捲
Hash Browned Potatoes yáng cōng chǎo mǎ líng shǔ	洋葱炒马铃薯 洋蔥炒馬鈴薯	doughnut tián tián qūan	甜甜圈 甜甜圈

 miscellaneous breakfast

glazed doughnut táng jiāng tián tián quān	糖浆甜甜圈 糖漿甜甜圈
miscellaneous wǔ huā bā mén; zá yàng	五花八门;杂样 五花八門;雜樣	chocolate doughnut qiǎo kè lì tián tián quān	巧克力甜甜圈 巧克力甜甜圈
pastry tián diǎn	甜点 甜點	Oatmeal mài piàn zhōu	麦片粥 麥片粥
rye bread kē mài miàn bāo	棵麦面包 棵麥麵包	Mush yǔ mǐ hú	玉米糊 玉米糊
toast kǎo miàn bāo piàn	烤面包片 烤麵包片	Cereal zǎo cān gǔ piàn	早餐谷片 早餐穀片
butter niú yóu; huáng yóu	牛油;黄油 牛油;黃油	Hot Corn Bread rè yǔ mǐ gāo	热玉米面糕 熱玉米麵糕
margarine rén zào niú yóu	人造牛油 人造牛油	English Muffins Yīng Guó sōng bǐng	英国松饼 英國鬆餅
cheese rǔ luò	乳酪 乳酪	Hot Cinnamon Rolls kǎo ròu guì tián juǎnr	烤肉桂甜卷儿 烤肉桂甜捲兒
peanut butter huā shēng jiàng	花生酱 花生醬		

26G

Sandwiches & Fast-food
三明治與快餐

fast-food	快餐;速食	Tuna Fish Sandwich	鲔鱼三明治
kuài cān; sù shí	快餐;速食	wěi yú sān míng zhì	鮪魚三明治
Taco	墨西哥玉米饼	Bologna Sandwich	肉肠三明治
Mò Xī Gē yù mǐ bǐng	墨西哥玉米餅	ròu cháng sān míng zhì	肉腸三明治
Hot Dog	热狗	Hot Beef Sandwich	牛肉卤汁三明治
rè gǒu	熱狗	niú ròu lǔ zhī sān míng zhì	牛肉滷汁三明治
Hamburger	汉堡包	Hot Pork Sandwich	猪肉卤汁三明治
hàn bǎo-bao	漢堡包	zhū ròu lǔ zhī sān míng zhì	豬肉滷汁三明治
Cheeseburger	乳酪汉堡包	Ham and Cheese Sandwich	火腿乳酪…
rǔ luò hàn bǎo-bao	乳酪漢堡包	huó tuí rǔ luò sān míng zhì	火腿乳酪…
Turkeyburger	火鸡汉堡包	Bacon Tomato Sandwich	咸肉西红柿…
huǒ jī hàn bǎo-bao	火雞漢堡包	xián ròu xī hóng shì …	鹹肉西紅柿…
Chickenburger	鸡汉堡包	Peanut butter/Jelly Sand.	花生酱果酱…
jī hàn bǎo-bao	雞漢堡包	huā shēng jiàng guǒ jiàng…	花生醬果醬…
Fishburger	鱼汉堡包	Salami Sandwich	义式肉肠三明治
yú hàn bǎo-bao	魚漢堡包	Yì shì ròu cháng sān míng zhì	義式肉腸三明治
Vegeburger	素汉堡包	Fried Chicken Leg	炸鸡腿
sù hàn bǎo-bao	素漢堡包	zhá jī tuǐ	炸雞腿
Minute Steak Sandwich	小牛排三明治	Fried Chicken Thigh	炸鸡上腿块
xiǎo niú pái sān míng zhì	小牛排三明治	zhá jī shàng tuǐ kuài	炸雞上腿塊
Ham Sandwich	火腿三明治	Fried Drumstick	炸棒棒腿
huó tuí sān míng zhì	火腿三明治	zhá bàng bàng tuǐ	炸棒棒腿
Club Sandwich	三层三明治	Fried Chicken Breast	炸鸡胸
sān céng sān míng zhì	三層三明治	zhá jī xiōng	炸雞胸
Chicken Sandwich	鸡肉三明治	Fried Chicken Wing	炸鸡翅（膀）
jī ròu sān míng zhì	雞肉三明治	zhá jī chì (bǎng)	炸雞翅（膀）
Chicken Salad Sandwich	鸡沙拉三明治	Fried Chicken Neck	炸鸡脖子
jī shā là sān míng zhì	雞沙拉三明治	zhá jī bó-zi	炸雞脖子
Ham 'n Egg Sandwich	火腿蛋三明治	Fried Chicken Gizzards	炸鸡胗
huó tuí dàn sān míng zhì	火腿蛋三明治	zhá jī zhēn	炸雞胗
Grilled Cheese Sandwich	烘乳酪三明治	lunch box	盒儿饭
hōng rǔ luò sān míng zhì	烘乳酪三明治	hér fàn	盒兒飯

In Vogue
時髦穿著

apparel; clothing chuān zhuó	穿著 穿著	**car coat** duǎn dà yī	短大衣 短大衣
custom-made dìng zuò-de	订做的 訂做的	**hood** dà yī-de zhào tóu mào	大衣的罩头帽 大衣的罩頭帽
ready-made clothes chéng yī	成衣 成衣	**parka** dài zhào tóu mào duǎn dà yī	带罩头帽短大衣 帶罩頭帽短大衣
clothes; wardrobe yī-fu	衣服 衣服	**down jacket** é yǔ róng wài tào	鹅羽绒外套 鵝羽絨外套
outfit zhuāng shù	装束 裝束	**outerwear** wài yī	外衣 外衣
fashion liú xíng shì yàng	流行式样 流行式樣	**cloak** dǒu-peng	斗蓬 斗蓬
in fashion zhèng liú xíng	正流行 正流行	**stole; wrap** pī jiān	披肩 披肩
out of fashion guò shí-le	过时了 過時了	**formal wear** shèng zhuāng	盛装 盛裝
style fēng gé	风格 風格	**tuxedo; black tie** nán xiáo lǐ fú	男小礼服 男小禮服
popular rén rén xǐ-huan	人人喜欢 人人喜歡	**tailcoat; white tie** yàn wěi fú	燕尾服 燕尾服
wear chuān	穿 穿	**cummerbund** (tuxedo) lǐ fú yāo dài	礼服腰带 禮服腰帶
coat; overcoat dà yī	大衣 大衣	**sash** (both sex) yāo dài	腰带 腰帶
topcoat wài tào	外套 外套	**gorgeous** huá lì-de	华丽的 華麗的
fur coat pí máor dà yī	皮毛儿大衣 皮毛兒大衣	**elegant** gāo yǎ	高雅 高雅
sea otter collared coat shuí tǎ pí lǐng dà yī	水獭皮领大衣 水獭皮領大衣	**evening gown** nǚ wán lǐ fú	女晚礼服 女晚禮服

a sparkle tū xiǎn; qiáng yǎn	凸显；抢眼 凸顯；搶眼
very striking tè bié	特别显眼 特別顯眼
wedding gown nǚ jié hūn lǐ fú	女结婚礼服 女結婚禮服
bridal veil xīn niáng pī shā	新娘披纱 新娘披紗
a suit yí tào xī zhuāng	一套西装 一套西裝
single-breasted suit dān pái kòur tào zhuāng	单排扣儿套装 單排扣兒套裝
double-breasted jacket shuāng pái kòur shàng yī	双排扣儿上衣 雙排扣兒上衣
coat; jacket xī zhuāng shàng yī	西装上衣 西裝上衣
sports jacket xiū xián jiá kè	休闲夹克 休閒夾克
blazer xiān sè xī zhuāng shàng yī	鲜色西装上衣 鮮色西裝上衣
elbow-patch jacket pí bǔ-ding zhóur shàng yī	皮补钉肘儿上衣 皮補釘肘兒上衣
leather jacket pí jiá kè	皮夹克 皮夾克
suede jacket jǐ pí jiá kè	麂皮夹克 麂皮夾克
reversible jacket zhèng fǎn liǎng chuān jiá kè	正反两穿夹克 正反兩穿夾克
quilted jacket mián jiá kè	棉夹克 棉夾克
lined gown jiá ǎo	夹袄 夾襖
pants; trousers kù-zi	裤子 褲子
slacks xī zhuāng kù	西装裤 西裝褲
knickerbockers dēng-long kù	灯笼裤 燈籠褲
casual wear biàn zhuāng	便装 便裝

informal wear qīng zhuāng	轻装 輕裝
tops shàng yī	上衣 上衣
vest bèi xīn	背心 背心
jeans niú zǎi kù	牛仔裤 牛仔褲
cowboy suit niú zǎi tào zhuāng	牛仔套装 牛仔套裝
uniform zhì fú	制服 制服
overalls gōng zuò fú	工作服 工作服 (連褲式)
gong fu suit gōng fū zhuāng	功夫装 功夫裝
gong fu shirt gōng fū shān	功夫衫 功夫衫
gong fu trousers gōng fú kù	功夫裤 功夫褲
gong fu head scarf gōng fū tóu jīn	功夫头巾 功夫頭巾
6-feet black sash gōng fū yāo dài	功夫腰带 功夫腰帶
cotton trouser-belt kù yāo dài	裤腰带 褲腰帶
trouser-bottom laces tuǐ dài	腿带 腿帶
gong fu shoes gōng fū xié	功夫鞋 功夫鞋
dress yáng zhuāng	洋装 洋裝
long sleeve dress cháng xiùr yáng zhuāng	长袖儿洋装 長袖兒洋裝
short sleeve dress duǎn xiùr yáng zhuāng	短袖儿洋装 短袖兒洋裝
sleeveless wú xiù-de	无袖的 無袖的
beaded dress xiù zhū yáng zhuāng	绣珠洋装 繡珠洋裝

Mandarin dress **qí páor**	旗袍儿 旗袍兒	V-neck sweater **jiān lǐngr máo yī**	尖领儿毛衣 尖領兒毛衣
gown; robe **cháng páor**	长袍儿 長袍兒	pullover **tào tóu róng yùn dòng yī**	套头绒运动衣 套頭絨運動衣
bare-back dress **luǒ bèi yáng zhuāng**	裸背洋装 裸背洋裝	skirt **qún-zi**	裙子 裙子
low cut dress **dī xiōng yáng zhuāng**	低胸洋装 低胸洋裝	kilt **yīng shì nán zhuāng qún**	英式男装裙 英式男裝裙
maternity clothes **yùn fù zhuāng**	孕妇装 孕婦裝	mini skirt **mí nǐ qún**	迷你裙 迷你裙（極短裙）
sack dress **bù dài zhuāng**	布袋装 布袋裝	maxi skirt **cháng qún**	长裙 長裙（極長裙）
negligee **luó shā jū jiā páo**	縲纱居家袍 縲紗居家袍	pleated skirt **bái jǐng qún**	百景裙 百景裙
lingerie **nǚ-ren nèi yī**	女人内衣 女人內衣	shirt **nán chèn shān**	男衬衫 男襯衫
jersey **jǐn shēn zhēn zhī yī**	紧身针织衣 緊身針織衣	blouse **nǚ chèn shān**	女衬衫 女襯衫
nightgown **nǚ shuì páo**	女睡袍 女睡袍	terry cloth shirt **máo jīn bù chèn shān**	毛巾布衬衫 毛巾布襯衫
robe **nán shuì páo**	男睡袍 男睡袍	T-shirt **hàn shān**	汗衫 汗衫
pajamas **shuì yī**	睡衣 睡衣	underwear **nèi yī kù**	内衣裤 內衣褲
raincoat **yǔ yī**	雨衣 雨衣	undershirt **nèi yī**	内衣 內衣
remove; take off (clothes) **tuō yī-fu**	脱衣服 脱衣服	under shorts **nèi kù**	内裤 內褲
wind breaker **fēng yī**	风衣 風衣	boxer shorts **sì jiǎo kù**	四角裤 四角褲
swimsuit **nǚ yóu yǒng zhuāng**	女游泳装 女游泳裝	jockey shorts **nán sān jiǎor kù**	男三角儿裤 男三角兒褲
swimming trunks **nán yǒng kù**	男泳裤 男泳褲	panties **nǚ sān jiǎor kù**	女三角儿裤 女三角兒褲
sweater **máo yī**	毛衣 毛衣	panty hose **kù wà**	裤袜 褲襪
turtleneck sweater **gāo lǐngr máo yī** (龜脖子)	高领儿毛衣 高領兒毛衣	girdle; corset **shù yāo**	束腰 束腰
mock-turtleneck sweater **yüán lǐngr máo yī**	圆领儿毛衣 圓領兒毛衣	shorts **duǎn kù**	短裤 短褲

slip; petticoat **chèn qún**	衬裙 襯裙	helmet **tóu kuī**	头盔 頭盔
bikini **nǔ hǎi tān duǎn kù**	女海滩短裤 女海灘短褲	gloves **shǒu tàor**	手套儿 手套兒
biniki **tún zhào**	臀罩 臀罩	mittens **lián zhí shǒu tàor**	连指手套儿 連指手套兒
Bermuda shorts **nán hù wài duǎn kù**	男户外短裤 男戶外短褲	socks **wà-zi**	袜子 襪子
bra; brassiere **nǎi zhàor**	奶罩儿 奶罩兒	stretch socks **shēn suō wà**	伸缩袜 伸縮襪
strapless bra **wú dài nǎi zhàor**	无带奶罩儿 無帶奶罩兒	stockings; nylons **sī wà**	丝袜 絲襪
falsie **yì rǔ**	义乳 義乳	wear out **chuān pò**	穿破 穿破
children apparel **tóng zhuāng**	童装 童裝	wearing an odd pair of socks **wà-zi chuān yí yàng yì zhī**	袜子穿一样 一只
bib **wéi zuǐr**	围嘴儿 圍嘴兒	purse **nǔ pí bāo**	女皮包 女皮包
diaper **niào bù; niào kù**	尿布；尿裤 尿布；尿褲	handbag **shǒu tí dài**	手提袋 手提袋
disposable diaper **zhǐ niào kù**	纸尿裤 紙尿褲	shoulder bag **bēi jiān dài**	背肩袋 揹肩袋
veil **miàn shā**	面纱 面紗	backbag **bèi bāo**	背包 背包
scarf **wéi bór**	围脖儿 圍脖兒	wallet **pí bāo; pí jiá**	皮包；皮夹 皮包；皮夾
head scarf **tóu jīn**	头巾 頭巾	shoes **xié**	鞋 鞋
handkerchief **shǒu jüànr**	手绢儿 手絹兒	dress shoes **lǐ fú xié**	礼服鞋 禮服鞋
belt **pí dài**	皮带 皮帶	leather shoes **pí xié**	皮鞋 皮鞋
suspenders **diào kù dài**	吊裤带 吊褲帶	black shoes **hēi pí xié**	黑皮鞋 黑皮鞋
hat **mào-zi**	帽子 帽子	brown shoes **huáng pí xié**	黄皮鞋 黃皮鞋
straw hat **cǎo màor**	草帽儿 草帽兒	suede shoes **jī pí xié**	麂皮鞋 麂皮鞋
cap **yā shí màor**	鸭舌帽儿 鴨舌帽兒	heels; high heels **gāo gēn xié**	高跟鞋 高跟鞋

flat heels; flats píng dǐ xié	平底鞋 平底鞋	sneakers yùn dòng xié	运动鞋 運動鞋
loafers biàn xié	便鞋 便鞋	jogging shoes màn pǎo xié	慢跑鞋 慢跑鞋
embroidered shoes xiù huār xié	绣花儿鞋 繡花兒鞋	spiked shoes dīng-zi xié	钉子鞋 釘子鞋
bead-embroidered shoes xiù zhū xié	绣珠鞋 繡珠鞋	tennis shoes wǎng qiúr xié	网球儿鞋 網球兒鞋
satin shoes duàn-zi xié	缎子鞋 緞子鞋	basketball shoes lán qiúr xié	篮球儿鞋 籃球兒鞋
brocade shoes zhī jǐn duàn xié	织锦缎鞋 織錦緞鞋	galoshes; rain boots yǔ xuē	雨靴 雨靴
canvas shoes fān bù xié	帆布鞋 帆布鞋	umbrella yǔ sǎn	雨伞 雨傘
shoes/donkey skin front shuāng liǎnr xié	双脸儿鞋 雙臉兒鞋	parasol yáng sǎn	阳伞 陽傘
cotton quilted shoes máo wō; mián xié	毛窝；棉鞋 毛窩；棉鞋	shoe last xié xüàn-tou	鞋楦头 鞋楦頭
boots xuē-zi	靴子 靴子	spike heel gāo gén xié-de hòu gēn	高跟鞋的後跟 高跟鞋的後跟
knee highs guò xī cháng tǒngr xuē	过膝长儿筒靴 過膝長筒兒靴	heel xié gēn	鞋跟 鞋跟
ankle boots duǎn tǒngr xuē	短筒儿靴 短筒兒靴	sole xié dǐr	鞋底儿 鞋底兒
sandals liáng xié	凉鞋 涼鞋	umbrella yǔ sǎn	雨伞 雨傘
		parasol yáng sǎn	阳伞 陽傘

Clothing Materials 衣料

clothing material **yī liàor**	衣料儿	衣料兒
fabric **bù liàor**	布料儿	布料兒
wool **yáng máo**	羊毛	羊毛
woolen material **máo liào-zi**	毛料子	毛料子
worsted **ní liàor**	呢料儿	呢料兒
melton **hòu ní-zi**	厚呢子	厚呢子
tartan; plaid **gé-zi ní**	格子呢	格子呢
serge **xié wén ní; bì jī**	斜纹呢；哔叽	斜紋呢；嗶嘰
blue serge **zàng qīng bì jī**	藏青哔叽	藏青嗶嘰
cassimere; cashmere **bó máo ní**	薄毛呢	薄毛呢
herring-bone woolen **rén zì ní**	人字呢	人字呢
small check tweed **xiǎo fāng gér ní**	小方格儿呢	小方格兒呢
whipcord **huá dá ní; mǎ kù ní**	华达呢；马裤呢	華達呢；馬褲呢
tweed **huā ní**	花呢	花呢
quilting **chèn lǐ róng**	衬里绒	襯裏絨
gabardine **jiā bì dīng**	加毕丁	加畢丁
mohair **máo hǎi**	毛海	毛海
cashmere **kāi sī mǐ**	开司米	開司米
cotton **mián-hua ; mián-de**	棉花；棉的	棉花；棉的
cloth **bù**	布	布
print fabric; patterned cloth **yìn huā bù**	印花布	印花布
polka dots cloth **yuán diǎn huā bù**	圆点花布	圓點花布
stripe fabric cloth **tiáo wén huā bù**	条纹花布	條紋花布
horizontal stripe cloth **héng tiáo bù**	横条布	橫條布
vertical stripe cloth **shù tiáo bù**	竖条布	豎條布
plaid cloth **gé-zi huā bù**	格子花布	格子花布
twill **xié wén bù**	斜纹布	斜紋布
denim **xié wén cū bù**	斜纹粗布	斜紋粗布
jean **xié wén má bù**	斜纹麻布	斜紋麻布
khaki **kǎ qí bù**	卡其布	卡其布

canvas **fān bù**	帆布 帆布		plush **cháng máor róng**	长毛儿绒 長毛兒絨
linen **má bù**	麻布 麻布		flannel **fǎ lán róng**	法兰绒 法蘭絨
pure silk **chún sī**	纯丝 純絲		corduroy **dēng xīn róng**	灯心绒 燈心絨
raw silk **shēng sī**	生丝 生絲		web (length of cloth) **pǐ**	疋 疋
rayon **rén zào sī**	人造丝 人造絲		foot; feet **chǐ**	尺 尺
nylon **ní lóng**	尼龙 尼龍		yard **mǎ**	码 碼
stretch nylon **shēn suō ní lóng**	伸缩尼龙 伸縮尼龍		single width **dān fúr**	单幅儿 單幅兒
spandex **tán-xing rén zào xiān wéi**	弹性人造纤维 彈性人造纖維		double width **shuāng fúr**	双幅儿 雙幅兒
orlon **ào lóng**	奥龙 奧龍		lace **huā biānr**	花边儿 花邊兒
pongee silk **fǔ chóu**	府绸 府綢		ribbon **duàn dàir**	缎带儿 緞帶兒
satin **duàn-zi**	缎子 緞子		fur **máo pí; pí cǎo**	毛皮；皮草 毛皮；皮草
brocade **zhī jǐn duàn**	织锦缎 織錦緞		mink **bái diāo pí**	白貂皮 白貂皮
embroidery **xiù huār liào-zi**	绣花儿料子 繡花兒料子		beaver **shuǐ tà pí**	水獭皮 水獺皮
camlet **yǔ shā**	羽纱 羽紗		leather **pí gé**	皮革 皮革
georgette; voile **tòu míng shā**	透明纱 透明紗		calf leather **xiǎo niú pí**	小牛皮 小牛皮
crepe **zhòu shā**	绉纱 縐紗		leatherette **rén zào pí gé**	人造皮革 人造皮革
chiffon **xué fǎng**	雪纺 雪紡		Naugahyde **zhì shā fā jiǎ pí**	制沙发假皮 製沙發假皮
tiffany **sī shā luó**	丝纱罗 絲紗羅		synthetic leather **hé chéng pí gé**	合成皮革 合成皮革
velvet **sī róng**	丝绒 絲絨			

color yán sè	颜色 顏色	loud colors cì yǎn-de yán sè	刺眼的颜色 刺眼的顏色
natural color běn sè	本色 本色	colorful huā huā lǜ lǜ-de	花花绿绿的 花花綠綠的
soft color róu sè	柔色 柔色	multicolored cǎi sè-de	彩色的 彩色的
rich color nóng sè	浓色 濃色	various colors gè zhǒng yán sè	各种颜色 各種顏色
transparent; limpid tòu míng-de	透明的 透明的	blue lán	蓝 藍
translucent; semiopaque bàn tòu míng-de	半透明的 半透明的	royal blue bǎo lán	宝蓝 寶藍
delicate color jiāo sè	娇色 嬌色	sky blue tiān lán	天蓝 天藍
dark; deep shēn; àn	深；暗 深；暗	dark blue shēn lán	深蓝 深藍
light dàn; qiǎn; qīng	淡；浅；轻 淡；淺；輕	pale blue cāng lán	苍蓝 蒼藍
pale cāng bái	苍白 蒼白	light blue qiǎn lán	浅蓝 淺藍
contrast color chèn sè	衬色 襯色	Prussian blue pú lǔ shì lán	普鲁士蓝 普魯士藍
matching color xiāng pèi-de yán sè	相配的颜色 相配的顏色	Ming blue zàng qīng sè	藏青色 藏青色
protective color bǎo hù sè	保护色 保護色	turquoise lán lǜ sè	蓝绿色 藍綠色
color shade; tone yán sè-zhi shēn qiǎn	颜色之深浅 顏色之深淺	Oriental red dà hóng	大红 大紅
colorless wú sè	无色 無色	red hóng	红 紅

cardinal color shēn hóng sè	深红色 深紅色	beige mǐ sè	米色 米色
scarlet xīng hóng sè	腥红色 腥紅色	canary color dàn huáng	淡黄 淡黃
rosy méi guī hóng	玫瑰红 玫瑰紅	khaki color kǎ jī sè	卡叽色 卡嘰色
maroon shēn zǎo hóng	深枣红 深棗紅	gray huī sè	灰色 灰色
pink fěn hóng	粉红 粉紅	silver gray yín huī	银灰 銀灰
yellow huáng	黄 黃	charcoal gray shēn huī	深灰 深灰
white bái	白 白	purple zǐ sè	紫色 紫色
black hēi	黑 黑	mauve dàn zǐ sè	淡紫色 淡紫色
pitch black qī hēi	漆黑 漆黑	purple bronze zǐ tóng sè	紫铜色 紫銅色
green lǜ	绿 綠	violet zǐ luó lán sè	紫罗兰色 紫羅蘭色
sap green mò lǜ	墨绿 墨綠	lavender ǒu hé sè	藕荷色 藕荷色
apple green píng guǒ lǜ	苹果绿 蘋果綠	tan hé pí fū sè	褐皮肤色 褐皮膚色
olive green gán lǎn lǜ	橄榄绿 橄欖綠	hazel hé yǎn jīng sè（東方人）	褐眼睛色 褐眼睛色
aquamarine shuǐ lǜ sè	水绿色 水綠色	auburn lì-zi sè	栗子色 栗子色
jade green cuì lǜ sè	翠绿色 翠綠色	coral color shān hú sè	珊瑚色 珊瑚色
milk white rǔ bái sè	乳白色 乳白色	orange color chéng sè	橙色 橙色
cream color nǎi yóu sè	奶油色 奶油色	brown zōng sè	棕色 棕色
golden color jīn sè	金色 金色		

27D
Tailoring Terms
剪裁師傅

fashion designer fú zhuāng shè jì shī	服装设计师 服裝設計師
tailor xī zhuāng cái-feng	西装裁缝 西裝裁縫
dressmaker nǔ zhuāng cái féng	女装裁缝 女裝裁縫
model mó tè ér	模特儿 模特兒
manikin chú chuāng mó tè ér	厨窗模特儿 廚窗模特兒
dummy chú chuāng jiǎ rén	厨窗假人 廚窗假人
a fitting; try on shì chuān	试穿 試穿
fit hé shēn	合身 合身
misfit bù hé shēn	不合身 不合身
in fashion; in style zhèng liú xíng	正流行 正流行
out of style guò shí-le	过时了 過時了
letting out fàng chū-lai	放出来 放出來
taking in shōu jìn-qù	收进去 收進去
too tight tài jǐn	太紧 太緊
too loose tài sōng	太松 太鬆

too narrow tài zhǎi	太窄 太窄
too wide; too broad tài kuān	太宽 太寬
too long tài cháng	太长 太長
takeup the hem zhé biān féng jìn-qù	折边缝进去 折邊縫進去
too short tài duǎn	太短 太短
let down the hem féng fènr fàng-chu-lai	缝份儿放出来 縫份兒放出來
too big tài dà	太大 太大
cut down the size bǎ chí-cun suō xiǎo	把尺寸缩小 把尺寸縮小
too small tài xiǎo	太小 太小
need to re-size děi yào chóng gái chí-cun	得要重改尺寸 得要重改尺寸
just right zhèng hǎo	正好 正好
to alter xiū gǎi	修改 修改
patch bǔ-ding; bǔ	补钉;补 補釘;補
mend féng bǔ; xīu bǔ	缝补;修补 縫補;修補
darn socks zhī bǔ wà-zi	织补袜子 織補襪子

English	Pinyin	简体	繁體
is torn	sī pò-le	撕破了	撕破了
sew	féng	缝	縫
sewing machine	féng rèn jī	缝纫机	縫紉機
housewives	chā zhēn bāor	插针包儿	插針包兒
pin	dà tóu zhēn	大头针	大頭針
needle	zhēn	针	針
safety pin	bié zhēn	别针	別針
thimble	dǐng zhēnr	顶针儿	頂針兒
thread	xiàn	线	線
thread a needle	chuān zhēn	穿针	穿針
paper pattern	zhǐ yàng-zi	纸样子	紙樣子
cutting	jiǎn cái	剪裁	剪裁
cut	fú zhuāng-de shì yàng	服装的式样	服裝的式樣
chalk line	fěn xiàn	粉线	粉線
measure	liáng	量	量
tape measure	pí chǐ	皮尺	皮尺
footage	chí mǎr	尺码儿	尺碼兒（長度）
size	chí-cun	尺寸	尺寸
length	cháng-du	长度	長度
small size	xiǎo hàor	小号儿	小號兒
medium size	zhōng hàor	中号儿	中號兒
large size	dà hàor	大号儿	大號兒
extra large size	tè dà hàor	特大号儿	特大號兒
body length	shēn cháng	身长	身長
shoulders' width	jiān kuān	肩宽	肩寬
waistline	yāo wéi	腰围	腰圍
bust line	xiōng wéi	胸围	胸圍
collar width	lǐng kuān	领宽	領寬
collar height	lǐng gāo	领高	領高
sleeve	xiù-zi	袖子	袖子
sleeve length	xiù cháng	袖长	袖長
armhole	xiù kǒng	袖孔	袖孔
cuff	xiù kǒur	袖口儿	袖口兒
cuff opening	xiù kǒur kuān dù	袖口儿宽度	袖口兒寬度
pinking shears	gǒu yá jiǎn-zi	狗牙剪子	狗牙剪子
woolen yarn	máo xiàn	毛线	毛線
hand weaving	yòng shǒu gōng zhī	用手工织	用手工織
crochet	zhēn zhī pǐn	针织品	針織品
a run in stocking	ní lóng wà tuō zhēn	尼龙袜脱针	尼龍襪脫針
needle point	cì xiù; xiù huār	刺绣；绣花儿	刺繡；繡花兒

iron	熨斗	yùn-dou
	熨斗	
ironing board	烫衣板儿	tàng yī bǎnr
	燙衣板兒	
zipper	拉链儿	lā liànr
	拉鏈兒	
zip it up	拉上拉链儿	lā-shang lā liànr
	拉上拉鏈兒	
unzip it	拉开拉链儿	lā-kai lā liànr
	拉開拉鏈兒	
buckle	皮带扣儿	pí dài kòur
	皮帶扣兒	
elastic cord	松紧带儿	sōng jǐn dàir
	鬆緊帶兒	
button	钮扣儿	niǔ kòur
	鈕扣兒	
button hole	钮扣儿孔	niǔ kòur kǒng
	鈕扣兒孔	
press stud	按钮扣儿	àn niǔ kòur
	按鈕扣兒	
frog (a button)	钮袢儿	niǔ pànr
	鈕袢兒	
hook (a button)	领钩儿	lǐng gōur
	領鉤兒	
eye (a button)	领钩圈儿	lǐng gōu qüānr
	領鉤圈兒	
3-button coat	三个扣子上衣	sān-ge kòu-zi shàng yī
	三個扣子上衣	
lapel	西装翻领儿	xī zhuāng fān lǐngr
	西裝翻領兒	
collar	领子	lǐng-zi
	領子	
ruffle collar	荷叶领儿	hé yè lǐngr
	荷葉領兒	
lace	花边儿；蕾丝	huā biānr; léi sī
	花邊兒；蕾絲	
lace collar	花边儿领子	huā biānr lǐng-zi
	花邊兒領子	
shoulder padding	垫肩	diàn jiān
	墊肩	

three-quarter sleeve	七分袖儿	qī fēn xiùr
	七分袖兒	
dolman sleeve	蝴蝶袖儿	hú dié xiùr
	蝴蝶袖兒	
top of trousers	裤腰	kù yāo
	褲腰	
seat; seat of trousers	裤裆	kù dāng
	褲襠	
bottom; expansion	下摆	xià bǎi
	下擺	
bottom of trousers	裤脚儿	kù jiǎor
	褲腳兒	
slit	开叉儿	kāi chàr
	開叉兒	
pocket	衣袋	yī dài
	衣袋	
concealed pocket	暗袋	àn dài
	暗袋	
flap pocket	有盖袋	yǒu gài dài
	有蓋袋	
patch pocket	贴补袋	tiē bǔ dài
	貼補袋	
slash pocket	斜袋	xié dài
	斜袋	
watch pocket	表袋	biǎo dài
	錶袋	
side pocket	手插袋	shǒu chā dài
	手插袋	
seam	衣缝儿	yī fèngr
	衣縫兒	
fringe	繸子(边缘)	suì-zi
	繸子(邊緣)	
tassels	缨子	yīng-zi
	纓子	
macrame	花边流苏	huā biān liú sū
	花邊流蘇	
sequins	闪亮圆片	shǎn liàng yüán piàn
	閃亮圓片	
knitting	针织	zhēn zhī
	針織	

| stitch | 针脚儿 |
| zhēn-jiǎor | 針腳兒 |

| label | 品牌标签儿 |
| pǐn pái biāo qiānr | 品牌標籤兒 |

| price tag | 价码儿标签 |
| jià mǎr biāo qiān | 價碼兒 標籤 |

| tuck; goffer | 打褶儿 |
| dǎ zhér | 打褶兒 |

| cuffed trousers | 翻裤脚儿 |
| fān kù jiǎor | 翻褲腳兒 |

| cuffless trousers | 平裤脚儿 |
| píng kù jiǎor | 平褲腳兒 |

| straight cut trousers | 直统儿裤子 |
| zhí tǒngr kù-zi | 直統兒褲子 |

| bell-bottom pants | 喇叭裤 |
| lǎ bā kù | 喇叭褲 |

| lining | 里子 |
| lǐ-zi | 裏子 |

| a slipknot | 活结 |
| huó jié | 活結 |

| a knot | 死结 |
| sǐ jié | 死結 |

barber shop **lí fǎ diàn**	理发店 理髮店	bald **tū tóu**	秃头 秃頭
barber's pole **hóng lán zhuǎn dòng dēng**	红蓝转动灯 紅藍轉動燈	wig **jiá fǎ**	假发 假髮
barber **lí fǎ shī**	理发师 理髮師	toupee **nán xiǎo piànr jiá fǎ**	男小片儿假发 男小片兒假髮
hair **tóu-fa**	头发 頭髮	human hair wig **zhēn tóu-fa-de jiá fǎ**	真头发的假发 真頭髮的假髮
haircut **lí fǎ**	理发 理髮	synthetic fiber wig **hé chéng xiān wéi jiá fǎ**	合成纤维假发 合成纖維假髮
hairstyle **fǎ xíng**	发型 髮型	pomade **tóu yóu**	头油 頭油
trim **jiǎn xiū**	剪修 剪修	hair oil **yè tǐ tóu yóu**	液体头油 液體頭油
let hair grow **xù fǎ**	蓄发 蓄髮	vaseline **fán shì lín yóu**	凡士林油 凡士林油
electric hair-chippers **diàn tuī-zi**	电推子 電推子	shave **guā hú-zi**	刮胡子 刮鬍子
thinning scissors **dǎ báo jiǎn-zi**	打薄剪子 打薄剪子	shaving knife **tì hú dāor**	剃胡刀儿 剃鬍刀兒
crewcut; butch **píng tóu**	平头 平頭	mustache **bā zì húr**	八字胡儿 八字鬍兒
part hair **fēn fǎ**	分发 分髮	goateed **liú shān yáng hú-zi**	留山羊胡子 留山羊鬍子
comb your hair **shū tóu**	梳头 梳頭	wearing long beard **liú cháng hú-zi**	留长胡子 留長鬍子
sideburn **bìn jiǎor**	鬓角儿 鬢角兒	bearded face **mán liǎn hú xǔ**	满脸胡须 滿臉鬍鬚
losing my hair **diào tóu-fa**	掉头发 掉頭髮		

Beauty Salon 美髮廳 28B

| beauty parlor; salon | 美发厅；美容院 |
| mèi fǎ tīng; měi róng yüàn | 美髮廳；美容院 |

| beautician | 美发师 |
| mèi fǎ shī | 美髮師 |

| hairdresser | 做发师 |
| zuò fǎ shī | 做髮師 |

| hairdressing | 做头发 |
| zuò tóu-fa | 做頭髮 |

| cutting & styling | 剪发与做发型 |
| jián fǎ yǔ zuò fǎ xíng | 剪髮與做髮型 |

| hairdo | 妇女的发型 |
| fù nǚ-de fǎ xíng | 婦女的髮型 |

| hair set | 妇女做发型 |
| fù nǚ zuò fǎ xíng | 婦女做髮型 |

| fine-tooth comb | 细齿梳子 |
| xì chǐ shū-ze | 細齒梳子 |

| coarse-tooth comb | 粗齿梳子 |
| cū chǐ shū-ze | 粗齒梳子 |

| card (for hair) | 钢丝刷 |
| gāng sī shūa | 鋼絲刷 |

| hair wash; shampoo | 洗发 |
| xí fǎ | 洗髮 |

| shampoo | 洗发精 |
| xí fǎ jīng | 洗髮精 |

| conditioner | 润发乳 |
| rùn fǎ rǔ | 潤髮乳 |

| scalp | 头皮 |
| tóu pí | 頭皮 |

| dandruff | 头皮屑 |
| tóu pí xiè | 頭皮屑 |

| rinse | 冲洗 |
| chōng xǐ | 冲洗 |

| hair drier | 吹干机 |
| chuī gān jī | 吹乾機 |

| dry with towel | 擦干 |
| cā gān | 擦乾 |

| blow dry | 吹干 |
| chuī gān | 吹乾 |

| straight hair | 直头发 |
| zhí tóu-fa | 直頭髮 |

| permanent wave | 电烫 |
| diàn tàng | 電燙 |

| electric curler | 电烫发棒 |
| diàn tàng fǎ bàng | 電燙髮棒 |

| hair curler | 卷发夹子 |
| jüán fǎ jiá-zi | 捲髮夾子 |

| natural wavy hair | 自然卷儿 |
| zì rán jüǎnr | 自然捲兒 |

| large curl | 大卷儿 |
| dà jüǎnr | 大捲兒 |

| kinky hair | 黑人卷曲发 |
| hē rén jüǎn qū fǎ | 黑人捲曲髮 |

| hair band | 发箍 |
| fǎ gū | 髮箍 |

| bobby pin; hairpin | 发夹；夹发针 |
| fǎ jiá; jiá fǎ zhēn | 髮夾；夾髮針 |

| hair net | 发网 |
| fá wǎng | 髮網 |

| dye; tint | 染发 |
| rǎn fǎ | 染髮 |

hair dye **rán fǎ jì**	染发剂 染髮劑	salt & pepper hair **huī bái fǎ**	灰白发 灰白髮
red hair **hóng fǎ**	红发 紅髮	silver gray hair **yín bái fǎ**	银白发 銀白髮
red headed **hóng fǎ nán rén**	红发男人 紅髮男人	white hair **bái fǎ**	白发 白髮
brunette **zōng fǎ**	棕发 棕髮	bangs **liú hǎir**	浏海儿 瀏海兒
blonde **jīn fǎ nǔ láng**	金发女郎 金髮女郎	fringe **liú sū**	流苏 流蘇
blond **jīn fǎ**	金发 金髮	braid; queue **biàn-zi**	辫子 辮子
black hair **hēi fǎ**	黑发 黑髮	ponytail **má wěi biàn**	马尾辫 馬尾辮
gray hair **huī fǎ**	灰发 灰髮	pigtail **dān tiáo biàn-zi**	单条辫子 單條辮子

make oneself looks pretty **dǎ-ban**	打扮 打扮	freckles **què bān**	雀斑 雀斑
cosmetics **huà zhuāng pǐn**	化妆品 化妝品	blackhead **hēi tóur fěn cì**	黑头儿粉刺 黑頭兒粉刺
make-up **huà zhuāng**	化妆 化妝	wrinkles **zhòu wén**	皱纹 皺紋
makeup case **huà zhuāng xiāng**	化妆箱 化妝箱	unfolded eyelid **dān yǎn pír**	单眼皮儿 單眼皮兒
vanity case **shū zhuāng hér**	梳妆盒儿 梳妝盒兒	folded eyelid **shuāng yǎn pír**	双眼皮儿 雙眼皮兒
oily skin **yóu xìng pí-fu**	油性皮肤 油性皮膚	slit-eyed **mī mī yǎn**	眯眯眼 瞇瞇眼
dry skin **gān xìng pí-fu**	干性皮肤 乾性皮膚	dimple **jiǔ wō**	酒窝 酒窩
neutral skin **zhōng xìng pí-fu**	中性皮肤 中性皮膚	do a facial **zuò liǎn**	做脸 做臉
sensitive skin **mín gǎn xìng pí-fu**	敏感性皮肤 敏感性皮膚	facial mask **miàn mó**	面膜 面膜
beauty spot **měi rén zhì**	美人痣 美人痣	cuticle removal **qù jiǎo zhí**	去角质 去角質
dimple **jiǔ wōr**	酒窝儿 酒窩兒	fruit acids **guǒ suān**	果酸 果酸
scar **chuāng bā**	疮疤 瘡疤	bleach cream **měi bái gāo**	美白膏 美白膏
pimple **qīng chūn dòu; miàn pào**	青春痘；面疱 青春痘；面皰	keep moisture **bǎo chí shī rùn**	保持湿润 保持濕潤
acne **fěn cì**	粉刺 粉刺	lotion **rǔ yè**	乳液 乳液
squeeze; extract **jǐ**	挤 擠（粉刺）	facial cream **miàn shuāng**	面霜 面霜

sun block **gé lí shuāng**	隔离霜 隔離霜	smear **yūn-chu lái-le**	晕出来了 暈出來了
suntan oil **fáng shài yóu**	防晒油 防曬油	cleansing cream **xiè zhuāng miàn shuāng**	卸妆面霜 卸妝面霜
ultraviolet ray **zǐ wài xiàn**	紫外线 紫外線	dandruff remover **qù tóu-pi shuǐ**	去头皮水 去頭皮水
powder foundation **fén dǐ**	粉底 粉底	hand lotion **hù shǒu shuāng**	护手霜 護手霜
powder (make up) **mì fěn; pū fěn**	蜜粉；扑粉 蜜粉；撲粉	perfume **xiāng shuǐr**	香水儿 香水兒
powder puff **fěn pūr**	粉朴儿 粉撲兒	atomizer **pēn xiāng shuǐr píng**	喷香水儿瓶 噴香水兒瓶
compact **fěn hér**	粉盒儿 粉盒兒	cologne **nán yòng xiāng shuǐ**	男用香水 男用香水
liquid powder **shuí fěn**	水粉 水粉	after shaving lotion **guā hú shuǐ**	刮胡水 刮鬍水
rouge **yān-zhi; sāi hóng**	胭脂；腮红 胭脂；腮紅	skin moisturizer **rùn fū gāo**	润肤膏 潤膚膏
eye shadow **yán yǐng gāo**	眼影膏 眼影膏	deodorant **qù hú chòu shuǐ**	去狐臭水 去狐臭水
eye liner **yǎn xiàn bǐ**	眼线笔 眼線筆	lanolin oil **mián yáng yóu**	绵羊油 綿羊油
eyelash curler **jüǎn jié máo qì**	卷睫毛器 捲睫毛器	manicure **xiū shóu zhī-jia**	修手指甲 修手指甲
false eyelashes **jiǎ jié máo**	假睫毛 假睫毛	pedicure **xiū jiǎo zhī-jia**	修脚指甲 修腳指甲
mascara **jié máo gāo**	睫毛膏 睫毛膏	cuticle nipper **xiū zhī-jia pí jiǎn-zi**	修指甲皮剪子 修指甲皮剪子
eyebrow **méi-mao**	眉毛 眉毛	nail scissors **zhī-jia jiǎn-zi**	指甲剪子 指甲剪子
eyebrow pencil **méi bǐ**	眉笔 眉筆	nail clippers **zhī-jia dāor**	指甲刀儿 指甲刀兒
eyebrow brush **méi shuā**	眉刷 眉刷	nail file **zhī-jia cuò**	指甲锉 指甲銼
tweezers **niè-zi**	镊子 鑷子	varnish toe-nail **mó jiǎo zhī-jia yóu**	抹脚指甲油 抹腳指甲油
lipstick **chún gāo; kǒu hóng**	唇膏；口红 唇膏；口紅	nail polish **zhī-jia yóu**	指甲油 指甲油
apply; put on **mǒ**	抹 抹	nail polish remover **qù guāng shuǐ**	去光水 去光水

Jewelry Store 首飾店 29B

English	Pinyin	简体	繁体
jewelry	shǒu-shi	首饰	首飾
jewel	zhū bǎo	珠宝	珠寶
jewel box	shǒu-shi xiāng	首饰箱	首飾箱
ring	jiè-zhi	戒指	戒指
earrings	ěr huán	耳环	耳環
chandelier earrings	cháng ěr huán	长耳环	長耳環
screw-back earrings	nǐng luó-si shì ěr huán	拧螺丝式耳环	擰螺絲式耳環
pierced ear	zhā-guo ěr-duo yǎnr	扎过耳朵眼儿	紮過耳朵眼兒
stud earrings	chā dòng shì ěr huán	插洞式耳环	插洞式耳環
hook earrings	gōu shì ěr huán	钩式耳环	鉤式耳環
pin; broach	bié zhēn	别针	別針
bracelet	zhuó-zi	镯子	鐲子
ankle bracelet	jiǎo zhuó	脚镯	腳鐲
arm bracelet	gē-bi gūr	胳臂箍儿	胳臂箍兒
necklace	xiàng liàn	项链	項鏈
choker	xiàng quān	项圈	項圈
pendant	zhuì-zi	坠子	墜子
chain	liàn-zi	链子	鍊子
locket	jī xīn zhuì-zi	鸡心坠子	雞心墜子
cuff links	xiù kòur	袖扣儿	袖扣兒
tie pin	lǐng dài jiá-zi	领带夹子	領帶夾子
collar pin	lǐng zhēn	领针	領針
mount	xiāng	镶	鑲
gem	bǎo shí	宝石	寶石
birthstone	shēng rì bǎo shí	生日宝石	生日寶石
cameo	fú diāo bǎo shí	浮雕宝石	浮雕寶石
ruby	hóng bǎo shí	红宝石	紅寶石
sapphire	lán bǎo shí	蓝宝石	藍寶石
aquamarine	shuǐ lán bǎo shí	水蓝宝石	水藍寶石
emerald	lù bǎo shí	绿宝石	綠寶石

turquoise **lǜ sōng shí**	绿松石 綠松石	coral **shān hú**	珊瑚 珊瑚
jade **cuì; yù**	翠；玉 翠；玉	tigereye **hú yǎn**	虎眼 虎眼
green jade **fěi cuì**	翡翠 翡翠	opal; cat's eye **māor yǎn**	猫儿眼 貓兒眼
white jade **bái yù**	白玉 白玉	diamond **zuàn shí**	钻石 鑽石
jasper **bì yù**	碧玉 碧玉	rhinestone **jiǎ zuàn shí**	假钻石 假鑽石
topaz **huáng yù**	黄玉 黃玉	genuine **zhēn-de; tiān rán-de**	真的；天然的 真的；天然的
onyx **hēi yù**	黑玉 黑玉	imitation **fǎng zhì pǐn**	仿制品 仿製品
zircon **fēng xìn zǐ yù**	风信子玉 風信子玉	luster **guāng zé**	光泽 光澤
rhodonite **fén shuǐ jīng**	粉水晶 粉水晶	glistening **shǎn guāng**	闪光 閃光
crystal **shuǐ jīng**	水晶 水晶	carat, karat (gem) **kè lā**	克拉 克拉
rock crystal **shí jīng**	石晶 石晶	platinum; white gold **bái jīn**	白金 白金
amethyst **zí shuǐ jīng**	紫水晶 紫水晶	gold **huáng jīn**	黄金 黃金
quartz **shí yīng**	石英 石英	18 karat gold **shí bā kāi jīn**	18 开金 18 開金
bloodstone **xiě shí suí**	血石髓 血石髓	gold foil **jīn bó**	金箔 金箔
mother of pearl **zhēn zhū mǔ**	珍珠母 珍珠母	gold foiled **bāo jīn**	包金 包金
pearl **zhēn zhū**	珍珠 珍珠	gilt; gold plated **dù jīn**	镀金 鍍金
cultured pearl **yǎng zhū**	养珠 養珠	ornamental gold **jīn shì**	金饰 金飾
simulated pearl **jiǎ zhū**	假珠 假珠	niello **tài guó hēi jīn**	泰国黑金 泰國黑金
agate **má nǎo**	玛瑙 瑪瑙	sterling silver **chún yín**	纯银 純銀
amber **hǔ pò**	琥珀 琥珀	costume jewelry **jiá shǒu-shi**	假首饰 假首飾

Souvenir & Curio Stores
土產珍品店

local products; ethnic products 土产		after-sales service	售後服務
tú chǎn	土產	shòu hòu fú wù	售後服務
souvenir store	土产店	price list	价目表
tú chǎn diàn	土產店	jià mù biǎo	價目表
souvenir	纪念品	sales invoice	售货发票
jì niàn pǐn	紀念品	shòu huò fā piào	售貨發票
antique	古玩	white jade carvings	白玉雕刻
gǔ wán	古玩	bái yù diāo kè	白玉雕刻
curio store	珍品店	green jade carvings	翡翠雕刻
zhēn pǐn diàn	珍品店	fěi cuì diāo kè	翡翠雕刻
handmade	手工做的	Jadeite Cabbage	翠玉白菜
shǒu gōng zuò-de	手工做的	cuì yù bái cài	翠玉白菜
handicrafts	手工艺品	Coral Ornaments	珊瑚雕刻
shǒu gōng yì pǐn	手工藝品	shān hú diāo kè	珊瑚雕刻
customer	顾客；主顾	precious snuff bottles	珍贵鼻烟壶
gù kè; zhǔ-gu	顧客；主顧	zhēn guì bí yān hú	珍貴鼻煙壺
wholesale	批发	cloisonne	景泰蓝瓶
pī fā	批發	jǐng tài lán píng	景泰藍瓶
retail	零售	cinnabar vaces	红朱砂雕漆瓶
líng shòu	零售	hóng zhū shā diāo qī píng	紅硃砂雕漆瓶
cash register	收银机	famous calligraphy/painting	名人字画
shōu yín jī	收銀機	míng rén zì huà	名人字畫
on consignment	寄售	invaluable; priceless	价值连城
jì shòu	寄售	jià zhí lián chéng	價值連城
mail order	邮购	ceramic	陶制品
yóu gòu	郵購	táo zhì pǐn	陶製品
express mail	快递	earthenware	陶器
kuài dì	快遞	táo qì	陶器
service	服务	porcelain	瓷制品
fú wù	服務	cí zhì pǐn	瓷製品

Jingde blue/white china **Jǐng Dé Qīng Huā Cí**	景德青花瓷 **景德青花瓷**	
glassware **bō-li qì**	玻璃器 玻璃器	
brassware **tóng qì**	铜器 銅器（黃銅）	
sterling silver ornaments **chún yín zhì pǐn**	纯银制品 純銀製品	
bronzeware **qīng tóng qì**	青铜器 青銅器	
brass polish **cā tóng yóu**	擦铜油 擦銅油	
lacquerware **qī qì**	漆器 漆器	
shell **bàng ké**	蚌壳 蚌殼	
inlay **xiāng qiàn**	镶嵌 鑲嵌	
snake skin purse **shí pí pí bāo**	蛇皮皮包 蛇皮皮包	
alligaeor skin belt **è yǔ pí pí dài**	鳄鱼皮皮带 鱷魚皮皮帶	
deer's horn specimen **lù jiǎo**	鹿角标本 鹿角標本	
animal specimens **biāo běn**	动物标本 動物標本	
ox horn carvings **niú jiǎo yì pǐn**	牛角艺品 牛角藝品	
ivory carvings **xiàng yá diāo kè**	象牙雕刻 象牙雕刻	
basketry **biān lán-zi shǒu-yi**	编篮子手艺 編籃子手藝	
leather articles **pí gé zhì pǐn**	皮革制品 皮革製品	
leather artwork **pí gé yì-shu pǐn**	皮革艺术品 皮革藝術品	
palace lantern **gōng dēng**	宫灯 宮燈	
wooden carving **mù kè**	木刻 木刻	

embroideries **cì xiù**	刺绣 刺繡	
screen **píng fēng**	屏风 屏風	
scroll **jüǎn zhóu**	卷轴 捲軸	
camphor chest **zhāng mù xiāng**	樟木箱 樟木箱	
teakwood table **yòu mù zhuō-zi**	柚木桌子 柚木桌子	
teakwood stand **yòu mù píng zuòr**	柚木瓶座儿 柚木瓶座兒	
teakwood plate stand **yòu mù pán zuòr**	柚木盘座儿 柚木盤座兒	
mahogany table **hóng mù jiā jù**	红木家俱 紅木傢俱	
grass mat **shuì xí**	睡席 睡蓆	
straw mat **cǎo xí**	草席 草蓆	
place mat **dān rén cān diànr**	单人餐垫儿 單人餐墊兒	
straw hat **cǎo màor**	草帽儿 草帽兒	
bamboo basket **zhú lán-zi**	竹篮子 竹籃子	
statue **diāo xiàng**	雕像 雕像	
incense burner **xiāng lú**	香炉 香爐	
paper lantern **zhǐ dēng-long**	纸灯笼 紙燈籠	
smoking set **yāng jǜ**	烟具 煙具	
wind chimes **fēng líng**	风铃 風鈴	
knit **zhēn zhī pǐn**	针织品 針織品	
woven work **biān zhì（zhī）pǐn**	编制（织）品 編製（織）品	

Souvenir & Curio Stores

Clocks & Watches 30B 鐘錶

English	Pinyin	简体	繁體
watch	biǎo	表	錶
wrist watch	shóu biǎo	手表	手錶
pocket watch	huái biǎo	怀表	懷錶
dial (watch)	biǎo méng-zi	表蒙子	錶蒙子
hour hand	shí zhēn	时针	時針
minute hand	fēn zhēn	分针	分針
second hand	miǎo zhēn	秒针	秒針
ticktack	dī dā shēng	滴答声	滴答聲
advance the watch 3 mins.	wǎng qián bō sān fēn zhōng	往前拨3分钟	往前撥3分鐘
set back the watch 3 mins.	wǎng hòu bō sān fēn zhōng	往後拨3分钟	往後撥3分鐘
keeps time	zhǔn	准	準
clock	zhōng	钟	
digital watch	shù zì shóu biǎo	数字手表	數字手錶
digital clock	shù zì zhōng	数字钟	數字鐘
alarm clock	nào zhōng	闹钟	鬧鐘

English	Pinyin	简体	繁體
watch band	biǎo dài	表带	錶帶
luminous watch	yè míng biǎo	夜明表	夜明錶
electronic clock	diàn zǐ zhōng	电子钟	電子鐘
time clock	dá kǎ zhōng	打卡钟	打卡鐘
cuckoo clock	bù gú niǎor zhōng	布谷鸟儿钟	布穀鳥兒鐘
★watch gains time (see P.389★表快没坏)	biáo lǎo-shi kuài	錶老是快(壞了)	
★watch loses time (see Group 44B★表慢没坏)	biáo lǎo-shi màn	錶老是慢(壞了)	
repair	xiū li	修理	修理
chime	zhōng xiǎng	钟响	鐘響
striking (hourly)	bào shí	报时	報時
waterproof	fáng shuǐ	防水	防水
shock-proof	fáng zhèn	防震	防震
spring (watch)	fā tiáo	发条	發條
to wind (watch)	shàng xián	上弦	上弦
self-winding watch	zì dòng shàng xián biǎo	自动上弦表	自動上弦錶

Entertainment & Hobbies 娱乐与嗜好

entertainment **yǘ lè**	娱乐 娛樂	mixed bath **xǐ yūan yāng yù**	洗鸳鸯浴 洗鴛鴦浴
hobby **shì hào**	嗜好 嗜好	body-body bath **xǐ tài guó yù**	洗泰国浴 洗泰國浴
window-shopping **guàng jiē**	逛街 逛街	massage **àn mó**	按摩 按摩
stroll **liū-da**	溜达 溜達	finger pressure **zhǐ yā**	指压 指壓
browse **guàng**	逛 逛	facial massage **liǎn bù àn mó**	脸部按摩 臉部按摩
swapmeet; flea market **tiào zǎo shì chǎng**	跳蚤市场 跳蚤市場	body massage **quán shēn àn mó**	全身按摩 全身按摩
joy ride **kāi chē dōu fēngr**	开车兜风儿 開車兜風兒	stretching (one's limbs) **shēn lǎn yāo**	伸懒腰 伸懶腰
chatting **xián tán; liáo tiānr**	闲谈；聊天儿 閒談；聊天兒	yawn **dǎ hā qiàn**	打哈欠 打哈欠
chewing the fat **xián-de wú liáo; guǐ chě**	闲得无聊；鬼扯 閒得無聊；鬼扯	toe massage **niē jiǎo**	捏脚 捏腳
sunbath **rì guāng yù**	日光浴 日光浴	drinking **hē jiǔ**	喝酒 喝酒
sulfur bath **liú huáng yù**	硫磺浴 硫磺浴	to get drunk **bú zuì bú sàn**	不醉不散 不醉不散
sauna **pào sān wēn nuǎn**	泡三温暖 泡三溫暖	I'm sober! **wǒ méi zuì**	我没醉！ 我沒醉！
ultrasonic bath **pào chāo yīn bō yù**	泡超音波浴 泡超音波浴	he had one to many **tā hē duō-le**	他喝多了！ 他喝多了！
spa **pào wēn qüán yù**	泡温泉浴 泡溫泉浴	hangover **sù zuì**	宿醉 宿醉
Turkish bath **pào Tú Er Qí Yù**	泡土耳其浴 泡土耳其浴	smoke a cigarette **chōu yān**	抽菸 抽菸

puff out ring of smoke **chōu yān tǔ yān qüānr**	抽菸吐菸圈儿 抽菸吐菸圈兒	gossip in a teahouse **chá guǎnr liáo tiānr**	茶馆儿聊天儿 茶館兒聊天兒
smoke a cigar **chōu xüě jiā**	抽雪茄 抽雪茄	go to a pub **qù jiǔ bà**	去酒吧 去酒吧
smoke a pipe **chōu yān dǒu**	抽菸斗 抽菸斗	chasing girls; courting **pào niūr**	泡妞儿 泡妞兒
chew tobacco **jiáo yān cǎo**	嚼菸草 嚼菸草	to hook guys **diào kǎi-zi**	吊凯子 吊凱子
chew betel nut **jiáo bīn láng**	嚼槟榔 嚼檳榔	go to a club **qù jù lè bù**	去俱乐部 去俱樂部
strike a match **huá huǒ chái**	划火柴 划火柴	sex up the men **gōu yǐn nán-ren**	勾引男人 勾引男人
lighter **dá huǒ jī**	打火机 打火機	go to a girlie winehouse **qù jiǔ jiā**	去酒家 去酒家
flint **dá huǒ shí**	打火石 打火石	go to a ballroom **qù wǔ tīng**	去舞厅 去舞廳
lighter fluid **dá huǒ jī yóu**	打火机油 打火機油	go to a brothel **guàng yáo-zi**	逛窑子 逛窯子
using narcotics **xī dú**	吸毒 吸毒	have sexual intercourse **qù dǎ pào; xìng jiāo**	去打炮；性交 去打砲；性交
smoking opium **chōu yā piàn yān**	抽鸦片菸 抽鴉片菸	making love **zuò ài**	做爱 做愛
smoke pot; joint; grass **chōu dà má yān**	抽大麻菸 抽大麻菸	fondle **ài fǔ; fǔ mō**	爱抚；抚摸 愛撫；撫摸
marihuana; weed; pot **dà má yān**	大麻菸 大麻菸	masturbation; jerk off **shǒu yín; zì wèi**	手淫；自慰 手淫；自慰
heroin **hǎi luò yīn**	海洛英 海洛英	oral sex; a blow job **kǒu jiāo; kǒu yín**	口交；口淫 口交；口淫
shooting morphine **dá mǎ fēi**	打吗啡 打嗎啡	to do sixty-nine **bí cǐ hù xiǎng kǒu jiāo**	彼此互相口交 彼此互相口交
Benzodiazepines **Lèi ān mián zhèn jìng jì**	类安眠镇静剂 類安眠鎮靜劑	sodomy **gāng jiāo**	肛交 肛交
pop E (ecstasy; MDMA) **chī yáo tóu wán**	吃摇头丸 吃搖頭丸	orgy **zá jiāo**	杂交 雜交
amphetamine; ice **ān fēi tā mìng**	安非他命 安非他命	having a ball **wánr-de tòng-kuai**	玩儿得痛快 玩兒得痛快
dropping pills **tūn mí-hun yào**	吞迷魂药 吞迷魂藥	paint the town red **fēng kuáng-di wánr**	疯狂地玩儿 瘋狂地玩兒
get high **qīng piāo piāo-de gǎn jüé**	轻飘飘的感觉 輕飄飄的感覺	singing **chàng gēr**	唱歌儿 唱歌兒

play musical instrument **wánr yüè qì**	玩儿乐器 玩兒樂器	play Chinese chess **xià xiàng qí**	下象棋 下象棋
paint pictures **huà huàr**	画画儿 畫畫兒	to play 'go' **xià wéi qí**	下围棋 下圍棋
paint landscapes on location **xiě shēng**	写生 寫生	to play checkers **wánr tiào qí**	玩儿跳棋 玩兒跳棋
take photos **shè yǐng**	摄影 攝影	play monopoly **wánr dà fù wēng**	玩儿大富翁 玩兒大富翁
collect stamps **jí yóu**	集邮 集郵	play bingo **wánr bīn guǒ**	玩儿宾果 玩兒賓果
collect coins **shōu jí yìng bì**	收集硬币 收集硬幣	play bridge **wánr qiáo pái**	玩儿桥牌 玩兒橋牌
collect match boxes **shōu jí huǒ chái hér**	收集火柴盒儿 收集火柴盒兒	work a crossword puzzle **tián zì yóu xì**	填字游戏 填字遊戲
collect match books **shōu jí zhí huǒ chái**	收集纸火柴 收集紙火柴	play a puzzle **wánr pīn tú yóu xì**	玩儿拼图游戏 玩兒拼圖遊戲
collect post cards **shōu jí míng xìn piànr**	收集明信片儿 收集明信片兒	the pieces **pīn tú suì kuàir**	拼图碎块儿 拼圖碎塊兒
listen to the radio **tīng shōu yīn jī**	听收音机 聽收音機	fit into (puzzle game) **bǎi-jin-qü; chā-jin-qü**	摆进去；插进去 擺進去；插進去
listen to music **tīng yīn yüè**	听音乐 聽音樂	fit into one another **kuài kuài hù xiāng róng hé**	块块互相容合 塊塊互相容合
watching TV **kàn diàn shì**	看电视 看電視	fight one's way out **kè fú wàn nán**	克服万难 克服萬難
see a movie **kàn diàn yǐngr**	看电影儿 看電影兒	quit the game **bù wánr-le**	不玩儿了 不玩兒了
read newspapers **kàn bào**	看报 看報	keep dogs (stray dogs) **yáng gǒu (lióu làng gǒu)**	养狗(流浪狗) 養狗(流浪狗)
read magazines **kàn huà bào**	看画报 看畫報	breed dogs; kennel **pèi gǒu; gǒu shè**	配狗；狗舍 配狗；狗舍
read novels **kàn xiǎo shuōr**	看小说儿 看小說兒	raise pigeons **yǎng gē-zi**	养鸽子 養鴿子
read comic books **kàn màn huàr shū**	看漫画儿书 看漫畫兒書	fish culture **yǎng yú**	养鱼 養魚
difficult question contest **yì zhì yóu xì**	益智游戏 益智遊戲	gardening **zhòng huār**	种花儿 種花兒
make model airplanes **zuò fē jī mó xíng**	做飞机模型 做飛機模型	dunging vegetable garden **cài yüán shí féi**	菜园施肥 菜園施肥
play chess **xià yáng xiàng qí**	下洋象棋 下洋象棋	practice flower arrangement **chā huā**	插花 插花

cooking **pēng rèn**	烹饪 烹飪	children's slide **liū huá tī**	溜滑梯 溜滑梯
knitting **dǎ máo xiàn**	打毛线 打毛線	rocking horse **qí mù mǎ**	骑木马 騎木馬
go to a concert **tīng yīn yüè huì**	听音乐会 聽音樂會	roller coaster **yǔn xiāo fēi chē**	云霄飞车 雲霄飛車
go to night clubs **qù yè zǒng huì**	去夜总会 去夜總會	merry-go-round **xüán zhuǎn mù mǎ**	旋转木马 旋轉木馬
see a circus **kàn mǎ xì**	看马戏 看馬戲	kite flying **fàng fēng zhēn**	放风筝 放風箏
see a stage show **kàn wǔ tái biáo yǎn**	看舞台表演 看舞臺表演	ride on the swings **dàng qiū qiān**	荡秋千 盪鞦韆
see a drama **kàn huà jù**	看话剧 看話劇	play at seesaw **wánr qiāo qiāo bǎn**	玩儿跷跷板 玩兒蹺蹺板
see an opera **kàn kē jù**	看歌剧 看歌劇	hopscotch **tiào fáng-zi**	跳房子 跳房子
★see Beijing opera **kàn jīng xì**	看京戏 看京戲	play marbles **tán bō-li qiúr**	弹玻璃球儿 彈玻璃球兒
see a puppet show **kàn mù ǒu xì**	看木偶戏 看木偶戲	play games **zuò yóu xì**	作游戏 作遊戲
travel **lǚ xíng**	旅行 旅行	play TV games **dǎ diàn dòng wán jù**	打电动玩具 打電動玩具
spend the day in the country **jiāo yóu**	郊游 郊遊	draw a chance **mō jiǎng**	摸奖 摸獎
lounging around **xián dàng**	闲荡 閒蕩	raffle **chōu qiānr**	抽签儿 抽籤兒
hanging around in the corners 街上逛荡 **jiē-shang guàng dàng** 街上逛蕩		buy a lottery ticket **mái jiǎng qüàn**	买奖券 買獎券
go on a picnic **qù yě cān**	去野餐 去野餐	won the lottery **zhòng cǎi qüàn-le**	中彩券了 中彩券了
fishing **diào yú**	钓鱼 釣魚	see a cock-fight **kàn dòu jī**	看斗鸡 看鬥雞
go to amusement park **qù yóu lè yüán**	去游乐园 去遊樂園	see a horse race **kàn sài mǎ**	看赛马 看賽馬
play hide-and-seek **wán zhuō mí cáng**	玩捉迷藏 玩捉迷藏	see a dog race **kàn sài gǒu**	看赛狗 看賽狗
make-believe playmates **bàn jiā jiā jiǔ**	扮家家酒 扮家家酒	see a bullfight **kàn dòu niú**	看斗牛 看鬥牛
rope skipping **tiào shéng**	跳绳 跳繩	go to casino **qù dú chǎng**	去赌场 去賭場

Movie Fan

影迷

English	Chinese (Simplified)	Chinese (Traditional)
take in a movie **kàn diàn yǐngr**	看电影儿	看電影兒
movie theatre **diàn yǐngr yüàn**	电影儿院	電影兒院
cineprojector; projector **fàng yìng jī**	放映机	放映機
screen **yín mù**	银幕	銀幕
Chinese titles (subtitles) **zhōng wén zì mù**	中文字幕	中文字幕
program synopsis **shuō míng shū**	说明书	說明書
poster **hǎi bào**	海报	海報
showing today **jīn rì fàng yìng**	今日放映	今日放映
next showing **xià qí fàng yìng**	下期放映	下期放映
today only **zuì hòu yì tiān**	最后一天	最後一天
morning show **záo chǎng**	早场	早場
matinee **rì chǎng**	日场	日場
evening show **wán chǎng**	晚场	晚場
late show **wǔ yè chǎng**	午夜场	午夜場
coming soon **jìn rì fàng yìng**	近日放映	近日放映
ticket office **piào fángr**	票房儿	票房兒
complimentary ticket **zèng qüàn**	赠券	贈券
ticket **rù chǎng qüàn**	入场券	入場券
adult **chéng nián rén**	成年人	成年人
reserved seat **duì hàor rù zuò**	对号儿入座	對號兒入座
refund the ticket **tuì piào**	退票	退票
stand in line **pái duì**	排队	排隊
cut in a line **chā duì**	插队	插隊
scalper ticket **huáng niú piào**	黄牛票	黃牛票
full house **kè mǎn**	客满	客滿
on the main floor **lóu xià zuò weì**	楼下座位	樓下座位
in the balcony **lóu shàng zuò weì**	楼上座位	樓上座位
odd number seat **dān hàor zuò weì**	单号儿座位	單號兒座位
even number seat **shuāng hàor zuò weì**	双号儿座位	雙號兒座位
row **pái**	排	排

front seat **qián pái zuòr**	前排座儿 前排座兒	war picture **zhàn zhēng piàn**	战争片 戰爭片
back seat **hòu pái zuòr**	后排座儿 後排座兒	horror film **kǒng bù piàn**	恐怖片 恐怖片
exit **ān qüán mén**	安全门 安全門	adult movie **chéng rén diàn yǐngr**	成人电影儿 成人電影兒
entrance **rù kǒu**	入口 入口	science fiction movie **kē huàn piàn**	科幻片 科幻片
usher **dài zuò yüán**	带座员 帶座員	thriller film **jǐn zhāng piàn**	紧张片 緊張片
coming attractions **yǜ gào piàn**	预告片 預告片	ethical **lún lǐ piàn**	伦理片 倫理片
main feature **zhèng piàn**	正片 正片	educational **jiào yǜ piàn**	教育片 教育片
silent movie **mò piàn**	默片 默片	newsreel **xīn wén piàn**	新闻片 新聞片
black & white picture **hēi bái piàn**	黑白片 黑白片	documentary film **jì lù piàn**	记录片 記錄片
colored picture **cǎi sè piàn**	彩色片 彩色片	commercial **guǎng gào piàn**	广告片 廣告片
blockbuster movie **jǜ piàn**	巨片 巨片	slides **huàn dēng piàn**	幻灯片 幻燈片
detective picture **zhēn tàn piàn**	侦探片 偵探片	cartoon **kǎ tōng piàn**	卡通片 卡通片
Western picture **xī bù piàn**	西部片 西部片	literary film **wén yì piàn**	文艺片 文藝片
musical **yīn yüè piàn**	音乐片 音樂片	affectional film **ài qíng piàn**	爱情片 愛情片
comedy picture **xǐ jǜ piàn**	喜剧片 喜劇片	pornographic (porno) film **qíng sè piàn**	情色片 情色片
farce **xiào jǜ piàn**	笑剧片 笑劇片	violence film **bào lì piàn**	暴力片 暴力片
actioner **dòng zuò piàn**	动作片 動作片	sword-fighting film **wǔ xiá piàn**	武侠片 武俠片
slapstick **nào jǜ**	闹剧 鬧劇	gong-fu movie **gōng fū piàn**	功夫片 功夫片
tragedy film **bēi jǜ piàn**	悲剧片 悲劇片	historical drama **gǔ zhuāng piàn**	古装片 古裝片
adventure picture **jīng xiǎn (tàn xiǎn) piàn**	惊险(探险)片 驚險(探險)片	modern drama **shí zhuāng piàn**	时装片 時裝片

Oscar Ao Sī Kǎ	奥斯卡 奧斯卡	dilemma zuǒ yòu wéi nán	左右为难 左右為難
Academy Award jīn xiàng jiǎng	金像奖 金像獎	child star tóng xīng	童星 童星
supervisor jiān zhì	监制 監製	idol ǒu xiàng	偶像 偶像
producer zhì piàn	制片 製片	movie fan yǐng mí	影迷 影迷
playwright jù zuò jiā	剧作家 劇作家	movie critic yǐng píng rén	影评人 影評人
director dǎo yǎn	导演 導演	charity show cí shàn gōng yǎn	慈善公演 慈善公演
movie star míng xīng	明星 明星	studio shè yǐng péng	摄影棚 攝影棚
cast yǎn yuán zhèn róng	演员阵容 演員陣容	cameraman shè yǐng shī	摄影师 攝影師
best movie zuì jiā yǐng piàn	最佳影片 最佳影片	mercury vapor lamp shuǐ yín dēng	水银灯 水銀燈
featuring yóu mǒu júer yǎn chū	由某角儿演出 由某角兒演出	reflector fǎn shè bǎn	反射板 反射板
starring zhú yǎn	主演 主演	location shooting pāi wài jǐng	拍外景 拍外景
leading role zhú jiǎor (júer)	主角儿 主角兒	interior shooting nèi jǐng	内景 內景
supporting role pèi jiǎor (júer)	配角儿 配角兒	screen test shì jìng	试镜 試鏡
stunt man tì-shen	替身 替身	N.G.; No Good chóng pāi	重拍 重拍
best leading actor zuì jiā nán zhú jiǎor	最佳男主角儿 最佳男主角兒	crank up shā qīng	杀青 殺青
best leading actress zuì jiā nǚ zhú jiǎor	最佳女主角儿 最佳女主角兒	preview yù yǎn	预演 預演
character actor xìng-ge yǎn yuán	性格演员 性格演員	editing jiǎn jiē	剪接 剪接
secretly videotaped tōu pāi lù yǐng	偷拍录影 偷拍錄影	footage (film) piàn cháng	片长 片長
risk a double-cross hēi chī hēi	黑吃黑 黑吃黑	dubbing pèi yīn	配音 配音

night club
yè zǒng huì
夜总会
夜總會

emcee; master of ceremonies
sī yí
司仪
司儀

ballroom (dance hall)
wǔ tīng
舞厅
舞廳

floor show
wǔ chí bíao yǎn
舞池表演
舞池表演

revolving stage
xuán zhuǎn shì wǔ tái
旋转式舞台
旋轉式舞臺

stage lift
wǔ tái shēng jiàng jī
舞台升降机
舞臺升降機

thrust stage
shēn zhǎn tái
伸展台
伸展臺

raised platform
shēng jiàng shì wǔ tái
升降式舞台
升降式舞臺

guest of honor
tè bié lái bīn
特别来宾
特別來賓

draw a large audience
xī yǐn dà pī guan zhòng
吸引大批观众
吸引大批觀眾

sound effect
yīn xiǎng xiào guǒ
音响效果
音響效果

spotlight
jù guāng dēng
聚光灯
聚光燈

floodlight
sǎn guāng dēng
散光灯
散光燈

synopsis
shuō míng shū
说明书
說明書

program schedule
jié mù biǎo
节目表
節目表

program director
jié mù biān pái rén
节目编排人
節目編排人

band
yüè duì
乐队
樂隊

balloon
qì qiú
气球
氣球

mirror ball
bō-li xuán zhuǎn qiúr
玻璃旋转球儿
玻璃旋轉球兒

dressing room
gēng yī shì
更衣室
更衣室

talk show
tuō kǒu xiù
脱口秀
脫口秀

stage show
wǔ tái biáo yǎn
舞台表演
舞臺表演

chorus line
gē wǔ tuán
歌舞团
歌舞團

ballet
bā léi wǔ
芭蕾舞
芭蕾舞

ballet shoes
bā léi wǔ xié
芭蕾舞鞋
芭蕾舞鞋

toeshoe
zhǐ jiān wǔ xié
趾尖舞鞋
趾尖舞鞋

tutu
bā léi wǔ yī
芭蕾舞衣
芭蕾舞衣

ballet breeches
bā léi wǔ kù
芭蕾舞裤
芭蕾舞褲

flamingo
Xī Bān Yá Wǔ
西班牙舞
西班牙舞

belly dance
dù pí wǔ
肚皮舞
肚皮舞

English	简体	Pinyin	繁體
line dance	大腿舞		大腿舞
dà tuí wǔ			
drag show	男扮女装表演		男扮女裝表演
nán bàn nǚ zhuāng biáo yǎn			
transvest show	反串表演		反串表演
fǎn chuàn biáo yǎn			
impersonation show	模仿表演		模仿表演
mó fǎng biáo yǎn			
impersonator	模仿艺人		模仿藝人
mó fǎng yì rén			
sex change performer	变性艺人		變性藝人
biàn xìng yì rén			
play a part in	扮演一个角色		扮演一個角色
bàn yǎn yí-ge jiǎo-se			
play the role of	扮演		扮演
bàn yǎn			
clown	小丑儿		小丑兒
xiáo chǒur			
circus	马戏团		馬戲團
mǎ xì tuán			
raise curtain	启幕		啟幕
qǐ mù			
announcer	报幕		報幕
bào mù			
background	背景		背景
bèi jǐng			
backstage off stage	后台		後臺
hòu taí			
scenery	布景		佈景
bù jǐng			
property	道具		道具
dào jù			
costumes	行头		行頭
xíng-tou			
Ladies and Gentlemen!	个位观众好！		個位觀眾好！
gè wèi guan zhòng hǎo			
The next number, is…	下一个节目是..		下一個節目是..
xià yí-ge jié mù, shì…			
tightrope dancer	走绳索		走繩索
zǒu shéng suǒ			

English	简体	Pinyin	繁體
life net	安全网		安全網
ān quán wǎng			
aerialist	空中特技		空中特技
kōng zhōng tè jì			
fly lines	飞行绳索		飛行繩索
fēi xíng shéng suǒ			
iron bar acrobatics	杠上杂耍		槓上雜耍
gàng shàng zá shuǎ			
rope-bicycling	单车走钢丝		單車走鋼絲
dān chē zǒu gāng sī			
trick cycling	单车绝技		單車絕技
dān chē jüé jì			
monocycle	独轮车		獨輪車
dú lún chē			
fire hoop	跳火圈儿		跳火圈兒
tiào huǒ qüān			
juggling	变戏法儿		變戲法兒
biàn xì fǎr			
iron bar bending	弯铁棒		彎鐵棒
wān tiě bàng			
slipping-the-bond	脱身术		脫身術
tuō shēn shù			
ventriloquist	腹语表演		腹語表演
fù yǔ biáo yǎn			
body-sawing	锯体表演		鋸體表演
jù tǐ biáo yǎn			
dwarf show	侏儒戏		侏儒戲
zhū rú xì			
monkey tricks	耍猴儿戏		耍猴兒戲
shuǎ hóur xì			
horse dance	马舞		馬舞
má wǔ			
dog show	狗群表演		狗群表演
gǒu qún biáo yǎn			
bear show	狗熊表演		狗熊表演
gǒu xióng biáo yǎn			
elephant show	大象表演		大象表演
dà xiàng biáo yǎn			
human pyramid building	叠罗汉		疊羅漢
dié luó hàn			

turn a somersault **fān gēn-tou**	翻跟头 翻跟頭	middle stall **zhōng zuòr**	中座儿 中座兒
trapeze act; air docking **kōng zhōng fēi rén**	空中飞人 空中飛人	back stall **hòu zuòr**	后座儿 後座兒
fire spitting **tù huǒ**	吐火 吐火	audience **tīng zhòng**	听众 聽眾
sword swallowing **tūn jiàn**	吞剑 吞劍	spectator **guān zhòng**	观众 觀眾
knife throwing **fēi dāo biáo yǎn**	飞刀表演 飛刀表演	clap **gú zhǎng**	鼓掌 鼓掌
plates juggling **shuǎ pán-zi**	耍盘子 耍盤子	applause **zhǎng shēng**	掌声 掌聲
mimic **kǒu jì**	口技 口技	the audience hooted **hè dào cǎi**	喝倒采 喝倒采
tongue twister **rào kǒu lìngr**	绕口令儿 繞口令兒	curtain falls **luò mù**	落幕 落幕
magic **mó shù**	魔术 魔術	intermission **zhōng chǎng xiū xí**	中场休息 中場休息
hypnotic **cuī mián shù**	催眠术 催眠術	audiences leave **guān zhòng fēn fēn lí xí**	观众纷纷离席 觀眾紛紛離席
striptease **tuō yī wǔ**	脱衣舞 脫衣舞	smoking room **xī yān shì**	吸烟室 吸煙室
burlesque show **dī jí luó tí wǔ**	低级裸体舞 低級裸體舞	cloakroom **yī maò jiān**	衣帽间 衣帽間
cover charge **jī běn fèi**	基本费 基本費	generator **fā diàn jī**	发电机 發電機
minimum charge **zuì dī xiāo fèi é**	最低消费额 最低消費額	fire staircase **táo shēng ān quán tī**	逃生安全梯 逃生安全梯
signal the waiter **hū huàn shì zhě**	呼唤侍者 呼喚侍者	fuel cell **rán liào diàn chí**	燃料电池 燃料電池
patronize a performance **péng chǎng**	捧场 捧場	incandescent lamp **bái chì dēng**	白炽灯 白熾燈
stage box **tè bié bāo xiāng**	特别包厢 特別包廂	incandescent light bulb **bái chì dēng pàor**	白炽灯泡儿 白熾燈泡兒
lodge **bāo xiāng**	包厢 包廂	fire hydrant **xiāo fáng shuān**	消防栓 消防栓
aisle **zuò páng zǒu dào**	座旁走道 座旁走道	fire extinguisher **miè huǒ qì**	灭火器 滅火器
front stall **qián zuòr**	前座儿 前座兒		

camera zhào xiàng jī	照相机 照相機	twin lenses shuāng jìng tóu	双镜头 雙鏡頭
digital camera shù wèi zhào xiàng jī	数位照相机 數位照相機	telephoto lens wàng yüǎn jìng tóu	望远镜头 望遠鏡頭
automatic surveying camera qüán zì dòng zhào xiàng jī	全自动照相机 全自動照相機	binocular wàng yüǎn jìng	望远镜 望遠鏡
infra-red camera hóng wài xiàn shè yǐng jī	红外线摄影机 紅外線攝影機	zoom lens shēn suō jìng tóu	伸缩镜头 伸縮鏡頭
spying needle jiān shì shè yǐng jī	监视摄影机 監視攝影機	wide-angle lens guáng jiǎor jìng tóu	广角儿镜头 廣角兒鏡頭
pinhole camera zhēn kǒng shè yǐng jī	针孔摄影机 針孔攝影機	fish-eye lens yǔ yǎn jìng tóu	鱼眼镜头 魚眼鏡頭
sound camera lù yīn zhào xiàng jī	录音照相机 錄音照相機	panoramic lens yì lǎn jìng tóu	一览镜头 一覽鏡頭
underwater camera shǔi zhōng zhào xiàng jī	水中照相机 水中照相機	zone-lens sān hé yī jìng tóu	三合一镜头 三合一鏡頭
instant camera (Polariod) jí kě pāi xiàng jī	即可拍相机 即可拍相機	yellow filter huáng sè lǜ guāng jìng	黄色滤光镜 黃色濾光鏡
disposable camera pāi wán jì diū shì xiàng jī	拍完即丢式相机 拍完即丟式相機	ultraviolet filter zǐ wài xiàn lǜ jìng	紫外线滤镜 紫外線濾鏡
miniature camera xiù zhēn zhào xiàng jī	袖珍照相机 袖珍照相機	distance jù lí	距离 距離
camera leather case xiàng jī pí tàor	相机皮套儿 相機皮套兒	range finder cè jù jìng	测距镜 測距鏡
shoulder strap kuà jiān pí dài	胯肩皮带 跨肩皮帶	telemeter cè jù biǎo	测距表 測距表
lens cap jìng tóu gài-zi	镜头盖子 鏡頭蓋子	shutter kuài ménr	快门儿 快門兒
single lens dān jìng tóu	单镜头 單鏡頭	diaphragm guāng qüānr	光圈儿 光圈兒

English	Pinyin	Simplified	Traditional
high-speed	kuài sù	快速	快速
low-speed	màn sù	慢速	慢速
focusing	duì guāng	对光	對光
out of focus	jiāo diǎn bù zhǔn	焦点不准	焦點不準
in focus	jiāo dián zhǔn	焦点准	焦點準
exposure meter	pù guāng biǎo	曝光表	曝光表
1/2 second exposure	1/2 miǎo pù guāng	1/2 秒曝光	1/2 秒曝光
double-exposure	shuāng chóng pù guāng	双重曝光	雙重曝光
unexposed	wèi pù guāng	未曝光	未曝光
over-exposure	pù guāng guò dù	曝光过度	曝光過度
under-exposure	pù guāng bù zú	曝光不足	曝光不足
overlap	chóng dié	重叠	重疊
light leak	lòu guāng	漏光	漏光
flash	shǎn guāng dēng	闪光灯	閃光燈
flash bulb	shǎn guāng dēng pàor	闪光灯泡儿	閃光燈泡兒
electronic flash	diàn zǐ shǎn guāng dēng	电子闪光灯	電子閃光燈
tripod	sān jiǎor jià	三脚儿架	三腳兒架
timer	zì pāi qì	自拍器	自拍器
loading film	zhuāng piàn	装片	裝片
a roll of film	yī juǎn jiāo juǎnr	一卷胶卷儿	一卷膠捲兒
exposures	zhào xiàng zhāng shù	照像张数	照像張數
36-exposure film	36 zhāng juǎn	36 张卷	36 張捲
super sensitive film	tè kuài jiāo juǎn	特快胶卷	特快膠捲
fine grain film	wéi lì jiāo juǎn	微粒胶卷	微粒膠捲
color film	cǎi sè jiāo juǎn	彩色胶卷	彩色膠捲
spindle	juǎn xīn zhóu	卷心轴	捲心軸
cut film	sǎn zhuāng dǐ piàn	散装底片	散裝底片
to wind	juǎn piàn	卷片	捲片
to rewind	dào piàn	倒片	倒片
background	bèi jǐng	背景	背景
indoor	shì nèi	室内	室內
outdoor	shì wài	室外	室外
take a photo	pāi zhào	拍照	拍照
vertical position	zhí-zhe pāi	直著拍	直著拍
horizontal position	héng-zhe pāi	横著拍	橫著拍
portrait	rén xiàng	人像	人像
bust photo	bàn shēn zhào piàn	半身照片	半身照片
profile	cè miàn yǐng xiàng	侧面影像	側面影像（剖面）
close-up	tè xiě jìng tóu	特写镜头	特寫鏡頭
take a pose	bǎi zī shì	摆姿势	擺姿勢

photogenic **shàng jìng tóu**	上镜头 上鏡頭		reduction **suō xiǎo**	缩小 縮小
full-length portrait **qüán shēn**	全身 全身		dark room **àn fáng**	暗房 暗房
Say "cheese"! **xiào yī-ge**	笑一个 笑一個		undeveloped film **wèi chōng-de dǐ piàn**	未冲的底片 未沖的底片
fight for a position **qiǎng jìng tóu**	抢镜头 搶鏡頭		to develop film **chōng dǐ piàn**	冲底片 沖底片
take a snapshot **zhào-zhang kuài xiàng**	照张快相 照張快相		developing **xián yǐng**	显影 顯影
recent photo **jìn zhào**	近照 近照		fixation **dìng yǐng**	定影 定影
nude photo **luó tǐ zhào**	裸体照 裸體照		negative **dǐ piàn**	底片 底片
cheesecake **lù tuǐ zhào**	露腿照 露腿照（美女）		sharp **qīng xī**	清晰 清晰
pornography **chūn gōng zhào piàn**	春宫照片 春宮照片		clear **qīng-chu**	清楚 清楚
bird's-eye view **niǎo kàn**	鸟瞰 鳥瞰		blur **mó-hu**	模糊 模糊
aerophotography **kōng zhōng shè yǐng**	空中摄影 空中攝影		print **jiā xǐ**	加洗 加洗
still life **jìng wù**	静物 靜物		retouch **xiū bǎn**	修版 修版
panorama **qüán jǐng**	全景 全景		glossy printing paper **guāng miàn xiàng zhǐ**	光面相纸 光面相纸
long shot **yüán jǐng**	远景 遠景		mat printing paper **bù miàn xiàng zhǐ**	布面相纸 布面相纸
night view **yè jǐng**	夜景 夜景		round-cornered picture **yüán jiǎo zhào piàn**	圆角照片 圓角照片
scenic photo **fēng jǐng zhào**	风景照 風景照		borderless picture **wú biān zhào piàn**	无边照片 無邊照片
photographic slide **huàn dēng piàn**	幻灯片 幻燈片		reflector **fǎn guāng qì**	反光器 反光器
photograph **xiàng piàn**	相片 相片		3D; three dimensional **lì tǐ**	立体 立體
enlargement **fàng dà**	放大 放大		2D; two dimensional **píng miàn**	平面 平面

stamp collecting; philately **jí yóu**	集邮 集郵	**mono-color** **dān sè**	单色 單色
piece; unit stamp **dān méi**	单枚 單枚	**perforated stamp** **yǒu chí kǒng yóu piào**	有齿孔邮票 有齒孔郵票
pair stamp **shuāng lián**	双连 雙連	**face value** **miàn zhí**	面值 面值
a block of four stamps **sì fāng lián**	四方连 四方連	**inverted stamp** **dào yìn piào**	倒印票 倒印票
whole sheet of stamps **qüán zhāng**	全张 全張	**top against bottom stamp** **duì dào yóu piào**	对倒邮票 對倒郵票
complete set of stamps **qüán tào**	全套 全套	**overprinted stamp** **jiā zì jiù piào**	加字旧票 加字舊票
souvenir sheet of stamps **xiǎo qüán zhāng**	小全张 小全張	**ungummed** **wú bèi jiāo**	无背胶 無背膠
complete sheet of stamps **dà qüán zhāng**	大全张 大全張	**first day postmark** **shǒu rì yóu chuō**	首日邮戳 首日郵戳
unused stamp **wèi yòng piào**	未用票 未用票	**commemorative postmark** **jì niàn yóu chuō**	纪念邮戳 紀念郵戳
used stamp **jiù piào**	旧票 舊票	**typography; relief printing** **tū bǎn**	凸版 凸版
postage-due stamp **qiàn zī jiù piào**	欠资旧票 欠資舊票	**intaglio** **āo bǎn**	凹版 凹版
rare stamp **zhēn guì yóu piào**	珍贵邮票 珍貴郵票	**lithographic** **píng bǎn**	平版 平版
very fine (superb) condition **shàng pǐn; jí pǐn**	上品；极品 上品；極品	**stamp catalogue** **yóu piào mù lù**	邮票目录 郵票目錄
watermark **shuǐ yìn**	水印 水印	**stamp album** **yóu piào bù**	邮票簿 郵票簿
vertical stamp **zhí lì cháng yóu piào**	直立长邮票 直立長郵票	**stamp tongs** **yóu piào qián**	邮票钳 郵票鉗

33A Music 音樂

music yīn yüè	音乐 音樂
classical music gú diǎn yīn yüè	古典音乐 古典音樂
jazz music jüé shì yüè	爵士乐 爵士樂
rock n' roll yáo gǔn yüè	摇滚乐 搖滾樂
rap song ráo shé gē	绕舌歌 繞舌歌
swing music yáo bǎi yüè	摇摆乐 搖擺樂
light music qīng yīn yüè	轻音乐 輕音樂
hot music rè ménr yīn yüè	热门儿音乐 熱門兒音樂
pop music liú xíng yīn yüè	流行音乐 流行音樂
soul music hēi-ren líng hún yüè	黑人灵魂乐 黑人靈魂樂
country music xiāng cūn yīn yüè	乡村音乐 鄉村音樂
ballad mín yáo	民谣 民謠
Latin music lā dīng yīn yüè	拉丁音乐 拉丁音樂
atonal music qiāo dǎ yīn yüè	敲打音乐 敲打音樂
vocal music shēng yüè	声乐 聲樂

symphony jiāo xiǎng yüè	交响乐 交響樂
conductor zhǐ huī	指挥 指揮
band yüè duì	乐队 樂隊
brass band guǎn yüè duì	管乐队 管樂隊
string band xián yüè duì	弦乐队 絃樂隊
orchestra guǎn xián yüè duì	管弦乐队 管弦樂隊
choir gē chàng duì	歌唱队 歌唱隊
concert yīn yüè huì	音乐会 音樂會
recital dān dú yǎn chàng huì	单独演唱会 單獨演唱會
solo dú chàng; dú yǎn	独唱；独演 獨唱；獨演
accompany bàn zòu	伴奏 伴奏
record (music) chàng piàn	唱片 唱片
CD; compact disc guāng pán piàn	光盘片 光盤片
DVD; digital video disc yǐng pán piàn	影盘片 影盤片
original edition yüán bǎn	原版 原版

pirated edition **dào bǎn**	盗版 盜版	serenade **xiǎo yè qǔ**	小夜曲 小夜曲
singing **chàng gēr**	唱歌儿 唱歌兒	march **jìn xíng qǔ**	进行曲 進行曲
sing a song **chàng shǒu gēr**	唱首歌儿 唱首歌兒	rhapsody **kuáng xiáng qǔ**	狂想曲 狂想曲
singer **gē shǒu**	歌手 歌手	lullaby; berceuse **cuī mián qǔ**	催眠曲 催眠曲
tenor **nán gāo yīn**	男高音 男高音	aria; lyric **shū qíng qǔ**	抒情曲 抒情曲
baritone **nán zhōng yīn**	男中音 男中音	love song **qíng gē**	情歌 情歌
bass **nán dī yīn**	男低音 男低音	folk song **mín gē**	民歌 民歌
soprano **nǚ gāo yīn**	女高音 女高音	notation **yüè pǔ**	乐谱 樂譜
mezzo soprano **nǚ zhōng yīn**	女中音 女中音	staff; stave **wǔ xiàn pǔ**	五线谱 五線譜
alto **nǚ dī yīn**	女低音 女低音	concert **yīn yüè huì**	音乐会 音樂會
national anthem **guó gē**	国歌 國歌	a hush fell on the audience **yā què wú shēng**	鸦雀无声 鴉雀無聲
popular music **liú xíng gē qǔ**	流行歌曲 流行歌曲	encore! **zài chàng yí-ge**	(首) 再唱一个！(欢呼) 再唱一個！
hit song **rè mén gē qǔ**	热门歌曲 熱門歌曲	have no ear for music **méi yǒu yīn yüè xì bāo**	没有音乐细胞 沒有音樂細胞

Musical Instrument
樂器
33B

play musical instrument **wánr yüè qì**	玩儿乐器 玩兒樂器	moon banjo (4-string) **yüè qín**	月琴 月琴
pipe (vertical flute) **xiāo**	箫 簫	drum **gǔ**	鼓 鼓
circular organ (16-20 pipes) **pái xiāo**	排箫 排簫	bass drum **dà gǔ**	大鼓 大鼓
flute (horizontal) **héng dí**	横笛 橫笛	bongos **zhǐ jiān gǔ**	指尖鼓 指尖鼓
horizontal lute (25-string) **sè**	瑟 瑟	tambourine **shóu gǔ; líng gǔ**	手鼓；铃鼓 手鼓；鈴鼓
reed organ (with 36 pipes) **yǘ**	竽 竽	drum stick **gǔ chuí**	鼓槌 鼓槌
tongued bell **duó**	铎 鐸	clappers **pāi bǎnr**	拍板儿 拍板兒
oboe (wind instrument) **guǎn**	管 管	gong **xiǎo luó**	小锣 小鑼
stone chime **biǎn qìng**	扁磬 扁磬	copper gong **tóng luó**	铜锣 銅鑼
Chinese clarinet **suǒ nà**	唢呐 嗩吶	bass gong **dà luó**	大锣 大鑼
Chinese zither (horizontal string) **gǔ zhēng**	古筝 古箏	cymbals **tóng bó**	铜钹 銅鈸
reed organ (13 bamboo pipes) **shēng**	笙 笙	bells **zhōng; líng**	锺；铃 鐘；鈴
Chinese fiddle (2-string) **èr hú; hú qínr**	二胡；胡琴儿 二胡；胡琴兒	piano **gāng qín**	钢琴 鋼琴
Chinese banjo (3-string) **sān xiánr**	三弦儿 三弦兒	organ **fēng qín**	风琴 風琴
vertical lute (4-string) **pí-pa**	琵琶 琵琶	electronic piano **diàn zǐ qín**	电子琴 電子琴

pipe organ **guǎn shì dà fēng qín**	管式大风琴 管式大風琴	musical stones **qìng**	磬 磬
harmonica **kǒu-qin**	口琴 口琴	castanets **Xī Bān Yá xiáng bǎn**	西班牙响板 西班牙響板
tremolo harmonica **chàn-yin kǒu-qin**	颤音口琴 顫音口琴	clarinet **shù dí**	竖笛 豎笛
modica **kǒu fēng qín**	口风琴 口風琴	saxophone **sà kè sī fēng**	萨克斯风 薩克斯風
violin; fiddle **xiǎo tí qín**	小提琴 小提琴	trumpet **xiáo lǎ-ba**	小喇叭 小喇叭
viola **zhōng tí qín**	中提琴 中提琴	tuba **dà lǎ-ba**	大喇叭 大喇叭
cello **dà tí qín**	大提琴 大提琴	bugle **lǎ-ba**	喇叭 喇叭
contrabass; bassfiddle **dī yīn dà tí qín**	低音大提琴 低音大提琴	horn **hào jiáo**	号角 號角
xylophone **mù qín**	木琴 木琴	trombone **shēn suō lǎ-ba**	伸缩喇叭 伸縮喇叭
ukulele **sì xián qín**	四弦琴 四弦琴	guitar **jí tā**	吉他 吉他
lyre **qī xián qín**	七弦琴 七弦琴	electronic guitar **diàn jí tā**	电吉他 電吉他
French horn **Fà Guó hào**	法国号 法國號	accordion **shǒu fēng qín**	手风琴 手風琴
triangle **sān jiáo tiě**	三角铁 三角鐵	concertina **shǒu fēng qín**	六角形手风琴 手風琴
metronome **jié pāi qì**	节拍器 節拍器	banjo **wǔ xián qín**	五弦琴 五弦琴
percussion instrument **dǎ jí yüè qì**	打击乐器 打擊樂器		

33 C Audio 音響

audio; sound **yīn xiǎng**	音响 音響	circuit **diàn lù; xiàn lù tú**	电路；线路图 電路；線路圖
sound effect **yīn xiào**	音效 音效	circuit diagram **xiàn lù tú**	线路图 線路圖
volume **yīn liàng**	音量 音量	accessory **líng jiàn**	零件 零件
sound control **yīn liàng kòng zhì qì**	音量控制器 音量控制器	stereophonic **lì tǐ shēng**	立体声 立體聲
turn volume up **nǐng dà**	拧大 擰大	loudspeaker **yáng shēng qì**	扬声器 揚聲器
turn volume down **níng xiǎo**	拧小 擰小	echo **huí shēng**	回声 回聲
loudspeaker **kuò yīn lǎ-ba**	扩音喇叭 擴音喇叭	quaver **zhàn yīn**	颤音 顫音
amplifier **kuò yīn qì**	扩音器 擴音器	decibel (dB; db) **fēn bèi**	分贝 分貝
balance control **píng héng kòng zhì**	平衡控制 平衡控制	signal **xùn hào**	讯号 訊號
Hi-Fi components **yīn xiáng zǔ hé**	音响组合 音響組合	sound track **yīn guǐ**	音轨 音軌
component **zǔ jiàn**	组件 組件	tuning **tiáo xié**	调谐 調諧
parts **líng jiàn**	零件 零件	FM; frequency modulation **tiáo pín**	调频 調頻
tone control **yīn diào kòng zhì**	音调控制 音調控制	FM tuner **tiáo pín tiáo xié qì**	调频调谐器 調頻調諧器
tweeter **gāo yīn**	高音 高音	4-track recording **sì shēng dào lù yīn**	四声道录音 四聲道錄音
woofer **dī yīn**	低音 低音	4-channel stereo **sì shēng dài lì tǐ yīn**	四声带立体音 四聲帶立體音

selector **xüǎn zé qì**	选择器 選擇器	negative pole **diàn chí-de yīn jí**	电池的阴极 電池的陰極
rectifier **zhěng liú qì**	整流器 整流器	insulating **jüé yüán**	绝缘 絕緣
sensitivity **líng mǐn dù**	灵敏度 靈敏度	insulator **jüé yüán qì**	绝缘器 絕緣器
super tweeter **chāo gāo yīn**	超高音 超高音	resistance **diàn zǔ**	电阻 電阻
transformer **biàn yā qì**	变压器 變壓器	resistor **diàn zǔ qì**	电阻器 電阻器
condenser **diàn róng qì**	电容器 電容器	rheostat **biàn zǔ qì**	变阻器 變阻器
condenser plate **xù diàn bǎn**	蓄电板 蓄電板	magic eye **diàn yǎn**	电眼 電眼
block **duàn lù**	断路 斷路	indicator light **zhǐ shì dēng**	指示灯 指示燈
out of order **gù zhàng**	故障 故障	charge **chōng diàn**	充电 充電
not working **huài-le**	坏了 壞了	knob **niǔ**	钮 鈕
leakage **lòu diàn**	漏电 漏電	push button **àn niǔr**	按钮儿 按鈕兒
short circuit **duǎn lù**	短路 短路	rewind (film) **dào piàn; dào dài**	倒片；倒带 倒片；倒帶
shocked **chù diàn**	触电 觸電	playback **lù fàng**	录放 錄放
proof plate **yàn diàn bǎn**	验电板 驗電板	microphone **mài kè fēng**	麦克风 麥克風
anode **yáng diàn**	阳电 陽電	earphone **ěr jī**	耳机 耳機
cathode **yīn diàn**	阴电 陰電	headphone **tóu tào ěr jī**	头套耳机 頭套耳機
positive pole **diàn chí-de yáng jí**	电池的阳极 電池的陽極		

Related Terms: Group 49C, 自己动手 Do It Yourself;
Group 10H, 家庭电器用品 Household Electric Appliances

33D

Dancing 跳舞

dancing	舞蹈；跳舞
wú dǎo；tiào wǔ	舞蹈；跳舞

go dancing	去跳舞
qǜ tiào wǔ	去跳舞

dancing party	舞会
wǔ huì	舞會

partner	舞伴
wǔ bàn	舞伴

escort	护花使者
hù huā shí zhě	護花使者

corsage	胸花
xiōng huā	胸花

square dance	方块舞
fāng kài wǔ	方塊舞

folk dance	土风舞
tǔ fēng wǔ	土風舞

hula	草裙舞
cǎo qǚn wǔ	草裙舞

tap dance	踢踏舞
tī-ta wǔ	踢踏舞

social dance	交际舞
jiāo-ji wǔ	交際舞

tango	探戈舞
tàn-ge wǔ	探戈舞

waltz	华尔滋舞
huá-er zī wǔ	華爾滋舞

samba	森巴舞
sēn-ba wǔ	森巴舞

rumba	伦巴舞
lún-ba wǔ	倫巴舞

mambo	曼波舞
màn-bo wǔ	曼波舞

cha-cha	恰恰舞
qiā-qia wǔ	恰恰舞

twist	扭扭舞
niū-niu wǔ	扭扭舞

rock & roll	摇滚舞
yáo-gun wǔ	搖滾舞

jitterbug	吉特巴舞
jí-te bā wǔ	吉特巴舞

disco	狄斯可舞
dī-si kě wǔ	狄斯可舞

fox trot	狐步舞
hú bù wǔ	狐步舞

aerobic dancing	有氧舞蹈
yóu yǎng wú dǎo	有氧舞蹈

modern dance	现代舞
xiàn dài wǔ	現代舞

limbo dance	凌波舞
líng bō wǔ	凌波舞

flamenco	西班牙舞
xī bān yá wǔ	西班牙舞

street dance	跳街头舞
tiào jiē tóu wǔ	跳街頭舞

advance the left foot	左脚往前移
zuó jiǎo wǎng qián yí	左腳往前移

move right foot backward	右脚往后退
yòu jiǎo wǎng hòu tuì	右腳往後退

象棋與洋象棋

Chinese chess **xiàng qí**	象棋 象棋	**elephants** **xiàng**	象 象
play chess **xià xiàng qí**	下象棋 下象棋	**chariots** **jǔ**	车 車
chessboard **qí pán**	棋盘 棋盤	**horse** **mǎ**	马 馬
boundary **chǔ hé hàn jiè**	楚河汉界 楚河漢界	**cannons** **pào**	炮 炮
separated squares **fāng gér**	方格儿 方格兒	**soldiers** **bīng**	兵 兵
diagonally **duì jiǎor xiàn**	对角儿线 對角兒線	**pawns** **zú**	卒 卒
matt **tián zì gér**	田字格儿 田字格兒	**promoted** **guò hé zú**	过河卒 過河卒
chessman **qí zǐr**	棋子儿 棋子兒	**move chessman** **zǒu qí**	走棋 走棋
red chessman **hóng qí zǐr**	红棋子儿 紅棋子兒	**first move** **xiān zǒu**	先走 先走
black chessman **hēi qí zǐr**	黑棋子儿 黑棋子兒	**forward** **qián jìn**	前进 前進
arrange chessmen **bǎi qí zǐr**	摆棋子儿 擺棋子兒	**retreat** **hòu tuì**	后退 後退
general **jiàng**	将 將	**leap** **tiào**	跳 跳
marshal **shuài**	帅 帥	**rank** **héng xíng**	横行 橫行
scholars **shì**	士 士	**file** **zòng xíng**	纵行 縱行
councilors **xiàng**	相 相	**diagonal** **xié xíng**	斜行 斜行

| take opposing chessman | 吃 | knight | 骑士：武士 |
| chī | 吃（子） | qí shì; wǔ shì | 騎士：武士 |

| gambit | 牺牲一卒 | pawn | 士兵 |
| xī shēng yī zú | 犧牲一卒 | shì bīng | 士兵 |

| check | 将"军" | embattle | 布局 |
| jiāng "jǔn" | 將"軍" | bù jú | 佈局 |

| stalemate | 棋子不能动 | strategy | 战略 |
| qí zǐ bù néng dòng | 棋子不能動 | zhàn lüè | 戰略 |

| smother | 死棋 | maneuver | 计诱 |
| sǐ qí | 死棋 | jì yòu | 計誘 |

| | | filler | 牺牲一子 |
| | | xī shēng yī zǐ | 犧牲一子 |

| | | opponent | 敌人 |
| | | dí rén | 敵人 |

| chess | 西洋象棋 | checkmate | 围攻 |
| xī yáng xiàng qí | 西洋象棋 | wéi gōng | 圍攻 |

| checker board | 西洋棋盘 | mate; check | 逼将 |
| xī yáng qí pán | 西洋棋盤 | bī jiàng | 逼將 |

| king | 国王 | win | 胜 |
| guó wáng | 國王 | shèng | 勝 |

| queen | 皇后 | lose | 败 |
| huáng hòu | 皇后 | bài | 敗 |

| bishop | 主教 | drawn | 和局 |
| zhǔ jiào | 主教（僧侣） | hé jú | 和局 |

| rook | 城堡形棋子 | | |
| chéng bǎo xíng qí zǐ | 城堡形棋子 | | |

34B

Go 围棋

go **wéi qí**	围棋	圍棋
go board **qí pán**	棋盘	棋盤
stone **qí zǐr**	棋子儿	棋子兒
go-to **hòu shǒu**	后手	後手
corner opening **dìng shì**	定式	定式
squeeze **jǐ**	挤	擠
throw in; pitch **pū**	扑	撲
diagonal jump weakness **xiàng yǎn**	象眼	象眼
shape **qí xíng**	棋形	棋形
variation **biàn huà**	变化	變化
opening **bù jú**	布局	佈局
guessing the stones **cāi zǐ**	猜子	猜子
extension **chāi**	拆	拆
proper move **bén shǒu**	本手	本手
eternal life **cháng shēng**	长生	長生
capture **chī**	吃	吃
occupy **zhàn jù**	占据	佔據
peek **cì**	刺	刺
invasion **dǎ rù**	打入	打入
big point **dà chǎng**	大场	大場
big Knight's move **dà fēi**	大飞	大飛
neutral point **dān guān**	单官	單官
block **dǎng**	挡	擋
snapback **dào pū**	倒扑	倒撲
territory **dì pán**	地盘	地盤
placement **diǎn**	点	點
settle **dìng xíng**	定型	定型
bridge under **dù**	渡	渡
cut **duàn**	断	斷
capturing race **duì shā**	对杀	對殺

English	Simplified/Traditional	English	Simplified/Traditional
bad move **è shǒu**	恶手 惡手	shortage of liberties **qì jǐn**	气紧 氣緊
knight's move **fēi**	飞 飛	handicap **ràng zǐ**	让子 讓子
even game **fēn xiān**	分先 分先	corner enclosure **shóu jiǎo**	守角 守角
shared liberty **gōng qì**	公气 公氣	bamboo joint **shuāng**	双 雙
corner approach **guà jiǎo**	挂角 掛角	remove from board **tí**	提 提
endgame **guān zǐ**	官子 官子	wedge **wā**	挖 挖
good point **háo diǎn**	好点 好點	star point **xīng wèi**	星位 星位
Influence **hòu shì**	厚势 厚勢	situation **xíng shì**	形势 形勢
tiger's mouth **hú kǒu**	虎口 虎口	positional judgement **xíng shì pàn duàn**	形势判断 形勢判斷
clamp **jiá**	夹 夾	ladder block **yǐn zhēng**	引征 引征
false eye **jiá yǎn**	假眼 假眼	ladder **zhēng zǐ**	征子 征子
diagonal **jiān**	尖 尖	middle game **zhōng pán**	中盘 中盤
descent **lì**	立 立	exchange **zhuǎn huàn**	转换 轉換
connect **lián**	连 連	loose ladder **huǎn zhēng**	缓徵 緩徵
good move **miào shǒu**	妙手 妙手	living group **huó qí**	活棋 活棋
territorial framework **mú yàng**	模样 模樣	vital point **jí suǒ**	急所 急所
internal liberty **nèi qì**	内气 內氣	life and death problem **sǐ huó tí**	死活题 死活題
crosscut **niǔ duàn**	扭断 扭斷	dead group **sǐ qí**	死棋 死棋
attach **pèng**	碰 碰	corner opening squeeze **dìng shì jǐ**	定式挤 定式擠
liberty **qì**	气 氣	one skip/point jump **yì jiān tiào**	一间跳 一間跳

compensatin for 2nd moveor	贴目	2 play handicap	让二子
tiē mù	貼目	**ràng èr zǐ**	讓二子
end game	收官	race to capture	攻杀
shōu guān	收官	**gōng shā**	攻殺
forcing move	先手	record	棋谱
xiān shǒu	先手	**qí pǔ**	棋譜
take/capture	提	decisive mistake	败著
tí	提	**bài zhāo**	敗著
point	目/点	knock-out	淘汰赛
mù; diǎn	目/點	**táo tài sài**	淘汰賽

play bridge **dǎ qiáo pái**	打桥牌 打橋牌	**guard** **jiě pái**	解牌 解牌
honey moon bridge **mì yüè qiáo pái**	蜜月桥牌 蜜月橋牌	**top card** **dǐng pái**	顶牌 頂牌
three-handed bridge **sān rén qiáo pái**	三人桥牌 三人橋牌	**trick** **sì jiā gè chū yì zhāng pái**	四家各出一张牌 四家各出一張牌
rubber **sān jú liǎng shèng**	三局两胜 三局兩勝	**tricks** **gòng shí sān cì "trick"**	共 13 次 trick 共 13 次 trick
shuffle **xǐ pái**	洗牌 洗牌	**lay down** **tān pái**	摊牌 攤牌
opener **kāi pái rén**	开牌人 開牌人	**slam** **mǎn guàn**	满贯 滿貫
deal **fā pái**	发牌 發牌	**make** **dé fēn**	得分 得分
dealer **fā pái rén**	发牌人 發牌人	**partial score** **yì bǎi fēn yǐ xià fēn-shu**	100 分以下分数 100 分以下分數
leader **chū pái rén**	出牌人 出牌人	**game** **jú**	局 局
discard **chū pái**	出牌 出牌	**game point** **dé yì bǎi fēn**	得一百分 得一百分
defender **fáng jiā**	防家 防家	**no trump** **wú wáng pái zǔ**	无王牌组 無王牌組
partner **huǒ bàn**	夥伴 夥伴	**no trump point** **wú wáng pái zǔ fēn-shu**	无王牌组分数 無王牌組分數
dummy **liàng pái huǒ bàn**	亮牌夥伴 亮牌夥伴	**one no trump** **dé sì-shi fēn**	得四十分 得四十分
trump **wáng pái**	王牌 王牌	**all higher no trumps** **dé sān-shi fēn**	得三十分 得三十分
honor card **zūn pái**	尊牌 尊牌	**two no trump** **dé qī-shi fēn**	得七十分 得七十分

three no trump **dé yì bǎi fēn**	得一百分 得一百分	singleton **shí sān pái-zhong yǒu yì dān huā**	十三牌中有一单花 十三牌中有一單花
round **wú jié guǒ-de jú**	无结果的"局" 無結果的"局"	doubleton **shí sān pái-zhong yǒu èr dān huā**	十三牌中有二单花 十三牌中有二單花
down **méi dé fēn**	没得分 沒得分	bidding **jiào pái**	叫牌 叫牌
point **diǎn shùr**	点数儿 點數兒	void **wú cǐ pái zǔ**	无此牌组 無此牌組
trump suit **wáng pái zǔ**	王牌组 王牌組	vulnerable **shèng yì jú-de nà fāng**	胜一局的那方 勝一局的那方
major suit **zhǔ pái zǔ**	主牌组 主牌組（30分）	finesse **kǎ pái**	卡牌 卡牌
spade suit **hēi táo zǔ**	黑桃组 黑桃組	double **shū yíng jiā beì**	输赢加倍 輸贏加倍
heart suit **hóng xīn zǔ**	红心组 紅心組	grand slam **dà mǎn guàn** (13副 trick)	大满贯 大滿貫
minor suit **fù pái zǔ**	副牌组 副牌組（20分）	little (small) slam **xiáo mǎn guàn** (12副 trick)	小满贯 小滿貫
diamond suit **fāng kuài zǔ**	方块组 方塊組	contract bridge **qì yūē qiáo pái**	契约桥牌 契約橋牌
club suit **méi huā zǔ**	梅花组 梅花組	auction bridge **wú qì yūē qiáo pái**	无契约桥牌 無契約橋牌
side suit **luàn pái zǔ**	乱牌组 亂牌組		

Nine Out Of Ten Gamblers Are Losers
十个赌九个输
shí-ge dǔ   jiǔ-ge shū

cricketfighting **dòu qū qǔr**	斗蛐蛐儿 鬥蛐蛐兒	a dime **yi máo qián měi jīn**	一毛钱美金 一毛錢美金
cockfighting **dòu jī**	斗鸡 鬥雞	a quarter **liǎng máo wǔ měi jīn**	两毛五美金 兩毛五美金
horse race **sài mǎ; páo mǎ**	赛马；跑马 賽馬；跑馬	change money **huàn qián**	换钱 換錢
dog race **sài gǒu**	赛狗 賽狗	dice **shǎi-zi**	骰子 骰子
bullfight **dòu niú**	斗牛 鬥牛	dice box **shǎi-zi hér**	骰子盒儿 骰子盒兒
bullring; arena **dòu niú chǎng**	斗牛场 鬥牛場	craps table **shǎi-zi tái**	骰子台 骰子台
slot machine **chī jiǎo-zi láo hǔ**	吃角子老虎 吃角子老虎	shoot dice **zhí shǎi-zi**	掷骰子 擲骰子
slot **tóu bì kǒu**	投币口 投幣口	blackjack **èr shí yī diǎnr**	二十一点儿 二十一點兒
insert coins **tóu bì**	投币 投幣	casino **dú chǎng**	赌场 賭場
pull the lever **lā shóu bǎ**	拉手把 拉手把	gambler **dǔ tú**	赌徒 賭徒
hit the jackpot **zhòng-le dà jiǎng**	中了大奖 中了大獎	gambling **dǔ bó**	赌博 賭博
token **daì bì**	代币 代幣	bouncer **bǎo biāo**	保镖 保鏢
a nickle **wǔ fēn qián měi jīn**	五分钱美金 五分錢美金	cut of the winning **chōu tóur**	抽头儿 抽頭兒

gambling table	赌台 / 赌台	**dǔ tái**
croupier	赌注收付员 / 赌注收付員	**dǔ zhuō shōu fù yuán**
pool	赌金 / 赌金	**dǔ jīn**
gambling debt	赌债 / 赌債	**dǔ zhài**
hit	要牌 / 要牌	**yào paí**
stay	停牌 / 停牌	**tìng paí**
double	赌注加倍 / 赌注加倍	**dǔ zhù jīa bèi**
split	分牌 / 分牌	**fēn paí**
blow	超过点数 (爆) / 超過點數（爆）	**chāo gùo dǐan shù** (baò)
roulette	轮盘赌 / 輪盤赌	**lún pán dǔ**
roulette wheel	轮盘 / 輪盤	**lún pán**
roulette ball	轮盘赌球 / 輪盤赌球	**lún pán dǔ qiú**
roulette table plan	轮盘赌表 / 輪盤赌表	**lún pán dú bǐao**
roulette player	轮盘赌徒 / 輪盤赌徒	**lún pán dú tú**
roulette bowl	托盘 / 托盤	**tuō pán**

croupier	收付赌注人 / 收付赌注人	**shōu fù dǔ zhù rén**
cross handle	十字柄 / 十字柄	**shí zì bǐng**
money rake	收付赌注耙子 / 收付赌注耙子	**shōu fù dǔ zhù pá-zi**
odd numbers; impair	单数儿;奇数儿 / 單數兒;奇數兒	**dān shùr; qí shùr**
even numbers; pair	双数儿;偶数儿 / 雙數兒;偶數兒	**shuāng shùr; ǒu shùr**
black	黑色号码儿 / 黑色號碼兒	**hēi sè hào mǎr**
red	红色号码儿 / 紅色號碼兒	**hóng sè hào mǎr**
banker	庄家 / 莊家	**zhuāng-jia**
stake on	下注 / 下注	**xià zhù**
bet	赌注 / 赌注	**dǔ zhù**
bottom money	孤注一掷 / 孤注一擲	**gū zhù yì zhí**
lost	输了 / 輸了	**shū-le**
lost 100 dollars	输了一百块 / 輸了一百塊	**hū-le yì bǎi kuài**
won	赢了 / 贏了	**yíng-le**
won 1000 dollars	赢了一千块 / 贏了一千塊	**yíng-le yì qiān kuài**

He Never Makes His Month Ends Meet.
老是混不整
lào-shi hùn-bu zhěng

Playing Poker
打撲克牌
35B

cards	纸牌	squeezer	有暗号儿牌
zhǐ pái	紙牌	**yǒu àn hàor pái**	有暗號兒牌
pack; deck	一副	cheat	洗牌作弊
yí fù	一副（52 張）	**xǐ pái zuò bì**	洗牌作弊
play cards	玩儿纸牌	reshuffle	重新洗牌
wánr zhǐ pái	玩兒紙牌	**chóng xīn xǐ pái**	重新洗牌
spade	黑桃儿	play poker	玩儿扑克牌
hēi táor	黑桃兒	**wánr pū kè pái**	玩兒撲克牌
heart	红心	deck	一组牌
hóng xīn	紅心	**yì zǔ pái**	一組牌
diamond	钻石	pone	切牌人
zuàn shí	鑽石	**qiē pái rén**	切牌人
club	梅花	stock	发剩牌
méi huā	梅花	**fā shèng pái**	發剩牌
king	国王	misdealed	发错牌
guó wáng	國王	**fā cuò pái**	發錯牌
queen	皇后	jape	醒牌
huáng hòu	皇后	**xǐng pái**	醒牌
jack	J；杰克；仆人	show down	摊牌
J; jié kè; pú-ren	J；傑克；僕人	**tān pái**	攤牌
ace	么点儿	deal	发牌
yāo diǎnr	么點兒	**fā pái**	發牌
pip	牌点子	cut	切牌
pái diǎn-zi	牌點兒	**qiē pái**	切牌
face card	人头牌	pull	抽牌
rén tóu pái	人頭牌	**chōu pái**	抽牌
court card	有花的花牌	lead	开牌
yǒu huā-de huā pái	有花的花牌	**kāi pái**	開牌
joker	丑角牌	discard	出牌
chóu jiǎo pái	丑角牌	**chū pái**	出牌

bid	叫牌	flush	同花
jiào pái	叫牌	tóng huā	同花
open bid	开叫	suit	一副同花牌
kāi jiào	開叫	yī fù tóng huā pái	一副同花牌
unbid	不叫	straight	顺子
bú jiào	不叫	shùn-zi	順子
pass	不要	straight flush	同花顺子
bú yào	不要	tóng huā shùn-zi	同花順子
follow	跟	royal flush	同花大顺
gēn	跟	tóng huā dà shùn	同花大順
biddable suit	可叫组	a pair	一对
kě jiào zǔ	可叫組	yí duì	一對
over call	盖叫	two pairs	两对
gài jiào	蓋叫	liǎng duì	兩對
revoke/pass	不跟了	three of a kind	三条
bù gēn-le	不跟了	sān tiáo	三條
double	加倍	four of a kind	四张一样
jiā bèi	加倍	sì zhāng yí yàng	四張一樣
re-double	再加倍	thrice	三张顺序牌
zài jiā bèi	再加倍	sān zhāng shùn xù pái	三張順序牌
over	再再加倍	full house	三头及一对
zài zài jiā bèi	再再加倍	sān tóu jí yī duì	三頭及一對
re-open	再开牌		
zài kāi pái	再開牌		

Preventing From Getting Senile
預防老人癡呆
yù fáng lǎo rén chī dāi

playing mahjong (136 or 144 tiles) 打麻将
dǎ má jiàng 打麻將

Bamboo Suit (9 tiles) 条子；索
Tiáo-zi; Suō 條子；索

Dot Suit; Circle Suit (9 tiles) 筒；饼
Tǒng; Bǐng 筒；餅

Character Suit (9 tiles) 万
Wàn (10 thousand) 萬

Terminal Tiles 么
Yāo 么

Without the 2 Terminal tiles 不带么
bú dài yāo 不帶么

The 13 orphans (all ones, nines or characters)
Shí Sān Yāo 十三么

Play a game of domino 打牌
dǎ pái 打牌

Play 8 rounds 打八圈儿
dǎ bā qüānr 打八圈兒

Short Of One Hand 三缺一
Sān Qüē Yī 三缺一

Your Prior Hand (left) 上家
shàng jiā 上家

Your Next Hand (right) 下家
xià jiā 下家

Opposite Hand 对面儿那家
duì miànr nèi jiā 對面兒那家

The Dealer; The Bank 庄家
Zhuāng-jia 莊家

Being The Bank 作庄
Zuò Zhuāng 作莊

Win a second term dealer 连庄
lián zhuāng 連莊

Shuffle the tiles 洗牌
xǐ pái 洗牌

Forming the wall of stacks 砌牌
qì pái 砌牌

Discard a tile 出牌
chū pái 出牌

Bet; Stake 赌注
dǔ zhù 賭注

Chips; dib 筹码儿
Chóu-mǎr 籌碼兒

Throw dice 掷骰子
zhí shǎi-zi 擲骰子

Eating 吃
Chī 吃

Dragon Suit 一条龙
Yì Tiáo Lóng 一條龍
(complete sequence from 1st to 9th tiles
in the same suit)

Seven, Robbing One 七抢一
Qī Qiǎng Yī 七搶一
(having 7 flowers, y ou automaticallywin
game whenever the 8th flower is exposed)

Eight Immortals 八仙过海
Bā Xiān Guò Hǎi 八仙過海
(an All Eight Flower tile hand)

Four Of The Same Tile 杠
Gàng 槓

A Hand Of Four Gàngs 四杠牌
Sì Gàng Pái 四槓牌

Exposed Gàng	明杠
Míng Gàng	明槓
(Each exposed Gàng)	

Each Hidden Gàng (unexposed) 暗杠
àn Gàng 暗槓

Robbed A Player's Gàng and Won 抢杠
Qiǎng Gàng 搶槓

Gàng Blossom 杠上开花
Gàng-shang Kāi Huā 槓上開花
(Drew a winning tile from the end of the wall after a Gàng)

Slam 满贯
Mǎn Guàn 滿貫
(some play 3 folds, 4 folds, 6 folds ......)

Three Fortune Triples 大三元
Dà Sān Yüán (black, red, green) 大三元

Two 3-Fortune Triples 小三元
Xiǎo Sān Yüán 小三元
(three fortune triples and a pair as mahjong)

Greater 4 Winds(4 wind triples) 大四喜
Dà Sì Xǐ 大四喜

Lesser 4 Winds 小四喜
Xiǎo Sì Xǐ 小四喜
(3 wind triples and a pair winds as mahjong)

In Waiting 听牌
Tìng Pái 聽牌
(waiting for one tile to win)

Sole Waiting 单听
DānTìng 單聽
(awaiting the only one necessary tile to win)

Heaven's Grace In Waiting 天听
Tiān Tìng 天聽
(awaiting one tile to win with opening hand)

Earth's Grace In Waiting 地听
Dì Tìng 地聽
(awaiting one tile to win after first discarded tile from opening hand)

your turn to take a card 抓牌
zhuā pái 抓牌

Self-Touch 自摸儿
Zì Mōr 自摸兒
(Self drew the winning tile from the wall.)

Winning; Winning Hand 和
Hú 和

Heaven's Grace 天和
Tiān Hú 天和
(to win by dealer on starting hand)

Earth's Grace 地和
Dì Hú 地和
(win a hand after drawing only one tile)

Pure Hand 门前清
Mén Qián Qīng 門前清
(Never took a discarded piece for Gàng 杠, Pèng 碰 or Chī 吃")

Pure Self-Touch 门前清自摸
Mén Qián Qīng Zì Mōr 門前清自摸
(both Pure Hand and Self-Touch.)

3 Hidden Triples 三暗坎儿
Sān àn Kǎnr 三暗坎兒
(hand contains 3 hidden triples)

Hidden Triples 四暗坎儿
Sì àn Kǎnr 四暗坎兒
(hand contains 4 hidden triples)

Full Beggar's Hand 全求
Qüán Qiú 全求
(entire hand formed from others' discarded cards, with only one hidden card left)

No Flowers 无花
Wú Huā 無花
(hand contains no flower or season cards)

All The Four-Season Flowers 春夏秋冬
Chūn Xià Qiū Dōng 春夏秋冬

Spring 春
Chūn 春

Summer 夏
Xià 夏

Autumn 秋
Qiū 秋

Winter 冬
Dōng 冬

Taking 碰
Pèng 碰
(three of a kind by taking one tile from the others and up them face up.)

Without Melding	不求人	**No Characters**	无字
Bù Qiú Rén	不求人	**Wú Zì**	無字

Pure Characters 全字
Quán Zì 全字

(hand contains no winds or dragons)

Flower Tiles 花牌
Huā Pái 花牌

Red Dragon Tile 红中
Hóng Zhōng 紅中

Wind Tiles 风牌
Fēng Pái 風牌
(corresponding to your "house" direction)

Green Dragon Tile 发财
Fā Cái 發財

White Extra Tile; blank 白板
Bái Bǎn 白板

East Wind 东风
Dōng Fēng 東風

2-Eye; Pair; Mahjong 两个眼；一对
liǎng-ge yǎn; yí duì 兩個眼；一對

South Wind 南风
Nán Fēng 南風

Plucking Moon From Bottom Of Sea
Hái Dǐ Lāo Yüè 海底撈月

West Wind 西风
Xī Fēng 西風

(Self-Touch 自摸儿 last tile and win)

North Wind 北风
Běi Fēng 北風

lay down tiles to show 摊牌
Tān Pái 攤牌

East Wind Game 东风圈
Dōng Fēng Qüān 東風圈
(The 1st Round, each round consisting of
four hands of play)

Calculate Points 算和
Suàn Hú 算和

Fundamental (basic) **Points** 底和
Dǐ Hú 底和

North Wind Game 北风圈
Běi Fēng Qüān 北風圈
(The 4th Round, each round consisting of
four hands of play)

Plain Win (fundamental points only) 平和
Píng Hú 平和

(One hand contains three sets of different
kind of sequences of tiles plus one pair (non
Wind or Dragon) tiles. (Dān Tìng 单听 or
Self-Touch 自摸儿 are not allowed)

All Four Cards Of Flowers 梅兰竹菊
Méi Lán Zhú Jǔ 梅蘭竹菊

Pure Characters 全字
Quán Zì 全字

Plum 梅
Méi 梅

Winning With 4 Pèngs 对对胡
Duì Duì Hú 對對胡

Orchid 兰
Lán 蘭

(all paired tiles)

Bamboo 竹
Zhú 竹

Seven-Pairs 七对
Qī duì 七對

Chrysanthemum 菊
Jǔ 菊

(One hand contains seven pairs)

Flush 清一色
qīng yí sè 清一色

2 doubles 两番
liǎng fān 兩番

(purely One Color Hand, completely from
one suit, including the pair)

3 doubles 三番
sān fān 三番

Unified One Color Hand 混一色
Hǔn Yí Sè 混一色
(all from same one suit plus character tiles)

Ancient Chinese Literary Classics
中國古代文學名著
1 Essays 文章 wén zhāng

古文觀止 Guǒ Wén Guān Zhǐ
Gems from Chinese Culture

A collection of approximately 200 Essays of the best essays of all times between the period of 400BC to 1700AD. This period covers from the second half of the 周 Zhōu dynasty through 秦 Qín，汉 Hàn, the period of the six dynasties, 唐 Tang，宋 Song till the end of the 明 Ming dynasty. These 200 selected essays cover the best composed by the known scholars of each of that period.

One who is well acquainted with a good portion of these essays is normally considered a "learned" person. If a high school graduate is able to recite ten of these collections, he/she may be considered to be well informed in Chinese literature.

FICTIONS　小说 Xiǎo Shuō

四大奇書
The four "Wonders" of the ancient Chinese fictions:

红楼梦	**The Red Chambers**	水浒传	**The 108 Brotherhood Heroes**
紅樓夢	**Hóng Lóu Mèng**	水滸傳	**Shuí Hǔ Zhuàn**
三国演义	**The Three Kingdoms**	西游记	**The Adventure Of A Monk's**
三國演義	**Sān Guó Yǎn Yì**	西遊記	**Xī Yóu Jì** Journey to India

OTHER WELL-KNOWN ANCIENT FACTIONS

西厢记 **Xī Xiāng Jì** The Romance of the West Chamber

西湖梦寻 **Xī Hú Mèng Xún** Looking for a Dream in the West Lake

孔雀东南飞 **Kǒng Qüè Dōng Nán Fēi** The Peacocks Fly to the Southeast

镜花缘 **Jìng Huā Yüán**　The Flower in the Mirror

琵琶记 **Pí Pá jì**　The Romance of the Lute

义侠记 **Yì Xiá jì**　The Romance of the Cavaliers

霍小玉传 **Huò Xiǎo Yǜ Zhuàn**　The Legend of Huó Xiǎo-yǜ

醒世因缘传 **Xǐng Shì Yīn Yüán Zhuàn**　The Rousing Story of Fated Love

宣和遗事 **Xüān Hé Yí Shì**　The Anecdotes of Xüān Hé

聊斋志异 **Liáo Zhāi Zhì Yì**　Strange Stories from a Chinese Studio

封神榜 **Fēng Shén Bǎng**　The Legend of Deification

老残游记 **Lǎo Cán Yóu Jì**　The Travels of Lǎo Cán

牡丹亭 **Mǔ Dān Tíng** (还魂记 Huán Hún Jì)　The Peony Pavilion

虬髯客传 **Qiú Rán Kè Zhuàn**　The Legend of the Curly-bearded Hero

儿女英雄传 **Er Nǚ Yīng Xióng Zhuàn**　The Story of a Heroine

金瓶梅 **Jīn Píng Méi**　The Three Women

官场现形记 **Guān Chǎng Xiàn Xíng jì**　Corruption stories of Government Officials

二十四孝 **Er Shí Sì Xiào**　Twenty-Four Stories of Filial Piety

六福客栈 **Liù Fú Kè Zhàn**　The Inn of the Sixth Happiness

四库全书 **Sì Kù Qüán Shū**　Imperial Collection of Four Divisions
(all possiblely collected literature for the past 4000 years)

2 The Chinese Classics
中国「经史子集」Zhōng Guó "Jīng Shí Zǐ Jí"

A 經 Jīng
(Classic Teachings)

四书 Sì Shū
THE FOUR BOOKS

论语 論語	The Analects of Confucius **Lún Yǔ**
孟子 孟子	The Teachings of Mencius **Mèng Zǐ**
大学 大學	The Great Learning **Dà Xüé**
中庸 中庸	The Doctrine of the Mean **Zhōng Yǒng**

五经 Wǔ Jīng
THE FIVE CLASSICS

诗经 詩經	Book of Odes (poetry) **Shī Jīng**
书经 書經	Book of Political Ethics **Shū Jīng**
易经 易經	Book of the Law of the Changes of Nature **Yì Jīng**
礼记 禮記	The Book of Rites **Lǐ Jì**
乐经 樂經	Book of Music (record lost) **Yüè Jīng**
孝经 孝經	Book of Filial piety **Xiào Jīng**

経、史、子、集

36 A

Jīng, Shǐ, Zǐ, Jí

B 史 Shǐ (Officially Recorded History)
(The following books are listed according to the dynasty orders)

春秋 The Spring & Autumn Annals
Chūn Qiū

左传 a commentary on the Spring and
Zuǒ Zhuàn   Autumn Annals

公羊传   One Hundred Family Name
Gōng Yáng Zhuàn   Primer

谷梁传   24 Stories of Filial Piety
Gǔ Liáng Zhuàn

尔雅   (ancient book containing com-
Ar Yǎ   mentaries on classics, names, etc.)

史记 The Book of History
Shǐ Jì

汉书 The History of the Hàn Dynasty
Hàn Shū

後汉书 The History of Later Hàn
Hòu Hàn Shū

三国志 The History of the Three King-
Sān Guó Zhì   doms

魏书 The Book of the Wèi Dynasty
Wèi Shū

西晋书 The Book of the Western Jìn
Xī Jìn Shū   Dynasty

东晋书 The Book of the Eastern Jìn
Dōng Jìn Shū   Dynasty

宋书 The Book of the Sòng Dynasty
Sòng Shū

齐书 The Book of the Qí Dynasty
Qí Shū

梁书 The Book of the Líang Dynasty
Liáng Shū   Autumn Annals

陈书 The Book of the Chén Dynasty
Chén Shū

隋书 The Book of the Suí Dynasty
Suí Shū

旧唐书 The Old Book of the Táng
Jiù Táng shū   Dynasty

新唐书 The New Book of the Táng
Xīn Táng Shū   Dynasty

旧五代史 The Old History of the Five
Jiù Wǔ Dài Shǐ   Dynasties Period

新五代史 The New Written History of
Xīn Wǔ Dài Shǐ the Five Dynasties Period

宋史 The History of the Sòng Dynasty
Sòng Shǐ

资治通鉴 General Mirror for the Aid of
Zī Zhì Tōng Jiàn   Government

辽史 The History of the Liáo Dynasty
Liáo Shǐ

金史 The History of the Jīn Dynasty
Jīn Shǐ

元史 The History of the Yüán Dynasty
Yüán Shǐ

明史 The History of the Míng Dynasty
Míng Shǐ

清史 The History of the Qīng Dynasty
Qīng Shǐ

文献通考 General Study of Literary
Wén Xiàn Tōng Kǎo   Record

C 子 Zǐ (The Teaching of Ancient Philosophers)

尸子 **Book of Shī Zǐ**
Shī Zǐ

孔子集语 **Complete Sayings of Confucius**
Kóng Zǐ Jí Yǔ

文子纘义 **Wén Zǐ Book of Righteousness**
Wén Zí ZuǎnYì

文中子 **Book of Wén Zhōng Zǐ**
Wén Zhōng Zǐ

老子(道德经 **Dào Dé Jīng) Book of Ethics**
Láo Zǐ

列子 **Book of Lìe Zǐ**
Lìe Zǐ

竹书纪年 **(an ancient chronicle bamboo**
Zhú Shū Jì Nián   **book)**

荀子 **Book of Xún Zǐ**
Xún Zǐ

晏子春秋 **Book of Yàn Zǐ**
Yàn Zǐ Chūn Qiū

庄子 **Book of Zhuāng Zǐ**
Zhuāng Zǐ

商君书 **Book of Shāng Jǔn**
Shāng Jǔn Shū

淮南子 **Book of Huái Nán Zǐ**
Huái Nán Zǐ

扬子法言 **The Yáng Zǐ Discussion on**
Yáng Zí Fǎ Yán   **Legalism**

贾子新书 **The New Book of Jiá Zǐ**
Jiá Zǐ Xīn Shū

管子 **Book of Guán Zǐ**
Guán Zǐ

墨子 **Book of Mò Zǐ**
Mò Zǐ

韩非子 **Book of Hán Fēi Zǐ**
Hán Fēi Zǐ

D 集 Jí (The Collection of Ancient Teaching)

二程全书 **The Complete Works of Er**
Er Chéng Qüán Shū Chéng

玄真子 **Xüán Zhēn Zǐ Collection**
Xüán Zhēn Zǐ

朱子全书 **The Complete Works of the**
Zhū Zǐ Qüán Shū   **Philosophers**

明夷待访录 **Míng Yí Collection**
Míng Yí Dài Fǎng Lù

象山全集 **The Complete Collection of**
Xiàng Shān Qüán Jí Xiàng Shān

阳明全书 **The Complete Works of Yáng**
Yáng Míng Qüán Shū   **Míng**

阳春集 **Yáng Chūn Collection**
Yáng Chūn Jí

尊前集 **Zūn Qián Collection**
Zūn Qián Jí

儿童古书 Er Tóng Gǔ Shū Ancient Classics For Children

三字经 **sān zì jīng Three Character Primer**
千字文 **qiān zì wén One Thousand Character Prime**
百家姓 **bǎi jiā xìng One Hundred Family Name Primer**

Chinese Characters
中國字

Chinese characters	中国字		**twist & warp right**	右拐钩儿	
Zhōng Guó zì	中國字		**yòu guǎi gōur**	右拐鉤兒 ㄥ	
simplified characters	简体字		**a horizontal and down hook**	平拐钩儿	
jiǎn tǐ zì	簡體字		**píng guǎi gōur**	平拐鉤兒 ㄱ	
calligraphy	中国书法		**write with one's might**	有力	
Zhōng Guó shū fǎ	中國書法		**yǒu lì**	有力	
calligraphist	书法家		**running handwriting**	行书	
shū fǎ jiā	書法家		**xíng shū**	行書	
Chinese brush script	中国毛笔字		**cursive handwriting; grass script**	草书	
Zhōng Guó máo bǐ zì	中國毛筆字		**cǎo shū**	草書	
penmanship	手写的字		**Han style calligraphy**	隶书	
shóu xiě-de zì	手寫的字		**lì shū**	隸書	
copy-book	字帖		**seal script**	篆书	
zì tiè	字帖		**háo shū**	篆書	
Sung-type	老宋体		**stone ink-rubbing**	石拓	
lǎo sòng tǐ	老宋體		**shí tà**	石拓	
regular script; text handwritin	正楷;楷书		**paleography**	古体文	
zhèng kǎi ; kǎi shū	正楷;楷書		**gú tǐ wén**	古體文	
character strokes	笔划		**(ox) carapace-bone script**	甲古文	
bǐ huà	筆劃		**jiá gǔ wén**	甲古文	
a horizontal stroke	一横儿		**pictograph**	象形文字	
yì héngr	一橫兒 一		**xiàng xíng wén zì**	象形文字	
a straight down stroke	一竖儿		**vertical scroll**	立轴儿	
yí shùr	一豎兒 丨		**lì zhóur**	立軸兒	
a falling left skim	一撇儿		**large size ; vertical scroll**	中堂	
yì piěr	一撇兒 丿		**zhōng táng**	中堂	
a falling right slant	一捺儿		**horizontal scroll**	横披	
yí nàr	一捺兒 乀		**héng pī**	橫披	
straight down with a left hook	一竖钩儿		**distich**	对联儿	
yí shù gōur	一豎鉤兒 亅		**duì liánr**	對聯兒	
falling right dot	顿点儿				
dùn diǎnr	頓點兒 丶				

Paintings

art museum **měi shù guǎn**	美术馆 美術館
Chinese painting **guó huà**	国画 國畫
brush painting **máo bǐ huà**	毛笔画 毛筆畫
Chinese writing brush **Zhōng Guó máo bǐ**	中国毛笔 中國毛筆
Chinese inkstone **yàn-tai**	砚台 硯臺
Chinese ink stick **mò**	墨 墨
bamboo paper; rice paper **xuān zhǐ**	宣纸 宣紙
heading **shàng kuǎnr**	上款儿 上款兒
complimentary close **xià kuǎnr**	下款儿 下款兒
chop **tú zhāng**	图章 圖章
red ink paste **yìn ní**	印泥 印泥
painter; artist **huà jiā**	画家 畫家
roller for scroll **jüǎn zhóur**	卷轴儿 卷軸兒
hanging scroll **guà zhóur**	挂轴儿 掛軸兒
landscape painting **shān shuǐ huà**	山水画 山水畫

do landscapes **huà shān shuǐ**	画山水 畫山水
depict human beings **huà rén wù**	画人物 畫人物
paint birds & flowers **huà huā niǎo**	画花鸟 畫花鳥
minute/finely detailed drawing **gōng bǐ huà**	工笔画 工筆畫
central brush-painting technique **zhōng fēng**	中锋 中鋒
Chinese outline drawing **bái miáo**	白描 白描
imitating Sùng Yüán landscapes **lín mó sòng yüán shān shuǐ**	临摹宋元 臨摹宋元山水
ink splashing painting **pō mò huà**	泼墨画 潑墨畫
picture delineated by fingers **zhǐ huà**	指画 指畫
modern art **xiàn dài měi shù**	现代美术 現代美術
psychodelic art **chāo xiàn shí měi shù**	超现实美术 超現實美術
surrealism **chāo xiàn shí pài**	超现实派 超現實派
futurism **xīn cháo pài**	新潮派 新潮派
futuristic painting **xīn cháo huà**	新潮画 新潮畫
expressionism **biǎo xiàn pài**	表现派 表現派

action painting **chōu xiàng biǎo xiàn pài**	抽象表现派 抽象表現派	portrait **rén xiàng**	人像 人像
inspiration **líng gǎn**	灵感 靈感	realistic portrait **xiě shí rén xiàng**	写实人像 寫實人像
inspired painter **líng gǎn huà jiā**	灵感画家 靈感畫家	self-portrait **zì huà xiàng**	自画像 自畫像
abstract painting **chōu xiàng huà**	抽象画 抽象畫	silhouette **cè miàn huà xiàng**	侧面画像 側面畫像
impressionism **yìn xiàng pài**	印象派 印象派	nudity **luó tǐ huà**	裸体画 裸體畫
neo-impressionism **xīn yìn xiàng pài**	新印象派 新印象派	pornography **sè qíng huà**	色情画 色情畫
impressionistic style **xiě yì huà**	写意画 寫意畫	still life **jìng wù huà**	静物画 靜物畫
graphic art **bǎn huà**	版画 版畫	moving forms **dòng tài huà**	动态画 動態畫
drawing **yòng yìng bǐ huà**	用硬笔画 用硬筆畫	Buddhist image **fó xiàng huà**	佛像画 佛像畫
cartoon **màn huà**	漫画 漫畫	mural **bì huà**	壁画 壁畫
illustrator **huà chā tú**	画插图 畫插圖	fan painting **shàn miàn huà**	扇面画 扇面畫
caricature **fěng cì huà**	讽刺画 諷刺畫	mounted paintings **biǎo huà**	裱画 裱畫
scribbling **tú yā; luàn huà**	涂鸦；乱画 塗鴉；亂畫	paper mounting **zhí biǎo**	纸裱 紙裱
sketch **sù miáo**	素描 素描	cloth mounting **bù biǎo**	布裱 布裱
painting **yòng máo bǐ huà**	用毛笔画 用毛筆畫	warped silk mounting **líng biǎo**	绫裱 綾裱
oil painting **yóu huà**	油画 油畫	glossy damask mounting **huā líng zhuāng biǎo**	花绫装裱 花綾裝裱
wash drawing **shuǐ mò huà**	水墨画 水墨畫	frame **huà kuāng**	画框 畫框
watercolor; aquarelles **shuí cǎi huà**	水彩畫 水彩畫	picture **xiàng piàn**	相片 相片
realism **xiě shí pài**	写实派 寫實派	framed paintings **xiāng kuāng-de huà**	镶框的画 鑲框的畫
figure drawing **rén wù huà**	人物画 人物畫	mount a picture **xiāng jìng kuāng**	镶镜框 鑲鏡框

English	Simplified/Pinyin	Traditional
frame a picture **zhuāng jìng kuāng**	装镜框	裝鏡框
hang paintings **guà huàr**	挂画儿	掛畫兒
to drive a nail **dīng-ge dīng-zi**	钉个钉子	釘個釘子
hand me the hammer **dì-wo chuí-zi**	递我锤子	遞我鎚子
give me a 4-inch nail **gěi-wo-ge sì cùn dīng**	给我个四寸钉	給我個四吋釘
blow (pound) it hard **shǐ jìn dīng**	使劲钉	使勁釘
crooked **wān-le**	弯了	彎了
a flat topped screw **píng tóur luó-si dīngr**	平头儿螺丝钉儿	平頭兒螺絲釘兒
measure it first **xiān liáng yí xiàr**	先量一下儿	先量一下兒

English	Simplified/Pinyin	Traditional
I want a smaller sized one **yào xiǎo-yi diǎnr-de**	要小一点儿的	要小一點兒的
a smaller one yet **zài xiǎo-yi diǎnr**	再小一点儿	再小一點兒
I need a screwdriver **wǒ yào-ge luó-si dāor**	我要个螺丝刀儿	我要個螺絲刀兒
the Philips screwdriver **yào shí zì tóur-de**	要十字头儿的	要十字頭兒的
not the regular kind **bú yào yī zì tóur-de**	不要一字头儿的	不要一字頭兒的
this is cement wall **zhè qiáng shì shuǐ ní-de**	这墙是水泥的	這牆是水泥的
need a steel nail **xū yào gāng dīng**	需要钢钉	需要鋼釘
lopsided **wāi-le; bú zhèng**	歪了；不正	歪了；不正
slanting; oblique **xié-le**	斜了	斜了

画

36
C

Paintings

37A Television 電視

television; TV **diàn shì**	电视 電視	report **bào dǎo**	报导 報導
satellite dish (卫星接受碟) **xiáo ěr-duo**	小耳朵 小耳朵	news report **xīn wén bào dǎo**	新闻报导 新聞報導
cable television **yǒu xiàn diàn shì**	有线电视 有線電視	weather report **qì xiàng bào gào**	气象报告 氣象報告
wireless TV **wú xiàn diàn shì**	无线电视 無線電視	anchorman **xīn wén bō bào yuán**	新闻播报员 新聞播報員
closed circuit TV **bì lù diàn shì**	闭路电视 閉路電視	anchorwoman **nǚ bō bào yuán**	女播报员 女播報員
digital television (DTV) **shù zì diàn shì**	数字电视 數字電視	telefilm **diàn shì yǐng piàn**	电视影片 電視影片
satellite (relay) station **wèi xīng diàn tái**	卫星电台 衛星電臺	quiz show **cāi mí jié mù**	猜谜节目 猜謎節目
TV network **diàn shì wǎng**	电视网 電視網	sports event **tǐ yù shí kuàng**	体育实况 體育實況
channel **pín dào**	频道 頻道	variety show **zòng yì jié mù**	综艺节目 綜藝節目
channel 14 **dì shí sì tái**	第十四台 第十四台	monotalk show **dān kǒu xiàng-sheng**	单口相声 單口相聲
stay tuned **qǐng wù zhuǎn tái**	请勿转台 請勿轉臺	2-man comic talk show **duì kǒu xiàng-sheng**	对口相声 對口相聲
prime time soap opera **bā diǎn dǎng**	八点档 八點檔	drama serial **lián xù jù**	连续剧 連續劇
program **jié mù**	节目 節目	drama installment **lián xù jù dān jí**	连续剧单集 連續劇單集
audience rating **shōu shì lǜ**	收视率 收視率	give-away show **yóu jiǎng jié mù**	有奖节目 有獎節目
viewer **guān zhòng**	观众 觀眾	panel show **zhuān yí tǎo lùn jié mù**	专题讨论节目 專題討論節目

interview show fǎng wèn jié mù	访问节目	訪問節目
kid show ér tóng jié mù	儿童节目	兒童節目
commercials shāng yè guǎng gào	商业广告	商業廣告
nursery rhyme tóng yáo	童谣	童謠
fluorescent screen yíng guāng mù	萤光幕	螢光幕
remote control yáo kòng qì	摇控器	搖控器
luminescent fā lěng guāng	发冷光	發冷光
gloom light yōu àn guāng	幽暗光	幽暗光
brightness liàng-du	亮度	亮度
not bright enough bú gòu liàng	不够亮	不夠亮
contrast control duì bǐ kòng zhì qì	对比控制器	對比控制器
unbalanced color yán-se bú zhèng	颜色不正	顏色不正
color not bright yán-se bù xiān yàn	颜色不鲜艳	顏色不鮮豔
on the red side yán-se piān hóng	颜色偏红	顏色偏紅
on the green side yán-se piān lǜ	颜色偏绿	顏色偏綠
unclear sound tīng-bu qīng-chu	听不清楚	聽不清楚
interference zá yīn tài duō	杂音太多	雜音太多
unclear picture huà miàn bù qīng-chu	画面不清楚	畫面不清楚
blurry mó-hu	模糊	模糊

snowing on the screen huà miàn shǎn dòng	画面闪动	畫面閃動
the picture is a mere blur huà miàn mó hú bùqīng	画面模糊不清	畫面模糊不清
blinking yì shǎn yì shǎn-de	一闪一闪的	一閃一閃的
appear horizontal lines chū héng dào-zi	出横道子	出橫道子
no video signal shōu-bu dào huà miàn	收不到画面	收不到畫面
no audio signal shōu-bu dào shēng-yin	收不到声音	收不到聲音
language switch yǔ yán zhuǎn huàn niǔr	语言转换钮儿	語言轉換鈕兒
program director jié mù dǎo bō	节目导播	節目導播
dress rehearsal cǎi pái	彩排	彩排
direct current (DC) zhí liú diàn	直流电	直流電
alternation current (AC) jiāo liú diàn	交流电	交流電
high voltage electricity gāo yā diàn	高压电	高壓電
power for industrial use gōng yè yòng diàn	工业用电	工業用電
dynamic electricity dòng diàn	动电	動電
static electricity jìng diàn	静电	靜電
voltage diàn yā	电压	電壓
power diàn lì	电力	電力
power of shortage diàn lì bù zú	电力不足	電力不足

Radio Station
廣播電台

radio **shōu yīn jī**	收音机 收音機	a megahertz **zhào hè**	兆赫 兆赫
broadcasting **guǎng bō**	广播 廣播	antenna **tiān xiàn**	天线 天線
network **guǎng bō wǎng**	广播网 廣播網	ground wire **dì xiàn**	地线 地線
AM (amplitude modulation) **tiáo fú**	调幅 調幅	sound wave **yīn bō**	音波 音波
FM (frequency modulation) **tiáo pín**	调频 調頻	microwave **wéi bō**	微波 微波
FM tuner **tiáo xié qì**	调谐器 調諧器	short-wave **duǎn bō**	短波 短波
tuning **tiáo xié**	调谐 調諧	tune in the radio **shōu tīng**	收听 收聽
AF (audio frequency) **yīn pín**	音频 音頻	tune out the radio **guān bì shōu yīn jī**	关闭收音机 關閉收音機
frequency control **pín lǜ kòng zhì**	频率控制 頻率控制	dial **kè dù pán**	刻度盘 刻度盤
magnetic field **cí chǎng**	磁场 磁場	master tape **mǔ dài**	母带 母帶
frequency **pín lǜ; zhōu lǜ**	频率；周率 頻率；周率	signal **xùn hào**	讯号 訊號
cycle **zhōu bō**	周波 周波	sound track **yīn guǐ**	音轨 音軌
kilocycle **qiān zhōu**	千周 千周	dry cell **gān diàn chí**	干电池 乾電池
megacycle **zhào zhōu**	兆周 兆周	cathode **yīn jí**	阴极 陰極
a kilohertz **qiān hè**	千赫 千赫	anode **yáng jí**	阳极 陽極

positively **dài zhèng diàn**	带正电 帶正電	atmospheric disturbance **kōng zhōng gān rǎo**	空中干扰 空中干擾
negatively **dài fù diàn**	带负电 帶負電	interference eliminator **gān ráo miǎn chú qì**	干扰免除器 干擾免除器
clock radio **nào zhōng shōu yīn jī**	闹钟收音机 鬧鐘收音機	scratch; ground noise **zá yīn**	杂音 雜音
wrist radio **shóu biǎo shōu yīn jī**	手表收音机 手錶收音機	noise filter **zá shēng lǜ qì**	杂声滤器 雜聲濾器
transistor radio **jīng tí guǎn shōu yīn jī**	晶体管收音机 晶體管收音機	reduction noise **qīng chú zá yīn**	清除杂音 清除雜音

Newspaper & Magazine

報紙與雜誌

newspaper bào zhǐ	报纸 報紙	star reporter míng jì zhě	名记者 名記者
magazine zá zhì	杂志 雜誌	keyhole reporter shè huì xīn wén jì zhě	社会新闻记者 社會新聞記者
paparazzo; paparazzi gǒu zǎi duì	狗仔队 狗仔隊	news source xīn wén lái yuán	新闻来源 新聞來源
news media xīn wén méi tǐ	新闻媒体 新聞媒體	first-hand news yī shǒur xiāo xí	一手儿消息 一手兒消息
banner head héng guàn dà biāo tí	横贯大标题 橫貫大標題	official announcement guān fāng xiāo xí	官方消息 官方消息
news flash tóu tiáo xīn wén	头条新闻 頭條新聞	semi-officialannouncement bàn guān fāng xiāo xí	半官方消息 半官方消息
local edition xīn wén běn dì bǎn	本地版 本地版	news release xīn wén gǎo	新闻稿 新聞稿
international edition guó jì bǎn	国际版 國際版	unofficial news fēi guān fāng xiāo xí	非官方消息 非官方消息
air edition háng kōng bǎn	航空版 航空版	hot news zuì xīn xiāo xí	最新消息 最新消息
overseas edition hǎi wài bǎn	海外版 海外版	well-informed xiāo xí líng tōng fāng miàn	消息灵通方面 消息靈通方面
press photographer shè yǐng jì zhě	摄影记者 攝影記者	learn about; contended jù wén; jù chēng	据闻;据称 據聞;據稱
staff writer tè pài jì zhě	特派记者 特派記者	reliable source kě kào fāng miàn	可靠方面 可靠方面
special correspondent tè tài yuán	特派员 特派員	(in) terms of reality yī jù shì shí	依据事实 依據事實
journalist zhuàn gǎo jì zhě	撰稿记者 撰稿記者	authoritative quán wēi fāng miàn	权威方面 權威方面
correspondent tōng xùn yuán	通讯员 通訊員	(in) regard to the facts gēn jù shì-qing zhēn xiàng	根据事情真相 根據事情真相

said to be **jù shuō**	据说 據說	round-up report **zòng hé bào dǎo**	综合报导 綜合報導
groundless **haó wú gēn jù**	毫无根据 毫無根據	newswoman **nǚ jì zhě**	女记者 女記者
hearsay **chuán wén**	传闻 傳聞	journalist **xīn wén cóng yè yuán**	新闻从业员 新聞從業員
rumor **yáo yán**	谣言 謠言	feature writer **tè yüē zhuàn shù**	特约撰述 特約撰述
international news **guó jì xīn wén**	国际新闻 國際新聞	columnist **zhuān lán zuò jiā**	专栏作家 專欄作家
domestic news **guó nèi xīn wén**	国内新闻 國內新聞	Dear Moly Mayfield **mǒu fū rén xìn xiāng**	某夫人信箱 某夫人信箱
highlight; newsbreak **zhòng yào xīn wén**	重要新闻 重要新聞	freelance writer **zì yóu zuò jiā**	自由作家 自由作家
local news **dì fāng xīn wén**	地方新闻 地方新聞	copywriter **zhù zuò qüán rén**	著作权人 著作權人
screamer **hōng dòng shè huì xīn wén**	轰动社会新闻 轟動社會新聞	news analyst **xīn wén píng lùn jiā**	新闻评论家 新聞評論家
exclusive (news) **dú jiā bào dǎo**	独家报导 獨家報導	commentator **shí shì píng lùn jiā**	时事评论家 時事評論家
dope story **nèi mù xīn wén**	内幕新闻 內幕新聞	editorial writer **shè píng zuò zhě**	社评作者 社評作者
news maker **xīn wén rén wù**	新闻人物 新聞人物	free lancer **zì yóu zhuàn gǎo rén**	自由撰稿人 自由撰稿人
follow up **zhuī zōng bào dǎo**	追踪报导 追蹤報導	bulldog edition **zuì zǎo-de zǎo bào**	最早的早报 最早的早報
scandal **chǒu wén**	丑闻 醜聞	morning paper **zǎo bào**	早报 早報
gossip column; titbit **huā biān xīn wén**	花边新闻 花邊新聞	noon paper **wǔ bào**	午报 午報
bring forth **gōng bù**	公布 公佈	evening paper **wǎn bào**	晚报 晚報
open secret **gōng kāi-de mì mì**	公开的秘密 公開的秘密	express **kuài bào**	快报 快報
known far and near **yüǎn jìn jiē zhī**	远近皆知 遠近皆知	extra **hàor wài**	号儿外 號兒外
play on words **wán nòng wén zì**	玩弄文字 玩弄文字	press (1 reporter)**jì zhě** 　　(2 agency)**tōng xǜn shè**	1 记者；2 通讯社 1 記者；2 通訊社
reputation **míng yù; míng shēng**	名誉；名声 名譽；名聲	special dispatch **zhuān diàn**	专电 專電

reference room zī liào shì	资料室 資料室	periodical dìng qí kān wù	定期刊物 定期刊物
clipping jiǎn bào	剪报 剪報	weekly (publication) zhōu kān	周刊 週刊
legend jiù wén	旧闻 舊聞	monthly (publication) yüè kān	月刊 月刊
frame news zhì zào xīn wén	制造新闻 製造新聞	chronicle news jì shì bào	记事报 記事報
shoddy news wèi zào-de xīn wén	伪造的新闻 偽造的新聞	review news píng shì bào	评事报 評事報
feature tè xiě	特写 特寫	local press běn dì bào	本地报 本地報
world news in brief shì jiè yào wén	世界要闻 世界要聞	weekly xīn wén zhōu bào	新闻周报 新聞週報
quirks in news shì jiè zhēn wén	世界珍闻 世界珍聞	essay duǎn wén	短文 短文
international links guó jì jiāo wǎng xīn wén	国际交往新闻 國際交往新聞	treatise cháng piān	长篇 長篇
society column shè jiāo xīn wén	社交新闻 社交新聞	advertising department guǎng gào bù	广告部 廣告部
ten top news shí dà xīn wén	十大新闻 十大新聞	AE (account executive) guǎng gào yè wù jīng lǐ	广告业务经理 廣告業務經理
man of the year fēng yún rén wù	风云人物 風雲人物	advertiser guǎng gào kè hù	广告客户 廣告客戶
people shí rén xíng zōng	时人行踪 時人行蹤	publicity company chuán bō gōng sī	传播公司 傳播公司
political news zhèng zhì xīn wén	政治新闻 政治新聞	advertising agency guǎng gào gōng sī	广告公司 廣告公司
economic front jīng jì dòng tài	经济动态 經濟動態	ad; advertisement guǎng gào; xüān chuán	广告；宣传 廣告；宣傳
Beijing vignettes běi jīng diǎn dī	北京点滴 北京點滴	advertising dēng guǎng gào	登广告 登廣告
news eyes xīn wén yǎn	新闻眼 新聞眼	display ad shāng pǐn shè jì guǎng gào	商品设计广告 商品設計廣告
news picture xīn wén zhào piàn	新闻照片 新聞照片	classified ad fēn lèi guǎng gào	分类广告 分類廣告
publish fā biǎo	发表 發表	whole page ad quán yè guǎng gào	全页广告 全頁廣告
appear pī lù	披露 披露	publicity yín qǐ gōng zhòng zhù yì	引起公众注意 引起公眾注意

Banking 银行 38A

bank yín háng	银行 銀行
banking yín háng yè wù	银行业务 銀行業務
national bank guó jiā yín háng	国家银行 國家銀行
state bank zhōu lì yín háng	州立银行 州立銀行
government treasury zhèng fǔ gōng kù	政府公库 政府公庫
provincial treasury shěng lì gōng kù	省立公库 省立公庫
provincial bank shěng lì yín háng	省立银行 省立銀行
city bank shì lì yín háng	市立银行 市立銀行
commercial bank shāng yè yín háng	商业银行 商業銀行
investment bank tóu zī yín háng	投资银行 投資銀行
export-import bank jìn chū kǒu yín háng	进出口银行 進出口銀行
trust bank xìn tuō yín háng	信托银行 信託銀行
medium & small business bank zhōng xiǎo qì yè yín hágn	中小企业银行 中小企業銀行
branch office fēn háng	分行 分行
information desk xún wèn chù	询问处 詢問處

closed zhàn tíng shòu lǐ	暂停受理 暫停受理
banking hours yíng yè shí jiān	营业时间 營業時間
automatic cash dispenser zì dòng tí kuǎn jī	自动提款机 自動提款機
automatic depositor zì dòng cún kuǎn jī	自动存款机 自動存款機
currency counting machine dián shǔ chāo piào jī	点数钞票机 點數鈔票機
teller guì tái zhí yüán	柜台职员 櫃檯職員
money qían	钱 錢
cash xiàn jīn	现金 現金
dollar yüán; kuài qián	元；块钱 元；塊錢
bill; banknote zhǐ chāo	纸钞 紙鈔
coin qián bì	钱币 錢幣
counterfeit note jiǎ chāo	假钞 假鈔
Renminbi (RMB) rén mín bì	人民币 人民幣
New Taiwan Dollar (NT$) xīn tái bì	新台币 新台幣
U.S. Currency (US$) měi jīn	美金 美金

Pound Sterling **yīng bàng**	英镑 英鎊	transfer **zhuǎn zhàng**	转帐 轉帳
Japanese Yuan **rì bì**	日币 日幣	receipt **shōu jù**	收据 收據
Deutsche Mark **mǎ kè**	马克 馬克	close account **jié qīng**	结清 結清
Euro **ōu yuán**	欧元 歐元	deposit slip **cún kuǎn dān**	存款单 存款單
receiving **shōu kuǎn**	收款 收款	deposit receipt **cún kuǎn shōu jù**	存款收据 存款收據
loan **fàng kuǎn**	放款 放款	foreign deposit **wài bì cún kuǎn**	外币存款 外幣存款
collection **dài shōu**	代收 代收	safe deposit vault **báo xiǎn kù**	保险库 保險庫
item collected for **dài shōu fèi yòng**	代收费用 代收費用	safe deposit box **báo xiǎn xiāng**	保险箱 保險箱
bank charges **yín háng shǒu xù fèi**	银行手续费 銀行手續費	depositor **cún kuǎn rén**	存款人 存款人
open an account **kāi hù tóu**	开户头 開戶頭	legal seal **yìn jiàn**	印鉴 印鑒
joint account **gòng yǒu hù tóu**	共有户头 共有戶頭	to stamp **gài zhāng**	盖章 蓋章
savings account **cún kuǎn hù tóu**	存款户头 存款戶頭	cosign **lián shǔ**	连署 連署
checking account **zhī piào hù tóu**	支票户头 支票戶頭	sign **qiān zì**	签字 簽字
current account **huó qí cún kuǎn**	活期存款 活期存款	signature **qiān míng**	签名 簽名
fixed account **dìng qí cún kuǎn**	定期存款 定期存款	check **zhī piào**	支票 支票
account number **zhàng hào**	帐号 帳號	checkbook **zhī piào bù**	支票簿 支票簿
account's name **hù míng**	户名 戶名	stub **zhī piào cún gēn**	支票存根 支票存根
bankbook **cún zhé**	存摺 存摺	blank check **kòng bái zhī piào**	空白支票 空白支票
deposit **cún kuǎn**	存款 存款	handling charge **shǒu xù fèi**	手续费 手續費
withdrawal **tí kuǎn**	提款 提款	pay to the order of **píng piào qí fù**	凭票祈付 憑票祈付

English	简体	繁體
block letter dà xiě shù zì	大写数字	大寫數字
certified check bǎo fù zhī piào	保付支票	保付支票
sight check jí qí piào	即期票	即期票
traveler's check lǚ xíng zhī piào	旅行支票	旅行支票
uncollected check tuō shōu zhī piào	托收支票	托收支票
deferred payment yán qí zhī fù	延期支付	延期支付
unclaimed wú rén qǔ kuǎn	无人取款	無人取款
rubber check kōng tóu zhī piào	空头支票	空頭支票
shortage bù zú	不足	不足
insufficient fund cún kuǎn bù zú	存款不足	存款不足
check bounced tuì piào	退票	退票
dishonored account jù jué wǎng lái hù	拒绝往来户	拒絕往來戶
forger of check mào qiān zhī piào	冒签支票	冒簽支票
third party check zhuán shǒu zhī piào	转手支票	轉手支票
cashier's check yín háng běn piào	银行本票	銀行本票
money order yín háng huì piào	银行汇票	銀行匯票
draft huì piào	汇票	匯票
drawer fā piào rén	发票人	發票人
bearer chí piào rén	持票人	持票人
assignor ràng yǔ rén	让与人	讓與人

English	简体	繁體
payee shòu kuǎn rén	受款人	受款人
assignee shòu ràng rén	受让人	受讓人
protest jù fù	拒付	拒付
stop payment zhǐ fù	止付	止付
transaction jiāo yì chú lǐ	交易处理	交易處理
void zuò fèi	作废	作廢
credit card xìn yòng kǎ	信用卡	信用卡
charge it shē zhàng	赊帐	賒帳
handy fāng biàn hǎo yòng	方便好用	方便好用
credit line xìn yòng é dù	信用额度	信用額度
bank statement yín háng jié dān	银行结单	銀行結單
monthly statement měi yuè jié dān	每月结单	每月結單
balance jié cún; yǔ é	结存；馀额	結存；餘額
confirmation of balance duì zhàng dān	对账单	對賬單
budget yù suàn	预算	預算
title (the bearer's name) tái tóu	抬头 (支票)	抬頭
to endorse bèi shū	背书	背書
non-negotiable bù néng zhuǎn ràng	不能转让	不能轉讓
words & figures differ jīn é bù fú	金额不符	金額不符
official rate guān jià	官价	官價

black market hēi shì	黑市 黑市	application for exchange shēn qǐng wài huì	申请外汇 申請外匯
receivable account yīng shōu wèi shōu kuǎn	应收未收款 應收未收款	bureau de change wài bì duì huàn chù	外币兑换处 外幣兌換處
is honored zhī piào yǐ duì xiàn	支票已兑现 支票已兌現	exchange rate huì lǜ	汇率 匯率
account closed hù tóu guān bì	户头关闭 戶頭關閉	floating fú dòng lǜ	浮动率 浮動率
canceled check yǐ duì xiàn fèi piào	已兑现废票 已兌現廢票	selling mài chū	卖出 賣出
post-dated check yuǎn qí zhī piào	远期支票 遠期支票	buying mǎi rù	买入 買入
stale check guò qí zhī piào	过期支票 過期支票	invest tóu zī	投资 投資
clearance piào jù jiāo huàn	票据交换 票據交換	currency huò bì	货币 貨幣
bill undue piào qí wèi dào	票期未到 票期未到	hard currency qiáng shì huò bì	强势货币 強勢貨幣
past due guò qí	过期 過期	legal tender fǎ dìng huò bì	法定货币 法定貨幣
cash a check duì xiàn	兑现 兌現	speculate wài bì tóu jī mǎi mài	外币投机买卖 外幣投機買賣
deposit transfer cún kuǎn zhuǎn ràng	存款转让 存款轉讓	marketable securities yǒu jià zhèng quàn	有价证券 有價證券
transfer debt zhuǎn zhàng zhī chū	转帐支出 轉帳支出	stock gǔ piào	股票 股票
overdraw; overdraft tòu zhī	透支 透支	common stock pǔ tōng gǔ	普通股 普通股
bank loan yín háng fàng kuǎn; róng zī	银行放款;融资 銀行放款；融資	fund jī jīn	基金 基金
international exchange guó jì huì duì	国际汇兑 國際匯兌	mutual funds gòng tóng jī jīn	共同基金 共同基金
domestic exchange guó nèi huì duì	国内汇兑 國內匯兌	secured loan dǐ yā fàng kuǎn	抵押放款 抵押放款
remittance huì kuǎn	汇款 匯款	credit loan xìn yòng fàng kuǎn	信用放款 信用放款
charge of remittance huì shuǐ	汇水 匯水	short term loan duǎn qí fàng kuǎn	短期放款 短期放款
foreign exchange wài huì	外汇 外匯	long term loan cháng qí fàng kuǎn	长期放款 長期放款

mortgage **dǐ yā**	抵押 抵押	annual rate **nián xí lù**	年息率 年息率
collateral **dān bǎo wù**	担保物 擔保物	mensal rate **yüè xí lù**	月息率 月息率
pledge **dǐ yā pǐn**	抵押品 抵押品	daily rate **rì xí lù**	日息率 日息率
property **zī chǎn**	资产 資產	round up the figure **sì shé wǔ rù**	四舍五入 四捨五入
real estate **bú dòng chǎn**	不动产 不動產	annum interest **nián xí**	年息 年息
real estate mortgage **bú dòng chán dǐ yā**	不动产抵押 不動產抵押	tighten money supply **chōu jǐn yín gēn**	抽紧银根 抽緊銀根
chattel mortgage **dòng chǎn dǐ yā**	动产抵押 動產抵押	deflation **tōng huò jǐn suō**	通货紧缩 通貨緊縮
down payment **shǒu qí fù kuǎn**	首期付款 首期付款	inflation **tōng hùo péng zhàng**	通货膨胀 通貨膨脹
installment payment **fēn qí fù kuǎn**	分期付款 分期付款	finance **cái zhèng**	财政 財政
monthly installment **àn yüè tān fù**	按月摊付 按月攤付	promissory note **jiè jù; běn piào**	借据；本票 借據；本票
redemption house **shú huí fáng wū**	赎回房屋 贖回房屋	compound interest **lì gǔn lì**	利滚利 利滾利
investment in enterprise **qì yè tóu zī**	企业投资 企業投資	guarantor **bǎo-ren**	保人 保人
lending rate **dài kuǎn lì lù**	贷款利率 貸款利率	debit **jiè fāng**	借方 借方
principal and interest **běn lì**	本利 本利	creditor **dài fāng**	贷方 貸方
interest **lì xí**	利息 利息	debt **zhài**	债 債
interest rate **lì lù**	利率 利率	bonus **hóng lì**	红利 紅利
prime rate **jī běn lì lù**	基本利率 基本利率		

Money Talks
有钱能使鬼推磨
yǒu qián néng shǐ guǐ tuī mò
(Money can make a ghost push the millstones for you like a donkey does)

Insurance Company 保險公司

English	简体	繁體
underwriter **báo xiǎn shāng**	保险商	保險商
insurance broker **báo xiǎn jīng jì rén**	保险经纪人	保險經紀人
examiner **chá hé yuán**	查核员	查核員
inspector **chá kān yuán**	查勘员	查勘員
applicant **shēn qǐng rén**	申请人	申請人
beneficiary **shòu yì rén**	受益人	受益人
the assured ; policyholder **bèi báo xiǎn rén**	被保险人	被保險人
policy applies to **báo xiǎn shì yòng yú**	保险适用於	保險適用於
named in the schedule **qīng dān zhōng rén míng**	清单中人名	清單中人名
against all risks (A.A.R.) **tóu báo qüán xiǎn**	投保全险	投保全險
comprehensive ins. **zòng hé báo xiǎn**	综合保险	綜合保險
group insurance **tuán tǐ báo xiǎn**	团体保险	團體保險
public liability **gōng gòng yì wài zé rèn**	公共意外责任	公共意外責任
life insurance **rén shòu báo xiǎn**	人寿保险	人壽保險
whole-life insurance **zhōng shēn rén shòu báo xiǎn**	终身人寿保险	

English	简体	繁體
health insurance **jiàn kāng báo xiǎn**	健康保险	健康保險
labor insurance **láo gōng báo xiǎn**	劳工保险	勞工保險
automobile insurance **qì chē xiǎn**	汽车险	汽車險
casualty insurance **yì wài xiǎn**	意外险	意外險
burglary (theft) insurance **qiè dào báo xiǎn**	窃盗保险	竊盜保險
industrial insurance **gōng yè báo xiǎn**	工业保险	工業保險
property insurance **chǎn wù báo xiǎn**	产物保险	產物保險
cargo insurance **huò wù báo xiǎn**	货物保险	貨物保險
official public bonds **gōng wù yuán báo zhèng xiǎn**	公务员保证险	
inland marine insurance **nèi lù shǔi yùn báo xiǎn**	内路水运保险	內路水運保險
marine insurance **shúi xiǎn**	水险	水險
fire insurance **húo xiǎn**	火险	火險
full insurance coverage **quán é báo xiǎn**	全额保险	全額保險
lump sum insurance **yí cì jiāo báo xiǎ**	一次缴保险	一次繳保險
coverage **báo xiǎn zǒng é**	保险总额	保險總額

insurance policy bǎo dān	保单 保單	liability fǎ lǜ péi cháng zé rèn	法律赔偿责任 法律賠償責任
the premium báo xiǎn fèi	保险费 保險費	deemed to be shì zuò	视作 視作
due to yīn yóu	因由 因由	default wéi yüē	违约 違約
consequential loss jiàn jiē sǔn shī	间接损失 間接損失	basis of this contract hé yuē zhǔn zé	合约准则 合約準則
declare shēng míng; shēn bào	声明；申报 聲明；申報	has paid to the corporation yǐ fù gōng sī	已付公司 已付公司
claim papers suǒ péi wén jiàn	索赔文件 索賠文件	in the manner yí cǐ fāng shì	以此方式 以此方式
cover lǐ péi fàn wéi	理赔范围 理賠範圍	no opposition wú rén fǎn duì	无人反对 無人反對
in accordance with yī jù	依据 依據	indemnify miǎn yǔ shòu fá	免於受罚 免於受罰
conditions tiáo jiàn	条件 條件	up to but not exceeding zuì duō bù chāo guò	最多不超过 最多不超過
return goods tuì huò	退货 退貨	amounts specified in schedule shù mù rú zǎi	数目如载 數目如載
get a refund tuì kuǎn	退款 退款	bodily injury rén shēn shòu shāng	人身受伤 人身受傷
covering note zhàn bǎo dān	暂保单 暫保單	damage to property cái chǎn shòu sǔn	财产受损 財產受損
subsidy bǔ zhù	补助 補助	group caused by fā shēng yǔ; qǐ yīn	发生於；起因 發生於；起因
reinsurance zhuǎn tóu bǎo	转投保 轉投保	any accident occurring rèn hé zāi huò fā shēng	任何灾祸发生 任何災禍發生
crushed yā suì-le	压碎了 壓碎了	policy period báo xiǎn qí jiān	保险期间 保險期間
damage sǔn hài	损害 損害（損壞）	occurring before during zài fā shēng qí jiān	在发生期间 在發生期間
loss sǔn shī	损失 損失	set forth in the agreement xié yì zhōng tí dào	协议中提到 協議中提到
defective items xiá cī pǐn	瑕疵品 瑕疵品	during the period set forth qí xiàn nèi tí chū	期限内提出 期限內提出
cost and insurance (C & I) báo xiǎn fèi zài nèi	保险费在内 保險費在內	renewal date xǜ yüē; xǜ dìng	续约；续订 續約；續訂
cost insurance freight (C.I.F) yǜn fèi báo xiǎn zài nèi	运费保险在内 運費保險在內	see attachment jiàn fù jiàn	见附件 見附件

保险公司

38
B

Insurance Company

339

disability insurance	残废险	殘廢險
cán fèi xiǎn		
disability benefit	残废给付	殘廢給付
cán fèi jǐ fù		
burglary insurance	窃盗险	竊盜險
qiè dào xiǎn		
corporate surety	公司保证人	公司保證人
gōng sī bǎo zhèng rén		
public property	公有产物	公有產物
gōng yóu chǎn wù		
claimant	索赔人	索賠人
suǒ péi rēn		
contingent beneficiary	第二受益人	第二受益人
dì èr shòu yì rén		
terminated insurance	停止保险	停止保險
tíng zhǐ báo xiǎn		
indemnity	赔偿	賠償
péi chǎng		
adjustment	理赔	理賠
lǐ péi		
age limits	年龄限制	年齡限制
nián líng xiàn zhì		
effective date	生效日期	生效日期
shēng xiào rì qí		
period of validity	有效期限	有效期限
yǒu xiào qí xiàn		
payment by installment	分期缴费	分期繳費
fēn qí jiǎo fèi		
minimum (net) premiu	最低保费	最低保費
zuì dī bǎo féi		
maximum coverage	最高承受额	最高承受額
zuì gāo chéng shòu é		
void	无效	無效
wú xiào		
cancellation	注销	註銷
zhù xiāo		
arson	纵火	縱火
zòng huǒ		
embezzlement	监守自盗	監守自盜
jiān shǒu zì dào		
investigation	调查	調查
diào chá		
concealment	隐瞒	隱瞞
yǐn mán		
innocent misrepresentation	误报	誤報
wù bào		
actual cash value	实际现金价值	實際現金價值
shí jì xiàn jīn jià zhí		
limit of liability	责任限度	責任限度
zé rèn xiàn dù		
per person	以人头计	以人頭計
yǐ rén tóu jì		
per accident	以案件计	以案件計
yǐ àn jiàn jì		
herein	在此袋中	在此袋中
zài cǐ dài zhōng		
enclosed	內附	內附
nèi fù		
whereas	鑑於	鑑於
jiàn yǘ		
incident	事故	事故
shì gù		
have occurred	业已发生	業已發生
yè yǐ fā shēng		
risk	风险	風險
fēng xiǎn		
as a consequence	其後果	其後果
qí hòu guǒ		
has made to	嘱托於	囑託於
zhǔ tuō yú		
hereinafter called	以下简称	以下簡稱
yǐ xià jiǎn chēng		
the corporation	该法人	該法人
gāi fǎ rén		
written proposal	书面提案	書面提案
shū miàn tí àn		
bearing the date	明列日期	明列日期
míng liè rì qí		
specified in the schedule	明确指出	明確指出
míng què zhǐ chū		

hereby tè cǐ; jiè cǐ	特此；藉此 特此；藉此	beneficiary shòu yì rén	受益人 受益人
modification xiū zhèng	修正 修正	natural disaster tiān zāi	天灾 天災
agrees to the extent shòu xiàn yú	受限於 受限於	fire disaster huǒ zāi	火灾 火災
deductible kě jián miǎn-de	可减免的 可减免的	intentional injury gù yì shāng hài	故意伤害 故意傷害
hazards ǒu fā wéi hài	偶发危害 偶發危害	in relation to guān yú	关於 關於
covering legal liability gài kuò fǎ lǜ zé rèn	盖括法律责任 蓋括法律責任	water damage insurance shuǐ zì báo xiǎn	水渍保险 水漬保險
refer to cān zhào	参照 參照	additional premium jiā báo fèi	加保费 加保費
endorsement bèi shū; qiān shǔ	背书；签署 背書；簽署	full settlement qǘan é péi fù	全额赔付 全額賠付
excluding bù bāo kuò	不包括 不包括	partial settlement bù fèn péi fù	部分赔付 部分賠付
irrevocable bù néng biàn gēng	不能变更 不能變更	evaluation; appraisal gū jià	估价 估價

International Trade

國際貿易

trade; trading	mào yì	贸易 / 貿易
import	jìn kǒu	进口 / 進口
export	chū kǒu; wài xiāo	出口；外销 / 出口；外銷
importer/exporter	jìng chū kǒu shāng	进出口商 / 進出口商
international trade	guó jì mào yì	国际贸易 / 國際貿易
foreign trade	duì wài mào yì	对外贸易 / 對外貿易
third party trade	sān jiǎo mào yì	三角贸易 / 三角貿易
processing trade for export	jiā gōng chū kǒu mào yì	加工出口贸易 / 加工出口貿易
processing trade for import	jiā gōng jìn kǒu mào yì	加工进口贸易 / 加工進口貿易
trade fair	shāng pín zhǎn xiāo huì	商品展销会 / 商品展銷會
purchases	cǎi gòu	采购 / 採購
deficiency	chì zì	赤字 / 赤字
goods in lots	zhěng pī huò wù	整批货物 / 整批貨物
counterfeit article	fǎng mào pǐn	仿冒品 / 仿冒品
prohibited goods	wéi jìn pǐn	违禁品 / 違禁品
commodity market	shāng pǐn shì chǎng	商品市场 / 商品市場
market price	shì jià	市价 / 市價
cash transactions	xiàn jīn jiāo yì	现金交易 / 現金交易
at sight	jiàn piào jí fù	见票即付 / 見票即付
invoice	fā huò qīng dān	发货清单 / 發貨清單
deposit	dìng jīn	定金 / 定金
merchandise	shāng pǐn	商品 / 商品
inquiry	xún jià	询价 / 詢價
catalogue	chán pǐn mù lù	产品目录 / 產品目錄
brochure	xüān chuán xiǎo cè	宣传小册 / 宣傳小冊
unit price	dān jià	单价 / 單價
sample	yàng pǐn	样品 / 樣品
pattern	tú àn; zhǐ yàng	图案；纸样 / 圖案；紙樣
seller's sample	mài fāng yàng pǐn	卖方样品 / 賣方樣品
buyer's sample	mǎi fāng yàng pǐn	买方样品 / 買方樣品

telemarketing diàn huà gòu wù	电话购物 電話購物	counter offer huán jià	还价 還價
a deal yì bǐ shēng-yi	一笔生意 一筆生意	bargain yì jià	议价 議價（協議）
buyer mái zhǔ	买主 買主	price break pián yí yì diǎnr	便宜一点儿 便宜一點兒
client kè hù	客户 客戶	coordination xié tiáo	协调 協調
consumer xiāo fèi zhě	消费者 消費者	correction gēng zhèng	更正 更正
end-user; ultimate user huò pǐn gòu mǎi zhě	货品购买者 貨品購買者	amend xiū zhèng	修正 修正
prospect qián zài gù kè	潜在顾客 潛在顧客	overcome kè fú	克服 克服
reputation xìn yù	信誉 信譽	conform fú hé	符合 符合
distributor jīng xiāo shāng	经销商 經銷商	confirm qùè dìng yí xià	确定一下 確定一下
agent dài lǐ shāng	代理商 代理商	order dìng huò	订货 訂貨
sole agency dú jiā dài lǐ	独家代理 獨家代理	place an order xià dìng dān	下订单 下訂單
credit bureau zhēng xìn suǒ	征信所 徵信所	piece jiàn	件 件
credit sale shē mài	赊卖 賒賣	minimum order zuì shǎo dìng huò liàng	最少订货量 最少訂貨量
patronage huì gù	惠顾 惠顧	maximum production zuì dà shēng chǎn liàng	最大生产量 最大生產量
cold call diàn fǎng	电访 電訪	foreign trade deficit mào yì nì chā	贸易逆差 貿易逆差
lead list diàn fǎng míng dān	电访名单 電訪名單	favorable balance of trade mào yì shùn chā	贸易顺差 貿易順差
follow up zhuī zōng	追踪 追蹤	cancel the order qǔ xiāo dìng dān	取消订单 取消訂單
estimation gū jià dān	估价单 估價單	back order qūe huò zhàn huǎn yùn jiāo	缺货暂缓运交 缺貨暫緩運交
quotation bào jià dān	报价单 報價單	export permit shū chū xǔ kě zhèng	输出许可证 輸出許可證
offer chū jià	出价 出價	export license chū kǒu pái zhào	出口牌照 出口牌照

pro forma invoice **yù gū fā huò dān**	预估发货单 預估發貨單	free alongside ship (F.A.S.) 船边交货价 **chuán-bian jiāo huò jià** 船邊交貨價
letter of credit (L/C) **xìn yòng zhuàng**	信用状 信用狀	shipping company / forwarder 船公司 **chuán gōng sī** 船公司
irrevocable **bù kě chè xiāo-de**	不可撤销的 不可撤銷的	sent by air 空运 **kōng yùn** 空運
method of payment **fù kuǎn fāng shì**	付款方式 付款方式	surface shipment 海运 **hǎi yùn** 海運
negotiate **jiāo shè**	交涉 交涉（押匯）	container ship 货柜船 **huò guì chuán** 貨櫃船
negotiating bank **yā huì yín háng**	押汇银行 押匯銀行	ship the goods 出货 **chū huò** 出貨
payment in advance **yù fù huò kuǎn**	预付货款 預付貨款	deliver the goods 交货 **jiāo huò** 交貨
cash with order **suí dìng dān fù xiàn**	随订单付现 隨訂單付現	shipping date 船期 **chuán qí** 船期
authorities **shòu quán**	授权 授權	delivery date 交货日期 **jiāo huò rì qí** 交貨日期
instructions **zhí yín shǒu cè**	指引手册 指引手冊	within 30 days 三十天内 **sān shí tiān nèi** 三十天內
documentary bills **yā huì piào**	押汇票 押匯票	on time 准时 **zhǔn shí** 準時
shipping documents **huò yùn dān jù**	货运单据 貨運單據	delay 延误 **yán wù** 延誤
packaging **bāo zhuāng**	包装 包裝	date extension 延迟 **yán chí** 延遲
net cost **chéng běn**	成本 成本	shipping delays 船期延误 **chuán qí yán wù** 船期延誤
freight **yùn fèi**	运费 運費	shipment details 装货明细 **zhuāng huò míng xì** 裝貨明細
cost and freight (C & F) **yùn fèi zài nèi**	运费在内 運費在內	immediate shipment 立即装船 **lì jí zhuāng chuán** 立即裝船
cost and insurance (C & I) **báo xiǎn fèi zài nèi**	保险费在内 保險費在內	date of shipment 装船日期 **zhuāng chuán rì qí** 裝船日期
cost insurance freight (C. I. F) **yùn fèi báo xiǎn zài nèi**	运费保险在内 運費保險在內	official exchange rate 公告外汇汇率 **gōng gào wài huì huì lǜ** 公告外匯匯率
free on truck (F.O.T.) **huò-che jiāo huò jià**	货车交货价 貨車交貨價	certificate of origin 原产地证明书 **yúan chǎn dì zhèng míng shū** 原產地證明書
free on board (F.O.B.) **chuán-shang jiāo huò jià**	船上交货价 船上交貨價	bill of entry 报税单 **bào shuì dān** 報稅單

export quarantine chū kóu jiǎn yì	出口检疫 出口檢疫	cargo zhuāng zǎi-de huò wù	装载的货物 裝載的貨物
marine insurance policy shuí xiǎn tóu bǎo dān	水险投保单 水險投保單	container huò guì	货柜 貨櫃
shipping invoice zhuāng yùn fā piào	装运发票 裝運發票	sales confirmation shòu huò qüè rèn shū	售货确认书 售貨確認書
shipping advice zhuāng chuán tōng zhī dān	装船通知单 裝船通知單	handling charges shǒu xǜ fèi	手续费 手續費
route háng xiàn	航线 航線	guarantee bǎo zhèng	保证 保證
smuggle zǒu sī	走私 走私	customhouse hǎi guān	海关 海關
smuggled goods zǒu sī huò	走私货 走私貨	customs broker bào guān háng	报关行 報關行
via; by route jīng yóu	经由 經由	customs documents hǎi guān wén jiàn	海关文件 海關文件
warrant cāng dān	仓单 倉單	customs duties guān shuì	关税 關稅
shipping terms yùn sòng tiáo jiàn	运送条件 運送條件	import tariff jìn kǒu shuì zé	进口税则 進口稅則
certificate of inspection jiǎn yàn zhèng míng shū	检验证明书 檢驗證明書	import duty rù kǒu shuì	入口税 入口稅
packing list zhuāng xiāng dān	装箱单 裝箱單	export duty chū kǒu shuì	出口税 出口稅
quantity shù liàng	数量 數量	unconditional wú tiáo jiàn-de	无条件的 無條件的
case mù bǎn xiāng	木板箱 木板箱	signature qiān shǔ	签署 簽署
carton zhí bǎn xiāng	纸板箱 紙板箱	documents against payment píng dān fù kuǎn	凭单付款 憑單付款
barrel xiàng mù tǒng	橡木桶 橡木桶	delivery order (D/O) hǎi guān tí huò dān	海关提货单 海關提貨單
in bulk rate dà pī huò-de jià lǜ	大批货的价率 大批貨的價率	document against acceptance píng huò dān qiān shōu	凭货单签收 憑貨單簽收
gross weight máo zhòng	毛重 毛重	loading charges zhuāng zǎi fèi	装载费 裝載費
net weight jìng zhòng	净重 淨重	bill of lading tí dān	提单 提單
quality pǐn zhí	品质 品質	bill of sale mài qì	卖契 賣契

What's Your Line Of Business
您是做哪行生意的？

English	Pinyin	简体	繁體
company (Co.) (co.)	gōng sī; shāng hào	公司；商号	公司；商號
enterprise	qì yè	企业	企業
corporation (Corp.)	cái tuán fǎ rén	财团法人	財團法人
incorporated (Inc.)	hé bìng cái tuán fǎ rén	合并财团法人	合併財團法人
merge; merged company	hé bìng; hé bìng gōng sī	合并；合并公司	合併；合併公司
legitimate business	hé fǎ shì yè	合法事业	合法事業
head office	zǒng gōng sī	总公司	總公司
proprietor	yè zhǔ	业主	業主
partner	hé huǒ rén	合夥人	合夥人
shareholder	gǔ dōng	股东	股東
share	gǔ fèn	股份	股份
limited (Ltd.)	yǒu xiàn	有限	有限
unlimited	wú xiàn	无限	無限
private company	sī rén háng hào	私人行号	私人行號
store	diàn	店（售货）	店
shop	pù-zi	铺子（修理）	鋪子

English	Pinyin	简体	繁體
business license	yíng yè zhí zhào	营业执照	營業執照
chamber of commerce	shāng huì	商会	商會
labor union	gōng huì	工会	工會
fishermen's association	yú huì	渔会	漁會
farmers' association	nóng huì	农会	農會
real estate company	fáng dì chǎn gōng sī	房地产公司	房地產公司
recruitment agency	wài láo zhòng jiè gōng sī	外劳仲介公司	外勞仲介公司
department store	bǎi huò gōng sī	百货公司	百貨公司
multilevel marketing	láo shǔ huì (duō cé cì chuan xiāo)	(多层次传销)老鼠会	老鼠會
shopping mall	dà mài chǎng	大卖场	大賣場
supermarket	chāo jí shì chǎng	超级市场	超級市場
grocery store	zá huò diàn	杂货店	雜貨店
convenience store	biàn lì shāng diàn	便利商店	便利商店
laundry shop	xǐ yī diàn	洗衣店	洗衣店
laundromat	zì dòng xǐ yī	自动洗衣店	自動洗衣店
dry cleaner	gān xǐ diàn	干洗店	乾洗店

optical company yǎn jìng háng	眼镜行 眼鏡行	hardware store wǔ jīn háng	五金行 五金行	
watch store zhōng biǎo háng	钟表行 鐘錶行	butchery ròu diàn	肉店 肉店	
furniture store jiā jù diàn	家俱店 家俱店	photo studio zhào xiàng guǎn	照相馆 照相館	
rattan ware store téng qì diàn	藤器店 藤器店	scientific apparatus store kē xué yí qì háng	科学仪器行 科學儀器行	
bamboo ware store zhú qì diàn	竹器店 竹器店	chemical supplies store huà gōng yuán liào háng	化工原料行 化工原料行	
handicraft store shǒu gōng yì pǐn diàn	手工艺品店 手工藝品店	second-hand clothing store gù yī diàn	估衣店 估衣店(二手衣)	
paint store yóu qī diàn	油漆店 油漆店	second-hand store jiù huò diàn	旧货店 舊貨店	
antique shop gǔ wàn diàn	古玩店 古玩店	flea market tiào zǎo shì chǎng	跳蚤市场 跳蚤市場	
curio shop wén wàn diàn	文玩店 文玩店	toy shop wán jù diàn	玩具店 玩具店	
stationery store wén jù diàn	文具店 文具店	bakery miàn bāo fáng	面包房 麵包房	
shoe store pí xié diàn	皮鞋店 皮鞋店	flower shop huā diàn	花店 花店	
drug store xī yào fáng	西药房 西藥房	fruit store shuí guǒ diàn	水果店 水果店	
herb medicine store zhōng yào diàn	中药店 中藥店	jewelry store zhū bǎo diàn	珠宝店 珠寶店	
bookstore shū diàn	书店 書店	consignment store wěi tuō háng	委托行 委託行	
dry goods store chóu duàn diàn	绸缎店 綢緞店	auction pāi mài háng	拍卖行 拍賣行	
haberdashery nán fú shì yòng pǐn diàn	男服饰用品店 男服飾用品店	aquarium shuǐ zú guǎn	水族馆 水族館	
men's wear store xī shuāng diàn	西装店 西裝店	breeding aquatics fán zhí yú miáo	繁殖鱼苗 繁殖魚苗	
tailor shop cái féng diàn	裁缝店 裁縫店	kennel gǒu yuán	狗园 狗園	
children's wear store tóng zhuāng diàn	童装店 童裝店	bird shop niǎor diàn	鸟儿店 鳥兒店	
dress shop; women's wear nǔ zhuāng diàn	女装店 女裝店	sporting goods shop tǐ yù yòng pǐn shè	体育用品社 體育用品社	

English	Simplified / Traditional	English	Simplified / Traditional
law office; law firm **lǜ shī shì wù suǒ**	律师事务所 律師事務所	clinic **zhén suǒ**	诊所 診所
public accountant **kuài jì shī shì wù suǒ**	会计师事务所 會計師事務所	cosmetic surgery clinic **zhěng róng zhén suǒ**	整容诊所 整容診所
sign shop **zhāo pái diàn**	招牌店 招牌店	hospital **yī yuàn**	医院 醫院
advertising co. **guǎng gào gōng sī**	广告公司 廣告公司	veterinary hospital **shòu yī yuàn**	兽医院 獸醫院
pawn shop; hock shop **dàng-pu**	当铺 當鋪	bath house **zǎo táng-zi**	澡堂子 澡堂子
unployment agency **zhī yè jiè shào suǒ**	职业介绍所 職業介紹所	spa **wēn quán yù chǎng**	温泉浴场 溫泉浴場
janitorial service **qīng jié fú wù shè**	清洁服务社 清潔服務社	manufacturing co. **zhì zào chǎng**	制造厂 製造廠
a small workshop (for certain trade) **zuō-fang**	作坊 作坊	air-conditioner repair shop **lěng qì gōng chéng háng**	冷气工程行 冷氣工程行
stock exchange **zhèng quàn jiāo yì suǒ**	证券交易所 證券交易所	farm **nóng chǎng**	农场 農場
cafeteria **zì zhù cān tīng**	自助餐厅 自助餐廳	piggery **yǎng zhū shè**	养猪舍 養豬舍
restaurant **fàn guǎnr**	饭馆儿 飯館兒	rabbit warren **yǎng tù chǎng**	养兔场 養兔場
café **xiǎo cān guǎnr**	小餐馆儿 小餐館兒	chicken farm **yǎng jī chǎng**	养鸡场 養雞場
motel **qì chē lǚ guǎn**	汽车旅馆 汽車旅館	raise ducks **yǎng yā**	养鸭 養鴨
hostel **zhāo dài suǒ**	招待所 招待所	apiculture; bee yard **yǎng fēng yè; fēng chǎng**	养蜂业；蜂场 養蜂業；蜂場
dancing hall **wǔ tīng**	舞厅 舞廳	sericulture **yǎng cán yè**	养蚕业 養蠶業
bar; tavern; pub **jiǔ bà; jiǔ guǎn**	酒吧；酒馆 酒吧；酒館	slaughter house **tú zái chǎng**	屠宰场 屠宰場
massage parlour **àn mó yuàn**	按摩院 按摩院	livestock farm **mù chǎng**	牧场 牧場
massage parlor house **sè qíng àn mó yuàn**	色情按摩院 色情按摩院	fish farm **yú wēn**	鱼塭 魚塭
brothel **jì nǚ hùr**	妓女户儿 妓女戶兒	bicycle repair shop **jiǎo tà chē xiū lǐ diàn**	脚踏车修理店 腳踏車修理店
whorehouse **yáo-zi**	窑子 窯子	motor cycle repair shop **mó tuō chē xiū lí chǎng**	摩托车修理厂 摩托車修理廠

garage; car repair shop **xiū chē chǎng**	修车厂 修車廠	retail store **líng shòu diàn**	零售店 零售店
insurance company **báo xiǎn gōng sī**	保险公司 保險公司	wholesale store **pī fā diàn**	批发店 批發店
building contractor **yíng zào chǎng**	营造厂 營造廠	filling station; gas station **jiā yóu zhàn**	加油站 加油站
building supply co. **jiàn cái háng**	建材行 建材行	agent **dài lǐ shāng**	代理商 代理商
sanitary equipment company **wèi yù shè bèi háng**	卫浴设备行 衛浴設備行	petroleum refinery **liàn yǒu chǎng**	炼油厂 煉油廠
kitchen equipment company **chú jù shè bèi háng**	厨具设备行 廚具設備行	steel mill **liàn gāng chǎng**	炼钢厂 煉鋼廠
glass store **bō-li diàn**	玻璃店 玻璃店	nuclear power plant **hé diàn chǎng**	核电厂 核電廠
electric appliance shop **diàn qì yòng pǐn háng**	电器用品行 電器用品行	plastic co. **sù jiāo gōng sī**	塑胶公司 塑膠公司
electrical shop **diàn liào háng**	电料行 電料行	engineering co. **jī xiè gōng sī**	机械公司 機械公司
plumbing service **shuí guǎn gōng chéng háng**	水管工程行 水管工程行	paper & pulp co. **zhǐ yè gōng sī**	纸业公司 紙業公司
bank **yín háng**	银行 銀行	aluminum co. **lǚ yè gōng sī**	铝业公司 鋁業公司
printing shop **yìn shuā chǎng**	印刷厂 印刷廠	fertilizer co. **féi liào gōng sī**	肥料公司 肥料公司
travel service **lǚ xíng shè**	旅行社 旅行社	fishery co. **shuí chǎn gōng sī**	水产公司 水產公司
billiard room; pool hall **zhuàng qiú chǎng**	撞球场 撞球場	mining co. **kuàng yè gōng sī**	矿业公司 礦業公司
Beijing opera theatre **jīng xì yüàn**	京戏院 京戲院	insurance co. **báo xiǎn gōng sī**	保险公司 保險公司
night club **yè zǒng huì**	夜总会 夜總會	cement co. **shuǐ ní gōng sī**	水泥公司 水泥公司
movie theatre **diàn yǐng yüàn**	电影院 電影院	petroleum corp. **shí yóu gōng sī**	石油公司 石油公司
theatre **jù yüàn**	剧院 劇院	funeral home **bìn yí guǎn**	殡仪馆 殯儀館
import/export co. **jìn chū kǒu háng**	进出口行 進出口行	mortuary **zàng yí shè**	葬仪社 葬儀社
trading co. **mào yì háng**	贸易行 貿易行	cemetery **fén dì**	坟地 墳地

您是做哪行生意的

39
B

What's Your Line Of Business?

Manufacturer Terms
39C
製造廠商

manufacturer **chǎng shāng**	厂商 廠商	board of directors **dǒng shì huì**	董事会 董事會
factory; manufactory **gōng chǎng**	工厂 工廠	the committee convened **zhào kāi wěi yüán huì**	召开委员会 召開委員會
cannery **guàn tóu chǎng**	罐头厂 罐頭廠	The committee voted **wěi yüán huì tóu piào**	委员会投票 委員會投票
foundry **zhù zào chǎng**	铸造厂 鑄造廠	vote against **tóu fǎn duì piào**	投反对票 投反對票
textile factory **fǎng zhī chǎng**	纺织厂 紡織廠	moderator **zhòng cái zhě**	仲裁者 仲裁者
artificial fiber co. **rén zào xiān wéi chǎng**	人造纤维厂 人造纖維廠	committee's recommendations **wěi yüán huì jiàn yì**	委员会建议 委員會建議
sugar corporation **táng chǎng**	糖厂 糖廠	company reorganization **gōng sī gái zǔ**	公司改组 公司改組
flour mill **miàn fén chǎng**	面粉厂 麵粉廠	fund raising **chóu mù jī jīn huó dòng**	筹募基金活动 籌募基金活動
paper mill **zào zhí chǎng**	造纸厂 造紙廠	stock market investments **gǔ piào shì chǎng tóu zī**	股票市场投资 股票市場投資
iron works **tiě gōng chǎng**	铁工厂 鐵工廠	managerial staffs **guán lǐ jiē céng yüán gōng**	管理阶层员工 管理階層員工
machinery manufacturing co. **jī qì zhì zào chǎng**	机器制造厂 機器製造廠	factory worker **gōng chǎng gōng-ren**	工厂工人 工廠工人
camphor factory **zhāng náo chǎng**	樟脑厂 樟腦廠	raw material **yüán liào**	原料 原料
timber mill **mù chǎng**	木厂 木廠	production **shēng chǎn**	生产 生產
lumber yard **mù cái háng**	木材行 木材行	production line **shēng chǎn xiàn**	生产线 生產線
investments **tóu zī**	投资 投資	output **shēng chǎn liàng**	生产量 生產量
investors **tóu zī rén**	投资人 投資人	productivity and cost **shēng chǎn hé xiāo fèi**	生产和消费 生產和消費

English	Pinyin	Simplified	Traditional
product	chán pǐn	产品	產品
stock	kù cún; cún huò	库存；存货	庫存；存貨
supplier	gōng yìng shāng	供应商	供應商
reputable	xìn yù hǎo	信誉好	信譽好
seasonable goods	jì jié xìng huò pǐn	季节性货品	季節性貨品
mass production	dà liàng shēng chǎn	大量生产	大量生產
increase production quotas	zēng jiā shēng chǎn pèi é	增加生产配额	增加生產配額
guarantee quality production	bǎo zhèng shēng chán pǐn zhí	保证生产品质	保證生產品質
inventory	cún huò qīng dān	存货清单	存貨清單
warehouse	cāng kù	仓库	倉庫
overstock	kù cún guò duō	库存过多	庫存過多
clear out everything	dōng-xi dū bān-chu-lai	东西都搬出来	東西都搬出來
oversupply	gōng yìng guò duō	供应过多	供應過多
had been put in progress	gōng zuò yí yǒu jìn zhǎn	工作已有进展	工作已有進展
take the average on	píng jūn jì suàn yíng kuī	平均计算盈亏	平均計算盈虧
overheads	kāi xiāo	开销	開銷
prime (capitalized) cost	chéng běn	成本	成本
brand （罐头食品）	pái-zi; pǐn pái	牌子；品牌	牌子；品牌
make （大型汽车冰箱）	chǎng pái; xíng	厂牌；型	廠牌；型
trademark	shāng biāo	商标	商標

English	Pinyin	Simplified	Traditional
label	biāo qiān; tiē zhǐ	卷标；贴纸	標籤；貼紙
logo	biāo zhì; shāng biāo	标志；商标	標誌；商標
slogan	biāo yǔ; kǒu hào	标语；口号	標語；口號
bar-code	diàn nǎo tiáo mǎ	电脑条码	電腦條碼
develop	yán fā	研发	研發
launch	tuī chū xīn chán pǐn	推出新产品	推出新產品
market research	shì chǎng diào chá	市场调查	市場調查
point of sale	xiāo shòu dì diǎn	销售地点	銷售地點
strike a bargain	tǎo jià huán jià	讨价还价	討價還價
distribution	jīng xiāo	经销	經銷
sales promotions	cù xiāo huó dòng	促销活动	促銷活動
sponsor	zàn zhù chǎng shāng	赞助厂商	贊助廠商
to increase profits	zēng jiā yíng shōu	增加盈收	增加盈收
economy on the decline	jīng jì shuāi tuì	经济衰退	經濟衰退
stock market plummeted	gǔ jià cǎn diē	股价惨跌	股價慘跌
pay off the debt	huán qīng zhài wù	还清债务	還清債務
remain in practice	zhào cháng zhí yè	照常执业	照常執業
could not continue	wú fǎ jīng yíng xià qù	无法经营下去	無法經營下去
go on a strike	bà gōng	罢工	罷工
declare oneself bankrupt	xüān gào pò chǎn	宣告破产	宣告破產

Office Terms
上班族群

headquarters **zǒng gōng sī**	总公司 總公司	office hours **bàn gōng shí jiān**	办公时间 辦公時間
branch-office **fēn gōng sī**	分公司 分公司	flexible working time **tán xìng shàng bān**	弹性上班 彈性上班
chief accountant **zǒng kuài jì shī**	总会计师 總會計師	wage; salary **xīn-shui**	薪水 薪水
Production Dept. **shēng chǎn bù mén**	生产部门 生產部門	annual salary **nián xīn**	年薪 年薪
Marketing Dept. **xíng xiāo bù mén**	行销部门 行銷部門	labor insurance **láo bǎo**	劳保 勞保
Purchasing Dept. **cǎi gòu bù mén**	采购部门 採購部門	health insurance **jiàn bǎo**	健保 健保
Research & Development **yán fā bù mén**	研发部门 研發部門	group insurance **tuán tǐ báo xiǎn**	团体保险 團體保險
Sales Department **xiāo shòu bù mén**	销售部门 銷售部門	subsidy **bǔ zhù**	补助 補助
tele-conferencing **diàn huà huì yì**	电话会议 電話會議	non-leave bonus **quán qín jiǎng jīn**	全勤奖金 全勤獎金
tele-marketing **diàn huà xíng xiāo**	电话行销 電話行銷	bonus **jiǎng jīn; fēn hóng**	奖金；分红 獎金；分紅
video-conferencing **shì xùn huì yì**	视讯会议 視訊會議	perk **jīn tiē**	津贴 津貼
listed company **shàng shì gōng sī**	上市公司 上市公司	file income tax return **bào suǒ dé shuì**	报所得税 報所得稅
personnel **quán tǐ zhí yuán**	全体职员 全體職員	recruit **zhāo mù yuán gōng**	招募员工 招募員工
staff **gāo jí zhú guǎn rén yuán**	高级主管人员 高級主管人員	resume **lǚ lì biǎo**	履历表 履歷表
reception desk **xún wèn chù**	询问处 詢問處	curriculum vitae **jiǎn lì**	简历 簡歷

to employ; hire **lù yòng**	录用 錄用	Xerox; make copies **yǐng yìn**	影印 影印
stipulate **guī dìng**	规定 規定	toner; carbon **tàn fěn**	碳粉 碳粉
absence without leave **wú gù kuàng zhí**	无故旷职 無故曠職	make it lighter **yán-se qiǎn-yì diǎnr**	颜色浅一点儿 顏色淺一點兒
retirement **tuì xiū**	退休 退休	fill the paper **zhuāng zhǐ**	装纸 裝紙
lay off **cái yuán; jiě gù**	裁员；解雇 裁員；解雇	paper got stuck **zhí kǎ-zhu-le**	纸卡住了 紙卡住了
fired **gé zhí**	革职 革職	10 reams of paper **shí líng zhǐ**	十令纸 十令紙
you are fired **nǐ bèi kāi chú**	你被开除 你被開除	office closed **xià bān-le**	下班了 下班了
financial crisis **cái wù wéi jī**	财务危机 財務危機	consult **zī xǔn**	谘询 諮詢
form of asking for leave **qǐng jià dān**	请假单 請假單	application **shēn qǐng shū**	申请书 申請書
maternity leave **chǎn jià**	产假 產假	notify **tōng zhī**	通知 通知
Personnel Office **rén shì chù**	人事处 人事處	interview **miàn shì**	面试 面試
personnel officer **rén shì zhú guǎn**	人事主管 人事主管	shorthand **sù jì**	速记 速記
promotion **shēng zhí**	升职 升職	interpret **kǒu yì**	口译 口譯
prospect **yuàn jǐng**	愿景 願景	translate **fān yì; bǐ yì**	翻译；笔译 翻譯；筆譯
handouts; circulars **chuán dān**	传单 傳單	project **jì huà**	计划 計劃
punch clock **dá kǎ zhōng**	打卡锺 打卡鐘	proposal **qì huà shū**	企划书 企劃書
punch in **shàng bān dá kǎ**	上班打卡 上班打卡	verbal report **kǒu tóu bào gào**	口头报告 口頭報告
punch out **xià bān dá kǎ**	下班打卡 下班打卡	written report **shū miàn bào gào**	书面报告 書面報告
punch card **dá kǎ piàn**	打卡片 打卡片	authorize **shòu quán yǔ**	授权于 授權於
Xerox (copy) machine **yǐng yìn jī**	影印机 影印機	delegation of authority **shòu quán**	授权 授權

bulletin gōng gào	公告 公告	follow up zhuī zōng	追踪 追蹤
bulletin board bù gào lán	布告栏 佈告欄	approval pī zhǔn	批准 批准
execution zhí xíng	执行 執行	written authorization shū miàn pī zhǔn	书面批准 書面批准
business is business gōng shì gōng bàn	公事公办 公事公辦	ratification pī zhǔn qiān fā	批准签发 批准簽發
judgment by matter duì shì bú duì rén	对事不对人 對事不對人	issued date hé fā rì qí	核发日期 核發日期
go by facts & figures jiù shì lùn shì	就事论事 就事論事	effective shēng xiào	生效 生效
impeachment tán hé	弹劾 彈劾	validity yǒu xiào qí jiān	有效期间 有效期間
resign; quit cí zhí	辞职 辭職	expiration date jié zhǐ rì qí	截止日期 截止日期
filing cabinet dǎng àn guì	档案柜 檔案櫃	certificate zhèng míng shū	证明书 證明書
folder wén jiàn jiā	文件夹 文件夾	verify jiàn dìng	鉴定 鑒定
file wén jiàn	文件 文件	manuscript yuán gǎo	原稿 原稿
relevant document yǒu guān wén jiàn	有关文件 有關文件	original copy zhèng běn	正本 正本
holder jüàn zōng	卷宗 卷宗	copy fù běn	副本 副本
document gōng wén	公文 公文	whereas jiàn yú	鉴于 鑒於
red tape guān yàng wén zhāng	官样文章 官樣文章	in view of yǒu jiàn yú	有鉴于 有鑒於
submit chéng dì	呈递 呈遞	regarding guān yú	关于 關於
backlog of documents jī yā gōng wén	积压公文 積壓公文	with reference to (re) yǒu guān yǔ	有关於 有關於
work overtime jiā bān	加班 加班	concerning tí jí	提及 提及
urgent jí jiàn	急件 急件	relevant to yǒu guān	有关 有關
priority yōu xiān	优先 優先	as per zūn fèng	遵奉 遵奉

announcement **xuān bù**	宣布 宣佈
as indicated **rú wén**	如文 如文
due to; owing to **yóu yǔ**	由于 由於
the said **shàng shù**	上述 上述
which quotes **lüè kāi**	略开 略開
in order to **yǐ biàn**	以便 以便
enable **shí xiàn**	实现 實現
facilitate **yǐ lì**	以利 以利
cause **dǎo zhì**	导致 導致
to avoid **yí miǎn**	以免 以免
pending **xuán ér wèi jüé**	悬而未决 懸而未決
postpone **yán qí**	延期 延期
assure you **bǎo zhèng**	保证 保證
heretofore; hereto **qì jīn wéi zhǐ**	迄今为止 迄今為止
herein **yú cǐ**	于此 於此
hereafter **sì hòu**	嗣后 嗣後
hereinafter **yǐ xià**	以下 以下
furthermore **zài zhě**	再者 再者
Gentlemen: **jìng qí zhě**	敬启者 敬啟者
in answer to **jìng fù**	敬覆 敬覆
personal and confidential **qīn qǐ**	亲启 親啟
your esteemed letter **zūn hán**	尊函 尊函
herewith **suí hán**	随函 隨函
enclosure **xìn fēng nèi fù jiàn**	信封内附件 信封內附件
attachment **fù jiàn**	附件 附件
P.S. (postscript) **fù yán**	附言 附言
tear up **sī huǐ**	撕毁 撕毀
burn up **shāo huǐ**	烧毁 燒毀
shredder **suì zhǐ qì**	碎纸机 碎紙機
blot out; cross out **tú diào**	涂掉 塗掉
throw away (dispose) **diū qì**	丢弃 丟棄
ask for a raise **qǐng qiú jiā xīn**	请求加薪 請求加薪
had a raise **jiā xīn-le**	加薪了 加薪了

Stationery Goods 文具用品

stationery goods wén jù	文具 文具	staples dìng shū zhēn	钉书针 釘書針
stationery xìn zhǐ	信纸 信紙	rubber stamp xiàng pí tú zhāng	橡皮图章 橡皮圖章
envelope xìn fēngr	信封儿 信封兒	stamp pad yìn ní tái	印泥台 印泥台
letterhead xìn zhǐ xián-tou	信纸衔头 信紙銜頭	paste water jiāng hú	浆糊 漿糊
printer yìn biǎo jī	印表机 印表機	glue jiāo shuǐ	胶水 膠水
calculator jì suàn jī （加减乘除）	计算器 計算器	adhesive tape jiāo zhǐ	胶纸 膠紙
copy machine fù yìn jī	复印机 復印機	Scotch tape dispenser jiāo zhí dǐ zuò	胶纸底座 膠紙底座
plastic coat press hù bèi jī	护贝机 護貝機	sticker nián xìng juàn biāo	黏性卷标 黏性標籤
punch clock dá kǎ zhōng	打卡锤 打卡鐘	pen gāng bǐ	钢笔 鋼筆
fax machine chuán zhēn jī	传真机 傳真機	ink mò shuǐ	墨水 墨水
scanner sǎo miáo qì	扫描器 掃描器	ball-point pen yuán-zi bǐ	原子笔 原子筆
paper shredder suì zhǐ jī	碎纸机 碎紙機	leak lòu shuǐ	漏水 漏水
hole puncher dǎ dòng jī	打洞机 打洞機	whiteout; Wite-out lì kě bái	立可白 立可白
stapler dìng shū jī	钉书机 釘書機	felt pen (permanent color) máo zhān bǐ	毛毡笔 毛氈筆
heavy duty stapler zhòng xíng dìng shū jī	重型钉书机 重型釘書機	whiteboard felt pen bái bǎn máo zhān bǐ	白板毛毡笔 白板毛氈筆

English	Pinyin	Simplified	Traditional
line marker (luminous)	yíng guāng huà xiàn bǐ	莹光划线笔	瑩光劃線筆
dermatography (wax crayon)	zhǐ jüǎn là bǐ	纸卷腊笔	紙捲蠟筆
wax crayon	xiǎo xüé shēng là bǐ	小学生腊笔	小學生蠟筆
pencil	qiān bǐ	铅笔	鉛筆
pencil lead	qiān bǐ xīn	铅笔芯	鉛筆芯
pencil sharpener	xiāo qiān bǐ dāor	削铅笔刀儿	削鉛筆刀兒
pin	dà tóu zhēn	大头针	大頭針
paper clip	huí wén zhēn	回纹针	迴紋針
thumb tack	tú dīngr	图钉儿	圖釘兒
push pin	chā tú dīng	插图钉	插圖釘
rubber band	xiàng pí qüānr	橡皮圈儿	橡皮圈兒
loose-leaf book	huó yè bù	活页簿	活頁簿
memo pad	bèi wàng jì shì bù	备忘记事簿	備忘記事簿
cellophane	bō lí zhǐ	玻璃纸	玻璃紙
cardboard	mǎ fèn zhǐ; yìng zhí bǎn	马粪纸；硬纸板	馬糞紙；硬紙板
brown paper	niú pí zhǐ	牛皮纸	牛皮紙
window envelope	kāi chuāng kǒu xìn fēng	开窗口信封	開窗口信封
ruler	chǐ	尺	尺
triangular rule	sān jiáo chǐ	三角尺	三角尺
compasses	yüán guī	圆规	圓規
drawing apparatus	huì tú yí qì	绘图仪器	繪圖儀器
drafting board	huì tú bǎn	绘图板	繪圖板
drawing paper	huà tú zhǐ	画图纸	畫圖紙
drawing pen	huà tú bǐ	画图笔	畫圖筆
pastel	là bǐ	腊笔	蠟筆
portfolio	jüàn zōng jiá	卷宗夹	卷宗夾
filing cabinet	dǎng àn guì	档案柜	檔案櫃
office chair	bàn gōng yǐ	办公椅	辦公椅
magazine rack	shū bào zá zhì jià	书报杂志架	書報雜誌架
printing	yìn shuā	印刷	印刷
business card	míng piàn	名片	名片
New Year's card	hè nián kǎ	贺年卡	賀年卡
Christmas card	shèng dàn kǎ	圣诞卡	聖誕卡
birthday card	shēng rì kǎ	生日卡	生日卡
Easter card	fù huó jié kǎ	复活节卡	復活節卡
invitation card	qíng tiě	请帖	請帖
wedding card	jié hūn qíng tiě	结婚请帖	結婚請帖
Thank You card	gǎn xiè kǎ	感谢卡	感謝卡
sympathy card (丧;患)	tong qíng	同情卡	同情卡

41A

Secretarial Terms
秘書術語

secretary **mì shū**	秘书 秘書	bold-face **cū tǐ**	粗体 粗體
typewrite **dǎ zì**	打字 打字	script **yīng wén kǎi shū**	英文楷书 英文楷書
type it up **dǎ chū lái**	打出来 打出來	abbreviation **suō xiě**	缩写 縮寫
lapse of pen **bǐ wù**	笔误 筆誤	punctuation mark **biāo diǎn fú hào**	标点符号 標點符號
typo; typing error **pái bǎn cuò wù**	排印错误 排印錯誤	comma **dòu diǎn**	逗点 逗點　（，）
margin **tiān dì zuǒ yòu liú bái**	天地左右留白 天地左右留白	period **jù diǎn**	句点 句點　（·）
duplicate **yí shì liǎng fèn**	一式两份 一式兩份	ringlet **xiǎo quān**	小圈 小圈　（。）
triplicate **yí shì sān fèn**	一式三份 一式三份	colon **mào hào**	冒号 冒號　（：）
letter **zì mǔ; xìn**	字母；信 字母；信	semi colon **fēn hào**	分号 分號　（；）
capital letter **dà xiě zì mǔ**	大写字母 大寫字母	question mark; interrogation **wèn hào**	问号 問號　（？）
lower case; small letter **xiáo xiě zì mǔ**	小写字母 小寫字母	exclamation mark **jīng tàn hào**	惊叹号 驚嘆號　（！）
roman **yīng wén zhèng tǐ zì**	英文正体字 英文正體字	hyphen **lián jiē hào**	连接号 連接號　（-）
italic **yīng wén xié tǐ zì**	英文斜体字 英文斜體字	slash **wáng zuǒ xié xiàn**	往左斜线 往左斜線　（/）
runic **yīng wén cū tǐ**	英文粗体 英文粗體	back slash **wǎng yòu xié xiàn**	往右斜线 往右斜線　（\）
block letter **yìn shuā tǐ zì mǔ**	印刷体字母 印刷體字母	parenthesis (复 theses) **guā húr** (kuò húr)	括弧儿 括弧兒　（ ）

358

brackets **fāng guā hàor**	方括号儿 方括號兒（[ ]）	registered trademark **zhù cè biāo jì**	注册标记 註冊標記（®）
quotation marks **yǐn hàor**	引号儿 引號兒（" "）	copyright **bǎn quán suó yǒu**	版权所有 版權所有（©）
umlaut (as ü) **shuāng diǎn**	双点 雙點 如（ü）	bar code **diàn nǎo tiáo mǎ**	电脑条码 電腦條碼
percentage mark **bǎi fēn hàor**	百分号儿 百分號兒（%）	per unit; at **měi dān wèi; měi jiàn**	每单位；每件 每單位；每件（@）
percent **bǎi fēn lǜ**	百分率 百分率	paragraph **yì xiǎo duàn**	一小段 一小段
fractions **jǐ fēn zhī jǐ**	几分之几 幾分之幾 如（⅝）	section **yì jié**	一节 一節 （§）
plus **jiā hàor**	加号儿 加號兒（+）	indentation **shǒu háng kòng yí zì**	首行空一字 首行空一字
minus **jiǎn hàor**	减号儿 減號兒（-）	underline **zì xià huà xiàn**	字下划线 字下劃線 （＿）
multiplication **chéng hàor**	乘号儿 乘號兒（×）	broken line **zhé xiàn**	折线 折線 （—）
division **chú hàor**	除号儿 除號兒（÷）	dotted line **diǎn xiàn**	点线 點線 （…）
equation; equal sign **děng hàor**	等号儿 等號兒（=）	mark of accent **zhòng yīn fú hàor**	重音符号儿 重音符號兒（ˋ）
decimal point **xiǎo shù diǎnr**	小数点儿 小數點兒 （.）	dieresis **fēn yīn fú hàor**	分音符号儿 分音符號兒 "naïve"（¨）
ampersand **yǐ jí**	以及 以及 （and &）	asterisk (5-pointed star) **xīng biāo**	星标 星標 （★）
caret **bǔ là zì fú hàor**	补落字符号儿 補落字符號兒（∧）	asterism **sān xīng biāo**	三星标 三星標（⁂ 或 ⁂）
ditto **tóng shàng**	同上 同上 （"或 do）	diesis **shuāng shí zì yuán**	双十字元 雙十字元 （‡）
number indicator **hào mǎr biāo jì**	号码儿标记 號碼兒標記 （#）	tilde **bō xíng hào**	波形号 波形號 （~）
index **zhǐ biāo**	指标 指標 （☞）	type-setting **pái bǎn**	排版 排版
English pound **yīng bàng**	英镑 英鎊（£）	column setting **zhí pái**	直排 直排
cent **fēn qián**	分钱 分錢（¢）	crossing setting **héng pái**	横排 横排
dollar **měi (jiā) yuán**	美（加）元 美（加）元（$）	border **huā biānr**	花边儿 花邊兒

Conference & Meeting
會議與開會

public relations **gōng guān**	公关 公關	leadership breakfast meeting **zǎo cān huì**	早餐会 早餐會	
conference **huì yì**	会议 會議	opening address **zhì kāi huì cí**	致开会词 致開會詞	
meeting **kāi huì**	开会 開會	administrative report **shī zhèng bào gào**	施政报告 施政報告	
grand opening **kāi mù**	开幕 開幕	keynote speech **zhèng cè yǎn shuō**	政策演说 政策演說	
opening ceremony **kāi mù dián lǐ**	开幕典礼 開幕典禮	work report **gōng zuò bào gào**	工作报告 工作報告	
ribbon cutting **jián cǎi**	剪彩 剪綵	permanent member **yóng jiǔ huì yüán**	永久会员 永久會員	
auditorium **lǐ táng**	礼堂 禮堂	full attendance **qüán tǐ chū xí**	全体出席 全體出席	
convention hall **huì yì shì**	会议室 會議室	absent **qüē xí**	缺席 缺席	
conference table **huì yì zhuō**	会议桌 會議桌	authorized personnel only **fēi qǐng mò rù**	非请莫入 非請莫入	
shareholders' meeting **gǔ dōng dà huì**	股东大会 股東大會	briefing **jiǎn bào**	简报 簡報	
executive council **lǐ shì huì**	理事会 理事會	body language **shēn tǐ yǔ yán**	身体语言 身體語言	
board of directors **dǒng shì huì**	董事会 董事會	guest speaker **lái bīn zhì cí**	来宾致词 來賓致詞	
board of supervisors **jiān shì huì**	监事会 監事會	thanks address **xiè cí**	谢词 謝詞	
regular session **cháng huì**	常会 常會	closing address **bì mù cí**	闭幕词 閉幕詞	
annual meeting **nián huì**	年会 年會	minute book **jì lù bù**	纪录簿 紀錄簿	

for your information **bèi chá**	备查 備查
initial and pass on **chuán yüè**	传阅 傳閱
for your comments **chéng hé**	呈核 呈核
please handle **zhuó bàn**	酌办 酌辦
for your approval **qǐng pī zhǔn**	请批准 請批准
investigate and report **chá míng jù bào**	查明具报 查明具報
for your file **cún jüàn**	存卷 存卷
for your reference **cān yüè**	参阅 參閱
please return to **qǐng guī huán**	请归还 請歸還
interpellation **zhí xǔn**	质询 質詢
reply **dá biàn**	答辩 答辯
oral answer **kǒu tóu dá fù**	口头答复 口頭答覆
written reply **shū miàn dá fù**	书面答复 書面答覆
compliment **gōng-wei**	恭维 恭維
agenda **yì chéng**	议程 議程
verbal advice **kǒu tóu jiàn yì**	口头建议 口頭建議
written advice **shū miàn jiàn yì**	书面建议 書面建議
proposal **tí àn; qì huà shū**	提案；企划书 提案；企劃書
draft **cǎo àn**	草案 草案
memorandum (memo) **bèi wàng lù**	备忘录 備忘錄

bill **fǎ àn**	法案 法案
motion **dòng yì**	动议 動議
incidental motion **lín shí dòng yì**	临时动议 臨時動議
urgent motion **jǐn jí dòng yì**	紧急动议 緊急動議
microphone **mài kè fēng**	麦克风 麥克風
flip chart **huó dòng guà tú**	活动挂图 活動掛圖
whiteboard **bái bǎn**	白板 白板
slide **huàn dēng piàn**	幻灯片 幻燈片
screen **píng mù**	屏幕 屏幕
overhead projector **gāo shè tóu yǐng jī**	高射投影机 高射投影機
parley **tán pàn**	谈判 談判
harmonize **xié tiáo**	协调 協調
arbitration **xié yì**	协议 協議
condition **qíng kuàng; zhuàng tài**	情况；状态 情況；狀態
terms **tiáo jiàn; tiáo kuǎn**	条件；条款 條件；條款
appendix **fù jiàn**	附件 附件
objection **yì yì**	异议 異議
research **yán-jiu**	研究 研究
debate **biàn lùn**	辩论 辯論
review **chóng xīn yán tǎo**	重新研讨 重新研討

group discussion xiáo zú tǎo lùn	小组讨论 小組討論	show of hands jǔ shóu biǎo jüé	举手表决 舉手錶決
discussion jián tǎo	检讨 檢討	unanimous yí zhì zàn chéng	一致赞成 一致贊成
contradict biàn bó	辩驳 辯駁	favor zàn chéng	赞成 贊成
break the ice dǎ pò jiāng jú	打破僵局 打破僵局	majority guò bàn shù	过半数 過半數
a blunt answer tǎn bái-de shuo	坦白的说 坦白的說	absolute majority jüé duì duō shù	绝对多数 絕對多數
criticize pī-ping	批评 批評	pass tōng guò	通过 通過
apology dào qiàn	道歉 道歉	minority shǎo shù-de	少数的 少數的
lay over gē zhì	搁置 擱置	veto fuǒ jüé	否决 否決
reach an agreement dá chéng xié yì	达成协议 達成協議	opposition fǎn duì	反对 反對
sign a contract qiān hé-tong	签合同 簽合同	protest kàng yì	抗议 抗議
fulfill lǚ xíng	履行 履行	null and void wú xiào	无效 無效
conclusion jié lùn	结论 結論	amendment xiū zhèng àn	修正案 修正案
vote tóu piào biǎo jüé	投票表决 投票表決	non-confidential bill bú xìn rèn àn	不信任案 不信任案
ballot wú jì míng tóu piào	无记名投票 無記名投票	conference abortion huì yì liú chǎn	会议流产 會議流產
casting vote jüé dìng piào	决定票 決定票	postpone yán qí	延期 延期
proxy vote dài lǐ tóu piào	代理投票 代理投票	review seminar jián tǎo huì	检讨会 檢討會
warrant; authorize shòu quán	授权 授權	adjourned sàn huì	散会 散會

Telephone Calls
打電話

您說您貴姓來著？
nín shuō nín guì xìng-lai-zhe
What did you say your name was?

public telephone **gōng yòng diàn huà**	公用电话 公用電話	**press the star key** **àn mǐ zì jiàn**	按米字键 按米字鍵（＊）
pay-phone **tóu bì diàn huà**	投币电话 投幣電話	**busy tone** **zhàn xiàn shēng**	占线声 占線聲
telephone booth **diàn huà tíng**	电话亭 電話亭	**line's busy** **jiǎng huà zhōng**	讲话中 講話中
international call **guó jì diàn huà**	国际电话 國際電話	**enter another number** **qiǎng bō qí tā hào mǎ**	请拨其他号码 請撥其他號碼
local call **shì nèi diàn huà**	市内电话 市內電話	**an emergency call** **yóu jǐn jí diàn huà**	有紧急电话 有緊急電話
toll call **àn shí jì fèi**	按时计费 按時計費	**please interrupt the call** **qǐng duì fāng guà duàn**	请对方挂断 請對方掛斷
make a phone call **dǎ diàn huà**	打电话 打電話	**connected** **jiē tōng**	接通了 接通了
insert **chā rù**	插入 插入	**dialing tune** **jiē tōng shēng**	接通声 接通聲
IC telephone card **diàn huà kǎ**	电话卡 電話卡	**telephone's ringing** **diàn huà xiǎng**	电话响 電話響
coin **yìng bì**	硬币 硬幣	**mobile (cellular) phone** **shǒu jī**	手机 手機
deposit coins **tóu bì**	投币 投幣	**answer the telephone** **jiē diàn huà**	接电话 接電話
collect-call **duì fāng fù fèi**	对方付费 對方付費	**no answer** **méi rén jiē**	没人接 沒人接
dial **bō hàor**	拨号儿 撥號兒	**is on temporary suspension** **zhàn tíng shǐ yòng**	暂停使用 暫停使用
press (push) button **àn jiàn**	按键 按鍵	**number's been changed to** **hào mǎr gǎi wéi**	号码儿改为 號碼兒改為
press the pound key **àn jǐng zì jiàn**	按井字键 按井字鍵（＃）	**has not been asigned yet** **kōng hàor**	空号儿 空號兒

private telephone **sī rén diàn huà**	私人电话 私人電話	video-phone **yǐng xiàng diàn huà**	影像电话 影像電話
extension **fēn jī**	分机 分機	teleconferencing **diàn huà huì yì**	电话会议 電話會議
May I ask… **qǐng wèn…**	请问… 請問…	video-conferencing **yǐng xiàng diàn huà huì yì**	影像电话会议 影像電話會議
…the nature of the call **yǒu shén-me guì shì**	有甚麼贵事？ 有甚麼貴事？	intercom **nèi bù duì jiǎng jī**	内部对讲机 內部對講機
It's personal. **shì sī shì**	是私事 是私事	detectaphone; bug **qiè tīng qì**	窃听器 竊聽器
hang up **guà duàn**	挂断 掛斷	tapping **qiè tīng**	窃听 竊聽
off the hook **méi guà hǎo**	没挂好 沒掛好	harassing calls **diàn huà são rǎo**	电话骚扰 電話騷擾
hold on **bié guà duàn**	别挂断 別掛斷（等候）	phone sex **diàn huà xìng aì**	电话性爱 電話性愛
One minute, please. **qǐng shāo děng**	请稍等 請稍等	fax; facsimile **chuán zhēn**	传真 傳真
area code **qū yù hào mǎr**	区域号码儿 區域號碼兒	telephone call recorder **lù yīn diàn huà**	录音电话 錄音電話
frequently called numbers **cháng yòng hào mǎr**	常用号码儿 常用號碼兒	I'm not available **bù fāng biàn jiē diàn huà**	不方便接电话 不方便接電話
information **chá hào tái**	查号台 查號臺	(after) at the tone **dū shēng hòu**	嘟声後 嘟聲後
telephone directory **diàn huà bù**	电话簿 電話簿	please leave a message **qǐng liú yán**	请留言 請留言
residential pages **zhù zhái hào bái yè zhǐ**	住宅号白页纸 住宅號白頁紙	call you back **géi nǐ huí diàn**	给你回电 給你回電
yellow pages **fēn lèi guǎng gào yè**	分类广告页 分類廣告頁	be back shortly **mǎ shàng huí lái**	马上回来 馬上回來
wireless telephone **wú xiàn diàn huà**	无线电话 無線電話	as soon as possible **jìn kuài**	尽快 盡快
answering machine **diàn huà dá lù jī**	电话答录机 電話答錄機	cancel the call **bú yòng dǎ-le (qǔ xiāo)**	不用打了（取消） 不用打了（取消）
conference call **huì yì diàn huà**	会议电话 會議電話	I have a call waiting. **wó yǒu chā bō**	我有插拨。 我有插撥。
multiple telephone **duō tái jí shāng diàn huà**	多台集商电话 多台集商電話		

Beat Telephone
dǎ diàn huà 打电话
(to make a telephone call)
(More on Group 4)

① My name is Mary Doe. I come from India.
wǒ-shì cóng Yìn Dù lái-de Dòu Mary
我是从印度来的窦玛丽。

② You have a call from Mr. Doe on line 4.
yǒu wèi Dòu xián-sheng zhǎo nín, zài dì sì
xiàn 有位窦先生找您，在第四线。

③ How and where can I get ahold of him?
wǒ zài nǎr ké yǐ lián-luo-shang-ta?
我在哪儿可以连络上他？

④ I'll try to locate him for you.
wó gěi nín dào chùr zhǎo-yi zhǎo-ta
我给您到处儿找一找他。

⑤ Can I take a massage?
nín yǒu shé-me shì yào jiāo-dai-ma?
您有什么事要交代吗？

⑥ I'm taking the next flight out for Japan.
wǒ zuò xià-yi bān fēi jī qù Rì Běn
我坐下一班飞机去日本。

⑦ Would you get Mr. John Doe on the line
for me, please?
qíng-ni tì-wó dǎ-ge diàn huà zhǒu Dòu Zhì
Áng xiān-sheng hǎo-ma?
请你替我打个电话找窦志昂先生好吗？

⑧ May I ask who's calling, please?
qǐng wèn, nín ná-li zhǎo?
请问，您哪里找？

⑨ What are your office hours?
guì gōng-si jí diǎn-zhong shàng xià bān?
贵公司几点锺上下班？

⑩ The manager is in a conference.
jīng lǐ zhèng-zai kāi huì
经理正在开会。

⑪ What time do you expect him back?
tā yǒu-mei yǒu shuō jí diǎn huí-lai?
他有没有说几点回来？

⑫ Punch the "star" key after the number dialed.
bō wán hào mǎr zài àn mǐ zì jiàn
拨完号码儿再按「米」字键

⑬ Punch the "pound" key after you've
completed your message.
liú yán hòu qǐng àn yí xiàr jǐng zì jiàn
留言後请按一下儿「井」字键。

⑭ Would you like to speak to her secretary?
nín gēn tā-de mì-shu jiǎng huà hǎo-ma?
您跟她的秘书讲话好吗？

⑮ What number do you dial for Germany?
qǐng wèn dǎ-dao Dé Guó zěn-me dǎ?
请问打到德国怎么打？

⑯ Mr. Doe has just stepped out the office.
Dòu xiān-sheng bú zài wèi-zi-shang
窦先生不在位子上。

⑰ Could you give me your number again?
néng bǎ nín-de diàn huà hào mǎr zài shuō-yi
biàn-ma? 能把您的电话号码儿再说一遍吗？

⑱ What is Mr. Doe's extension number?
Dòu xiān-sheng-de fēn jī hào már jǐ hào?
窦先生的分机号码儿几号？

⑲ I'm returning Mr. Doe's call.
Dòu xiān-sheng dǎ diàn huà zhǎo-wo,
bù zhī-dao yǒu shé-me shì
窦先生打电话找我，不知道有什么事。

⑳ My phone number remain unchanged. wǒ
diàn huà hào mǎr méi gǎi 我电话号码儿没改

㉑ Can you give me his office phone number?
nǐ ké-yi géi-wo tā bàn gōng shì diàn huà-ma?
你可以给我他办公室电话吗？

㉒ Can you page Mr. John Doe for me?
nǐ néng tì-wo guǎng bō-yi xiàr, zhǎo Dòu
Zhì Áng xiān-sheng-ma?
你能替我广播一下儿找窦志昂先生吗？

㉓ "Paging for Mr. John Doe" please.
Dòu Zhì Áng xiān-sheng, yǒu rén zhǎo
窦志昂先生，有人找！

Computer Terms
電腦用語

computer diàn nǎo; jì suàn jī	电脑；计算机 電腦；計算機
turn on the computer bǎ diàn nǎo kāi jī	把电脑开机 把電腦開機
start up kāi jī	开机 開機
click the "start menu" àn kāi shǐ jiàn	按「开始」键 按「開始」鍵
computer boots up diàn nǎo qǐ dòng	电脑起动 電腦起動
monitor screen diàn nǎo yíng mù	电脑萤幕 電腦螢幕
appear on screen yíng mù-shang chū xiàn	萤幕上出现 螢幕上出現
desktop zhuō miàn	桌面 桌面
images tú xiàng	图像 圖像
left button yòu jiàn	右键 右鍵
cursor; arrow jiàn tóu	箭头 箭頭
point at desired item duì zhǔn zhèng què fú hào	对准正确符号 對準正確符號
folders bāo-fu; mù lù jiā	包袱；目录夹 包袱；目錄夾
communicate with computer yǔ diàn nǎo hù dòng	与电脑互动 與電腦互動
click the mouse àn yí xià huá shǔ	按一下滑鼠 按一下滑鼠

double-click àn liǎng xià	按两下 按两下
to open an icon dǎ-kai tú xiàng jì hào	打开图像记号 打開圖像記號
blank word document kōng wén jiàn dǎng	空文件档 **空文件檔**
applications chéng shì gōng jù	程式工具 **程式工具**
a unique file gè bié dǎng àn	各别档案 各別檔案
installed onto computer guàn rù diàn nǎo	灌入电脑 灌入電腦
accesse qǔ chū shǐ yòng	取出使用 取出使用
insert into disk drive chā rù guāng pán cáo	插入光盘槽 插入光盤槽
read the disk dú qǔ guāng pán	读取光盘 讀取光盤
recycle bin;trash huí shōu tǒng; lā jī tǒng	回收桶;垃圾桶 回收桶;垃圾桶
active desktop zhuō miàn shǐ yòng zhōng	桌面使用中 桌面使用中
operate cāo zuò	操作 操作
convert zhuǎn huàn	转换 轉換
files dǎng àn	档案 檔案
save the document; save; store cún dǎng	存档 存檔

open file kāi dǎng àn	开档案 開檔案	pop-up tán chū xiǎo chuāng kǒu	弹出小窗口 彈出小窗口
computer broke down diàn nǎo huài-le	电脑坏了 電腦壞了	cursor yóu biāo	游标 遊標
Won't start dǎ-bu kāi	打不开 打不開	click on the icons diǎn xuǎn xiǎo tú shì	点选小图示 點選小圖示
file lock suó mǎ; suó dǎng	锁码;锁档 鎖碼;鎖檔	data zī liào	资料 資料
decode; decipher jié mǎ	解码 解碼	dataset zī liào jiá	资料夹 資料夾
password mì mǎr	密码儿 密碼兒	database shù jù kù (zī liào kù)	数据库 資料庫
set up shè dìng	设定 設定	press àn	按 按
keyboard jiàn pán	键盘 鍵盤	shift yí dòng	移动 移動
key àn jiàn; jiàn-zi	按键;键子 按鍵;鍵子	reads data dú qǔ zī liào	读取资料 讀取資料
key-in shū rù	输入 輸入	computing yùn suàn	运算 運算
input devices shū rù zhuāng zhì	输入装置 輸入裝置	backup copy bèi fèn dǎng àn	备份档案 備份檔案
enter shū rù jiàn	输入键 輸入鍵	preview yù lǎn	预览 預覽
number pad shù zì jiàn	数字键 數字鍵	color this paragraph black fǎn hēi zhè yí duàn	反黑这一段 反黑這一段
delete; erase shān chú	删除 刪除	align duì qí	对齐 對齊
exit tiào chū; dēng chū	跳出;登出 跳出;登出	alphabetic sorting zì mǔ pái xù fǎ	字母排序法 字母排序法
crash; locked down dàng jī	当机 當機	automatic numbering zì dòng biān hàor	自动编号儿 自動編號兒
console kòng zhì tái	控制台 控制臺	manual numbering shǒu gōng biān hàor	手工编号儿 手工編號兒
command zhǐ lìng	指令 指令	consequent numbering yán xù biān hàor	延续编号儿 延續編號兒
short cuts kuài jié jiàn (jié jìng jiàn)	快捷键 捷徑鍵	designing tools shè jì gōng jù	设计工具 設計工具
voice demand shēng kòng	声控 聲控	add a frame jiā kuāng xiàn	加框线 加框線

English	Pinyin	简体	繁體
border and shading	kuāng xiàn jí wáng dǐ	框线及网底	框線及網底
blank	kòng bái	空白	空白
symbol	fú hàor	符号儿	符號兒
title	pái bǎn-de shū míng	排版的书名	排版的書名
fonts	zì xíng	字型	字型
input fonts into system	gùan zì tǐ	灌字体	灌字體
slim the style of font	bǎ zì xíng biàn zhǎi	把字型变窄	把字型變窄
widen the style of font	bǎ zì xíng biàn kuān	把字型变宽	把字型變寬
bold	cū tǐ zì	粗体字	粗體字
fine	xì tǐ zì	细体字	細體字
italicize	xié tǐ huà	斜体化	斜體化
shadow these letters	zhè xiē zì jiā yīn yǐng	这些字加阴影	這些字加陰影
flowing animation	dòng huà	动画	動畫
cleaning out garbage files	qīng chú lā jī dǎng àn	清除垃圾档案	清除垃圾檔案
reacting	xiǎng yìng	响应	響應
slow to respond	fǎn yìng hěn màn	反应很慢	反應很慢
response time	fǎn yìng shí jiān	反应时间	反應時間
unreadable code	luàn mǎ	乱码	亂碼
caps lock	suǒ dìng dà xiě zì mǔ	锁定大写字母	鎖定大寫字母
outdated	guò qí	过期	過期
overload	chāo zǎi	超载	超載
jump all over the page	zhěng huà miàn dū tiào dòng	整画面都跳动	整畫面都跳動
debug	chú cuò	除错	除錯
save key	chú cún niǔ	储存钮	儲存鈕
save the file as you go	biān zuò biān cún dǎng	边做边存档	邊做邊存檔
log file	bèi fèn dǎng	备份档	備份檔
save data onto disk	bǎ zī liào cún jìn	把资料存进	把資料存進
access data from disk	cóng cí pán qǔ chū zī liào	从磁盘取出资料	從磁盤取出資料
space	kòng gé jiàn	空格键	空格鍵
backspace	tuì gé jiàn	退格键	退格鍵
tab key (tabulate)	wǎng hòu tiào gé jiàn	往后跳格键	往後跳格鍵
exit the document	guān diào wén jiàn	关掉文件	關掉文件
escape	tuì chū jiàn	退出键	退出鍵
execution	zhí xíng	执行	執行
function keys	gōng néng jiàn	功能键	功能鍵
F1; help	shuō míng jiàn	说明键	說明鍵
(remove) pull the disc out	qǔ chū cí pán	取出磁盘	取出磁盤
(CD) compact disc	guāng pán	光盘	光盤
CDRW	kě chóng fù shǐ yòngCD	可重复使用光盘	可重複使用光盤
track	cí dào	磁道	磁道

device **zhuāng zhì**	裝置 裝置	embedded **jiā jìn-qù; qiàn rù**	加进去；嵌入 加進去；嵌入
file on drive B **dǎng àn zài B cáo**	档案在B槽 檔案在B槽	digitalization **shù zì huà**	数字化 數位化
floppy disk **ruǎn pán; cí pán**	软盘；磁盘 軟盤；磁盤	computer science **diàn nǎo kē xué**	电脑科学 電腦科學
known brand discs **míng pái cí pán**	名牌磁盘 名牌磁盤	IT information technology **xìn xí jì shù xué**	信息技术学 資訊技術學
defective disc **cí pán sún hǔi**	磁盘损毁 磁盤損毀	binary code **èr jìn zhì shù mǎ**	二进制数码 二進制數碼
surface was scratched **biǎo céng mó sǔn**	表层磨损 表層磨損	bit; digit **shù yuán wèi**	数元位 數元位
repair file **xiū fù dǎng àn**	修复档案 修復檔案	byte memory **nèi cún zì jié**	内存字节 內存字節
rewrite **fù xiě**	复写 複寫	gigabytes **qiān zhào wèi**	千兆位 千兆位
RW (rewritable) **kě fù xiě**	可复写 可複寫	megabytes **zhào wèi**	兆位 兆位
format **gé shì huà**	格式化 格式化	**Computer literacy** **diàn nǎo shǐ yòng néng lì**	电脑使用能力 電腦使用能力
print screen **dǎ yìn píng mù huà miàn**	打印屏幕画面 打印屏幕畫面	computer-literate **huì cāo zuò diàn nǎo**	会操作电脑 會操作電腦
rearrang the hard drive **chóng zǔ yìng pán**	重组硬盘 重組硬盤	select boot device **xǔan zé kāi jī zhuāng zhì**	选择开机装置 選擇開機裝置
computer engineer **diàn nǎo gōng chēng shī**	电脑工程师 電腦工程師	normal boot **zhèng cháng kāi jī chéng shì**	正常开机程式 正常開機程式
computer programmer **diàn nǎo chéng shì shī**	电脑程序师 電腦程式師	logged **jiā zǎi kāi jī dǎng àn**	加载开机档案 加載開機檔案
computer hardware specialist **diàn nǎo wéi hù yuán**	电脑维护员 電腦維護員	safe mode **ān qúan mó shì**	安全模式 安全模式
word processing **wén shū chú lǐ**	文书处理 文書處理	step-by-step confirmation **qùe rèn měi yì bù zòu**	确认每一步骤 確認每一步驟
graphic **huì tú**	绘图 繪圖	did not finish loading **jiā zǎi wèi wán chéng**	加载未完成 加載未完成
drawing utilities **huì tú ruán tǐ**	绘图软体 繪圖軟體	previous attempt **céng cháng shì guò**	曾尝试过 曾嘗試過
		shutdown (turn off) computer **guān diàn nǎo**	关电脑 關電腦

电脑硬體

hardware **yìng jiànr; yìng tǐ**	硬件儿；硬体 **硬件兒；硬體**	transistor **jīng tǐ guǎn; diàn jīng tǐ**	晶体管 電晶體
PC; personal computer **gè rén diàn nǎo**	个人电脑 個人電腦	semi-conductor **bàn dáo tǐ**	半导体 半導體
pocket computer **mí nǐ diàn nǎo**	迷你电脑 迷你電腦	memory **jì yì tǐ**	记忆体 記憶體
laptop computer **bǐ jì běn xíng diàn nǎo**	笔记本型电脑 筆記本型電腦	RAM-random access memories **diàn nǎo zhǔ jī jì yì tǐ**	电脑主机记忆体 電腦主機記憶體
calexico **wú xiàn tōng xùn xīn piàn**	无线通讯芯片 無線通訊晶片	ROM - read only memory **zhǐ dú jì yì tǐ**	只读存储器 只讀記憶體
ODEM **dú lì xíng xīn piàn zǔ**	独立型芯片组 獨立型晶片組	memory capacity **nèi cún róng liàng**	内存容量 內存容量
Montara-GM **zhěng hé xíng xīn piàn zǔ**	整合型芯片组 整合型晶片組	temporary storage units **zhàn cún nèi cún**	暂存内存 暫存內存
upgrade **shēng jí**	升级 升級	memory stick **nèi cún tiáo; jì yì tiáo**	内存条 記憶條
gadget **xiáo qiǎo-de jī jiàn**	小巧的机件 小巧的機件	interface **jiē kǎo**	接口 接口
device **yí qì; zhuāng zhì**	仪器；装置 儀器；裝置	slot **chā cáo**	插槽 插槽
similar device **lèi sì yí qì**	类似仪器 類似儀器	main boards (motherboards) **zhǔ jī bǎn**	主机板 主機板
casing **jī kér**	机壳儿 機殼兒	central processing unit (CPU) **zhōng yāng chú lǐ qì**	中央处理器 中央處理器
printed circuit board **diàn lù bǎn**	电路板 電路板	CD burner; CD recorder **shāo lù jī**	烧录机 燒錄機
(IC) integrated circuit **jī tǐ diàn lù**	集成电路 積體電路	CD drive **guāng qǜ**	光驱 光碟機
integrated circuit board **jī tǐ diàn lù bǎn**	集成电路板 積體電路板	burn data onto CD **shāo lù zī liào dào CD**	烧录资料到 CD 燒錄資料到 CD

hard drive (disc; disk) **yìng pán; guāng pán**	硬盘；光盘	硬盤；光盤
hard drive capacity **yìng pán róng liàng**	硬盘容量	硬盤容量
malfunction **yì cháng yùn zuò**	异常运作	異常運作
graphics **yǐng xiàng**	影像	影像
graphic card **huì tú kǎ**	绘图卡	繪圖卡
3D graphic games **lì tǐ dòng huà yóu xì**	立体动画游戏	立體動畫遊戲
graphic accelerator **huì tú jiā sù qì**	绘图加速器	繪圖加速器
sound card **shēng kǎ; yīn xiào kǎ**	声卡 音效卡	
monitor **píng mù xiǎn shì qì**	屏幕显示器	屏幕顯示器
gas plasma display **diàn jiāng xiǎn shì qì**	电浆显示器	電漿顯示器
resolution **fēn biàn lǜ**	分辨率	解析度

low resolution **fēn biàn lǜ tài dī**	分辨率太低	解析度太低
mouse button **shǔ biāo jiàn**	鼠标键	滑鼠鍵
mouse **shǔ biāo**	鼠标	滑鼠
mouse-pad **shǔ biāo diàn**	鼠标垫	滑鼠墊
cordless mouse **wú xiàn shǔ biāo**	无线鼠标	無線滑鼠
cordless keyboard **wú xiàn jiàn pán**	无线键盘	無線鍵盤
printed circuit board **yìn shuā diàn lù bǎn**	印刷电路板	印刷電路板
color printer **cǎi sè dǎ yìn jī**	彩色打印机	彩色打印機
scanner **sǎo miáo qì**	扫描仪	掃描器
optical recognition **guāng xué biàn shì**	光学辨识	光學辨識
flash connector **dà mǔ gē (suí shēn guāng pán)** 大姆哥	大姆哥（随身光盘）	

Computer Software
電腦軟體

條條道路通羅馬
tiáo tiáo dào lù tōng luó mǎ
There's more than one way to skin a cat

software **ruǎn jiànr; ruán tǐ**	软件儿；软体 **軟件兒；軟體**	program design **shè jì chéng xù**	设计程序 設計程式
evaluation version **shì yòng bǎn**	试用版 試用版	install a program **ān zhuāng chéng xù**	安装程序 安裝程式
install software **guàn ruán tǐ**	灌软体 灌軟體	(\) sub directory **zǐ mù lù**	子目录 子目錄
computer system **diàn nǎo xì-tong**	电脑系统 電腦系統	windows folder **chuāng kǎo zī liào jiá**	窗口资料夹 視窗資料夾
system environment **xì-tong huán jìng**	系统环境 系統環境	word processor **wén shū chú lǐ ruán tǐ**	文书处理软体 文書處理軟體
operating system (abbreviated OS)操作系统 **cāo zuò xì-tong**	操作系統	the program of GB code **GB** (gigabyte) **mǎ**	GB 码 GB 碼
computer utility **gōng yòng chéng xù**	公用程序 公用程式	KK phonetic alphabet **KK yīn biāo**	KK 音标 KK 音標
bootstrap **qǐ dòng chéng xù**	启动程序 啟動程式	input method **shū rù fǎ**	输入法 輸入法
application program **yìng yòng chéng xù**	应用程序 應用程式	Chinese phonetic **pǔ tōng huà zhù yīn**	普通话注音 普通話注音
program **chéng xù**	程序 程式	simplified character **jiǎn huà zì**	简化字 簡化字
programming language **chéng xù yǔ yén**	程序语言 程式語言	traditional character **fán tǐ zì**	繁体字 繁體字
software programs **ruán tǐ chéng xù**	软体程序 軟體程式	phonetic symbol input **zhù yīn shū rù fǎ**	注音输入法 注音輸入法
anti-virus program **fáng dú chéng xù**	防毒程序 防毒程式	. exe files **zhí xíng dǎng**	执行档 執行檔

English	Simplified / Pinyin	Traditional

. doc files
wén jiàn dǎng
文件档
文件檔

Microsoft Word
wēi ruǎn wén zì ruán tǐ
微软文字软体
微軟文字軟體

RO (read only)
wéi dú
唯读
唯讀

compressed file; zip files
yā suō dǎng
压缩档
壓縮檔

winzip
yā suō jí jiě yā suō
压缩及解压缩
壓縮及解壓縮

open compressed file
jiě kāi yā suō dǎng
解开压缩档
解壓縮檔

how to unzip
rú hé jiě yā suō
如何解压缩
如何解壓縮

click the zip file
dián xüǎn yā suō dǎng
点选压缩档
點選壓縮檔

unzip automatically
zì dòng jiě yā suō
自动解压缩
自動解壓縮

select file location
xüǎn zé dǎng àn wèi zhì
选择档案位置
選擇檔案位置

stop (按 s)
tíng zhǐ kāi qí dǎng àn
停止开启档案
停止開啟檔案

continue (按 c)
jì xǜ kāi qí dǎng àn
继续开启档案
繼續開啟檔案

exclude (按 e)
lüè guò dǎng àn
略过档案
略過檔案

data processing
shù jǔ chù lǐ
数据处理
數據處理

integrated circuit
jī tǐ diàn lù
积体电路
積體電路

quarantine (按 q)
gé lí dǎng àn
隔离档案
隔離檔案

reduce your risk
jiàn dī fēng xiǎn
减低风险
減低風險

virtual reality
xū nǐ shí jìng
虚拟实境
虛擬實境

plug-in
wài guà chéng xǜ
外挂程序
外掛程式

computer animation
diàn nǎo dòng huà
电脑动画
電腦動畫

movie clips
yǐng piàn jiǎn jiē
影片剪接
影片剪接

media
méi tǐ
媒体
媒體

multimedia
duō méi tǐ
多媒体
多媒體

multimedia tools
duō méi tǐ gōng jù
多媒体工具
多媒體工具

Microsoft Windows
wēi ruǎn chuāng kǒu
微软窗口
微軟視窗

machine-oriented language
jī qì yǔ yán
机器语言
機器語言

MIS management information system
xìn xí guán lǐ xì-tong
信息管理系统
資訊管理系統

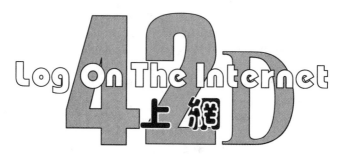

Log On The Internet 上網

你的　电子邮件　几号？
nǐ-de　diàn zǐ yóu jiàn　jǐ hào

What is your e-mail account?

How to get on line? zé-me shàng wǎng	怎麼上网？ 怎麼上網？
log in; log in the internet shàng wǎng	上网 上網
website wǎng zhàn	网站 網站
my website is … wó-de wǎng zhàn shì …	我的网站是… 我的網站是…
gate website; portal site rù kóu wǎng zhàn	入口网站 入口網站
website address wǎng zhǐ	网址 網址
account established jiàn lì zhàng hào	建立帐号 建立帳號
internet language wǎng lù yòng yǔ	网路用语 網路用語
on line trading wǎng lù jiāo yì	网路交易 網路交易
trading stocks on internet wǎng lù gǔ piào jiāo yì	网路股票交易 網路股票交易
invest on internet wǎng lù tóu zī	网路投资 網路投資
turn on your computer dǎ-kai diàn nǎo	打开电脑 打開電腦
find a website brokerage zháo wǎng zhàn qián kè	找网站揹客 找網站揹客
open an account kāi-ge hù tóu	开个户头 開個戶頭
personal identification shēn fèn zhèng míng	身份证明 身份證明
password is required xū yào mì mǎ	需要密码 需要密碼
protect your privacy bǎo hù yǐn sī	保护隐私 保護隱私
protect your security ān quán cuò shī	安全措施 安全措施
the site offers you services wǎng zhàn tí gong fú wù	网站提供服务 網站提供服務
a number of topics yí xì liè tí cái	一系列题材 一系列題材
to work on kāi shǐ yùn zuò	开始运作 開始運作
once you finish with yí dàn wán chéng zuò yè	一旦完成作业 一旦完成作業
proceed to log out lì jí guān diào wǎng lù	立即关掉网路 立即關掉網路
for security reason yǐ cè ān quán	以策安全 以策安全
online shopping wǎng lù gòu wù	网路购物 網路購物
won't do you any harm méi yǒu fēng xiǎn	没有风险 沒有風險

discussion about internet **tǎo lùn shàng wǎng wèn tí**	讨论上网问题 討論上網問題
ICQ (I seek you.) **wǎng shàng chuán hū**	网上传呼 網上傳呼
chat over Internet **wǎng shàng liáo tiān**	网上聊天 網上聊天
chat room **liáo tiān shì**	聊天室 聊天室
webcam **wǎng lù shè yǐng jī**	网路摄影机 網路攝影機
cybersex Syndicate **wǎng lù xìng ài jí tuán**	网路性爱集团 網路性愛集團
websex; internet sex **wǎng lù xìng ài**	网路性爱 網路性愛
self-taking (photo) **zì pāi** (zhào xiàng)	自拍（照相） 自拍（照相）
nude photo **luǒ zhào**	裸照 裸體
expose your private part **pù lù sī chù**	暴露私处 暴露私處
host (computer) **zhǔ jī**	主机 主機
web host **wǎng zhàn zhàn zhǎng**	网站站长 網站站長
home page **shǒu yè**	首页 首頁
counter (computer) **jì shù qì**	计数器 計數器
server name (computer) **fú wù qì míng chēng**	服务器名称 伺服器名稱
ID account; user name **yòng hù zhàng hào**	用户帐号 用戶帳號
password (computer) **mì mǎ**	密码 密碼
search engine (computer) **sōu xǘn yǐn qíng**	搜寻引擎 搜尋引擎
searching; surf **sōu xǘn**	搜寻 搜尋
surfs the net; searching the internet **shàng wáng zhǎo**	上網找
update (computer) **gēng xīn**	更新 更新
download **xià zǎi**	下载 下載
downloaded for a fee. **fù fèi xià zǎi**	付费下载 付費下載
downloaded free **miǎn fèi xià zǎi**	免费下载 免費下載
disk quota **zū yòng kōng jiān**	租用空间 租用空間
E-mail **diàn zǐ you jiàn**	電子郵件 電子郵件
on-line **zài xiàn-shang**	在线上 在線上
cookies (computer) **wǎng lù zhàn cún jì lù**	网路暂存纪录 網路暫存紀錄
mail servers **yóu jiàn fú wù qì**	邮件服务器 郵件伺服器
e-mail manager **yóu jiàn tōng xǜn ruán tǐ**	邮件通讯软体 郵件通訊軟體
scan mail **sǎo miáo yóu jiàn ruán tǐ**	扫瞄邮件软体 掃瞄郵件軟體
scan e-mails **sǎo miáo diàn zǐ yóu jiàn**	扫描電子邮件 掃描電子郵件
send; forward e-mail **jì diàn zǐ yóu jiàn**	寄電子邮件 寄電子郵件
receive e-mail **shōu diàn zǐ yóu jiàn**	收電子邮件 收電子郵件
open e-mails **dā kāi diàn zǐ yóu jiàn**	打开電子邮件 打開電子郵件
e-mail messages **yóu jiàn xǜn xí**	邮件讯息 郵件訊息
Yahoo messager **yá hǔ jí tōng ruán tǐ**	雅虎即通软体 雅虎即通軟體
attachment **fù jiàn**	附件 附件
address book **tōng xǜn lù**	通讯录 通訊錄
through e-mails **jīng yóu yóu jiàn chuán sòng**	经由邮件传送 經由郵件傳送

auto preview function yù lǎn gōng néng	预览功能 預覽功能	circulated xún huán; liú chuán	循环；流传 循環；流傳
virus bìng dú	病毒 病毒（電腦）	auto protect zì dòng fáng hù	自动防护 自動防護
infected with a virus zhòng dú	中毒 中毒（電腦）	targeted to attack yǐ gōng jí wéi mù biāo	以攻击为目标 以攻擊為目標
virus found fā xiàn bìng dú	发现病毒 發現病毒	crack (computer) pò jiě mì mǎ	破解密码 破解密碼
detected a virus fā xiàn yì zhǒng bìng dú	发现一种病毒 發現一種病毒	uncleanable (computer) wú fǎ qīng chú	无法清除 無法清除
melissa 332 yì zhǒng bìng dú	一种病毒 一種病毒	user interface (computer) shǐ yòng zhě jiè miàn	使用者界面 使用者界面
install ān zhuāng	安装 安裝	on-line-real-time system xiàn-shang jí shí xì-tong	线上实时系统 線上即時系統
current anti-virus software zuì xīn fáng dú ruán tǐ	最新防毒软体 最新防毒軟體	T/P system diàn zǐ chuán sòng xì-tong	电子传送系统 電子傳送系統
Norton Antivirus nuò dùn fáng dú ruán tǐ	诺顿防毒软体 諾頓防毒軟體	information retrieval system xìn xí huí fù xì-tong	信息回复系统 資訊回復系統
virus definition codes bìng dú mǎ	病毒码 病毒碼	data transmission system zī liào chuán shū xì-tong	数据传输系统 資料傳輸系統
virus scan sǎo dú	扫毒 掃毒	digital-analog converter shù wèi mó nǐ zhuǎn huàn	数字模拟转换 數位類比轉換
viruses attack bìng dú gōng jí	病毒攻击 病毒攻擊	Internet hacker wǎng lù hēi kè	网路黑客 網路駭客
viruses spread bìng dú kuò sàn	病毒扩散 病毒擴散	internet frauds wǎng lù zhà qī	网路诈欺 網路詐欺
slowly spreading màn mān-de kuò sàn	慢慢的扩散 慢慢的擴散	forged personal identification wèi zào shēn fèn	伪造身分 偽造身分
thru (computer) jìn rù suó yǒu-de	进入所有的 進入所有的	credibility of information xìn yòng zī xùn	信用资讯 信用資訊
systems xì-tong	系统 系統	netnews wǎng lù lùn tán	网路论坛 網路論壇
operating system cāo zuò xì-tong	操作系统 操作系統	online credit card application xiàn shàng shēn qǐng xìn yòng kǎ	线上申请信用卡 線上申請信用卡
a fair amount of work hǎo fèi shì	好费事 好費事	presentation over Internet wǎng shàng jiǎn bào wén gǎo	网上演示文稿 網上簡報文稿
get it straightened out bǎ tā zhéng lí hǎo	把它整理好 把它整理好	conferenceing over Internet wǎng shàng huì yì	网上会议. 網上會議.
checked/disinfected system xì tǒng xiāo dú wán bì	系统消毒完毕 系統消毒完畢	brief discussion jiǎn bào	简报 簡報

English	简体 / 繁體	Pinyin
maintenance service	维修服务 / 維修服務	wéi xiū fú wù
integrated services	整合服务 / 整合服務	zhěng hé fú wù
interactive lessons	互动式教学 / 互動式教學	hù dòng shì jiāo xüé
remote classes	远距离教学 / 遠距離教學	yüǎn jù lí jiāo xüé
fiber optic cable	光纤电缆 / 光纖電纜	guāng xiān diàn lǎn
twisted pair cable	双绞线 / 雙絞線	shuāng jiǎo xiàn
Infrared	红外线传输 / 紅外線傳輸	hóng wài xiàn chuán shū
DNS (domain name server)	区域名称服务器 / 區域名稱伺服器	qū yù míng chēng fú wù qì
ISP (inter. service provider)	网路服务提供者 / 網路服務提供者	wǎng lù fú wù tí gōng zhě
junk mail	垃圾邮件 / 垃圾郵件	lā jī yóu jiàn
text messaging	文字简迅 / 文字簡迅	wén zì jiǎn xùn
through website	透过网站 / 透過網站	tòu guò wǎng zhàn
logout; log out	关掉网路 / 關掉網路	guān diào wǎng lù
cheaper and convenient	便宜又方便 / 便宜又方便	pián-yi yòu fāng-bian
electronic news letters	电子报 / 電子報	diàn zǐ bào
OSI (open system interconnection)	网路国际标准 / 網路國際標準	wǎng lù guó jì biāo zhǔn
packet (computer)	讯息包 / 訊息包	xùn xí bāo
Uniform Resource Locator	网址定位 / 網址定位	wáng zhǐ dìng wèi
TCP (transmission control protocol)	传输控制 / 傳輸控制	chuán shū kòng zhì
IP (internet protocol)	网路通讯协议 / 網路通訊協定	wǎng lù tōng xùn xié yì
web space	網域空間 / 網域空間	wǎng yǜ kōng jiān
RTCC (real-time computer complex)	实时电脑总部 / 即時電腦總部	shí shí diàn nǎo zǒng bù
ATM (asynchronous transfer mode)	非同步传输模式 / 非同步傳輸模式	fēi tóng bù chuán shū mó shì
IOCS (input-output control system)	输出入控制 / 輸出入控制	shū chū rù kòng zhì
BIOS (basic input-output system)	基本输出入系统 / 基本輸出入系統	jī běn shū chū rù xì-tong
ADSL (asymmetric digital subscriber link)	宽频数据机 / 寬頻數據機	kuān pín shù jù jī
IS (intergrated services)	整合服务 / 整合服務	zhěng hé fú wù
DN (digital network)	数位网路 / 數位網路	shù wèi wǎng lù
multimedia	多媒体 / 多媒體	duō méi tǐ
terminal	终端机；屏幕 / 終端機；屏幕	zhōng duān jī; píng mù
shared processor	共用处理器 / 共用處理器	gòng yòng chú lǐ qì
computer network	电脑网路 / 電腦網路	diàn nǎo wǎng lù
internet	网际网路 / 網際網路	wǎng jì wǎng lù
intranet	企业内部网路 / 企業內部網路	qì yè nèi bù wǎng lù
Ethernet	乙太网路 / 乙太網路	yǐ tài wǎng lù
LAN (local area network)	地区网路 / 地區網路	dì qū wǎng lù
bandwidth (computer)	网路频宽 / 網路頻寬	wǎng lù pín kuān
broadband	宽频网路 / 寬頻網路	kuān pín wǎng lù
modem	调制解调器 / 數據機（窄频）	tiáo zhì jiě tiáo qì
humanized designs	人性化设计 / 人性化設計	rén xìng huà shè jì

digitalized **shù zì huà**	数字化 數位化	
integrated services **zhěng hé fú wù**	整合服务 整合服務	
cable modem **lǎn xiàn shù jù jī**	缆线数据机 纜線數據機	
fixed network **gù wǎng**	固网 固網	
virtual **xū nǐ**	虚拟 虛擬	
platform (computer) **jiāo liú píng tái**	交流平台 交流平臺	
communications platform **tōng xùn píng tái**	通讯平台 通訊平臺	
FTP (file transfer) **dǎng àn chúan shū**	档案传输 檔案傳輸	
P (protocol) **xié yì**	协议 協定	

WWW (world wide web) **qüán qiú zī xùn wǎng**	全球资讯网 全球資訊網
SMTP (simple mail transfer) **jiǎn xìn jiǎn chuán**	简信简传 簡信簡傳
HTTP (hypertext transfer) **chāo wén jiàn chuán sòng**	超文件传送 超文件傳送
PPP (point to point) **diǎn duì diǎn tōng xùn**	点对点通讯 點對點通訊
absolute program loader **dìng wèi chéng xù jiā zǎi qì**	定位程序加载器 定位程序加載器
DAT (dynamic address translation) **dòng tài dì zhǐ zhuǎn huàn**	动态地址转换 動態地址轉換
dynamic relocation **dòng tài fù dìng wèi**	动态复定位 動態重定位
indirect address (computer) **jiàn jiē xún zhǐ**	间接寻址 間接定址
relative address (computer) **xiāng duì dì zhǐ**	相对地址 相對位址
IE (internet explorer) **wēi ruǎn shì chuāng gōng jù**	微软视窗工具 微軟視窗工具

Post Office 郵局 43 A

post office **yóu jú**	邮局 郵局	air mail **háng kōng xìn**	航空信 航空信
addressor; sender **jì xìn rén**	寄信人 寄信人	registered mail **guà hào xìn**	挂号信 掛號信
addressee; receiver **shōu xìn rén**	收信人 收信人	register (with acknowledgement of receipt) 双挂号 **shuāng guà hào** 雙掛號	
last name; family name **xìng**	姓 姓	acknowledgement of receipt 挂号回单 **guà hào huí dān** 掛號回單	
first name; given name **míng**	名 名	sea mail **hǎi yóu**	海邮 海郵（邮件）
full name **xìng míng; quán míng**	姓名；全名 姓名；全名	miscarry **wù tóu**	误投 誤投
please forward **qíng zhuǎn jì**	请转寄 請轉寄	miscarried mail **wù tóu xìn jiàn**	误投信件 誤投信件
in care of (c/o) **zhuǎn jiāo**	转交 轉交	insured letter **báo xiǎn xìn jiàn**	保险信件 保險信件
kindness of **dài jiāo**	带交 帶交	domestic mail **guó nèi yóu jiàn**	国内邮件 國內郵件
postcard **míng xìn piànr**	名信片儿 名信片兒	international mail **guó wài yóu jiàn**	国外邮件 國外郵件
surface mail; ordinary mail **píng xìn**	平信 平信	local mail **běn dì xìn jiàn**	本地信件 本地信件
urgent mail **jí jiàn**	急件 急件	out of city mail; outgoing mail 外埠信件 **wài hù xìn jiàn** 外埠信件	
deliver **tóu dì**	投递 投遞	postal money order **yóu zhèng huì piào**	邮政汇票 郵政匯票
special delivery **kuài dì**	快递 快遞	money order **huì piào**	汇票 匯票
prompt delivery **xiàn shí zhuān sòng**	限时专送 限時專送	commercial circular **shāng yè chuán dān**	商业传单 商業傳單

English	中文 (简)	中文 (繁)
affix stamp tiē yóu piào	贴邮票	贴邮票
tax stamp yìn huā	印花	印花
postage paid in bulk yóu zī zǒng fù	邮资总付	郵資總付
stamp vending machine shòu yóu piào jī	售邮票机	售郵票機
postage yóu zī	邮资	郵資
postpaid; postage paid yóu zī yǐ fù	邮资已付	郵資已付
business reply mail miǎn tiē yóu xìn jiàn	免贴邮信件	免貼郵信件
return postage guaranteed miǎn tiē yóu piào	免贴邮票	免貼郵票
bulk rate dà zōng yóu jiàn	大宗邮件	大宗郵件
belt conveyor chuán sòng dài	传送带	傳送帶
last pickup mò bān shōu xìn	末班收信	末班收信
postage due qiàn zī	欠资	欠資
postmark yóu chuō	邮戳	郵戳
legal attest letter cún zhèng xìn hán	存证信函	存證信函
certified mail huí tiáo guà hào xìn	回条挂号信	回條掛號信
postal remittance yóu zhèng huà bō	邮政划拨	郵政劃撥
postal savings yóu zhèng cún kuǎn	邮政存款	郵政存款
transfer savings deposits huà bō chú jīn	划拨储金	劃撥儲金
cash on delivery (C.O.D.) huò dào shōu kuǎn	货到收款	貨到收款
air letter háng kōng yóu jiǎn	航空邮简	航空郵簡
mail order yóu gòu	邮购	郵購
parcel post yóu bāo	邮包	郵包
tag bāo guǒ diào pái	包裹吊牌	包裹吊牌
printed matter yìn shuā pǐn	印刷品	印刷品
overweight guò zhòng	过重	過重
brown paper envelope niú pí zhǐ xìn fēng	牛皮纸信封	牛皮紙信封
insured letter bào zhí yóu jiàn	报值邮件	報值郵件
insured and registered letter bào zhí guà hào xìn	报值挂号信	報值掛號信
mail yóu jiàn	邮件	郵件
aerogram háng kōng yóu jiǎn	航空邮简	航空郵簡
post-office box (P.O.Box) yóu zhèng xìn xiāng	邮政信箱	郵政信箱
letter box (for receipt of mail) xìn xiāng	信箱	信箱
mail box (for posting mail) yóu tǒng	邮筒	郵筒
stamp yóu piào	邮票	郵票
self-addressed envelope huí yóu xìn fēngr	回邮信封	回郵信封
mail carrier; mailman yóu chāi	邮差	郵差
sorter jiǎn xìn yuán	拣信员	揀信員
perforated dài chí kǒng-de	带齿孔的	帶齒孔的
memorial stamp jì niàn yóu piào	纪念邮票	紀念郵票
memorial postmark jì niàn yóu chuō	纪念邮戳	紀念郵戳

zip code **yóu zhèng biān mǎ**	邮政编码 **郵遞區號**	fragile **yì suì**	易碎 易碎
return address **huí xìn dì zhǐ**	回信地址 回信地址	handle with care **qīng fàng**	轻放 輕放
destination **mù dì dì**	目的地 目的地	do not drop **wù shuāi**	勿摔 勿摔
change of address **gǎi dì zhǐ**	改地址 改地址	this side up **cǐ duān xiàng shàng**	此端向上 此端向上
address insufficient **dì zhǐ bù qüán**	地址不全 地址不全	lay flat **píng fàng**	平放 平放
address unknown **dì zhǐ bù míng**	地址不明 地址不明	photo inside **nèi yǒu zhào piàn**	内有照片 內有照片
moved **qiān yí**	迁移 遷移	do not bend **qǐng wù zhé dié**	请勿折叠 請勿折疊
no such number **bìng wú cǐ chù**	并无此处 並無此處	do not fold **qǐng wù zhé sǔn**	请勿折损 請勿折損
undelivered mail **wú fǎ tóu dì yóu jiàn**	无法投递邮件 無法投遞郵件	keep in cool place **qǐng zhì lěng chù**	请置冷处 請置冷處
general delivery **qīn zì yóu jú qǔ xìn**	亲自邮局取信 親自郵局取信	keep refrigeration **qǐng lěng cáng**	请冷藏 請冷藏

Where Do You Live?
住哪兒？

Where do you live? **nǐ zhù nǎr?**	你住那儿？ 你住那兒？
residence **zhù zhái**	住宅 住宅
house **jū suǒ**	居所 居所
home **jiā**	家 家
household **jū jiā; jīa tíng**	居家；家庭 居家；家庭
location **zuò luò; dì diǎn**	座落；地点 座落；地點
address **dì zhǐ**	地址 地址
live **zhù**	住 住
stay **zhàn zhù**	暂住 暫住
suburb; rural area **jiāo qū**	郊区 郊區
residential area **zhù zhái qū**	住宅区 住宅區
uptown **fēi shāng yè qū**	非商业区 非商業區
commercial area **shāng yè qū**	商业区 商業區
industrial area **gōng yè qū**	工业区 工業區
community **shè qū**	社区 社區

skid row **pín mín qū**	贫民区 貧民區
located (in; on) **dì diǎn zài**	地点在 地點在
down town **shì zhōng xīn**	市中心 市中心
central located **dì diǎn shì zhōng**	地点适中 地點適中
one block **yī jiē zhī jù**	一街之距 一街之距
vicinity **fù jìn**	附近 附近
neighbourhood **jiē-fang; jìn lín**	街坊；近邻 街坊；近鄰
neighbor **lín jū**	邻居 鄰居
City **chéng; běn shì**	城；本市 城；本市
County **jùn**	郡 郡
municipality **zhí xiá shì**	直辖市 直轄市
village **cūn**	村 村
direction **fāng xiàng**	方向 方向
east (E.) **dōng**	东 東
west (W.) **xī**	西 西

south (S.) **nán**	南 南	curb **mǎ lù biānr**	马路边儿 馬路邊兒
north (N.) **běi**	北 北	gutter **mǎ lù biānr shuǐ gōu**	马路边儿水沟 馬路邊兒水溝
northwest **xī běi**	西北 西北	up stair **lóu shàng**	楼上 樓上
southeast **dōng nán**	东南 東南	down stair **lóu xià**	楼下 樓下
side **biān**	边 邊	floor **lóu céng; dì bǎn**	楼层；地板 樓層；地板
Boulevard (Blvd.) **lín yìn dà dào**	林荫大道 林蔭大道	First floor **yī lóu**	一楼 一樓
Terrace **shān pō xiàng dào**	山坡巷道 山坡巷道	Eighth floor **bā lóu**	八楼 八樓
Road (Rd.) **mǎ lù; dà dào**	马路；大道 馬路；大道	room **shì; fáng jiān**	室；房间 室；房間
Street (St.) **héng jiē**	横街 橫街	Room 303 (Rm.303) **sān líng sān shì**	三零三室 三零三室
Avenue (Ave.) **shù jiē**	竖街 豎街	Apartment 8-1(dash one) **gōng yù bā hào zhī yī**	公寓八号之一 公寓八號之一
Lane **hú tòngr; xiàng**	胡同儿；巷 胡同兒；巷	top floor **dǐng lóu**	顶楼 頂樓
Sub-lane; Alley **xiǎo hú tòngr; nòng**	小胡同儿；弄 小胡同兒；弄	basement **dì xià shì**	地下室 地下室
Section (Sec.) **duàn**	段 段	front **qián**	前 前
District **qū**	区 區	in front of **-de qián-bian**	的前边 的前邊
House Number **mén pái hào mǎr**	门牌号码儿 門牌號碼兒	back **hòu**	後 後
dash one (-1) **zhī yī**	之一 之一	behind; in the back of **-de hòu-bian**	的後边 的後邊
go straight down **yì zhí zǒu**	一直走 一直走	left **zuǒ**	左 左
down the street **wǎng qián zǒu jiù shì**	往前走就是 往前走就是	on your left-hand side **zài nǐ zuǒ-bian**	在你左边 在你左邊
three doors down **wǎng qián zǒu dì sān jiā**	往前走第三家 往前走第三家	right **yòu**	右 右
two blocks from here **guò liǎng tiáo mǎ lù jiù shì**	过两条马路就是 過兩條馬路就是	on your right **yòu-bian**	右边 右邊

English	简体	繁體
front door qián mén	前门	前門
back door; rear door hòu mén	后门	後門
side door páng mén	旁门	旁門
entrance rù kǒu	入口	入口
exit chū kǒu	出口	出口
situated on northern sided block zuò běi	坐北	坐北
house facing south cháo nán	朝南	朝南
house exposed to west fáng-zi xī shài	房子西晒	房子西曬
house exposed to east fáng-zi dōng shài	房子东晒	房子東曬
facing the street miàn duì jiào táng	面对教堂	面對教堂
rent zū; zū jīn	租；租金	租；租金
rent paid in advance yù fù zū jīn	预付租金	預付租金
key money dǐng fèi	顶费	頂費
rental deposit yā zū; yā jīn	押租；押金	押租；押金
lease zū yüē	租约	租約
office bàn gōng shì	办公室	辦公室
dormitory sù shè	宿舍	宿舍
unfurnished room bú dài jiā jù fáng jiān	不带家俱房间	不帶家俱房間
furnished room dài jiā jù fáng jiān	带家俱房间	帶家俱房間
kitchenette dài chuī dān rén fáng	带炊单人房	帶炊單人房
utilities included shuǐ diàn méi qì zài nèi	水电煤气在内	水電煤氣在內
public housing guó mín zhù zhái	国民住宅	國民住宅
condominium gòng yǒu gōng yù	共有公寓	共有公寓
apartment house gōng yù dà shà	公寓大厦	公寓大廈
apartment; a flat gōng yù	公寓	公寓
loft kāi fàng shì dà gé lóu	开放式大阁楼	開放式大閣樓
penthouse lóu dǐng wū	楼顶屋	樓頂屋
attic dǐng lóu; gé lóu	顶楼；阁楼	頂樓；閣樓
bungalow píng fáng	平房	平房
villa; cottage home bié shù	别墅	別墅
guest room kè fáng	客房	客房
basement dì xià shì	地下室	地下室
vault dì xià chú cáng shì	地下储藏室	地下儲藏室
storeroom; storage room chú cáng shì	储藏室	儲藏室
maid's room yōng rén fáng	佣人房	傭人房
laundry room xǐ yī shì	洗衣室	洗衣室
cellar dì jiào; jiǔ jiào	地窖；酒窖	地窖；酒窖

Related Terms: Group 50, 建築與建材 Construction & Building Materials

nowadays **zhè nián tóur**	这年头儿 這年頭兒	**The year of Rat** **shǔ nián**	鼠年 鼠年
calendar **rì lì**	日历 日曆	**The year of Ox** **niú nián**	牛年 牛年
Western calendar **gōng lì**	公历 公曆	**The year of Tiger** **hǔ nián**	虎年 虎年
solar calendar **yáng lì**	阳历 陽曆	**The year of Rabbit** **tù nián**	兔年 兔年
lunar calendar **yīn lì; nóng lì**	阴历；农历 陰曆；農曆	**The year of Dragon** **lóng nián**	龙年 龍年
according to the almanac **gēn jù lì shū**	根据历书 根據曆書	**The year of Snake** **shé nián**	蛇年 蛇年
The 10 Heavenly Stems **tiān gān**	天干 天干	**The year of Horse** **mǎ nián**	马年 馬年

The ten Heavenly Stems "**tiāngān**" the single-character names of which are used as serial mumbers, and in combination with the set of twelve Earthly Branches ("**dìzhǐ**") used in sequential 2-character combination to designate years, months, days, etc.
The 10 Celestial Stems used with the 12 Terrestrial Branches to form a cycle of sixty.

The year of Ram (Lamb) **yáng nián**	羊年 羊年
The year of Monkey **hóu nián**	猴年 猴年
The year of Cock **jī nián**	鸡年 雞年
The year of Dog **gǒu nián**	狗年 狗年
The year of Boar **zhū nián**	猪年 豬年
12-year sexagenary cycle **shí èr nián lún**	十二年轮 十二年輪
dynasty **cháo dài**	朝代 朝代
century **bǎi nián; shì jì**	百年；世纪 百年；世紀

The 12 Earthly Branches **dì zhī**	地支 地支
12 animal signs **shí èr shēng xiào**	十二生肖 十二生肖

new era xīn jì yüán	新纪元 新紀元	two months (See P.67★) liǎng-ge yüè	两个月 兩個月
centennial; centenary bǎi nián jì niàn	百年纪念 百年紀念	January yī yüè	一月 一月
decade shí nián	十年 十年	February èr yüè	二月 二月
annually nián nián	年年 年年	March sān yüè	三月 三月
year nián	年 年	April sì yüè	四月 四月
this year jīn nián	今年 今年	May wǔ yüè	五月 五月
next year míng nián	明年 明年	June liù yüè	六月 六月
last year qù nián	去年 去年	July qī yüè	七月 七月
years ago háo jǐ nián yǐ qián	好几年以前 好幾年以前	August bā yüè	八月 八月
is dead sǐ-le	死了 死了	September jiǔ yüè	九月 九月
death sǐ wáng	死亡 死亡	October shí yüè	十月 十月
died sǐ yú	死于 死於	November shí yī yüè	十一月 十一月
died before 40 dé niáu	得年 得年	December shí èr yüè	十二月 十二月
died between 40~60 xiǎng niáu	享年 享年	date rì qí	日期 日期
died over 60 xiǎng shòu	享寿 享壽	first; No. 1 yī hào; dì yī	一号；第一 一號；第一
years old suì	岁 歲	second; No. 2 èr hào; dì èr	二号；第二 二號；第二
leap year rùn nián	润年 潤年	third; No. 3 sān hào; dì sān	三号；第三 三號；第三
leap month rùn yüè	润月 潤月	fourth; No. 4 sì hào; dì sì	四号；第四 四號；第四
month yüè	月 月	fifth; No. 5 wǔ hào; dì wǔ	五号；第五 五號；第五
one month (See P.67★) yí-ge yüè	一个月 一個月	sixth; No. 6 liù hào; dì liù	六号；第六 六號；第六

seventh; No. 7 **qī hào; dì qī**	七号；第七 七號；第七	Wednesday **xīng qí sān**	星期三 星期三
eighth; No. 8 **bā hào; dì bā**	八号；第八 八號；第八	Thursday **xīng qí sì**	星期四 星期四
ninth; No. 9 **jiǔ hào; dì jiǔ**	九号；第九 九號；第九	Friday **xīng qí wǔ**	星期五 星期五
tenth; No. 10 **shí hào; dì shí**	十号；第十 十號；第十	Saturday **xīng qí liù**	星期六 星期六
eleventh; No. 11 **shí yī hào; dì shí yī**	十一号；第十一 十一號；第十一	Sunday **xīng qí rì**	星期日 星期日
twelfth; No. 12 **shí èr hào; dì shí èr**	十二号；第十二 十二號；第十二	every week **měi xīng qí**	每星期 每星期
thirteenth; No. 13 **shí sān hào; dì shí sān**	十三号；第十三 十三號；第十三	weekly **měi zhōu-de**	每周的 每週的
fifteenth; No. 15 **shí wǔ hào; dì shí wǔ**	十五号；第十五 十五號；第十五	weekend **zhōu mò**	周末 週末
nineteenth; No. 19 **sí jiǔ hào; dì shí jiǔ**	十九号；第十九 十九號；第十九	week days **zhōu yī zhì zhōu wǔ**	周一至周五 週一至週五
twentieth; No. 20 **èr shí hào; dì èr shí**	二十号；第二十 二十號；第二十	this week **bǎn xīng qí**	本星期 本星期
thirtieth; No. 30 **sān shí hào; dì sān shí**	三十号；第三十 三十號；第三十	this coming Wednesday **bǎn xīng-qi sān**	本星期三 本星期三
fiftieth; No. 50 **wǔ shí hào; dì wǔ shí**	五十号；第五十 五十號；第五十	last week **shàng xīng qí**	上星期 上星期
ninety first; No. 91 **jiǔ-shi yī hào; dì jiǔ-shi yī**	九十一号；第九十一 九十一號；第九十一	last Saturday **shàng xīng-qi liù**	上星期六 上星期六
ninety second; No. 92 **jiǔ-shi èr hào; dì jiǔ-shi èr**	九十二号；第九十二 九十二號；第九十二	2 weeks ago Friday **shàng shàng xīng-qi wǔ**	上上星期五 上上星期五
one hundred third; No. 103 **yī bǎi líng sān hào**	一百零三号 一百零三號	3 weeks ago Monday **shàng shàng shàng xīng-qi yī**	上上上星期一 上上上星期一
one hundred fourth; No. 104 **yī bǎi líng sì hào**	一百零四号 一百零四號	next week **xià xīng qí**	下星期 下星期
week **xīng qí; zhōu**	星期；周 星期；週	next Sunday **xià xīng-qi rì**	下星期日 下星期日
day **tiān**	天 天	2 weeks from Thursday **xià xià xīng-qi sì**	下下星期四 下下星期四
Monday **xīng qí yī**	星期一 星期一	3 weeks from Tuesday **xià xià xià xīng-qi èr**	下下下星期二 下下下星期二
Tuesday **xīng qí èr**	星期二 星期二	6 weeks from today **zài guò liù-ge xīng qí**	再过六个星期 再過六個星期

| two months ago | 两个月以前 | tomorrow night | 明天夜里 |
| liǎng-ge yüè yǐ qián | 兩個月以前 | míng-tian yè-li | 明天夜裏 |

| this month | 本月 | day after tomorrow | 后天 |
| běn yüè | 本月 | hòu-tian | 後天 |

| last month | 上月 | 3 days from today | 大后天 |
| shàng yüè | 上月 | dà hòu-tian | 大後天 |

| two months ago | 上上月 | 4 days from today | 再过四天 |
| shàng shàng yüè | 上上月 | zài guò sì-tian | 再過四天 |

| next month | 下个月 | today | 今儿个；今天 |
| xià-ge yüè | 下個月 | jīnr-ge; jīn-tian | 今兒個；今天 |

| two months from now | 下下月 | at noon | 今天中午 |
| xià xià yüè | 下下月 | jīn-tian zhōng-wu | 今天中午 |

| every month | 每月 | this morning | 今儿早上 |
| měi yüè | 每月 | jīnr zǎo-shang | 今兒早上 |

| monthly | 按月的 | this afternoon | 今天下午 |
| àn yüè-de | 按月的 | jīn-tian xià-wu | 今天下午 |

| two months later | 两个月以后 | this evening | 今儿晚上 |
| liǎng-ge yüè yǐ hòu | 兩個月以後 | jīnr wǎn-shang | 今兒晚上 |

| two months from now | 再过两个月 | tonight | 今天夜里 |
| zài guò liǎng-ge yüè | 再過兩個月 | jīn tian yè-li | 今天夜裏 |

| lately | 近来 | midnight | 半夜十二点 |
| jìn lái | 近來 | bàn yè shí èr diǎn | 半夜十二點 |

| recently | 最近 | yesterday | 昨天；昨儿个 |
| zuì jìn | 最近 | zuó-tian; zuór-ge | 昨天；昨兒個 |

| everyday | 天天；每天 | yesterday morning | 昨儿早上 |
| tiān tiān; měi tiān | 天天；每天 | zuór zǎo-shang | 昨兒早上 |

| daily | 每天的 | yesterday evening | 昨儿晚上 |
| měi tiān-de | 每天的 | zuór wǎn-shang | 昨兒晚上 |

| every other day | 每隔一天 | last night | 昨天夜里 |
| měi gé yì tiān | 每隔一天 | zuó tiān yè-li | 昨天夜裏 |

| every three days | 每隔三天 | 4 days ago | 四天以前 |
| měi gé sān tiān | 每隔三天 | sì tiān yǐ qián | 四天以前 |

| on alternate days | 隔天轮流 | day before yesterday | 前天 |
| gé tiān lún liú | 隔天輪流 | qián-tian | 前天 |

| tomorrow | 明儿个；明天 | 3 days ago | 大前天 |
| míngr-ge; míng-tian | 明兒個；明天 | dà qián-tian | 大前天 |

| tomorrow morning | 明儿早上 | a few days ago | 前几天 |
| míngr zǎo-shang | 明兒早上 | qián-ji tiān | 前幾天 |

| tomorrow evening | 明儿晚上 | long time ago | 好久以前 |
| míngr wǎn-shang | 明兒晚上 | hǎo-jiu yǐ qián | 好久以前 |

Times & Appointments

時間與約談

| date | 约会 |
| yuē-hui | 約會（情人） |

| rendezvous | 幽会 |
| yōu huì | 幽會 |

| engagement | 约会 |
| yuē-hui | 約會 |

| business engagement | 约会 |
| yuē-hui | 約會（洽谈公事） |

| appointment | 约谈 |
| yuē tán | 約談 |

| make an appointment | 预约时间会面 |
| yù yuē shí jiān huì miàn | 預約時間會面 |

| dinner engagement | 饭局 |
| fàn jú | 飯局 |

| not being punctual | 不守时刻 |
| bù shǒu shí kè | 不守時刻 |

| be punctual | 守时 |
| shǒu shí | 守時 |

| previous engagement | 事先已有约会 |
| shì xiān yí yǒu yuē-hui | 事先已有約會 |

| previously | 先前 |
| xiān qián | 先前 |

| priority | 在先；居前 |
| zài xiān; jū qián | 在先；居前 |

| I'll take a rain check. | 下次一定来 |
| xià cì yí dìng lái | 下次一定來 |

| make it another day | 改天 |
| gǎi tiān | 改天 |

| let me host | 我来做东 |
| wǒ lái zuò dōng | 我來做東 |

| Well, if you insist. | -哪我就不客气了 |
| -na wǒ jiù bú kè-qi-le | -哪我就不客氣了 |

| We go Dutch. | 咱们各付各的 |
| zán-men gè fù gè-de | 咱們各付各的 |

| time | 时间 |
| shí jiān | 時間 |

| while you | 当你… |
| dāng-ni… | 當你… |

| when | 当；的时候 |
| dāng; -de shí-hòu | 當；的時候 |

| now | 现在 |
| xiàn zài | 現在 |

| then | 彼时 |
| bǐ shí | 彼時 |

| was; were | 当时 |
| dāng shí | 當時 |

| what time | 几点 |
| jí dǐan | 幾點 |

| o'clock | 点锺 |
| diǎn zhōng | 點鐘 |

| ★hour | 小时；钟头 |
| xiǎo shí; zhōng tóu | 小時；鐘頭 |

| quarter (15 minutes) | 一刻 |
| yí kè | 一刻 |

| two hours and five minutes | 两小时零五分 |
| liáng xiǎo shí líng wǔ fēn | 兩小時零五分 |

| three and a half hours | 三个半小时 |
| sān-ge bàn xiǎo shí | 三個半小時 |

| ★ watch is fast (see P.282 ★ 老是快，坏了) | |
| biǎo kuài | 錶快 (没坏) |

| set back | 往回拨 |
| wǎng huí bō | 往回撥 |

| ★ watch is slow (see Group 30B ★ 老是慢，坏了) | |
| biǎo màn | 錶慢 (没坏) |

move forward **wǎng qián bō**	往前拨 往前撥	my working hours are... **wǒ-de shàng bān shí jiān**	我上班时间是... 我上班時間是...
correct time **zhèng qüè shí jiān**	正确时间 正確時間	day shift **rì bān**	日班 日班
local time **dāng dì shí jiān**	当地时间 當地時間	night shift **yè bān**	夜班 夜班
standard time **biāo zhǔn shí jiān**	标准时间 標準時間	graveyard shift **dà yè bān**	大夜班 大夜班
Greenwich standard time **gé lín wēi zhì shí jiān**	格林威治时间 格林威治時間	switch shifts **huàn yí xiàr bān**	换一下儿班 換一下兒班
on time; prompt **zhǔn shí**	准时 準時	change shift **diào bān**	调班 調班
in time **jí shí; zhèng qiǎo**	及时；正巧 及時；正巧	adjust time **duì zhōng; duì biǎo**	对锺；对表 對鐘；對錶
during the day **bái-tian**	白天 白天	three-O-one (3：01) **sān diǎn yì fēn**	三点一分 三點一分
in the morning (A.M.)★ **yú shàng-wu**	于上午 於上午	three-O-nine (3：09) **sān dián jiǔ fēn**	三点九分 三點九分
at noon **yú zhōng-wu shí èr diǎn**	于中午十二点 於中午十二點	three-ten (3：10) **sān diǎn shí fēn**	三点十分 三點十分
in the afternoon (P.M.)★ **yú xià-wu**	于下午 於下午	two o'clock sharp **liáng dián zhěng**	两点整 兩點整
in the evening **wǎn-shang**	晚上 晚上	five fifteen (5：15) **wú diǎn yí kè**	五点一刻 五點一刻
at night **yè-li**	夜里 夜裏	eight forty-five (8：45) **bā diǎn sān kè**	八点三刻 八點三刻
at midnight **yú wǔ yè shí èr diǎn**	于午夜十二点 於午夜十二點	eight forty-six (8：46) **bā diǎn sì shí liù fēn**	八点 46 分 八點 46 分
at 6 o'clock **yú liù diǎn-zhong**	于六点锺 於六點鐘	twelve thirty (12：30) **shí èr diǎn bàn**	十二点半 十二點半
business hours **yíng yè shí jiān**	营业时间 營業時間	twelve fifty-one (12：51) **shí èr dián wǔ shí yī fēn**	12 点 51 分 12 點 51 分
what're your office hours **nǐ jí diǎn shàng xià bān**	你几点上下班 你幾點上下班	three minutes to five **chà sān fēn wú diǎn**	差三分五点 差三分五點
24-hour service **èr shí sì xiǎo shí yíng yè**	24 小时营业 24 小時營業	three of five **chà sān fēn wú diǎn**	差三分五点 差三分五點
daylight saving time **xià lìng shí jiān**	夏令时间 夏令時間	three pass five **wú diǎn sān fēn**	五点三分 五點三分

See Group 4, 一二三 One Two Three and Group 30B, 鐘錶 Clocks & Watches.

Holidays & Special Occasions
假日與節慶

holiday **jià rì**	假日 假日	Dragon Boat Festival **duān wǔ jié**	端午节 端午節
occasions **jié qìng; shèng diǎn**	节庆;盛典 節慶;盛典	Seventh day of the Seventh Month **qī yüè qī**	七月七 七月七
vacation **jià qí**	假期 假期	Ghost Festival **zhōng yüán jié**	中元节 中元節
celebration **qìng zhù**	庆祝 慶祝	Mid-Autumn Festival **zhōng qiū jié**	中秋节 中秋節
day off **xiū xí bú shàng bān**	休息不上班 休息不上班	Double Nine Festival **chóng yáng jié**	重阳节 重陽節
Solar New Year's Eve **xīn nián yè**	新年夜 新年夜（陽曆）	Valentine's Day **qíng rén jié**	情人节 情人節
Solar New Year's day **yüán dàn**	元旦 元旦	Good Friday **yē sū shòu nàn rì**	耶苏受难日 耶穌受難日
Lunar New Year's Eve **chú xì**	除夕 除夕	Easter **fù huó jié**	复活节 復活節
Lunar New Year's Day **dà nián chū yī**	大年初一 大年初一	All Saint's Day **wàn shèng jié**	万圣节 萬聖節
Spring Festival **chūn jié**	春节 春節	Halloween **guǐ jié** （萬聖節前夕）	鬼节 鬼節
Lantern Festival **dēng jié; yüán xiāo jié**	灯节;元宵节 燈節;元宵節	Thanks Giving Day **gǎn ēn jié**	感恩节 感恩節
Tomb Sweeping Day **qīng-míng; sǎo mù jié**	清明;扫墓节 清明;掃墓節	Christmas **shèng dàn jié**	圣诞节 聖誕節
cemetery **fén dì**	坟地 墳地	The Lord's Day **zhǔ rì**	主日 主日
memorial service **zhuī dào huì**	追悼会 追悼會	Judgment Day **shì jiè mò rì**	世界末日 世界末日
Memorial Day **zhèn wáng jiàng shì jì niàn rì**	阵亡将士纪念日 陣亡將士紀念日	National Day **guó qìng rì**	国庆日 國慶日

Farmer's Day nóng mín jié	农民节 農民節	**exhibition** zhán lǎn huì	展览会 展覽會
April Fool's Day yú rén jié	愚人节 愚人節	**Happy anniversary** zhōu nián jì nián kuài lè	周年纪念快乐 週年紀念快樂
Arbor Day zhí shù jié	植树节 植樹節	**Merry Christmas** shèng dàn jié kuài lè	圣诞节快乐 聖誕節快樂
Labor Day láo gōng jié	劳工节 勞工節	**Happy New Year** xīn nián kuài lè	新年快乐 新年快樂
Independence Day dú lì jì niàn rì	独立纪念日 獨立紀念日	**Seasonal Greetings!** nín guò jié hǎo	您过节好！ 您過節好！
Women's Day fù nǚ jié	妇女节 婦女節	**Welcome!** huān yíng	欢迎！ 歡迎！
Mother's Day mǔ qīng jié	母亲节 母親節	**a dinner of welcome** jiē fēng xǐ chén	接风洗尘 接風洗塵
Father's Day fù qīng jié	父亲节 父親節	**welcome reception** huān yíng huì	欢迎会 歡迎會
Children's Day ér tóng jié	儿童节 兒童節	**farewell party** huān sòng huì	欢送会 歡送會
Teacher's Day jiào shī jié	教师节 教師節	**athletic meet** yùn dòng huì	运动会 運動會
social obligation yìng-chou	应酬 應酬	**shower party** zhǔn xīn niáng chá huì	准新娘茶会 準新娘茶會
social activity shè jiāo huó dòng	社交活动 社交活動	**celebration party** qìng zhù yàn huì	庆祝宴会 慶祝宴會
parties gè zhǒng jiāo yí huì	各种交谊会 各種交誼會	**Homecoming Day** fǎn xiào jié	返校节 返校節
graduation bì yè dián lǐ	毕业典礼 畢業典禮	**house warming party** qiān jǔ yàn huì	迁居宴会 遷居宴會
ribbon cutting ceremony jián cǎi dián lǐ	剪彩典礼 剪綵典禮	**Happy Housewarming!** qiáo qiān zhī xǐ	乔迁之喜！ 喬遷之喜！
ground breaking ceremony pò tǔ dián lǐ	破土典礼 破土典禮	**carnival** yóu yüán huì	游园会 遊園會
birthday shēng-ri	生日 生日	**anniversary** zhōu nián jì niàn	周年纪念 週年紀念
wedding day jié hūn rì	结婚日 結婚日		

Wedding Anniversary
結婚週年紀念

wedding anniversary	結婚周年纪念	lace wedding an. (13yr.)	花边婚
jié hūn zhōu nián jì niàn	結婚週年紀念	**huā biān hūn**	花邊婚（13 年）
paper wedding an. (1yr.)	纸婚	ivory wedding an. (14yr.)	象牙婚
zhǐ hūn	紙婚（1 年）	**xiàng yá hūn**	象牙婚（14 年）
cotton wedding an. (2yr.)	棉婚	crystal wedding an. (15yr.)	水晶婚
mián hūn	棉婚（2 年）	**shuǐ jīng hūn**	水晶婚（15 年）
leather wedding an. (3yr.)	革婚	china wedding an. (20yr.)	瓷婚
gé hūn	革婚（3 年）	**cí hūn**	瓷婚（20 年）
silk wedding an. (4yr.)	丝婚	silver wedding an. (25yr.)	银婚
sī hūn	絲婚（4 年）	**yín hūn**	銀婚（25 年）
wood wedding an. (5yr.)	木婚	pearl wedding an. (30yr.)	珍珠婚
mù hūn	木婚（5 年）	**zhēn zhū hūn**	珍珠婚（30 年）
iron wedding an. (6yr.)	铁婚	coral wedding an. (35yr.)	珊瑚婚
tiě hūn	鐵婚（6 年）	**shān hú hūn**	珊瑚婚（35 年）
copper wedding an. (7yr.)	铜婚	ruby wedding an. (40yr.)	红宝石婚
tóng hūn	銅婚（7 年）	**hóng bǎo shí hūn**	紅寶石婚（40 年）
electric appliance wedding an. (8yr.)	电器婚	sapphire wedding an. (45yr.)	蓝宝石婚
diàn qì hūn	電器婚（8 年）	**lán bǎo shí hūn**	藍寶石婚（45 年）
pottery wedding an. (9yr.)	陶器婚	golden wedding an. (50yr.)	金婚
táo qì hūn	陶器婚（9 年）	**jīn hūn**	金婚（50 年）
tin wedding an. (10yr.)	锡婚	emerald wedding an. (55yr.)	绿宝石婚
xí hūn	錫婚（10 年）	**lǜ bǎo shí hūn**	綠寶石婚（55 年）
steel wedding an. (11yr.)	钢婚	diamond wedding an. (60yr.)	钻石婚
gāng hūn	鋼婚（11 年）	**zuàn shí hūn**	鑽石婚（60 年）
linen wedding an. (12yr.)	麻布婚	diamond wedding an. (75yr.)	钻石婚
má bù hūn	麻布婚（12 年）	**zuàn shí hūn**	鑽石婚（75 年）

Going Abroad 45A 出國

passport **hù zhào**	护照	護照
entry visa **rù jìng qiān zhèng**	入境签证	入境簽證
going abroad **chū guó**	出国	出國
traveling **lǚ xíng**	旅行	旅行
round-the-world trip **huán qiú lǚ xíng**	环球旅行	環球旅行
on vacation **dù jià**	渡假	渡假
baggage; luggage **xíng-li**	行李	行李
flight bag; overnight bag **lǚ xíng dài**	旅行袋	旅行袋
suitcase **pí xiāng**	皮箱	皮箱
trunk **dà-xing tiě lǚ xíng xiāng**	大型铁旅行箱	大型鐵旅行箱
carryall; holdall **dà fān bù dài**	大帆布袋	大帆布袋
carry-ons **xiǎo guàn xǐ bāor**	小盥洗包儿	小盥洗包兒
carry-on baggage **shǒu tí xíng-li**	手提行李	手提行李
wheeled garment bag **lā gán lǚ xíng xiāng**	拉杆旅行箱	拉桿旅行箱
personal effects **suí shēn rì yòng pǐn**	随身日用品	隨身日用品
briefcase **gōng shì bāo**	公事包	公事包

inbound traveler **rù jìng lǚ kè**	入境旅客	入境旅客
outbound traveler **chū guó lǚ kè**	出国旅客	出國旅客
tourist guide **dǎo yóu**	导游	導遊
bilingual tourist guide **shuāng yǔ dǎo yóu**	双语导游	雙語導遊
multi-lingual guide **duō zhóng yǔ yán dǎo yóu**	多种语言导游	多種語言導遊
tour brochure **guān guāng shǒu cè**	观光手册	觀光手冊
sight-seeing tour **guān guāng lǚ xíng**	观光旅行	觀光旅行
tourism **guān guāng shì yè**	观光事业	觀光事業
group tour **tuán tí lǚ yóu**	团体旅游	團體旅遊
independent travel **zì zhù lǚ xíng**	自助旅行	自助旅行
accommodation **zhù sù wèn tí**	住宿问题	住宿問題
five-day tour **wǔ rì yóu**	五日游	五日遊
package deal **qún tàor bāo bàn**	全套儿包办	全套兒包辦
helicopter tour **zhí shēng jī yóu lǎn**	直升机游览	直升機遊覽
on second thought(s) **wǒ zài yì xiǎng**	我再一想	我再一想
changed my mind **gǎi biàn zhǔ yì-le**	改变主意了	改變主意了

business tour; biz tour **shāng wù kǎo chá**	商务考察 商務考察
visit relatives **tàn qīn**	探亲 探親
family reunion **yì jiā tuán yüán**	一家团圆 一家團圓
exciting **xīng fèn-de bù dé liǎo**	兴奋得不得了 興奮得不得了
for an employment **yìng pìn**	应聘 應聘
traveler; passenger **lǚ kè**	旅客 旅客
tourist **guān guāng kè**	观光客 觀光客
travel service; ticket agent **lǚ xíng shè**	旅行社 旅行社
travel insurance **lǚ yóu bǎo xiǎn**	旅游保险 旅遊保險
itinerary **lǚ chéng biǎo**	旅程表 旅程表
transportation **jiāo tōng gōng jù**	交通工具 交通工具
sightseeing bus; tour bus **yóu lǎn chē**	游览车 遊覽車
double-decker bus **shuāng céng bā shì**	双层巴士 雙層巴士
pick you up **qù jiē-nin**	去接您 去接您
take you to Hangzhou **sòng-nin qù Háng-Zhōu**	送您去杭州 送您去杭州
bring you back **jiē nín huí-lai**	接您回来 接您回來
to your hotel **sòng-dao nín-de lǚ guǎn**	送到您的旅馆 送到您的旅館
pick-up time **jiē kè shí jiān**	接客时间 接客時間
guaranteed departure **zhǔn shí chū fā**	准时出发 準時出發
city & suburb tour **shì jiāo lǚ yóu**	市郊旅游 市郊旅遊

take in a city tour **běn shì zhī lǚ**	本市之旅 本市之旅
city map **jiē dào dì tú**	街道地图 街道地圖
free at leisure **zì yóu huó dòng**	自由活动 自由活動
take a cruise **dào chù qiáo-yi qiáo**	到处瞧一瞧 到處瞧一瞧
I'm lost **wǒ mí lù-le**	我迷路了 我迷路了
take this opportunity **chèn zhè-ge jī huì**	趁这个机会 趁這個機會
why not **hé fáng**	何妨 何妨
take in a movie **qù kàn-chang diàn yǐngr**	去看场电影儿 去看場電影兒
window shopping **guàng jiē**	逛街 逛街
sounds inviting **tīng-zhe mǎn yòu rén-de**	听著满诱人的 聽著滿誘人的
sounds good **tīng qǐ-lai bú cuò**	听起来不错 聽起來不錯
take your time **màn mānr lái**	慢慢儿来 慢慢兒來
show you **ràng-ni qiáo-qiao**	让你瞧瞧 讓你瞧瞧
downtown **shì zhōng xīn**	市中心 市中心
uptown **zhù zhái qǚ**	住宅区 住宅區
go for a joy ride **qù dōu fēngr**	去兜风儿 去兜風兒
around town **shì nèi**	市内 市內
night-life **yè shēng huó**	夜生活 夜生活
thrill **xīn qí cì jī-de shìr**	新奇刺激的事儿 新奇刺激的事兒
night market **yè shì**	夜市 夜市

Scenic Spots & Traditions

45 B

觀光

go on a tour **guān guāng**	观光 觀光	
to visit; touring **qù wánr**	去玩儿 去玩兒	
visit public places **cān guān**	参观 參觀	
natural beauty spots **gāo shān méi jǐng**	高山美景 高山美景	
scenic spot; scenery **fēng jǐng qū**	风景区 風景區	
sightseeing **yóu shān wán shuǐ**	游山玩水 遊山玩水	
waterfall **pù bù**	瀑布 瀑布	
sightseeing; a passing glance **zóu mǎ kàn huā**	走马看花 走馬看花	
famous places **míng shèng**	名胜 名勝	
historic site **gǔ jī**	古迹 古蹟	
ruins **fèi xū**	废墟 廢墟	
ancient ruins **gǔ dài fèi xū**	古代废墟 古代廢墟	
traditions **chuán tǒng jiàn zhú**	传统建筑 傳統建築	
historic sights **shǐ jī-zhi lǚ**	史迹之旅 史蹟之旅	
looks great **hǎo bàng; piào liàng**	好棒；漂亮 好棒；漂亮	
enjoy **jìn qíng xiǎng shòu**	尽情享受 盡情享受	

luxury resort **háo huá xiū xián qǔ**	豪华休闲区 豪華休閒區
summer resort **bì shǔ shèng dì**	避暑胜地 避暑勝地
winter resort **huá xǖe shèng dì**	滑雪胜地 滑雪勝地
art museum **yì shù guǎn**	艺术馆 藝術館
historic museum **lì shǐ bó wù guǎn**	历史博物馆 歷史博物館
traditional festival **chuán tǒng jié qìng**	传统节庆 傳統節慶
tour rates **lǚ yóu fèi-yong biǎo**	旅游费用表 旅遊費用表
worth it **huá-de lái**	划得来 劃得來
worthwhile **zhí-de yí kàn**	值得一看 值得一看
night view **yè jǐng**	夜景 夜景
pedicab **sān lún chē**	三轮车 三輪車
prospect; post card **fēng jǐng kǎ**	风景卡 風景卡
take a snapshot **pāi-ge kuài zhào**	拍个快照 拍個快照
public place **gōng gòng cháng suǒ**	公共场所 公共場所
elevator **diàn tī**	电梯 電梯
escalator **diàn shǒu fú tī**	电手扶梯 電手扶梯

balloon advertisement dà qì qiú guǎng gào	大气球广告 大氣球廣告	roller-blade skating rink zhí pái lún liū bīng chǎng	直排轮溜冰场 直排輪溜冰場
billboard dà xíng guǎng gào pái	大型广告牌 大型廣告牌	arena lù tiān jìng jì chǎng	露天竞技场 露天競技場
sign zhāo-pai	招牌牌 招牌牌	bench cháng dèng	长凳 長凳
canvas advertisement fán bù guǎng gào	帆布广告 帆布廣告	carnival jiā nián huá huì	嘉年华会 嘉年華會
plaque biǎn; biǎn pái	匾；匾牌 匾；匾牌	palace gōng diàn	宫殿 宮殿
exhibition zhán lǎn huì	展览会 展覽會	fountain pēn shuǐ chí	喷水池 噴水池
library tú shū guǎn	图书馆 圖書館	bronze statue tóng xiàng	铜像 銅像
museum bó wù guǎn	博物馆 博物館	monument jì niàn bēi	纪念碑 紀念碑
zoo dòng wù yuán	动物园 動物園	pagoda tǎ	塔 塔
botanical garden zhí wù yuán	植物园 植物園	pavilion tíng-zi	亭子 亭子
park gōng yuán	公园 公園	veranda huí láng	回廊 迴廊
recreation center yù lè zhōng xīn	育乐中心 育樂中心	bridge qiáo	桥 橋
fisherman's wharf yú rén mǎ-tou	渔人码头 漁人碼頭	elevated bridge; viaduct lù qiáo	陆桥 陸橋
seashore hǎi bīn	海滨 海濱	pedestrian overpass tiān qiáo	天桥 天橋
beach shā tān	沙滩 沙灘	suspension bridge diào qiáo	吊桥 吊橋
hot spring wēn quán	温泉 溫泉	toilet; lavatory gōng gòng cè suǒ	公共卫生间 公共廁所
spa kuàng quán yù chǎng	矿泉浴场 礦泉浴場	men's room nán cè suǒ	男卫生间 男廁所
sulfur spring bath liú huáng yù chí	硫磺浴池 硫磺浴池	ladies' room nǚ cè suǒ	女卫生间 女廁所
amusement park ér tóng lè yuán	儿童乐园 兒童樂園	dustbin lā jī xiāng	垃圾箱 垃圾箱
bowling alley bǎo líng qiú guǎn	保龄球馆 保齡球館	neon light ní hóng dēng	霓虹灯 霓虹燈

Air Stewardess 空姐

airport **fēi jī chǎng**	飞机场	飛機場
concourse **jī chǎng dà tīng**	机场大厅	機場大廳
airlines **háng kōng gōng sī**	航空公司	航空公司
air route **háng xiàn**	航线	航線
airplane **feī jī**	飞机	飛機
transport plane **yùn shū jī**	运输机	運輸機
chartered plane **bāo jī**	包机	包機
private plane **zhuān jī**	专机	專機
jet engine **pēn shè yǐn qíng**	喷射引擎	噴射引擎
jet airliner **pēn shè kè jī**	喷射客机	噴射客機
supersonic transport **chāo yīn bō kè jī**	超音波客机	超音波客機
domestic flight **guó nèi bān jī**	国内班机	國內班機
international flight **guó jì bān jī**	国际班机	國際班機
international departure lobby **jī chǎng chū jìng dà shà**	机场出境大厦	機場出境大廈
direct (non-stop) flight **zhí dá bān jī**	直达班机	直達班機

schedule **shí jiān biǎo**	时间表	時間表
take-off **qǐ fēi**	起飞	起飛
flight number **bān cì**	班次	班次
departure time **qǐ fēi shí jiān**	起飞时间	起飛時間
arrival time **dào dá shí jiān**	到达时间	到達時間
flying time **fēi chéng shí jiān**	飞程时间	飛程時間
local time **dāng dì shí jiān**	当地时间	當地時間
one way **dān chéng**	单程	單程
round trip **lái huí**	来回	來回
stand-by ticket **hòu bǔ kè jī piào**	候补客机票	候補客機票
open ticket **wèi dìng jī wèi**	未订机位	未訂機位
non-transferable **jī piào bù zhǔn zhuǎn ràng**	机票不准转让	機票不准轉讓
non-reroutable **bù zhǔn zhuǎn huàn lù xiàn**	不准转换路线	不准轉換路線
confirmation **qüè dìng jī wèi**	确定机位	確定機位
reservation **dìng zuò-wei**	订座位	訂座位

English	Chinese (Simplified / Traditional)
seat assignment **xǖan dìng zuò-wei**	选定座位 選定座位
window-seat **kào chuāng zuò-wei**	靠窗座位 靠窗座位
center seat **zhōng jiān zuò-wei**	中间座位 中間座位
aisle seat **kào zǒu dào zuò-wei**	靠走道座位 靠走道座位
airline ticket **fēi jī piào**	飞机票 飛機票
flying insurance **fēi xíng báo xiǎn**	飞行保险 飛行保險
travel accident insurance **lǚ yóu píng ān xiǎn**	旅游平安险 旅遊平安險
air-travel insurancec **háng kōng lǚ yóu xiǎn**	航空旅游险 航空旅遊險
valid until **yǒu xiào qí-jian zhì**	有效期间至… 有效期間至…
invalid **guò qí-le**	过期了 過期了
to cancel **qǔ xiāo**	取消 取消
check in **bàn tuó shǒu xǔ**	办妥手续 辦妥手續
incoming passenger **jìn-lai-de lǚ kè**	进来的旅客 進來的旅客
outgoing passenger **chū-qu-de lǚ kè**	出去的旅客 出去的旅客
transit passenger **guò jìng lǚ kè**	过境旅客 過境旅客
passenger list **lǚ kè míng dān**	旅客名单 旅客名單
to receive (meet) someone **jiē rén**	接人 接人
to greet someone **yíng jiē kè-ren**	迎接客人 迎接客人
to see someone off **jī chǎng sòng rén**	机场送人 機場送人
tourist passport **guān guāng hù zhào**	观光护照 觀光護照
tourist visa / visitor visa **guān guāng qiān zhèng**	观光签证 觀光簽證
formality **shǒu xù**	手续 手續
passport **hù zhào**	护照 護照
permanent residence card **yóng jiǔ jǖ liú zhèng**	永久居留证 永久居留證（綠卡）
visa **qiān zhèng**	签证 簽證
health certificate **huáng pí shū**	黄皮书 黃皮書
birth certificate **chū shēng zhèng míng**	出生证明 出生證明
police certificate **liáng mín zhèng**	良民证 良民證
vaccination certificate **zhòng dòu zhèng míng**	种痘证明 種痘證明（接種）
quarantine **jiǎn yì**	检疫 檢疫
quarantine certificate **jiǎn yì zhèng míng**	检疫证明 檢疫證明
to emigrate **yí mín guó wài**	移民国外 移民國外
to immigrate **wài lái-de yí mín**	外来的移民 外來的移民
overstay **yù qí jǖ liú**	逾期居留 逾期居留
date of birth **shēng-ri**	生日 生日
place of birth **chū shēng dì**	出生地 出生地
nationality **guó jí**	国籍 國籍
destination **mù-di dì**	目的地 目的地
sex **xìng bié**	性别 性別
age **nián líng**	年龄 年齡

marital status **jié hūn fǒu**	结婚否 結婚否	board (airplane) **shàng fēi jī**	上飞机 上飛機
military status **bīng yì qíng kuàng**	兵役情况 兵役情況	runway; airstrip **pǎo dào**	跑道 跑道
name of spouse **pèi ǒu xìng míng**	配偶姓名 配偶姓名	is taking off **qǐ fēi**	起飞 起飛
education **jiào yù chéng dù**	教育程度 教育程度	departure **chū fā**	出发 出發
firearms license number **qiāng zhào hào mǎ**	枪照号码 槍照號碼	outgoing flight **chū jìng bān jī**	出境班机 出境班機
curriculum vitae **lǚ lì biǎo**	履历表 履歷表	incoming flight **rù jìng bān jī**	入境班机 入境班機
present address **xiàn zài dì zhǐ**	现在地址 現在地址	cabin **jī cāng**	机舱 機艙
permanent address **yóng jiǔ dì zhǐ**	永久地址 永久地址	cabin door **jī cāng mén**	机舱门 機艙門
security screening **ān quán jiǎn chá**	安全检查 安全檢查	first class **tóu děng zuò wèi**	头等座位 頭等座位
metal detector **jīn shǔ zhēn chá jī**	金属侦察机 金屬偵察機	tourist class **pǔ-tong zuò wèi**	普通座位 普通座位
body check **sōu shēn**	搜身 搜身	economic class **jīng-ji cāng**	经济舱 經濟艙
baggage compartment **xíng-li cāng**	行李舱 行李艙	fasten **xì jǐn**	系紧 繫緊
baggage inspection **xíng-li jiǎn chá**	行李检查 行李檢查	seat belt **ān quán dài**	安全带 安全帶
smuggler **zǒu sī zhě**	走私者 走私者	oxygen mask **yǎng qì miàn zhào**	氧气面罩 氧氣面罩
hazardous material **wéi jìn pǐn**	违禁品 違禁品	life jacket; life vest **jiù shēng yī**	救生衣 救生衣
baggage room **xíng-li jì cún chù**	行李寄存处 行李寄存處	tray table **zuò-wei huó-dong cān zhuō**	座位活动餐桌 座位活動餐桌
locker room **tóu bì jì cún shì**	投币寄存室 投幣寄存室	table light **zuò qián zhuō dēng**	座前桌灯 座前桌燈
boarding gate **dēng jī rù kǒu chù**	登机入口处 登機入口處	reading light **kàn shū dēng**	看书灯 看書燈
air bridge **dēng jī tī**	登机梯 登機梯	earphone **ěr jī**	耳机 耳機
boarding pass **lǚ kè dēng jī zhèng**	旅客登机证 旅客登機證	headsets **tào tóu-shi ěr jī**	套头式耳机 套頭式耳機

| earphone outlet | 耳机插座儿 |
| ěr jī chā zuòr | 耳機插座兒 |

| fixed to the armrest | 安在扶手上面 |
| ān-zai fú-shou-shang-mian | 安在扶手上面 |

| serve lunch | 开饭 |
| kāi fàn | 開飯（中飯） |

| dinner cart | 餐车 |
| cān chē | 餐車 |

| vegetarian | 吃素者 |
| chī sù zhě | 吃素者 |

| Cognac; brandy | 白兰地酒 |
| bái lán dì jiǔ | 白蘭地酒 |

| a refill | 续杯；再加满 |
| xù bēi; zài jiā mǎn | 續杯；再加滿 |

| cool air | 冷气；冷风 |
| lěng qì; lěng fēng | 冷氣；冷風 |

| blow in my direction | 朝向我吹 |
| cháo xiàng wǒ chuī | 朝向我吹 |

| airsick | 晕机 |
| yūn jī | 暈機 |

| motion sickness pill | 晕机药 |
| yūn jī yào | 暈機藥 |

| nausea | 有呕吐感 |
| yóu ǒu tù gǎn | 有嘔吐感 |

| disposal bag | 废物袋 |
| fèi wù dài | 廢物袋 |

| pre-moist towelette | 湿纸巾 |
| shī zhǐ jīn | 濕紙巾 |

| call button | 呼人按钮儿 |
| hū rén àn niǔr | 呼人按鈕兒 |

| blindfold | 眼罩 |
| yǎn zhào | 眼罩 |

| relax | 放松 |
| fàng sōng | 放鬆 |

| rest | 休息 |
| xiū-xi | 休息 |

| sleep | 睡觉 |
| shuì jiào | 睡覺 |

| take a nap (snooze) | 打个盹儿 |
| dǎ-ge dǔnr | 打個盹兒 |

| get forty winks | 睡一会儿 |
| shuì-yi huǐr　　（白天） | 睡一會兒 |

| one more pillow | 再给个枕头 |
| zài gěi-ge zhěn-tou | 再給個枕頭 |

| blanket | 毛毯 |
| máo tǎn | 毛毯 |

| slippers | 拖鞋 |
| tuō xié | 拖鞋 |

| ground staff | 地勤人员 |
| dì qín rén yuán | 地勤人員 |

| cabin crew | 机上人员 |
| jī shàng rén yuán | 機上人員 |

| command pilot; captain | 机长 |
| jī zhǎng | 機長 |

| pilot | 正驾驶 |
| zhèng jià shǐ | 正駕駛 |

| copilot | 副驾驶 |
| fù jià shǐ | 副駕駛 |

| stewardess | 空中小姐 |
| kōng zhōng xiáo jiě | 空中小姐 |

| steward | 空中少爷 |
| kōng zhōng shào-ye | 空中少爺 |

| attendant | 机上服务生 |
| jī-shang fú wù shēng | 機上服務生 |

| put on the rack | 放在架子上 |
| fàng-zai jià-zi-shang | 放在架子上 |

| pull the seat out | 把座位拉出来 |
| bǎ zuò-wei lā-chu-lai | 把座位拉出來 |

| lean back | 往后靠 |
| wǎng hòu kào | 往後靠 |

| adjust my seat | 调整我的座位 |
| tiáo-zheng wǒ-de zuò-wei | 調整我的座位 |

| reclining button | 仰椅背的按钮儿 |
| yáng yǐ bèi-de àn niǔr | 仰椅背的按鈕兒 |

| up straight your seat | 把椅背推直 |
| bá yǐ bèi tuī zhí | 把椅背推直 |

| tables in lock position | 把桌子收回去 |
| bǎ zhuō-zi shōu-hui-qù | 把桌子收回去 |

| put out your cigarette(s) | 把香烟熄灭 |
| bǎ xiāng yān xí miè | 把香煙熄滅 |

turn off your cellphone	关上您的手机	restricted area	禁区
guān-shang nín-de shǒu jī	關上您的手機	jìn qū	禁區
all electronic devices	所有的电子仪器	apron area	停机坪
suó yǒu-de diàn zǐ yí qì	所有的電子儀器	tíng jī píng	停機坪
in-flight	飞行中	boarding-ramp	登机梯
fēi xíng zhōng	飛行中	dēng jī tī	登機梯
re-boarding	中途换机	ramp bus	机坪载客车
zhōng tú huàn jī	中途換機	jī píng zài kè chē	機坪載客車
intermediate stop	中间站	airport bus	机场巴士
zhōng jiān zhàn	中間站	jī chǎng bā shì	機場巴士
duty free shop	免税商店	excess baggage	超重行李
miǎn shuì shāng diàn	免税商店	chāo zhòng xíng-li	超重行李
transit pass	过境登机证	excess baggage ticket	超重行李票
guò jìng dēng jī zhèng	過境登機證	chāo zhòng xíng-li piào	超重行李票
stopover	中途停留	bound baggage	过境寄存行李
zhōng tú tíng liú	中途停留	guò jìng jì cún xíng-li	過境寄存行李
refueling	加油	baggage claim	提取行李
jiā yóu	加油	tí qǔ xíng-li	提取行李
connecting flight	转接班机	belt conveyor carousel	行李运送带
zhuǎn jiē bān jī	轉接班機	xíng-li yùn sòng dài	行李運送帶
emergency landing	紧急降落	tag (for baggage)	行李签
jǐn jí jiàng luò	緊急降落	xíng-li qiān	行李籤
taxiway	滑行道	baggage cart	行李小推车
huá xíng dào	滑行道	xíng-li xiǎo tuī chē	行李小推車
land marking	地面标帜	delayed (airplane)	误点
dì miàn biāo zhì	地面標幟	wù diǎn	誤點
landing light	著陆灯	ahead of schedule	提前
zhuó lù dēng	著陸燈	tí qián	提前
runway light	跑道灯	the estimate arrival time	误点到达
pǎo dào dēng	跑道燈	wù diǎn dào dá	誤點到達
under carriage wheel	起落轮	arrival	到达
qǐ luò lún	起落輪	dào dá	到達
nose landing wheel	鼻轮	time difference	时差
bí lún	鼻輪	shí chā	時差
retractable landing gear	伸缩起落架	jet lag	时差失调感
shēn suō qǐ luò jià	伸縮起落架	shí chā shī tiáo gǎn	時差失調感
landing	著陆	I'm fatigued.	我累死了！
zhuó lù	著陸	wǒ lèi-si-le	我累死了！

| pier; dock | 码头 | ship | 船；鉴 |
| **mǎ-tou** | 碼頭 | **chuán; jiàn** | 船；鑑 |

| seaport | 海港；海港市 | cargo hold | 货舱 |
| **hái gǎng; hái gǎng shì** | 海港；海港市 | **huò cāng** | 貨艙 |

| harbour | 港；避风港 | cabin | 客舱 |
| **gǎng; bì fēng gǎng** | 港；避風港 | **kè cāng** | 客艙 |

| harbour pilot | 领港员 | first-class cabin | 头等客舱 |
| **líng gǎng yuán** | 領港員 | **tóu děng kè cāng** | 頭等客艙 |

| passenger steamer | 客轮 | second-class cabin | 二等客舱 |
| **kè lún** | 客輪 | **èr děng kè cāng** | 二等客艙 |

| freighter; cargo ship | 货轮 | economy class cabin | 经济舱 |
| **huò lún** | 貨輪 | **jīng jì cāng** | 經濟艙 |

| liner | 定期船 | bunk | 床位 |
| **dìng qí chuán** | 定期船 | **chuáng wèi** | 床位 |

| tramp ship | 不定期船 | hammock | 吊铺 |
| **bú dìng qí chuán** | 不定期船 | **diào pù** | 吊鋪 |

| civilian ship | 民船 | hatch | 舱口盖 |
| **mín chuán** | 民船 | **cāng kǒu gài** | 艙口蓋 |

| merchant ship | 商船 | tank | 水槽 |
| **shāng chuán** | 商船 | **shuǐ cáo** | 水槽 |

| yacht; float | 游艇 | compass | 指南针 |
| **yóu tǐng** | 遊艇 | **zhǐ nán zhēn** | 指南針 |

| ferry; ferryboat | 渡船 | pelorus | 方位盘 |
| **dù chuán** | 渡船 | **fāng wèi pán** | 方位盤 |

| sailboat | 帆船 | rhumb line | 罗盘方位线 |
| **fān chuán** | 帆船 | **luó pán fāng wèi xiàn** | 羅盤方位線 |

| junk | 中国帆船 | anchor | 锚 |
| **zhōng guó fān chuán** | 中國帆船 | **máo** | 錨 |

| boat | 小船 | mast | 桅杆 |
| **xiǎo chuán** | 小船 | **wéi gān** | 桅杆 |

flagstaff	旗杆	life buoy	救生圈
qí gǎn	旗桿	jiù shēng qüān	救生圈
hoist flag	悬旗	life jacket	救生衣
xüán qí	懸旗	jiù shēng yī	救生衣
siren	汽笛	captain	船长
qì dí	汽笛	chuán zhǎng	船長
oar	桨	chief officer	大副
jiǎng	槳	dà fù	大副
chain	锁链	second officer	二副
suǒ liàn	鎖鏈	èr fù	二副
gangway	船扶梯	chief engineer	轮机长
chuán fú tī	船扶梯	lún jī zhǎng	輪機長
folding ladder	折梯	second engineer	二管轮
zhé tī	摺梯	èr guǎn lún	二管輪
rope ladder	绳梯	fishing boat	渔船
shéng tī	繩梯	yǘ chuán	漁船
skylight	天窗	salvage boat	海难救助船
tiān chuāng	天窗	hǎi nàn jiù zhù chuán	海難救助船
ventilation	通风	swell; surge	大浪;浪涛汹涌
tōng fēng	通風	dà làng; làng tāo xiōng yǒng	大浪;浪濤洶湧
deck	甲板	the crew; crew members	全体船员
jiá bǎn	甲板	qüán tǐ chuán yüán	全體船員
clearance	出港许可	seaman; sailor	水手;水兵
chū gǎng xǘ kě	出港許可	shuí shǒu; shuǐ bīng	水手;水兵
unloading	卸货	lifeguard	救生员
xiè huò	卸貨	jiù shēng yüán	救生員
loading	装货	boatman	船夫
zhuāng huò	裝貨	chuán fū	船夫
beacon; lighthouse	灯塔	rolling	左右摇摆
dēng tǎ	燈塔	zuǒ yòu yáo bǎi	左右搖擺
signal light	信号灯	survivor	生还者
xìn hào dēng	信號燈	shēng huán zhě	生還者
searchlight	探照灯	oarsman	划桨手
tàn zhào dēng	探照燈	huá jiáng shǒu	劃槳手
navigation	航海	draught; draft	吃水
háng hǎi	航海	chī shuǐ	吃水（船）
navigator	领航员	water-line	吃水线
lǐng háng yüán	領航員	chī shuǐ xiàn	吃水線
lifeboat	救生船	S.O.S.	求救信号
jiù shēng chuán	救生船	qiú jiù xìn hào	求救信號

steamer qì chuán	汽船 汽船	
tugboat tuō chuán	拖船 拖船	
oil tanker; oiler yóu lún	油轮 油輪	
cargo-passenger ship kè huò lún	客货轮 客貨輪	
pirate ship; sea rover hǎi dào chuán	海盗船 海盜船	
knot; sea mile lí; hái lǐ	浬；海里 浬；海里	
floating crane qǐ zhòng chuán	起重船 起重船	
luff nì fēng	逆风 逆風	
berth nag tíng bó	停泊 停泊	
stowaway tōu dù	偷渡 偷渡	
vessel chuán bó	船舶 船舶	
container ship purpose huò guì chuán	货柜船 貨櫃船	
dock at the pier tíng kào mǎ-tou	停靠码头 停靠碼頭	
very enjoyable trip hǎo wánr-de lǚ chéng	好玩儿的旅程 好玩兒的旅程	
disembark dēng àn	登岸 登岸	
go ashore shàng àn	上岸 上岸	
paddle (boat) duán jiǎng chuán	短桨船 短槳船	
mail boat; mail liner yóu lún	邮轮 郵輪	
tail wind shùn fēng	顺风 順風	
alongside kào àn	靠岸 靠岸	

warship zhàn jiàn	战舰 戰艦	
rubber boat xiàng pí tǐng	橡皮艇 橡皮艇	
canoe dú mù zhōu	独木舟 獨木舟	
refrigerating ship lěng cáng chuán	冷藏船 冷藏船	
carrier shū sòng jiàn	输送舰 輸送艦	
coast-guard ship xún luó jiàn	巡逻舰 巡邏艦	
cruiser xún yáng jiàn	巡洋舰 巡洋艦	
stateroom tè děng fáng	特等房 特等房	
top light wéi dǐng xìn hào dēng	桅顶信号灯 桅頂信號燈	
sail fān	帆 帆	
rudder duò	舵 舵	
oar jiǎng	桨 槳	
anchor shank pāo máo	抛锚 抛錨	
weigh anchor qǐ máo	起锚 起錨	
funnel yān-cong	烟囱 煙囪	
ventilator tōng fēng jī	通风机 通風機	
steering engine cāo duò jī	操舵机 操舵機	
steam engine zhēng qì jī	蒸汽机 蒸汽機	
propeller tuī jìn qì	推进器 推進器	
passenger's ladder lǚ kè tī	旅客梯 旅客梯	

oscillate **bǎi dòng**	摆动 擺動	boatswain **shuí shóu zhǎng**	水手长 水手長
dipping **shàng xià dòng**	上下动 上下動	superintendent officer **zǒng chuán zhǎng**	总船长 總船長
row boat **huá chuán**	划船 划船	superintendent engineer **zǒng lún jī zhǎng**	总轮机长 總輪機長
route **háng xiàn**	航线 航線	diver **qián shuǐ yuán**	潜水员 潛水員
distance **háng chéng**	航程 航程	floating dock **fú wù**	浮坞 浮塢
coxswain **tíng zhǎng; duò-shou**	艇长；舵手 艇長；舵手	forklift **duī gāo jī**	堆高机 堆高機
quartermaster **cāo duò shǒu**	操舵手 操舵手	oil storage tank **zhǔ yóu cáo**	贮油槽 貯油槽
chief operator **bào wù zhǔ rèn**	报务主任 報務主任	rummaging **hǎi guān sōu chá**	海关搜查 海關搜查
electric engineer **diàn jī shī**	电机师 電機師	procedures completed **bàn wán shǒu xù**	办完手续 辦完手續
motorman **jī gōng zhǎng**	机工长 機工長	motion sickness **yūn**（**chē; chuán; fēi jī**）	晕(车、船、飞机) 暈(車、船、飛機)
inform the quartermaster **tōng zhī bǔ jí zhǎng**	通知补给长 通知補給長	seasick **yūn chuán**	晕船 暈船
steward **nán shì**　　　（船；飛機）	男侍 男侍		

Customs Declaration

出國海關申報

He	open one eye	close one eye	let it go.
他	睁一只眼	闭一只眼	就算了
tā	zhēng-yi zhī yǎn	bì-yi zhī yǎn	jiù suàn-le

(He just looked at the other way.)

English	简体	繁體
immigration yí mín jú	移民局	移民局
customs declaration hǎi guān shēn bào	海关申报	海關申報
duty guān shuì	关税	關稅
dutiable shàng guān shuì	上关税	上關稅
fill out the form tián biǎo	填表	填表
go through customs tōng guò hǎi guān	通过海关	通過海關
customs formalities hǎi guān shǒu xù	海关手续	海關手續
customs tariff shuì zé	税则	稅則
tax shuì	税	稅
assess kè shuì	课税	課稅
tax evasion táo shuì	逃税	逃稅
evade duty lòu shuì	漏税	漏稅
duty-free articles miǎn shuì wù pǐn	免税物品	免稅物品
drawback; tax return tuì shuì	退税	退稅

English	简体	繁體
inspection jiǎn chá	检查	檢查
accompany luggage suí shēn xíng-li	随身行李	隨身行李
personal effects sī rén wù-pin	私人物品	私人物品
unlock the suitcase dǎ-kai xiāng suǒ	打开箱锁	打開箱鎖
brand-new qüán xīn	全新	全新
luxury shē-chi pǐn	奢侈品	奢侈品
prohibited articles wéi jìn wù pǐn	违禁物品	違禁物品
stowaway tōu dù	偷渡	偷渡
smuggle zǒu sī	走私	走私
false declaration xū bào shuì é	虚报税额	虛報稅額
hold kòu yā	扣押	扣押
confiscate mò shōu	没收	沒收
fine fá jīn	罚金	罰金
release fàng guān	放关	放關

Customs Searching Party

海關抄班

coast guard qì sī rén yuán	缉私人员 緝私人員	customs affairs hǎi guān shì wù	海关事物 海關事物
customs inspector hǎi guān dū chá yuán	海关督察员 海關督察員	manifest zài huò dān	载货单 載貨單
aboard your ship (vessel) dēng shàng guì chuán	登上贵船 登上貴船	store list cāng dān	仓单 倉單
have access to your vessel yǒu quán dēng guì jiàn	有权登贵舰 有權登貴艦	draft indication shuǐ jiǎo	水脚（船） 水腳（船）
searching party chāo bān	抄班 抄班	lacking one item quē shǎo yí xiàng	缺少一项 缺少一項
have been informed jiē dào mì bào	接到密报 接到密報	captain's signature chuán zhǎng qiàn shǔ	船长签署 船長簽署
possibility kě néng xìng	可能性 可能性	not to raise the gangway bié diào-qi fú tī	别吊起扶梯 別吊起扶梯
illegal merchandise wéi jìn pǐn	违禁品 違禁品	lower the gangway bǎ fú tī jiàng dī	把扶梯降低 把扶梯降低
appreciate your full cooperation pài rén yì tóng chāo chá	一同抄查 派人一同抄查	luggage compartment xíng-li shì	行李室 行李室
empty the water tank chōu gān shuǐ guì	抽乾水柜 抽乾水櫃	don't break the seals bié nòng huài fēng-tiao	别弄坏封条 別弄壞封條
raise / check the anchor lā-qi tiě máo jiǎn chá	拉起铁锚检查 拉起鐵錨檢查	or there will be a problem huì yǒu má-fan-de	会有麻烦的 會有麻煩的
all compartments available dǎ-kai suó yǒu chú guì	打开所有橱柜 打開所有櫥櫃	in obedience of regulations fǒu zé wéi guī	否则违规 否則違規
inspect foot lockers jiǎn chá sī rén yī guì	检查私人衣柜 檢查私人衣櫃	open and check the hold jiǎn chá huò cāng	检查货舱 檢查貨艙
responsible for duì cǐ fù zé	对此负责 對此負責	articles were found chá huò wù jiàn	查获物件 查獲物件
sealing wax huǒ qī	火漆 火漆	to sign qiān míng	签名 簽名
seal the supply room tiē fēng chǔ cáng shì	贴封储藏室 貼封儲藏室	witness signature jiàn zhèng rén qiān míng	见证人签名 見證人簽名

Hotel Services
旅館服務

hotel **lǚ guǎn**	旅馆 旅館	page **guǎng bō zhǎo rén**	广播找人 廣播找人
motel **qì chē lǚ guǎn**	汽车旅馆 汽車旅館	reservation **dìng fáng jiān**	订房间 訂房間
seaside resort **hǎi biān dù jià cūn**	海边渡假村 海邊渡假村	full occupancy **kè mǎn**	客满 客滿
a pleasure tourism **xiū xián lǚ yóu**	休闲旅游 休閒旅遊	room available **yǒu fáng jiān**	有房间 有房間
go vacationing **dù jià**	渡假 渡假	no vacancy **méi kòng fáng**	没空房 沒空房
go home on furlough **huí guó xiū jià**	回国休假 回國休假	make arrangements **ān-pai**	安排 安排
on season; peak season **wàng jì**	旺季 旺季	satisfactory **lìng rén mǎn yì**	令人满意 令人滿意
off season **dàn jì**	淡季 淡季	confirm **qüè rèn yí xià**	确认一下 確認一下
boarding house **gōng shí sù-de tào fáng**	供食宿的套房 供食宿的套房	rates **fáng zū jià mù biǎo**	房租价目表 房租價目表
courtesy car **lǚ guǎn jiē sòng chē**	旅馆接送车 旅館接送車	check in **guì tái dēng jì**	柜台登记 櫃檯登記
hotel accommodation **lǚ guǎn shè shī**	旅馆设施 旅館設施	registration card **lǚ kè dēng jì kǎ**	旅客登记卡 旅客登記卡
lobby **lǚ guǎn dà tīng**	旅馆大厅 旅館大廳	luggage; baggage **xíng-li**	行李 行李
lounge **lǚ kè xiū xián tīng**	旅客休闲厅 旅客休閒廳	bags **bāo-guo; bāo bāo**	包裹；包包 包裹；包包
coffee shop **kā fēi tīng**	咖啡厅 咖啡廳	suitcase **pí xiāng**	皮箱 皮箱
buffet dinner **xī shì zì zhù cān**	西式自助餐 西式自助餐	briefcase **gōng shì bāo**	公事包 公事包

has a nice view **shì-ye hǎo**	视野好 視野好	snore **dǎ hū-lu; dǎ hān**	打呼噜；打鼾 打呼嚕；打鼾
stay overnight **guò yè**	过夜 過夜	yawn **dǎ há-qian**	打哈欠 打哈欠
single room **dān rén fāng**	单人房 單人房	doze off; nod **dǎ kē-shuì**	打瞌睡 打瞌睡
double room **shuāng rén fáng**	双人房 雙人房	not sleepy **bú kùn**	不困 不睏
adjoining rooms **hù tōng-de fáng jiān**	互通的房间 互通的房間	cannot fall asleep **shuì-bu zhuó**	睡不著 睡不著
connecting door **hù tōng mén**	互通门 互通門	has fallen asleep **shuì zháo-le**	睡著了 睡著了
triple bed room **sān rén fáng**	三人房 三人房	soundly asleep **hū hū dà shuì**	呼呼大睡 呼呼大睡
single bed **dān rén chuáng**	单人床 單人床	my foot is asleep **wǒ-de jiǎo má-le**	我的脚麻了 我的腳麻了
double bed **shuāng rén chuáng**	双人床 雙人床	fingers are numb with cold **shǒu zhí-tou dòng má-le**	手指头冻麻了 手指頭凍麻了
twin bed **duì chuáng**	对床 對床	rest for a while **xiū-xi-yi xiàr**	休息一下儿 休息一下兒
extra bed **jiā-zhang chuáng**	加张床 加張床	Do Not Disturb **qǐng wù dá rǎo**	请勿打扰 請勿打擾
folding cot **zhé dié shì fān bù chuáng**	折叠式帆布床 折叠式帆布床	morning call; wake-up call **jiào xǐng qǐ chuáng**	叫醒起床 叫醒起床
key deposit **yào-shi yā jīn**	钥匙押金 鑰匙押金	satisfied **mǎn yì**	满意 滿意
extra charge **lìng wài shōu fèi**	另外收费 另外收費	suite **tào fáng**	套房 套房
sleepy **kùn**	睏 睏	Suite 6 **dì liù hào tào fáng**	第六号套房 第六號套房
sleep **shuì jiào**	睡觉 睡覺	Room 808 **bā líng bā hào fáng jiān**	八零八号房间 八零八號房間
hit the sack **qù shuì jiào**	去睡觉 去睡覺	down the hall **shùn-zhe zǒu dào wǎng qián zǒu**	顺著走道往前走 順著走道往前走
take a nap **dǎ-ge dǔnr**	打个盹儿 打個盹兒	turn left **zuó zhuǎn**	左转 左轉
had a forty winks **shuì-le-yi xiàr**	睡了一下儿 睡了一下兒	turn right **yòu zhuǎn**	右转 右轉
didn't sleep a wink **yì wǎn-shang méi hé yǎ**	一晚上没阖眼 一晚上沒闔眼	1st door to your left **zuǒ-bian dì yī-ge mén**	左边第一个门 左邊第一個門

English	Chinese (Simplified / Traditional)	Pinyin
the last door	最后一个门 / 最後一個門	zuì hòu yí-ge mén
2nd door from the last	倒数第二个门 / 倒數第二個門	dào shǔ dì èr-ge mén
on your right	在你的右手 / 在你的右手	zài nǐ-de yòu shǒu
payment in advance	预付 / 預付	yù fù
discount	折扣 / 折扣	zhé-kou
check out	结帐退房 / 結帳退房	jié zhàng tuì fáng
complaint	抱怨 / 抱怨	bào-yüan
got a problem	出了问题 / 出了問題	chū-le wèn tí
call to my attention	引起我的注意 / 引起我的注意	yǐn-qi wǒ-de zhù yì
shortly	马上 / 馬上	mǎ shàng
cashier	出纳 / 出納	chū nà
suggest	建议 / 建議	jiàn yì
valuables	贵重物品 / 貴重物品	guì zhòng wù pǐn
safe deposit	旅馆保险箱 / 旅館保險箱	lǘ guǎn báo xiǎn xiāng
here's your key	这是您的钥匙 / 這是您的鑰匙	zhè-shi nín-de yào-shi
long distance call	长途电话 / 長途電話	cháng tú diàn huà
collect call	对方付费 / 對方付費	duì-fang fù fèi
dial directly	直拨 / 直撥	zhí bō
dial 9 first	先拨 9 / 先撥 9	xiān bō jiǔ
stationery	信封儿信纸 / 信封兒信紙	xìn fēngr xìn zhǐ
bring me	给我拿来 / 給我拿來	géi-wo ná-lai
more stamps	多给几张邮票 / 多給幾張郵票	duō-gei jǐ-zhang yóu piào
mail it for me	替我寄 / 替我寄	tì-wo jì
send it airmail	寄航空信 / 寄航空信	jì háng kōng xìn
insured	把它保险 / 把它保險	bǎ-ta báo xiǎn
room service	客房服务 / 客房服務	kè fáng fú wù
tip	小费 / 小費	xiǎo fèi
bellboy	行李服务生 / 行李服務生	xíng-li fú wù shēng
make up the room	打扫房间 / 打掃房間	dá-sao fáng jiān
maid	女仆 / 女僕	nǚ pú
valet service	洗烫服务 / 洗燙服務	xǐ tàng fú wù
have it dry cleaned	把它干洗 / 把它乾洗	bǎ-ta gān xǐ
have it pressed; ironed	把它熨好 / 把它熨好	bǎ-ta yùn hǎo
one-hour service	一小时做好 / 一小時做好	yì xiǎo shí zuò hǎo
I appreciate it	感激不尽 / 感激不盡	gǎn jī bú jìn
I'd appreciate it	则感激不尽 / 則感激不盡	zé gǎn jī bú jìn
recommend	推荐 / 推薦	tuī jiàn
shampoo & set	洗头和做头发 / 洗頭和做頭髮	xǐ tóu hé zuò tóu-fa
beauty salon	美容院 / 美容院	měi róng yüàn
good service	服务周到 / 服務周到	fú wù zhōu dào

Train Station & Subway
火車與地鐵

train	火车	express	快车
huǒ chē	火車	**kuài chē**	快車
train station	火车站	local train	普通车
huǒ chē zhàn	火車站	**pǔ tōng chē**	普通車
concourse	火车站大厅	through train; non-stop train	直达车
huǒ chē zhàn dà tīng	火車站大廳	**zhí dá chē**	直達車
entrance	入口	catch the train	赶搭火车
rù kǒu	入口	**gǎn dā huǒ chē**	趕搭火車
exit	出口	missed the train	没赶上车
chū kǒu	出口	**méi gǎn shàng chē**	沒趕上車
railway	铁路	freight train	货车
tiě lù	鐵路	**huò chē**	貨車
subway; metro; MRT	地下铁道	cargo train	货运车
dì xià tiě dào	地下鐵道	**huò yùn chē**	貨運車
railway tunnel	铁路隧道	freight charge	运费
tiě lù suì dào	鐵路隧道	**yùn fèi**	運費
elevated train	高架火车	coach	客车
gāo jià huǒ chē	高架火車	**kè chē**	客車
overpass	天桥	tourist train	观光号
tiān qiáo	天橋	**guān guāng hào**	觀光號
railroad crossing	平交道	diner; dining train	火车餐车
píng jiāo dào	平交道	**huǒ chē cān chē**	火車餐車
north-bound train	北上火车	sleeper	卧车
běi shàng huǒ chē	北上火車	**wò chē**	臥車
up train	上行火车	compartment; coach	车厢
shàng xíng huǒ chē	上行火車	**chē xiāng**	車廂
south-bound train	南下火车	lower berth	下铺
nán xià huǒ chē	南下火車	**xià pù**	下舖
down train	下行火车	upper berth	上铺
xià xíng huǒ chē	下行火車	**shàng pù**	上舖

information service fú wù tái	服务台 服務台	fare chē fèi	车费 車費
coin locker yìng bì cún wù xiāng	硬币存物箱 硬幣存物箱	waiting room hòu chē shì	候车室 候車室
message board liú yán bǎn	留言板 留言板	puncher jiǎn piào yuán	剪票员 剪票員
lost and found shī wù zhāo lǐng chù	失物招领处 失物招領處	platform yüè tái	月台 月臺
time table shí jiān biǎo	时间表 時間表	initial station qí diǎn zhàn	起点站 起點站
train time table huǒ chē shí kè biǎo	火车时刻表 火車時刻表	departure sign chū fā biāo zhì	出发标志 出發標誌
delay wù diǎn	误点 誤點	departure qǐ chéng; kāi chē	起程；开车 起程；開車
ticket office; ticket booth shòu piào chù	售票处 售票處	locomotive huǒ chē tóu	火车头 火車頭
economy class pǔ tōng piào	普通票 普通票	engine driver huǒ chē sī jī	火车司机 火車司機
half fare bàn piào	半票 半票	station master zhàn zhǎng	站长 站長
free pass miǎn piào	免票 免票	conductor chē zhǎng	车掌 車掌
one-way ticket dān chéng piào	单程票 單程票	seat zuò-wei	座位 座位
return ticket huí chéng piào	回程票 回程票	aisle zǒu dào	走道 走道
round trip ticket lái huí piào	来回票 來回票	aisle seat zǒu dào zuò-wei	走道座位 走道座位
season ticket dìng qí piào	定期票 定期票	window seat kào chuāng zuò-wei	靠窗座位 靠窗座位
party ticket tuán tǐ piào	团体票 團體票	reserved seat duì hào rù zuò	对号入座 對號入座
berth ticket wò pù piào	卧铺票 臥鋪票	baggage rack xíng-li jià	行李架 行李架
first class ticket tóu děng piào	头等票 頭等票	slide window huá chuāng	滑窗 滑窗
second class ticket èr děng piào	二等票 二等票	ticket checker yàn piào yuán	验票员 驗票員
baggage check xíng-li piào	行李票 行李票	attendant chē tóng	车僮 車僮

slip carriage **bù tíng chē zhàn**	不停车站 不停車站	overrunning fare **yüè zhàn chē fèi**	越站车费 越站車費
junction station **huàn chē zhàn**	换车站 換車站	baggage room **xíng-li fáng**	行李房 行李房
intermediate station **zhōng jiān zhàn**	中间站 中間站	consignor **tuō yùn rén**	托运人 託運人
home signal **jìn zhàn hào zhì**	进站号志 進站號誌	consignee **shòu huò rén**	受货人 受貨人
arrival station **dào zhàn**	到站 到站	label **tiē jüàn biāo; tiē biāo qiān**	贴卷标 貼標籤
arrival on time **zhǔn shí dào zhàn**	准时到站 準時到站	pick-up luggage **qǔ xíng-li**	取行李 取行李
terminal station **zhōng diǎn zhàn**	终点站 終點站	to haul **bān yùn**	搬运 搬運
stopover **zhōng tú xià chē**	中途下车 中途下車	porter **jiǎo fū**	脚夫 腳夫
alight; get off **xià chē**	下车 下車	derail **chū guǐ**	出轨 出軌
excess fare **yüè zhàn bǔ piào**	越站补票 越站補票	signal man **hào zhì gōng**	号志工 號誌工

bus gōng gòng qì chē	公共汽车 公共汽車	lower deck xià céng	下层 (车、船) 下層
highway bus cháng tú bā shì	长途巴士 長途巴士	seating zuò-wei	座位 座位
Grayhound Bus huī gǒu cháng tú bā shì	灰狗长途巴士 灰狗長途巴士	standing zhàn-zhe	站著 站著
bus driver gōng chē jià shǐ	公车驾驶 公車駕駛	strap; hanging ring chē nèi-de diào huán	车内的吊环 車內的吊環
express bus zhí dá chē	直达车 直達車	a main traffic artery jiāo tōng gàn xiàn	交通干线 交通幹線
touring bus yóu lǎn chē	游览车 遊覽車	highway gōng lù	公路 公路
Take Ten! xiū-xi shí fēn zhōng	休息十分钟 休息十分鐘	safety island; terrace ān quán dǎo	安全岛 安全島
Departing! yào kāi-le	要开了(车、船) 要開了	bus stop gōng chē zhàn pái	公车站牌 公車站牌
microbus xiǎo xíng bā shì	小型巴士 小型巴士	East-bounding bus wǎng dōng kāi-de bā shì	往东开的巴士 往東開的巴士
street car; tramcar diàn chē	电车 電車	West-bounding bus wǎng xī kāi-de bā shì	往西开的巴士 往西開的巴士
school bus xiào chē	校车 校車	South-bounding bus wǎng nán kāi-de bā shì	往南开的巴士 往南開的巴士
company bus jiāo tōng chē	交通车 交通車	North-bounding bus wǎng běi kāi-de bā shì	往北开的巴士 往北開的巴士
dial-a-bus diàn huà zhāo bā shì	电话招巴士 電話招巴士	going downtown kāi wǎng shì zhōng xīn	开往市中心 開往市中心
double-decker bus shuāng céng bā shì	双层巴士 雙層巴士	going uptown kāi wǎng zhù zhái qū	开往住宅区 開往住宅區
upper deck shàng céng chē	上层 (车、船) 上層	transfer zhuǎn chē	转车 轉車

transfer ticket zhuǎn chē piào	转车票 轉車票	
crowded on the bus chē shàng rén hěn duō	车上人很多 車上人很多	
didn't make a stop guò zhàn méi tíng	过站没停 過站沒停	
next bus's coming xià bān chē mǎ shàng dào	下一班车马上到 下一班車馬上到	
every 20 minutes měi èr shí fēn zhōng	每二十分钟 每二十分鐘	
bus leaves in 6 minutes zài liù fēn zhōng kāi chē	再六分鐘开车 再六分鐘開車	
every hour on the hour měi zhéng diǎn yì bān chē	每整点一班车 每整點一班車	
in the direction of; toward cháo; xi	朝；向 朝；向	
go in a w estward direction wǎng xī kāi	往西开 往西開	
is bound for the beach kāi wáng hǎi bīn	开往海滨 開往海濱	
shove tuī jǐ	推挤 推擠	
stand in line pái duì	排队 排隊	
Don't hold the line bié dǎng-zhe bíé-ren	别挡著别人 別擋著別人	
Get on! (bus) shàng chē	上车（公车） 上車	
Get in! (car) jìn-lai	进来（轿车） 進來	

Get off! (bus) xià chē	下车（公车） 下車
Get out! (car) xià chē	下车（轿车） 下車
Move up, please qíng wǎng qián zǒu	请往前走 請往前走
What's the fare? chē piào duō-shao qián	车票多少钱 車票多少錢
Stop, please qíng tíng chē	请停车 請停車
When we get there. dào zhàn shí	到站时 到站時
Notify me, please qǐng tōng zhī-wo yí xiàr	请通知我一下儿 請通知我一下兒
Yes, ma'am. shì-de xiáo jiě	是的，小姐 是的，小姐
offer seats ràng zuòr	让座儿 讓座兒
bus station gōng chē zhàn	公车站 公車站
bus depot gōng chē zǒng zhàn	公车总站 公車總站
ticket booth piào tíng	票亭 票亭
token; bus token gōng chē chéng chē bì	公车乘车币 公車乘車幣

vehicle **chē liàng**	车辆 車輛	**sports car** **pǎo chē**	跑车 跑車
automobile **qì chē**	汽车 汽車	**convertible car** **chǎng péng qì chē**	敞篷汽车 敞篷汽車
private car **zì yòng chē**	自用车 自用車	**racing car** **sài chē**	赛车 賽車（競賽車）
brand new car **qüán xīn qì chē**	全新汽车 全新汽車	**jeep** **jí pǔ chē**	吉普车 吉普車
used car **èr shǒu chē**	二手车 二手車	**station wagon** **lǚ xíng kè huò chē**	旅行客货车 旅行客貨車
jalopy **lǎo-ye chē**	老爷车 老爺車	**moving van** **jiā jù bān yùn chē**	家俱搬运车 傢俱搬運車
hot rod **gǎi zhuāng chē**	改装车 改裝車	**tractor** **qiān yǐn chē**	牵引车 牽引車
lemon car (unqualified) **bù hé gé-de qì chē**	不合格的汽车 不合格的汽車	**trailer** **huó dòng fáng wū tuō chē**	活动房屋拖车 活動房屋拖車
trade-in car **zhé jià huàn xīn chē**	折价换新车 折價換新車	**taxi; cab** **jì chéng chē**	计程车 • 計程車
warranty **bǎo zhèng shū**	保证书 保證書	**cable car** **lǎn chē**	缆车 纜車
coupe **shuāng zuò xiǎo qì chē**	双座小汽车 雙座小汽車	**bus** **góng gòng qì chē**	公共汽车 公共汽車
compact car **qīng biàn xiǎo jiào chē**	轻便小轿车 輕便小轎車	**streetcar** **diàn chē**	电车 電車
sedan **jiào chē**	轿车 轎車	**carriage** **mǎ chē**	马车 馬車
limousine **dà lǐ chē**	大礼车 大禮車	**tricycle** **sān lún chē**	三轮车 三輪車
bullet-proof sedan **fáng dàn qì chē**	防弹汽车 防彈汽車	**motorcycle** **mó tuō chē**	摩托车 摩托車

hard hat	ān qüán mào; tóu kuī	安全帽；头盔	安全帽；頭盔
scooter	qīng jī chē	轻机车	輕機車
mini-bike	mí nǐ jī chē	迷你机车	迷你機車
bicycle	zì xíng chē	自行车	自行車
minivan	qī rén xiǎo bā shì	七人小巴士	七人小巴士
pickup	xiǎo huò chē	小货车	小貨車
truck	dà huò chē	大货车	大貨車
heavy truck	zhòng xíng kǎ chē	重型卡车	重型卡車
container car	huò guì chē	货柜车	貨櫃車
refrigeration truck	lěng cáng chē	冷藏车	冷藏車
camion	jūn yòng kǎ chē	军用卡车	軍用卡車
fuel truck	yùn yóu chē	运油车	運油車
mobile machinery shop	gōng chéng chē	工程车	工程車
concrete mixer	shuǐ ní jiǎo bàn chē	水泥搅拌车	水泥攪拌車
squeez-crete	hùn níng tǔ bèng chē	混凝土泵车	混凝土泵車
trolley	kōng zhōng diào yùn chē	空中吊运车	空中吊運車
tow car	tuō chē	拖车	拖車
bulldozer	duī tǔ jī	堆土机	堆土機
belt conveyer	yùn shū dài	运输带	運輸帶
ditcher	wā gōu jī	挖沟机	挖溝機
backhoe	chú tǔ jī	锄土机	鋤土機
dump truck	qīng dào chē	倾倒车	傾倒車
road roller	yā lù jī	压路机	壓路機
stack machine	duī gāo jī	堆高机	堆高機
derrick	qǐ zhòng jī	起重机	起重機
crane	qǐ zhòng jī diào chē	起重机吊车	起重機吊車
street sprinkler	sá shuǐ chē	洒水车	灑水車
squad car	jǐng chē	警车	警車
police motorcade	jǐng chē duì	警车队	警車隊
patrol car	xún luó chē	巡逻车	巡邏車
ambulance	jiù hù chē	救护车	救護車
mail car	yóu chē	邮车	郵車
rubbish collector	lā jī chē	垃圾车	垃圾車
fire engine	jiù huǒ chē	救火车	救火車

Traffic Regulations
交通規則

No Passing jìn zhǐ chāo chē	禁止超车 禁止超車	No Entry bù zhǔn shǐ rù	不准驶入 不准駛入
Keep In Lane jìn zhǐ yüè xiàn	禁止越线 禁止越線	No Through Traffic jìn zhǐ tōng xíng	禁止通行 禁止通行
oncoming traffic duì miàn lái chē	对面来车 對面來車	Detour rào dào xíng shǐ	绕道行驶 繞道行駛
failure to yield lái-bu jí shǎn bì	来不及闪避 來不及閃避	Hampers Ahead qián yǒu zhàng wù	前有障物 前有障物
make way for ràng kāi lù	让开路 讓開路	in the way zǔ ài; dǎng lù	阻碍；挡路 阻礙；擋路
Slow Down màn-shi-lai	慢下来 慢下來	Narrow Bridge Ahead qián yóu zhǎi qiáo	前有窄桥 前有窄橋
Keep Right kào yòu	靠右 靠右	Hump Bridge Ahead qián yóu gǒng qiáo	前有拱桥 前有拱橋
No Horn jìn àn lǎ-ba	禁按喇叭 禁按喇叭	Tunnel Ahead qián miàn suì dào	前面隧道 前面隧道
No Turns jìn zhǐ zhuǎn wān	禁止转弯 禁止轉彎	Workmen Ahead qián miàn shī gōng	前面施工 前面施工
take the wrong turn zhuǎn cuò-le wān	转错了弯 轉錯了彎	Cross Road jiāo chā gàn dào	交叉干道 交叉幹道
No U-turn bù zhǔn huí zhuǎn	不准回转 不准迴轉	Road Junction sān chā lù kǒu	三叉路口 三叉路口
No Left Turn bù zhǔn zuó zhuǎn	不准左转 不准左轉	Narrow Road zhǎi lù	窄路 窄路
Stop tíng chē zài qǐ	停车再起 停車再起	Zigzag Path yáng cháng xiǎo jìng	羊肠小径 羊腸小徑
Railroad Crossing xiǎo xīn huǒ chē	小心火车 小心火車	Rough Road dào lù bù píng	道路不平 道路不平
Dead End; Road Closed cǐ lù bù tōng	此路不通 此路不通	Slippery When Wet dì shī lù huá	地湿路滑 地濕路滑

Dangerous Curves **wéi xiǎn wān lù**	危险弯路 危險彎路	**School Zone** **xüé xiào dì qǖ**	学校地区 學校地區
Dangerous Down Grade **wéi xiǎn xià pō**	危险下坡 危險下坡	**Hospital Zone** **yī yüàn dì qǖ**	医院地区 醫院地區
Steep Hill **shàng pō**	上坡 上坡	**Residential Zone** **zhù zhái qǖ**	住宅区 住宅區
Down Hill **xià pō**	下坡 下坡	**Silent Zone** **níng jìng dì qǖ**	宁静地区 寧靜地區
Winding Road **wān qǖ lù**	弯曲路 彎曲路	**No Jaywalking** **jìn zhǐ chuān yüè mǎ lù**	禁止穿越马路 禁止穿越馬路
No Parking **jìn zhǐ tíng chē**	禁止停车 禁止停車	**Pedestrian Crossing** **dāng xīn xíng rén**	当心行人 當心行人
Restricted Waiting **bù zhǔn zhì liú**	不准滞留 不准滯留	**Children** **xiǎo xīn ér tóng**	小心儿童 小心兒童
No Double Parking **jìn zhǐ bìng pái tíng chē**	禁止并排停车 禁止併排停車		

Driving Abroad
48C
国外開車

driver **jià shǐ; sī jī**	驾驶；司机 駕駛；司機	**premium gasoline** **gāo jí qì yóu**	高级汽油 高級汽油
chauffeur **sī jiā sī jī**	私家司机 私家司機	**super gasoline** **tè jí qì yóu**	特级汽油 特級汽油
pick up **jiē rén**	接人 接人	**unleaded (no lead) gas** **wú qiān qì yóu**	无铅汽油 無鉛汽油
a car-pool (共乘一车) **lún liú kāi chē shàng bān**	轮流开车上班 輪流開車上班	**engine oil** **jī yóu**	机油 機油
slowpoke driver **kāi màn chē-de rén**	开慢车的人 開慢車的人	**battery fluid** **diàn chí shuǐ**	电池水 電池水
seating capacity **xiàn zuò**	限座 限座	**traffic police** **jiāo tōng jǐng chá**	交通警察 交通警察
back-seat driver **yì-jian duō-de chéng kè**	意见多的乘客 意見多的乘客	**traffic control** **jiāo tōng guǎn zhì**	交通管制 交通管制
hitchhike **gōng lù lán chē dā biàn**	公路拦车搭便 公路攔車搭便	**traffic sign** **jiāo tōng biāo zhì**	交通标志 交通標誌
joyride **jià chē dōu fēngr**	驾车兜风儿 駕車兜風兒	**traffic regulation** **jiāo tōng guī zé**	交通规则 交通規則
jaywalker **luàn chuān mǎ lù-de rén**	乱穿马路的人 亂穿馬路的人	**traffic light** **hóng lǜ dēng**	红绿灯 紅綠燈
service/ filling station **jiā yóu zhàn**	加油站 加油站	**red light** **hóng dēng**	红灯 紅燈
gasoline; gas **qì yóu**	汽油 汽油	**green light** **lǜ dēng**	绿灯 綠燈
self-serve **zì xíng jiā yóu**	自行加油 自行加油	**amber/yellow light** **huáng dēng**	黄灯 黃燈
fill her up **bǎ qì yóu jiā mǎn**	把汽油加满 把汽油加滿	**elevated bridge** **gāo jià qiáo**	高架桥 高架橋
regular gasoline **pǔ tōng qì yóu**	普通汽油 普通汽油	**elevated road** **gāo jià dào lù**	高架道路 高架道路

freeway (FWY) **gāo sù gōng lù**	高速公路 高速公路	zebra stripe **bān mǎ xiàn**	斑马线 斑馬線
superhighway **chāo jí gāo sù gōng lù**	超级高速公路 超級高速公路	sidewalk **xíng rén biàn dào**	行人便道 行人便道
turnpike **shōu fèi gāo sù gōng lù**	收费高速公路 收費高速公路	pedestrian **xíng rén**	行人 行人
toll **guò lù fèi**	过路费 過路費	highway sign **gōng lù pái**	公路牌 公路牌
pay a toll **fù guò lù fèi**	付过路费 付過路費	milestone **lǐ chéng bēi**	里程碑 里程碑
tollgate **shōu fèi zhàn**	收费站 收費站	road sign **lù biāo; lù pái**	路标；路牌 路標；路牌
loop road **huí chē dào**	回车道 迴車道	street sign **jiē pái**	街牌 街牌
passing bay **ràng chē wān**	让车弯 讓車彎	double park **bìng pái tíng chē**	并排停车 併排停車
rest area **xiū xí zhàn**	休息站 休息站	parking **tíng chē**	停车 停車(停車位)
tunnel **suì dào**	隧道 隧道	parking area **tíng chē qū**	停车区 停車區
underpass **dì xià dào**	地下道 地下道	parking meter **tíng chē jì shí qì**	停车计时器 停車計時器
pedestrian overpass **tiān qiáo; xíng rén lù qiáo**	天桥；行人陆桥 天橋；行人陸橋	parking lot **tíng chē chǎng**	停车场 停車場
intersection; cross road **shí zì lù kǒu**	十字路口 十字路口	multi-story garage **lì tǐ tíng chē chǎng**	立体停车场 立體停車場
eight-lane traffic **bā xiàn dào**	八线道 八線道	auto shift **zì dòng pái dǎng**	自动排档 自動排檔
two-lane traffic **shuāng chē dào**	双车道 雙車道	starting handle **shǒu yáo fā dòng**	手摇发动 手搖發動
quick lane **kuài chē dào**	快车道 快車道	ignite **fā dòng**	发动 發動
slow traffic lane **màn chē dào**	慢车道 慢車道	start **qǐ dòng**	起动 起動
one-way street **dān xíng dào**	单行道 單行道	step on accelerator **cǎi yóu ménr**	踩油门儿 踩油門兒
on ramp **zài xié pōr shàng**	在斜坡儿上 在斜坡兒上	gear shift **tóu dǎng**	头档 頭檔
off ramp **lí kāi xié pō**	离开斜坡 離開斜坡	intermediate gear **èr dǎng**	二档 二檔

third gear **sān dǎng**	三档 三檔	
top gear **gāo sù dǎng**	高速档 高速檔	
straight **zhí zǒu; wǎng qián**	直走；往前 直走；往前	
pressed for time **gǎn shí jiān**	赶时间 趕時間	
drive faster **kāi kuài yì diǎnr**	开快一点儿 開快一點兒	
turning **zhuǎn xiàng**	转向 轉向	
turn right **yòu zhuǎn**	右转 右轉	
turn left **zuó zhuǎn**	左转 左轉	
cutting in **zhōng jiān chā duì**	中间插队 中間插隊	
road barrier **lù zhàng**	路障 路障	
about **diào tóu; huí zhuǎn**	调头；回转 調頭；迴轉	
short-cut **chāo jìn lù**	抄近路 抄近路	
yield; give way **ràng lù**	让路 讓路	
right of way **yōu xiān xíng shǐ**	优先行驶 優先行駛	
change up **jiā sù**	加速 加速	
speed variable **biàn sù**	变速 變速	
change down **jiǎn sù**	减速 減速	
neutral gear **kōng dǎng**	空档 空檔	
reversing gear **dào chē dǎng**	倒车档 倒車檔	
reversing turn **dào tuì zhuǎn wān**	倒退转弯 倒退轉彎	

engage handbrake **lā-shou shā chē**	拉手煞车 拉手煞車
emergency brake **jǐn jí shā chē**	紧急煞车 緊急煞車
engine failure **jī jiàn shī líng**	机件失灵 機件失靈
brake failure **shā chē bù líng**	煞车不灵 煞車不靈
brake fluid **shā chē yóu**	煞车油 煞車油
car broke down **pāo máo**	抛锚 拋錨
my car had stalled **chē fā dòng bù qǐ lái**	車發動不起來 車發動不起來
conked-out **fā dòng shī líng**	发动失灵 發動失靈
engine failure **yǐn qíng gù zhàng**	引擎故障 引擎故障
turn off engine **xí huǒ**	熄火 熄火
pull over **kào biān tíng**	靠边停 靠邊停
pull to the curb **kào mǎ lù biānr tíng**	靠马路边儿停 靠馬路邊兒停
red highway flare **pāo máo xìn hào dēng**	抛锚信号灯 拋錨信號燈
load limit **zài zhòng xiàn zhì**	载重限制 載重限制
overloading **chāo zài**	超载 超載
speed limit **sù dù xiàn zhì**	速度限制 速度限制
excessive speed **chāo sù**	超速 超速
illegal passing **wéi guī chāo chē**	违规超车 違規超車
go through stop light **chuǎng hóng dēng**	闯红灯 闖紅燈
disobeying traffic light **qiǎng huáng dēng**	抢黄灯 搶黃燈

random honking **luàn àn lǎ-ba**	乱按喇叭 亂按喇叭	collision **zhuàng chē**	撞车 撞車
illegal parking **rèn yì tíng chē**	任意停车 任意停車	head-on-collision **yíng mìan xiāng zhuàng**	迎面相撞 迎面相撞
got a ticket **kāi gào fā dān**	开告发单 開告發單	knock over; ram **zhuàng dǎo**	撞倒 撞倒
towaway **tuō diào**	拖吊 拖吊	car accident **chē huò**	车祸 車禍
identification card (I.D.) **shēn fèn zhèng**	身份证 身份證	run over **yā guò**	压过 壓過
fine **fá kuǎn**	罚款 罰款	knock down **zhuàng sǐ**	撞死 撞死
license revoke **zhí zhào diào xiāo**	执照吊销 執照吊銷	casualties **shāng wáng**	伤亡 傷亡
suspended **zhí zhào kòu yā**	执照扣押 執照扣押	a chain collision **lián huán zhuàng**	连环撞 連環撞
license plate **chē pái**	车牌 車牌	hit-run driver **sī jī zhuàng rén ér táo**	司机撞人而逃 司機撞人而逃
driver's license **jià shǐ zhí zhào**	驾驶执照 駕駛執照	all-risk insurance **bǎo qüán xiǎn**	保全险 保全險
international driver's license **guó jì jià shǐ zhí zhào**	国际驾驶执照 國際駕駛執照	car insurance policy **qì chē báo xiǎn dān**	汽车保险单 汽車保險單
learning permit **xüé xí zhí zhào**	学习执照 學習執照	rush hours **jiān fēng shí jiān**	尖峰时间 尖峰時間
driving without a license **wú zhào jià shǐ**	无照驾驶 無照駕駛	traffic; traffic flow **jiāo tōng liàng**	交通量 交通量
careless driving **cū xīn jià shǐ**	粗心驾驶 粗心駕駛	traffic jam **jiāo tōng yōng jǐ**	交通拥挤 交通擁擠
dangerous driving **wéi xiǎn jià shǐ**	危险驾驶 危險駕駛	jampacked; clogged up **sāi chē**	塞车 塞車
drive under influence **jiǔ zuì jià shǐ**	酒醉驾驶 酒醉駕駛	get stuck in traffic **kǎ-zai chē zhèn zhōng**	卡在车阵中 卡在車陣中
breath tester **jiǔ cè qì**	酒测器 酒測器	traffic could not move **chē-zi dòng-tan bù dé**	车子动弹不得 車子動彈不得
slight impact **qīng wéi zhuàng pèng**	轻微撞碰 輕微撞碰	over crowded **yōng jǐ bù kān**	拥挤不堪 擁擠不堪
crashed into **zhuàng rù**	撞入 撞入		

Auto Body & Parts
車身與零件

auto; automobile qì chē	汽车 汽車（簡稱）	driving light zhào yüǎn dēng	照远灯 照遠燈
body chē shēn	车身 車身	turning light fāng xiàng dēng	方向灯 方向燈
parts líng jiàn	零件 零件	flasher; blinker shǎn guāng dēng	闪光灯 閃光燈
accessories fù jiàn	附件 附件	back light dào chē dēng	倒车灯 倒車燈
frame chē jià	车架 車架	rear blinker zhuǎn wān zhǐ shì dēng	转弯指示灯 轉彎指示燈
chassis dǐ pán	底盘 底盤	fog light wù dēng	雾灯 霧燈
base assembly dǐ ké	底壳 底殼	dome lamp dǐng dēng	顶灯 頂燈
bumper báo xǐng gàng	保险杠 保險槓	stop light tíng chē dēng	停车灯 停車燈
flagstaff qí gǎn	旗杆 旗桿	hood chē tóu zhào	车头罩 車頭罩
rearview mirror zhào hòu jìng	照后镜 照後鏡	horn lǎ-ba	喇叭 喇叭
side mirror cè jìng	侧镜 側鏡	front spoiler dǎng fēng bǎn	挡风板 擋風板
headlight qián zhào dēng	前照灯 前照燈	windshield dǎng fēng chuāng	挡风窗 擋風窗
taillight wěi dēng; hòu dēng	尾灯；后灯 尾燈；後燈	sun visor zhē yáng bǎn	遮阳板 遮陽板
dim light àn guāng dēng	暗光灯 暗光燈	glare shield dǎng guāng bǎn	挡光板 擋光板
dimmer biàn dēng guāng	变灯光 變燈光	safety glass ān qüán bō-li	安全玻璃 安全玻璃

layered glass jiá céng bō-li	夹层玻璃 夾層玻璃		trunk hòu xíng-li xiāng	后行李箱 後行李箱
shatterproof glass fáng suì bō-li	防碎玻璃 防碎玻璃		trunk lip xíng-li xiāng gài	行李箱盖 行李箱蓋
antenna mast tiān xiàn gǎn	天线杆 天線桿		top chē dǐng	车顶 車頂
windshield wiper yǔ guā-zi	雨刮子 雨刮子		luggage carriage chē dǐng xíng-li jià	车顶行李架 車頂行李架
wiper control yǔ guā-zi kāi guān	雨刮子开关 雨刮子開關		main shaft zhǔ zhóu	主轴 主軸
ventilating glass qián dōu fēng chuāng	前兜风窗 前兜風窗		shift biàn sù gǎn	变速杆 變速桿
side vent sān-jiaor chuāng	三角儿窗 三角兒窗		brake shā chē	煞车 煞車
front seat qián-zuòr	前座儿 前座兒		hydraulic brake yóu shā chē	油煞车 油煞車
power seat huó dòng zuò-wei	活动座位 活動座位		hand brake shǒu shā chē	手煞车 手煞車
seat belt zuò yǐ ān qüán dài	座椅安全带 座椅安全帶		foot brake jiǎo shā chē	脚煞车 腳煞車
headrest zuò-shang kào tóu zhěn	座上靠头枕 座上靠頭枕		gas saver shěng yóu qì	省油器 省油器
power window diàn dòng chuāng	电动窗 電動窗		starter (car) fā dòng qì	发动器 發動器
auto stereo qì chē shōu yīn jī	汽车收音机 汽車收音機		clutch lí hé qì	离合器 離合器
auto TV qì chē diàn shì jī	汽车电视机 汽車電視機		pedal tà bǎnr	踏板儿 踏板兒
steering wheel fāng xiàng pán	方向盘 方向盤		accelerator yóu ménr	油门儿 油門兒
glove compartment shǒu tàor zá wù xiāng	手套儿杂物箱 手套兒雜物箱		carburetor huà yóu qì	化油器 化油器
accelerator pedal yóu-menr tà-banr	油门儿踏板儿 油門兒踏板兒		engine yǐn qíng	引擎 引擎
tonneau hòu chē shēn	后车身 後車身		cylinder qì gāng	汽缸 汽缸
back seat hòu-zuòr	后座儿 後座兒		crankshaft qū zhóu	曲轴 曲軸
grab handles tóu dǐng wò-ba	头顶握把 頭頂握把		flywheel fēi lún	飞轮 飛輪

English	简体 / 繁體	Pinyin
ring gear	环齿 / 環齒	huán chǐ
housing	飞轮壳儿 / 飛輪殼兒	fēi lún kér
piston	活塞 / 活塞	huó sāi
speedometer	速度表 / 速度表	sù dù biǎo
odometer	计程表 / 計程表	jì chéng biǎo
thermometer	温度计 / 溫度計	wēn dù jì
volt meter	电压表 / 電壓表	diàn yā biǎo
gas gauge	汽油表 / 汽油表	qì yóu biǎo
oil gauge	机油表 / 機油表	jī yóu biǎo
valve	气门 / 氣門	qì mén
spring (elastic)	弹簧 / 彈簧	tán huáng
camshaft	偏心轴 / 偏心軸	piān xīn zhóu
ball bearing	钢珠轴承 / 鋼珠軸承	gāng zhū zhóu chéng
chain	链条 / 鏈條	liàn tiáo
sproket	偏心轴齿轮 / 偏心軸齒輪	piān xīn zhóu chǐ lún
oil pump	机油帮浦 / 機油幫浦	jī yóu bāng-pu
fuel pump	汽油帮浦 / 汽油幫浦	qì yóu bāng-pu
oil filter	机油滤清器 / 機油濾清器	jī yóu lǜ qīng qì
air cleaner	空气滤清器 / 空氣濾清器	kōng qì lǜ qīng qì
regulator	调节器 / 調節器	tiáo jié qì

English	简体 / 繁體	Pinyin
ventilator	通风器 / 通風器	tōng fēng qì
oil breather	机油通气系统 / 機油通氣系統	jī yóu tōng qì xì-tong
manifold	回气管 / 迴氣管	huí qì guǎn
choke	风门 / 風門	fēng mén
muffler	消音器 / 消音器	xiāo yīn qì
radiator	水箱 / 水箱	shuǐ xiāng
fan	风扇 / 風扇	fēng shàn
fan belt	风扇皮带 / 風扇皮帶	fēng shàn pí dài
fuel tank	油箱 / 油箱	yóu xiāng
generator	发电机 / 發電機	fā diàn jī
spark plug	火星塞 / 火星塞	huǒ xīng sāi
cable (wire)	电缆 / 電纜	diàn lǎn
transmission	变速箱 / 變速箱	biàn sù xiāng
front axle	前轴 / 前軸	qián zhóu
spindle	轮轴 / 輪軸	lún zhóu
drive shaft	驱动轴 / 驅動軸	qū dòng zhóu
rear axle	后轴 / 後軸	hòu zhóu
gear	齿轮 / 齒輪	chǐ lún
wheel	车轮 / 車輪	chē lún
hub; nave	轮壳 / 輪殼	lún ké

brake drum **lún gǔ**	轮鼓 輪鼓	tubeless tire **wú nèi tāi lún tāi**	无内胎轮胎 無內胎輪胎
wheel rim **lún biān gāng qüān**	轮边钢圈 輪邊鋼圈	jet nozzle **qì zuǐr**	汽嘴儿 汽嘴兒
rim **lún yán gāng qüān**	轮沿钢圈 輪沿鋼圈	fender **dǎng ní bǎnr**	挡泥板儿 擋泥板兒
wheel hub **chē zhóu ké**	车轴壳 車軸殼	piston pin **huó sāi zhóu**	活塞轴 活塞軸
tire **chē tāi**	车胎 車胎	dip rod **liáng yóu gǎn**	量油杆 量油桿
tire casing **wài tāi**	外胎 外胎	bolt **luó sī mǔr**	螺丝母儿 螺絲母兒
inner tube **nèi tāi**	内胎 內胎	stud **luó sī zhùr**	螺丝柱儿 螺絲柱兒
spare tire **bèi tāi**	备胎 備胎	nut **luó sī màor**	螺丝帽儿 螺絲帽兒
solid tire **shí xīn lún tāi**	实心轮胎 實心輪胎	washer **diàn qüānr**	垫圈儿 墊圈兒
snow tire **xüě lù lún tāi**	雪路轮胎 雪路輪胎	wheel cover **lún gài**	轮盖 輪蓋

Tools & hardware
工具與五金

lathe **chē chuáng**	车床 車床	power shovel **dòng lì chǎn**	动力铲 動力鏟
toolbox **gōng jù xiāng**	工具箱 工具箱	jackhammer **qì yā záo-zi**	气压凿子 氣壓鑿子
hardware **wǔ jīn**	五金 五金	drill **zuàn**	钻 鑽
pliers **qián-zi**	钳子 鉗子	electric drill **diàn zuàn**	电钻 電鑽
cutting pliers **láo hǔ qián-zi**	老虎钳子 老虎鉗子	plane **bào-zi**	刨子 鉋子
rivet **jiǎo dīng**	铰钉 鉸釘	whetstone **mó dāo shí**	磨刀石 磨刀石
screw **luó-si dīng**	螺丝钉 螺絲釘	file **cuò**	锉 銼
steel nail **gāng dīng**	钢钉 鋼釘	saw **jù**	锯 鋸
nail **dīng-zi**	钉子 釘子	jigsaw **xiàn jù**	线锯 線鋸
3-inch nails **sān cùn dīng**	三寸钉 三吋釘	hook **gōu-zi**	钩子 鉤子
hammer **chuí-zi**	锤子 錘子	shovel **chǎn-zi**	铲子 鏟子
pick hammer **jiān tóur chuí-zi**	尖头儿锤子 尖頭兒錘子	rake **pá-zi**	耙子 耙子
mallet **dà tóu chuí**	大头槌 大頭槌	hoe **chú-tou**	锄头 鋤頭
chisel **záo-zi**	凿子 鑿子	mattock **jiān zuǐ chú**	尖嘴锄 尖嘴鋤
awl **zhuī-zi**	锥子 錐子	screwdriver **gǎi zhuī luó-si qǐ-zi**	改锥;螺丝启子 改錐;螺絲啟子
wheelbarrow **dú lún shǒu tuī chē**	独轮手推车 獨輪手推車	Philips screwdriver **shí zì luó-si dāo**	十字螺丝刀 十字螺絲刀

washer **diàn quānr**	垫圈儿 墊圈兒	sandpaper **shā zhǐ**	砂纸 砂紙
stud **luó-si zhù**	螺丝柱 螺絲柱	corrugated box **wǎ léng zhǐ xiāng**	瓦楞纸箱 瓦楞紙箱
nut **luó-si mǔ**	螺丝母 螺絲母	cardboard box **yìng zhǐ xiāng**	硬纸箱 硬紙箱
bolt **luó shuān**	螺栓 螺栓	pick; pickaxe **shí zì gǎo**	镐 鎬
axe **fǔ tóu**	斧头 斧頭	hacksaw **gōng jù**	弓锯 弓鋸
hatchet **duán bǐng xiáo fǔ-tou**	短柄小斧头 短柄小斧頭	ink trough **mò dǒu**	墨斗 墨斗
level **shuǐ píng chǐ (yí)**	水平尺（仪） 水平尺（儀）	plumb line **chuí xiàn**	锤线 錘線
tape measure **jüán chǐ**	卷尺 捲尺	wire cutter **gāng sī jiǎn**	钢丝剪 鋼絲剪
ruler **chǐ**	尺 尺	flat-head pliers **píng tóu qián-zi**	平头钳子 平頭鉗子
T-square **dīng zì chǐ**	丁字尺 丁字尺	sieve **shāi-zi**	筛子 篩子
protractor **fēn dù qì**	分度器 分度器	screening **guò shāi**	过筛 過篩
crowbar; lever **tiě qiào bàng**	铁撬棒 鐵撬棒	tweezers **niè-zi**	镊子 鑷子
claw-hammer **bá dīng chuí**	拔钉锤 拔釘錘	rope **shéng-zi**	绳子 繩子
tire lever **qiào lún tāi bàng**	撬轮胎棒 撬輪胎棒	string **xì shéngr**	细绳儿 細繩兒
double end wrench **shuāng tóur bān-zi**	双头儿扳子 雙頭兒扳子	pail **tí tǒng**	提桶 提桶
open end wrench **kāi kǒu bān-zi**	开口扳子 開口扳子	bucket **shuí tǒng**	水桶 水桶
monkey wrench **huó bān-shou**	活扳手 活扳手	container **guàn-zi; róng qì**	罐子；容器 罐子；容器
Stillson wrench **shuí guǎn bān-zi**	水管扳子 水管扳子	ladder **tī-zi**	梯子 梯子
adjustable wrench **wàn néng bān-shou**	万能扳手 萬能扳手	welding mask **diàn hàn yǎn zhàor**	电焊眼罩儿 電焊眼罩兒
hinges **hé yè; jiǎo liàn**	合叶；铰炼 合葉；鉸煉		

Do It Yourself
自己動手

damaged	huài-le	坏了 / 壞了
there's a hole in it	pò-le-ge kū-long	破了个窟窿 / 破了個窟窿
loose	sōng-le	松了 / 鬆了
dirty	zāng-le	脏了 / 髒了
wear off	yòng huài-le	用坏了 / 用壞了
abrased	mó huài-le	磨坏了 / 磨壞了
nick	kē hén	刻痕 / 刻痕
crack	liè fèngr	裂缝儿 / 裂縫兒
crazing	liè wén	裂纹 / 裂紋
scratch	guā hén	刮痕 / 刮痕
distorted	biàn xíng-le	变形了 / 變形了
discolored	biàn sè-le	变色了 / 變色了
bended	wān-le	弯了 / 彎了
elongate	bǎ-ta lā cháng	把它拉长 / 把它拉長
blunt	mó dùn-le	磨钝了(用久) / 磨鈍了
dull	chí dùn	钝;不快了 / 鈍;不快了
sharpen	mó kuài	磨快;磨利 / 磨快;磨利
sharp	fēng lì	锋利 / 鋒利
is torn	sī-le	撕了 / 撕了
lopsided; not straight	wāi-le; bú zhèng	歪了;不正 / 歪了;不正
slant	qīng xié; wāi-zhe	倾斜;歪著 / 傾斜;歪著
warpped	juǎn-le; qiào qǐ lái-le	卷了;翘起来了 / 捲了;翹起來了
strip	bō guāng	剥光 / 剝光
abrasion	mó sǔn	磨损 / 磨損
corrosion	fǔ shí	腐蚀 / 腐蝕
weathering	fēng huà	风化 / 風化
deterioration	làn-le	烂了 / 爛了
overaged	lǎo jiù-le	老旧了 / 老舊了
dented	zhuàng biě-le	撞瘪了 / 撞癟了
bumped	zhuàng shàng-le	撞上了 / 撞上了
came off	tuō luò-le; diào-xia-lai-le	脱落了;掉下来了 / 脫落了;掉下來了
got stuck	kǎ zhù-le; yǎo zhù-le	卡住了;咬住了 / 卡住了;咬住了

439

English	Pinyin	Simplified	Traditional
bound up	chán zhù-le; bǎng zhù-le	缠住了；绑住了	纏住了；綁住了
gnawed	jiǎo huài-le; yǎo duàn-le	搅坏了；咬断了	攪壞了；咬斷了
bubbled up	qǐ pào-le	起泡了	起泡了
rusted	shēng xiù-le	生锈了	生鏽了
molded	fā méi-le	发霉了	發黴了
verminated	zhǎng chóng-le	长虫了	長蟲了
deteriorated	biàn zhí-le	变质了	變質了
brake went wrong	shā chē shī líng	煞车失灵	煞車失靈
clogged	dǔ zhù-le	堵住了	堵住了
spilled	sǎ-le	洒了	灑了
tune-up	jiǎn xiū	检修	檢修
alter	xiū gǎi	修改	修改
overhaul	dà xiū	大修	大修
disassemble	chāi-kai	拆开	拆開
install	ān zhuāng	安装	安裝
fix up	tiáo xiū; nòng láo	条修；弄牢	條修；弄牢
attach	fù jiā yǘ; bǎng zài	附加於；绑在	附加於；綁在
cast	zhù zào	铸造	鑄造
weld	hàn jiē	焊接	焊接
solder	diàn hàn	电焊	電焊

English	Pinyin	Simplified	Traditional
plate	diàn dù	电镀	電鍍
alignment	chē lún dìng wèi	车轮定位	車輪定位
repaired tube	bǔ nèi tāi	补内胎	補內胎
reclaim usable parts	chāi líng jiàn yòng	拆零件用	拆零件用
sheet metal	bǎn jīn	板金	板金
spray	pēn qī	喷漆	噴漆
polish	mó guāng	磨光	磨光
waxing	dǎ là	打腊	打蠟
upkeep; check up	báo-yang	保养	保養
car wash	xǐ chē	洗车	洗車
tighten	nòng jǐn	弄紧	弄緊
loosen	fàng sōng	放松	放鬆
lubrication	shàng yóu	上油	上油
lubricant	rùn huá yóu	润滑油	潤滑油
engine oil	jī yóu	机油	機油
grease gun	huáng yóu qiāng	黄油枪	黃油槍
grease	huáng yóu	黄油	黃油
fuel	rán liào	燃料	燃料
adhere	nián	黏	黏
replace	bǔ huàn; bǔ quē	补换；补缺	補換；補缺

change **huàn**	换 換	garage **xiū chē chǎng**	修车厂 修車廠
renew **jiàn xīn; zhěng xīn**	见新；整新 見新；整新	repair shop **wéi xiū chǎng**	维修厂 維修廠
match **xiāng pèi**	相配 相配	repair works **xiū lǐ**	修理 修理
fill one in **bǔ yí-ge**	补一个 補一個	auto-mechanic **xiū chē shī fù**	修车师傅 修車師傅
blow out **bào tāi**	爆胎 爆胎	wrecked car **zhuàng huài-de chē-zi**	撞坏的车子 撞壞的車子
brake drum **lún gǔ**	轮鼓 輪鼓	damaged parts **sǔn huài-de bù-fen**	损坏的部分 損壞的部分
flat tire **lún tāi xiè qì**	轮胎泄气 輪胎泄氣	car lift **jǔ chē jià**	举车架 舉車架
tire gauge **liáng qì biǎo**	量汽表 量汽表	creeper **xiū chē táng bǎnr**	修车躺板儿 修車躺板兒
pressure **yā lì**	压力 壓力	auto crane **qǐ zhòng jī**	起重机 起重機
unsaturated vapor **qì bù zú**	气不足 氣不足	jack **qiān jīn dǐng**	千斤顶 千斤頂
tire pump **dǎ qì tǒng**	打气筒 打氣筒	car wax **qì chē là**	汽车腊 汽車蠟
inflate **dǎ qì**	打气 打氣	distress sign **sān jiáo fǎn guāng biāo zhì**	三角反光标志 三角反光標誌
punctured **zā pò-le**	扎破了 紮破了	trouble light **xiū chē dēng**	修车灯 修車燈
leaking air **lòu qì**	漏气 漏氣	ammeter **diàn liú biǎo**	电流表 電流錶
patching **bǔ tāi**	补胎 補胎	positive plate **zhèng jí piàn**	正极片 正極片
airtight **mì bì-de**	密闭的 密閉的	negative plate **fù jí piàn**	负极片 負極片
assembling plant **zhuāng pèi gōng chǎng**	装配工厂 裝配工廠	auto battery **qì chē diàn píng**	汽车电瓶 汽車電瓶
assemble **zhuāng pèi**	装配 裝配	electrolyte **diàn píng yào shuǐ**	电瓶药水 電瓶藥水
ran out of **cún huò yòng guāng-le**	存货用光了 存貨用光了	storage battery **xù diàn chí**	蓄电池 蓄電池

Related Terms: Group 33C, 音响 Audio;
Group 10H, 家庭电器用品 Household Electric Appliances

Real Estate & Building Maetrials

房地產與建材

English	简体	繁體
construction **jiàn zhú**	建筑	建築
materials **jiàn cái**	建材	建材
building **lóu fáng; dà lóu**	楼房；大楼	樓房；大樓
high-rises **dà gāo lóu**	大高楼	大高樓
skycraper **mó tiān lóu**	摩天楼	摩天樓
castle **chéng bǎo**	城堡	城堡
palace **huáng gōng**	皇宫	皇宮
mansion **dà shà; dǐ**	大厦；邸	大廈；邸
duplex **shuāng pīn shì lóu fang**	双拼式楼房	雙拼式樓房
split-level house **shān pō cuò céng shì lóu**	山坡错层式楼	山坡錯層式樓
separate entrance **mén hù dú lì**	门户独立	門戶獨立
one unit **yí hù**	一户	一戶
a 10-storied building **shí céng gāo lóu**	十层高楼	十層高樓
a flat **yì zhěng céng lóu**	一整层楼	一整層樓
gate **dà jiē mén**	大街门	大街門

English	简体	繁體
revolving door **xuán zhuǎn mén**	旋转门	旋轉門
elevator; lift **diàn tī**	电梯	電梯
odd stop (elevator) **féng dān diàn tī**	逢单电梯	逢單電梯
even stop (elevator) **féng shuāng diàn tī**	逢双电梯	逢雙電梯
escalator **diàn fú tī**	电扶梯	電扶梯
is out of order **huài-le**	坏了	壞了
use the stairway **qíng zǒu lóu tī**	请走楼梯	請走樓梯
stairway; stairs; staircase **lóu tī**	楼梯	樓梯
banister; handrail **lóu tī fú-shou**	楼梯扶手	樓梯扶手
platform **píng tái**	平台	平臺
balcony **yáng tái**	阳台	陽臺
steps **jiē tī; tái jiē**	阶梯；台阶	階梯；臺階
front steps **dà mén tái jiēr**	大门台阶儿	大門臺階兒
door **mén**	门	門
doorframe **mén kuāng**	门框	門框

English	Simplified	Traditional
sliding door **lā ménr**	拉门儿	拉門兒
screen door **shā ménr**	纱门儿	紗門兒
folding door **zhé ménr**	摺门儿	摺門兒
doorknob; door handle **mén shǒu-ba**	门把手	門把手
skylight; dormer window **tiān chuāng**	天窗	天窗
window **chuāng-hu**	窗户	窗戶
venetian blinds **bǎi yè chuāng**	百叶窗	百葉窗
bamboo shade **zhú lián**	竹帘	竹簾
wall-size window **dà xíng luò dì chuāng**	大型落地窗	大型落地窗
a pane of glass **yí shàn bō-li**	一扇玻璃	一扇玻璃
tempered glass **qiáng huà bō-li**	强化玻璃	強化玻璃
ceiling **tiān huā bǎn**	天花板	天花板
roof garden **wū dǐng huā yüán**	屋顶花园	屋頂花園
build; construct **jiàn zào**	建造	建造
remodeling; renovate **zhuāng xiū**	装修	裝修
wooden material **mù liào**	木料	木料
lumber **mù-cai**	木材	木材
wood plank **mù bǎn**	木板	木板
thickness **hòu dù**	厚度	厚度
plywood **sān jiá bǎn**	三夹板	三夾板

English	Simplified	Traditional
four (feet) by eight **sì chǐ cháng bā chǐ kuān**	四尺长八尺宽	四呎長八呎寬
parquet floor **pīn huā dì bǎn**	拼花地板	拼花地板
roof **wū dǐng**	屋顶	屋頂
roof ridge **wū jǐ**	屋脊	屋脊
eaves **wū yán**	屋檐	屋簷
beam **fáng liáng**	房梁	房樑
pillar **zhù-zi**	柱子	柱子
stone **shí**	石	石
marble **dà lǐ shí**	大理石	大理石
roof tile **wǎ**	瓦	瓦
land **tǔ dì**	土地	土地
ground **dì miàn**	地面	地面
concrete foundation **shuǐ ní dì jī**	水泥地基	水泥地基
tile **dì zhuān; cí zhuān**	地砖；瓷砖	地磚；瓷磚
brick **zhuān**	砖	磚
cement **shuǐ ní**	水泥	水泥
lime **shí huī**	石灰	石灰
paint **yóu qī**	油漆	油漆
tung oil **tóng yóu**	桐油	桐油
rosin; colophony **sōng xiāng**	松香	松香

English	Pinyin	Chinese (Simplified)	Chinese (Traditional)
retinal; rosin oil	sōng xiāng yóu	松香油	松香油
turpentine	sōng jié yóu	松节油	松節油
graphite	shí mò	石墨	石墨
con crete	hǔn níng tǔ	混凝土	混凝土
pitch; asphalt; tar	lì qīng; bó yóu	沥青;柏油	瀝青;柏油
wall	qiáng	墙	牆
wall foundation	qiáng jī	墙基	牆基
bounding wall	wéi qiáng	围墙	圍牆
partition	gé jiān	隔间	隔間
passage way	tōng dào	通道	通道
hall; hallway	guò dào	过道	過道
porch; corridor	zǒu láng	走廊	走廊
yard	yüàn-zi	院子	院子
courd yard	tíng yüàn	庭院	庭院
backyard	hòu yüànr	後院儿	後院兒
awning	liáng péng; yáng peng	凉蓬;阳蓬	涼蓬;陽蓬
canopy	tiān péng; yǔ péng	天棚;雨棚	天棚;雨棚
veranda	liáng tái; yóu láng	凉台;游廊	涼臺;遊廊
pergola	tíng-zi	亭子	亭子
rail	lán gān	栏杆	欄杆

English	Pinyin	Chinese (Simplified)	Chinese (Traditional)
lotus pond	hé huā chí	荷花池	荷花池
fountain	pēn qüán	喷泉	噴泉
garden	huā yüán	花园	花園
rockery	jiǎ shān	假山	假山
swimming pool	yóu yǒng chí	游泳池	游泳池
chimney	yān cōng	烟囱	煙囱
hydrant	xiāo fáng shuān	消防栓	消防栓
ditch	yīn gōu	阴沟	陰溝
drainage	xià shuǐ dào	下水道	下水道
farmhouse	nóng shè	农舍	農舍
fence	lí-ba	篱笆	籬笆
bamboo fence	zhú lí-ba	竹篱笆	竹籬笆
hedge	shù lí-ba	树篱笆	樹籬笆
barn	gǔ cāng	谷仓	穀倉
log cabin; wooden house	mù wū	木屋	木屋
tin roof shack	tiě pí wū	铁皮屋	鐵皮屋
warehouse	cāng kù	仓库	倉庫
stable	mǎ fáng	马房	馬房
garage	chē fáng; chē kù	车房;车库	車房;車庫
a lot	yí kuài tǔ dì	一块土地	一塊土地

property owner yè zhǔ	业主 業主	real estate bú dòng chǎn	不动产 不動產
land owner dì zhǔ	地主 地主	house property fáng chǎn	房产 房產
title of ownership suó yǒu qüán zhuàng	所有权状 所有權狀	transfer guò hù	过户 過戶
contract qì yüē	契约 契約	register of transfer guò hù dēng jì	过户登记 過戶登記
blue print lán tú	蓝图 藍圖	execution of contract qì yüē shēng xiào	契约生效 契約生效
decoratuon zhuāng huáng	装潢 裝潢	mortgage yā; dǐ yā	押；抵押 押；抵押
contract hé-tong	合同 合同	trust deed diǎn qì	典契 典契
party A jiǎ fāng	甲方 甲方	redemption shú huí fáng wū	赎回房屋 贖回房屋
party B yǐ fāng	乙方 乙方	witness jiàn zhèng rén	见证人 見證人
duplicate fù běn	副本 副本	delinquency huǐ yüē	毁约 毀約
personal property sī chǎn; dì chǎn	私产；地产 私產；地產	option xù yüē	续约 續約
movable effects dòng chǎn	动产 動產	default wéi yüē	违约 違約

Related Terms: Group 43B, 住哪儿？Where do you live?
Group 49B, 工具与五金 Tools & Hardware

An Appointment
With A Doctor
掛號看病

hospital yī yüàn	医院 醫院	medical record number bìng lì hào mǎr	病历号码儿 病歷號碼兒
clinic zhén suǒ	诊所 診所	which department nǎ-yi kē	哪一科 哪一科
patient bìng rén	病人 病人	is booked up for today jīn tiān guà hào yí mǎn	今天挂号已满 今天掛號已滿
sick; ill bìng-le	病了 病了	make an appointment with guà X dài-fu-de hào	…挂 X 大夫的号 掛 X 大夫的號
outpatient mén zhěn bìng rén	门诊病人 門診病人	not diagnosing patients toda tā jīn-tian bú kàn zhěn	y他今天不看诊 他今天不看诊
I want to see the doctor wǒ yòu kàn bìng	我要看病 我要看病	the physician in charge zhǔ zhì yī shī	主治医师 主治醫師
which doctor nǎ wèi yī shī	哪位医师？ 哪位醫師？	Dr. X is diagnosing today X dài-fu jīn-tian zhú zhěn	X 大夫今天主诊 X 大夫今天主診
make an appointment guà hào	挂号 掛號	make pre-appointments yǜ yüē guà hào	预约挂号 預約掛號
first visit chū zhěn	初诊 初診	I used to see Dr. X. wó yǐ qián shì kàn X dài-fu	我以前是看 X 大夫 我以前是看 X 大夫
registration chū zhěn guà hào (dēng jì)	初诊挂号(登记) 初診掛號	not very professional bú tài zhuān yè	不太专业 不太專業
fill out your personal data tián chū zhěn biǎo	填初诊表 填初診表	change my appointment gǎi yí xià yǜ yüē shí jiān	改一下预约时间 改一下預約時間
identification card (ID) shēn-fen zhèng	身分证 身分證	with another doctor huàn qí tā yī shēng	换其他医生 換其他醫生
medical insurance card jiàn báo kǎ	健保卡 健保卡	designated doctor zhǐ dìng yī shēng	指定医师 指定醫師
have insurance yǒu báo xiǎn	有保险 有保險	for your illness nǐ-de bìng yīng gāi	你的病应该… 你的病應該…
subsequent visit fù zhěn	复诊 複診	your appointment is yǜ yüē guà hào rì qí	预约挂号日期 預約掛號日期

for next Friday (See P.387)	订在下星期五	pill	药丸儿
dìng-zai xià xīng qí wǔ	訂在下星期五	yào wánr	藥丸兒
eight-fifteen A.M. (See P.390)	下午八点一刻	tablet; troche	药片儿; 锭
xià-wu bā-dian yí kè	下午八點一刻	yào piànr; dìng	藥片兒; 錠
cancel the appointment	取消挂号	capsule	胶囊
qǔ xiāo guà hào	取消掛號	jiāo náng	膠囊
couldn't come	有事没能来	julep	糖浆药水
yǒu shì méi néng lái	有事沒能來	táng jiāng yào shuǐ	糖漿藥水
didn't show up	没露面儿	shake before use	服前摇瓶
méi lòu miànr	沒露面兒	fú qián yáo píng	服前搖瓶
after your diagnosis	看完病以后	tablespoonful	一满汤匙
kàn wán bìng yǐ hòu	看完病以後	yì mǎn tāng chí	一滿湯匙
pay at the Cashier's	到收费处付费	fasting	空腹
dào shōu fèi chù fù fèi	到收費處付費	kōng fù	空腹
want to see an oculist	要看眼科医生	before breakfast	早餐前服用
yào kàn yǎn kē yī shēng	要看眼科醫生	zǎo cān qián fú yòng	早餐前服用
see a psychiatrist	看心理医师	before going to bed	睡前服用
kàn xīn lǐ yī shī	看心理醫師	shuì qián fú yòng	睡前服用
see an E.N.T. doctor	看耳鼻喉科医生	AC (ante cibum)	饭前
kàn ěr bí hóu kē yī shēng	看耳鼻喉科醫生	fàn qián	飯前
see a pediatrician	看小儿科医生	before meal	饭前服用
kàn xiǎo ér kē yī shēng	看小兒科醫生	fàn qián fú yòng	飯前服用
internal medicine department	内科门诊	PC (post cibum)	饭后
nèi kē mén zhěn	內科門診	fàn hòu	飯後
please take a seat	请坐下来	after meal	饭后服用
qǐng zuò-xia-lai	請坐下來	fàn hòu fú yòng	飯後服用
please wait here	请在这儿等	2hrs. P.C. (post cibum)	饭后两小时
qǐng zài zhèr děng	請在這兒等	fàn hòu liǎng xiǎo shí	飯後兩小時
you'll be called	医生会叫你的	between meals	两餐之间服用
yī shēng huì jiào-ni-de	醫生會叫你的	liǎng cān zhī jiān fú yòng	兩餐之間服用
to apply; to smear	敷药; 涂抹	every other hour	每隔一小时
fū yào; tú mǒ	敷藥; 塗抹	měi gé yì xiǎo shí	每隔一小時
ointment	药膏	twice a day	每日两次
yào gāo	藥膏	měi rì liǎng cì	每日兩次
not to be taken	忌食	three times a day	每日三次
jì shí	忌食	měi rì sān cì	每日三次
see indication	见说明书	alternate day	隔日
jiàn shuō míng shū	見說明書	gé rì	隔日
internal use	内服	alternate night	隔夜
nèi fú	內服	gé yè	隔夜

Outpatient, Emergency Cases & Hospitalization

門診、急診與住院

| medical center | 医疗中心 | wheelchair | 轮椅 |
| yī liáo zhōng xīn | 醫療中心 | lún yǐ | 輪椅 |

| general hospital | 综合医院 | ambulance | 救护车 |
| zòng hé yī yüàn | 綜合醫院 | jiù hù chē | 救護車 |

| sanitarium | 疗养院 | critical care | 紧急病患处 |
| liáo yǎng yüàn | 療養院 | jǐn jí bìng huàn chù | 緊急病患處 |

| reception desk | 询问处 | car accident | 车祸 |
| xún wèn chù | 詢問處 | chē huò | 車禍 |

| outpatient clinic | 门诊部 | hospitalization | 住院 |
| mén zhěn bù | 門診部 | zhù yüàn | 住院 |

| waiting room | 候诊室 | accident victims | 事故伤患 |
| hòu zhěn shì | 候診室 | shì gù shāng huàn | 事故傷患 |

| emergency case | 急诊 | in case of fire | 万一失火 |
| jí zhěn | 急診 | wàn yī shī huǒ | 萬一失火 |

| emergency hospital | 急诊室 | fire broke out | 发生大火 |
| jí zhěn shì | 急診室 | fā shēng dà huǒ | 發生大火 |

| sign the application | 申请表签字 | caught on fire | 著火了 |
| shēn qíng biǎo qiān zì | 申請表簽字 | zháo huǒ-le | 著火了 |

| the Relief | 救济单位 | self-immolation | 自焚 |
| jiù-ji dān wèi | 救濟單位 | zì fén | 自焚 |

| city sanitation department | 市卫生局 | the calls for help | 求救讯号 |
| shì wèi shēng jú | 市衛生局 | qiú jiù xùn hào | 求救訊號 |

| first aid | 急救 | use stairwell to leave | 爬逃生梯离开 |
| jí jiù | 急救 | pá táo shēng tī lí kāi | 爬逃生梯離開 |

| first aid kit | 急救包 | the tragic accident | 不幸意外 |
| jí jiù bāo | 急救包 | bú xìng yì wài | 不幸意外 |

| artificial respiration | 人工呼吸 | suffered from | 遭受 |
| rén gōng hū xī | 人工呼吸 | zāo shòu | 遭受 |

| stretchers | 担架 | burn by fire | 烧伤 |
| dān jià | 擔架 | shāo shāng | 燒傷 |

third degree burn sān dù tàng shāng	三度烫伤 三度燙傷
superficial burn biǎo pí shāo shāng	表皮烧伤 表皮燒傷
scalded by boiling water tàng shāng	烫伤 燙傷
a pain killer zhǐ tòng yào	止痛药 止痛藥
the rescue teams jiù nàn duì yüán	救难队员 救難隊員
the victim bìng huàn; shāng huàn	病患；伤患 病患；傷患
sympathy for the victims tóng qíng shòu nàn zhě	同情受难者 同情受難者
survivors of the disaster zāi nàn shēng huán zhě	灾难生还者 災難生還者
killed from fume immolation wǎ sī zhòng dú	瓦斯中毒 瓦斯中毒
alcoholism; alcoholic jiǔ jīng zhòng dú	酒精中毒 酒精中毒
poured acid on him bèi pō liú (yán) suān	被泼硫（盐）酸 被潑硫（鹽）酸
was stabbed bèi tǒng-le yì dāo	被捅了一刀 被捅了一刀
was beaten to death huó huó-de gěi dá-si-le	活活的给打死了 活活的給打死了
SARS jí xìng hū xī dào zhèng hòu qún	急性呼吸道症候群 急性呼吸道症候群
commited suicide zì shā	自杀 自殺
took poison fú dú	服毒 服毒
committed harakiri qiē fù	切腹 切腹
cut his own wrist gē wàn	割腕 割腕
strangled before help could reach him sòng yī qián jiù lēi-si-le	送医前就勒死了 送醫前就勒死了
hung oneself shàng diào	上吊 上吊

abused oneself zì cán	自残 自殘
shot oneself kāi qiāng zì shā	开枪自杀 開槍自殺
Russian roulette suicide É shì Zuǒ Lún zì shā	俄式左轮自杀 俄式左輪自殺
jumped from a bridge tiào hé	跳河 跳河
jumped from a building tiào lóu	跳楼 跳樓
fracture of bone gǔ zhé	骨折 骨折
unconsciousness hūn mí bù xǐng	昏迷不醒 昏迷不醒
concussion nǎo zhèn dàng	脑震荡 腦震盪
brain death náo sǐ	脑死 腦死
was struck by lightning bèi shǎn diàn jí zhòng-le	被闪电击中了 被閃電擊中了
my heart gave a violent bound Xīn měng tiào-yi-xia	心猛跳了一下 心猛跳了一下
died instantly dāng cháng sǐ wáng	当场死亡 當場死亡
unconscious bù xǐng rén shì	不省人事 不省人事
regained consciousness xǐng guò-lai-le	省过来了 省過來了
recuperate fù yüán zhōng	复原中 復原中
recovered kāng fù-le	康复了 康復了
resuscitated jiù huó-le	救活了 救活了
is dying yào sǐ	要死 要死
in critical condition bìng qíng wéi jí	病情危急 病情危急
struggling to survive yǔ sǐ shén bó dòu	与死神搏斗 與死神搏鬥

bedridden wò bìng zài chuáng	卧病在床	臥病在床
died of cancer sǐ yǔ ái zhèng	死於癌症	死於癌症
blood transfusion shū xiě	输血	輸血
oxygen tank yǎng qì tǒng	氧气桶	氧氣桶
oxygen mask yǎng qì zhào	氧气罩	氧氣罩
liquid air yè tǐ kōng qì	液体空气	液體空氣

住院 hospitalization

pay in advance xiān fù; yù fù	先付；预付	先付；預付
room charges zhù yuàn fèi	住院费	住院費
boarding fees shàn fèi	膳费	膳費
medicine charges yào fèi	药费	藥費
hospital charges yī yào fèi	医药费	醫藥費
doctor's bill yī shī fèi	医师费	醫師費
diagnosis fees zhěn chá fèi	诊察费	診察費
injection fees zhù shè fèi	注射费	注射費
X-ray charges X guāng fèi	X 光费	X 光費
E.E.G. charges yàn nǎo bō fèi	验脑波费	驗腦波費
E.K.G. charges xīn diàn tú fèi	心电图费	心電圖費
cardiac catheterization fees xīn dǎo guǎn jiǎn chá fèi	心导管检查费	心導管檢查費

endoscopy charges nèi shì jìng jiǎn chá fèi	内视镜检查费	內視鏡檢查費
material fees cái liào fèi	材料费	材料費
treatment charges zhì liáo fèi	治疗费	治療費
rehabilitation therapy fù jiàn zhì liáo fèi	复健治疗费	復健治療費
laboratory fees jiǎn yàn fèi	检验费	檢驗費
pathology exam fees bìng lí jiǎn chá fèi	病理检查费	病理檢查費
operation fees shǒu shù fèi	手术费	手術費
operating room charges shǒu shù fáng fèi	手术房费	手術房費
anesthesia fees má zuì fèi	麻醉费	麻醉費
narcotic fees má zuì yào pǐn fèi	麻醉药品费	麻醉藥品費
assistant doctor fees zhù lǐ yī shī fèi	助理医师费	助理醫師費
nursing care fees hù lǐ fèi	护理费	護理費
certificate fees zhěn duàn zhèng míng shū fèi	诊断证明书费	診斷證明書費
special nurse fee tè bié hù-shi fèi	特别护士费	特別護士費
consultation fees huì zhěn fèi	会诊费	會診費
hemodialysis fees xiě yè tòu xī fèi	血液透析费	血液透析費
physical exam fees jiàn kāng jiǎn chá fèi	健康检查费	健康檢查費
miscellaneous fees zá xiàng fèi yòng	杂项费用	雜項費用
has been discharged (ward) chū yuàn-le	出院了	出院了
recuperating at home zài jiā yǎng bìng	在家养病	在家養病

Practicing Medicine Abroad
出國行醫

medical ward **bìng fáng**	病房 病房	ache **téng**	疼 疼（由內部發出）
isolation ward **gé lí bìng fáng**	隔离病房 **隔離病房**	sore **suān tòng**	酸痛 酸痛
intensive care unit **jiā hù bìng fáng**	加护病房 加護病房	vomiting **ǒu tù**	呕吐 嘔吐
public ward **pǔ tōng bìng fáng**	普通病房 普通病房	feel nauseous **ě xīn**	噁心 噁心
private ward **tè bié bìng fáng**	特别病房 特別病房	chilly feeling **fā lěng**	发冷 發冷
admission **zhù yüàn shǒu xù**	住院手续 住院手續	shivering **fā dǒu**	发抖 發抖
is hospitalized **zhù yüàn-le**	住院了 住院了	inflammation **fā yán**	发炎 發炎
sickbed **bìng chuáng**	病床 **病床**	instrument cabinet **shǒu shù qì cái guì**	手术器材柜 手術器材櫃
clinic chart **bìng lì**	病历 病歷	cotton holder **mián-hua zhōng**	棉花盅 棉花盅
superintendent of nurse **hù lí zhǔ rèn**	护理主任 護理主任	alcohol **jiǔ jīng**	酒精 酒精
head nurse **hù-shi zhǎng**	护士长 護士長	sanitary cotton **wèi shēng mián-hua**	卫生棉花 衛生棉花
nurse **hù-shi**	护士 護士	absorbent cotton; cotton wool 药棉花 **yào mián-hua**	藥棉花
resident doctor **zhù yüàn yī shēng**	住院医生 住院醫生	sterile gauze **xiāo dú shā bù**	消毒纱布 消毒紗布
intern **jiàn xí yī shēng**	见习医生 見習醫生	adhesive tape **jiāo bù**	胶布 膠布
consultation **huì zhěn**	会诊 會診	ice bag **bīng dài**	冰袋 冰袋

English	Chinese (Simplified)	Chinese (Traditional)
icecap bīng mào	冰帽	冰帽
ice pillow bīng zhěn	冰枕	冰枕
hot water bag rè shuǐ dài	热水袋	熱水袋
give him a shot dǎ-yi zhēn	打一针	打一針
injection zhù shè	注射	注射
syringe dǎ zhēn tǒng	打针筒	打針筒
needle zhēn tóu	针头	針頭
hypodermic injection pí xià zhù shè	皮下注射	皮下注射
intravenous injection jìng mài zhù shè	静脉注射	靜脈注射
an intravenous drip dá diǎn dī	打点滴	打點滴
normal saline shēng lǐ yán shuǐ	生理盐水	生理鹽水
glucose; dextrose pú-tao táng	葡萄糖	葡萄糖
iron element tiě zhí	铁质	鐵質
smallpox vaccine niú dòu miáo	牛痘苗	牛痘苗
cholera vaccine huò luàn jùn miáo	霍乱菌苗	霍亂菌苗
pertussis vaccine bǎi rì ké jùn miáo	百日咳菌苗	百日咳菌苗
Bacillus Calmette-Guerin kǎ jiè miáo	卡介苗	卡介苗
virus lǜ guò xìng bìng dú	滤过性病毒	濾過性病毒
transplant yì tǐ yí zhí	异体移植	異體移植
blood xiě	血	血
take a blood sample chōu xiě	抽血	抽血
blood type; blood group xiě xíng	血型	血型
plasma xiě jiāng	血浆	血漿
dextran dài xiě jiāng	代血浆	代血漿
swell; swollen zhǒng; zhǒng-le	肿;肿了	腫;腫了
change the dressing huàn yào	换药	換藥
mind healing jīng shén zhì liáo	精神治疗	精神治療
electrotherapy diàn qì zhì liáo	电气治疗	電氣治療
natural healing zì rán zhì liáo	自然治疗	自然治療
treatment zhì liáo	治疗	治療
cure zhì bìng	治病	治病
diarrhoea; loose bowels xiè dù	泻肚	瀉肚
suffer from constipation dà biàn bù tōng	大便不通	大便不通
therapy of regularity biàn mì yào	便秘药	便秘藥
bedpan biàn pén	便盆	便盆
urinal niào hú	尿壶	尿壺
healed zhì hǎo-le	治好了	治好了
is well bìng hǎo-le	病好了	病好了
Speedy Recovery! sù yù	速愈	速癒
Get Well Soon! zǎo rì fù yuán	早日复原	早日復原

The Human Body

身體各部

general appearance **wài mào**	外貌 外貌	spinal disk **jí zhuī diàn gǔ**	脊椎垫骨 脊椎墊骨
human body **shēn tǐ**	身体 身體	bone **gǔ-tou**	骨头 骨頭
physique **tǐ gé**	体格 體格	skeleton **gǔ gé**	骨骼 骨骼
naked **luó tǐ**	裸体 裸體	lymph gland **lín bā xiàn**	淋巴腺 淋巴腺
organs **qì guān**	器官 器官	skull **tóu lú**	头颅 頭顱
blood **xiě**	血 血	head **nǎo-dai; tóu**	脑袋；头 腦袋；頭
blood vessel **xié guǎn**	血管 血管	scalp **tóu pí**	头皮 頭皮
pulse **mài**	脉 脈	hair (head) **tóu-fa**	头发 頭髮
flesh **ròu**	肉（人） 肉（人）	body hair **tǐ máo**	体毛 體毛
muscle **jī ròu**	肌肉 肌肉	skin **pí**	皮 皮
ligament **jīn**	筋 筋	light complexion **bái pí-fu**	白皮肤 白皮膚
nerve **shén jīng**	神经 神經	dark complexion **hēi pí-fu**	黑皮肤 黑皮膚
tissue **zǔ zhī**	组织 組織	forehead **qián é**	前额 前額
spine **jí zhuī**	脊椎 脊椎	brain **nǎo-zi**	脑子 腦子
vertebra **dān gēn jí zhuī gǔ**	单根脊椎骨 單根脊椎骨	brain capsule **nǎo suǐ**	脑髓 腦髓

English	Pinyin	Simplified	Traditional
face	liǎn	脸	臉
cheek	sāi bāng-zi	腮帮子	腮幫子
dimple	jiǔ wōr	酒窝儿	酒窩兒
temple	tài yáng xüè	太阳穴	太陽穴
eyebrow	méi-mao	眉毛	眉毛
eyelash	jié máo	睫毛	睫毛
eye	yǎn-jing	眼睛	眼睛
tear	yǎn lèi	眼泪	眼淚
eyeball	yǎn qiú	眼球	眼球
eyelid	yán liǎn	眼睑	眼瞼
nose	bí-zi	鼻子	鼻子
philtrum	rén zhōng	人中	人中
lip	zuǐ chún	嘴唇	嘴唇
mouth	zuǐ	嘴	嘴
tongue	shé-tou	舌头	舌頭
taste buds	wèi lěi	味蕾	味蕾
tooth (teeth 复数)	yá	牙	牙
jaw	è	颚	顎
ear	ěr-duo	耳朵	耳朵
earlobe	ěr chuí	耳垂	耳垂
neck	bó-zi	脖子	脖子
collarbone; clavicle	suó gǔ	锁骨	鎖骨
throat	hóu lóng	喉咙	喉嚨
chin	xià-ba	下巴	下巴
lower jaw	xià è	下颚	下顎
Adam's apple	hóu jié	喉结	喉結
whisker	hú xū	胡须	鬍鬚
trunk	shàng shēn; qū gàn	上身；躯干	上身；軀幹
breast	xiōng bù	胸部	胸部
chest	qián xiōng táng	前胸膛	前胸膛
thorax	xiōng qiāng	胸腔	胸腔
diaphragm	héng gé mó	横膈膜	橫膈膜
back	hòu bèi	后背	後背
lung	fèi	肺	肺
windpipe	qì guǎn	气管	氣管
a breast; a bosom	rǔ fáng	乳房	乳房
breast fold	rǔ gōu	乳沟	乳溝
nipple	rǔ tóu	乳头	乳頭
heart	xīn	心	心
cardiac	xīn kǒu	心口	心口

rib lè gǔ	肋骨 肋骨	
waist yāo	腰 腰	
abdomen fù bù	腹部 腹部	
liver gān	肝 肝	
pancreas yí zàng	胰脏 胰臟	
gall bladder dǎn náng	胆囊 膽囊	
spleen pí zàng	脾脏 脾臟	
navel; belly button dù qí	肚脐 肚臍	
belly dù-zi	肚子 肚子	
stomach wèi	胃 胃	
bowels cháng-zi	肠子 腸子	
appendix máng cháng	盲肠 盲腸	
rectum zhí cháng	直肠 直腸	
duodenum shí èr zhǐ cháng	十二指肠 十二指腸	
large intestine dà cháng	大肠 大腸	
crotch kuà bù	胯部 胯部	
groin shǔ xī	鼠蹊 鼠蹊	
inguinal fù gǔ gōu	腹股沟 腹股溝	
pelvis gǔ pén	骨盆 骨盆	
sexual organs xìng qì guān	性器官 性器官	

private parts sī chù; yīn bù	私处；阴部 私處；陰部	
vagina nǚ xìng shēng zhí qì	女性生殖器 女性生殖器	
pussy; cunt; a piece bī	屄 屄	
penis yáng jù; xiǎo biàn	阳具；小便 陽具；小便	
cock; Dick; Peter jī-ba	鸡巴 雞巴	
the balanus; glans penis guī tóu	龟头 龜頭	
wienie xiǎo jī jī	小鸡鸡 小雞雞	
kidney shèn; yāo-zi	肾；腰子 腎；腰子	
bladder páng guāng	膀胱 膀胱	
urethra niào dào	尿道 尿道	
buttock; butt pì-gu	屁股 屁股	
hip tún gǔ	臀骨 臀骨	
anus gāng mén	肛门 肛門	
asshole pì yǎnr	屁眼儿 屁眼兒	
limb; extremity sì zhī	四肢 四肢	
upper extremity shàng zhī	上肢 上肢	
shoulders jiān bǎng	肩膀 肩膀	
shoulder blade; scapula jiān jiá gǔ	肩胛骨 肩胛骨	
ridge bèi jǐ	背脊 背脊	
arm gē-bo	胳膊 胳膊	

armpit	胳肢窝；腋窝	lower extremity	下肢
gē zhī wō; yè wō	胳肢窩；腋窩	xià zhī	下肢
elbow	胳膊肘儿	thigh	大腿
gē-bo zhǒur	胳膊肘兒	dà tuǐ	大腿
wrist	手腕子	knee	膝
shǒu wàn-zi	手腕子	xī	膝
hand	手	knee cap; patella	膝盖
shǒu	手	xī gài	膝蓋
palm	手掌	joint	关节
shóu zhǎng	手掌	guān jié	關節
hand back	手背	leg	腿
shǒu bèi	手背	tuǐ	腿
finger	手指头	ankle	脚腕子；踝
shǒu zhí-tou	手指頭	jiǎo wàn-zi; huái	脚腕子；踝
thumb	大拇指	foot; feet	脚；脚丫子
dà mú zhǐ	大拇指	jiǎo; jiǎo yā-zi	脚；脚丫子
thumbpit	虎口	instep	脚背
hú kǒu	虎口	jiǎo bèi	脚背
index finger	食指	foot sole	脚板
shí zhǐ	食指	jiáo bǎn	脚板
middle finger	中指	arch of the foot	脚掌心
zhōng zhǐ	中指	jiáo zhǎng xīn	脚掌心
ring finger	无名指	heel	后脚跟
wú míng zhǐ	無名指	hòu jiǎo gēn	後脚跟
little finger	小指	toe	脚指头
xiáo zhǐ	小指	jiǎo zhí-tou	脚指頭
knuckle	指节	hallux toe	大脚趾
zhǐ jié	指節	dà jiáo zhǐ	大脚趾
fingerprint	指纹	second toe	二脚趾
zhǐ wén	指紋	èr jiáo zhǐ	二脚趾
whorl of finger	手指涡纹	middle toe	中脚趾
shóu zhǐ wō wén	手指渦紋	zhōng jiáo zhǐ	中脚趾
fingertip	指尖	fourth toe	无名趾
zhǐ jiān	指尖	wú míng zhǐ	無名趾
nail	指甲	little toe	小脚趾
zhī-jia	指甲	xiáo jiáo zhǐ	小脚趾
hangnail	指甲旁刺	toenail	脚指甲
zhī-jia páng cì	指甲旁刺	jiǎo zhī-jia	脚指甲
fist	拳头	bare foot	光脚
qǔan-tou	拳頭	guāng jiǎo	光脚

Dept. Of Internal Medicine, Diseases & Cancer
內科, 疾病與癌症

internal medicine **nèi kē**	内科 內科	disease **jí bìng**	疾病 疾病
physician; doctor **yī shēng; yī shī**	医生;医师 醫生;醫師	have a cold **zhāo liáng-le; shāng fēng**	著凉了;伤风 著涼了;傷風
internist **nèi kē yī shēng**	内科医生 內科醫生	fever; have a temperature **fā shāo**	发烧 發燒
scale **bàng chèng**	磅秤 磅秤	cough **ké-sou**	咳嗽 咳嗽
forehead lamp **é tóu dēng**	额头灯 額頭燈	vertigo **tóu yūn**	头晕 頭暈
clinical thermometer **tǐ wēn jì**	体温计 體溫計	headache **tóu tòng**	头痛 頭痛
rectal thermometer **gāng mén tǐ wēn jì**	肛门体温计 肛門體溫計	acute disease **jí xìng bìng**	急性病 急性病
stethoscope **tīng zhěn qì**	听诊器 聽診器	chronic disease **màn xìng bìng**	慢性病 慢性病
pulse **mài bó**	脉膊 脈膊	carriers of disease **dài yüán zhě**	带原者 帶原者
sphygmometer; pulsimete **mài bó jì**	脉搏计 脈搏計	infectious disease **chuán rǎn bìng**	传染病 傳染病
blood pressure **xiě yā**	血压 血壓	contagious **huì chuán rǎn-de**	会传染的 會傳染的
sphygmomanometer **xiě yā jì**	血压计 血壓計	epidemic **liú xíng xìng chuán rǎn bìng**	流行性传染病 流行性傳染病
hypotension **dī xiě yā**	低血压 低血壓	bird flu **qín liú gǎn**	禽流感 禽流感
hypertension **gāo xiě yā**	高血压 高血壓	suffered from malaria **dá bǎi-zi; nüè jí bìng**	打摆子;疟疾病 打擺子;瘧疾病
suffer from **huàn; dé; shēng**	(病) 患;得;生 患;得;生	SARS(Severe Airway Respiratory Syndrome) 严重呼吸道窘迫症候群 **yán zhòng hū xī dào jiǒng pò zhèng hòu qún**	

twitch; jerk	抽搐；痉挛
chōu chù; jìng lüán	抽搐；痙攣
ALD	肾上腺质白退化症
shèn shàng xiàn zhí bái tuì huà zhèng	
germs	细菌
xì jùn	細菌
attack (germs)	感染
gán rǎn	感染
prevent (cold)	预防
yù fáng	預防（感冒）
bad clod	重感冒
zhòng gǎn mào	重感冒
flu; influenza	流行性感冒
liú xíng xìng gǎn mào	流行性感冒
contagious disease widespread	传染病扩散中
chuán rǎn bìng kuò sàn zhōng	傳染病擴散中
diagnosis	诊断书
zhěn duàn shū	診斷書
rendered his diagnosis	作出诊断
zuò chū zhěn duàn	作出診斷
prescription	处方
chǔ fāng	處方
secondary	续发性
xù fā xìng	續發性
migraine	偏头痛
piān tóu tòng	偏頭痛
hearbeat	心跳
xīn tiào	心跳
tachycardia	心跳过速
xīn tiào guò sù	心跳過速
electrocardiogram	心电图
xīn diàn tú	心電圖
heart disease	心脏病
xīn zàng bìng	心臟病
arrhythmia	心律不整
xīn lǜ bù zhěng	心律不整
heart failure	心脏衰竭
xīn zàng shuāi jié	心臟衰竭
valvular disease	心瓣病
xīn bàn bìng	心瓣病

heartburn; vexation	心痛
xīn tòng	心痛
angina pectoris	心绞痛
xīn jiǎo tòng	心絞痛
infarct	血管梗塞
xié guán gěng sè	血管梗塞
vascular sclerosis	血管硬化
xié guǎn yìng huà	血管硬化
cardiac paralysis	心脏麻痹
xīn zàng má bì	心臟痲痹
myocardial infarction	心肌梗塞
xīn jī gěng sè	心肌梗塞
acute myocardial infarction	急性心肌梗塞
jí xìng xīn jī gěng sè	急性心肌梗塞
cholesterol	胆固醇
dǎn gù chún	膽固醇
capillary	微血管
wéi xiě guǎn	微血管
anemia	贫血
pín xiě	貧血
septic poisoning	败血症
bài xǐe zhèng	敗血症
artery	动脉
dòng mài	動脈
main artery; aorta	大动脉；主动脉
dà dòng mài; zhǔ dòng mài	大動脈；主動脈
vein	静脉
jìng mài	靜脈
large intestine	大肠
dà cháng	大腸
small intestine	小肠
xiǎo cháng	小腸
rectum	直肠
zhí cháng	直腸
duodenum	十二指肠
shí èr zhǐ cháng	十二指腸
duodenal ulcer	十二指肠溃疡
shí èr zhǐ cháng kuì yáng	十二指腸潰瘍
enterodynia	肠痛
cháng tòng	腸痛

intestinal perforation **cháng chuān kǒng**	肠穿孔 腸穿孔	colic **fù jiǎo tòng**	腹绞痛 腹絞痛
intestinal hemorrhage **cháng chū xiě**	肠出血 腸出血	diarrhoea **fù xiè**	腹泻 腹瀉
appendicitis **máng cháng yán**	盲肠炎 盲腸炎	deprivation **tuō shuǐ**	脱水 脱水
acute appendicitis **jí xìng máng cháng yán**	急性盲肠炎 急性盲腸炎	cerebral disease **nǎo bìng**	脑病 腦病
peritoneum **fù mó**	腹膜 腹膜	encephalitis **nǎo yán**	脑炎 腦炎
peritonitis **fù mó yán**	腹膜炎 腹膜炎	meningitis **nǎo mó yán**	脑膜炎 腦膜炎
diaphragm **héng gé mó**	横隔膜 橫隔膜	brain hemorrhage **nǎo yì xiě**	脑溢血 腦溢血
rugae **wèi bì**	胃壁 胃壁	stroke **zhòng fēng; nǎo chōng xiě**	中风；脑充血 中風；腦充血
digestion **xiāo huà**	消化 消化	hemiplegia **bàn shēn bù suí**	半身不遂 半身不遂
digestive system **xiāo huà xì-tong**	消化系统 消化系統	paralysis **tān huàn**	瘫痪 癱瘓
indigestion **xiāo huà bù liáng**	消化不良 消化不良	cerebral paralysis **dà nǎo má bì**	大脑麻痹 大腦痳痹
metabolism **xīn chén dài xiè**	新陈代谢 新陳代謝	cerebral embolism **nǎo shuān sāi zhèng**	脑栓塞症 腦栓塞症
fasting **jìn shí**	禁食 禁食	gout **tòng fēng zhèng**	痛风症 痛風症
vitamin deficiency **qūē fá wéi tā mìng**	缺乏维他命 缺乏維他命	hepatic artery **gān dòng mài**	肝动脉 肝動脈
hyperacidity **wèi suān guò duō**	胃酸过多 胃酸過多	cirrhosis **gān yìng huà**	肝硬化 肝硬化
stomachache **wèi tòng**	胃痛 胃痛	hepatitis **gān yán**	肝炎 肝炎
gastric ulcer **wèi kuì yáng**	胃溃疡 胃潰瘍	nephralgia **shèn bìng**	肾病 腎病
gastric perforation **wèi chuān kǒng**	胃穿孔 胃穿孔	acute nephritis **jí xìng shèn yán**	急性肾炎 急性腎炎
gastric hemorrhage **wèi chū xiě**	胃出血 胃出血	renal calculus **shèn jié shí**	肾结石 腎結石
abdominal pain **dù-zi tòng**	肚子痛 肚子痛	bile; gall **dǎn zhī**	胆汁 膽汁

gall bladder dǎn náng	胆囊 膽囊
jaundice huáng dǎn bìng	黄疸病 黃疸病
icterus index huáng dǎn zhǐ shù	黄疸指数 黃疸指數
cholelithiasis dǎn jié shí	胆结石 膽結石
cystitis; inflammation of the bladder páng guāng yán	膀胱炎 膀胱炎
tuberculosis (TB) fèi jié hé	肺结核 肺結核
consumption fèi bìng	肺病 肺病
pneumonia fèi yán	肺炎 肺炎
vomit blood tù xiě	吐血 吐血
hemoptysis ká xiě	咳血 咳血
vital capacity fèi huó liàng	肺活量 肺活量
pulmonary edema fèi shuí zhǒng	肺水肿 肺水腫
pleurisy xiōng mó yán	胸膜炎 胸膜炎
emphysema qì zhǒng	气肿 氣腫
tracheitis qì guǎn yán	气管炎 氣管炎
bronchitis zhī qì guǎn yán	支气管炎 支氣管炎
bronchiectasis zhī qì guǎn kuò zhāng	支气管扩张 支氣管擴張
pant qì chuǎn	气喘 氣喘
asthma xiāo chuǎn	哮喘 哮喘
progression bìng qíng háo zhuǎn	病情好转 病情好轉

癌症 cancer

cancer (see P.478★,PET) ái　（测癌：正子扫瞄摄影）	癌 癌
sarcoma ròu liú	肉瘤 肉瘤
benignancy liáng xìng	良性 良性
malignant è xìng	恶性 惡性
chemotherapy huà xué liáo fǎ	化学疗法 化學療法
terminal cancer patient ái zhèng mò qí	癌症末期 癌症末期
cancer cells metastasis ái xì bāo zhuǎn yí	癌细胞转移 癌細胞轉移
days are numbered lái rì bù duō	来日不多 來日不多
bronchial tumour zhī qì guán zhǒng liú	支气管肿瘤 支氣管腫瘤
mutation tú biàn	突变 突變
necrosis gǔ jǔ; huài sǐ ròu	骨疽;坏死肉 骨疽;壞死肉
cancer of the esophagus shí dào ái	食道癌 食道癌
gastric carcinoma wèi ái	胃癌 胃癌
pancreatic carcinoma yí zàng ái	胰脏癌 胰臟癌
liver cancer gān ái	肝癌 肝癌
leukemia xiě ái	血癌 血癌
lung cancer fèi ái	肺癌 肺癌
neuroma shén jīng liú	神经瘤 神經瘤

Surgery & Orthopedics 外科與骨科

surgery **wài kē**	外科 外科
surgeon **wài kē yī-sheng**	外科医生 外科醫生
severe wound **zhòng shāng**	重伤 重傷
slight wound **qīng shāng**	轻伤 輕傷
external use **wài fū yào**	外敷药 外敷藥
wound **chuàng shāng**	创伤 創傷
vital injury **zhì mìng shāng**	致命伤 致命傷
scratch **zhuā pò**	抓破 抓破
raw **cā pò pí**	擦破皮 擦破皮
slip wound **dié shāng**	跌伤 跌傷
fall wound **zhuì shāng**	坠伤 墜傷
contuse **dǎ shāng**	打伤 打傷
stab wound **dāo shāng**	刀伤 刀傷
puncture wound **cì shāng**	刺伤 刺傷
bullet wound **dàn shāng**	弹伤 彈傷
bruise **yū shāng**	瘀伤 瘀傷

dull pain **àn shāng**	暗痛 暗痛

 骨科 orthopedics

knee struck against the chair **xī gài zhuàng-shang yǐ-z i**	膝盖撞上椅子 膝蓋撞上椅子
osteocope **jǔ xìng gǔ tòng**	剧性骨痛 劇性骨痛
coccygodynia **wéi gǔ tòng**	尾骨痛 尾骨痛
chondromatosis **ruán gǔ liú bìng**	软骨瘤病 軟骨瘤病
spondylexarthrosis **jí zhuī tuō wèi**	脊椎脱位 脊椎脫位
costectomy **lè gǔ qiē chú**	肋骨切除 肋骨切除
osteoma **nǎo ké liú**	脑壳瘤 腦殼瘤
surgical ward **wài kē bìng fáng**	外科病房 外科病房
operating room **shǒu shù shì**	手术室 手術室
undergo an operation **dòng shǒu shù**	动手术 動手術
major operation **dà shǒu shù**	大手术 大手術
minor operation **xiáo shǒu shù**	小手术 小手術
plastic surgery **zhěng xíng wài kē**	整形外科 整形外科

cosmetic surgery **zhěng róng shǒu shù**	整容手术 整容手術	a pair of scissors **yì-ba jiǎn-zi**	一把剪子 一把剪子
operating coat (cap) **shǒu shù yī (mào)**	手术衣（帽） 手術衣（帽）	a pair of tweezers **yí-ge niè-zi**	一个镊子 一個鑷子
nose jobs **lóng bí**	隆鼻 **隆鼻**	forceps **yī yìng qián-zi**	医用钳子 醫用鉗子
surgical gloves **shǒu shù shǒu tào**	手术手套 手術手套	comminuted fracture **fěn suì gǔ zhé**	粉碎骨折 粉碎骨折
harelip **tù chún**	兔唇 兔唇	skeletal traction **gǔ zhé jiē hé**	骨折接合 骨折接合
facelift **lā pí**	拉皮 拉皮	sciatic **zuò gǔ**	坐骨 坐骨
breast augmentation **lóng rǔ**	隆乳 隆乳	osteoporosis **gǔ zhí shū sōng**	骨质疏松 骨質疏鬆
the 3 measurements **sān wéi**	三围 三圍（女）	calcium deficiency **qūē gài zhí**	缺钙质 缺鈣質
bust measurement **xiōng wéi**	胸围 胸圍	spongy bone **sōng zhí gǔ**	松质骨 鬆質骨
waist measurement **yāo wéi**	腰围 腰圍	compact bone **mì zhí gǔ**	密质骨 密質骨
measurement of hips **tún wéi**	臀围 臀圍	reduction of fracture synthesis **jiē gǔ**	接骨 接骨
figure **shēn duàn**	身段 身段	dislocation **tuō jiù**	脱臼 脫臼
curves **qū xiàn**	曲线 曲線	shoulder joint dislocation **jiān gǔ tuō jiù**	肩骨脱臼 肩骨脫臼
tummy tucks **suō fù**	缩腹 **縮腹**	dislocated jaw **xià bā tuō jiù**	下巴脱臼 下巴脫臼
shadowless lamp **wú yǐng zhào míng dēng**	无影照明灯 無影照明燈	bleeding **liú xiě**	流血 流血
surgical instrument **kāi dāo yòng jù**	开刀用具 開刀用具	blood transfusion **shū xiě**	输血 輸血
percussion hammer **kòu zhěn chuí**	叩诊锤 叩診錘	sutures **féng xiàn**	缝线 縫線
anesthetization **má zuì**	麻醉 麻醉	remove the stitches **chāi xiàn**	拆线 拆線
narcotic anaesthetic **má zuì yào**	麻醉药 麻醉藥	sterilize **xiāo dú**	消毒 消毒
bone saw **gǔ jù**	骨锯 骨鋸	bandaging **bāo zā**	包扎 包紮

bandage **bēng dài**	绷带 繃帶	chondritis **ruán gǔ yán**	软骨炎 軟骨炎
elastic bandage **tán xìng bēng dài**	弹性绷带 彈性繃帶	rickets **kòu lóu bìng**	佝偻病 佝僂病
bandelette **xiǎo bēng dài**	小绷带 小繃帶	periostitis **gǔ mó yán**	骨膜炎 骨膜炎
Sayre's jacket **shí gāo bèi xīn**	石膏背心 石膏背心	marrow; bone marrow **gǔ suí**	骨髓 骨髓
cradle fracture **gǔ zhé zhī jià**	骨折支架 骨折支架	osteomyelitis **gǔ suí yán**	骨髓炎 骨髓炎
gypsum cast **shí gāo mó**	石膏模 石膏模	bone marrow transplant **gǔ suí yí zhí**	骨髓移植 骨髓移植
in traction **diào tuǐ**	吊腿 吊腿	caries **gǔ kuì yáng**	骨溃疡 骨潰瘍
artificial limb **yì zhī**	义肢 義肢	myelitis **jí suí yán**	脊髓炎 脊髓炎
stump **mù tuǐ**	木腿 木腿	gout **gǔ jié tòng**	骨节痛 骨節痛
numb **má mù**	麻木 麻木	osteo-arthritis **guān jié yán**	关节炎 關節炎
deformed **cán fèi-le**	残废了 殘廢了	rheumatism **fēng shī**	风湿 風濕
titubation **pán shān bù xíng**	蹒跚步行 蹣跚步行	gonarthritis **xī guān jié yán**	膝关节炎 膝關節炎
limp **yì qué yì guǎi-de**	一瘸一拐的 一瘸一拐的	bony spur **gǔ cì**	骨刺 骨刺
lame **bó jiǎo; qué-zi**	跛脚；瘸子 跛腳；瘸子	prolapse of the anus **tuō gāng**	脱肛 脱肛
walking stick **guǎi gùnr; shǒu zhàng**	拐棍儿；手杖 拐棍兒；手杖	hernia **shàn qì; xiǎo cháng qì**	疝气；小肠气 疝氣；小腸氣
crutches **guǎi**	拐 拐	hemorrhoids; piles **zhì chuāng**	痔疮 痔瘡
sprain **niǔ shāng**	扭伤 扭傷	internal piles **nèi zhì**	内痔 內痔
ligament **jīn**	筋 筋	external piles **wài zhì**	外痔 外痔
osteitis **gǔ yán**	骨炎 骨炎	anal fistula **zhì lòu**	痔漏 痔瘻
osteomalacia **ruán gǔ bìng**	软骨病 軟骨病	kyphosis; hunchback **tuó bèi**	驼背 駝背

Dentistry 牙科

Dentistry **yá kē**	牙科 牙科		**enamel** **yá cí**	牙磁 牙磁
dentist **yá yī shēng**	牙医生 牙醫生		**sordes; dental calculus** **yá gòu**	牙垢 牙垢
clinic chair **yá kē zhěn liáo yǐ**	牙科诊疗椅 牙科診療椅		**polishing brush** **diàn mó yá shuā**	电磨牙刷 電磨牙刷
dentistry examination **yá yī jiǎn chá**	牙医检查 牙醫檢查		**saliva ejector** **shù kóu shuǐ jī**	漱口水机 漱口水機
tooth; teeth **yá**	牙 牙		**toothache** **yá tòng**	牙痛 牙痛
front teeth **mén yá**	门牙 門牙		**antiodontalgic** **yá chí zhǐ tòng yào**	牙齿止痛药 牙齒止痛藥
upper teeth **shàng yá**	上牙 上牙		**decayed tooth** **zhù yá**	蛀牙 蛀牙
lower teeth **xiè yá**	下牙 下牙		**pulp** **yá suí**	牙随 牙隨
crown **chǐ guān**	齿冠 齒冠		**puplitis** **yá suí yán**	牙随炎 牙隨炎
tooth fang of root **yá gēn**	牙根 牙根		**edentated** **diào yá**	掉牙 掉牙
bicuspid **jiù chǐ**	臼齿 臼齒		**halitosis; bad breath** **kǒu chòu**	口臭 口臭
molar **cáo yá; dà jiù chǐ**	槽牙；大臼齿 槽牙；大臼齒		**saliva** **kóu shuǐ**	口水 口水
odontoscope **jiǎn yá jìng**	检牙镜 檢牙鏡		**slobber** **liú kóu shuǐ**	流口水 流口水
noma; cancrum oris **yá gān**	牙疳 牙疳		**gum** **yá yín; yá chuáng**	牙龈；牙床 牙齦；牙床
dentine **yá zhí**	牙质 牙質		**gum gingivitis** **yá yín yán**	牙龈炎 牙齦炎

gum infection antiseptic **yá yín kàng jùn yào shuǐ**	牙龈抗菌药水 牙齦抗菌藥水
periodontosis **yá zhōu bìng**	牙周病 牙周病
periodontitis **yá zhōu yán**	牙周炎 牙周炎
odontrrhagia **yá cáo chū xiě**	牙槽出血 牙槽出血
pyorrhea **chǐ cáo nóng lòu**	齿槽脓漏 齒槽膿漏
aphtha **kuǒ chuāng**	口疮 口瘡
oral cavity **kuǒ qiāng**	口腔 口腔
stomatitis **kuǒ qiāng yán**	口腔炎 口腔炎
drill **yá kē zuān kǒng jī**	牙科钻孔机 牙科鑽孔機
orthodontia **jiǎo zhèng yá chǐ**	矫正牙齿 矯正牙齒
bridge **jīn shǔ qiáo jià**	金属桥架 金屬橋架
canine tooth **hǔ yá**	虎牙 虎牙
bucktooth **bào yá; liáo yá**	暴牙;獠牙 暴牙;獠牙
change tooth **huàn yá**	换牙 換牙
odontiasis **zhǎng yá**	长牙 長牙
extracted tooth **bá yá**	拔牙 拔牙
extraction forceps **bá yá qián**	拔牙钳 拔牙鉗
ethyl chloride **zhǐ tòng shuǐ**	止痛水 止痛水

filling tooth **bǔ yá; tián yá**	补牙;填牙 補牙;填牙
grinding **mó yá**	磨牙 磨牙
gypsum cast **shí gāo mó**	石膏模 石膏模
impression tray **yìn yá mó-zi**	印牙模子 印牙模子
toothless **wú yá**	无牙 無牙
screw porcelain **zhí yá**	植牙 植牙
braces **yá tào**	牙套 牙套
false tooth **jiǎ yá**	假牙 假牙
denture **yì fù jiǎ yá**	一副假牙 一副假牙
porcelain tooth **cí yá**	磁牙 磁牙
framework **jiǎ yá jià**	假牙架 假牙架
denture base **yá tuō**	牙托 牙托
color guide **yá sè yàng běn**	牙色样本 牙色樣本
odontexesis **xǐ yá**	洗牙 洗牙
space between the teeth **yá fèngr**	牙缝儿 牙縫兒
had gaps in the teeth **yá yǒu qūē fèngr**	牙有缺缝儿 牙有缺縫兒
grate the teeth **shuì mèng mó yá**	睡梦磨牙 睡夢磨牙

Ophthalmology & Eyeglasses 眼科與眼鏡

ophthalmology yǎn kē	眼科 眼科	blepharitis liǎn yüán yán	睑缘炎 瞼緣炎
oculist; eye-doctor yǎn kē yī shēng	眼科医生 眼科醫生	palpebritis yán liǎn yán	眼睑炎 眼瞼炎
eyes yǎn-jing	眼睛 眼睛	hordeolum liǎn xiàn yán	睑腺炎 瞼腺炎
eyelashes jié máo	睫毛 睫毛	fundus; eye ground yán dǐ	眼底 眼底
trichiasis jié máo dào zhǎng	睫毛倒长 睫毛倒長	corner of the eyes yán jiǎo	眼角 眼角
blear yǎn jí	眼疾 眼疾	eyepit yǎn kuàng	眼眶 眼眶
eyes sore yǎn tòng	眼痛 眼痛	eyeball yǎn qiú	眼球 眼球
asthenopia yǎn jīng pí láo	眼睛疲劳 眼睛疲勞	lens yǎn qiú jīng tǐ	眼球晶体 眼球晶體
congestion chōng xiě	充血 充血	white of eye yǎn bái	眼白 眼白
haemophthalmos yǎn nèi chū xiě	眼内出血 眼內出血	eyewink; wink your eyes zhá yǎn	眨眼 眨眼
hydrophthalmos yǎn shuí zhǒng	眼水肿 眼水腫	lachrymal gland lèi xiàn	泪腺 淚腺
eyelid yǎn pí	眼皮 眼皮	tear yǎn lèi	眼泪 眼淚
twitching of the eye yǎn tiào	眼跳 眼跳	secretion of eye; discharge yán shǐ; fēn mì wù	眼屎；分泌物 眼屎；分泌物
eyelid edema yǎn pí fú zhǒng	眼皮浮肿 眼皮浮腫	foreign body yǎn yì wù	眼异物 眼異物
lid hyperemia yán liǎn chōng xiě	眼睑充血 眼瞼充血	ophthalmia yǎn-jing fā yán	眼睛发炎 眼睛發炎

eyeball abscess **yǎn zhū nóng chuāng**	眼珠脓疮 眼珠膿瘡	collyrium **xí yǎn yào**	洗眼药 洗眼藥
dacryocystitis **lèi náng yán**	泪囊炎 淚囊炎	eyecup **xí yǎn bēi**	洗眼杯 洗眼杯
nebula **jiǎo mó yǚn yì**	角膜云翳 角膜雲翳	eye drops **yǎn yào shuǐ**	眼药水 眼藥水
retinopathy **shì wǎng mó bìng**	视网膜病 視網膜病	ophthalmic ointment **yǎn yào gāo**	眼药膏 眼藥膏
xerosis; xeroma **yǎn gān zào**	眼干燥 眼乾燥	pupil **tóng kǒng**	瞳孔 瞳孔
ocular lubricant ointment **gān sè yǎn yào gāo**	乾涩眼药膏 乾澀眼藥膏	miosis **tóng kǒng suō xiǎo**	瞳孔缩小 瞳孔縮小
arteriosclerosis **xiǎo dòng mài yìng huà**	小动脉硬化 小動脈硬化	myotics **suō tóng kǒng yào**	缩瞳孔药 縮瞳孔藥
ophthalmic ward **yǎn kē bìng fáng**	眼科病房 眼科病房	mydriasis **tóng kǒng fàng dà**	瞳孔放大 瞳孔放大
sensitiveness to light **wèi guāng**	畏光 畏光	mydriatic **tóng kǒng fàng dà yào**	瞳孔放大药 瞳孔放大藥
photophobia **wèi guāng zhèng**	畏光症 畏光症	intraocular pressure **yǎn yā**	眼压 眼壓
protruding eyes **tū yǎn**	凸眼 凸眼	visual acuity intraocular pressure **shì lì yǎn yā**	视力眼压 視力眼壓
strabismus **xié yǎn**	斜眼 斜眼	cataract **bái nèi zhàng**	白内障 白內障
emmetropia **zhèng shì**	正视 正視	cataract removal **bái nèi zhàng gē chú**	白内障割除 白內障割除
cockeyed; crosseyed **dòu jī yǎn**	斗鸡眼 鬥雞眼	enucleation **yǎn qiú zhāi chú shù**	眼球摘除术 眼球摘除術
blind **xiā yǎn**	瞎眼 瞎眼	artificial eye **jiá yǎn**	假眼 假眼
ablepsia **shī míng**	失明 失明	trachoma **shā yǎn**	沙眼 沙眼
hemiopia **bàn máng**	半盲 半盲	cornea **jiǎo mó**	角膜 角膜
sty **zhēn-yan**	针眼 針眼	keratitis **jiǎo mó yán**	角膜炎 角膜炎
pannus **xié guǎn yì**	血管翳 血管翳	corneal transplantation **jiǎo mó yí zhí**	角膜移植 角膜移植
nystagmus **yǎn qiú zhèn chàn zhèng**	眼球震颤症 眼球震顫症	corneal ulcer **jiǎo mó kuì yáng**	角膜溃疡 角膜潰瘍

orbit tumor yán zhǒng liú	眼肿瘤 眼腫瘤	
conjunctiva jié mó	结膜 結膜	
conjunctivitis jié mó yán	结膜炎 結膜炎	
pink-eye jí xìng jié mó yán	急性结膜炎 急性結膜炎	
chalazion liǎn pí xiàn náng zhǒng	睑皮腺囊肿 瞼皮腺囊腫	
iris hóng mó	虹膜 虹膜	
iritis hóng mó yán	虹膜炎 虹膜炎	
iridectomy hóng mó qiē chú shù	虹膜切除术 虹膜切除術	
retina shì wǎng mó	视网膜 視網膜	
blind spot shì wǎng mó máng diǎn	视网膜盲点 視網膜盲點	
optic nerve shì shén jīng	视神经 視神經	
train one's eyes yǎn-jing guò dù pí láo	眼睛过度疲劳 眼睛過度疲勞	
vision defect shì jüé bù liáng	视觉不良 視覺不良	
blurred vision yǎn huā	眼花 眼花	
diplopia; double vision fù shì; shuāng chóng yǐng xiàng	复视；双重影像 複視；雙重影像	
optic atrophy shì lì wěi suō	视力萎缩 視力萎縮	
color blind sè máng	色盲 色盲	
nyctalopia yè máng zhèng	夜盲症 夜盲症	
glaucoma qīng guāng yǎn	青光眼 青光眼	
narrow angle glaucoma bì suǒ xìng qīng guāng yǎn	闭锁性青光眼 閉鎖性青光眼	

wide angle glaucoma kāi fàng xìng qīng guāng yǎn	开放性青光眼 開放性青光眼	
undergo an operation jiē shòu shǒu shù	接受手术 接受手術	
xeroma gān yǎn bìng	干眼病 乾眼病	
hemeralopia yè shì zhèng	夜视症 夜視症	
errors of refraction qū guāng bú zhèng	屈光不正 屈光不正	
muscae volitantes fēi yíng zhèng	飞蝇症 飛蠅症	
epiphora; dacryops lèi lòu zhèng	泪漏症 淚漏症	

spectacles; eyeglasses yǎn jìngr	眼镜儿 眼鏡兒	
optical glasses píng guāng yǎn jìngr	平光眼镜儿 平光眼鏡兒	
excellent eyesight shì lì fēi cháng hǎo	视力非常好 視力非常好	
exceptionally bad shì lì hěn chā	视力很差 視力很差	
prescripted glasses yǒu dù shùr yǎn jìngr	有度数儿眼镜儿 有度數兒眼鏡兒	
high degree dù shùr shēn	度数儿深 度數兒深	
low degree dù shùr qiǎn	度数儿浅 度數兒淺	
your left eye is 1.25 nǐ zuó-yan shì yī diǎn èr wǔ	你左眼是1.25 你左眼是1.25	
power of the left lens is +4.5 zuǒ piàn shì sì dán wǔ dù	左片是4.5度 左片是4.5度	
the lens powers are different liǎng piàn dù shù bù tóng	两片度数不同 兩片度數不同	
I have a 20/20 vision wǒ liáng yǎn dū-shi èr diǎn líng	我两眼都是2.0 我兩眼都是2.0	

what is your lens power **nǐ jìng piàn duō-shao dù**	你镜片多少度 你鏡片多少度	soft lenses **ruǎn piàn yǎn jìngr**	软片眼镜儿 軟片眼鏡兒（隱形）
determine the style **jüé-ding kuǎn shì**	决定款式 決定款式	sight; visual sense **shì jüé**	视觉 視覺
spectacle frame **yǎn jìngr kuāng**	眼镜儿框 眼鏡兒框	vision **shì lì**	视力 視力
spectacle lens **yǎn jìngr piàn**	眼镜儿片 眼鏡兒片	dacryoadenitis **lèi xiàn yán**	泪腺炎 涙腺炎
farsighted; hyperopia **yüǎn-shi yǎn**	远视眼 遠視眼	dacryorrhea **jiàn fēng liú lèi**	见风流泪 見風流淚
distant glasses **yüǎn shì yǎn jìngr**	远视眼镜儿 遠視眼鏡兒	look **kàn**	看 看
nearsighted; short-sighted **jìn-shi yǎn**	近视眼 近視眼	see **kàn jiàn**	看见 看見
nearsighted glasses **jìn shì yǎn jìngr**	近视眼镜儿 近視眼鏡兒	cannot see **kàn bú jiàn**	看不见 看不見
reading glasses **kàn shū yǎn jìngr**	看书眼镜儿 看書眼鏡兒	foggy **mó-hu**	模糊 模糊
astigmatism **sǎn guāng**	散光 散光	gritting dim **shì lì mó-hu**	视力模糊 視力模糊
double vision **chóng shì**	重视 重視	test chart **shì lì cè tú biǎo**	视力测图表 視力測圖表
I see things in double **kàn-jian liǎng-ge yǐng-zi**	看见两个影子 看見兩個影子	ophthalmoscope **shì lì cè jìng piàn**	视力测镜片 視力測鏡片
presbyopia **lǎo huā yǎn**	老花眼 老花眼	test lens frame **shì lì cè jìng jià**	视力测镜架 視力測鏡架
glasses for the aged **lǎo huā jìng**	老花镜 老花鏡	vision correction **jiǎo zhèng shì lì**	矫正视力 矯正視力
bifocal glasses **shuāng jiāo jü yǎn jìngr**	双焦距眼镜儿 雙焦距眼鏡兒	optometry **yàn guāng**	验光 驗光
sunglasses **tài yáng yǎn jìngr**	太阳眼镜儿 太陽眼鏡兒	optometrist **yàn guāng shī**	验光师 驗光師
my glasses have got glass lenses **jìng piàn shì bō-li-de**	镜片是玻璃的 鏡片是玻璃的	focus **jiāo-dian**	焦点 焦點
safety glass lenses **ān qüán bō-li jìng piàn**	安全玻璃镜片 安全玻璃鏡片	blinkers **hù mù jìng**	护目镜 護目鏡
contact lenses **yǐn-xing yǎn jìngr**	隐形眼镜儿 隱形眼鏡兒	magnifying glass **fàng dà jìng**	放大镜 放大鏡
hard lenses **yìng piàn yǎn jìngr**	硬片眼镜儿 硬片眼鏡兒（隱形）	telescope **wàng yüǎn jìng**	望远镜 望遠鏡

57 A Ear 耳

E.N.T. examination **ěr bí hóu kē jiǎn chá**	耳鼻喉科检查	耳鼻喉科檢查
otology **ěr kē**	耳科	耳科
otologist **ěr kē yī shī**	耳科医师	耳科醫師
ear **ěr-duo**	耳朵	耳朵
earhole **ér kǒng**	耳孔	耳孔
eardrum **ěr mó**	耳膜	耳膜
earwax **ér shǐ**	耳屎	耳屎
earache **ěr tòng**	耳痛	耳痛
tinnitus **ěr míng**	耳鸣	耳鳴
otorrhea **ěr lòu**	耳漏	耳漏
otitis **ěr yán**	耳炎	耳炎
otitis externa **wài ěr yán**	外耳炎	外耳炎
otitis media **zhōng ěr yán**	中耳炎	中耳炎
middle ear **zhōng ěr**	中耳	中耳
vertigo **xuàn yūn**	眩晕	眩暈
deafness; deaf **ěr lóng**	耳聋；聋子	耳聾；聾子
partimutism **lóng yǎ zhèng**	聋哑症	聾啞症
otomycosis **wài ěr méi jùn bìng**	外耳霉菌病	外耳黴菌病
mumps; King's evil **zhà-sai; ěr xià xiàn yán**	炸腮；耳下腺炎	炸腮；耳下腺炎
acousma; phonism **huàn tīng**	幻听	幻聽
hearing **tīng jüé**	听觉	聽覺
audio acuity **tīng lì jiǎn chá**	听力检查	聽力檢查
listen **tīng**	听	聽
hear **tīng jiàn**	听见	聽見
hard-of-hearing **ěr bèi; zhòng tīng**	耳背；重听	耳背；重聽
cannot hear **tīng bú jiàn**	听不见	聽不見
otoscope **jián ěr jìng**	检耳镜	檢耳鏡
earplugs **ěr sāi-zi**	耳塞子	耳塞子
hearing aid **zhù tīng qì**	助听器	助聽器

bridge of the nose **bí liáng**	鼻梁 鼻樑	coryza **bí mó yán**	鼻膜炎 鼻膜炎
nasal cavity **bí qiāng**	鼻腔 鼻腔	allergic rhinitis **guò mǐn xìng bí yán**	过敏性鼻炎 過敏性鼻炎
nostril **bí kǒng**	鼻孔 鼻孔	polypus **bí ròu ròu liú**	鼻肉肉瘤 鼻肉肉瘤
conchitis **bí jiǎ yán**	鼻甲炎 鼻甲炎	smell **xiù jué**	嗅觉 嗅覺
atomizer **pēn wù qì**	喷雾器 噴霧器	anosmia **xiù jué sàng shī zhèng**	嗅觉丧失症 嗅覺喪失症
epistaxis; nose bleeding **liú bí xiě**	流鼻血 流鼻血	breath; respiration **hū xī**	呼吸 呼吸
errhine **cuī pēn-ti yào**	催喷嚏药 催噴嚏藥	hay fever **huā fěn zhèng**	花粉症 花粉症
forehead mirror **qián é fǎn guāng jìng**	前额反光镜 前額反光鏡	catarrh **bí nián mó yán**	鼻黏膜炎 鼻黏膜炎
rhinoscope; nasoscope **jiǎn bí qiāng jìng**	检鼻腔镜 檢鼻腔鏡	nasal mucus **bí-ti; bí shuǐ**	鼻涕；鼻水 鼻涕；鼻水
spray pipe **pēn wù zuǐr**	喷雾嘴儿 噴霧嘴兒	running nose; snivel **liú bí shuǐ**	流鼻水 流鼻水
needless jet syringe **pēn shè zhù shè qì**	喷射注射器 噴射注射器	sneeze **dǎ pēn-ti**	打喷嚏 打噴嚏
brandy nose **jiǔ zāo bí-zi**	酒糟鼻子 酒糟鼻子	stuffy nose **bí-zi bù tōng**	鼻子不通 鼻子不通
paranasal sinus **bí dòu**	鼻窦 鼻竇	nasal congestion **bí sāi**	鼻塞 鼻塞
nasosinusitis **bí dòu yán**	鼻窦炎 鼻竇炎		

57 Throat 喉 C

throat **hóu lóng**	喉咙 喉嚨	stomatitis **kǒu qiāng yán**	口腔炎 口腔炎
larynx **hóu tóu**	喉头 喉頭	oral mucosa **kǒu qiāng nián mó**	口腔黏膜 口腔黏膜
Adam's apple **hóu jié**	喉结 喉結	esophagitis **shí dào yán**	食道炎 食道炎
laryngoscope **hóu jìng**	喉镜 喉鏡	thyroid gland; thyroid **jiǎ zhuàng xiàn**	甲状腺 甲狀腺
mouth **zuǐ; kǒu**	嘴；口 嘴；口	vocal cord **shēng dài**	声带 聲帶
lips **zuǐ chún**	嘴唇 嘴唇	windpipe **qì guǎn**	气管 氣管
oral cavity; mouth cavity **kǒu qiāng**	口腔 口腔	bronchus **zhī qì guǎn**	支气管 支氣管
mouth mirror **kǒu qiāng jìng**	口腔镜 口腔鏡	whoop **xiāo chuǎn shēng**	哮喘声 哮喘聲
tongue **shé-tou**	舌头 舌頭	salivary gland **tuò yè xiàn**	唾液腺 唾液腺
uvula **xiǎo shé**	小舌 小舌	spit **tǔ kóu shuǐ**	吐口水 吐口水
glossitis **shé yán**	舌炎 舌炎	saliva; sputum **tuò yè**	唾液 唾液
taste buds **wèi lěi**	味蕾 味蕾	phlegm **tán**	痰 痰
taste **wèi jüé**	味觉 味覺	spiting **tǔ tán**	吐痰 吐痰
spatula **yā shé bǎnr**	压舌板儿 壓舌板兒	clear your throat **bǎ tán dōu qīng chú diào**	把痰都清除掉 把痰都清除掉
cheilosis **kó jiǎo yán**	口角炎 口角炎	hack **gān ké**	干咳 乾咳

English	Pinyin	简体	繁體
have a sore throat	hóu lóng tòng	喉咙痛	喉嚨痛
throat-itchy	hóu lóng yǎng	喉咙痒	喉嚨癢
strangled an impulse to cough	rěn-zhu ké-sou	忍住咳嗽	忍住咳嗽
pharyngitis	yān tóu yán	咽头炎	咽頭炎
laryngitis	hóu tóu yán	喉头炎	喉頭炎
hiccup; burp	dǎ gér	打嗝儿	打嗝兒
dysphonia	fā yīn kùn nán	发音困难	發音困難
tonsillitis	biǎn táo xiàn yán	扁桃腺炎	扁桃腺炎
gullet	shí dào	食道	食道
scarlet fever	hóu shā; xīng hóng rè	喉痧;猩红热	喉痧;猩紅熱

pediatrics **xiǎo ér kē**	小儿科 小兒科	acquired osteogenesis imperfect **xiān tiān xìng chéng gǔ bù quán**	先天性成 骨不全
pediatrician **xiǎo ér kē yī shī**	小儿科医师 小兒科醫師	IQ (intelligence quotient) **zhì shāng**	智商 智商
pediatrics ward **xiǎo ér kē bìng fáng**	小儿科病房 小兒科病房	amentia; mental deficiency **zhì néng bù zú**	智能不足 智能不足
midwife **zhù chǎn shì**	助产士 助產士	hermaphrodite **yīn yáng rén**	阴阳人 陰陽人
birth certificate **chū shēng zhèng míng shū**	出生证明书 出生證明書	precocity child **zǎo shú-de hái-zi**	早熟的孩子 早熟的孩子
preemie; premature infant **záo chǎn ér**	早产儿 早產兒	hyperactive child **guò dòng ér**	过动儿 過動兒
incubator **záo chǎn ér bǎo yù xiāng**	早产儿保育箱 早產兒保育箱	infantile autism **zì bì zhèng**	自闭症 自閉症
resistance **dǐ kàng lì**	抵抗力 抵抗力	vaccination **jiē zhǒng**	接种 接種
gene **jī yīn; yí chuán yīn zǐ**	基因;遗传因子 基因;遺傳因子	immune **miǎn yì-de**	免疫的 免疫的
DNA (deoxyribonucleic acid) **rǎn sè tǐ jī yīn zǔ chéng**	染色体基因组成 染色體基因組成	contagious **chuán rǎn xìng-de**	传染性的 傳染性的
gene mutation **jī yīn tú biàn**	基因突变 基因突變	infection **gán rǎn**	感染 感染
heredity **yí chuán**	遗传 遺傳	syndrome **bìng fā zhèng**	并发症 併發症
hereditary disease **yí chuán bìng**	遗传病 遺傳病	measles **má zhěn**	麻疹 麻疹
Down syndrome **táng shì zhèng**	唐氏症 唐氏症	small pox **tiān huā**	天花 天花
poliomyelitis; polio **xiǎo ér má bì zhèng**	小儿麻痹症 小兒麻痹症	chicken pox **shuǐ dòu**	水痘 水痘

cholera **huò luàn**	霍乱 霍亂	
dysentery **lā lì-ji**	拉痢疾 拉痢疾	
enterovirus **cháng bìng dú**	肠病毒 腸病毒	
tonsillitis **biǎn táo xiàn yán**	扁桃腺炎 扁桃腺炎	
mumps **sāi xiàn yán**	腮腺炎 腮腺炎	
diphtheria **bái hóu**	白喉 白喉	
mucus **nián yè**	黏液 黏液	
rash **zhěn-zi**	疹子 疹子	
gamma globulin **xiě qiú dàn bái**	血球蛋白 血球蛋白	
whooping cough remedy **bǎi rì ké yào**	百日咳药 百日咳藥	
caugh drop **ké sòu táng dìng**	咳嗽糖锭 咳嗽糖錠	
caugh syrup; cough mixture **ké sòu táng jiāng**	咳嗽糖浆 咳嗽糖漿	
progression **bìng qíng háo zhuǎn**	病情好转 病情好轉	
choking **yē-zhu-le**	噎住了 噎住了	
suffocation **zhì xí; mèn-si**	窒息；闷死 窒息；悶死	
dyspnea **hū xī kùn nán**	呼吸困难 呼吸困難	
stool sample **fèn biàn yàng běn**	粪便样本 糞便樣本	
parasite **jì shēng chóng**	寄生虫 寄生蟲	

pinworm **ráo chóng**	蛲虫 蟯蟲	
roundworm; ascarid **huí chóng**	蛔虫 蛔蟲	
hookworm **gōu chóng**	钩虫 鉤蟲	
filaria **xiě sī chóng**	血丝虫 血絲蟲	
tapeworm; cestode **tiáo chóng**	条虫 條蟲	
ova **chóng luǎn**	虫卵 蟲卵	
santonin **huí chóng qū chú yào**	蛔虫驱除药 蛔蟲驅除藥	
nutrition **yíng yǎng**	营养 營養	
mineral **kuàng wù zhí**	矿物质 礦物質	
malnutrition; dystrophy **yíng yǎng bù liáng**	营养不良 營養不良	
urine **niào; xiǎo biàn**	尿；小便 尿；小便	
urinate; pee **niào niào; sā niào; xiǎo biàn**	尿尿；撒尿；小便 尿尿；撒尿；小便	
stool **shǐ; dà biàn; fèn**	屎；大便；粪 屎；大便；糞	
bowels movement **lā shǐ; pái biàn; dà biàn**	拉屎；排便；大便 拉屎；排便；大便	
diaper **niào bù**	尿布 尿布	
lay a fart; break wind **fàng pì**	放屁 放屁	
stink; smelly **chòu**	臭 臭	

Obstetrics & Gynecology

婦產科

obstetrics **chǎn kē**	产科 產科	Seasonale **jì jīng wán**	季经丸 季經丸
obstetrician **chǎn kē yī shēng**	产科医生 產科醫生	oviduct **shū luǎn guǎn**	输卵管 輸卵管
gynecology **fù kē**	妇科 婦科	ovum; ova **luǎn zǐ**	卵子 卵子
gynecologist **fù kē yī shēng**	妇科医生 婦科醫生	ovulation **pái luǎn**	排卵 排卵
gynecopathy **fù nǚ bìng**	妇女病 婦女病	egg cell **luǎn xì bāo**	卵细胞 卵細胞
emmenia; menses **yuè jīng**	月经 月經	ovary **luǎn cháo**	卵巢 卵巢
menstruation; period **pái yuè jīng; jīng qí**	排月经：经期 排月經：經期	ovaritis **luǎn cháo yán**	卵巢炎 卵巢炎
emmeniopathy **yuè jīng bù tiáo**	月经不调 月經不調	castrate (women) **gē chú luǎn cháo**	割除卵巢 割除卵巢
menorrhagia **yuè jīng guò duō**	月经过多 月經過多	uterus; womb **zǐ gōng**	子宫 子宫
menostaxis **jīng qí qiān yán**	经期迁延 經期遷延	mole **zǐ gōng liú**	子宫瘤 子宫瘤
menstrual disorder **yuè jīng shī tiáo**	月经失调 月經失調	cervical cancer **zǐ gōng jǐng ái**	子宫颈癌 子宫頸癌
suppressed menstruation; amenorrhoea **jīng bì**	 經閉	cervical smear **zǐ gōng jīng mǒ piàn**	子宫颈抹片 子宫頸抹片
irregularity of menstruation **yuè jīng bú shùn**	月经不顺 月經不順	cervical erosion **zǐ gōng jǐng mí làn**	子宫颈糜烂 子宫頸糜爛
menstruous **gěi yuè jīng nòng zāng-le**	给月经弄脏了 給月經弄髒了	intra-uterine device **zǐ gōng bì yùn qì**	子宫避孕器 子宫避孕器
dysmenorrhea **tòng jīng**	痛经 痛經	contraceptive drugs **bì yùn yào**	避孕药 避孕藥

contraception bì yùn	避孕 避孕	lutein huáng tǐ sù	黄体素 黃體素
birth control jié yù	节育 節育	estimated date of delivery yù chǎn qí	预产期 預產期
celiosalpingectomy shū luán guǎn qiē chú	输卵管切除 輸卵管切除	postpartum depression chǎn hòu yōu yù zhèng	产後忧郁症 產後憂鬱症
infertility bú yùn zhèng	不孕症 不孕症	breast milk ; breast-feed mú nǎi ; wèi mú nǎi	母奶；喂母奶 母奶；餵母奶
ligation jié zā	结扎 結紮	breast pump mú nǎi xī qǔ qì	母奶吸取器 母奶吸取器
twins shuāng bāo tāi	双胞胎 雙胞胎	extrauterine pregnancy zǐ gōng wài yùn	子宫外孕 子宮外孕
triplets sān bāo tāi	三胞胎 三胞胎	dilatation of curettage guā zǐ-gong	刮子宫 刮子宮
quadruplets sì bāo tāi	四胞胎 四胞胎	fetus tāi ér	胎儿 胎兒
vesicular mole pú táo tāi	葡萄胎 葡萄胎	premature delivery záo chǎn	早产 早產
take a pregnancy test zuò huái yùn jiǎn chá	做怀孕检查 做懷孕檢查	antenatal training tāi jiào	胎教 胎教
the result is negative jié guǒ chéng yīn xìng	结果呈阴性 結果呈陰性	version tāi wèi dào zhuǎn	胎位倒转 胎位倒轉
the result is positive jié guǒ chéng yáng xìng	结果呈阳性 結果呈陽性	hasten child delivery cuī shēng	催生 催生
pregnant huái yùn	怀孕 懷孕	labor pains zhèn tòng	阵痛 陣痛
morning sickness yùn tù	孕吐 孕吐	amnion fluid yáng shuǐ	羊水 羊水
antenatal examination chǎn qián jiǎn chá	产前检查 產前檢查	umbilical cord qí dài	脐带 臍帶
three-monthpregnant sān-ge yùe-de yùn	三个月的孕 三個月的孕	placenta tāi pán	胎盘 胎盤
is expecting her baby dài chǎn	待产 待產	midwife jiē shēng pó	接生婆 接生婆
due to delivery yào shēng-le	要生了 要生了	deliver a child jiē shēng	接生 接生
amniocentesis yáng mó chuān cì shù	羊膜穿刺术 羊膜穿刺術	delivery fees jiē shēng fèi	接生费 接生費
ultrasonic waves chāo yīn bō	超音波 超音波	spontaneous labor zì rán fēn miǎn	自然分娩 自然分娩

general anaesthesia **qüán shēn má zuì**	全身麻醉 全身麻醉	climacteric **gēng nián qí**	更年期 更年期
caesarean operation **pǒu fù shēng chǎn**	剖腹生产 剖腹生產	hormone **hè ěr méng**	荷尔蒙 荷爾蒙
dystocia **nǎn chǎn**	难产 難產	hormone injections **dǎ hè ěr méng zhēn**	打荷尔蒙针 打荷爾蒙針
gave birth to a boy **shēng-le-ge nán háir**	生了个男孩儿 生了個男孩兒	sexual organs **xìng qì guān**	性器官 性器官
abortion **duò tāi**	堕胎 墮胎	vagina **yīng dào**	阴道 陰道
abortion; miscarriage **liú chǎn**	流产 流產	labia majora; labium maju **dà yīn chún**	大阴唇 大陰唇
vacuum aspiration **zhēn kōng xī yǐn shù**	真空吸引术 真空吸引術	labium minus; nympha **xiǎo yīn chún**	小阴唇 小陰唇
hysterectomy **gē chú zǐ gōng shù**	割除子宫术 割除子宮術	maidenhead; hyman **chù nǔ mó**	处女膜 處女膜
conization **zǐ gōng jǐng qiē chú shù**	子宫颈切除术 子宮頸切除術	clitoris **yīn dì**	阴蒂 陰蒂
celiosalpingectomy **shū luán guǎn qiē chú**	输卵管切除 輸卵管切除	vaginitis **yīn dào yán**	阴道炎 陰道炎
infertility **bú yùn zhèng**	不孕症 不孕症	vaginal itching **yīn dào yǎng**	阴道痒 陰道癢
artificial insemination **rén gōng shòu yùn**	人工受孕 人工受孕	leucorrhea **bái dài**	白带 白帶
test-tube baby **shì guǎn yīng ér**	试管婴儿 試管嬰兒	candidiasis **niàn zhū jùn bìng**	念珠菌病 念珠菌病
fertilize **shòu jīng**	受精 受精	douche bag **fù nǔ guàn xǐ dài**	妇女灌洗袋 婦女灌洗袋
fertilized egg; zygote **shòu jīng luǎn**	受精卵 受精卵	theloncus **rǔ tóu liú**	乳头瘤 乳頭瘤
embryo **pēi tāi**	胚胎 胚胎	thelitis **rǔ tóu yán**	乳头炎 乳頭炎
in vitro **zài bō-li qì nèi**	在玻璃器内 在玻璃器內	mastitis **rǔ xiàn yán**	乳腺炎 乳腺炎
implant **yí zhí rù**	移植入 移植入	lump **yìng kuài**	硬块 硬塊
surrogate mother **dài lǐ yùn mǔ**	代理孕母 代理孕母	breast cancer **rǔ ái**	乳癌 乳癌
gynaecological examination **fù kē jiǎn chá**	妇科检查 婦科檢查	mastectomy **rǔ fáng qiē chú**	乳房切除 乳房切除

dermatology pí fū kē	皮肤科 皮膚科	onychomycocis huī zhí-jia	灰指甲 灰指甲
dermatologist pí fū kē yī shī	皮肤科医师 皮膚科醫師	sweat hàn	汗 汗
skin disease; dermatosis pí fū bìng	皮肤病 皮膚病	sudoriferous gland hàn xiàn	汗腺 汗腺
dermatitis pí fū yán	皮肤炎 皮膚炎	hidrosis hàn duō	汗多 汗多
skin allergy pí fū mín gǎn	皮肤敏感 皮膚敏感	hand sweat disease shǒu chū hàn zhèng	手出汗症 手出汗症
dry skin gān xìng pí fū	干性皮肤 乾性皮膚	body odor (B.O.) hú chòu	狐臭 狐臭
oily skin yóu xìng pí fū	油性皮肤 油性皮膚	pimple qīng chūn dòu; miàn pào	青春痘；面疱 青春痘；面皰
sensitive skin mín gǎn xìng pí fū	敏感性皮肤 敏感性皮膚	acne fěn cì	粉刺 粉刺
combination skin zòng hé xìng pí fū	综合性皮肤 綜合性皮膚	blackhead; comedo hēi tóur fěn cì	黑头儿粉刺 黑頭兒粉刺
neurodermatitis shéng jīng xìng pí fū yán	神经性皮肤炎 神經性皮膚炎	doxycycline dòu liáo huán sù dìng	痘疗环素锭 痘療環素錠
leprosy má fēng bìng	麻疯病 痲瘋病	clindanycin phosphate dòu liáo yào shuǐ	痘疗药水 痘療藥水
athlete's foot xiāng gáng jiǎo	香港脚 香港腳	freckle qüè bān	雀斑 雀斑
beriberi jiǎo-qi bìng	脚气病 腳氣病	erythema hóng bān	红斑 紅斑
corn jiǎo jī-yan	脚鸡眼 腳雞眼	Hydroquinone zhì hēi bān yào	治黑斑药 治黑斑藥
corn-remover jiǎo jī-yan yào shuǐ	脚鸡眼药水 腳雞眼藥水	age spots; seborrhea lǎo rén bān	老人斑 (皮肤角化) 老人斑 (皮膚角化)

pus **nóng**	脓 膿	psoriasis **niú pí xiǎn**	牛皮癣 牛皮癬
maturated **shēng nóng**	生脓 生膿	pityriasis **shé pí xiǎn**	蛇皮癣 蛇皮癬
abscess **nóng pào**	脓疱 膿皰	abrasion **cā shāng**	擦伤 擦傷
blister **qǐ pào**	起泡 起泡	chilblains; frostbite **dòng chuāng**	冻疮 凍瘡
swelling **zhǒng**	肿 腫	puffy **xū zhǒng**	虚肿 虛腫
dropsy **shuǐ zhǒng**	水肿 水腫	edema; dropsy **fú zhǒng; shuǐ zhǒng**	浮肿;水肿 浮腫;水腫
rash **zhěn-zi**	疹子 疹子	resolution **xiāo zhǒng**	消肿 消腫
eczema **shī zhěn**	湿疹 濕疹	bulla **shuǐ páo**	水庖 水庖
scabies **jiè**	疥 疥	pustule **nóng páo**	脓庖 膿庖
scabies ointment **jiè chuāng gāo**	疥疮膏 疥瘡膏	ploypus flesh **xí ròu; ròu yá**	息肉;肉芽 息肉;肉芽
itching **yǎng**	痒 癢	scabbing **zhǎng gē-da**	长疙瘩 長疙瘩
scratching **são yǎng**	搔痒 搔癢	mole **zhì**	痣 痣
boil **dīng**	疔 疔	scar **bā**	疤 疤
prickly heat **fèi-zi**	痱子 痱子	to form a scar **jié bā**	结疤 結疤
measles **má zhěn; shā-zi**	麻疹;痧子 麻疹;痧子	sarcoma **ròu liú**	肉瘤 肉瘤
varicella; chickenpox **shuǐ dòu; jī dòu**	水痘;鸡痘 水痘;雞痘	neoplasm **zhǒng liú**	肿瘤 腫瘤
smallpox **tiān huā**	天花 天花	benign tumor **liáng xìng liú**	良性瘤 良性瘤
pockmark **má-zi**	麻子 麻子	skin cancer **pí-fu ái**	皮肤癌 皮膚癌
tinea **xiǎn**	癣 癬	fatty tumor **zhī fáng liú**	脂肪瘤 脂肪瘤
ringworm **jīn qiān xiǎn**	金钱癣 金錢癬	Kaposi's Sarcoma **kǎ pō xī ròu liú**	卡波西肉瘤 卡波西肉瘤

aortitis dà dòng mài yán	大动脉炎 大動脈炎		hair (head) tóu-fa	头发 頭髮
aneurysm dòng mài liú	动脉瘤 動脈瘤		canities bái fǎ zhèng	白发症 白髮症
varix jìng mài liú	静脉瘤 靜脈瘤		psilosis tuō fǎ zhèng	脱发症 脫髮症
skin; derma pí; pí fū	皮；皮肤 皮；皮膚		alopecia tū fǎ zhèng	秃发症 禿髮症
epidermis biǎo pí	表皮 表皮		scalp tóu pí	头皮 頭皮
it gives me goose pimples qǐ jī pī gē-da	起鸡皮疙瘩 起雞皮疙瘩		itching scalp tóu pí yǎng	头皮痒 頭皮癢
creepy feeling máo gú sǒng rán	毛骨悚然 毛骨悚然		seborrhea tóu pí zhī yì	头皮脂溢 頭皮脂溢
adipose zhī fáng	脂肪 脂肪		losing hair; shedding diào tóu-fa	掉头发 掉頭髮
flash ròu	肉 肉（人類）		dandruff tóu pí xiè	头皮屑 頭皮屑
muscle jī ròu	肌肉 肌肉		dandruff remover qù tóu pí shuǐ	去头皮水 去頭皮水
hair (body) máo; tǐ máo	毛；体毛 毛；體毛		antiseptic tar (抗菌焦油) tóu pí yào shuǐ	头皮药水 頭皮藥水
complexion fū sè	肤色 膚色		medicated soap yào zào	药皂 藥皂
sunburn pí fū shài hóng	皮肤晒红 皮膚曬紅		medicated shampoo yào jì xí fǎ jīng	药剂洗发精 藥劑洗髮精
suntan rì guāng yù; shài hēi	日光浴；晒黑 日光浴；曬黑		hair lustrous tóu-fa guāng liàng	头发光亮 髮 光亮
suntan lotion fáng shài yóu	防晒油 防曬油			
decortication; skin peels off tuō pí	脱皮 脫皮			
senile lentigo pí fū jiǎo huà	皮肤角化 皮膚角化			
hyperkeratotic skin pí fū gān liè	皮肤乾裂 皮膚乾裂			
Urea and Hydrocortisone jiǎo zhí shī zhěn bìng	角质湿疹药 角質濕疹藥			
skin-printing pí fū yìn shuā	皮肤印刷 皮膚印刷			

Venereal Disease 性病

venereal disease (V.D.) **xìng bìng**	性病	性病
sexual intercourse **xìng jiāo**	性交	性交
congestion **chōng xiě**	充血	充血
erection; got a hard-on **bó qǐ**	勃起	勃起
contagious **chuán rǎn**	传染	傳染
condom **báo xiǎn tàor**	保险套儿	保險套兒
one of his blood donators **tā-de yí-ge jüān xiě rén**	他的一个捐血人	他的一個捐血人
AIDS(acquired immune deficiency syndrome) **ài zī bìng**	爱滋病	
is an AIDS patient **shì ài zī bìng huàn**	是爱滋病患	是愛滋病患
tender pain **chù tòng**	触痛	觸痛
syphilitic disease **huā liǔ bìng**	花柳病	花柳病
gonorrhea; gonococcus **lín bìng; lín bìng jùn**	淋病；淋病菌	淋病；淋病菌
lymphatic gland **lín bā xiàn**	淋巴腺	淋巴腺
syphilis **méi dú**	梅毒	梅毒
bubo **yǔ kǒu**	鱼口	魚口（淋巴腺腫）
venereal ulcer **xià gān**	下疳	下疳
genitalia **shēng zhí qì**	生殖器	生殖器
penis **yáng jù; xiǎo biàn**	阳具；小便	陽具；小便
phallus **yīn jīng**	阴茎	陰莖
glans penis **guī tóu**	龟头	龜頭
balanoposthitis **bāo pí yán**	包皮炎	包皮炎
testis; testicle **gāo wán**	睾丸	睾丸
castrate (men) **qù shì; qiē chú gāo wán**	去势；切除睾丸	去勢；切除睾丸
scrotum **yīn náng**	阴囊	陰囊
seminal vesicle **jīng náng**	精囊	精囊

urologist **mì niào kē yī shēng**	泌尿科医生 泌尿科醫生	**anuria** **wú niào zhèng**	无尿症 無尿症
prostate gland **shè hù xiàn**	摄护腺 攝護腺（前列腺）	**dysuria** **xiǎo biàn kùn nán**	小便困难 小便困難
prostatitis **shè hù xiàn féi dà**	摄护腺肥大 （前列腺炎）攝護腺肥大	**urinage** **niào shī jìn**	尿失禁 尿失禁
carcinoma of prostate **shè hù xiàn aí**	摄护腺癌 （前列腺癌）攝護腺癌	**foreskin; prepuc** **bāo pí**	包皮 包皮
vesiculitis **jīng náng yán**	精囊炎 精囊炎	**phimosis** **bāo jīng ;bāo pí guò cháng**	包茎；包皮过长 包莖；包皮過長
orchitis **gāo wán yán**	睾丸炎 睾丸炎	**circumcise** **gē bāo pí**	割包皮 割包皮
urethra **niào dào**	尿道 尿道	**spermatorrhea; wet dream** **mèng yí**	梦遗 夢遺
infections of urinary **niào dào chuán rǎn bìng**	尿道传染病 尿道傳染病	**premature ejaculation** **zǎo xiè**	早泄 早泄
urethritis **niào dào yán**	尿道炎 尿道炎	**sperm duct** **shū jīng guǎn**	输精管 輸精管
uremia; uraemia **niào dú zhèng**	尿毒症 尿毒癥	**ejaculatory duct** **shè jīng guǎn**	射精管 射精管
dialysis **xǐ shèn**	洗肾 洗腎	**ejaculation** **shè jīng**	射精 射精
hematuria; haematuria **xiě niào zhèng**	血尿症 血尿症	**semen; seminal fluid** **jīng yè**	精液 精液
strangury **niào jí**	尿急 尿急	**sperm** **jīng chóng**	精虫 精蟲
frequent micturition **niào pín**	尿频 尿頻	**impotence** **yáng wěi**	阳萎 陽萎
urinary incontinence **niào shī jìn**	尿失禁 尿失禁	**can't get a hard on** **yìng-bu qǐ lái**	硬不起来 硬不起來
enuresis **yí niào zhèng**	遗尿症 遺尿症	**philters; aphrodisiac** **chūn yào**	春药 春藥

Psychiatry & Neurology

精神病與神經病

English	简体	繁體
psychiatry **jīng shén**	精神病	精神病
psychiatrist **jīng shén bìng yī shī**	精神病医师	精神病醫師
neurologist **shén jīng bìng yī shī**	神经病医师	神經病醫師
neurology **shén jīng bìng (kē)**	神经病 (科)	神經病 (科)
neuralgia **shén jīng tòng**	神经痛	神經痛
neurasthenia **shén jīng shuāi ruò**	神经衰弱	神經衰弱
hyperaesthesia **shén jīng guò mǐn**	神经过敏	神經過敏
mental hospital **jīng shén bìng yüàn**	精神病院	精神病院
psychiatric ward **jīng shén bìng fáng**	精神病房	精神病房
nuthouse; lunatic asylum **fēng rén yüàn**	疯人院	瘋人院
psychosis; insane **jīng shén cuò luàn**	精神错乱	精神錯亂
disorders of consciousness **shén jīng shī cháng**	神经失常	神經失常
insanity **fēng kuáng**	疯狂	瘋狂
lunatic **fēng diān**	疯癫	瘋癲
nut; cuckoo **fēng-zi**	疯子	瘋子
psychologist; shrink **xīn lǐ yī shī**	心理医师	心理醫師
epilepsy **yáng jiǎo fēng**	羊角疯	羊角瘋
heredity **yí chuán**	遗传	遺傳
had a seizure **bìng fā**	病发	病發
shock **xiū kè**	休克	休克
coma **hūn mí**	昏迷	昏迷
syncope; faint **hūn jüé; hūn dǎo-le**	昏厥；昏倒了	昏厥；昏倒了
dizziness **hūn xüàn**	昏眩	昏眩
nerve **shén jīng**	神经	神經
nervous **jǐn zhāng bù ān**	紧张不安	緊張不安
nervous breakdown **jīng shén bēng kuì**	精神崩溃	精神崩潰
neurological examination **shén jīng jiǎn chá**	神经检查	神經檢查
neuropathy **shén jīng xì bìng**	神经系病	神經系病
neurosis **shén jīng zhèng**	神经症	神經症
neuritis **shén jīng yán**	神经炎	神經炎

autism zì bì zhèng	自闭症 自閉症	
idiocy; amentia bái chī	白痴 白癡	
mental retardation zhì zhàng	智障 智障	
insomnia shī mián zhèng	失眠症 失眠症	
frozen shoulder wǔ shí jiān	五十肩 五十肩	
stiff shoulders jiān suān tòng	肩酸痛 肩酸痛	
spur gǔ cì	骨刺 骨刺	
hysteria fā shén jīng; xiē sī dí lǐ	发神精；歇斯底里 發神精；歇斯底里	
schizophrenia jīng shén fēn liè zhèng	精神分裂症 精神分裂症	
Parkinsonism pà jīn sēn diān xián zhèng	帕金森癫痫症 帕金森癲癇症	
delirium fā fēng	发疯 發瘋	
hypnotism cuī mián shù	催眠术 催眠術	
Alzheimer's disease chī dāi zhèng	痴呆症 癡呆症	
senile lǎo rén chī dāi zhèng	老人痴呆症 老人癡呆症	
amnesia shī yì zhèng	失忆症 失憶症	
hump; feel low (blue) qíng xù dī cháo	情绪低潮 情緒低潮	
poor in spirit jīng shén bù hǎo	精神不好 精神不好	
Panic Attacks kǒng huāng zhèng	恐慌症 恐慌症	
Phobias kǒng jù zhèng	恐惧症 恐懼症	
sensitive mín gǎn zhèng	敏感症 敏感症	

paranoid state huàn xiǎng	幻想 幻想	
paranoia wàng xiǎng zhèng	妄想症 妄想症	
emotional disease qíng xù bìng	情绪病 情緒病	
melancholia; depression yōu yù zhèng	忧郁症 憂鬱症	
Anxiety Disorder zào yù zhèng	躁郁症(焦虑) 躁鬱症(焦慮)	
Obsessions qiáng pò zhèng (guǐ mí)	强迫症(鬼迷) 強迫症(鬼迷)	
soliloquize; talk to oneself zì yán zì yǔ	自言自语 自言自語	
stutter kuǒ jí	口吃 口吃	
Marfan Syndrome zhī zhū rén zhèng hòu qún	蜘蛛人症候群 蜘蛛人症候群	
Lesch-Nyhan Syndrome zì huǐ róng mào zhèng hòu qún	自毁容貌症候群 自毀容貌症候群	
noctambulation mèng yóu zhèng	梦游症 夢遊症	
nightmare mèng yè	梦魇 夢魘	
kleptomania tōu qiè kuáng	偷窃狂 偷竊狂	
abnormal; metamorphosis biàn tài	变态 變態	
masochism nüè dài kuáng	虐待狂 虐待狂	
chorea wú dǎo zhèng	舞蹈症 舞蹈症	
myasthenia gravis zhòng zhèng jī wú lì zhèng	重症肌无力症 重症肌無力症	
notalgia bèi tòng	背痛 背痛	
lumbago yāo suān	腰酸 腰酸	
spasm; cramp chōu jīn	抽筋 抽筋	

Physical Checkup & Laboratory

健康檢查與化驗室

health checkup jiàn kāng jiǎn chá	健康检查 健康檢查	ureter X-ray shū niào guǎn X guāng	输尿管 X 光 輸尿管 X 光
height shēn gāo	身高 身高	bladder X-ray páng guāng X guāng shè yǐng	膀胱 X 光摄影 膀胱 X 光攝影
weight tǐ zhòng	体重 體重	flat plate (K.U.B.) X-ray fù bù X guāng shè yǐng	腹部 X 光摄影 腹部 X 光攝影
blood pressure xiě yā	血压 血壓	gastrointestinal (GI) X-ray xiāo huà dào shè yǐng	消化道摄影 消化道攝影
body temperature tǐ wēn	体温 體溫	upper GI X-ray shàng xiāo huà dào shè yǐng	上消化道摄影 上消化道攝影
pulse mài bó	脉搏 脈搏	upper endoscopy cháng wèi jìng jiǎn chá	肠胃镜检查 腸胃鏡檢查
respiration; respire hū xī	呼吸 呼吸	supersonic (ultrasonic) waves chāo yīn bō	超音波 超音波
skinfold niē pí zhī fáng hòu dù	捏皮脂肪厚度 捏皮脂肪厚度	electrocardiogram xīn diàn tú	心电图 心電圖
hematology xiě yè fēn xī	血液分析 血液分析	pulmonary function fèi gōng néng	肺功能 肺功能
haemophilia xié yǒu bìng	血友病 血友病	vital capacity fèi huó liàng	肺活量 肺活量
★PET pistron emulsion tomography zhèng zǐ sǎo miáo shè yǐng	正子扫瞄摄影 正子掃瞄攝影	GYN examination fù kē jiǎn chá	妇科检查 婦科檢查
hepatitis B surface antigen B xíng gān yán kàng yuán	B型肝炎抗原 (HBs-Ag) B型肝炎抗原	urine and stool analysis niào jí fèn biàn jiǎn chá	尿及粪便检查 尿及糞便檢查
proctological examination zhí cháng jiǎn chá	直肠检查 直腸檢查	thermograph hóng wài xiàn sǎo miáo	红外线扫瞄 紅外線掃瞄
chest X-ray xiōng bù X guāng shè yǐng	胸部 X 光摄影 胸部 X 光攝影	ultra-red ray hóng wài xiàn	红外线 紅外線
kidney X-ray shèn zàng X guāng shè yǐng	肾脏X光摄影 腎臟X光攝影	ultraviolet ray zǐ wài xiàn	紫外线 紫外線

laboratory

laboratory (lab.)
shí yàn shì
实验室
實驗室

clinical laboratory
huà yàn shì
化验室
化驗室

technician
jì shù yuán
技术员
技術員

X-ray room
X guāng shì
X 光室
X 光室

perspective view
tòu shì
透视
透視

hold your breath
tíng zhǐ hū xī
停止呼吸
停止呼吸

negative
zhèng cháng; méi bìng
正常；没病
正常；沒病

positive
què dìng yǒu bìng
确定有病
確定有病

roentgenology
X guāng lǐ liáo
X 光理疗
X 光理療

DNA (deoxyribonucleic acid)
rǎn sè tǐ/jī yīn zǔ hé tǐ
染色体 基因组合体
染色體/基因組合體

glass bell jar
bō lí zhōng zhào
玻璃盅罩
玻璃盅罩

section cutting
qiē piàn
切片
切片

microtome
qiē piàn jī
切片机
切片機

analysis
fēn xī
分析
分析

chemicals
huà xué yào pǐn
化学药品
化學藥品

hematology; blood test
xiě yè jiǎn chá
血液检查
血液檢查

corpuscle
xiě qiú
血球
血球

R.B.C.; erythrocyte
hóng xiě qiú
红血球
紅血球

W.B.C.; leucocyte
bái xiě qiú
白血球
白血球

plasma
xiě jiāng
血浆
血漿

cell
xì bāo
细胞
細胞

hemoglobin
xiě sè sù
血色素
血色素

serum
xiě qīng
血清
血清

congealed blood
níng xiě
凝血
凝血

occult blood
qián xiě
潜血
潛血

blood sedimentation rate
xiě yè chén jiàng lǜ
血液沈降率
血液沈降率

bleeding time
chū xiě shí jiān
出血时间
出血時間

coagulation time
níng xiě shí jiān
凝血时间
凝血時間

platelet count
xiě xiáo bǎn jì suàn
血小板计算
血小板計算

blood sugar
xiě táng
血糖
血糖

glucagon
gāo xiě táng
高血糖
高血糖

hematuria; haematuria
xiě niào zhèng
血尿症
血尿症

uric acid
niào suān
尿酸
尿酸

creatine
jī suān
肌酸
肌酸

coagulation
níng jié wù
凝结物
凝結物

sediment
chén diàn
沈淀
沈澱

cholesterol detection
dǎn gù chún cè dìng
胆固醇测定
膽固醇測定

triglyceride
sān suān gān yóu zhǐ
三酸甘油酯
三酸甘油酯

steroid **lèi gù chún**	类固醇 類固醇	remaine in shape **shēn tǐ qíng kuàng liáng hǎo**	身体情况良好 身體情況良好
albuminuria **dàn bái niào**	蛋白尿 蛋白尿	pathological laboratory **bìng lǐ huà yàn shì**	病理化验室 病理化驗室
lipuria **zhī fáng niào**	脂肪尿 脂肪尿	clinical **lín chuáng-de**	临床的 臨床的
lipoprotein **zhī dàn bái**	脂蛋白 脂蛋白	clinical chemistry **lín chuáng huà xüé**	临床化学 臨床化學
high-density **gāo mì dù**	高密度 高密度	clinical pathology **lín chuáng bìng lǐ xüé**	临床病理学 臨床病理學
low-density **dī mì dù**	低密度 低密度	is dead **sǐ -le**	死了 死了
pus cell **nóng xì bāo**	脓细胞 膿細胞	remains (of the dead) **yí tǐ**	遗体 遺體
blood smear for parasites **jì shēng chóng yàn xiě**	寄生虫验血 寄生蟲驗血	donate one's remains **jüan zèng yí tǐ**	捐赠遗体 捐贈遺體
hepatic (liver) function test **gān gōng néng cè dìng**	肝功能测定 肝功能測定	corpse **shī tǐ**	尸体 屍體
bile pigment **dǎn zhī sè sù**	胆汁色素 膽汁色素	frozen section **lěng dòng jiān**	冷冻间 冷凍間
bilirubin detection **dǎn hóng sù cè dìng**	胆红素测定 膽紅素測定	human anatomy **rén tǐ jiě pōu**	人体解剖 人體解剖
gastric juice analysis **wèi yè fēn xī**	胃液分析 胃液分析	anthropotomy **rén tǐ jiě pōu xüé**	人体解剖学 人體 解剖學
erosion **wèi suān fǔ shí**	胃酸腐蚀 胃酸腐蝕	coffin; casket **guān cai**	棺材 棺材
culture of bacteria **péi-yang xì jùn**	培养细菌 培養細菌	morgue **tài píng jiān**	太平间 太平間
quarantine **jiǎn yì**	检疫 檢疫	pay last respects to the remains **xiàng yí tǐ gào bié**	向遗体 告别
immunization **miǎn yì**	免疫 免疫	memorial service **zhuī dào huì**	追悼会 追悼會
urine examination **xiǎo biàn jiǎn yàn**	小便检验 小便檢驗	incinerator **fén huà lú**	焚化炉 焚化爐
stool routine exam **dà biàn jiǎn chá**	大便检查 大便檢查	cremate; incinerate **huǒ huà; huǒ zàng**	火化；火葬 火化；火葬
pregnancy test **yùn fù jiǎn yàn**	孕妇检验 孕婦檢驗	funerary ern **gǔ huī wèng**	骨灰瓮 骨灰甕
metabolism **xīn chén dài xiè**	新陈代谢 新陳代謝	burial in the sea **shuǐ zàng**	水葬 水葬

pharmacy; drug store **yào fáng**	药房 藥房	insufflate **chuī qì fǎ**	吹气法 吹氣法
prescription **chǔ fāng jiān**	处方笺 處方箋	ointment **yào gāo**	药膏 藥膏
doctor's order **yī shēng zhǐ shì**	医生指示 醫生指示	plaster **gāo-yao**	膏药 膏藥
drug **yào-pin**	药品 藥品	salve; unguent **ruǎn gāo**	软膏 軟膏
ampoule **xiǎo píngr zhēn jì**	小瓶儿针剂 小瓶兒針劑	zinc ointment **xīn gāo**	锌膏 鋅膏
international unit (I.U.) **guó jì dān wèi**	国际单位 國際單位	liniment **chá jì**	搽剂 搽劑
high unit **gāo dān wèi**	高单位 高單位	to apply; to smear **tú mǒ**	涂抹 塗抹
dose **yào jì**	药剂 藥劑	not to be taken **wài yòng yào, jì shí**	外用药，忌食 外用藥，忌食
dosage **jì liàng**	剂量 劑量	tranquilizer; sedative **zhèn jìng jì**	镇静剂 鎮靜劑
adult **chéng-ren**	成人 成人	sleeping pill **ān mián yào**	安眠药 安眠藥
children **xiǎo háir**	小孩儿 小孩兒	stimulant **xìng fèn yào**	兴奋药 興奮藥
pastil **kǒu hán yào**	口含药 口含藥	anti hypnotic **fáng shuì yào**	防睡药 防睡藥
scent drug **xiù jì**	嗅剂 嗅劑	diaphoretic **fā hàn yào**	发汗药 發汗藥
solvent **róng jì**	溶剂 溶劑	anti hidrotics **zhǐ hàn yào**	止汗药 止汗藥
inhalation **xī rù jì**	吸入剂 吸入劑	antipyretic **zhèn tòng yào**	镇痛药 鎮痛藥

specific; a wonder drug tè xiào yào	特效药 特效藥	philter; pet pill zhuàng yáng yào	壮阳药 壯陽藥
heart stimulant qiáng xīn jì	强心剂 強心劑	Viagra wēi ěr gāng	威尔钢 威爾鋼（壯陽藥）
neurotic bú nǎo yào	补脑药 補腦藥	testosterone nán xìng hé ěr méng	男性荷尔蒙 男性荷爾蒙
appetizer kāi wèi yào	开胃药 開胃藥	estrogen nǚ xìng hé ěr méng	女性荷尔蒙 女性荷爾蒙
antemetic cuī tù yào	催吐药 催吐藥	toxic dose zhòng dú liàng	中毒量 中毒量
expectorant huà tán yào	化痰药 化痰藥	lethal dose zhì sǐ liàng	致死量 致死量
galactagogue cuī rǔ yào	催乳药 催乳藥	antiphlogistic xiāo yán yào	消炎药 消炎藥
anti galactic zhǐ rǔ yào	止乳药 止乳藥	repellent xiāo zhǒng yào	消肿药 消腫藥
diuretics lì niào yào	利尿药 利尿藥	ether yǐ mí	乙醚 乙醚
laxative tablet syrup tōng biàn jì	通便剂 通便劑	supplementation yíng yǎng bǔ chōng	营养补充 營養補充
Metamucil biàn mì tōng	便秘通 便秘通	antibiotics kàng shēng sù	抗生素 抗生素
cathartics qīng cháng jì	清肠剂 清腸劑	antiarthritics zhì guān jié yán yào	治关节炎药 治關節炎藥
purgative xiè yào	泻药 瀉藥	antirheumatics zhì fēng shī yào	治风湿药 治風濕藥
castor oil bì má yóu	篦麻油 篦麻油	quack drug-fake medicine jiǎ yào	假药 假藥
insulin yí dǎo sù	胰岛素 胰島素	deterioration drug biàn zhí yào	变质药 變質藥
enzyme xiào sù	酵素 酵素	sterilizing shā jùn zuò yòng	杀菌作用 殺菌作用
sterility bú yùn yào	不孕药 不孕藥	collateral action; side effect fù zuò yòng	副作用 副作用
contraceptive bì yùn yào	避孕药 避孕藥	potency yào xiào	药效 藥效
birth-control pill bì yùn wán	避孕丸 避孕丸	non toxic wú dú	无毒 無毒
aphrodisiac chūn yào	春药 春藥	toxic yǒu dú	有毒 有毒

sulphur	硫磺	cyanocobalamin	维他命 B12
liú huáng	硫磺	wéi tā mìng B12	維他命 B12
borax	硼砂	Pangamic acid	维他命 B15
péng shā	硼砂	wéi tā mìng B15	維他命 B15
carbolic acid	碳酸	vitamin C	维他命 C
tàn suān	碳酸	wéi tā mìng C	維他命 C
traumatic	外伤药	ascorbic acid (vitamin C)	抗坏血酸
wài shāng yào	外傷藥	kàng huài xiě suān	抗壞血酸（維他命C）
styptic	止血药	tocopherol acetate (vitamin E)	维他命 E
zhí xiě yào	止血藥	wéi tā mìng E	維他命 E
quinine	圭宁;金鸡纳霜	multi vitamin	多种维他命
guī níng; jīn jī nà shuāng	圭寧;金雞納霜	duō zhǒng wéi tā mìng	多種維他命
anaesthetic; narcotic	麻醉药	vitamin K	维他命 K
má zuì yào	麻醉藥	wéi tā mìng K	維他命K
antiseptic; preservative	防腐剂	mineral substance	矿物质
fáng fǔ jì	防腐劑	kuàng wù zhí	礦物質
cotton bud; swab	棉花棒	fish oil	鱼油
mián huā bàng	棉花棒	yǔ yóu	魚油
hydrogen peroxide	双氧水	cod liver oil	鱼肝油
shuāng yáng shuǐ	雙氧水	yǔ gān yóu	魚肝油
iodine	碘酒	calcium tablet	钙片
dián jiǔ	碘酒	gài piàn	鈣片
mercurochrome liquid	红药水	liver extract	肝精
hóng yào shuǐ	紅藥水	gān jīng	肝精
gentian violet liquid	紫药水	chicken essence	鸡精
zǐ yào shuǐ	紫藥水	jī jīng	雞精
petrolatum vaseline	凡士林	narcotics; drug	毒品
fán shì lín	凡士林	dú pǐn	毒品
tonic	补药	heroin	海洛英
bǔ yào	補藥	hǎi luò yīn	海洛英
vitamin	维他命	opium	鸦片
wéi tā mìng	維他命	yā piàn	鴉片
retinol (vitamin A)	维他命 A	morphine	吗啡
wéi tā mìng A	維他命 A	mǎ fēi	嗎啡
B complex	综合维他命 B	marijuana; weed; grass	大麻菸
zòng hé wéi tā mìng B	綜合維他命 B	dà má yān	大麻菸
thiamin (vitamin B1)	维他命 B1	amphetamine (drug)	安非他命
wéi tā mìng B1	維他命 B1	ān fēi tā mìng	安非他命（毒品）
riboflavin (vitamin B2)	维他命 B2	hallucinogen (drug)	迷幻药
wéi tā mìng B2	維他命 B2	mí huàn yào	迷幻藥（毒品）

acidhead (drug) **yáo tóu wán**	摇头丸 搖頭丸（毒品）	antidote **jiě dú yào**	解毒药 解毒藥
pentazocine (drug) **sūn wù kōng**	孙悟空 孫悟空（毒品）	antidysenteric **zhǐ lì yào**	止痢药 止痢藥
superglue (drug) **qiáng lì jiāo**	强力胶 強力膠（毒品）	antitoxin **kàng dú sù**	抗毒素 抗毒素
codeine (drug) **kě dài yīn**	可待因 可待因（毒品）	aspirin **ā sī pǐ líng**	阿司匹灵 阿司匹靈
niacin **yān jiǎn suān**	烟硷酸 煙鹼酸	aureomycin **jīn méi sù**	金霉素 金黴素
addicted **shàng yǐn-le**	上瘾了 上癮了	bactericide **shā jùn yào**	杀菌药 殺菌藥
ephedrine **má huáng sù**	麻黄素 麻黃素	biochemistry analysis **shēng huà xué fēn xī**	生化学分析 生化學分析
caffeine **kā fēi yīn**	咖啡因 咖啡因	boracic solution **péng suān shuǐ**	硼酸水 硼酸水
ammonia **ā mò ní yǎ; ān**	阿莫尼亚；氨 阿莫尼亞；氨	calcium glucose **pú-tao táng gài**	葡萄糖钙 葡萄糖鈣
absorbefacient **xī shōu jì**	吸收剂 吸收劑	camphor **zhāng nǎo**	樟脑 樟腦
acetone **bǐng tóng**	丙酮 丙酮	cerate **zhī là hé jì**	脂腊合剂 脂蠟合劑
acid phosphatase **suān xìng lín suān**	酸性磷酸 酸性磷酸	chloroform **lǜ fǎng**	氯仿 氯仿
absolute alcohol **chún jiǔ jīng**	纯酒精 純酒精	chloromycetin **lǜ méi sù**	绿霉素 綠黴素
denatured alcohol **biàn xìng jiǔ jīng**	变性酒精 變性酒精	cimetidine **kàng wèi kuì yáng yào**	抗胃溃疡药 抗胃潰瘍藥
androgens **xióng xìng jī sù**	雄性激素 雄性激素	citronella oil **xiāng máo yóu**	香茅油 香茅油
gonadotropin **cù xìng xiàn jī sù**	促性腺激素 促性腺激素	demulcent **huǎn hé jì**	缓和剂 緩和劑
cortisone **shèn shàng xiàn pí zhí sù**	肾上腺皮质素 腎上腺皮質素	deodorant **chú tǐ chòu lù**	除体臭露 除體臭露
anodyne **zhèn tòng jì**	镇痛剂 鎮痛劑	depilatory cream **tuō máo yào shuāng**	脱毛药霜 脫毛藥霜
anti-diabetics **zhì táng niào bìng yào**	治糖尿病药 治糖尿病藥	digestive **xiāo huà j**	消化剂 消化劑
arsenic antidote **pī shuāng jiě dú yào**	砒霜解毒药 砒霜解毒藥	dispensary **yī yuàn yào fáng**	医院药房 醫院藥房

dispensing **pèi yào**	配药 配藥	
emmenagogue **tōng jīng yào**	通经药 通經藥	
emulsion **rǔ jì**	乳剂 乳劑	
febrifuge **tuì shāo yào**	退烧药 退燒藥	
fertility pill **shòu yùn yào**	受孕药 受孕藥	
fractional dose **jì liàng shǎo**	剂量少 劑量少	
fungicide **shā jùn jì**	杀菌剂 殺菌劑	
glycerin **gān yóu**	甘油 甘油	
hemopoietics **bú xiě yào**	补血药 補血藥	
herb **cǎo yào**	草药 草藥	
hormone **hé ěr méng**	荷尔蒙 荷爾蒙	
inhalant medicine **xiù yào**	嗅药 嗅藥	
lactose **rǔ táng**	乳糖 乳糖	
lecithin **luǎn lín zhī**	卵磷脂 卵磷脂	
lipoprotein **zhī dàn bái**	脂蛋白 脂蛋白	
liquid medicine **yào shuǐ**	药水 藥水	
lozenge **zhǐ ké táng**	止咳糖 止咳糖	
menthol **bò-he yóu**	薄荷油 薄荷油	
mercurous chloride **gān gǒng**	甘汞 甘汞	
microorganism **wéi shēng wù**	微生物 微生物	

mildew drug **méi yào wù**	霉药物 黴藥物	
nutrient injection **bǔ zhēn**	补针 補針	
painkiller **zhǐ tòng yào**	止痛药 止痛藥	
parasiticide **qū chóng jì**	驱虫剂 驅蟲劑	
paste **hú**	糊 糊	
potash **tàn suān jiǎ; cáo jiǎn**	碳酸钾；草硷 碳酸鉀；草鹼	
powdered medicine **yào fěn**	药粉 藥粉	
scabies ointment **jiè chuāng yào gāo**	芥疮药膏 芥瘡藥膏	
seasick pill **yūn chuán yào**	晕船药 暈船藥	
serological examination **xiě qīng jiǎn yàn**	血清检验 血清檢驗	
sleeping inhalant **mí yào**	迷药 迷藥	
sodium iodide **diǎn huà jiǎ**	碘化钾 碘化鉀	
sterile cotton pad **shā mián diàn**	纱棉垫 紗棉墊	
stomachic powder; peptic **zhù xiāo huà yào**	助消化药 助消化藥	
streptomycin **liàn méi sù**	链霉素 鏈黴素	
sugar coated **wài bāo táng yī**	外包糖衣 外包糖衣	
sulfonal **cuī mián yào**	催眠药 催眠藥	
suppositories **shuān jì**	栓剂 栓劑	
suppository vaginal **yīn dào-de shuān jì**	阴道的栓剂 陰道的栓劑	
synthetic drugs **rén gōng hé chéng yào**	人工合成药 人工合成藥	

triglyceride **sān suān gān yóu zhǐ**	三酸甘油酯 三酸甘油酯	oxytocic **cuī shēng jì**	催生剂 催生劑
turpentine oil **sōng jié yóu**	松节油 松節油	antispasmodic **zhì jìng lüán yào**	治痉挛药 治痙攣藥
urine and stool analysis **niào hé fèn biàn fēn xī**	尿和粪便分析 尿和糞便分析	antiemetic **zhǐ tù yào**	止吐药 止吐藥
urine sugar analysis paper **niào táng fēn xī zhǐ**	尿糖分析纸 尿糖分析紙	calcium gluconate **gài pú-tao táng suān**	钙葡萄糖酸 鈣葡萄糖酸
vaccine **yì miáo**	疫苗 疫苗	dextran **pú táo jù táng**	葡萄聚糖 葡萄聚糖
valium **ān mián zhèn dìng yào**	安眠镇定药 安眠鎮定藥	cold medicine **gǎn mào yào**	感冒药 感冒藥
vulneraries **shāng yào**	伤药 傷藥	diet pill **jiǎn féi yào**	减肥药 減肥藥
salicylic acid **shuǐ yáng suān**	水杨酸 水楊酸	Mentholatum **màn xiù léi dūn**	曼秀雷敦 曼秀雷敦
ntidiarrheal drugs **zhǐ xiè yào**	止泻药 止瀉藥	preservative **fáng fǔ jì**	防腐剂 防腐劑
helminthagogue **qū cháng chóng jì**	驱肠虫剂 驅腸蟲劑	trichogen **shēng fǎ jì**	生发剂 生髮劑
Epsom salts **xiè yán**	泻盐 瀉鹽	Penicillin **pán ní xī lín**	盘尼西林 盤尼西林
glucide **táng jīng; tián jīng**	糖精；甜精 糖精；甜精	lymph vaccine **lín bā yì miáo**	淋巴疫苗 淋巴疫苗
abortigenic **duò tāi jì**	堕胎剂 墮胎劑		

Medical Equipment
醫療器材

medical equipment **yī liáo qì cái**	医疗器材 醫療器材	glass plate **bō-li bǎnr**	玻璃板儿 玻璃板兒
well equipped **shè bèi wán shàn**	设备完善 設備完善	spatula **bàn yào dāor**	拌药刀儿 拌藥刀兒
medical instrument **yī liáo yí qì**	医疗仪器 醫療儀器	spoon **chí**	匙 匙
apparatus **yí qì**	仪器 儀器	curette **guā chí**	刮匙 刮匙
dispensing scale **yào chèng**	药秤 藥秤	spreader **tān yào dāo**	摊药刀 攤藥刀
balance (scale) **tiān píng**	天平 天平	mortar **yào jiù**	药臼 藥臼
iron stand **tiě jià**	铁架 鐵架	pestle **yào chǔ**	药杵 藥杵
iron ring **tiě quān**	铁圈 鐵圈	stirring rod **jiǎo bàng**	搅棒 攪棒
iron tripod **tiě sān jiǎo**	铁三角 鐵三角	strainer **qù zhā lǜ bù**	去渣滤布 去渣濾布
drop bottle **dī yào-shui píngr**	滴药水瓶儿 滴藥水瓶兒	scalder **zhǔ fèi qì**	煮沸器 煮沸器
drop rod **dī yào-shui bàng**	滴药水棒 滴藥水棒	wheel chair **lún yǐ**	轮椅 輪椅
vial; phial **yào píngr**	药瓶儿 藥瓶兒	spittoon **tán yǘ**	痰盂 痰盂
matrass **cháng jǐng yuán qiú píng**	长颈圆球瓶 長頸圓球瓶	corn plaster **jī yǎn diàn**	鸡眼垫 雞眼墊
measure glass **liáng bēi**	量杯 量杯	piles cushion **zhì-chuāng diàn**	痔疮垫 痔瘡墊
graduation **liáng bēi kē dù**	量杯刻度 量杯刻度	ear syringe **xí ěr qì**	洗耳器 洗耳器

English	Pinyin	Chinese
nose syringe	xǐ bí qì	洗鼻器 / 洗鼻器
esophagoscope	shí dào jìng	食道镜 / 食道鏡
hypodermic syringe	dǎ zhēn jī-tong	打针唧筒 / 打針唧筒
plastic syringe	sù jiāo zhēn tóu	塑胶针头 / 塑膠針頭
endoscope	nèi shì jìng	内视镜 / 內視鏡
bronchoscope	zhī qì guǎn jìng	支气管镜 / 支氣管鏡
hernia belt	shàn qì dài	疝气带 / 疝氣帶
drainer	pái nóng guǎn	排脓管 / 排膿管
pus tray	zhì nóng pán	置脓盘 / 置膿盤
microscope	xiǎn wéi jìng	显微镜 / 顯微鏡
electron microscope	diàn-zi xiǎn wéi jìng	电子显微镜 / 電子顯微鏡
concave mirror	aō miàn jìng	凹面镜 / 凹面鏡
convex mirror	tū miàn jìng	凸面镜 / 凸面鏡
TV camera	diàn shì shè yǐng jī	电视摄影机 / 電視攝影機
galvanoscope	yàn diàn liú qì	验电流器 / 驗電流器

English	Pinyin	Chinese
body protractor	rén tǐ zēng gāo jī	人体增高机 / 人體增高機
radiator	fàng rè qì	放热器 / 放熱器
air pump	chōu qì jī	抽气机 / 抽氣機
lift-pump	chōu shuǐ jī	抽水机 / 抽水機
germinator	fā yá qì	发芽器 / 發芽器
purifier	jīng liàn (tí chún) qì	精链(提纯器) / 精鍊(提純器)
rubber tube	jiāo guǎn	胶管 / 膠管
catheter	dǎo niào guǎn	导尿管 / 導尿管
computerized tomography	duàn céng shè yǐng jī	断层摄影机 / 斷層攝影機
enema	guàn cháng qì	灌肠器 / 灌腸器
slipper bed pan	bìng rén biàn pán	病人便盘 / 病人便盤
female urinal	nǔ yòng niào pán	女用尿盘 / 女用尿盤
male urinal	nán yòng niào hú	男用尿壶 / 男用尿壺
urinal bag	niào dài	尿袋 / 尿袋
douche bag	nǔ yòng guàn xǐ dài	女用灌洗袋 / 女用灌洗袋

Group 64, 健康检查与化验室 Physical Checkup & Laboratory;
Related Terms: Group 78, 科学常识 Science

67 Herbal Medicine 草藥

herb medicine **cǎo yào**	草药 草藥	mint oil **bò-he yóu**	薄荷油 薄荷油
herb doctor **zhōng yī shī**	中医师 中醫師	menthol **bò-he nǎo**	薄荷脑 薄荷腦
gallipot **zhōng yào yào guàn**	中药药罐 中藥藥罐	aromatic oil **xiāng yóu**	香油 香油
herb **cáo běn zhí wù**	草本植物 草本植物	tiger balm **wàn jīn yóu**	万金油 萬金油
suffer from excessive internal heat **shàng huǒ**	上火 上火	hereditary secret formula **zǔ chuán mì fāng**	祖传秘方 祖傳秘方
symptoms **zhèng zhuàng**	症状 症狀	proprietary medicine **mì fāng chéng-yao**	秘方成药 秘方成藥
inflammation of nasal cavities **bí qiāng fā yán**	鼻腔发炎 鼻腔發炎	nostrum **wàn néng yào**	万能药 萬能藥
inflammation of oral cavities **kǒu qiāng fā yán**	口腔发炎 口腔發炎	revitalizing tonic **zī yǎng yào gāo**	滋养药膏 滋養藥膏
constipation **biàn mì**	便秘 便秘	panacea **wàn yìng yào**	万应药 萬應藥
conjunctivitis **jié mó yán**	结膜炎 結膜炎	catholicon **wàn líng yào**	万灵药 萬靈藥
reduce excessive internal heat **jiàng huǒ**	降火 降火	myrrh **mò yào**	没药 沒藥
stimulant **tí shén**	提神 提神	moxibustion; moxa treatment **jiǔ; ài jiǔ**	灸;艾灸 灸;艾灸
sedative **qīng huǒ**	清火 清火	capsule **dān**	丹 丹
refrigerant **sàn rè**	散热 散熱	refining **liàn**	炼 煉
camphor oil **zhāng-nao yóu**	樟脑油 樟腦油	alchemy **liàn dān**	炼丹 煉丹

pulvis **yào sǎn**	药散 藥散	ginseng **rén-shen**	人参 人參
trituration **fěn mò**	粉末 粉末	Korean ginseng **Gāo-li shēn**	高丽参 高麗參
grinding **yán mòr**	研末儿 研末兒	clarified **bái ròu yáng shēn**	白肉洋参 白肉洋參
bray **dǎo suì**	捣碎 搗碎	American ginseng **xī-yang shēn**	西洋参 西洋參
pulverization **dǎo-cheng fěn**	捣成粉 搗成粉	monkey bezoar **hóu zǎo**	猴枣 猴棗
decocting **jiān**	煎 煎	horse bezoar **mǎ bǎo**	马宝 馬寶
dose **yí jì yào**	一剂药 一劑藥	bear's gall **xióng dǎn**	熊胆 熊膽
sifting **shāi**	筛 篩	seal penis **hái gǒu biān**	海狗鞭 海狗鞭
filtering **lù**	滤 濾	Penis cervi **méi lù biān**	梅鹿鞭 梅鹿鞭
gruff **yào zhā**	药渣 藥渣	margarita **zhēn zhū yún mǔ**	珍珠云母 珍珠雲母
disguise **yào yǐn-zi**	药引子 藥引子	polygonum **shǒu wū**	首乌 首烏
vapor **xūn yào**	熏药 燻藥	polygonum multiflorum **hé shǒu wū**	何首乌 何首烏
brew **pào zhì**	泡制 泡制	deer young antler **lù róng**	鹿茸 鹿茸
medicine liquor **jìn jiǔ**	浸酒 浸酒	isinglass **yú jiāo**	鱼胶 魚膠
herb soup **tāng yào**	汤药 湯藥	armadillo scale **shān jiǎ piàn**	山甲片 山甲片
herb tea **yào chá**	药茶 藥茶	rhinoceros horn **xī niú jiǎo**	犀牛角 犀牛角
pill **wán yào**	丸药 丸藥	chamois horn **líng yáng jiǎo**	羚羊角 羚羊角
bolus **dà wán yào**	大丸药 大丸藥	tiger's bone **hú gǔ**	虎骨 虎骨
pellet **xiǎo yào wánr**	小药丸儿 小藥丸兒	os draconian **wǔ huā lóng gǔ**	五花龙骨 五花龍骨
wax capsule **là ké**	腊壳 蠟殼	cuttlebone **mò yú gǔ**	墨鱼骨 墨魚骨

hippocampus **dà hái mǎ**	大海马 大海馬	pyrethrum **chú chóng cǎo**	除虫草 除蟲草
gecko **dà gé**	大蛤 大蛤	safflower **hóng huā**	红花 紅花
toad venoms **dú chán chú**	毒蟾蜍 毒蟾蜍	crocus **fān hóng huā**	番红花 番紅花
cicada shell **chán tuì**	蝉蜕 蟬蛻	saffron **zàng hóng huā**	藏红花 藏紅花
anise **dà huí xiāng**	大茴香 大茴香	feverfew **bái jú huā**	白菊花 白菊花
cumin **xiǎo huí xiāng**	小茴香 小茴香	honey-suckle **jīn yín huā**	金银花 金銀花
fennei **huí xiāng**	茴香 茴香	cassia **guì pí**	桂皮 桂皮
musk; thyme **shè xiāng**	麝香 麝香	dried orange-peel **chén pí**	陈皮 陳皮
grace herb **yǔn xiāng**	芸香 芸香	pomegranate bark **shí-liu pí**	石榴皮 石榴皮
agalloch **chén xiāng**	沈香 沈香	mulberry root bark **sāng bái pí**	桑白皮 桑白皮
clove **dīng-xiang**	丁香 丁香	lichen **dì gǔ pí**	地骨皮 地骨皮
resin **sōng-xiang**	松香 松香	simarouba **kǔ mù pí**	苦木皮 苦木皮
star anise **bā jiǎo**	八角 八角	rhodium **hóng xiāng mù**	红香木 紅香木
cinnamon **ròu guì**	肉桂 肉桂	sweet basil **sū yè**	苏叶 蘇葉
cardamom **dòu kòu**	豆蔻 豆蔻	dried waterlily leaf **gān hé yè**	干荷叶 乾荷葉
zinnia **bǎi-ri cǎo**	百日草 百日草	loquat leaf **pí-pa yè**	枇杷叶 枇杷葉
plantain **chē qián cǎo**	车前草 車前草	peppermint leaves **bò-he yè**	薄荷叶 薄荷葉
liquorice **gān cǎo**	甘草 甘草	absinth **kǔ ài**	苦艾 苦艾
sage **xiāng cǎo**	香草 香草	vulgaris **ài yè**	艾叶 艾葉
gromwell **zí cǎo**	紫草 紫草	aconite root **wū tóu gēn**	乌头根 烏頭根

gentian root **lóng dǎn gēn**	龙胆根 龍膽根	
turmeric **jiāng huáng**	姜黄 薑黃	
shrubby **má huáng**	麻黄 麻黃	
rhubarb horse-tails **dà huáng**	大黄 大黃	
orpiment **xióng-huang**	雄黄 雄黃	
bezoar **niú huáng**	牛黄 牛黃	
digitalis **dì huáng**	地黄 地黃	
coptis **huáng lián**	黄莲 黃蓮	
reed rhizome **lú gēn**	芦根 蘆根	
medlar **góu qǐ-zi**	枸杞子 枸杞子	
gall **mò shí zǐ**	没食子 沒食子	
plantain seed **chē qián zǐ**	车前子 車前子	
tuckahoe **fú líng**	茯苓 茯苓	
angelica **dāng guī**	当归 當歸	
betel nut **bīng-lang**	槟榔 檳榔	
caladium **bèi mǔ**	贝母 貝母	
apricot kernel **xìng rén**	杏仁 杏仁	
gingko; ginkgo **bái guǒr; yín xìngr**	白果儿；银杏儿 白果兒；銀杏兒	
theophylline **chá jiǎn**	茶硷 茶鹼	
arsenic **pī shuāng**	砒霜 砒霜	

nitre **xiāo**	硝 硝	
white arsenic **bái xìn shí**	白信石 白信石	
red arsenic **hóng xìn shí**	红信石 紅信石	
alum **bái fán**	白矾 白礬	
vitriol **lǜ fán**	绿矾 綠礬	
cinnabar **zhū-sha**	朱砂 朱砂	
quicksilver **shuǐ yín**	水银 水銀	
gypsum **shí gāo**	石膏 石膏	
talcum **huá-shi fěn**	滑石粉 滑石粉	
deliquescent **shōu shī**	收湿 收濕	
desiccation **qù shī**	去湿 去濕	
divergence **fā sàn**	发散 發散	
relief of constipation **tōng biàn**	通便 通便	
diuresis **lì niào**	利尿 利尿	
emollient **rùn fū jì**	润肤剂 潤膚劑	
anti-rheum plaster **gǒu pí gāo**	狗皮膏 狗皮膏	
concentration **shōu gāo**	收膏 收膏	
ointment **yào gāo**	药膏 藥膏	
plaster **gāo-yao**	膏药 膏藥	
poultice **xiāo zhǒng gāo-yao**	消肿膏药 消腫膏藥	

adhesive plaster **shōu kǒu gāo-yao**	收口膏药 收口膏藥	abrism **xiāng sī dòu**	相思豆 相思豆
camphor **bīng piàn; lóng nǎo**	冰片；龙脑 冰片；龍腦	quisqualis indica **shǐ jūn zǐ**	使君子 使君子
contraindication **jìn jì**	禁忌 禁忌	encommiae ulmoide **dù zhòng**	杜仲 杜仲
diet **jì kǒu**	忌口 忌口	ligusticum wallichii **chuān qióng**	川芎 川芎
ganoderma lucidum **líng zhī**	灵芝 靈芝	zanthoxylum **chuān jiāo**	川椒 川椒
rehmanniae **shēng dì**	生地 生地	bigarabe **kǔ chéng**	苦橙 苦橙
rehmanniae vaporata **shú dì**	熟地 熟地	zizyphus vulgaris **suān zǎo rénr**	酸枣仁儿 酸棗仁兒
herbaepimedii **yín yáng huò**	淫羊藿 淫羊藿	sterculia scaphigera **péng dà hǎi**	彭大海 彭大海

68 Acupuncture 针灸

acupuncture **zhēn jiǔ**	针灸 針灸	symphysion **lián hé xüè**	联合穴 聯合穴
acupuncturist **zhēn jiǔ dài-fu**	针灸大夫 針灸大夫	meridian **jīng luò**	经络 經絡
cauterizing **jiú fǎ**	灸法 灸法	needle **zhēn**	针 針
vital point **xüè dào**	穴道 穴道	fine needle **háo zhēn**	毫针 毫針
point **xüè**	穴 穴	ear acupuncture **ěr zhēn**	耳针 耳針
ophryon **méi xüè**	眉穴 眉穴	triangular needle **sān léng léng zhēn**	三棱棱针 三稜稜針
obelion **dǐng xüè**	顶穴 頂穴	staying needle **pí ròu zhēn**	皮肉针 皮肉針
auriculare **ěr xüè**	耳穴 耳穴	plum-flower needle **méi huā zhēn**	梅花针 梅花針
genion **ké xüè**	颏穴 頦穴（下巴颏）	moxa **ài; ài hāo**	艾；艾蒿 艾；艾蒿
gnathion **hé xüè**	颌穴 頜穴	moxibustion **ài jiǔ**	艾灸 艾灸
temple **tài-yang xüè**	太阳穴 太陽穴	fumigation **xūn-fa**	熏法 燻法
zygion **è xüè**	轭穴 軛穴	chiropractor **tuī ná**	推拿 推拿
metopion **é xüè**	额穴 額穴	kneading **róu niē-fa**	揉捏法 揉捏法
stephanion **guàn xüè**	冠穴 冠穴	cupping **bá guàn-zi**	拔罐子 拔罐子
stenion **xiá xüè**	狭穴 狹穴	acupressure **zhǐ yā; àn mó**	指压；按摩 指壓；按摩

Athletic Terms
運動術語

sports yùn-dong	运动 運動	decisive point jüé shèng diǎn	决胜点 決勝點
athletic terms yùn-dong shù yǔ	运动术语 運動術語	athletic meet yùn-dong huì	运动会 運動會
athletics tǐ yù	体育 體育	see a sports contest kàn yùn-dong huì	看运动会 看運動會
athlete; sportsman yùn-dong yüán	运动员 運動員	Olympic Games ào lín pǐ kè jìng sài	奥林匹克竞赛 奧林匹克競賽
amateur sportsman yè yǔ yùn dòng	业馀运动 業餘運動	torch light shèng huǒ	圣火 聖火
stadium tǐ yù jìng sài chǎng	体育竞赛场 體育競賽場	Asian Games yà yùn huì	亚运会 亞運會
sports field yùn dòng chǎng	运动场 運動場	Area Games qū yùn huì	区运会 區運會
arena jìng jì chǎng	竞技场 競技場	International Games guó jì sài	国际赛 國際賽
gym; gymnasium tǐ yù guǎn	体育馆 體育館	open competition gōng kāi sài	公开赛 公開賽
fitness center jiàn shēn fáng	健身房 健身房	invitation match yāo qǐng sài	邀请赛 邀請賽
warm-up nuǎn shēn yùn dòng	暖身运动 暖身運動	visiting team kè duì	客队 客隊
fundamental movement jī-ben dòng zuò	基本动作 基本動作	duel meet duì kàng sài	对抗赛 對抗賽
physical strength tǐ lì	体力 體力	elimination system táo tài zhì	淘汰制 淘汰制
physical ability tǐ néng	体能 體能	fair play gōng píng jìng zhēng	公平竞争 公平競爭
physical constitution tǐ zhí	体质 體質	tournament lián sài	联赛 聯賽

exhibition game **biáo yǎn sài**	表演赛 表演賽	third place; ternary **jì jūn**	季军 季軍
professional player **zhí yè yùn dòng yüán**	职业运动员 職業運動員	fourth place; rear ward **diàn jūn**	殿军 殿軍
semi-professional player **bàn zhí yè yùn dòng yüán**	半职业运动员 半職業運動員	prize **jiáng-pin**	奖品 獎品
amateur player **yè yǘ yùn dòng yüán**	业馀运动员 業餘運動員	gold medal **jīn pái**	金牌 金牌
decathlon **shí xiàng yùn dòng**	十项运动 十項運動	silver medal **yín pái**	银牌 銀牌
record holder **jì lù bǎo chí zhě**	纪录保持者 紀錄保持者	bronze medal **tóng pái**	铜牌 銅牌
world record **shì jiè jì lù**	世界纪录 世界紀錄	trophy **yín bēi**	银杯 銀盃
national record **qüán guó jì lù**	全国纪录 全國紀錄	silver shield **yín dùn**	银盾 銀盾
broke the record **dǎ pò jì lù**	打破记录 打破記錄	tapestry flag **jǐn qí**	锦旗 錦旗
to watch a ball game **kàn sài qiú**	看赛球 看賽球	citation **jiǎng zhuàng**	奖状 獎狀
try-out **xüǎn bá; yù xüǎn**	选拔；预选 選拔；預選	coach **jiào liàn**	教练 教練
preliminary heat **yù sài**	预赛 預賽	referee, judge **cái pàn yüán**	裁判员 裁判員
final contest; final heat **jüé sài**	决赛 決賽	announcer **bào gào yüán**	报告员 報告員
win **yíng**	赢 贏	stopwatch **páo biǎo**	跑表 跑錶
won **yíng-le**	赢了 贏了	time keeper **jì shí yüán**	计时员 計時員
lose **shū**	输 輸	scoreboard **jì fēn bǎn**	计分板 計分板
lost **shū-le**	输了 輸了	default **qì qüán**	弃权 棄權
champion **guàn jūn**	冠军 冠軍	disqualification **qǔ xiāo zī gé**	取消资格 取消資格
runner-up **yǎ jūn**	亚军 亞軍		

Track Events 径赛

track events **jìng sài**	径赛 徑賽	100-meter dash; hectometer **pǎo bái mǐ**	跑百米 跑百米
track & field area **tián jìng chǎng**	田径场 田徑場	speed up; acceleration **jiā sù**	加速 加速
oval **jìng sài chǎng**	径赛场 徑賽場	turning mark **zhé huí-de biāo zhì**	折回的标帜 折回的標幟
running **pǎo**	跑 跑	decisive point **jüé shèng diǎn**	决胜点 決勝點
torch **huǒ jù**	火炬 火炬	hurdles **lán**	栏 欄
inner lane (course) **nèi qüān**	内圈 內圈	low hurdles **dī lán**	低栏 低欄
outer lane (course) **wài qüān**	外圈 外圈	intermediate hurdles **zhōng lán**	中栏 中欄
inter boundary **pǎo nèi dào**	跑内道 跑內道	high hurdles **gāo lán**	高栏 高欄
outer boundary **pǎo wài dào**	跑外道 跑外道	run the low hurdles **dī lán sài pǎo**	低栏赛跑 低欄賽跑
on your marks **gè jiù gè wèi**	各就各位 各就各位	trail **zhuī gǎn**	追赶 追趕
stopwatch **má biǎo**	马表 馬錶	long distance race **zháng chéng pǎo**	长程跑 長程跑
get set **yǜ bèi**	预备 預備	middle distance race **zhōng chéng pǎo**	中程跑 中程跑
standing **lì zī**	立姿 立姿	false start **tōu bù**	偷步 偷步
crouching **dūn zī**	蹲姿 蹲姿	starting line **qí pǎo xiàn**	起跑线 起跑線
start **qí pǎo**	起跑 起跑	starting hole **qí pǎo dòng**	起跑洞 起跑洞

unfair start qí pǎo bù gōng	起跑不公 起跑不公	straightaway zhí xìan pǎo dào	直线跑道 直線跑道
early-start detector záo pǎo cè dìng qì	早跑测定器 早跑測定器	turn yuán xíng pǎo dào	圆形跑道 圓形跑道
spiked shoes dīng xié	钉鞋 釘鞋	lane; line pǎo dào xiàn	跑道线 跑道線
marathon race mǎ lā sōng sài pǎo	马拉松赛跑 馬拉松賽跑	one lap pǎo yì qüān	跑一圈 跑一圈
long distance race cháng jù lí sài pǎo	长距离赛跑 長距離賽跑	preliminary contest yù sài	预赛 預賽
baton jiē lì bàng	接力棒 接力棒	foot race; walking race jìng zǒu	竞走 競走
baton pass jiē bàng	接棒 接棒	jogging màn pǎo	慢跑 慢跑
baton-passing area (zone) jiē bàng qū	接棒区 接棒區	sprint; short distance race duán pǎo	短跑 短跑
relay runner jiē bàng zhě	接棒者 接棒者	dash race sài pǎo	赛跑 賽跑
relay race jiē lì sài pǎo	接力赛跑 接力賽跑	obstacle chase race zhàng ài sài pǎo	障碍赛跑 障礙賽跑
medley relay hùn hé jiē lì sài	混合接力赛 混合接力賽	obstacle course zhàng ài pǎo dào	障碍跑道 障礙跑道
impulse zhōng lì	冲力 衝力	cross-country race yüè yě sài pǎo	越野赛跑 越野賽跑
to breast the tape chōng guò zhōng diǎn	冲过终点 衝過終點	to trail wěi suí rén hòu	尾随人後 尾隨人後
the finish; goal zhōng diǎn	终点 終點	leg guard hù-tui	护腿 護腿
finish line zhōng diǎn xiàn	终点线 終點線	kneecap; kneepad hù xī	护膝 護膝
terminal post zhōng diǎn zhù	终点柱 終點柱	parade yóu xíng	游行 遊行
home stretch zuì hòu sài chéng	最後赛程 最後賽程	cheering squad; rooters lā lā duì	拉拉队 拉拉隊
gasp chuǎn qì	喘气 喘氣	banner qí zhì	旗帜 旗幟
starting pistol fā lìng qiāng	发令枪 發令槍	yell nà hǎn	呐喊 吶喊
track; course pǎo dào	跑道 跑道	go, go! jiā yóu	加油 加油

field events **tián sài**	田赛 田賽	barbell; lever-bell **jǔ zhòng yǎ líng**	举重哑铃 舉重啞鈴
pennant **jiǎng qí; sān jiǎo qí**	奖旗;三角旗 奬旗;三角旗	discus throw **rēng tié bǐng**	扔铁饼 扔鐵餅
school banner **xiào qí**	校旗 校旗	javelin throw **rēng biāo qiāng**	扔标枪 扔標槍
weight-lifting **jǔ zhòng**	举重 舉重	hammer throw **shuǎi liàn qiú**	甩炼球 甩鍊球
the weightlifter **jǔ zhòng xüán-shou**	举重选手 舉重選手	shot put; putting **tuī qiān qiú**	推铅球 推鉛球
to stay in shape **bǎo chí liáng hǎo zhuàng kuàng**	保持良好状况 保持良好狀況	skipping rope **tiào shéng**	跳绳 跳繩
hand snatch **zhuā jǔ**	抓举 抓舉	broad jump pit **shā kēng**	沙坑 沙坑
hand military press **tuī jǔ**	推举 推舉	take-off line **qǐ tiào xiàn**	起跳线 起跳線
two-arm snatch **shuāng bì jí jǔ**	双臂急举 雙臂急舉	high jump **tiào gāo**	跳高 跳高
standing lateral raise **lì shì cè jǔ**	立式侧举 立式側舉	high jump standard **tiào gāo jià**	跳高架 跳高架
lying lateral raise **wò shì tuī jǔ**	卧式推举 臥式推舉	standing high jump **lì dìng tiào gāo**	立定跳高 立定跳高
hercule set **wò lì qì**	握力器 握力器	pole vault; pole jump **chēng gān tiào**	撑竿跳 撑竿跳
erector **jǔ zhòng qì**	举重器 舉重器	broad (long) jump **tiào yǔan**	跳远 跳遠
chest expander **kuò xiōng qì**	扩胸器 擴胸器	standing broad jump **lì dìng tiào yǔan**	立定跳远 立定跳遠
dumbbell **yǎ líng**	哑铃 啞鈴	hop, step & jump **sān jí tiào yǔan**	三级跳远 三級跳遠

gymnastics; physical exercise **tǐ cāo**	体操 體操	to pull up **bǎ shēn tǐ xiàng shàng lā**	把身体向上拉 把身體向上拉
morning exercise **chén cāo**	晨操 晨操	horizontal balance **shuǐ píng píng héng**	水平平衡 水平平衡
exerciser **tǐ cāo qì xiè**	体操器械 體操器械	balance beam **píng héng tái**	平衡台 平衡台
gymnastic **jiàn shēn shù**	健身术 健身術	balance exercise **píng héng yùn dòng**	平衡运动 平衡運動
workout (training) **jiàn shēn**	健身 健身	trapeze **diào dān jià qiū qiān**	吊单架秋千 吊單架秋千
competition **jìng jì**	竞技 競技	mat tumbling **diàn shàng yùn dòng**	垫上运动 墊上運動
warm up **nuǎn shēn cāo**	暖身操 暖身操	pyramid building **dié luó hàn**	叠罗汉 疊羅漢
fitness exercise **jiàn shēn cāo**	健身操 健身操	shoulder stand **jiān bèi dào lì**	肩背倒立 肩背倒立
body building **liàn shēn tǐ**	练身体 練身體	one-hand balance **dān shǒu dào lì**	单手倒立 單手倒立
pep **huó lì**	活力 活力	squatting; crouching **dūn xià**	蹲下 蹲下
horizontal bar **dān gàng**	单杠 單槓	bend trunk forwards **shàng tǐ qián wān**	上体前弯 上體前彎
parallel bars **shuāng gàng**	双杠 雙槓	bend trunk backwards **shàng tǐ hòu dǎo**	上体后倒 上體後倒
uneven bars **dà shuāng gàng**	大双杠 大雙槓	springboard **tán huáng bǎn**	弹簧板 彈簧板
horse **mù mǎ**	木马 木馬	jump **tiào**	跳 跳
rope quoit **diào huán**	吊环 吊環	rope jumping **tiào shéng**	跳绳 跳繩

hula hoop **hū lā qüān**	呼拉圈 呼拉圈	stride position **chá tuǐ zī shì**	踏腿姿势 踏腿姿勢
vault box **tiào xiāng**	跳箱 跳箱	official exercise **guī dìng dòng zuò**	规定动作 規定動作
vaulting horse **ān mǎ**	鞍马 鞍馬	sit-ups **yǎng wò qǐ zuò**	仰卧起坐 仰臥起坐
roll over back **gǔn fān guò bèi**	滚翻过背 滾翻過背	front support/arms bent **fú dì**	伏地 伏地
pole climbing **pá gān**	爬竿 爬竿	push-ups **fú dì tǐng shēn**	伏地挺身 伏地挺身
relaxing movement **sōng chí yùn dòng**	松弛运动 鬆弛運動	side support position **cè shì tǐng shēn**	侧式挺身 側式挺身
calisthenics **jiàn méi tǐ cāo**	健美体操 健美體操	one hand push up **dān shǒu fú dì tǐng shēn**	单手伏地挺身 單手伏地挺身
rhythmic gymnastic **yùn lǜ tǐ cāo**	韵律体操 韻律體操	knee raising **xī gài píng tí**	膝盖平提 膝蓋平提
mass drill **tuán tǐ cāo**	团体操 團體操	stride position **shuāng tuǐ shēn kāi**	双腿伸开 雙腿伸開
aerobic exercise **yóu yǎng yùn dòng**	有氧运动 有氧運動	colored ribbon dance **shuái cǎi dài**	甩彩带 甩彩帶（彩帶舞）
anaerobic exercise **wú yǎng yùn dòng**	无氧运动 無氧運動	yoga **yǔ jiā**	瑜珈 瑜珈
neck exercise **jǐng bù yùn dòng**	颈部运动 頸部運動	karma yoga **wú wǒ yǔ jiā**	无我瑜珈 無我瑜珈
hands on the hips **shuāng shǒu chā yāo**	双手叉腰 雙手叉腰	bodily yoga **tǐ lì yǔ jiā**	体力瑜珈 體力瑜珈
deep knee bend **shuāng xī xià dūn**	双膝下蹲 雙膝下蹲	jnana yoga **zhì huì yǔ jiā**	智慧瑜珈 智慧瑜珈
bend the trunk sideways **shàng tí zuǒ yòu wān**	上体左右弯 上體左右彎	service, faith & wisdom **qín wù xìn yǎng zhì huì**	勤务信仰智慧 勤務信仰智慧
grasp your neck **liáng shǒu bào tóu**	两手抱头 兩手抱頭	raja-yoga **zì zhì yǔ jiā**	自制瑜珈 自制瑜珈
with heel raised **tóng shí zú gēn tí qǐ**	同时足跟提起 同時足跟提起	tapas; sandhana **xīu-xing**	修行 修行
abdominal exercise **fù bù yùn dòng**	腹部运动 腹部運動	kundalini **xhén jīng yùn dòng**	神经运动 神經運動
alternative exercise **wǎng fù yùn dòng**	往复运动 往復運動	yama **jìn jiè**	禁戒 禁戒
basic position **jī běn zī shì**	基本姿势 基本姿勢	waist twisting **niǔ yāo yùn dòng**	扭腰运动 扭腰運動

Martial Arts 武術 70 B

martial art **wǔ shù**	武术	武術
kung fu **gōng-fu**	功夫	功夫
meditation **dǎ zuò**	打坐	打坐
shadow boxing **tài jí quán**	太极拳	太極拳
eight trigrams boxing **bā duàn jǐn**	八段锦	八段錦
internal work **nèi gōng**	内功	內功
external work **wài gōng**	外功	外功
feat of strength (deep breathing) **qì gōng**	气功	氣功
rage; energy of life **qì**	气	氣
practice breathing **tiáo qì**	调气	調氣
deep breathing **shēn hū xī**	深呼吸	深呼吸
shallow breathing **qiǎn hū xī**	浅呼吸	淺呼吸
to feel suffocated **bì qì**	闭气	閉氣
hitting vital point **diǎn xùè**	点穴	點穴
practicing iron ore palm **tiě shā zhǎng**	铁砂掌	鐵砂掌
three jointed pike **sān jié gùn**	三节棍	三節棍
regimen **yǎng shēng fǎ**	养生法	養生法
the lower part of abdomen **dān tián**	丹田	丹田
cross legs sit **pán tuí dǎ zuò**	盘腿打坐	盤腿打坐
akimbo **liáng shǒu chā yāo**	两手叉腰	兩手叉腰
hand slap **tuī-shou**	推手	推手
grappling **qín-shou**	擒手	擒手
hand wrestling **bāi wàn-zi**	掰腕子	掰腕子
to have a tumble **fān gēn-tou**	翻跟头	翻跟頭
boxing & kicking **quán dǎ jiǎo tī**	拳打脚踢	拳打腳踢
dagger **bí-shou**	匕首	匕首
spear **huā qiāng**	花枪	花槍
double-edged straight sword **jiàn**	剑	劍
bamboo epee **zhú jiàn**	竹剑	竹劍
knobkerrie **yüán tóu bàng**	圆头棒	圓頭棒
pike; lance **cháng máo**	长矛	長矛
emprise **wǔ xiá**	武侠	武俠

competition in martial skills **bí wǔ**	比武 比武	
challenge **tiǎo zhàn shū**	挑战书 挑戰書	
life and death duel **shēng sǐ dòu**	生死斗 生死鬥	
achillean **dāo qiāng bú rù**	刀枪不入 刀槍不入	
hercules **dà lì shì**	大力士 大力士	
aggressor **xiān xià shóu zhě**	先下手者 先下手者	
fundamental movement posture **jī běn bù fǎ**	基本步法 基本步法	
stationary work **zhàn gōng**	站功 站功	
starting-leg posture **lì dìng shì**	立定式 立定式	
back-loaded posture **zuò bù shì**	坐步式 坐步式	
front-loaded posture **gōng bù shì**	弓步式 弓步式	
leg work **tuǐ gōng**	腿功 腿功	
single-leg bending & rising **tí tuǐ**	提腿 提腿	
inner-leg kick; toe kick **tī tuǐ**	踢腿 踢腿	
heel kick **chuài tuǐ**	踹腿 踹腿	
hip turning **tún tuǐ**	臀腿 臀腿	
single-leg squatting posture **xià kuà shì**	下跨式 下跨式	
quick reaction **yìng biàn fǎ**	应变法 應變法	
direction of striking position **qüán shì fāng wèi**	拳势方位 拳勢方位	
24 direction position **luó jīng fāng wèi**	罗经方位 羅經方位	

action **dǎ; dòng zuò**	打；动作 打；動作	
waving hands in the clouds **yǘn shǒu**	云手 雲手	
bending backward **hòu yǎng**	后仰 後仰	
bending forward **qián fǔ**	前俯 前俯	
bending backward & turning **yáng zhuǎn**	仰转 仰轉	
kneeling/body bend backward **guì yǎng**	跪仰 跪仰	
leg stretching **bān tuǐ**	扳腿 扳腿	
hooking hands **gōu shǒu**	勾手 勾手	
floating up and down **chén fú**	沉浮 沉浮	
inertia **chèn shì qián jìn**	趁势前进 趁勢前進	
squatting down like snake **shé shēn xià shì**	蛇身下势 蛇身下勢	
golden pheasant on one leg **jīn jī dú lì**	金鸡独立 金雞獨立	
sweep the lotus with one leg **shí zì bǎi lián**	十字摆莲 十字擺蓮	
step forward to 7 stars **shàng bù qī xīng**	上步七星 上步七星	
step back ride on tigerback **tuì bù kuà hǔ**	退步跨虎 退步跨虎	
firm footing **lì dì rú shēng gēn**	立地如生根 立地如生根	
deflect momentum of 1000 lbs. with a trigger force of four ozs. **sì liǎng bō qiān jīn**	四两拨千斤 四兩撥千斤	
conquering unyielding with the yield- ing **yǐ róu kè gāng**	以柔克钢 以柔克鋼	

boxing qüán jí	拳击 拳擊	prize ring jǐn biāo sài	锦标赛 錦標賽
boxing terminology qüán jí shù yǔ	拳击术语 拳擊術語	excited bái rè zhàn	白热战 白熱戰
in shape shēng lóng huó hǔ; bèi zhàn	生龙活虎；备战 生龍活虎；備戰	crown fight wèi miǎn zhàn	卫冕战 衛冕戰
boxer; pugilist qüán jí shǒu	拳击手 拳擊手	10–round shí huí hé	十回合 十回合
boxing contest (match) qüán jí sài	拳击赛 拳擊賽	Thai boxing Tài Guó qüán	泰国拳 泰國拳
boxing coach qüán shī	拳师 拳師	sand bag; punching sack shā dài	砂袋 砂袋
professional boxer zhí yè qüán shī	职业拳师 職業拳師	punching ball liàn jí lí-xing qiú	练击梨形球 練擊梨形球
heavyweight zhòng liàng jí	重量级 重量級	punching bag liàn qüán pí dài	练拳皮袋 練拳皮袋
light heavyweight cì zhòng liàng jí	次重量级 次重量級	boxer's head-guard qüán-shi hù tóu tào	拳师护头套 拳師護頭套
middleweight zhōng liàng jí	中量级 中量級	mouthpiece hù chǐ tào	护齿套 護齒套
welterweight cì zhōng liàng jí	次中量级 次中量級	boxing gloves; muffler qüán jí shǒu-taor	拳击手套儿 拳擊手套兒
lightweight qīng liàng jí	轻量级 輕量級	hand-bandage shǒu bēng-dai	手绷带 手繃帶
featherweight yǔ liàng jí; cì qīng liàng	羽量级；次轻量 羽量級；次輕量	sparring partner liàn qüán-de duì-shou	练拳的对手 練拳的對手
flyweight yíng liàng jí; cì zùi qīng liàng	蝇量级；次最轻量 蠅量級；次最輕量	shadow boxing (boxing) dǎ kōng qüán	打空拳 打空拳
bantamweight chú liàng jí; zùi qīng liàng	雏量级；最轻量 雛量級；最輕量	antagonist; opponent duì-shou	对手 對手

weight-in **guò bàng**	过磅 過磅	knock down **dá dǎo**	打倒 打倒
left hook **zuǒ gōu quán**	左钩拳 左鉤拳	break apart **fēn kāi**	分开 分開
right hook **yòu gōu quán**	右钩拳 右鉤拳	shiner **yǎn-jing dǎ qīng**	眼睛打青 眼睛打青
hook blow **gōu jí**	钩击 鉤擊	mourner **dá zhóng yǎn-jing**	打肿眼睛 打腫眼睛
facer **dǎ jí liǎn bù**	打击脸部 打擊臉部	to bloody one's nose **dǎ liú bí xiě**	打流鼻血 打流鼻血
long jab; long straight **zhí jí**	直击 直擊	feinting **shēng dōng jí xī**	声东击西 聲東擊西
infighting **jìn jí**	近击 近擊	ducking **dī tóu qiǎn bì**	低头潜避 低頭潛避
offensive blow **jìn gōng quán**	进攻拳 進攻拳	ducking and crouching **dūn fú shǎn bì**	蹲伏闪避 蹲伏閃避
short straight (jab) **duǎn jí**	短击 短擊	belt (hit below the belt) **àn zhōng shāng rén**	暗中伤人 暗中傷人
bash blow **měng jí**	猛击 猛擊	portsider **guàn yòng zuǒ quán**	惯用左拳 慣用左拳
dynamite blow **tòng jí**	痛击 痛擊	cross wrist **qiē-shou**	切手 切手
sweeping blow **sǎo jí**	扫击 掃擊	to win by retirement **bú zhàn ér shèng**	不战而胜 不戰而勝
attack position **jìn gōng**	进攻 進攻	throw the white towel **zhōng-tu tuì chū**	中途退出 中途退出
guard position **shǒu shì**	守势 守勢	wide margin **gāo xià xuán shū**	高下悬殊 高下懸殊
dodge **shǎn bì**	闪避 閃避	tied; evenly matched **bù fēn shèng fù**	不分胜负 不分勝負
elbow block **zhóu dǎng**	肘挡 肘擋	victory after defeated **zhuǎn bài wéi shèng**	转败为胜 轉敗為勝
forearm block **qián bì dǎng**	前臂挡 前臂擋	to win by decision **pàn jüé huò shèng**	判决获胜 判決獲勝
intercept **yíng jí**	迎击 迎擊	knock out **jí dǎo**	击倒 擊倒
slugged **jí zhòng**	击中 擊中	win by knockout (KO) **dá dǎo huò shèng**	打倒获胜 打倒獲勝
knocked senseless **dǎ yǔn**	打晕 打暈	count out (counting to ten) **xüān gào dǎ bài** （數到十）	宣告打败 宣告打敗

wrestling **shuāi jiǎo**	摔角 摔角	**violation** **fàn guī**	犯规 犯規
to wrestle **jiǎo lì**	角力 角力	**black belt** **hēi dài**	黑带 黑帶
sumo; sumo wrestling **xiāng pū**	相扑 相撲	**decision** **cái jüé**	裁决 裁決
taekwondo **tái qüán dào**	跆拳道 跆拳道	**half point** **bàn shèng**	半胜 半勝
karate (Empty hand) **kōng shǒu dào**	空手道 空手道	**one point** **yí shèng**	一胜 一勝
garrote; scrag **è hóu**	扼喉 扼喉	**win by default** **bú sài ér shèng**	不赛而胜 不賽而勝
scrag **niǔ jíng fǎ**	扭颈法 **扭頸法**	**judo** **róu dào**	柔道 柔道
strangling technique **lēi jíng fǎ**	勒颈法 勒頸法	**judo terminology** **róu dào shù yǔ**	柔道术语 柔道術語
clinching **hù è**	互扣 互扣	**throwing technique** **shuāi fǎ**	摔法 **摔法**
close buttock; waust throw **lán yāo bào zhí**	拦腰抱掷 攔腰抱擲	**grappling** **zhuā láo**	抓牢 抓牢
legs coiled against the other's **chán tuǐ**	缠腿 纏腿	**head-twist** **niǔ tóu**	扭头 扭頭
squeezing the abdomen **yā fù**	压腹 壓腹	**tripping** **bàn jiāo**	绊跤 絆跤
body crash **yòng shēn-ti zhuàng**	用身体撞 用身體撞	**tripping kick** **gōu tuǐ**	钩腿 鉤腿
nearly fall **bàn dǎo**	半倒 半倒	**foot sweep** **sáo tuǐ**	扫腿 掃腿
take down **shuāi dǎo**	摔倒 摔倒	**back-drop** **fǎn shuāi**	反摔 反摔
headlong **dào zāi cōng**	倒栽葱 倒栽蔥	**bare-handed; barefisted** **chì shǒu kōng qüán**	赤手空拳 赤手空拳

basketball game **lán qiú sài**	篮球赛 籃球賽	division line **fēn chǎng xiàn**	分场线 分場線
play a game **dá chǎng qiú**	打场球 打場球	free throw lane **lán xià jìn qū**	篮下禁区 籃下禁區
backboard **lán bǎn**	篮板 籃板	free throw line **fá qiú xiàn**	罚球线 罰球線
rebound **lán bǎn qiú**	篮板球 籃板球	frontcourt **qián chǎng**	前场 前場
rim **lán kuāng**	篮框 籃框	half court **bàn chǎng**	半场 半場
basket **qiú lán**	球篮 球籃	outer perimeter **sān fēn xiàn wài**	三分线外 三分線外
league **lián méng**	联盟 聯盟	three-point line **sān fēn xiàn**	三分线 三分線
NBA(Natnl. Basketball Asso.) **quán měi lán qiú xié huì**	全美篮球协会 全美籃球協會	center **zhōng fēng**	中锋 中鋒
playoff games **jì hòu sài**	季後赛 季後賽	bench player **hòu bǔ qiú yuán**	後补球员 後補球員
full court game **dǎ quán chǎng**	打全场 打全場	forward **qián fēng**	前锋 前鋒
score **dé fēn**	得分 得分	guard **hòu wèi**	后卫 後衛
semi-final **zhǔn jué sài**	准决赛 準決賽	opponent **duì-shou**	对手 對手
What's the score? **jí bí jǐ**	几比几 幾比幾	point guard **kòng qiú hòu wèi**	控球后卫 控球後衛
Who won? **shuí yíng-le**	谁赢了 誰贏了	shooting guard **dé fēn hòu wèi**	得分后卫 得分後衛
score tied; draw **píng shǒu**	平手 平手	power forward **dà qián fēng**	大前锋 大前鋒

small forward xiǎo qián fēng	小前锋 小前鋒	crossover kuà xià yùn qiú	跨下运球 跨下運球
fundamentals jī běn dòng zuò	基本动作 基本動作	cover; screen yǎn hù	掩护 掩護
passes chuán qiú	传球 傳球	fast break kuài gōng	快攻 快攻
two-hand overhead pass shuāng shǒu guò tóu chuán qiú	双手过头传球 雙手過頭傳球	shot clock jìn gōng shí jiān	进攻时间 進攻時間
footwork jiǎo bù yí dòng	脚步移动 腳步移動	guide the offenses zhú dǎo jìn gōng	主导进攻 主導進攻
field goal chū shǒu dé fēn	出手得分 出手得分	miss on possession cuò shī dé fēn jī huì	错失得分机会 錯失得分機會
flashy moves shǎn shuò-de dòng zuò	闪烁的动作 閃爍的動作	offensive rebound jìn gōng lán bǎn	进攻篮板 進攻籃板
assist zhù gōng	助攻 助攻	on the run lián xù dé fēn	连续得分 連續得分
close shot jìn jǜ lí shè qiú	近距离射球 近距離射球	openings for attack gōng jí kòng dǎng	攻击空档 攻擊空檔
long shot yüǎn tóu	远投 遠投	turnover shī wù	失误 失誤
shoot long distance shot shè wài xiàn	射外线 射外線	defense fáng shǒu	防守 防守
three point shots sān fēn qiú	三分球 三分球	double-team bāo jiá	包夹 包夾
hook shots gōu shè	勾射 勾射	press yā pò	压迫 壓迫
lay-ups shàng lán	上篮 上籃	steal chāo jié	抄截 抄截
shoot hoops tóu lán	投篮 投籃	dominate chēng bà	称霸 稱霸
nothing but net kōng xīn tóu lán	空心投篮 空心投籃	field goal percentage chū shǒu mìng zhòng lǜ	出手命中率 出手命中率
dunk shot qiáng lì guàn lán	强力灌蓝 強力灌籃	free throw percentage fá qiú mìng zhòng lǜ	罚球命中率 罰球命中率
reverse dunks fán shǒu guàn lán	反手灌篮 反手灌籃	team qiú duì	球队 球隊
Ally-oop kōng zhōng jiē qiú guàn lán	空中接球灌篮 空中接球灌籃	coach jiào liàn	教练 教練
dribbling yùn qiú	运球 運球	strategy cè lüè	策略 策略

tempo jié zòu	节奏 節奏	personal foul gè rén fàn guī	个人犯规 個人犯規
agility jī dòng xìng	机动性 機動性	team foul tuán duì fàn guī	团队犯规 團隊犯規
set patterns ān pái jìn gōng mó shì	安排进攻模式 安排進攻模式	technical foul jì shù fàn guī	技术犯规 技術犯規
man-to-man defense rén dīng rén fáng shǒu	人盯人防守 人盯人防守	center jump zhōng quān tiào qiú	中圈跳球 中圈跳球
zone defense qū yù fáng shǒu	区域防守 區域防守	double dribble liǎng cì yùn qiú	两次运球 兩次運球
playing mental game dǎ xīn lǐ zhàn	打心理战 打心理戰	get knocked bèi zhuàng dǎo	被撞倒 被撞倒
psychological effects xīn lǐ yíng xiǎng	心理影响 心理影響	goaltending gān rǎo dé fēn	干扰得分 干擾得分
ball hug dú xíng xiá	独行侠 獨行俠	hold lā chě	拉扯 拉扯
personal athletic skills gè rén jì qiǎo	个人技巧 個人技巧	free throw fá qiú	罚球 罰球
team spirit tuán duì jīng shén	团队精神 團隊精神	jump ball tiào qiú	跳球 跳球
teamwork tuán tǐ hé zuò	团体合作 團體合作	out of bound; out side chū jiè	出界 出界
chemistry among players qiú yüán jiān-de mò qì	球员间的默契 球員間的默契	push tuī jǐ	推挤 推擠
turn the game around niú zhuǎn jú shì	扭转局势 扭轉局勢	traveling zǒu bù	走步 走步
rule guī zé	规则 規則	trip bàn dǎo	绊倒 絆倒
time-out zhàn tíng	暂停 暫停	violation wéi lì	违例 違例
sub situation huàn rén	换人 換人	three-second violation sān miǎo wéi lì	三秒违例 三秒違例
body contact shēn tǐ jiē chù	身体接触 身體接觸	referee cái pàn	裁判 裁判
disqualification qǔ xiāo zī gé	取消资格 取消資格	make a bad call pàn jüé bù gōng	判决不公 判決不公
foul fàn guī	犯规 犯規	eliminated táo tài	淘汰 淘汰
offensive foul jìn gōng fàn guī	进攻犯规 進攻犯規	slap　　　　(庆贺) hù xiāng jí zhǎng	互相击掌 互相擊掌

baseball bàng qiú	棒球 棒球	home base bén lěi	本垒 本壘
sponge ball; softball ruǎn bàng qiú	软棒球 軟棒球	single hit yī lěi ān dǎ	一垒安打 一壘安打
baseball game bàng qiú sài	棒球赛 棒球賽	double hit èr lěi ān dǎ	二垒安打 二壘安打
stadium bàng qiú chǎng	棒球场 棒球場	triple hit sān lěi ān dǎ	三垒安打 三壘安打
grandstand lù tiān kàn tái	露天看台 露天看臺	home run ;homer qüán lěi dǎ	全垒打 全壘打
umpire cái pàn	裁判 裁判	strike hǎo qiú	好球 好球
coach jiào liàn	教练 教練	strike zone hǎo qiú qū	好球区 好球區
little league shào bàng duì	少棒队 少棒隊	ball huài qiú	坏球 壞球
senior little league qīng shào bàng duì	青少棒队 青少棒隊	wild pitch bào tóu	暴投 暴投
cheer squad lā lā duì	啦啦队 啦啦隊	three strikes sān hǎo qiú	三好球 三好球
onlookers còu rè-nao-de rén	凑热闹的人 湊熱鬧的人	three balls sān huài qiú	三坏球 三壞球
loudly applauded dà shēng gú zhǎng	大声鼓掌 大聲鼓掌	four balls sì huài qiú	四坏球 四壞球
first base yī lěi	一垒 一壘	legal pitch hé fǎ tóu qiú	合法投球 合法投球
second base èr lěi	二垒 二壘	full count mǎn qiú shù	满球数 滿球數
third base sān lěi	三垒 三壘	pick-off chù shā chū jú	触杀出局 觸殺出局

walk (four balls) **bǎo sòng shàng lěi**	保送上垒 保送上壘 (四壞球)	棒球赛
free pass (hit by pitcher's ball) **bǎo sòng shàng lěi**	保送上垒 保送上壘 (觸身球)	
return to one's base **tuì huí yüán lěi**	退回原垒 退回原壘	
out; outs **chū jǘ; chū jǘ rén shù**	出局；出局人数 出局；出局人數	
force out **cì shā**	刺杀 刺殺	
assist **zhù shā**	助杀 助殺	
grounded out **fēng shā**	封杀 封殺	
flied out **jiē shā**	接杀 接殺	
strike out **sān zhèn chū jǘ**	三振出局 三振出局	
double play **shuāng shā**	双杀 雙殺	
triple play **sān shā**	三杀 三殺	
safe **ān qüán shàng lěi**	安全上垒 安全上壘	
bases loaded **mán lěi**	满垒 滿壘	
infield fly ball **nèi yě fēi qiú**	内野飞球 內野飛球	
infield **nèi yě**	内野 內野	
outfield **wài yě**	外野 外野	
fair ball; fair territory **jiè nèi qiú**	界内球 界內球	
foul ball **jiè wài qiú**	界外球 界外球	
pitcher **tóu-shou**	投手 投手	
screw-armer; southpaw **zuó piě-zi tóu-shou**	左撇子投手 左撇子投手	

pitcher's foot fault **tóu-shou jiǎo fàn-gui**	投手脚犯规 投手腳犯規	72 B
no-hitter **wú ān dá bǐ sài**	无安打比赛 無安打比賽	
catcher **bú-shou**	捕手 捕手	Baseball Game
passed ball **bú-shou lòu jiē**	捕手漏接 捕手漏接	
battery **tóu bú zǔ hé**	投捕组合 投捕組合	
batter **dǎ jí shǒu**	打击手 打擊手	
pinch hitter **dài dǎ**	代打 代打	
designated hitter **zhǐ dìng dǎ jí**	指定打击 指定打擊	
batting average **dǎ-ji lǜ**	打击率 打擊率	
base man **shóu lěi yüán**	守垒员 守壘員	
fielding average **shǒu bèi lǜ**	守备率 守備率	
error **wù chā**	误差 誤差	
infielder **nèi yé shǒu**	内野手 內野手	
outfielder **wài yé shǒu**	外野手 外野手	
pitching ball **tóu qiú**	投球 投球	
pop-up **shàng shēng qiú**	上升球 上昇球	
overarm throw **shàng tóu**	上投 上投	
curve ball **qū xiàn qiú**	曲线球 曲線球	
fastball **kuài sù qiú**	快速球 快速球	
slider **huá qiú**	滑球 滑球	

sinker xià zhuì qiú	下坠球 下墜球	earned run average dé diǎn lǜ	得点率 得點率
rising curve ball shàng qū qiú	上曲球 上曲球	swing and missing huī bàng luò kōng	挥棒落空 揮棒落空
sinking curve ball xià qū qiú	下曲球 下曲球	base running páo lěi	跑垒 跑壘
sinking curve ball wài qū qiú	外曲球 外曲球	base sliding huá lěi	滑垒 滑壘
knuckle ball màn biàn-huà qiú	慢变化球 慢變化球	base stealing (s.b.) dào lěi	盗垒 盜壘
line drive zhí fēi qiú	直飞球 直飛球	caught stealing dào lěi bèi zhuō	盗垒被捉 盜壘被捉
screw ball xüán zhuǎn qiú	旋转球 旋轉球	returning to base tuì huí yüán lěi	退回原垒 退回原壘
ground ball gǔn dì qiú	滚地球 滾地球	mitten shǒu tào	手套 手套
high fly ball gāo fēi qiú	高飞球 高飛球	cage; mask miàn zhào	面罩 面罩
lineup dǎ jí zhèn róng	打击阵容 打擊陣容	protector xiōng jiǎ	胸甲 胸甲
runs batted in dá diǎn	打点 打點	baseball bat qiú bàng	球棒 球棒
switch hit shuāng xiàng huàn shǒu dá	双向换手打 雙向換手打	leg guard hù xī	护膝 護膝
swing bat huī bàng	挥棒 揮棒	bullpen tóu-shou liàn tóu qū	投手练投区 投手練投區
fair territory ān dǎ qū	安打区 安打區	dugout xüán-shou xiū xí qū	选手休息区 選手休息區
foul territory jiè wài qiú qū	界外球区 界外球區	exhausted and fell fast asleep lèi-de hū hū dà shuì	累得呼呼大睡 累得呼呼大睡
long swing cháng dǎ	长打 長打	inning jú	局 局
short swing; bunt duán dǎ	短打 短打	scoreboard jì fēn bǎn	计分板 計分板
sacrifice hit xī shēng dǎ	牺牲打 犧牲打	ended with é jú	结局 結局
tag up chù lěi	触垒 觸壘	cancelled due to rain yīn yǔ qǔ xiāo	因雨取消 因雨取消
earned run dé diǎn	得点 得點	rowdy behaviors cháo chǎo nào nào	吵吵闹闹 吵吵鬧鬧

soccer **zú qiú**	足球 足球	**left full back** **zuǒ hòu wèi**	左后卫 左後衛
soccer game **zú qiú sài**	足球赛 足球賽	**right wing** **yòu fēng**	右锋 右鋒
football field **zú qiú chǎng**	足球场 足球場	**right inside forward** **yòu nèi fēng**	右内锋 右內鋒
goalmouth **qiú mén kǒu**	球门口 球門口	**right half back** **yòu qián wèi**	右前卫 右前衛
goal net **qiú mén wǎng**	球门网 球門網	**right full back** **yòu hòu wèi**	右后卫 右後衛
goal line **jüé shèng xiàn**	决胜线 決勝線	**goal keeper** **shǒu mén yuán**	守门员 守門員
touch line **biān xiàn**	边线 邊線	**referee** **cái pàn yuán**	裁判员 裁判員
halfway line **zhōng xiàn**	中线 中線	**warming up** **rè shēn zhǔn bèi**	热身准备 熱身準備
center spot **zhōng diǎn**	中点 中點	**penalty kick** **shí èr mǎ qiú**	十二码球 十二碼球
penalty area **fá qiú qū**	罚球区 罰球區	**free kick** **zì yóu qiú**	自由球 自由球
corner kick area **jiǎo qiú qū**	角球区 角球區	**corner kick** **jiǎo qiú**	角球 角球
center forward **zhōng fēng**	中锋 中鋒	**kick-off** **kāi qiú**	开球 開球
left wing **zuǒ fēng**	左锋 左鋒	**stopping** **tíng qiú**	停球 停球
left inside forward **zuǒ nèi fēng**	左内锋 左內鋒	**kick** **tī**	踢 踢
left half back **zuǒ qián wèi**	左前卫 左前衛	**head passing** **tóu dǐng chuán qiú**	头顶传球 頭頂傳球

English	Chinese (Simplified)	Chinese (Traditional)
drop kick / luò dì tī qiú	落地踢球	落地踢球
toe kick / zú jiān tī	足尖踢	足尖踢
feint; dummy / jiǎ dòng zuò	假动作	假動作
overhead hook / dào gōu	倒钩	倒鉤
fly kick / fēi tuǐ	飞腿	飛腿
line up / liè zhèn	列阵	列陣
dodging / shǎn bì	闪避	閃避
dead ball / sǐ qiú	死球	死球
goal shooting / shè mén	射门	射門
rush net / chōng wǎng	冲网	沖網
block tackle / lán jié	拦截	攔截
dive across / fēi shēn lán jié	飞身拦截	飛身攔截
fumble / shī shǒu	失手	失手
fumble in goal / shī shǒu rù wǎng	失手入网	失手入網
miskick; fumble / lòu qiú	漏球	漏球
no goal / wèi rù wǎng	未入网	未入網
offside / yüè wèi	越位	越位
throw-in / fā jiè wài qiú	发界外球	發界外球
penalty area / fá qiú qǖ	罚球区	罰球區
hacking / bàn jiǎo	绊脚	絆腳
intentional tripping / yǒu yì bàn jiǎo	有意绊脚	有意絆腳
unintentional tripping / wú yì bàn jiǎo	无意绊脚	無意絆腳
rough / cū bào xíng wéi	粗暴行为	粗暴行為
caution; warning / jǐng gào	警告	警告
taken name by referee / bèi cái pàn jì míng	被裁判记名	被裁判記名
leave the court / shàn zì lí chǎng	擅自离场	擅自離場
marching order; expelled / qǖ zhú lí chǎng	驱逐离场	驅逐離場
out of play; time out / zhàn tíng	暂停	暫停
interval / xiū-xi	休息	休息
half time / bàn-chang	半场	半場
first half / qián bàn-chang	前半场	前半場
second half / hòu bàn-chang	后半场	後半場
injury time / shāng tíng bǔ shí	伤停补时	傷停補時
penalty kick / fá qió	罚球	罰球
on the scoreboard / shǒu kāi jì lù	首开记录	首開記錄
fitness form / diān fēng zhuàng tài	颠峰状态	顛峰狀態
lopsided win; one side game / yí miàn dǎo	一面倒	一面倒
deadlock / shí lì xiāng dāng	实力相当	實力相當
draw / píng shǒu	平手	平手
narrow victory / xiǎn shèng	险胜	險勝

football game **gán lǎn qiú sài**	橄榄球赛 橄欖球賽	**forward man** **qián wèi**	前卫 前衛
rugby **Yīng shì gán lǎn qiú**	英式橄榄球 英式橄欖球	**full back** **hòu wèi**	后卫 後衛
team manager **qiú duì jīng lǐ**	球队经理 球隊經理	**wing three quarter** **yì fēng**	翼锋 翼鋒
football player **gán lǎn qiú xüán-shou**	橄榄球选手 橄欖球選手	**center three quarter** **zhèng fēng**	正锋 正鋒
Super Ball **Shì-jie guàn jūn dà sài**	世界冠军大赛 世界冠軍大賽	**kick off** **kāi qiú**	开球 開球
contest **bǐ sài**	比赛 比賽	**touch down** **dá zhèn**	达阵 達陣
contestants **bǐ sài xüán-shou**	比赛选手 比賽選手	**saving ball** **shā qiú**	杀球 殺球
is challenging **yóu tiǎo zhàn xìng**	有挑战性 有挑戰性	**try ball** **jìn qiú**	进球 進球
gained the upper hand **zhàn-le shàng fēng**	占了上风 佔了上風	**tackle ball** **bào qiú**	抱球 抱球
superior odds **yōu shì**	优势 優勢	**dribbling ball** **pán qiú**	盘球 盤球
easy to win the game **róng-yi yíng dé bǐ sài**	容易赢得比赛 容易贏得比賽	**free kick** **zì yóu tī**	自由踢 自由踢
winning streak **yíng qiú qì-shi gāo zhàng**	赢球气势高涨 贏球氣勢高漲	**hacking** **tī jìng**	踢胫 踢脛
football team's victory **gán lǎn qiú duì dé shèng**	橄榄球队得胜 橄欖球隊得勝	**gridiron** **gán lǎn qiú chǎng**	橄榄球场 橄欖球場
get a grip on **zhǎng wò**	掌握 掌握	**goal** **qiú mén**	球门 球門
on the situation **qüán jú**	全局 全局	**touch line** **biān xiàn**	边线 邊線

dummy **yòu bì**	诱避 誘避	defense team players **fáng duì yüán**	防队员 防隊員
grounding ball **yā qiú chù dì**	压球触地 壓球觸地	linebackers **zhǔ fáng yüán**	主防员 主防員
direct touch **zhí qiú chù dì**	直球触地 直球觸地	nose tackles **fáng wèi zhōng fēng**	防卫中峰 防衛中峰
knocking violation **jí qiú wéi lì**	击球违例 擊球違例	defensive ends **fáng yì**	防翼 防翼（邊上防守員）
drop goal **pèng qiú rù mén**	碰球入门 碰球入門	defensive tackles **fáng zǔ yüán**	防阻员 防阻員
line out **jiè wài qiú**	界外球 界外球	defensive backs **zhǔ fáng wèi**	主防卫 主防衛
scrimmage **bìng liè zhēng qiú**	并列争球 並列爭球	comebacks **jǐao wèi**	角卫 角衛
shoulder pad **hù jiān**	护肩 護肩	rookie **dì yī nían-de xīn duì yüán**	第一年的新队员 第一年的新隊員
head harness **hù tóu zhào**	护头罩 護頭罩	toss the ball to start **kāi qiú**	开球 開球
offense team **gōng duì**	攻队 攻隊	downs **jìn cì**	进次 進次
offense team players **gōng duì yüán**	攻队员 攻隊員	1st downs **dì yī jìn**	第一进 第一進
quarterback **sì fēn wèi**	四分卫 四分衛（隊指揮）	2nd downs **dì èr jìn**	第二进 第二進
running backs **gōng fáng wèi**	攻防卫 攻防衛	3rd downs **dì sān jìn**	第三进 第三進
half back **bàn fēn wèi**	半分卫 半分衛	4th downs　（球歸對方） **dì sì jìn**（四次總數未過十碼）	第四进 第四進
wide receivers **yüǎn jīe yüán**	远接员 遠接員	touchdown (6 points) **góng rù fáng qū**　（得六分）	攻入防区 攻入防區
tight ends **zuǒ yòu yì**	左右翼 左右翼	extra point (add 1 point) **jīa yì fēn**　（TD 後球踢在兩杠之間過橫樑）	加一分
guards **zuǒ yòu wèi**	左右卫 左右衛	field goal (3 points)　球踢在兩杠之間入門 **qiú tī-zai liǎng gàng-zhi jiān rù mén**（3分）	
tackles **qín bào; lán zǔ yüán**	擒抱；拦阻员 擒抱；攔阻員	end zone **fáng qū**	防区 防區
center **zhōng fēng**	中峰 中峰	goalline **fáng qū xìan**	防区线 防區線
defense team **fáng duì**	防队 防隊	snap　（即為活球） **qíu lí zhōng fēng shǒu**	球离中锋手 球離中鋒手

live ball huó qíu	活球 活球	laid flat on his back píng tǎng-zai dì-shang	平躺在地上 平躺在地上
dead ball sǐ qíu	死球 死球	made a great effort fèn lì yī bó	奋力一搏 奮力一搏
loose ball shī kòng qíu	失控球 失控球（活球）	relieved the starting pitcher huàn xià xiān fā tóu-shou	换下先发投手 換下先發投手
interception bèi duì fāng lán jié	被对方拦截 被對方攔截	a replacement pitcher jiù yüán tóu-shou	救援投手 救援投手
shutout zú zhǐ duì-fang dé fēn	阻止对方得分 阻止對方得分	fill in for him tián bǔ tā-de wèi zhì	填补他的位置 填補他的位置
fumble shī shǒu sōng qíu	失手松球 失手鬆球（成活球）	team's poor morale qiú duì shì qì dī mí	球队士气低迷 球隊士氣低迷
foul fàn gūi	犯规 犯規	excel biǎo xiàn tú chū	表现突出 表現突出
personal foul (15-yd penalty) qīn rén fàn qūi	侵人犯规 侵人犯規	the opposing team duì-shou duì	对手队 對手隊
clipping (15-yd penalty) yóu hòu xià fāng zǔ rén fàn gūi	由后下方阻人犯规 由後下方阻人犯規	opponents duì-shou	对手 對手
holding (penalty 10 yards) jiū rén fàn gūi	揪人犯规 揪人犯規	fight against duì kàng	对抗 對抗
fair catch jīe qíu bú dòng	接球不动 接球不动	experience a hard struggle yī chǎng xīn kǔ fèn zhàn	一场辛苦奋战 一場辛苦奮戰
line of scrimmage zhōng lì qū (雙方各有自己的虛線不得越過)	中立区（两虚线之间）	falls short expectations wèi dá-dao yù qí chéng-ji	未达到预期成绩 未達到預期成績
punt yüǎn tī (踢後即为活球)	球尖平行，掉下时以脚背这踢 平時用於 4th downs	schedule extra practice ān pái é wài liàn xí	安排额外练习 安排額外練習
punter (全賽中只负责此一踢) yüǎn tī yüán	远踢员（不作别事） 遠踢員	beat off their efforts jí bài shì qì	击败士气 擊敗士氣
kicker (全賽中只负责此一踢) tī qíu shè mén shǒu (專踢 field goal)	踢球射门手 踢球射門手	win the game yíng dé shèng lì	赢得胜利 贏得勝利
safety (penalty 2 points) zuò mén	坐门（对方加两分） （在自己禁区被对方阻倒）	bear /beat (break) the record pò jì lù	破纪录 破紀錄
conversion (2 points) bìan gōng jìn qǔ	变攻禁区（加两分） 變攻禁區	contestant cān sài zhě	参赛者 參賽者
most likely lose hén kě néng huì shī bài	很可能会失败 很可能會失敗	run at their full speed quán lì chōng cì	全力冲刺 全力衝刺
hit hard on the field chǎng shàng shòu-le zhòng jí	场上受了重击 場上受了重擊	a tie; deadlock shuāng fāng píng shǒu	双方平手 雙方平手

Tennis Tournament
網球錦標賽

play tennis **dá wǎng qiú**	打网球 打網球	lawn tennis **cǎo dì wǎng qiú**	草地网球 草地網球
tournament **jǐn biāo sài**	锦标赛 錦標賽	hard court **yìng dì wǎng qiú chǎng**	硬地网球场 硬地網球場
seeded player **zhóng zǐ duì yüán**	种子队员 種子隊員	clay court **ní tú wǎng qiú chǎng**	泥土网球场 泥土網球場
tennis player **wǎng qiú xüǎn-shou**	网球选手 網球選手	half-court line **bàn-chang xiàn**	半场线 半場線
representing a team **xüǎn-shou**	选手 選手	center mark **zhōng xīn diǎn**	中心点 中心點
tennis racket **wǎng qiú pāi**	网球拍 網球拍	line tape **jiè-xian dài**	界线带 界線帶
racket press **qiú pāi jiā**	球拍夹 球拍夾	drive **chōu jí; sǎo jí**	抽击；扫击 抽擊；掃擊
racket cover **qiú pāi tào**	球拍套 球拍套	serving; serve **kāi qiú; fā qiú**	开球；发球 開球；發球
frame **qiú pāi kuāng**	球拍框 球拍框	return to service **huí jí fā qiú**	回击发球 回擊發球
racket strings; gut **qiú pāi xián**	球拍弦 球拍絃	spin **gǔn fā qiú**	滚发球 滾發球
eight-sided racket **bā jiǎo xíng pāi bǐng**	八角形拍柄 八角形拍柄	side-spin **cè gǔn**	侧滚 側滾
backhand grip **fán shǒu wò pāi**	反手握拍 反手握拍	slice **xiāo qió**	削球 削球
forehand grip **zhèng shǒu wò pāi**	正手握拍 正手握拍	slice-spin **xié gǔn**	斜滚 斜滾
tennis ball **wǎng qiú**	网球 網球	back-spin **bèi gǔn**	背滚 背滾
tennis court **wǎng qiú chǎng**	网球场 網球場	bad bounce **tán huí qiú**	弹回球 彈回球
indoor (real) tennis **zhì-nei wǎng qiú**	室内网球 室內網球	mid-air return **lán jí**	拦击 攔擊

fault kāi qiú chū jiè	开球出界 開球出界	undercut xià qiē qiú	下切球 下切球
over head service guò dǐng fā qiú	过顶发球 過頂發球	topspin shàng xüán qiú	上旋球 上旋球
advantage in fā qiú rén lǐng xiān	发球人领先 發球人領先	forehead (slice) drive zhèng shǒu qiē jí	正手切击 正手切擊
reserve; receiving jiē qiú	接球 接球	pick-up dōu qǐ	兜起 兜起
net play; rushing the net dǐ xiàn zhàn shù	底线战术 底線戰術	half volley dōu jí	兜击 兜擊
net play; rushing the net jìn wǎng zhàn shù	近网战术 近網戰術	drop shot guò wǎng jí luò qiú	过网急落球 過網急落球
advantage out jiē qiú rén lǐng xiān	接球人领先 接球人領先	single game dān dǎ sài	单打赛 單打賽
spin ball; reel xüán zhuǎn qiú	旋转球 旋轉球	single court dān dǎ qiú chǎng	单打球场 單打球場
reel jüàn xiàn zhóu qiú	卷线轴球 捲線軸球	double game shuāng dǎ sài	双打赛 雙打賽
smash shā qiú; měng jí	杀球；猛击 殺球；猛擊	double court shuāng dǎ qiú chǎng	双打球场 雙打球場
to chop kǎn jí; qiē dǎ	砍击；切打 砍擊；切打	mixed double game hùn hé shuāng dǎ	混合双打 混合雙打
short smash duǎn pū shā qiú	短扑杀球 短撲殺球	David cup guó jiā bēi	国家杯 國家盃
forehand drive zhèng pāi	正拍 正拍	foot fault judgement sī zú cái pàn	司足裁判 司足裁判
volley qiú luò dì qián jí huí	球落地前击回 球落地前擊回	net cord umpire sī wǎng cái pàn	司网裁判 司網裁判
overhead (volley) smash yóu gāo pū shā	由高扑杀 由高撲殺	foot fault cǎi xiàn fàn guī	踩线犯规 踩線犯規
lob tiāo gāo qiú	挑高球 挑高球	net ball chù wǎng	触网 觸網
drive chōu qiú	抽球 抽球	edge ball chù xiàn	触线 觸線
flat drive píng chōu	平抽 平抽	a set yì pán	一盘 一盤
forehand stroke zhèng shóu sǎo jí	正手扫击 正手掃擊	love líng fēn	零分 零分
backhand stroke fán shǒu jí	反手击 反手擊		

72 Golf Tournament
高爾夫球錦標賽

golf **gāo ěr fū qiú**	高尔夫球 高爾夫球	golf bag **qiú gǎn dài**	球杆袋 球桿袋
tournament **jǐn biāo sài**	锦标赛 錦標賽	bag stand **gǎn dài jià**	杆袋架 桿袋架
clubhouse; golf club **gāo ěr fū jù lè bù**	高尔夫俱乐部 高爾夫俱樂部	golf cart **qiú jù tuī chē**	球具推车 球具推車
golfer **gāo ěr fū qiú yüán**	高尔夫球员 高爾夫球員	electric golf cart **qiú chǎng zuò chē**	球场座车 球場座車
top-notch golfer **gāo ěr fū qiú míng shǒu**	高尔夫球名手 高爾夫球名手	hole **dòng**	洞 洞
golf course **gāo ěr fū qiú chǎng**	高尔夫球场 高爾夫球場	pin **qiú dòng qí gān**	球洞旗竿 球洞旗竿
golf shoes **gāo ěr fū qiú xié**	高尔夫球鞋 高爾夫球鞋	tee **qiú zuò; kāi qiú**	球座；开球 球座；開球
club **gāo ěr fū qiú bàng**	高尔夫球棒 高爾夫球棒	tee marker **qiú zuò biāo jì**	球座标记 球座標記
cleek; cleik **tiě-gou qiú bàng**	铁钩球棒 鐵鉤球棒	to tee off **cóng qiú zuò dǎ chū**	从球座打出 從球座打出
putter **duǎn qiú bàng**	短球棒 短球棒	caddie; caddy **qiú tong**	球僮 球僮
putter **qīng jí bàng**	轻击棒 輕擊棒	caddie house **qiú tóng xiū xí chù**	球僮休息处 球僮休息處
chip shot **qiē jí**	切击 切擊	fairway **qiú dào**	球道 球道
stance **jí qiú zī-shi**	击球姿势 擊球姿勢	fairway marker **qiú dào hào mǎr pái**	球道号码儿牌 球道號碼兒牌
club-head **qiú gǎn tóu**	球杆头 球桿頭	dogleg (hole) **qǔ xíng qiú dào**	曲形球道 曲形球道
club-head cover **gǎn tóu tào**	杆头套 桿頭套	fairway bunker **qiú dào zhàng ài**	球道障碍 球道障礙

out-of-bounds (OB) **yüè jiè**	越界 越界	
short hole **duǎn jù lí dòng**	短距离洞 短距離洞	
tree hazard **zhàng ài shù**	障碍树 障礙樹	
water hazard **zhàng ài shuǐ chí**	障碍水池 障礙水池	
long hole **cháng jù lí dòng**	长距离洞 長距離洞	
middle-distance hole **zhōng jù lí dòng**	中距离洞 中距離洞	
baff **guā dì yì jī qiú gāo fēi**	括地一击球高飞 括地一擊球高飛	
approache **xhàng zhōng-da dì-qü dǎ**	向终打地区打 向終打地區打	
fringe of the green **zhōng-da dì-qü biān yüán**	终打地区边缘 終打地區邊緣	
sand trap; green bunker **zhōng-da dì-qü kēng wā**	终打地区坑洼 終打地區坑窪	
hole-in-one **yí-ci jiù zhòng**	一次就中 一次就中	
loft **gāo jí qiú**	高击球 高擊球	
marker **luò qiú dì diǎn jì-hao**	落球地点记号 落球地點記號	
foursome **èr dùi èr bǐ sài**	二对二比赛 二對二比賽	

par **biāo zhún gǎn shù**	标准杆数 標準桿數	
match play **rù dòng shù jüé shèng fù**	入洞数决胜负 入洞數決勝負	
medal play **zuì dī gān jüé shèng fù**	最低杆决胜负 最低桿決勝負	
play off **pīng shǒu yán cháng sài**	平手延长赛 平手延長賽	
tie **hé jǘ**	和局 和局	
green; putting green **guó lǐng; zhōng dǎ qǖ**	果岭；终打区 果嶺；終打區	
rough **luàn cǎo qǖ**	乱草区 亂草區	
flag pole **qí gān**	旗竿 旗竿	
yardage marker **mǎ shù bǎn**	码数板 碼數板	
putting **gǎn qiú**	赶球 趕球	
bogey （高於標準桿） **yì gǎn rù dòng**	一杆入洞 一桿入洞	
birdie （低於標準桿） **yì gǎn rù dòng**	一杆入洞 一桿入洞	
eagle （低於标准杆） **liáng gǎn rù dòng**	两杆入洞 兩桿入洞	

72G

Volleyball 排球

volleyball **pái qiú**	排球 排球	
volleyball court **pái qiú chǎng**	排球场 排球場	
front line center **qián pái zhōng**	前排中 前排中	
second line center **èr pái zhōng**	二排中 二排中	
second line left **èr pái zuǒ**	二排左 二排左	
second line right **èr pái yòu**	二排右 二排右	
serve **kāi qiú**	开球 開球	
serving order **fā qiú cì xù**	发球次序 發球次序	
fault **fā qiú chū jiè**	发球出界 發球出界	
serve again **chóng xīn fā qiú**	重新发球 重新發球	
under-hand serve **dī shǒu fā qiú**	低手发球 低手發球	
sidearm serve **cè miàn fā qiú**	侧面发球 側面發球	
over-hand serve **yáng shǒu fā qiú**	扬手发球 揚手發球	
stop volley **jié qiú**	截球 截球	
follow **shùn shì yā qiú**	顺势压球 順勢壓球	

dead ball **sǐ qiú**	死球 死球	
volleyball net **pái qiú wǎng**	排球网 排球網	
over net **yüè wǎng**	越网 越網	
recovering from net **wǎng jiù qiú**	网救球 網救球	
punching **yüè qǐ jiē qiú**	击球 躍起接球	
punching **jí qiú**	击球 擊球	
setting-up **tuō qiú**	托球 托球	
netman sets up spike **tuō qiú rén**	托球人 托球人	
spkie **kòu qiú**	扣球 扣球	
smash **shā qiú**	杀球 殺球	
blocking **fēng qiú**	封球 封球	
dribbling **lián jí**	连击 連擊	
step on the line **chū jiè**	出界 出界	
double fault **liǎng cì shī wù**	两次失误 兩次失誤	
point **dé fēn**	得分 得分	

72H Badminton 羽毛球

badminton **yǔ máo qiú**	羽毛球	羽毛球
play badminton **dá yǔ máo qiú**	打羽毛球	打羽毛球
badminton match **yǔ máo qiú sài**	羽毛球赛	羽毛球賽
badminton court **yǔ máo qiú chǎng**	羽毛球场	羽毛球場
bird **yǔ qiú**	羽球	羽球
racket **qiú pāi**	球拍	球拍
racket press **qiú pāi jiā**	球拍夹	球拍夾
singles **dān dǎ**	单打	單打
singles' line **dān dǎ biān xiàn**	单打边线	單打邊線
doubles **shuāng dǎ**	双打	雙打
doubles' line **shuāng dǎ biān xiàn**	双打边线	雙打邊線
serve **kāi qiú**	开球	開球
inside (short) serve line **nèi kāi qiú xiàn**	内开球线	內開球線
forehead stroke **zhèng shǒu jí**	正手击	正手擊
bachhand stroke **fán shǒu jí**	反手击	反手擊
right serve (service) court **yòu kāi qiú chǎng**	右开球场	右開球場
left serve (service) court **zuǒ kāi qiú chǎng**	左开球场	左開球場
outside service line **wài kāi qiú xiàn**	外开球线	外開球線
serving side **kāi qiú yì fāng**	开球一方	開球一方
receiving side **jiē qiú yì fāng**	接球一方	接球一方
high serve **gāo fā qiú**	高发球	高發球
low serve **dī fā qiú**	低发球	低發球
smash **shā qiú**	杀球	殺球
drop shot **guò wǎng zhí luò qiú**	过网直落球	過網直落球
underhand pass **dí shǒu chuán qiú**	低手传球	低手傳球
outside **chū jiè**	出界	出界
game **jú**	局	局

Table Tennis
(ping-pong)
乒乓球

play table tennis dǎ pīng pāng qiú	打乒乓球 打乒乓球	orthodox grip zhèng què ná qiú pāi	正确拿球拍 正確拿球拍
ping-pong table pīng pāng qiú zhuō	乒乓球桌 乒乓球桌	good server fā qiú háo shǒu	发球好手 發球好手
ping-pong court qiú tái	球台 球檯	tip the paddle qiú chù pāi	球触拍 球觸拍
ping-pong ball pīng pāng qiú	乒乓球 乒乓球	let ball fā qiú chù wǎng	发球触网 發球觸網
clap-board; paddle pīng pāng qiú pāi	乒乓球拍 乒乓球拍	serve again chóng fā qiú	重发球 重發球
server fā qiú rén	发球人 發球人	lose one's serve fā qiú shī wù	发球失误 發球失誤
striker jiē qiú rén	接球人 接球人	change server huàn fā qiú	换发球 換發球
crack hand yī liú háo shǒu	一流好手 一流好手	receive jiē qiú	接球 接球
mixed double game hùn hé shuāng dǎ	混合双打 混合雙打	drop-shot wǎng qián qiú	网前球 網前球
singles dān dǎ	单打 單打	net ball zhōng jiān chù wǎng qiú	中间触网球 中間觸網球
singles shuāng dǎ	双打 雙打	forehand ball zhèng shǒu qiú	正手球 正手球
combination hùn dǎ	混打 混打	high-return yǐ gāo qiú huán jí	以高球还击 以高球還擊
support; net brace wǎng jià	网架 網架	lob gāo huǎn qiú	高缓球 高緩球
sponge rubber paddle hǎi mián jiāo bǎn	海绵胶板 海綿膠板	dead ball tíng qiú	停球 停球
serve fā qiú	发球 發球	smash kòu qiú	扣球 扣球

English	Simplified / Pinyin	Traditional
bottom-spin dī xuán zhuǎn qiú	低旋转球	低旋轉球
half volley kuài dǎng	快挡	快擋
deuce píng diǎn	平点	平點
even; drawn píng shǒu	平手	平手
break another's serve duì-shou fā qiú ér dé fēn	对手发球而得分	對手發球而得分
serve point fā qiú dé fēn	发球得分	發球得分
home court běn fāng tái miàn	本方台面	本方檯面
half court bàn biān chǎng	半边场	半邊場
foot-work bù fǎ	步法	步法
net ball chù wǎng	触网	觸網
edge ball chù xiàn	触线	觸線
cover ball chù tái	触台	觸檯
plain (flush) hit píng jí	平击	平擊
counter fǎn jí	反击	反擊
attack gōng jí	攻击	攻擊
back-spin; slice qiē qiú	切球	切球
reciprocal slice qiē qiú huán-yi qiē qiú	切球还以切球	切球還以切球
short-range slice jìn xiāo	近削	近削

English	Simplified / Pinyin	Traditional
deep ball cháng qiú	长球	長球
top-spin chōu qiú	抽球	抽球
drive chōu jí	抽击	抽擊
revolving top-spin chōu zhuǎn qiú	抽转球	抽轉球
quick return jí tuī qiú	急推球	急推球
back-spin tuì hòu xuán zhuǎn	退后旋转	退後旋轉
liner biān qiú	边球	邊球
curve zhuǎn qiú lù	转球路	轉球路
block dǎng qiú	挡球	擋球
spin ball xüán zhuǎn qiú	旋转球	旋轉球
backhand fán shǒu qiú	反手球	反手球
backhand slide fán shóu yüǎn xiāo	反手远削	反手遠削
rally hù xiāng lián xừ duì dǎ	互相连续对打	互相連續對打
bounce; bound tiào qiú	跳球	跳球
flick; tap qīng jí	轻击	輕擊
defence gōng shǒu	攻守	攻守
hat-thick zhí luò sān pán	直落三盘	直落三盤
one-side game yí miàn dǎo	一面倒	一面倒

bowling dá bǎo líng qiú	打保龄球 打保齡球	headpin; kingpin yī hào tóu píng	一号头瓶 一號頭瓶
bowling alley bǎo líng qiú guǎn	保龄球馆 保齡球館	corner pin yǔ píng; jiǎo píng	隅瓶；角瓶 隅瓶；角瓶
bowling ball bǎo líng qiú	保龄球 保齡球	straight ball zhí xiàn qiú	直线球 直線球
bowling bag bǎo líng qiú dài	保龄球袋 保齡球袋	curve hú xíng qiú	弧形球 弧形球
bowling shoes bǎo líng qiú xié	保龄球鞋 保齡球鞋	backup huí xuán qiú; fēi díe qiú	回旋球；飞碟球 迴旋球；飛碟球
bowling match bǎo líng qiú bǐ sài	保龄球比赛 保齡球比賽	hook zuǒ qū qiú	左曲球 左曲球
bowler bǎo líng qiú shǒu	保龄球手 保齡球手	slice yòu qū qiú	右曲球 右曲球
lane qiú dào	球道 球道	gutter ball wù rù gōu qiú	误入沟球 誤入溝球
gutter qiú gōu	球沟 球溝	cherry liǎng cì jǐn qián píng dǎo	两次仅前瓶倒 兩次僅前瓶倒
gutter ball gǔn-ru qiú gōu-de qiú	滚入球沟的球 滾入球溝的球	brooklyn yì wài quán dǎo	意外全倒 意外全倒
return rack huí qiú jià	回球架 回球架	pocket kǒu dài	口袋 口袋（二瓶之間距）
automatic pinsetting zì dòng zhì píng	自动置瓶 自動置瓶	spare liǎng qiú jí dǎo quán bù	两球击倒全部 兩球擊倒全部
spot; aiming marker miáo zhǔn jì-haor	瞄准记号儿 瞄準記號兒	strike yí cì quán dǎo	一次全倒 一次全倒
foul cǎi xiàn fàn guī	踩线犯规 踩線犯規	double liǎng cì lián xù quán dǎo	两次连续全倒 兩次連續全倒
follow-trough zhuī zōng	追踪 追蹤	turkey sān cì lián xù quán dǎo	三次连续全倒 三次連續全倒

Billiards (shoot pool)
撞球兒

English	中文 (简)	中文 (繁)
billiard **tái qiú**	台球	檯球
pool hall; billiard room **zhuàng qiú chǎng; dàn zǐ fáng**	撞球场;弹子房	撞球場;彈子房
shoot pool **zhuàng qiú; dǎ dàn zǐ**	撞球;打弹子	撞球;打彈子
billiard ball **tái qiú; dàn zǐ**	台球儿;弹子	檯球兒;彈子
billiard table **zhuàng qiú tái**	撞球台	撞球檯
cushion **qiú tái xiàng pí biān**	球台橡皮边	球臺橡皮邊
billiard match **zhuàng qiú sài**	撞球赛	撞球賽
billiardist **zhuàng qiú-shou**	撞球手	撞球手
cueist **zhuàng qiú gāo-shou**	撞球高手	撞球高手
triangle **sān jiǎo qì**	三角器	三角器
ball rack **qiú jià**	球架	球架
pocket **qiú dài**	球袋	球袋
corner pocket **jiǎo luò qiú dài**	角落球袋	角落球袋
side pocket **cè miàn qiú dài**	侧面球袋	側面球袋
cue; stick **zhuàng qiú gān**	撞球杆	撞球桿
cue tip **qiú gān jiān**	球杆尖	球桿尖
cue rack **zhuàng qiú gān jià**	撞球杆架	撞球桿架
cue ball **mǔ qiú; bái-se qiú**	母球;白色球	母球;白色球
chalk (for cue) **lán sè fén bǐ kuàir**	蓝色粉笔块儿	藍色粉筆塊兒
an inning **yì jǘ**	一局	一局
nine-ball **jiǔ qiú luò dài**	九球落袋	九球落袋
snooker **dǎ zhí xiàn qiú**	打直线球	打直線球
screw shot **xüán zhuǎn jí fǎ**	旋转击法	旋轉擊法
top stroke **dǐng jí fǎ**	顶击法	頂擊法
masse **chuí zhí zhuàng qiú fǎ**	垂直撞球法	垂直撞球法
carom **yì jí lián zhuàng liǎng qiú**	一击连撞两球	一擊連撞兩球
twist **huí tán; héng xiàng xüán zhuǎn**	回弹;横向旋转	回彈;橫向旋轉
losing hazard **dǎ chū-de qiú rù dài**	打出的球入袋	打出的球入袋
winning hazard **bèi zhuàng-de qiú rù dài**	被撞的球入袋	被撞的球入袋
cannon; carom **lián zhuàng liǎng qiú**	连撞两球	連撞兩球

527

72 Ice Hockey 冰球兒

play ice-hockey **dǎ bīng qiúr**	打冰球儿	打冰球兒
ice-hockey **bīng qiúr; qū gùn qiú**	冰球儿；曲棍球	冰球兒；曲棍球
hockey game **qū gùn qiú sài**	曲棍球赛	曲棍球賽
field hockey **lù shàng qū gùn qiú**	陆上曲棍球	陸上曲棍球
hockey stick **qū gùn qiú bàng**	曲棍球棒	曲棍球棒
ice-hockey skates **qū gùn liū bīng xié**	曲棍溜冰鞋	曲棍溜冰鞋
roller hockey **lún shì xié qū gùn qiú**	轮式鞋曲棍球	輪式鞋曲棍球
goal keeper **shǒu mén**	守门	守門
goalie; goalkeeper **shǒu mén yüán**	守门员	守門員
face mask **miàn zhào**	面罩	面罩
forward **qián fēng**	前锋	前鋒
center halfback (forward) **zhōng jiān; zhōng fēng**	中坚；中锋	中堅；中鋒
halfback **qián wèi**	前卫	前衛
fullback **hòu wèi**	后卫	後衛
left inner **zuǒ fēng**	左锋	左鋒
right wing **yòu yì**	右翼	右翼
center zone **zhōng qū**	中区	中區
center face-off spot **zhōng jiān fā qiú diǎn**	中间发球点	中間發球點
seven-yard line **qī mǎ xiàn**	七码线	七碼線
bully off **kāi qiú**	开球	開球
carrying **dài qiú**	带球	帶球
corner hit **jí jiǎo qiú**	击角球	擊角球
cross-check **zú dǎng**	阻挡	阻擋
tripping **bàn rén**	绊人	絆人
goal area **mén nèi qū**	门内区	門內區
shooting circle **dǎ jí qüān**	打击圈	打擊圈
striking circle **jí qiú qüān**	击球圈	擊球圈
high stick **gāo jí**	高击	高擊
to shoot **shè mén**	射门	射門
roll-in the cage (goal) **gǔn rù qiú mén**	滚入球门	滾入球門

outdoor sports **hù wài yùn dòng**	户外运动 戶外運動	bungee jumping **gāo kōng tán tiào**	高空弹跳 高空彈跳
mountain climbing **dēng shān**	登山 登山	croquet **chuí qiú**	槌球 槌球
mountain hiking **pá shān**	爬山 爬山	fishing (rod) **diào yú (gān)**	钓鱼（竿） 釣魚（竿）
hiking **jiàn xíng**	健行 健行	rowing **huá chuán**	划船 划船
camping **lù yíng**	露营 露營	boat racing **sài chuán**	赛船 賽船
sleeping bag **shuì dài**	睡袋 睡袋	shell racing **qīng tǐng sài**	轻艇赛 輕艇賽
compass **zhǐ nán zhēn**	指南针 指南針	Dragon Boat Racing **lóng zhōu sài**	龙舟赛 龍舟賽
tent **zhàng-peng**	帐篷 帳篷	sailing **jià fān chuán**	驾帆船 駕帆船
hammock **diào chuáng**	吊床 吊床	canoeing **jià dú mù zhōu**	驾独木舟 駕獨木舟
campfire **yíng huǒ**	营火 營火	yachting **chéng yóu tǐng**	乘游艇 乘遊艇
tug of war **bá hé**	拔河 拔河	surfing **chōng làng**	冲浪 衝浪
car race **sài chē**	赛车 賽車	surfboard **chōng làng bǎn**	冲浪板 衝浪板
floored the pedal **yóu ménr cǎi dào dǐ**	油门儿踩到底 油門兒踩到底	to water ski **huá shuǐ**	滑水 滑水
bicycle race ; cycling **zì xíng chē jìng sài**	自行车竞赛 自行車競賽	aquaplane **chéng huá shuí bǎn**	乘滑水板 乘滑水板
motercycle race **mó-tuo chē jìng sài**	摩托车竞赛 摩托車競賽		

(See 31A 娛樂 與 嗜好 Entertainment & Hobbies)

Horseback Riding & Horse Racing
騎馬與賽馬

horseback riding qí mǎ yùn-dong	骑马运动 騎馬運動	riding crop wò quān shì duǎn biān	握圈式短鞭 握圈式短鞭
riding on the horseback qí mǎ	骑马 騎馬	horsemanship; equestrianism mǎ shù	马术 馬術
polo mǎ qiú	马球 馬球	equestrian skill jīng tōng mǎ jì	精通马技 精通馬技
hunting dǎ liè	打猎 打獵	haute ecole chāo jí mǎ shù	超级马术 超級馬術
riding suit qí zhuāng	骑装 騎裝	riding academy qí shù xué xiào	骑术学校 騎術學校
riding habit nǚ qí zhuāng	女骑装 女騎裝	manege mǎ shù xùn liàn	马术训练 馬術訓練
jockette; equestrienne nǚ qí shì	女骑士 女騎士	schooling lane liàn má chǎng	练马场 練馬場
riding master qí shù shī	骑术师 騎術師	horsebreaker; roughrider xùn mǎ shī	驯马师 馴馬師
riding hood dài mào-zi pī jiān	带帽子披肩 帶帽子披肩	trotting course xiǎo bù pǎo dào	小步跑道 小步跑道
riding coat chéng mǎ yòng wài yī	乘马用外衣 乘馬用外衣	racecourse for flat race píng dì sài má pǎo dào	平地赛马跑道 平地賽馬跑道
jodhpurs; riding breeches mǎ kù	马裤 馬褲	an obstacle zhàng ài	障碍 障礙
jockey cap qí mǎ mào	骑马帽 騎馬帽	a fence (an obstacle) lí zhàng	篱障 籬障
riding jacket qí mǎ jiá kè	骑马夹克 騎馬夾克	steeplechase course zhàng ài sài má pǎo dào	障碍赛马跑道 障礙賽馬跑道
riding boots mǎ xūē	马靴 馬靴	stockade zhà-lan	栅栏 柵欄
horsewhip mǎ biān	马鞭 馬鞭	the hurdle tiào lán	跳栏 跳欄

English	Pinyin	简体	繁體
a spur	mǎ cì	马刺	馬刺
stirrup	mǎ dèng	马镫	馬鐙
horseblock	tà tái	踏台	**踏臺**
horse racing	sài mǎ; páo mǎ	赛马；跑马	**賽馬**；**跑馬**
racehorse	bǐ sài yòng mǎ	比赛用马	比賽用馬
paddock	xiǎo xíng diào má chǎng	小型调马场	小型調馬場
the favorite	háo mǎ	好马	好馬
jockey ; horseman	qí shǒu; sài mǎ shī	骑手；赛马师	騎手；賽馬師
racecourse; the turf	sài má chǎng	赛马场	賽馬場
dopesheet	sài má jiǎn bào	赛马简报	賽馬簡報
race card	sài má cì xǜ biǎo	赛马次序表	賽馬次序表
starting gate	chū fā mén	出发门	出發門
starting flag	chū fā qí	出发旗	出發旗
the referee's stand	cái pàn tái	裁判台	裁判台
lottery ticket	cǎi piào	彩票	彩票
rain check	xià yǔ yán qí piào	下雨延期票	下雨延期票
finish line	zhōng diǎn xiàn	终点线	終點線
horse parlor	sài mǎ dú chǎng	赛马赌场	賽馬賭場
tote board	zǒng é jì suàn jī	总额计算机	總額計算機
totalizator	dǔ jīn jì suàn jī	赌金计算机	賭金計算機

English	Pinyin	简体	繁體
stable	mǎ fang; mǎ jiù	马房；马厩	馬房；馬廄
a manger	mǎ cáo	马槽	馬槽
horse gear	mǎ jù	马具	馬具
saddle	mǎ ān; ān-zi	马鞍；鞍子	馬鞍；鞍子
weight cloth	ān yī	鞍衣	鞍衣
saddle cloth with lead plates	qiān bǎn ān yī	铅板鞍衣	鉛板鞍衣
horse cloth	mǎ bèi	马被	馬被
tendon boot	tuǐ jiàn tào	腿腱套	腿腱套
horse collar	má jǐng qūan	马颈圈	馬頸圈
rein	jiāng shéng	缰绳	韁繩
checkrein	lēi mǎ jiāng shéng	勒马缰绳勒	勒馬韁繩
gag-bit	xián tiě; lēi kǒu qì	衔铁；勒口器	銜鐵；勒口器
blinkers; blinders	má yǎn zhàor	马眼罩儿	馬眼罩兒
horse's hoof	mǎ tí	马蹄	馬蹄
horseshoe	má zhǎng; mǎ tí tiě	马掌；马蹄铁	馬掌；馬蹄鐵
a sulky	dān rén mǎ chē	单人马车	單人馬車
spread fences	shuāng chóng lí-ba	双重篱笆	雙重籬笆
hedge-jump over water	tiào shuǐ gōu	跳水沟	跳水溝
the bank (an obstacle)	tí pō zhàng ài wù	堤坡障碍物	堤坡障礙物
the ditch and hedge	háo gōu lí zhàng	濠沟篱障	濠溝籬障

Archery & Shooting
射箭與射擊

archery **shè jiàn**	射箭 射箭	**clout** **shè zhòng**	射中 射中
archer **gōng jiàn shǒu**	弓箭手 弓箭手	**at the target** **miáo zhún bǎ xīn**	瞄准靶心 瞄準靶心
sharpshooter; marksman **shén jiàn shǒu**	神箭手 神箭手	**landed very far from it** **jiàn lí bǎ xīn tài yuǎn**	箭离靶心太远 箭離靶心太遠
archery range **shè jiàn chǎng**	射箭场 射箭場		
crossbow; large bow **nǔ**	弩 弩		
arch; bow **gōng**	弓 弓	**shooting** **shè jí**	射击 射擊
bowstring **gōng xián**	弓弦 弓弦	**gunnery meeting** **shè jí bǐ sài**	射击比赛 射擊比賽
arrow **jiàn**	箭 箭	**firearms** **qiāng zhī**	枪枝 槍枝
arrowhead **jiàn-tóur**	箭头儿 箭頭兒	**pistol** **shǒu qiāng**	手枪 手槍
shaft **jiàn gàn**	箭干 箭幹	**automatic pistol** **zì dòng shǒu qiāng**	自动手枪 自動手槍
quiver **jiàn dài**	箭袋 箭袋	**rifle** **bù qiāng**	步枪 步槍
poisoned arrow **dú jiàn**	毒箭 毒箭	**army rifle** **jūn yòng bù qiāng**	军用步枪 軍用步槍
drawing the bow **zhāng gōng**	张弓 張弓	**small-bore rifle** **xiǎo xíng bù qiāng**	小型步枪 小型步槍
target **jiàn bǎ**	箭靶 箭靶	**high power rifle** **dà kǒu jìng bù qiāng**	大口径步枪 大口徑步槍
bull's eye; clout **bǎ xīn**	靶心 靶心	**carbine** **kǎ bīn qiāng**	卡宾枪 卡賓槍

over-and-under shotgun shuāng guǎn qiāng	双管枪 雙管槍
free pistol zì yóu shì shǒu qiāng	自由式手枪 自由式手槍
free rifle zì yóu shì bù qiāng	自由式步枪 自由式步槍
defense pistol zì wèi shǒu qiāng	自卫手枪 自衛手槍
slides huá tào	滑套 滑套
chamber dàn táng	弹膛 彈膛
trigger bān jī	扳机 扳機
caliber; bore kǒu jìng	口径 口徑
ball cartridge shí dàn	实弹 實彈
blank cartridge kōng dàn	空弹 空彈
shooting range bá chǎng; shè chéng	靶场；射程 靶場；射程
freak target jiá bǎ	假靶 假靶
moving target yí dòng bǎ	移动靶 移動靶
rotating target xüán zhuán bǎ	旋转靶 旋轉靶
line of sight miáo zhǔn xiàn	瞄准线 瞄準線
trap fàng bǎ jī	放靶机 放靶機
firing position shè jí zī-shi	射击姿势 射擊姿勢
assigned stance guī dìng zī-shi	规定姿势 規定姿勢
setting the trigger bān jī shàng huáng	扳机上簧 扳機上簧
hang fire yán chí fā huǒ	延迟发火 延遲發火

magazine dàn yào kù	弹药库 彈藥庫
gun qiāng	枪 槍
revolver zuǒ lún shǒu qiāng	左轮手枪 左輪手槍
air rifle qì qiāng	气枪 氣槍
service pistol zhì shì shǒu qiāng	制式手枪 制式手槍
sporting rifle liè qiāng	猎枪 獵槍
shotgun sǎn dàn qiāng	散弹枪 散彈槍
double barreled shotgun shuāng guǎn qiāng	双管枪 雙管槍
charge; load zhuāng dàn	装弹 裝彈
loaded gun shàng táng qiāng	上镗枪 上鏜槍
firing pin zhuàng zhēn	撞针 撞針
bullet; cartridge zǐ dàn	子弹 子彈
front sight qián miáo zhǔn qì	前瞄准器 前瞄準器
aiming miáo zhǔn	瞄准 瞄準
practice range liàn xí bá chǎng	练习靶场 練習靶場
fire fā shè	发射 發射
hit shè zhòng; mìng zhòng	射中；命中 射中；命中
dead bird zhòng bǎ	中靶 中靶
lost bird; miss méi zhòng bǎ	没中靶 沒中靶
cease fire　　　（口令） tíng zhǐ shè jí	停止射击 停止射擊

summer resorts **bì shǔ shèng dì**	避暑胜地 避暑勝地	
beach **hǎi bīn**	海滨 海濱	
bathing beach **hái shuǐ yù chǎng**	海水浴场 海水浴場	
insolation; sunbath **rì guāng yù**	日光浴 日光浴	
beach parasol **hǎi bīn yáng sǎn**	海滨阳伞 海濱陽傘	
hammock **diào chuáng**	吊床 吊床	
bask **shài tài-yang**	晒太阳 曬太陽	
suntan **pí fū shài hēi**	皮肤晒黑 皮膚曬黑	
dabble **xì shuǐ**	戏水 戲水	
synchronized swimming **shuǐ shàng bā lěi**	水上芭蕾 水上芭蕾	
aquatic meet **shuǐ shàng yùn dòng huì**	水上运动会 水上運動會	
water polo **shuǐ qiú**	水球 水球	
duck in water **pào-zai shuí-li**	泡在水里 泡在水裡	
swimming **yóu yǒng**	游泳 游泳	
swimming pool **yóu yǒng chí**	游泳池 游泳池	

natatorium; indoor pool **shì nèi yǒng chí**	室内泳池 室內泳池	
bathhouse **gēng yī shì**	更衣室 更衣室	
swimming suit **yǒng yī**	泳衣 泳衣	
swimming cap **yǒng mào**	泳帽 泳帽	
swimming trunks **yǒng kù**	泳裤 泳褲	
swimming fins **wá xié**	蛙鞋 蛙鞋	
swim meet **yóu yóng bǐ sài**	游泳比赛 游泳比賽	
medley relay **hǔn hé jiē lì**	混和接力 混和接力	
cross harbor race **yóu yǒng dù hái bǐ sài**	游泳渡海比赛 游泳渡海比賽	
free-style; crawl stroke **zì yóu shì**	自由式 自由式	
butterfly stroke **hú dié shì**	蝴蝶式 蝴蝶式	
backstroke **yáng yǒng**	仰泳 仰泳	
frog style; frontstroke **wā shì**	蛙式 蛙式	
breast stroke **fú yǒng**	俯泳 俯泳	
side stroke swimming **cè yǒng**	侧泳 側泳	

English	简体 / 繁體	English	简体 / 繁體

dog paddle
gǒu pá shì; hú yóu
狗爬式；胡游
狗爬式；胡遊

ventilation
huàn qì
换气
換氣

I have a cramp
wǒ chōu jīn-le
我抽筋了
我抽筋了

dive
qián shuǐ; tiào shuǐ
潜水；跳水
潛水；跳水

releas the cramp
chōu jīn zěn-me bàn
抽筋怎麼办
抽筋怎麼辦

skin-dive
luó tǐ qián shuǐ
裸体潜水
裸體潛水

tuck
bào xī tiào
抱膝跳
抱膝跳

skin-diving
fú qián
浮潜
浮潛

buoyancy
fú lì
浮力
浮力

hydroscope
qián shuí yǎn jìng
潜水眼镜
潛水眼鏡

sinking
xià chén
下沈
下沈

aqualung; scuba
shuǐ fèi
水肺
水肺

life guard
hǎi tān jiù shēng yuán
海滩救生员
海灘救生員

oxygen cylinder (air tank)
kōng qì tǒng
空气筒
空氣筒

rescue facilities
jiù shēng shè bèi
救生设备
救生設備

deep-sea dive
shēn hǎi qián shuǐ
深海潜水
深海潛水

artificial respiration
rén gōng hū xī
人工呼吸
人工呼吸

scuba-diving
dài shuǐ fèi qián shuǐ
戴水肺潜水
戴水肺潛水

life buoy; rubber ring
jiù shēng quān
救生圈
救生圈

flippers
qián shuǐ wā jiǎo
潜水蛙脚
潛水蛙腳

holding
bì qì
闭气
閉氣

surfboard
chōng làng bǎn
冲浪板
衝浪板

belly-flop
dǎ dù pí
打肚皮（跳水）
打肚皮

face mask
shuǐ jìng
水镜
水鏡

spring board
tiào bǎn
跳板
跳板

earplug
ěr sāi
耳塞
耳塞

vaulting platform
tiào tái
跳台
跳臺

nose bug
bí jiá
鼻夹
鼻夾

reversed dive
fǎn shēn tiào
反身跳
反身跳

snorkel
hū xī guǎn
呼吸管
呼吸管

curl dive
juǎn shēn tiào
卷身跳
捲身跳

swimming course
yǒng dào
泳道
泳道

fancy dive
huā shì tiào shuǐ
花式跳水
花式跳水

foot bath
xí jiǎo chí
洗脚池
洗腳池

whip arms (swan) dive
zhāng bì tiào shuǐ
张臂跳水
張臂跳水

water wings
bǎng jiān fú dài
绑肩浮袋
綁肩浮袋

gainer dive
dào zāi gēn-tou tiào
倒栽跟头跳
倒栽跟頭跳

73E Ice Skating 溜冰

ice skating **bīng dāo liū bīng**	冰刀溜冰 冰刀溜冰	figure skating **huā shì huá bīng**	花式溜冰 花式溜冰
skating rink **liū bīng chǎng**	溜冰场 溜冰場	backward **hòu tuì**	后退 後退
hardrail **fú-shou gǎn**	扶手杆 扶手桿	skating backward **dào tuì liū**	倒退溜 倒退溜
blade **bīng dāo**	冰刀 冰刀	turning backward **hòu tuì zhuǎn xiàng**	后退转向 後退轉向
figure blade skates **huā shì bīng dāo xié**	花式冰刀鞋 花式冰刀鞋	dead break **jí tíng**	急停 急停
speed blade skates **kuài sù bīng dāo xié**	快速冰刀鞋 快速冰刀鞋	compass **xüán yüán qüān**	旋圆圈 旋圓圈
inside edge **nèi rèn**	内刃 內刃	ice skaters **liū bīng xüán-shou**	溜冰选手 溜冰選手
outside edge **wài rèn**	外刃 外刃	get ahead of **lǐng xiān; chāo qián**	领先；超前 領先；超前
ice skates **bīng dāo liū bīng xié**	冰刀溜冰鞋 冰刀溜冰鞋	spin; rotation **xüán zhuǎn**	旋转 旋轉
skating shoes **huá bīng xié**	滑冰鞋 滑冰鞋	free-skiting specs **yǎn jìng xíng**	眼镜形 眼鏡形
roller skates **lún shì liū bīng xié**	轮式溜冰鞋 輪式溜冰鞋	jump **tiào**	跳 跳
roller skating **lún shì liū bīng**	轮式溜冰 輪式溜冰	counter; turn **fán zhuǎn**	反转 反轉
roller blading **liū zhí pái lún**	溜直排轮 溜直排輪	dead-stop **jí tíng**	急停 急停
in-line skating **zhí pái lún**	直排轮 直排輪	flying jump **fēi tiào**	飞跳 飛跳
free figure **zì yóu huā shì**	自由花式 自由花式		

skiing huá xuě	滑雪 滑雪	bob-sleigh xuě chē	雪车 雪車
down hill race xià shān huá sài	下山滑赛 下山滑賽	snow browing xuě shàng jí tíng	雪上急停 雪上急停
herring boning fēn tuǐ huá xíng	分腿滑行 分腿滑行	side slipping cè huá	侧滑 側滑
street running zhí xiàn huá pǎo	直线滑跑 直線滑跑	ski-jumping huá xuě tiào yuè	滑雪跳跃 滑雪跳躍
crouch running qū shēn huá pǎo	屈身滑跑 屈身滑跑	round head stick yuán tóu zhàng	圆头杖 圓頭杖
telemark qū xī xuán zhuǎn	屈膝旋转 屈膝旋轉	flight tiào yuè fēi xíng	跳跃飞行 跳躍飛行
avalanche xuě bēng	雪崩 雪崩	toboggan qiāo	橇 橇
safety strap ān quán jié hé dài	安全结合带 安全結合帶	seat prop zhò wèi zhī jià	座位支架 座位支架
sled / horn-shaped runners jiǎo xíng huá jià xuě qiāo	角型滑架雪橇 角型滑架雪橇	ski binding xuě jī dǐ jié	雪屐底结 雪屐底結
skeleton sled dī jià xuě qiāo	低架雪橇 低架雪橇	ski press xuě jī zhěng xíng qì	雪屐整形器 雪屐整形器
ski zhì huá tiě	制滑铁 制滑鐵	ski wax xuě jī là	雪屐腊 雪屐蠟
toboggan biǎn píng dí xuě qiāo	扁平底雪橇 扁平底雪橇	ski boot xuě xuē	雪靴 雪靴
fore-tightener qián bù jiá bǎn	前部夹板 前部夾板	snow goggles xuě jìng	雪镜 雪鏡
stock (ring) jī tuō (quān)	屐托 屐托（圈）	sled; toboggan xuě qiāo	雪橇 雪橇
sealskin hǎi bào pí	海豹皮 海豹皮（登高裝置）	sled runner xuě qiāo huá xíng bǎn	雪橇滑行板 雪橇滑行板

toe strap (iron) **zhǐ dài** (tiě)	趾带 趾帶（鐵）	downhill racing **yóu shān dǐng huá xià jìng sài**	由山顶滑下竞赛 由山頂滑下競賽
bobsled **lián qiāo**	连橇 連橇	long-distance ski jump **cháng jù lí huá xüě tiào yüè**	长距离滑雪跳越 長距離滑雪跳越
touring ski **pǔ tōng xüě jī**	普通雪屐 普通雪屐	to schuss **zhí xiàn gāo sù huá xíng**	直线高速滑行 直線高速滑行
ski pole **huá xüě zhàng**	滑雪杖 滑雪杖	cross-country skiing **yüè yě huá xüě**	越野滑雪 越野滑雪
gliding ski **huá xüě jī**	滑雪屐 滑雪屐	skimeister **huá xüě zhuān jiā**	滑雪专家 滑雪專家
snow ring **huá xüě gǎn lún**	滑雪杆轮 滑雪桿輪	approach **huá luò bǎn**	滑落板 滑落板
course **huá xüě dào**	滑雪道 滑雪道	ski-jump; take-off platform **huá luò tiào chù; qǐ tiào diǎn**	滑落跳处；起跳点 滑落跳處；起跳點
foot plate **jiǎo pán**	脚盘 腳盤	leaning **qīng cè**	倾侧 傾側
ankle gaiter **jiǎo huái báng-tui**	脚踝绑腿 腳踝綁腿	banked turn **qīng cè zhuǎn wān**	倾侧转弯 傾側轉彎
jumping ski **tiào yüè xüě jī**	跳跃雪屐 跳躍雪屐	christiania **aò sī lù shì xüán zhuǎn**	奥斯路式旋转 奧斯路式旋轉
steering wheel **cāo zòng lún**	操纵轮 操縱輪	jump-turn **tiào yüè zhuǎn wān**	跳越转弯 跳越轉彎
spiral spring **luó xüán tán huáng**	螺旋弹簧 螺旋彈簧	amble **huǎn bù huá xíng**	缓步滑行 緩步滑行
racing ski **sài pǎo xüě jī**	赛跑雪屐 賽跑雪屐	reversng; kick-turp **tī xüán shì**	踢旋式 踢旋式
slalom ski **wān dào huá jiàng xüě jī**	弯道滑降雪屐 彎道滑降雪屐	traverse **héng huá**	横滑 橫滑
to herringbone **rén zì xíng pá dēng**	人字形爬登 人字形爬登	(to) slalom (race) **wān dào huá xüě sài**	弯道滑雪赛 彎道滑雪賽
downhill runngig **yóu shān dǐng huá xià**	由山顶滑下 由山頂滑下	ski lift **song huá xüé kè shàng shān diào jù**	送滑雪客上山吊具 送滑雪客上山吊具
stem-amble **nì xíng**	逆行 逆行		
side-step **cè bù pá dēng**	侧步爬登 側步爬登		

fencing **xī yáng jiàn**	西洋剑 西洋劍	**to cut at the cheek** **miàn jiá cì jí**	面颊刺击 面頰刺擊
fencing terrain **bǐ jiàn chǎng**	比剑场 比劍場	**sudden thrust of the head** **tú jí tóu bù**	突击头部 突擊頭部
heeless fencing shoes **wú gēn jiàn xūē**	无跟剑靴 無跟劍靴	**outsided cut at the head** **yóu wài cè jí tóu**	由外侧击头 由外側擊頭
fencing jacket **wǔ jiàn yī**	舞剑衣 舞劍衣	**to smash** **zhí pī**	直劈 直劈
fencing breeches **wǔ jiàn duǎn kù**	舞剑短裤 舞劍短褲	**to lunge** **cì**	刺 刺
sword **jiàn**	剑 劍	**high cuts** **shàng cì shì**	上刺式 上刺式
foil **liàn xí yòng dùn tóu jiàn**	练习用钝头剑 練習用鈍頭劍	**low cuts** **xià cì shì**	下刺式 下刺式
épée **wú rèn jiàn**	无刃剑 無刃劍	**straight thrust** **zhí cì**	直刺 直刺
swashbuckler **xǔ kuā jiàn shǒu**	虚夸剑手 虛誇劍手	**to pierce; hit** **cì rù**	刺入 刺入
on-guard position **fáng bèi zī-shi**	防备姿势 防備姿勢	**to cut at the flank** **héng fù cì rù**	横腹刺入 橫腹刺入
attack position **gōng jí zī-shi**	攻击姿势 攻擊姿勢	**cut at the chest** **cì xiōng**	刺胸 刺胸
chest protector **hù xiōng**	护胸 護胸	**cross piece** **jiāo chā bǐng huán**	交叉柄环 交叉柄環
neck guard **hù jǐng**	护颈 護頸	**circling crossing of swords** **huí zhuǎn jiāo fēng**	回转交锋 迴轉交鋒
to practice fencing **liàn jiàn**	练剑 練劍	**to parry** **dǎng-kai**	挡开 擋開
crossing swords **dòu jiàn**	门剑 鬥劍	**to riposte** **dǎng hòu huán cì**	挡后还刺 擋後還刺

74A

Birds 鸟類 A

bird **niǎor**	鸟儿 鳥兒	dove; pigeon **gē-zi**	鸽子 鴿子
birdie **xiáo niǎor**	小鸟儿 小鳥兒（暱稱）	carrier-pigeon **chuán xìn gē**	传信鸽 傳信鴿
phoenix **fèng-huang**	凤凰 鳳凰	squab **rǔ gē**	乳鸽 乳鴿
hummingbird **fēng niǎor**	蜂鸟儿 蜂鳥兒	swallow **yàn-zi**	燕子 燕子
teal; garganey **shuǐ yā**	水鸭 水鴨	flycatcher **jīng yàn**	京燕 京燕
canary **jīn sī qüè**	金丝雀 金絲雀	swallow (bird nest) **jīn sī yàn**	金丝燕 金絲燕（燕窩）
lark **bǎi líng niǎor**	百灵鸟儿 百靈鳥兒	petrel **hǎi yàn**	海燕 海燕
magpie **xǐ-qüè**	喜鹊 喜鵲	tern **yàn ōu**	燕鸥 燕鷗
sparrow **má qüè**	麻雀 麻雀	wild geese **dà yàn**	大雁 大雁
oriole **huáng yīng**	黄莺 黃鶯	woodpecker **zhuó mù niǎo**	啄木鸟 啄木鳥
quail **ān-chun**	鹌鹑 鵪鶉	a redhead **hóng tóu zhuó mù niǎo**	红头啄木鸟 紅頭啄木鳥
bamboo pheasant **zhú jī**	竹鸡 竹雞	toucan **jǜ zuǐ niǎo**	巨嘴鸟 巨嘴鳥
hazel grouse **sōng jī**	松鸡 松雞	crane **hè**	鹤 鶴
peacock **xióng kǒng-qüe**	雄孔雀 雄孔雀	white crane **bái hè**	白鹤 白鶴
peahen **cí kǒng-qüe**	雌孔雀 雌孔雀	stork **guàn**	鹳 鸛
peacock display **kǒng qüè kāi píng**	孔雀开屏 孔雀開屏	egret **bái lù**	白鹭 白鷺

ibis zhū lù	朱鹭 朱鷺	kingfisher cuì niǎo; yǘ gǒu	翠鸟；鱼狗 翠鳥；魚狗
flamingo hóng huǒ hè	红火鹤 紅火鶴	thunder bird léi niǎo	雷鸟 雷鳥
egret bái lù sī	白鹭丝 白鷺絲	penguin qì é	企鹅 企鵝
sea gull hǎi ōu	海鸥 海鷗	swan tiān é	天鹅 天鵝
gull shā ōu	沙鸥 沙鷗	goose é	鹅 鵝
eagle lǎo yīng	老鹰 老鷹（大型）	pelican táng é	塘鹅 塘鵝
hawk lǎo yīng	老鹰 老鷹（小型）	duck yā-zi	鸭子 鴨子
eaglet xiǎo yīng	小鹰 小鷹	duckling xiǎo yā	小鸭 小鴨
vulture tū yīng	秃鹰 禿鷹	mallard lù tóu yě yā	绿头野鸭 綠頭野鴨
buzzard hóng tóu měi zhōu yīng	红头美洲鹰 紅頭美洲鷹	teal shuǐ yā	水鸭 水鴨
snakebird shé tí niǎo	蛇鹈鸟 蛇鵜鳥	oviparity luǎn shēng	卵生 卵生
roc dà péng	大鹏 大鵬	a brood of chickens yì wō xiǎo jī	一窝小鸡 一窩小雞
kite yüān	鸢 鳶	artificial incubation rén gōng fū dàn	人工孵蛋 人工孵蛋
owl māo tóu yīng	猫头鹰 貓頭鷹	rooster gōng jī	公鸡 公雞
eagle-owl māo xiāo	猫枭 貓梟	hen mǔ jī	母鸡 母雞
pintail cháng wěi fú	长尾凫 長尾鳧	leghorn lái hēng jī	来亨鸡 來亨雞
horned owl jiǎo xiāo; xiāo	角鸮；枭 角鴞；梟	guinea zhū jī	珠鸡 珠雞
eatbird māo shēng niǎo	猫声鸟 貓聲鳥	golden pheasant jǐn jī	锦鸡 錦雞
falcon liè yīng	猎鹰 獵鷹	turtle dove bān jiū	斑鸠 斑鳩
wild fowl liè niǎo	猎鸟 獵鳥	crow wū yā	乌鸦 烏鴉

mandarin duck **yūān-yang**	鸳鸯 鴛鴦	star finch **xiǎo wén niǎor**	小纹乌儿 小紋鳥兒
fowl **qín lèi**	禽类 禽類	bee-eater (bird) **shí fēng niǎor**	食蜂乌儿 食蜂鳥兒
poultry **jiā qín**	家禽 家禽	linnet **hóng què**	红雀 紅雀
ostrich **tuó niǎo**	驼鸟 駝鳥	nightingale **yè yīng**	夜莺 夜鶯
rhea **sān zhǐ tuó niǎo**	三趾驼鸟 三趾駝鳥	thrush **huà méi**	画眉 畫眉
turkey **huǒ jī**	火鸡 火雞	beak **niǎor zuǐ**	鸟儿嘴 鳥兒嘴
pheasant **zhì; yě jī**	雉；野鸡 雉；野雞	comb **ròu guàn**	肉冠 肉冠
migratory birds **hòu niǎo**	候鸟 候鳥	wing **chì bǎng**	翅膀 翅膀
parrot **yīng wǔ**	鹦鹉 鸚鵡	flap **zhèn chì**	振翅 振翅
macaw **jīn gāng yīng wǔ**	金刚鹦鹉 金剛鸚鵡	feather **yǔ máo**	羽毛 羽毛
parakeet **xiǎo yīng wǔ**	小鹦鹉 小鸚鵡	birds molt; moult **niǎor tuō máo**	鸟儿脱毛 鳥兒脫毛
Chinese bulbul **bái tóu wēng**	白头翁 白頭翁	claw **zhuǎ-zi**	爪子 爪子
starling **ōu lüè niǎo**	欧掠鸟 歐掠鳥	bird's tail **niǎor yǐ-ba**	鸟儿尾巴 鳥兒尾巴
cuckoo **bù gú niǎo; dù juān**	布谷鸟；杜鹃 布穀鳥；杜鵑	chain for the birds **niǎor liàn-zi**	鸟儿炼子 鳥兒鍊子
robin; redbreast **zhī gēng niǎo**	知更鸟 知更鳥	birdcage **niǎor lóng-zi**	鸟儿笼子 鳥兒籠子
bluebird **lán zhī gēng niǎo**	篮知更鸟 藍知更鳥	bird nest **niǎor wō**	鸟儿窝 鳥兒窩
bluejay **guān lán yā**	冠篮鸦 冠籃鴉	bird seed **niǎor shí**	鸟儿食 鳥兒食
lovebirds **bǐ yì niǎo**	比翼鸟 比翼鳥	fledgling; nestling **chú niǎo**	雏鸟 雛鳥
goldfinch **jīn chì niǎo**	金翅鸟 金翅鳥	regurgitate **fǎn chú**	反刍 反芻
mynah **bā gēr**	八哥儿 八哥兒	bird flu **qín liú gǎn** (see poultry 家禽)	禽流感 禽流感

zoo dòng wù yüán	动物园 動物園	hide; leather shòu pí; gé	兽皮；革 獸皮；革
animal dòng wù	动物 動物	hair (animal hair) máo (shòu máo)	毛（兽毛） 毛（獸毛）
beast yě shòu	野兽 野獸	fur shòu pí máo	兽皮毛 獸皮毛
cub yòu shòu	幼兽（熊狮虎鲸鲨） 幼獸（熊獅虎鯨鯊）	specimen biāo běn yàng pǐn	标本样品 標本樣品
quadrupeds zǒu shòu	走兽 走獸	stuffed animal dòng wù biāo běn	动物标本 動物標本
to adventure tàn xiǎn	探险 探險	stuffed wildlife yě shēng dòng wù biāo běn	野生动物标本 野生動物標本
explore tàn suǒ	探索 探索	mammal bú rǔ dòng wù	哺乳动物 哺乳動物
explorers tàn xiǎn jiā	探险家 探險家	carnivorous animal ròu shí dòng wù	肉食动物 肉食動物
the wilderness kuāng yě huāng liāo	旷野荒郊 曠野荒郊	herbivorous animal cǎo shí dòng wù	草食动物 草食動物
endangered animals xī yǒu dòng wù	稀有动物 稀有動物	creature shēng wù	生物 生物
wildlife yě shēng dòng wù	野生动物 野生動物	dumb creature xià děng dòng wù	下等动物 下等動物
stranded in the desert kùn zài shā mò	困在沙漠 困在沙漠	vivitarity tāi shēng	胎生 胎生
prevent from dying out yǐ fáng jüé zhǒng	以防绝种 以防絕種	oviparous animal luǎn shēng dòng wù	卵生动物 卵生動物
(in) need of assistance xū yào yüán zhù	需要援助 需要援助	gentle animal wēn xùn dòng wù	温驯动物 溫馴動物
die of hunger è sǐ	饿死 餓死	tamed tīng huà; xùn fú-de	听话；驯服的 聽話；馴服的
die of thirst ké-sǐ	渴死 渴死	livestock shèng chù	牲畜 牲畜

English	Pinyin	Simplified	Traditional

cat
māo
猫
貓

kitten
yòu māo
幼猫
幼貓

Kittie! Kittie!
māo mī
猫咪！
貓咪！（呼唤）

Persian cat
bō sī māo
波斯猫
波斯貓

Siamese cat
xiān luó māo
暹罗猫
暹羅貓

dog
gǒu
狗
狗

Doggie! Doggie!
gǒu góu!
狗狗！
狗狗！（呼唤）

held in its mouth
diāo-zhe
叼著
叼著

puppy
yòu quǎn
幼犬
幼犬

mordant dog
huì yǎo rén-de gǒu
会咬人的狗
會咬人的狗

Scotch terrier
duán-tui jüǎn máor gǒu
短腿卷毛儿狗
短腿捲毛兒狗

gray hound
liè gǒu
猎狗
獵狗

Dachshund
là cháng gǒu
腊肠狗
臘腸狗

pointer
bān diǎn liè gǒu
斑点猎狗
斑點獵狗

German shepherd
Dé Guó mù yáng gǒu
德国牧羊狗
德國牧羊狗

Great Dane
dà dān gǒu
大丹狗
大丹狗

bulldog
niú tóu gǒu
牛头狗
牛頭狗

Doberman pinscher
dù bīn gǒu
杜宾狗
杜賓狗

Cocker Spaniel (long ear)
Xī Bān Yá liè gǒu (cháng-er)
西班牙猎狗
西班牙獵狗

French poodle
guì bīn gǒu
贵宾狗
貴賓狗

Pekingese (dog)
hā bā gǒu
哈巴狗
哈巴狗

Chow Chow (dog)
sōng shī gǒu
松狮狗
鬆獅狗

Finnish Spitz
hú-li gǒu
狐狸狗
狐狸狗

pocket dog
xiù-zhen gǒu
袖珍狗
袖珍狗

Chihuahua
Jí wá-wa
吉娃娃
吉娃娃

Sharpie
shā pí gǒu
沙皮狗
沙皮狗

Police dog
jíng quǎn
警犬
警犬

seeing-eye dog
dǎo máng quǎn
导盲犬
導盲犬

anthropoid
rén yüán
人猿
人猿

ape
yüán
猿
猿

howling monkey
hǒu yüán
吼猿
吼猿

orangutan; orangoutang
xīng-xing
猩猩
猩猩

baboon
fèi-fei
狒狒
狒狒

gorilla
dà xīng xīng
大猩猩
大猩猩

chimpanzee
hēi xīng-xing
黑猩猩
黑猩猩

gibbon
cháng bì yüán
长臂猿
長臂猿

spider monkey
zhī zhū yüán
蜘蛛猿
蜘蛛猿

lemur
hú hóu
狐猴
狐猴

flying lemur
fēi xíng hú hóu
飞行狐猴
飛行狐猴

monkey
hóu-zi
猴子
猴子

horse **mǎ**	马 馬	
colt; foal **xiáo mǎ**	小马 小馬	
pony **ái zhǒng xiáo mǎ**	矮种小马 矮種小馬	
llama **tuó mǎ**	驼马 駝馬	
zebra **bān mǎ**	斑马 斑馬	
unicorn **qí lín**	麒麟 麒麟	
donkey; ass **lǘ**	驴 驢	
mule **luó-zi**	骡子 騾子	
rhinoceros **xī niú**	犀牛 犀牛	
buffalo; bison **yě niú**	野牛 野牛	
dairy cattle; milch cow **rǔ niú**	乳牛 乳牛	
a herd of cattle **yì qǔn niú**	一群牛 一群牛	
cow **mǔ niú**	母牛 母牛	
bull **gōng niú**	公牛 公牛	
bullock; ox **yān niú**	阉牛 閹牛	
calf **xiǎo niú**	小牛 小牛	
buffalo **shuǐ niú**	水牛 水牛	
yak; zebu **lí niú**	犁牛 犛牛	
sheep **mián yáng**	绵羊 綿羊	
antelope **líng yáng**	羚羊 羚羊	

addax; antelope **xüán jiǎo líng yáng**	旋角羚羊 旋角羚羊	
goat **shān yáng**	山羊 山羊	
ram **gōng yáng**	公羊 公羊	
ewe **mǔ yáng**	母羊 母羊	
lamb **xiǎo yáng**	小羊 小羊	
deer **lù**	鹿 鹿	
musk deer **shè xiāng lù**	麝香鹿 麝香鹿	
giraffe **cháng jǐng lù**	长颈鹿 長頸鹿	
spotted deer **méi huā lù**	梅花鹿 梅花鹿	
elk; moose **mí lù; dà jiǎo lù**	麋鹿；大角鹿 麋鹿；大角鹿	
muntjac; barking deer **qiāng lù**	羌鹿 羌鹿	
elephant **xiàng**	象 象	
trunk **xiàng bí-zi**	象鼻子 象鼻子	
bear **xióng**	熊 熊	
wombat **dài xióng**	袋熊 袋熊	
panda **māo xióng**	猫熊 貓熊	
giant panda **dà xióng māo; dà māo xióng**	大熊猫；大猫熊 大熊貓；大貓熊	
koala bear **wú wěi xióng**	无尾熊 無尾熊	
tiger **hǔ**	虎 虎	
lion **shī-zi**	狮子 獅子	

liger **shī hǔ**	狮虎 獅虎	raccoon **huǎn xióng**	浣熊 浣熊
leopard **jīn qián bào**	金钱豹 金錢豹	skunk **yòu; chòu yòu**	鼬；臭鼬 鼬；臭鼬
panther **hēi bào**	黑豹 黑豹	marmot; ground hog **tǔ bō shǔ**	土拨鼠 土撥鼠
bobcat; lynx **shān māo**	山猫 山貓	mole **tián shǔ**	田鼠 田鼠
jackal **chái; hú láng**	豺；胡狼 豺；胡狼	rat **láo-shu**　（大）	老鼠 老鼠
wolf **láng**	狼 狼	mouse **hào-zi**　（小）	耗子 耗子
weasel **huáng-shu láng**	黄鼠狼 黃鼠狼	squirrel **sōng shǔ**	松鼠 松鼠
fox **hú-li**	狐狸 狐狸	guinea pig **tiān zhú shǔ**	天竺鼠 天竺鼠
silver fox **yín hú**	银狐 銀狐	kangaroo **dài shǔ**	袋鼠 袋鼠
masked (gem-faced) **civet** **guǒ-zi lí**	果子狸 果子狸	camel **luò-tuo**	骆驼 駱駝
mink **diāo**	貂 貂	dromedary **dān fēng luò-tuo**	单峰骆驼 單峰駱駝
bat **biān fú**	蝙蝠 蝙蝠	bactrain camel **shuāng fēng luò-tuo**	双峰骆驼 雙峰駱駝
fruit bat **shí guǒ biān fú**	食果蝙蝠 食果蝙蝠	porcupine **háo zhū**	豪猪 豪豬
vampire (bat) **xī xiě biān fú**	吸血蝙蝠 吸血蝙蝠	pig; hog **zhū**	猪 豬
anteater **shí yǐ shòu**	食蚁兽 食蟻獸	boar **yě zhū**	野猪 野豬
platypus **yā zuǐ shòu**	鸭嘴兽 鴨嘴獸	rabbit **tù-zi**	兔子 兔子
pangolin **chuān shān jiǎ**	穿山甲 穿山甲	hare **yě tù**	野兔 野兔
hedgehog **cì-wei**	刺猬 刺蝟	ran wild everywhere **dào chù luàn cuàn**	到处乱窜 到處亂竄
badger; brock **huān**	獾 獾	living beings **yǒu shēng mìng-de dòng wù**	有生命的动物 有生命的動物

74C

Aquatic Animals
水族動物

aquatic animals **shuǐ zú**	水族 水族	stingray **hōng**	魟 魟
gold fish **jīn yú**	金鱼 金魚	starfish **hǎi xīng**	海星 海星
tropical fish **rè dài yú**	热带鱼 熱帶魚	shark **shā yú; jiāo**	鲨鱼；鲛 鯊魚；鮫
fresh-water fish **dàn shuǐ yú**	淡水鱼 淡水魚	rockfish- **shí yú**	石鱼 石魚
deep-sea fish **shēn hǎi yú**	深海鱼 深海魚	whale **jīng yú**	鲸鱼 鯨魚
a school of fish **yì qún yú**	一群鱼 一群魚	dolphin; sea hog **bái hǎi tún**	白海豚 白海豚
fry (in schools) **yú miáo**	鱼苗 魚苗	sea otter **hǎi tà**	海獭 海獺
loach **ní-qiu**	泥鳅 泥鰍	seal; sea calf **hǎi bào**	海豹 海豹
eel (see P. 209 & P. 226 seafood) **mán yú**	鳗鱼 鰻魚	fur seal; ursine seal **hái gǒu**	海狗 海狗
conger eel; conger pike **hǎi mán**	海鳗 海鰻	nutria; coypu **hé lí shǔ**	河狸鼠 河狸鼠
sea snake **hǎi shé**	海蛇 海蛇	beaver **hǎi lí**	海狸 海狸
catfish **nián yú**	鲶鱼 鯰魚	walrus; morse **hǎi xiàng**	海象 海象
skipper **fēi yú**	飞鱼 飛魚	sea lion **hǎi shī**	海狮 海獅
devilfish **dà yáo yú**	大鹞鱼 大鷂魚	manatee; sea cow **hǎi niú**	海牛 海牛
sea horse **hái mǎ**	海马 海馬	hippopotamus **hé mǎ**	河马 河馬
sea-jelly **shuí-mu**	水母 水母	shellfish **jiǎ ké lèi**	甲壳类 甲殼類

Amphibians
雨棲類

English	简体	繁體
amphibious animals **liǎng qī dòng wù**	两栖动物	兩棲動物
cold-blooded creature **léng xiě dòng wù**	冷血动物	冷血動物
dragon **lóng**	龙	龍
dinosaur **kǒng lóng**	恐龙	恐龍
snake **shé**	蛇	蛇
to hibernate **dōng mián**	冬眠	冬眠
ecdysis; molt **tuì pí; tuō kér**	蜕皮；脱壳儿	蛻皮；脫殼兒
boa constrictor **mǎng**	蟒	蟒
poison snake **dú shé**	毒蛇	毒蛇
non-poison snake **wú dú shé**	无毒蛇	無毒蛇
python **jǐn shé**	锦蛇	錦蛇
banded krait **yǔ sǎn jié shé**	雨伞节蛇	雨傘節蛇
hundred-pacer **bǎi bù shé**	百步蛇	百步蛇
rattlesnake **xiáng wěi shé**	响尾蛇	響尾蛇
bamboo snake **zhú jié shé**	竹节蛇	竹節蛇

English	简体	繁體
cobra **yǎn jìng shé**	眼镜蛇	眼鏡蛇
bullfrog **niú wā**	牛蛙	牛蛙
toad **lài há-ma**	癞蛤蟆	癩蛤蟆
frog **qīng wā**	青蛙	青蛙
tadpole (蝌蚪) **há-ma gū-duor** (kē dǒu)	蛤蟆骨朵儿	蛤蟆骨朵兒
snail **guā niú**	蜗牛	蝸牛
conch **hǎi luó**	海螺	海螺
green trutle; sea turtle **hǎi guī**	海龟	海龜
turtle **guī; wū guī**	龟；乌龟	龜；烏龜
tortoise **lù guī**	陆龟	陸龜
soft-shelled turtle **biē**	鳖	鱉
lizard **xī yì**	蜥蜴	蜥蜴
chameleon **biàn sè xī yì**	变色蜥蜴	變色蜥蜴
alligator **xiǎo è yú**	小鳄鱼	小鱷魚
crocodile **dà è yú**	大鳄鱼	大鱷魚

insect **kūn chóng**	昆虫 昆蟲	ant **má yǐ**	蚂蚁 螞蟻
insect specimen **kūn chóng biāo běn**	昆虫标本 昆蟲標本	termite **bái yǐ**	白蚁 白蟻
fly **cāng-yíng**	苍蝇 蒼蠅	winged ant **fēi yǐ**	飞蚁 飛蟻
fruit fly **guǒ yíng**	果蝇 果蠅	firefly; lightning bug **yíng huǒ chóng**	萤火虫 螢火蟲
maggot **qū**	蛆 蛆	noctiluca **fú yóu yè guāng chóng**	浮游夜光虫 浮游夜光蟲
mosquito; gnat **wén-zi**	蚊子 蚊子	bee **mì fēng**	蜜蜂 蜜蜂
larva; larvae **yòu chóng**	幼虫 幼蟲	wasp **huáng fēng**	黄蜂 黃蜂
wiggler; wriggler **jié jüé**	孑孓 孑孓	hornet nest **dà huáng fēng fēng wō**	大黄蜂蜂窝 大黃蜂蜂窩
butterfly **hú dié**	蝴蝶 蝴蝶	locust **mà-zha; huáng-chong**	蚂蚱；蝗虫 螞蚱；蝗蟲
moth (worm) **zhù-chong**	蛀虫 蛀蟲	grasshopper **xiǎo zhà měng**	小蚱蜢 小蚱蜢
silverfish (worm) **yī chóng; dù chóng**	衣虫；蠹虫 衣蟲；蠹蟲	long-horned grasshoppe **guà-de biǎnr**	挂的扁儿 掛的扁兒（尖頭蚱蜢）
bookworm; booklouse **shū chóngr**	书虫儿 書蟲兒	walking stick (worm) **zhú jié chóng**	竹节虫 竹節蟲
moth (flying) **é**	蛾 蛾	praying mantis **táng láng**	螳螂 螳螂
pupa; nymph **yǒng**	蛹 蛹	dragonfly **qīng tíng**	蜻蜓 蜻蜓
ecdysis (cicada) (snake) **tuō kér; tuì pí**	脱壳儿；蜕皮 脫殼兒；蛻皮	spider **zhī-zhu**	蜘蛛 蜘蛛

orb spider **qiú-xíng zhī-zhu**	球形蜘蛛 球形蜘蛛	snapper; springtail **kē tóu chóng; tán wěi chóng**	磕头虫；弹尾虫 磕頭蟲；彈尾蟲
daddy longlegs **máng zhī-zhu**	盲蜘蛛 盲蜘蛛	silkworm **cán**	蚕 蠶
wolf spider **duō máo dà zhī-zhu**	多毛大蜘蛛 多毛大蜘蛛	louse **shī-zi**	虱子 蝨子
cobweb **zhī-zhu wǎng**	蜘蛛网 蜘蛛網	flea **tiào-zao**	跳蚤 跳蚤
centipede **wú-gong**	蜈蚣 蜈蚣	katydid; long-horned grasshopper **guō guōr**	蝈蝈儿 蟈蟈兒
gecko; house lizard **bì hǔ**	壁虎 壁虎	cricket **qǔ qǔr; xī shuài**	蛐蛐儿；蟋蟀 蛐蛐兒；蟋蟀
scorpion **xiē-zi**	蝎子 蠍子	cicada **chán; zhī liǎo**	蝉；知了 蟬；知了
cockroach **zhāng-lang**	蟑螂 蟑螂	demoiselle **dòu niáng**	豆娘 豆娘
worm **rú chóng**	蠕虫 蠕蟲	tiger moth **pū-deng ér**	扑灯蛾儿 撲燈蛾兒
beetle **jiǎ chóng**	甲虫 甲蟲	mollusca **ruán tǐ dòng wù**	软体动物 軟體動物
tortoise beetle **guī jiǎ chóng**	龟甲虫 龜甲蟲	cutworm **é máo chóng**	蛾毛虫 蛾毛蟲
tumblebug **fèn jīn guī**	粪金龟 糞金龜	caterpillar **máo-mao chóng; dié chóng**	毛毛虫；蝶虫 毛毛蟲；蝶蟲
dung beetle **shǐ-ke làng**	屎壳螂 屎殼螂	clothes moth **zhù chóng**	蛀虫 蛀蟲
cockchafer; dorbeetle **jīn guī-zi**	金龟子 金龜子	gastropod **fù zú dòng wù**	腹足动物 腹足動物
stinkbug **chòu zhuāng xiàng chóng**	臭桩象虫 臭椿象蟲	snail **guā niú**	蜗牛 蝸牛
long-horned beetle **tiān niú**	天牛 天牛	reptiles **pá xíng dòng wù**	爬行动物 爬行動物
weevil **xiàng bí chóng**	象鼻虫 象鼻蟲	arthropod **jié zú dòng wù**	节足动物 節足動物
bug **xiǎo pá chóng**	小爬虫 小爬蟲	amoeba **biàn xíng chóng**	变形虫 變形蟲
bedbug **chòu-chong**	臭虫 臭蟲	millepede **qiān zú chóng; mǎ lù**	千足虫；马陆 千足蟲；馬陸
ladybug **piáo chóng; hóng niáng**	瓢虫；红娘 瓢蟲；紅娘	earthworm **qiū yǐn**	蚯蚓 蚯蚓

horticulture **yuán yì**	园艺 園藝	flower stem; stalk **huā gěng**	花梗 花梗
lawn mower **jián cǎo qī**	剪草机 剪草機	pluck flowers **zhāi huā**	摘花 摘花
adequate water **zú gòu-de shuǐ fèn**	足够的水分 足夠的水分	flower arrangement **chā huā**	插花 插花
seed **zhǒng zi**	种子 種子	a frog (for flowers) **chā huā zuòr**	插花座儿 插花座兒
to germinate; to sprout **fā yá**	发芽 發芽	vase **huā píngr**	花瓶儿 花瓶兒
blossom; bloom **huā kāi**	花开 花開	artificial flower **rén zào huā**	人造花 人造花
wilt **huā xiè**	花谢 花謝	cherry blossom **yīng huā**	樱花 櫻花
flower bud **huā gū-duor**	花骨朵儿 花骨朵兒	plum blossom **là méi**	腊梅 臘梅
flower **huā duǒ**	花朵 花朵	chrysanthemum **jú huā**	菊花 菊花
petal **huā bàn**	花瓣 花瓣	orchid **lán huā**	兰花 蘭花
flower bud **huā lěi**	花蕾 花蕾	gardenia **zhī huā**	栀花 梔花
flower fragrance **huā xiāng**	花香 花香	camellia **chá huā**	茶花 茶花
pistil **cí ruǐ**	雌蕊 雌蕊	osmanthus **guì huā**	桂花 桂花
stamen **xióng ruǐ**	雄蕊 雄蕊	hydrangea **xiù qiú huā**	绣球花 繡球花
pollen **huā fěn**	花粉 花粉	pomegranate blossom **shí-liu huā**	石榴花 石榴花
flowering branch **huā zhī**	花枝 花枝	balsam **fèng xiān huā**	凤仙花 鳳仙花

English	简体	繁體
daffodil; narcissus shuǐ xiān huā	水仙花	水仙花
begonia hǎi táng huā	海棠花	海棠花
morning glory qiān niú huā	牵牛花	牽牛花
coxcomb jī guàn huā	鸡冠花	雞冠花
calla lily mǎ tí lán	马蹄兰	馬蹄蘭
violet zǐ luó lán	紫罗兰	紫羅蘭
fringed iris hú dié huā	蝴蝶花	蝴蝶花
jasmine mò-li huā	茉莉花	茉莉花
peony mǔ-dan huā	牡丹花	牡丹花
herbaceous peony sháo-yao huā	芍药花	芍藥花
tulip yù jīn xiāng	郁金香	鬱金香
rose méi-gui huā	玫瑰花	玫瑰花
lily flower bǎi hé huā	百合花	百合花
oleander jià zhú táo	夹竹桃	夾竹桃
sunflower xiàng rì kuí	向日葵	向日葵
tuberose yè lái xiāng	夜来香	夜來香
lotus lián huā	莲花	蓮花
water lily shuǐ fú lián	水浮莲	水浮蓮
carnation kāng nǎi xīn	康乃馨	康乃馨
azalea dù jüān huā	杜鹃花	杜鵑花
hibiscus fú róng huā	芙蓉花	芙蓉花
lilac zǐ dīng xiāng	紫丁香	紫丁香
petunia lǎ-ba huā	喇叭花	喇叭花
poinsettia shèng dàn hóng	圣诞红	聖誕紅
anthurium huǒ hè huā	火鹤花	火鶴花
dandelion pú gōng yīng	蒲公英	蒲公英
cactus xiān rén zhǎng	仙人掌	仙人掌
sensitive plant; mimosa hán xiū cǎo	含羞草	含羞草
evergreen wàn nián qīng	万年青	萬年青
bouquet huā shù	花束	花束
flower basket huā lán	花篮	花籃
lei huā chuàn	花串	花串
wreath huā qüān	花圈	花圈
corsage xiōng huā	胸花	胸花
grass cǎo	草	草
straw gān cǎo	干草	乾草
moss qīng tái	青苔	青苔
flower pot huā pén	花盆	花盆
potted plant pén huā	盆花	盆花
miniture garden pén jǐng	盆景	盆景

75B Plants 植物

botanical garden **zhí wù yǔan**	植物园 植物園	weeping willow **chuí liǔ**	垂柳 垂柳
plant; vegetation **zhí wù**	植物 植物	elm tree **yǔ shù**	榆树 榆樹
trees **shù**	树 樹	banyan **róng shù**	榕树 榕樹
shrubs; bushes **guàn mù**	灌木 灌木	phoenix tree **wú-tong**	梧桐 梧桐
arbor **qiáo mù**	乔木 喬木	oak **xiàng shù**	橡树 橡樹
pine **sōng shù**	松树 松樹	rubber tree **xiàng jiāo shù**	橡胶树 橡膠樹
umbrella pine **jīn sōng**	金松 金松	cork tree **ruǎn mù shù**	软木树 軟木樹
masson pine **má wěi sōng**	马尾松 馬尾松	mahogany **táo huā xīn mù shù**	桃花心木树 桃花心木樹
cypress **bó shù**	柏树 柏樹	lacquer (varnish) tree **qī shù**	漆树 漆樹
fir **shān**	杉 杉	birch **huá shù**	桦树 樺樹
hemlock **tiě shān**	铁杉 鐵杉	olive tree **gán lǎn shù**	橄榄树 橄欖樹
hornbeam tree **jiǎo shù**	角树 角樹	cassia tree **guì shù**	桂树 桂樹
mulberry tree **sāng shù**	桑树 桑樹	cinnamon **guì pí shù**	桂皮树 桂皮樹
pagoda tree **huái shù**	槐树 槐樹	linden **pú tí shù**	菩提树 菩提樹
willow **liǔ shù**	柳树 柳樹	abele **bái yáng**	白扬 白楊

boxtree **huáng yáng shù**	黄扬树 黃楊樹	camphor tree **zhāng shù**	樟树 樟樹
sassafrase **huáng zhāng**	黄樟 黃樟	incense wood tree **chén xiāng shù**	沉香树 沉香樹
bougainlaea **jiǔ chóng gě**	九重葛 九重葛	poppies **yīng sù**	罂粟 罌粟
sagebrush **shān ài shù**	山艾树 山艾樹	reeds **lú wěi**	芦苇 蘆葦
yaupon; holly tree **dōng qīng shù**	冬青树 冬青樹	bamboo **zhú-zi**	竹子 竹子
gum tree **yóu juā lì shù**	油加利树 油加利樹	rattan **téng-zi**	藤子 藤子
laurel; bay **yüè guì shù**	月桂树 月桂樹	bark **shù pí**	树皮 樹皮
gingko; maidenhair tree **yín xìng shù**	银杏树 銀杏樹	trunk **shù gàn**	树干 樹幹
silk cotton tree; kapok **mù mián shù**	木棉树 木棉樹	branch **shù zhī**	树枝 樹枝
butternut tree **bái hé-tao shù**	白胡桃树 白胡桃樹	root **gēn**	根 根
umbrella tree **sǎn shù**	伞树 傘樹	leaf **shù yè**	树叶 樹葉
Eutrema wasabi **shān kuí**	山葵 山葵	shoot **shù yá**	树芽 樹芽
ivy **cháng chūn téng**	长春藤 長春藤	seedling **yòu miáo**	幼苗 幼苗
coconut palm **yé-zi shù**	椰子树 椰子樹	slip; a slip **jiē zhī; chā zhī**	接枝；插枝 接枝；插枝
palm **zōng lǘ shù; zōng shù**	棕榈树；棕树 棕櫚樹；棕樹	photosynthesis **guāng hé zuò yòng**	光合作用 光合作用
betel palm **bīn-lang shù**	槟榔树 檳榔樹	chlorophyl **yè lǜ sù**	叶绿素 葉綠素
maple **fēng shù**	枫树 楓樹	auxin **zhí wù shēng zhǎng sù**	植物生长素 植物生長素
shaddock tree **yòu-zi shù**	柚子树 柚子樹	plant hormone **zhí wù jī sù**	植物激素 植物激素
teak tree (teakwood) **yóu mù shù**	柚木树 柚木樹	annual ring **nián lún**	年轮 年輪
sandalwood tree **tán xiāng mù shù**	檀香木树 檀香木樹	fertilizer **féi liào**	肥料 肥料

76A

Climate & Weather
氣候與天氣

English	简体	繁體
climate **qì-hou**	气候	氣候
weather **tiān-qi**	天气	天氣
season **jì**	季	季
spring **chūn-tian**	春天	春天
summer **xià-tian**	夏天	夏天
autumn **qiū-tian**	秋天	秋天
winter **dōng-tian**	冬天	冬天
sunny day; clear day **qíng tiān**	晴天	晴天
fair-weather; fine day **hǎo tiān-qi**	好天气	好天氣
freezing point **bīng diǎn**	冰点	冰點
5 below zero **líng xià wǔ dù**	零下五度	零下五度
degree **dù**	度	度
weather report **qì xiàng bào gào**	气象报告	氣象報告
weather forecast **tiān qì yù cè**	天气预测	天氣預測
muggy weather **mēn rè-de tiān-qi**	闷热的天气	悶熱的天氣
dry; arid **gān zào**	干燥	乾燥
a drought; aridity **gān hàn**	干旱	乾旱
moldy weather **huáng méi tiān**	黄梅天	黃梅天
cloud **yún-cai**	云彩	雲彩
cloudy **yīn tiān**	阴天	陰天
mostly cloudy **duō shí yīn tiān**	多时阴天	多時陰天
partly cloudy **duō yún shí qíng**	多云时晴	多雲時晴
rainy day **yǔ tiān**	雨天	雨天
windy day **guā fēng tiān**	刮风天	颳風天
temperature **wēn-du**	温度	溫度
18 to 22 degrees centigrade **shè-shi shí bā zhì èr-shi èr dù**	摄氏 18 至 22 度	攝氏 18 至 22 度
Fahrenheit (Fahr.) **Huá shì hán shǔ biǎo**	华氏寒暑表	華氏寒暑表
expected high is 90 degrees **yù cè gāo wēn jiǔ shí dù**	预测高温 90 度	預測高溫 90 度
overnight low will be **zhěng yè dī wēn**	整夜低温为	整夜低溫為
in the high seventy's **qī-shi liù dù yǐ shàng**	七十六度以上	七十六度以上
humidity **shī-du**	湿度	濕度
moisture **shī-qi**	湿气	濕氣

English	简体	繁體
humidity 70 percent **shī qì bǎi fēn-zhi qī shí**	湿气百分之70	濕氣百分之70
hot **rè**	热	熱
warm & comfortable **nuǎn-huo**	暖和	暖和
cold spell **hán liú**	寒流	寒流
It's freezing! **háo lěng**	好冷	好冷
cold **lěng**	冷	冷
chilly **liáng**	凉	涼
cool & comfortable **liáng-kuai**	凉快	涼快
breeze **wéi fēng**	微风	微風
begin with strong winds **kāi shǐ guā kuáng fēng**	开始刮狂风	開始刮狂風
typhoon **tái fēng**	台风	颱風
tornado **lóng juǎn fēng**	龙卷风	龍捲風
whirlwind **xüàn-fēng**	旋风	旋風
after the tornado hit **lóng juǎn fēng qīn xí hòu**	龙卷风侵袭后	龍捲風侵襲後
favorable wind **shùn fēng**	顺风	順風
head wind **nì fēng**	逆风	逆風
hurricane **jù fēng dài yǔ**	飓风带雨	颶風帶雨
hurricane hit the shore **jù fēng sì nüè hǎi àn**	飓风肆虐海岸	颶風肆虐海岸
house were torn to pieces **fáng wū sī-cheng suì piàn**	房屋撕成碎片	房屋撕成碎片
raining **xià yǔ**	下雨	下雨
rain; rainfall **yǔ; yǔ liàng**	雨；雨量	雨；雨量
storm **bào fēng yǔ**	暴风雨	暴風雨
heavy rainfall **háo yǔ**	豪雨	豪雨
torrential rain **bào yǔ**	暴雨	暴雨
downpour **qīng pén dà yǔ**	倾盆大雨	傾盆大雨
rainning cats and dogs **dà yǔ rú zhù**	大雨如注	大雨如注
shower **zhèn yǔ**	阵雨	陣雨
drizzling **máo máo yǔ**	毛毛雨	毛毛雨
snowing **xià xüě**	下雪	下雪
fog; foggy **wù; xià wù**	雾；下雾	霧；下霧
frost **shuāng**	霜	霜
dew **lù-shui**	露水	露水
smog **yān wù**	烟雾	煙霧
hail; hailed **báo-zi; xià báo-zi**	雹子；下雹子	雹子；下雹子
thunder **léi; dǎ léi**	雷；打雷	雷；打雷
lightning; lightning strike **shǎn diàn; tiān dǎ léi pī**	闪电;天打雷霹	閃電;天打雷霹
bad weather struck **tiān-qi tū-ran zhuǎn huài**	天气突然转坏	天氣突然轉壞
rainbow **hóng; cǎi hóng**	虹；彩虹	虹；彩虹
sky began to clear up **tiān-qì fàng qíng**	天气放晴	天氣放晴
sun came out **tài-yang chū lái-le**	太阳出来了	太陽出來了

Geography 地理

English	简体	繁體
earth **dì qiú; dà dì**	地球；大地	地球；大地
map **dì tú**	地图	地圖
relief map **lì tǐ mó xíng dì tú**	立体模型地图	立體模型地圖
world **shì jiè**	世界	世界
globe **dì qiú yí**	地球仪	地球儀
geography **dì lǐ**	地理	地理
island **dǎo**	岛	島
continent **dà lù**	大陆	大陸
desert **shā mò**	沙漠	沙漠
the frigid zone **hán dài**	寒带	寒帶
the temperate zone **wēn dài**	温带	溫帶
subtropics zone **yǎ rè dài**	亚热带	亞熱帶
the tropic zone **rè dài**	热带	熱帶
Pacific **tài píng yáng**	太平洋	太平洋
Atlantic **dà xī yáng**	大西洋	大西洋
Indian **yìn dù yáng**	印度洋	印度洋
Arctic **běi bīng yáng**	北冰洋	北冰洋
Asia **yǎ zhōu**	亚洲	亞洲
Africa **fēi zhōu**	非洲	非洲
Europe **ōu zhōu**	欧洲	歐洲
Australia **ào zhōu**	澳洲	澳洲
North America **běi měi zhōu**	北美洲	北美洲
South America **nán měi zhōu**	南美洲	南美洲
Antarctica **nán jí zhōu**	南极洲	南極洲
hemisphere **bàn qiú**	半球	半球
equator **chì dào**	赤道	赤道
longitude **jīng dù**	经度	經度
latitude **wěi dù**	纬度	緯度
earth's axis **dì zhóu**	地轴	地軸
pole **dì qiú jí; zhóu jí**	地球级；轴极	地球級；軸極

prime meridian zí wǔ xiàn	子午线 子午線	mountain range shān mài	山脉 山脈
North Pole běi jí	北极 北極	mountain slope shān pō	山坡 山坡
South Pole nán jí	南极 南極	the foot of hill shān jiǎo	山脚 山腳
plateau gāo yüán	高原 高原	clouds and mists in the mountains 山岚 shān lán 山嵐
plain (earth) píng yüán	平原 平原	mountain pass shān kǒu	山口 山口
basin (earth) pén dì	盆地 盆地	mountain valley shān gǔ	山谷 山谷
low-lying parts (land) dī wā chù	低洼处 低窪處	lofty mountains shān yüè	山岳 山嶽
floods; flood disaster hóng shuǐ; shuǐ zāi	洪水;水灾 洪水;水災	ridge of a mountain shān jǐ	山脊 山脊
tsunami; seismic sea wave hǎi xiào	海啸 海嘯	half way up the mountain shān yāo	山腰 山腰
earthquake dì zhèn	地震 地震	volcano huǒ shān	火山 火山
strong magnitude earthquake 强震 qiáng zhèn 強震		on the verge of erupting jí jiāng bào fā (火山)	即将爆发 即將爆發
weak magnitude earthquake 轻度地震 qīng dù dì zhèn 輕度地震		volcano erupted hǔo shān bào fā	火山爆发 火山爆發
after shock yǔ zhèn	馀震 餘震	lava huǒ shān róng yán	火山熔岩 火山熔岩
landslip; landslide shān bēng	山崩 山崩	flame huǒ yàn	火焰 火焰
snowslide; avalanche xuě bēng	雪崩 雪崩	fire huǒ	火 火
mudflows and landslides tǔ shí liú	土石流 土石流	smoke yān	烟 煙
mountain shān	山 山	valley shān jiàn	山涧 山澗
hill xiǎo shān; qiū	小山;丘 小山;丘	gorge shān xiá	山峡 山峽
peak shān fēng	山峰 山峰	ocean yáng	洋 洋
caves dòng xuè; shān dòng	洞穴;山洞 洞穴;山洞	canal yùn hé	运河 運河

sea **hǎi**	海 海	steep **xūán yái qiào bì**	悬崖峭壁 懸崖峭壁
tide **cháo**	潮 潮	cliff **hǎi biān xūán yái**	海边悬崖 海邊懸崖
high tide **zhàng cháo**	涨潮 漲潮	tunnel **suì dào**	隧道 隧道
wave **bō làng**	波浪 波浪	beach **hǎi tān**	海滩 海灘
ripple **bō wén**	波纹 波紋	shore **àn**	岸 岸
lake **hú**	湖 湖	embankment **tí**	堤 堤
river **hé**	河 河	dam **bà**	坝 壩
stream **xī**	溪 溪	the current is very rapid **shuǐ liú hěn jí**	水流很急 水流很急
bay; gulf **hǎi wān**	海湾 海灣	rock **yán shí**	岩石 岩石
harbor **gǎng**	港 港	stone **shí-tou**	石头 石頭
pool **chí**	池 池	marble **dà lǐ shí**	大理石 大理石
pond **táng**	塘 塘	pebble **luǎn shí**	卵石 卵石
spring (water) **qūán**	泉 泉	sand **shā**	沙 沙
well **jǐng**	井 井	mud **ní**	泥 泥
hot spring **wēn qūán**	温泉 溫泉	soil **tǔ**	土 土
waterfall **pù bù**	瀑布 瀑布	clay **nián tǔ**	黏土 黏土
cascade **shuǐ lián**	水帘 水簾	dust **chén tǔ**	尘土 塵土
strait **hǎi xiá**	海峡 海峽	ash **huī**	灰 灰
cape; promontory **hái jiǎo**	海角 海角	loess **huáng tǔ**	黄土 黃土
mountaineer **dēng shān duì yūán**	登山队员 登山隊員	mine **kuàng**	矿 礦

76C

Astronomy 天文

universe **jǔ zhòu**	宇宙 宇宙	air **kōng qì**	空气 空氣
astronomy **tiān wén xüé**	天文学 天文學	sun **tài-yang**	太阳 太陽
observatory **tiān wén tái**	天文台 天文臺	sunrise **rì chū**	日出 日出
planetarium **tiān xiàng yí**	天象仪 天象儀	sunset **rì luò**	日落 日落
astrology **zhān xīng xué**	占星学 占星學	solar eclipse **rì shí**	日蚀 日蝕
heaven **tiān**	天 天	moon **yüè-liang**	月亮 月亮
celestial body **tiān tǐ**	天体 天體	moon surface **yüè qiú biǎo miàn**	月球表面 月球表面
sky **tiān kōng**	天空 天空	Sea of Tranquility **níng jìng hǎi**	宁静海 寧靜海
space **tài kōng**	太空 太空	moon wanes **yüè kuī**	月亏 月虧
outer space **wài tài kōng**	外太空 外太空	full moon **mǎn yüè**	满月 滿月
light-year **guāng nían**	光年 光年	lunar eclipse **yüè shí**	月蚀 月蝕
cosmic year (200 million) **yǔ zhòu nían**	宇宙年 宇宙年（兩億年）	total eclipse **quán shí**	全蚀 全蝕
aerosphere **dà qì céng**	大气层 大氣層	Mercury **shuǐ xīng**	水星 水星
atmosphere **dà qì**	大气 大氣	Venus **jīn xīng**	金星 金星
pressure **yā lì**	压力 壓力	Mars **huǒ xīng**	火星 火星

Earth **dì qiú**	地球 地球	
horizon **dì píng xiàn**	地平线 地平線	
Jupiter **mù xīng**	木星 木星	
Saturn **tǔ xīng**	土星 土星	
Neptune **hǎi wáng xīng**	海王星 海王星	
Uranus **tiān wáng xīng**	天王星 天王星	
Pluto **míng wáng xīng**	冥王星 冥王星	
revolution **gōng zhuǎn**	公转 公轉	
rotation **zì zhuǎn**	自转 自轉	
orbit **guǐ dào**	轨道 軌道	
Milky Way; Galaxy **yín hé**	银河 銀河	
the galactic nebula **yín hé xīng yǔn**	银河星云 銀河星雲	
extragalactic nebula **yín hé wài xīng yǔn**	银河外星云 銀河外星雲	
black hole; collapsar **tài kōng hāi dòng**	太空黑洞 太空黑洞	
star **xīng**	星 星	

star cluster **xīng tuán**	星团 星團	
shooting star; meteor **liú xīng**	流星 流星	
shower of meteor **liú xīng yǔ**	流星雨 流星雨	
make a wish **xǔ-ge yuàn**	许个愿 許個願	
equation of time **shí chà**	时差 時差	
parallax **shì chà**	视差 視差	
satellite **wèi xīng**	卫星 衛星	
fixed star **héng xīng**	恒星 恆星	
sidereal period **héng xīng zhōu qí**	恒星周期 恆星週期	
comet **huì xīng**	慧星 慧星	
planet **xíng xīng**	行星 行星	
meteorite **yǔn xīng**	殒星 殞星	
the Dipper **béi dǒu xīng**	北斗星 北斗星	
polaris **běi jí xīng**	北极星 北極星	

法律常識
Turn big problems into small problems
and small problems into no problems.
"大事化小，小事化無"
dà shì huà xiǎo, xiǎo shì huà wú

supreme court zuì gāo fǎ yuàn	最高法院 最高法院	notary public gōng zhèng rén	公证人 公證人
superior (high) court gāo déng fǎ yuàn	高等法院 高等法院	council of the grand justice dà fǎ guān huì yì	大法官会议 大法官會議
district court dì fāng fǎ yuàn	地方法院 地方法院	judge fǎ guān	法官 法官
civil court mín shì fǎ tíng	民事法庭 民事法庭	preliminary hearing diào chá tíng	调查庭 調查庭
criminal court xíng shì fǎ tíng	刑事法庭 刑事法庭	grand jury dà péi shěn tuán	大陪审团 大陪審團
family court jiā shì fǎ tíng	家事法庭 家事法庭	jury péi shěn tuán	陪审团 陪審團
martial court jūn shì fǎ tíng	军事法庭 軍事法庭	juror péi shěn yuán	陪审员 陪審員
juvenile court shào nián fǎ tíng	少年法庭 少年法庭	enforce the law fairly gōng zhèng zhí fǎ	公正执法 公正執法
international court of justice guó jì fǎ tíng	国际法庭 國際法庭	chief prosecutor jiǎn chá zhǎng	检察长 檢察長
Federal court lián bāng fǎ tíng	聯邦法庭 聯邦法庭	clerk shū-ji guān	书记官 書記官
State court zhōu fǎ tíng	州法庭 州法庭	solicitor (England) fǎ wù guān	法务官 法務官
small claims court xiǎo é suǒ cháng fǎ tíng	小額索償法庭 小額索賠法庭	scribe (England) lù-shi	录事 錄事
traffic court jiāo tōng fǎ tíng	交通法庭 交通法庭	court bailiff fá jǐng	法警 法警
bankruptcy court pò chán fǎ tíng	破產法庭 破產法庭	lynching chù yǐ sī xíng	处以私刑 處以私刑
liable to a lawsuit rě shàng guān-si	惹上官司 惹上官司	bar association lù-shi gōng huì	律师公会 律師公會
collegiate bench of judges hé yì tíng	合议庭 合議庭	bar examination lù-shi zī gé kǎo shì	律师资格考试 律師資格考試

English	简体	繁體
counselor fǎ lǜ gù wèn	法律顾问	法律顧問
attorney; lawyer lǜ shī	律师	律師
plaintiff lawyer yüán gào lǜ shī	原告律师	原告律師
defense attorney; advocate biàn hù lǜ shī	辩护律师	辯護律師
power of attorney shòu qüán shū	授权书	授權書
title of ownership suó yǒu qüán shū	所有权书	所有權書
draw a contract cǎo ní hé yüē	草拟合约	草擬合約
trial brief sù shū	诉书	訴書
lawsuit sù sòng	诉讼	訴訟
civil suit mín shì sù sòng	民事诉讼	民事訴訟
criminal suit xíng shì sù sòng	刑事诉讼	刑事訴訟
criminal case xíng shì àn jiàn	刑事案件	刑事案件
criminal activity fàn fǎ-de xíng wéi	犯法的行为	犯法的行為
What is the charge? wǒ fàn-le shén-me fǎ	我犯了甚么法?	我犯了甚麼法?
prosecute qǐ sù	起诉	起訴
the accused bèi qǐ sù-de rén	被起诉的人	被起訴的人
indictment qǐ sù shū	起诉书	起訴書
sue kòng gào	控告	控告
counterclaim fǎn sù	反诉	反訴
appellant shàng sù rén	上诉人	上訴人

English	简体	繁體
plaintiff suitor yüán gào; qǐ sù rén	原告；起诉人	原告；起訴人
defendant bèi gào	被告	被告
court expense sù sòng fèi yòng	诉讼费用	訴訟費用
routine lì xíng gōng shì	例行公事	例行公事
subpoena chuán piào; chuán huàn	传票；传唤	傳票；傳喚
in session zhèng zài kāi tíng	正在开庭	正在開庭
maintain order bǎo chí zhì xǜ	保持秩序	保持秩序
solemn silence; quiet sù jìng	肃静	肅靜
swear by the Bible yǐ shèng jīng fā shì	以圣经发誓	以聖經發誓
marriage vows jié hūn shì cí	结婚誓词	結婚誓詞
common law wife tóng jǚ rén	同居人	同居人
paternity suit shēng fù qüè rèn sù sòng	生父确认诉讼	生父確認訴訟
DNA test (see Group 64 lab) rǎn sè tǐ jiǎn yàn	染色体检验	染色體檢驗
adopt líng yǎng; guò jì	领养；过继	領養；過繼
alimony shàn yǎng fèi	赡养费	贍養費
custody of the child zí nǚ jiān hù qüán	子女监护权	子女 監護權
arraign chuán xǜn	传讯	傳訊
appear in court chū tíng	出庭	出庭
personal presence qīn zì chū tíng	亲自出庭	親自出庭
default bú dào àn	不到案	不到案

English	中文 (简)	中文 (繁)
witness zhèng-ren	證人	證人
take the stand; testify in court chū tíng zuò zhèng	出庭作證	出庭作證
oath xūan shì	宣示	宣示
emigration yí jū guó wài	移居國外	移居國外
immigration wài lái yí mín	外來移民	外來移民
naturalization guī huà	归化	歸化
deportation hearing qū zhú chū jìng shěn chá	驅逐出境審查	驅逐出境審查
parties to a lawsuit dāng shì rén	当事人	當事人
direct examination zhí jiē pán jié	直接盘诘	直接盤詰
cross examination duì-fang lù-shi pán jié	對方律師盤詰	對方律師盤詰
leading question àn shì pán jié	暗示盤詰	暗示盤詰
evidence zhèng-jū	證据	證據
court exhibit chéng tíng zhèng wù	呈庭證物	呈庭證物
documentary evidence shū miàn zhèng-jū	书面證据	書面證據
circumstantial evidence páng zhèng	旁證	旁證
contrary evidence fǎn zhèng	反證	反證
valid evidence zhèng jù què shí	證據確實	證據確實
lack of evidence zhèng jù bù zú	證據不足	證據不足
destroy evidence huǐ miè zhèng jù	毀滅證據	毀滅證據
proviso dàn shū; fù dài tiáo jiàn	但書；附帶条件	但書；附帶條件

English	中文 (简)	中文 (繁)
null & void wú xiào	無效	無效
objection fǎn duì	反對	反對
sustained fǎn duì chéng lì	反對成立	反對成立
overruled fǎn duì wú xiào	反對無效	反對無效
contempt of court miǎo shì fǎ tíng	藐視法庭	藐視法庭
ordinance fǎ guī	法規	法規
regulation tiáo lì	條例	條例
delinquent wéi fǎ	違法	違法
alleged shè xián	涉嫌	涉嫌
suspect xián yí fàn	嫌疑犯	嫌疑犯
accessory cóng fàn (zòng fàn)	從犯	從犯
accomplice gòng fàn; tóng móu	共犯；同謀	共犯；同謀
scapegoat tì rén dǐng zuì	替人頂罪	替人頂罪
juvenile offender shào nián fàn	少年犯	少年犯
caught red-handed xiàn xíng fàn	現行犯	現行犯
caught on the spot xiàn chǎng jiù qín	現場就擒	現場就擒
court found him guilty pàn tā yǒu zuì	判他有罪	判他有罪
ex-convict qián kē fàn	前科犯	前科犯
criminal xíng shì fàn	刑事犯	刑事犯
unintentional criminal guò shī fàn	过失犯	過失犯

prisoner **qiú fàn**	囚犯 囚犯	
parolee **jiǎ shì fàn**	假释犯 假釋犯	
crime motive **fàn zùi dòng jī**	犯罪动机 犯罪動機	
without prejudice **bú dài piān jiàn**	不带偏见 不帶偏見	
unawares; negligent **wú yì zhōng; lěng-bu fáng**	无意中;冷不防 無意中; 冷不防	
self-defense **zì wèi**	自卫 自衛	
surrender; confess; give up **zì shǒu**	自首 自首	
intentional **xù yì zhǐ kòng**	蓄意指控 **蓄意指控**	
malicious prosecution **wū gào**	诬告 誣告	
perjury; misrepresentation **wěi zhèng zuì**	伪证罪 偽證罪	
frame-up **xiàn hài**	陷害 陷害	
forgery **wěi zào wén shū**	伪造文书 偽造文書	
representation **chén shù**	陈述 陳述	
oral confession **kǒu gòng**	口供 口供	
transcript **bǐ lù**	笔录 筆錄	
discovery **sōu zhèng**	搜证 搜證	
take deposition **lù kǒu-gong**	录口供 錄口供	
bribery **huì lù zuì**	贿赂罪 賄賂罪	
alibi **rén bú zài xiàn chǎng**	人不在现场 人不在現場	
How do you plead? **zhāo gòng bù zhāo**	招供不招？ 招供不招？	

plead guilty; guilty **rèn zuì; yǒu zuì**	认罪；有罪 認罪；有罪	
plead not guilty; innocent **bú rèn zuì; wú zuì**	不认罪；无罪 不認罪；無罪	
general denial **qüán pán fǒu rèn**	全盤否認 **全盤否認**	
defend **bèi gào dá biàn**	被告答辩 被告答辯	
contradict; a plea **kàng biàn**	抗辩 **抗辯**	
closure **biàn lùn zhōng jié**	辩论终结 辯論終結	
sum up **zǒng jié**	总结 總結	
legal loophole **fǎ lǜ lòu dòng**	法律漏洞 法律漏洞	
retract testimony **fān gòng**	翻供 翻供	
reopen case **fān àn**	翻案 翻案	
misdemeanor **qīng zuì**	轻罪 輕罪	
felony **zhòng zuì**	重罪 重罪	
trial **shěn pàn**	审判 審判	
preliminary hearing **chū shěn**	初审 初審	
trial de novo **fù shěn**	覆审 **覆審**	
take legal action **tí chū sù sòng**	提出訴訟 **提出訴訟**	
dismissal of the case **bó huí sù sòng**	駁回訴訟 **駁回訴訟**	
jury has reached a verdict judgement **péi shěn tuán cái jüé**	陪審團裁決	
condemn **dìng zuì**	定罪 定罪	
verdict **cái dìng**	裁定 裁定	

recession tuì tíng	退庭 退庭	retainer yù fù lǜ shī fèi	预付律师费 預付律師費
sentence pàn jüé	判决 判決	bankrupt pò chǎn	破产 破產
written judgment pàn jüé shū	判决书 判決書	attach chá fēng; kòu yā	查封；扣押 查封；扣押
court ruling monetary award cái wù cái pàn	财務裁判 財務裁判	judicial sale yī fǎ pāi mài	依法拍卖 依法拍賣
arbitration zhòng cái	仲裁 仲裁	lawful heir fǎ dìng jì chéng rén	法定继承人 法定繼承人
incorrect ruling wù pàn	误判 誤判	will trust probate court yí zhǔ xìn tuō rèn zhèng fǎ tíng	遺囑信託認證 法庭
rejection bó huí	驳回 駁回	death taxes; legacy taxes yí chǎn shuì	遗产税 遺產稅
commute jiǎn xíng	减刑 減刑	minor wèi chéng nián zhě	未成年者 未成年者
on probation huǎn xíng	缓刑 緩刑	legal guardian jiān hù rén	监护人 監護人
fine fá huán	罚锾 罰鍰	detention;take into custody jǚ liú	拘留 拘留
appeal shàng sù	上诉 上訴	bail bǎo shì jīn	保释金 保釋金
recover won the case shèng sù	胜诉 勝訴	fixed-term imprisonment yǒu qí tú xíng	有期徒刑 有期徒刑
suit defeated lost the case bài sù	败诉 敗訴	life sentence wú qí tú xíng	无期徒刑 無期徒刑
mediation; conciliate tiáo tíng	调停 調停	court order fǎ yüàn zhǐ lìng	法院指令 法院指令
intermediator; go-between tiáo jiě rén	调解人 調解人	death penalty sǐ xíng	死刑 死刑
compromise hé jiě ; tuǒ xié	和解；妥协 和解；妥協	disfranchise chǐ duó gōng qüán	褫夺公权 褫奪公權
private settlement sī jiě	私解 私解	jail; prison jiān yù	监狱 監獄
a win-win deal shuāng yíng jǚ miàn	双赢局面 雙贏局面	handcuffs shǒu kào	手铐 手銬
award for emotional distress jīng shén péi cháng	精神赔偿 精神賠償	fetters; shackles jiǎo liào	脚镣 腳鐐
reparation wù zhí péi cháng	物质赔偿 物質賠償	club jǐng gùn	警棍 警棍

on parole **huò jiǎ shì**	获假释 獲假釋	election fraud **xuǎn jǔ bì duān**	选举弊端 選舉弊端
jail breaking **yüè yù**	越狱 越獄	play confidence game **jīn guāng dǎng zhà qī**	金光党诈欺 金光黨詐欺
scaled the wall **fān qiáng**	翻墙 翻牆	patent right **zhuān lì quán**	专利权 專利權
fugitive **táo fàn**	逃犯 逃犯	copyright **zhù zuò quán**	著作权 著作權
on the lam; at large **zài táo; xiāo yáo fǎ wài**	在逃;消遥法外 在逃;消遥法外	corruption **tān wū zuì**	贪污罪 貪汙罪
get off with it **táo-guo sī fǎ zhì cái**	逃过司法制裁 逃過司法制裁	clean-handed **wú zuì; qīng lían-de**	无罪;清廉的 無罪;清廉的
in pursuit of the fugitive **zhuī bǔ táo fàn**	追捕逃犯 追捕逃犯	libel charge **fěi bàng zuì**	诽谤罪 誹謗罪
fugitive surrender **táo fàn tóu xiáng**	逃犯投降 逃犯投降	adultery **tōng jiān zuì**	通奸罪 通姦罪
got away; got away with **tuō táo; táo bì chěng fá**	脱逃;逃避惩罚 脫逃;逃避懲罰	rape **qiáng jiān zuì**	强奸罪 強姦罪
pardon **tè shè**	特赦 特赦	seduce **yòu jiān**	诱奸 誘姦
reformatory **gǎn huà yüàn**	感化院 感化院	statutory rape **yǔ wèi chéng nián tōng jiān**	与未成年通奸 與未成年通姦
juvenile delinquent **shào nián fàn zuì**	少年犯罪 少年犯罪	sodomy **jī jiān**	鸡奸 雞姦
committed the crime **fàn-le zuì**	犯了罪 犯了罪	indecent exposure **wěi xiè pù lù**	猥亵暴露 猥褻暴露
decide the outcome of the case **xià dá pàn jüé**	下达判决 下達判決	attempt **wèi suì**	未遂 未遂
conviction **pàn zuì**	判罪 判罪	drug addict **xī dú zhě**	吸毒者 吸毒者
prosecuted him **duì tā pàn xíng**	对他判刑 對他判刑	in possession of narcotics **chí yǒu dú pǐn**	持有毒品 持有毒品
charge for **kòng gào; zhǐ kòng**	控告;指控 控告;指控	gambling charge **dǔ bó zuì**	赌博罪 賭博罪
assault and battery **shāng hài zuì**	伤害罪 傷害罪	robbery **qiǎng jié**	抢劫 搶劫
intimidation **kǒng hè zuì**	恐吓罪 恐嚇罪	blackmail **lè suǒ zuì**	勒索罪 勒索罪
fraud; swindle; scam **zhà qī**	诈欺 詐欺	work undercover **wò dǐ**	卧底 臥底

notify the police tōng zhī jǐng fāng	通知警方 通知警方
under arrest dái bǔ guī àn	逮捕归案 逮捕歸案
trapped by police bèi jǐng fāng bāo wéi	被警方包围 被警方包圍
in search of bank robbers sōu xún yín háng qiáng fěi	搜寻银行抢匪 搜尋銀行搶匪
multiple murder of a family miè mén xiě àn	灭门血案 滅門血案
solved the crime pò-le àn	破了案 破了案
evidence of guilt fàn zuì zhèng jù	犯罪证据 犯罪證據
eyewitness mù jí zhě	目击者 目擊者
kidnapping bǎng jià zuì	绑架罪 綁架罪
ransom money shú kuǎn	赎款 贖款
slain sī piào	撕票 撕票
murder móu shā	谋杀 謀殺
assassination àn shā; xíng cì	暗杀；行刺 暗殺；行刺
homicide shā rén zuì; shā rén fàn	杀人罪；杀人犯 殺人罪；殺人犯
manslaughter guò shī shā rén	过失杀人 過失殺人
attempted suicide qì tú zì shā	企图自杀 企圖自殺
loot zāng kuǎn	赃款 臟款
stolen goods zāng wù	赃物 臟物

larceny tōu qiè	偷窃 偷竊
habitual thief guàn qiè	惯窃 慣竊
shoplifter shùn shǒu qiān yáng	顺手牵羊 順手牽羊
smuggler zǒu sī zhě	走私者 走私者
double cross hēi chī hēi	黑吃黑 黑吃黑
stowaway tōu dù	偷渡 偷渡
illegal immigrant fēi fǎ rù jìng	非法入境 非法入境
tip-off gào mì	告密 告密
stool pigeon; informer xiàn mín	线民 線民
impeach jián jǔ	检举 檢舉
wanted tōng qì	通缉 通緝
search warrant sōu suǒ piào	搜索票 搜索票
warrant jū bǔ zhuàng	拘捕状 拘捕狀
trap yòu bǔ	诱捕 誘捕
bugging qiè tīng	窃听 竊聽
bug qiè tīng qì	窃听器 竊聽器
lie detector cè huǎng qì	测谎器 測謊器
waiver qì quán	弃权 棄權

"不了了之 bù liáo liǎo zhī"
Settling a matter by leaving it unsettled.

science **kē xué**	科学 科學	photometer **guāng dù jì**	光度计 光度計
chemistry **huà xué**	化学 化學	balance **tiān-ping**	天平 天平
physics **wù lǐ xüé**	物理学 物理學	counterweight **fá mǎ**	砝码 砝碼
gene **jī yīn; yí chuán yīn zǐ**	基因;遗传因子 基因；遺傳因子	spectrometer **fēn guāng jìng**	分光镜 分光鏡
genetic engineering **jī yīn yí chuán gōng chéng**	基因遗传工程 基因遺傳工程	refractometer **qū guāng jìng**	屈光镜 屈光鏡
high technology; hi tech **gāo kē jì**	高科技 高科技	prism **léng jìng**	棱镜 棱鏡
chemical equation **huà xué fāng chéng shì**	化学方程式 化學方程式	convex mirror **tū miàn jìng**	凸面镜 凸面鏡
Fahrenheit (32°-212°) **huá shì**	华氏 華氏	biconvex mirror **shuāng tū jìng**	双凸镜 雙凸鏡
Celsius (0°-100°) **shè shì**	摄氏 攝氏	concave mirror **āo miàn jìng**	凹面镜 凹面鏡
boiling point **fèi diǎn**	沸点 沸點	biconcave mirror **shuāng āo jìng**	双凹镜 雙凹鏡
freezing point **bīng diǎn**	冰点 冰點	microscope **xiǎn wéi jìng**	显微镜 顯微鏡
5 degrees below zero **líng xià wǔ dù**	零下五度 零下五度	binocular microscope **shuāng tǒng xiǎn wéi jìng**	双筒显微镜 雙筒顯微鏡
thermometer **wēn dù jì**	温度计 溫度計	ultra microscope **xiàn wài xiǎn wéi jìng**	限外显微镜 限外顯微鏡
hydrometer **bǐ zhòng jì**	比重计 比重計	theorem **dìng lǐ**	定理 定理
colorimeter **bǐ sè jì**	比色计 比色計	laws of motion **yùn dòng dìng lù**	运动定律 運動定律
barometer **qì yā jì**	气压计 氣壓計	gravitation **wàn yóu yǐn lì**	万有引力 萬有引力

conservation of mass zhí liàng bú miè	质量不灭 質量不滅	narrow necked bottle xì jǐng píng	细颈瓶 細頸瓶
center of gravity zhòng lì zhōng xīn	重力中心 重力中心	dropping bottle dī píng	滴瓶 滴瓶
attraction xī lì	吸力 吸力	filtering flask guò lǜ píng	过滤瓶 過濾瓶
relativity xiāng duì lùn	相对论 相對論	squiring bottle pēn shuǐ píng	喷水瓶 噴水瓶
potential energy shì néng; wèi néng	势能；位能 勢能；位能	specific gravity bottle bǐ zhòng píng	比重瓶 比重瓶
projectile motion pāo wù xiàn yǔ dòng	抛物线运动 抛物線運動	cryophorus níng bīng qì	凝冰器 凝冰器
rectilinear motion zhí xiàn yǔ dòng	直线运动 直線運動	graduated bottle kè dù píng	刻度瓶 刻度瓶
centripetal force xiàng xīn lì	向心力 向心力	pipette ; pipet qiú xíng xī guǎn	球形吸管 球形吸管
centrifugal force lí xīn lì	离心力 離心力	measuring pipette kè dù xī guǎn	刻度吸管 刻度吸管
centrifugal globe lí xīn qiú	离心球 離心球	burette dī guǎn	滴管 滴管
centrifugal separator lí xīn jī	离心机 離心機	adapter jiē guǎn	接管 接管
apparatus yí qì	仪器 儀器	graduated cup liáng bēi	量杯 量杯
test tube shì guǎn	试管 試管	crucible gān guō	坩锅 坩鍋
beaker shāo bēi	烧杯 燒杯	crucible tongs gān guō jiá-zi	坩锅夹子 坩鍋夾子
conical beaker zhuī xíng shāo bēi	锥形烧杯 錐形燒杯	test-tube clam shì guǎn jiá	试管夹 試管夾
boiling flask píng dǐ shāo píng	平底烧瓶 平底燒瓶	funnel lòu dǒu	漏斗 漏斗
balloon flask qiú xíng shāo píng	球形烧瓶 球形燒瓶	separatory funnel fēn yè lòu dǒu	分液漏斗 分液漏斗
retorts bottle qū jǐng píng	曲颈瓶 曲頸瓶	funnel stand lòu dǒu jià	漏斗架 漏斗架
two-neck bottle shuāng jǐng píng	双颈瓶 雙頸瓶	asbestos pad shí mián diàn	石绵垫 石綿墊
wide mouth bottle dà kǒu píng	大口瓶 大口瓶	asbestos paper shí mián zhǐ	石绵纸 石綿紙

filter paper lǜ zhǐ	滤纸 濾紙	chemical element huà xué yuán sù	化学元素 化學元素
universal clamp huó yòng jiá	活用夹 活用夾	rare element xī yǒu yuán sù	稀有元素 稀有元素
pinch cock tán huáng jiá	弹簧夹 彈簧夾	radioactive element fàng shè xìng yuán sù	放射性元素 放射性元素
tilter qīng jià	倾架 傾架	radioactive contamination fàng shè xìng wū rǎn	放射性污染 放射性污染
alcohol lamp jiǔ jīng dēng	酒精灯 酒精燈	isotope tóng wèi sù	同位素 同位素
blasted spirit lamp jiǔ jīng pēn dēng	酒精喷灯 酒精噴燈	laser léi shè	雷射 雷射
mortar & pestle yán bō jí niǎn chuí	研砵及碾槌 研砵及碾槌	humidity shī dù	湿度 濕度
induction sphere gǎn yìng qiú	感应球 感應球	mist bó wù; shī qì	薄雾；湿气 薄霧；濕氣
induction coil gǎn yìng xiàn quān	感应线圈 感應線圈	steam; vapor zhēng qì	蒸气 蒸氣
induction coefficient gǎn yìng xì shù	感应系数 感應係數	water vapor shuǐ zhēng qì	水蒸气 水蒸氣
electromagnetic induction diàn cí gǎn yīng	电磁感应 電磁感應	gas; gaseous matter qì-ti	气体 氣體
radiation fú shè	辐射 輻射	air bubble qì pào	气泡 氣泡
magnet cí tiě	磁铁 磁鐵	distillation zhēng liú	蒸馏 蒸餾
electromagnet diàn cí tǐ	电磁体 電磁體	liquid; fluid yè-ti	液体 液體
horseshoe magnet mǎ tí xíng cí tiě	马蹄型磁铁 馬蹄型磁鐵	dissolution róng jiě	溶解 溶解
tuning fork yīn chā	音叉 音叉	hydrolysis shuí jiě	水解 水解
tuning fork hammer yīn chā chuí	音叉槌 音叉槌	solubility róng jiě dù	溶解度 溶解度
vacuum tube zhēn kōng guǎn	真空管 真空管	content róng jī	容积 容積
vacuity; a vacuum zhēn kōng-de	真空的 真空的	capacity róng liàng	容量 容量
capillarity tube máo xì xiàn xiàng guǎn	毛细现象管 毛細現象管	infusion pào jìn; jìn jì	泡浸；浸剂 泡浸；浸劑

shaking apparatus **yáo dòng qì**	摇动器 搖動器	fixative **gù dìng jì**	固定剂 固定劑
precipitate (ppt.) **chén diàn**	沈淀 沈澱	efflorescence **fēng huà**	风化 風化
evaporation **zhēng fā**	蒸发 蒸發	emulsification **rǔ huà**	乳化 乳化
solid; solid body **gù-ti**	固体 固體	concentration **nóng suō**	浓缩 濃縮
combustion **rán shāo**	燃烧 燃燒	fermentation **fā xiào**	发酵 發酵
sublimation **shēng huá**	升华 昇華	density **mì dù**	密度 密度
decomposition **fēn jiě**	分解 分解	specific gravity **bǐ zhòng**	比重 比重
fission **fēn liè**	分裂 分裂	volume **tǐ jī**	体积 體積
fusion **róng hé**	融合 融合	neutrino **wéi zhōng zǐ**	微中子 微中子
combination **huà hé**	化合 化合	organic matter **yǒu jī wù**	有机物 有機物
compound **huà hé wù**	化合物 化合物	inorganic matter **wú jī wù**	无机物 無機物
hydrate **shuǐ huà wù**	水化物 水化物	spirit level **shuǐ píng yí**	水平仪 水平儀
hydride **qīng huà wù**	氢化物 氫化物	celestial globe **tiān qiú yí**	天球仪 天球儀
cyanide **qīng huà wù**	氰化物 氰化物	terrestrial globe **dì qiú yí**	地球仪 地球儀
iodide **diǎn huà wù**	碘化物 碘化物	outer space **wài tài kōng**	外太空 外太空
carbide **tàn huà wù**	碳化物 碳化物	take off into space **shè rù tài kōng**	射入太空 射入太空
carbohydrate **tàn shuǐ huà hé wù**	碳水化合物 碳水化合物	astronauts lift off **tài kōng rén shēng kōng**	太空人升空 太空人升空
qualitative analysis **dìng xìng fēn xī**	定性分析 定性分析	in quest of the universe **xún zhǎo yǔ zhòu ào mì**	寻找宇宙奥秘 尋找宇宙奧秘
quantitative analysis **dìng liàng fēn xī**	定量分析 定量分析	the theory of gravity **dì xīn yǐn lì lǐ lùn**	地心引力理论 地心引力理論
primary color **yüán sè**	原色 原色	air pressure **kōng qì yā lì**	空气压力 空氣壓力

collision ball apparatus **pèng jí yí**	碰击仪 碰擊儀	antimony **tì**	锑 Sb 銻
surface tension apparatus **biǎo miàn zhàng lì**	表面胀力 表面脹力	nickel **niè**	镍 Ni 鎳
metal **jīn-shu**	金属 金屬	aluminum **lǔ**	铝 Al 鋁
heavy metal **zhòng jīn-shu**	重金属 重金屬	barium **bèi**	钡 Ba 鋇
alloy **hé jīn**	合金 合金	strontium **sī**	锶 Sr 鍶
element **yuán sù**	元素 元素	calcium **gài**	钙 Ca 鈣
gold **jīn**	金 Au 金	magnesium **měi**	镁 Mg 鎂
silver **yín**	银 Ag 銀	manganese **měng**	锰 Mn 錳
mercury **gǒng; shuǐ yín**	汞；水银 Hg 汞；水銀	cobalt **gǔ**	钴 Ca 鈷
copper **tóng**	铜 Cu 銅	zinc **xīn**	锌 Zn 鋅
brass **huáng tóng**	黄铜 黃銅	potassium **jiǎ**	钾 K 鉀
bronze **qīng tóng**	青铜 青銅	sodium **nà**	钠 Na 鈉
iron **tiě**	铁 Fe 鐵	phosphor **lín**	磷 P 磷
crude iron; pig iron **shēng tiě**	生铁 生鐵	iodine **diǎn**	碘 I 碘
cast iron **zhù tiě**	铸铁 鑄鐵	silicon **xì**	矽 Si 矽
wrought iron **duàn tiě**	锻铁 鍛鐵	arsenic **shēn**	砷 As 砷
steel **gāng**	钢 鋼	carbon **tàn**	炭 C 炭
stainless steel **bú xiù gāng**	不锈钢 不銹鋼	radium **léi**	镭 Ra 鐳
tin **xí**	锡 Sn 錫	tungsten **wū**	钨 W 鎢
lead **qiān**	铅 Pb 鉛	chromium **gè**	铬 Cr 鉻

titanium **tài**	钛 Ti 鈦	calcium carbonate **tàn suān gài**	碳酸钙 碳酸鈣
americium **měi**	镅 Am 鎇	citric acid **níng méng suān**	柠檬酸 檸檬酸
plutonium **bù**	钚 Pu 鈈	boric acid **péng suān**	硼酸 硼酸
thorium **tǔ**	钍 Th 釷	borax **péng shā**	硼砂 硼砂
uranium **yóu**	铀 U 鈾	hydrochloric acid **yán suān**	盐酸 鹽酸
sulfur **liú**	硫 S 硫	picric acid **kǔ wèi suān**	苦味酸 苦味酸
sulphur **liú huáng**	硫磺 硫磺	nitric acid **xiāo suān**	硝酸 硝酸
chlorine **lù**	氯 Cl 氯	sulfuric acid **liú suān**	硫酸 硫酸
fluorine **fú**	氟 F 氟	king water; aqua regia **wáng shuǐ**	王水 王水
nitrogen **dàn**	氮 N 氮	oxalic acid **cǎo suān**	草酸 草酸
neon **nǎi**	氖 Ne 氖	phosphoric acid **lín suān**	磷酸 磷酸
krypton **kè**	氪 Kr 氪	glacial acetic acid **bīng cù suān**	冰醋酸 冰醋酸
xenon **shān**	氙 Xe 氙	salicylic acid **shuǐ yáng suān**	水杨酸 水楊酸
hydrogen **qīng**	氢 H 氫	lactic acid **rǔ suān**	乳酸 乳酸
oxygen **yǎng**	氧 O 氧	formic acid **yǐ suān**	蚁酸 蟻酸
carbon monoxide **yì yǎng huà tàn**	一氧化碳 一氧化碳	gallic acid **mò shí zǐ suān**	没食子酸 沒食子酸
carbon dioxide **èr yǎng huà tàn**	二氧化碳 二氧化碳	tartaric acid **jiǔ shí suān**	酒石酸 酒石酸
ozone **chòu yǎng**	臭氧 臭氧	sodium thiosulfuric acid **liú dài liú suān nà**	硫代硫酸钠 硫代硫酸鈉
ammonia **ān; ā mó ní yǎ**	氨；阿摩尼亚 氨；阿摩尼亞	sodium bicarbonate **tàn suān qīng nà**	碳酸氢钠 碳酸氫鈉
carbolic acid **shí tàn suān**	石碳酸 石碳酸	gypsum **shí gāo**	石膏 石膏

caustic soda	苛性钠；烧硷	ethyl alcohol	乙醇
kē xìng nà; shāo jiǎn	苛性鈉；燒鹼	yǐ chún	乙醇
soda ash	碱	paraffin	石腊
jiǎn	鹼	shí là	石臘
alkali	硷性	calcium carbide	电石
jiǎn xìng	鹼性	diàn shí	電石
neutral	中性	atom	原子
zhōng xìng	中性	yuán zǐ	原子
acid	酸；酸性	nuclear	核子
suān; suān xìng	酸；酸性	hé zǐ	核子
polyethylene	聚乙烯	nucleus	原子核
jù yǐ xī	聚乙烯	yuán zǐ hé	原子核
poly chlorinated biphenyl	多氯联苯	nano meter	奈米
duō lù lián běn	多氯聯苯	nài mǐ	奈米
urea; carbamide	尿素	proton	质子
niào sù	尿素	zhí zǐ	質子
plastic	塑胶	molecule	分子
sù jiāo	塑膠	fēn zǐ	分子
acrylic	压克力	particle	质点
yā kè lì	壓克力	zhí diǎn	質點
styrofoam	保丽龙	neutron	中子
bǎo lì lóng	保麗龍	zhōng zǐ	中子
acetone	丙酮	pestrom	正子
bǐng tóng	丙酮	zhèng zǐ	正子
acetylene	乙炔	electron	电子
yǐ qüē	乙炔	diàn zǐ	電子
benzene	苯	ion	离子
běn	苯	lí zǐ	離子
ether	乙醚	cation	阳离子
yǐ mí	乙醚	yáng lí zǐ	陽離子
aldehyde	醛	anion	阴离子
qüán	醛	yīn lí zǐ	陰離子
formaldehyde	甲醛	Alternative Light Source	另类光源科技
jiǎ qüán	甲醛	lìng lèi guāng yüán kē jì	另類光源科技
methyl alcohol	甲醇	UltraLite (ULS)	另类光源扫瞄器
jiǎ chún	甲醇	lìng lèi guāng yüan sǎo miáo qì	

Related Terms: Group 66, 医疗器材 Medical Equipment;
Group 64, 健康检查与化验室 Physical Checkup & Laboratory

Countries & Their People
世界各國與人民

cuontry **guó**	国 國	mainlander **dà lù rén**	大陆人 大陸人
nation **mín zú**	民族 民族	Eskimo **Ài Sī Jī Mó Rén**	爱斯基摩人 愛斯基摩人
Allied Nations **méng guó**	盟国 盟國	Orient **dōng fāng**	东方 東方
United Nations **Lián Hé Guó**	联合国 聯合國	Oriental **Dōng Fāng Rén**	东方人 東方人
language **yǔ yán**	语言 語言	Jew **Yóu Tài Rén**	犹太人 猶太人
Chinese national language **Zhōng Guó Guó Yǔ**	中国国语 中國國語	Jewish **Yóu Tài-de**	犹太的 猶太的
Mandarin Chinese **pǔ tōng huà**	普通话 普通話	Continent **dà zhōu; dà lù**（七大洲）	大洲；大陆 大洲；大陸
dialect **fāng yán**	方言 方言	continental **dà lù-de**　　（七大洲）	大陆的 大陸的
slang **lí yǔ**	俚语 俚語	Afghanistan **Ā Fù Hàn**	阿富汗 阿富汗
colloquial **bái huà**	白话 白話	Afghanistani **Ā Fù Hàn Rén**	阿富汗人 阿富汗人
vulgar language **xià-liu huà**	下流话 下流話	Africa **Fēi Zhōu**	非洲 非洲
foreign countries **wài guó**	外国 外國	African **Fēi Zhōu Rén**	非洲人 非洲人
foreigner **wài-guo rén**	外国人 外國人	Albania **Ā Er Bā Ní Yǎ**	阿尔巴尼亚 阿爾巴尼亞
native **běn dì rén**	本地人 本地人	Algeria **Ā Er Jí Lì Yǎ**	阿尔及利亚 阿爾及利亞
aborigines **yüán zhù mín**	原住民 原住民	America **Měi Guó**	美国 美國

American Měi-gou Rén	美国人 美國人	Austrian Ào-di Lì Rén	奥地利人 奥地利人
American Samoa Méi Shǔ Sà Mó Yǎ	美属萨摩亚 美屬薩摩亞	Azerbaijan Yǎ Sài Bài Rán	亚塞拜然 亞塞拜然
Andorra Ān Dào Er	安道尔 安道爾	Bahamas Bā Hā Mǎ	巴哈马 巴哈馬
Angola Ān Gē Lā	安哥拉 安哥拉	Bahrain Bā Lín	巴林 巴林
Anguilla Ān Guī Lā	安圭拉 安圭拉	Baker Island Bèi Kè Dǎo	贝克岛 貝克島
Antarctica Nán Jí Zhōu	南极洲 南極洲	Bangladesh Mèng Jiā Lā	孟加拉 孟加拉
Antigua Ān Dì Kǎ	安地卡 安地卡	Barbados Bā Bèi Duō	巴贝多 巴貝多
Arabia Ā Lā Bó	阿拉伯 阿拉伯	Barbuda Bā Bù Dá	巴布达 巴布達
Arabian Ā Lā Bó Rén	阿拉伯人 阿拉伯人	Belorussia Bái È Luó Sī	白俄罗斯 白俄羅斯
Arctic Ocean Běi Bīng Yáng	北冰洋 北冰洋	Belgium Bǐ Lì Shí	比利时 比利時
Argentina Ā Gēn Tíng	阿根廷 阿根廷	Belgian Bǐ Lì Shí Rén	比利时人 比利時人
Argentine Ā Gēn Tíng Rén	阿根廷人 阿根廷人	Belize Bèi Lǐ Sī	贝里斯 貝里斯
Armenia Yá Měi Ní Yǎ	亚美尼亚 亞美尼亞	Benin Bèi Nán	贝南 貝南
Armenian Yá Měi Ní Yǎ Rén	亚美尼亚人 亞美尼亞人	Bermuda Bǎi Mù Dá	百慕达 百慕達
Aruba Ā Lù Bā	阿路巴 阿路巴	Bhutan Bù Dān	不丹 不丹
Ashmore Ā Shì Mó Kǎ	阿士摩卡 阿士摩卡	Bolivia Bō Lì Wéi Yǎ	玻利维亚 玻利維亞
Atlantic Ocean Dà Xī Yáng	大西洋 大西洋	Bolivian Bō Lì Wéi Yǎ Rén	玻利维亚人 玻利維亞人
Australia Ào Dà Lì Yǎ	澳大利亚 澳大利亞	Bosnia Bō Shì Ní Yǎ	波士尼亚 波士尼亞
Australian Ào Dà Lì Yǎ Rén	澳大利亚人 澳大利亞人	Bosnian Bō Shì Ní Yǎ Rén	波士尼亚人 波士尼亞人
Austria Ào Dì Lì	奥地利 奥地利	Botswana Bō Zhá Nà	波箚那 波劄那

| Brazil | 巴西 | Chadian | 查德人 |
| Bā Xī | 巴西 | Chá Dé Rén | 查德人 |

| Brazilian | 巴西人 | Chile | 智利 |
| Bā Xī Rén | 巴西人 | Zhì Lí | 智利 |

| British Indian O. Terr. | 英属印度 | Chilean | 智利人 |
| Yīng Shǔ Yìn Dù | 英屬印度 | Zhì Lí Rén | 智利人 |

| Brunei | 汶莱 | China | 中国 |
| Wén Lái | 汶萊 | Zhōng Guó | 中國 |

| Bulgaria | 保加利亚 | Chinese | 中国人 |
| Bǎo Jiā Lì Yǎ | 保加利亞 | Zhōng-guo Rén | 中國人 |

| Burkina Faso | 布吉纳法索 | Christmas Island | 圣诞岛 |
| Bù Jí Nà Fá Suǒ | 布吉納法索 | Shèng Dàn Dǎo | 聖誕島 |

| Burma | 缅甸 | Cocos Islands | 可可斯群岛 |
| Miǎn Diàn | 緬甸 | Ké Kě Sī Qǔn Dǎo | 可可斯群島 |

| Burmese | 缅甸人 | Colombia | 哥伦比亚 |
| Miǎn Diàn Rén | 緬甸人 | Gē Lún Bǐ Yà | 哥倫比亞 |

| Burundi | 浦隆地 | Colombian | 哥伦比亚人 |
| Pǔ Lóng Dì | 浦隆地 | Gē Lún Bǐ Yà Rén | 哥倫比亞人 |

| Caicos Islands | 开科斯群岛 | Comoros | 葛摩 |
| Kāi Kē Sī Qǔn Dǎo | 開科斯群島 | Gě Mó | 葛摩 |

| Cambodia | 柬埔寨 | Congo | 刚果 |
| Jián Pǔ Zhài | 柬埔寨 | Gāng Guǒ | 剛果 |

| Cambodian | 柬埔寨人 | Congolese | 刚果人 |
| Jián Pǔ Zhài Rén | 柬埔寨人 | Gāng Guǒ Rén | 剛果人 |

| Cameroon | 喀麦隆 | Cook Islands | 柯克群岛 |
| Kē Mài Lóng | 喀麥隆 | Kē Kè Qǔn Dǎo | 柯克群島 |

| Cameroonian | 喀麦隆人 | Coral Sea Islands | 珊瑚海 |
| Kē Mài Lóng Rén | 喀麥隆人 | Shān Hú Hǎi | 珊瑚海 |

| Canada | 加拿大 | Costa Rica | 哥斯大黎加 |
| Jiā Ná Dà | 加拿大 | Gē Sī Dà Lí Jiā | 哥斯大黎加 |

| Canadian | 加拿大人 | Costa Rican | 哥斯大黎加人 |
| Jiā Ná Dà Rén | 加拿大人 | Gē Sī Dà Lí Jiā Rén | 哥斯大黎加人 |

| Cape Verde | 维德角 | Croatia | 克罗埃西亚 |
| Wéi Dé Jiǎo | 維德角 | Kè Luó Ai Xī Yǎ | 克羅埃西亞 |

| Cayman Islands | 开曼群岛 | Cuba | 古巴 |
| Kāi Màn Qǔn Dǎo | 開曼群島 | Gǔ Bā | 古巴 |

| Central African Republic | 中非 | Cuban | 古巴人 |
| Zhōng Féi | 中非 | Gǔ Bā Rén | 古巴人 |

| Chad | 查德 | Cyprus | 赛普勒斯 |
| Chá Dé | 查德 | Sài Pǔ Lè Sī | 賽普勒斯 |

Czech Republic **Jié Kè Gòng Hé Guó**	捷克共和国 捷克共和國	**Estonian** **Ài Shā Ní Yǎ Rén**	爱沙尼亚人 愛沙尼亞人
Czechoslovakian **Jié Kè Rén**	捷克人 捷克人	**Ethiopia** **Yī Suǒ Ou Bí Yǎ**	衣索欧比亚 衣索歐比亞
Denmark **Dān Mài**	丹麦 丹麥	**Ethiopian** **Yī Suǒ Ou Bí Yǎ Rén**	衣索欧比亚人 衣索歐比亞人
Danish **Dān Mài Rén**	丹麦人 丹麥人	**Europa Island** **Yóu Luó Pà Dǎo**	尤罗帕岛 尤羅帕岛
Djibouti **Jí Bù Dì**	吉布地 吉布地	**Falkland Islands** (Malvinas) **Fú Kè Lán Qǔn Dǎo**	福克兰群岛 福克蘭群島
Dominica **Duō Mǐ Ní Kè**	多米尼克 多米尼克	**Faroe** **Fà Luó Qǔn Dǎo**	法罗群岛 法羅群島
Dominican Republic **Duō Míng Ní Jiā**	多明尼加 多明尼加	**Faroese** **Fà Luó Rén**	法罗人 法羅人
Dominican **Duō Míng Ní Jiā Rén**	多明尼加人 多明尼加人	**Fijian** **Fěi Jì Rén**	斐济人 斐濟人
East Timor **Dōng Dì Wén**	东帝汶 東帝汶	**Finland** **Fēn Lán**	芬兰 芬蘭
Ecuador **È Guā Duō Er**	厄瓜多尔 厄瓜多爾	**Finnish** **Fēn Lán Rén**	芬兰人 芬蘭人
Ecuadorian **È Guā Duō Er Rén**	厄瓜多尔人 厄瓜多爾人	**France** **Fà Guó**	法国 法國
Egypt **Āi Jí**	埃及 埃及	**French** **Fà-guo Rén**	法国人 法國人
Egyptian **Āi Jí Rén**	埃及人 埃及人	**French Guyana** **Fà Shǔ Gài Yǎ Nà**	法属盖亚纳 法屬蓋亞納
El Salvador **Sà Er Wǎ Duō**	萨尔瓦多 薩爾瓦多	**French Guiana** **Fà Shǔ Guī Yǎ Nà**	法属圭亚那 法屬圭亞那
El Salvadorian **Sà Er Wǎ Duó Rén**	萨尔瓦多人 薩爾瓦多人	**Gabon** **Jiā Péng**	加彭 加彭
England; Britain **Yīng Guó**	英国 英國	**Gabonese** **Jiā Péng Rén**	加彭人 加彭人
Englishman; British **Yīng-guo Rén**	英国人 英國人	**Gambia** **Gān Bí Yǎ**	甘比亚 甘比亞
Equatorial Guinea **Chì Dào Jǐ Nèi Yǎ**	赤道几内亚 赤道幾內亞	**Gaza Strip** **Jiā Sà Zǒu Láng**	加萨走廊 加薩走廊
Eritrea **È Lì Chuí Yǎ**	厄利垂亚 厄利垂亞	**Georgia** **Qiáo Zhì Yǎ**	乔治亚 喬治亞
Estonia **Ài Shā Ní Yǎ**	爱沙尼亚 愛沙尼亞	**Germany** **Dé Guó**	德国 德國

| German | 德国人 | Hollander | 荷兰人 |
| Dé-guo Rén | 德國人 | Hé Lán Rén | 荷蘭人 |

| Ghana | 迦纳 | Holy See | 教廷 |
| Jiā Nà | 迦納 | Jiào Tíng | 教廷 |

| Gibraltar | 直布罗陀 | Honduras | 宏都拉斯 |
| Zhí Bù Luó Tuó | 直布羅陀 | Hóng Dū Lā Sī | 宏都拉斯 |

| Greece | 希腊 | Honduran | 宏都拉斯人 |
| Xī Là | 希臘 | Hóng Dū Lā Sī Rén | 宏都拉斯人 |

| Greek | 希腊人 | Hongkong | 香港 |
| Xī Là Rén | 希臘人 | Xiāng Gǎng | 香港 |

| Greenland | 格陵兰 | Hongkong S.A.R. | 香港特区 |
| Gé Líng Lán | 格陵蘭 | Xiāng Gǎng Tè Qū | 香港特區 |

| Grenada | 格瑞那达 | Howland Island | 豪兰岛 |
| Gé Ruì Nà Dá | 格瑞那達 | Háo Lán Dǎo | 豪蘭島 |

| Grenadines | 格瑞那达人 | Hungary | 匈牙利 |
| Gé Ruì Nà Dá Rén | 格瑞那達人 | Xiōng Yá Lì | 匈牙利 |

| Guadeloupe | 哥德普洛 | Hungarian | 匈牙利人 |
| Gē Dé Pǔ Luò | 哥德普洛 | Xiōng Yá Lì Rén | 匈牙利人 |

| Guam | 关岛 | Iceland | 冰岛 |
| Guān Dǎo | 關島 | Bīng Dǎo | 冰島 |

| Guatemala | 瓜地马拉 | India | 印度 |
| Guā Dì Mǎ Lā | 瓜地馬拉 | Yìn Dù | 印度 |

| Guinea | 几内亚 | Indian | 印度人 |
| Jǐ Nèi Yǎ | 幾內亞 | Yìn Dù Rén | 印度人 |

| Guinea-Bissau | 比索 | Indonesia | 印尼 |
| Bí Suǒ | 比索 | Yìn Ní | 印尼 |

| Guyana | 盖亚纳 | Indonesian | 印尼人 |
| Gài Yǎ Nà | 蓋亞納 | Yìn Ní Rén | 印尼人 |

| Guyanese | 盖亚纳人 | Iran | 伊朗 |
| Gài Yǎ Nà Rén | 蓋亞納人 | Yī Lǎng | 伊朗 |

| Haiti | 海地 | Iranian | 伊朗人 |
| Hǎi Dì | 海地 | Yī Lǎng Rén | 伊朗人 |

| Haitian | 海地人 | Iraq | 伊拉克 |
| Hǎi Dì Rén | 海地人 | Yī Lā Kè | 伊拉克 |

| Heard & McDonald Islands | 赫德岛 | Iraqi | 伊拉克人 |
| Hè Dé Dǎo | 赫德島 | Yī Lā Kè Rén | 伊拉克人 |

| Hercegovina | 赫塞哥维纳 | Ireland | 爱尔兰 |
| Hè Sài Gē Wéi Nà | 赫塞哥維納 | Ài Er Lán | 愛爾蘭 |

| Holland | 荷兰 | Irish | 爱尔兰人 |
| Hé Lán | 荷蘭 | Ài Er Lán Rén | 愛爾蘭人 |

Israel	以色列	Kingman Reef	京曼岛
Yǐ Sè Liè	以色列	Jīng Màn Dǎo	京曼島
Israeli	以色列人	Kiribati	吉里巴斯
Yǐ Sè Liè Rén	以色列人	Jí Lǐ Bā Sī	吉裏巴斯
Italy	义大利	Korea	韩国
Yì Dà Lì	義大利	Hán Guó	韓國
Italian	义大利人	Korean	韩国人
Yì-da Lì Rén	義大利人	Hán-guo Rén	韓國人
Ivory Coast	象牙海岸	Kuwait	科威特
Xiàng Yá Hǎi An	象牙海岸	Kē Wēi Tè	科威特
Ivory Coaster	象牙海岸人	Kuwaiti	科威特人
Xiàng Yá Hǎi An Rén	象牙海岸人	Kē Wēi Tè Rén	科威特人
Jamaica	牙买加	Kirghizstan	吉尔吉斯坦
Yá Mǎi Jiā	牙買加	Jí Er Jí Sī Tǎn	吉爾吉斯坦
Jamaican	牙买加人	Laos	寮国
Yá Mǎi Jiā Rén	牙買加人	Liáo Guó	寮國
Jan Mayen	央棉岛	Laotian	寮国人
Yāng Mián Dǎo	央棉島	Liáo Guó Rén	寮國人
Japan	日本	Latvia	拉脱维亚
Rì Běn	日本	Lā Tuō Wéi Yǎ	拉脱維亞
Japanese	日本人	Latvian	拉脱维亚人
Rì Běn Rén	日本人	Lā Tuō Wéi Yǎ Rén	拉脱維亞人
Jarvis Island	加维斯岛	Lebanon	黎巴嫩
Jiā Wéi Sī Dǎo	加維斯島	Lí Bā Nèn	黎巴嫩
Jersey	泽西岛	Lebanese	黎巴嫩人
Zé Xī Dǎo	澤西島	Lí Bā Nèn Rén	黎巴嫩人
Johnston Atoll	詹斯顿岛	Lesotho	赖索托
Zhān Sī Dùn Dǎo	詹斯頓島	Lài Suǒ Tuō	賴索托
Jordan	约旦	Liberia	赖比瑞亚
Yuē Dàn	約旦	Lài Bǐ Ruì Yǎ	賴比瑞亞
Jordanian	约旦人	Liberian	赖比瑞亚人
Yuē Dàn Rén	約旦人	Lài Bǐ Ruì Yǎ Rén	賴比瑞亞人
Kazakhstan	哈萨克	Libya	利比亚
Hā Sà Kè	哈薩克	Lì Bí Yǎ	利比亞
Kazakh	哈萨克人	Libyan	利比亚人
Hā Sà Kè Rén	哈薩克人	Lì Bí Yǎ Rén	利比亞人
Kenya	肯亚	Liechtenstein	列支敦斯登
Kén Yǎ	肯亞	Liè Zhī Dūn Sī Dēng	列支敦斯登
Kenyan	肯亚人	Lithuania	立陶宛
Kén Yǎ Rén	肯亞人	Lì Táo Wǎn	立陶宛

Lithuanian **Lì Táo Wǎn Rén**	立陶宛人 立陶宛人	**Mauritania** **Máo Lì Tǎ Ní Yǎ**	茅利塔尼亚 茅利塔尼亞
Luxemburg **Lú Sēn Bǎo**	卢森堡 盧森堡	**Mauritanian** **Máo Lì Tǎ Ní Yǎ Rén**	茅利塔尼亚人 茅利塔尼亞人
Luxemburger **Lú Sēn Bǎo Rén**	卢森堡人 盧森堡人	**Mauritius** **Mó Lǐ Xī Sī**	模里西斯 模裏西斯
Macao S.A.R. **Ào Mén Tè Qū**	澳门特区 澳門特區	**Mauritian** **Mó Lǐ Xī Sī Rén**	模里西斯人 模裏西斯人
Macao **Ào Mén**	澳门 澳門	**Mexico** **Mò Xī Gē**	墨西哥 墨西哥
Macanese **Ào Mén Rén**	澳门人 澳門人	**Mexican** **Mò Xī Gē Rén**	墨西哥人 墨西哥人
Macedonia **Mǎ Qí Dùn**	马其顿 馬其頓	**Micronesia** **Mì Kè Luó Ní Xī Yǎ**	密克罗尼西亚 密克羅尼西亞
Macedonian **Mǎ Qí Dùn Rén**	马其顿人 馬其頓人	**Midway Islands** **Zhōng Tú Dǎo**	中途岛 中途島
Madagascar **Mǎ Dá Jiā Sī Jiā**	马达加斯加 馬達加斯加	**Moldova** **Mó Er Duō Wǎ**	摩尔多瓦 摩爾多瓦
Malagasy Republic **Mǎ Lā Jiā Xī**	马拉加西 馬拉加西	**Monaco** **Mó Nà Gē**	摩纳哥 摩納哥
Malagasy **Mǎ Lā Jiā Xī Rén**	马拉加西人 馬拉加西人	**Mongolia** **Méng Gǔ**	蒙古 蒙古
Malawi **Mǎ Lā Wēi**	马拉威 馬拉威	**Mongolian** **Méng-gu Rén**	蒙古人 蒙古人
Malawian **Mǎ Lā Wēi Rén**	马拉威人 馬拉威人	**Montserrat** **Méng Tè Sè Lā Tè Dǎo**	蒙特色拉特岛 蒙特色拉特島
Malaysia **Mǎ Lái Xī Yǎ**	马来西亚 馬來西亞	**Morocco** **Mó Luò Gē**	摩洛哥 摩洛哥
Malaysian **Mǎ Lái Sī Yǎ Rén**	马来西亚人 馬來西亞人	**Moroccan** **Mó Luò Gē Rén**	摩洛哥人 摩洛哥人
Maldives **Má Er Dì Fū**	马尔地夫 馬爾地夫	**Mozambique** **Mò Sān Bǐ Kè**	莫三比克 莫三比克
Mali **Mǎ Lì**	马利 馬利	**Myanmar** **Miǎn Diàn**	缅甸 緬甸
Malta **Má Er Tā**	马尔他 馬爾他	**Namibia** **Nà Mǐ Bí Yǎ**	纳米比亚 納米比亞
Isle of Man **Màn Chéng Dǎo**	曼城岛 曼城島	**Nauru** **Nuò Lǔ**	诺鲁 諾魯
Marshall Islands **Mǎ Shào Er Qún Dǎo**	马绍尔群岛 馬紹爾群島	**Navassa Island** **Nà Wǎ Sà Dǎo**	那瓦萨岛 那瓦薩島

Nepal **Ní Bó Er**	尼泊尔 尼泊爾	**Outer Mongolia** **Wài Méng Gǔ**	外蒙古 外蒙古
Nepalese **Ní Bó Er Rén**	尼泊尔人 尼泊爾人	**Outer Mongolian** **Wài Méng-gu Rén**	外蒙古人 外蒙古人
Netherland Antilles **Hé Shǔ An Tì Liè Sī**	荷属安替列斯 荷屬安替列斯	**Pakistan** **Bā Jī Sī Tǎn**	巴基斯坦 巴基斯坦
Netherlands **Hé Lán**	荷兰 荷蘭	**Pakistani** **Bā Jī Sī Tǎn Rén**	巴基斯坦人 巴基斯坦人
Dutch **Hé Lán Rén**	荷兰人 荷蘭人	**Palau Islands** **Bó Liú**	帛琉 帛琉
New Caledonia **Xīn Kà Lǐ Duō Ní Yǎ**	新喀里多尼亚 新喀裏多尼亞	**Palmyra Atoll** **Pà Mài Lā Dǎo**	帕迈拉岛 帕邁拉島
New Zealand **Niǔ Xī Lán**	纽西兰 紐西蘭	**Panama** **Bā Ná Mǎ**	巴拿马 巴拿馬
New Zealander **Niǔ Xī Lán Rén**	纽西兰人 紐西蘭人	**Panamanian** **Bā Ná Mǎ Rén**	巴拿马人 巴拿馬人
Nicaragua **Ní Jiā Lā Guā**	尼加拉瓜 尼加拉瓜	**Papua New Guinea** **Bā-bu Yá Niú Jǐ-nei Yǎ**	巴布亚纽几内亚 巴布亞紐幾內亞
Nicaraguan **Ní Jiā Lā Guā Rén**	尼加拉瓜人 尼加拉瓜人	**Paraguay** **Bā Lā Guī**	巴拉圭 巴拉圭
Niger **Ní Rì**	尼日 尼日	**Peru** **Mì-lu Gòng Hé Guó**	秘鲁共和国 秘魯共和國
Nigerien **Ní Rì Rén**	尼日人 尼日人	**Peruvian** **Mì-lu Rén**	秘鲁人 秘魯人
Nigeria **Nài Jí Lì Yǎ**	奈及利亚 奈及利亞	**Philippines** **Fēi-lü Bīn**	菲律宾 菲律賓
Nigerian **Nài Jí Lì Yǎ Rén**	奈及利亚人 奈及利亞人	**Filipino** **Fēi-lü Bīn Rén**	菲律宾人 菲律賓人
Norfolk Island **Nuò Fú Kè Dǎo**	诺福克岛 諾福克島	**Poland** **Bō Lán**	波兰 波蘭
North Korea **Běi Hán**	北韩 北韓	**Polish** **Bō Lán Rén**	波兰人 波蘭人
Northern Mariana Isl. **Běi Má Lǐ An Nà**	北马里安纳 北馬裏安納	**Polynesia** **Bō Lǐ Ní Xī Yǎ**	玻里尼西亚 玻裏尼西亞
Norway **Nuó Wēi**	挪威 挪威	**Polynesian** **Bō Lǐ Ní Xī Yǎ Rén**	玻里尼西亚人 玻裏尼西亞人
Norwegian **Nuó Wēi Rén**	挪威人 挪威人	**Portugal** **Pú-tao Yá**	葡萄牙 葡萄牙
Oman **Ā Màn**	阿曼 阿曼	**Portuguese** **Pú-tao Yá Rén**	葡萄牙人 葡萄牙人

Puerto Rico **Bō Duō Lí Gè**	波多黎各 波多黎各	Singaporean **Xīn Jiā Pō Rén**	新加坡人 新加坡人
Puerto Rican **Bō Duō Lí Gè Rén**	波多黎各人 波多黎各人	Slovakia **Sī Luò Fá Kè**	斯洛伐克 斯洛伐克
Qatar **Kǎ Dá**	卡达 卡達	Slovakian **Sī Luò Fá Kè Rén**	斯洛伐克人 斯洛伐克人
Reunion **Liú Ní Wàng**	留尼旺 留尼旺	Slovenia **Sī Luò Wéi Ní Yǎ**	斯洛维尼亚 斯洛維尼亞
Romania **Luó Mǎ Ní Yǎ**	罗马尼亚 羅馬尼亞	Slovenian **Sī Luò Wéi Ní Yǎ Rén**	斯洛维尼亚人 斯洛維尼亞人
Romanian **Luó Mǎ Ní Yǎ Rén**	罗马尼亚人 羅馬尼亞人	Solomon Islands **Suǒ-luo Mén Qún Dǎo**	索罗门群岛 索羅門群島
Russia **É Guó; È Guó**	俄国 俄國	Somalia **Suó Mǎ Lì Yǎ**	索马利亚 索馬利亞
Russian **É Guó Rén; È Guó Rén**	俄国人 俄國人	Somali **Suó Mǎ Lì Yǎ Rén**	索马利亚人 索馬利亞人
Ruanda **Lú An Dá**	卢安达 盧安達	South Africa **Nán Fēi**	南非 南非
Ruandan **Lú An Dá Rén**	卢安达人 盧安達人	South African **Nán Fēi Rén**	南非人 南非人
Samoa **Sà Mó Yǎ**	萨摩亚 薩摩亞	South Georgia **Nán Qiáo Zhì Yǎ**	南乔治亚 南喬治亞
Samoan **Sà Mó Yǎ Rén**	萨摩亚人 薩摩亞人	S, Sandwich Islands **Nán Sān-míng-zhì Qún Dǎo**	南三明治群岛 南三明治群島
San Marino **Shèng Mǎ Lì Nuò**	圣马利诺 聖馬利諾	Spain **Xī Bān Yá**	西班牙 西班牙
Saudi Arabia **Shā Wū Dì Ā Lā Bó**	沙乌地阿拉伯 沙烏地阿拉伯	Spaniard **Xī Bān Yá Rén**	西班牙人 西班牙人
Saudi Arabian **Shā Wū Dì Ā Lā Bó Rén**	沙乌地阿拉伯人 沙烏地阿拉伯人	Sri Lanka **Sī Lǐ Lán Kǎ**	斯里兰卡 斯裏蘭卡
Senegal **Sài Nèi Jiā Er**	塞内加尔 塞內加爾	St. Lucia **Shèng Lù Xī Yǎ**	圣露西亚 聖露西亞
Senegalese **Sài Nèi Jiā Er Rén**	塞内加尔人 塞內加爾人	St. Tome **Shèng Duō Měi**	圣多美 聖多美
Seychelles **Sài Xí Er Qún Dǎo**	塞席尔群岛 塞席爾群島	St. Vincent **Shèng Wén Sēn**	圣文森 聖文森
Sierra Leone **Shī Zi Shān**	狮子山 獅子山	Sudan **Sū Dān**	苏丹 蘇丹
Singapore **Xīn Jiā Pō**	新加坡 新加坡	Sudanese **Sū Dān Rén**	苏丹人 蘇丹人

Surinam **Sū Lì Nán**	苏利南 蘇利南		**Tuvalu** **Tǔ Wá Lǔ**	吐瓦鲁 吐瓦魯
Swaziland **Shí Wǎ Jì Lán**	史瓦济兰 史瓦濟蘭		**Uganda** **Wū Gān Dá**	乌干达 烏幹達
Sweden **Ruì Diǎn**	瑞典 瑞典		**Ukraine** **Wū Kè Lán**	乌克兰 烏克蘭
Swedish **Ruì Diǎn Rén**	瑞典人 瑞典人		**Ukrainian** **Wū Kè Lán Rén**	乌克兰人 烏克蘭人
Switzerland **Ruì Shì**	瑞士 瑞士		**United Arab Emirates** **A Lā Bó Dà Gōng Gúo**	阿拉伯大公国 阿拉伯大公國
Swiss **Ruì Shì Rén**	瑞士人 瑞士人		**United Kingdom** **Dà Yīng Lián Hé Wáng Guó**	大英联合王国 大英聯合王國
Syria **Xù Lì Yǎ**	叙利亚 敘利亞		**United States** **Měi Lì Jiān Hé Zhòng Gúo**	美利坚合众国 美利堅合眾國
Syrian **Xù Lì Yǎ Rén**	叙利亚人 敘利亞人		**Uruguay** **Wū Lā Guī**	乌拉圭 烏拉圭
Tajikistan **Tǎ Jí Kè**	塔吉克 塔吉克		**Uruguayan** **Wū Lā Guī Rén**	乌拉圭人 烏拉圭人
Tanzania **Tǎn Shàng Ní Yǎ**	坦尚尼亚 坦尚尼亞		**Uzbekistan** **Wū Zī Bié Kè Sī Tǎn**	乌兹别克斯坦 烏茲別克斯坦
Thailand **Tài Guó**	泰国 泰國		**Vanuatu** **Wàn Nà Dù**	万那杜 萬那杜
Thai **Tài Guó Rén**	泰国人 泰國人		**Vatican** **Fàn Dì Gāng**	梵帝岗 梵帝崗
Togo **Duō Gē**	多哥 多哥		**Rome** **Luó Mǎ**	罗马 羅馬
Tonga **Dōng Jiā**	东加 東加		**Venezuela** **Wěi Nèi Ruì Lā**	委内瑞拉 委內瑞拉
Trinidad-Tobago **Qiān Lǐ Dá Tuō Bā Gē**	千里达托巴哥 千里達托巴哥		**Venezuelan** **Wěi Nèi Ruì Lā Rén**	委内瑞拉人 委內瑞拉人
Tunisia **Tú Ní Xī Yǎ**	突尼西亚 突尼西亞		**Vietnam** **Yüè Nán**	越南 越南
Tunisian **Tú Ní Xī Yǎ Rén**	突尼西亚人 突尼西亞人		**Vietnamese** **Yüè Nán Rén**	越南人 越南人
Turkey **Tú Er Qí**	土耳其 土耳其		**Virgin Islands** (British) **Wéi Er Jīng Qún Dǎo**	维尔京群岛 維爾京群島（英）
Turkish **Tú Er Qí Rén**	土耳其人 土耳其人		**Virgin Islands** (US) **Wéi Er Jīng Qún Dǎo**	维尔京群岛 維爾京群島（美）
Turkmenistan **Tǔ Kù Màn**	土库曼 土庫曼		**Wake Island** **Wēi Kè Dǎo**	威克岛 威克島

Wallis; Valais	瓦利斯	black people	黑人
Wǎ Lì Sī	瓦利斯	hēi-ren	黑人
Yemen	叶门	Caucasian	白种人
Yè Mén	葉門	bái zhǒng rén	白種人
Yugoslavia	南斯拉夫	Orientals	东方人
Nán Sī Lā Fū	南斯拉夫	Dōng Fāng Rén	東方人
Yugoslavian	南斯拉夫人	Asian	亚洲人
Nán Sī Lā Fū Rén	南斯拉夫人	Yǎ Zhōu Rén	亞洲人
Zambia	尚比亚	Latin	拉丁民族人
Shàng Bí Yǎ	尚比亞	Lā Dīng Mín Zú Rén	拉丁民族人
Zimbabwe	辛巴威	African	非洲人
Xīn Bā Wēi	辛巴威	Fēi zhōu Rén	非洲人
ethnic group	人种	American Indians	美洲印地安人
rén zhǒng	人種	měi zhōu yìn dì ān rén	美洲印地安人

Military Terms
军中術語

English	Simplified / Traditional	Pinyin		English	Simplified / Traditional	Pinyin
national anthem	国歌 / 國歌	guó gē		army corps	军 / 軍	jūn
national flag	国旗 / 國旗	guó qí		division	师 / 師	shī
flagpole; flag post	旗杆 / 旗桿	qí gān		brigade	旅 / 旅	lǚ
hoist a flag	升旗 / 升旗	shēng qí		regiment	团 / 團	tuán
lower (haul down) a flag	降旗 / 降旗	jiàng qí		battalion	营 / 營	yíng
fly a flag at half-mast	降半旗 / 降半旗	jiàng bàn qí		company	连 / 連	lián
armed forces	三军 / 三軍	sān jūn		platoon	排 / 排	pái
marine corps	海军陆战队 / 海軍陸戰隊	hǎi jūn lù zhàn duì		squad (11 men, U..S..)	班 / 班	bān
air base	空军基地 / 空軍基地	kōng jūn jī dì		enlist	入伍 / 入伍	rù wǔ
M.P. station	宪兵分队 / 憲兵分隊	xiàn bīng fēn duì		draft	征兵 / 征兵	zhēng bīng
air-raid alert	空袭警报 / 空襲警報	kōng xí jǐng bào		discharged	退伍 / 退伍	tuì wǔ
guerrilla; guerilla	游击队 / 遊擊隊	yóu jí duì		honorary discharged	荣誉退伍 / 榮譽退伍	róng yù tuì wǔ
commando	突击队 / 突擊隊	tú jí duì		retired	退休 / 退休	tuì xiū
emergency unit	冲锋队 / 衝鋒隊	chōng fēng duì		messenger	传令兵 / 傳令兵	chuán lìng bīng
flying-column	特攻队 / 特攻隊	tè gōng duì		replacement	补充兵 / 補充兵	bǔ-chong bīng
troops	军队 / 軍隊	jūn duì		reservist	后备军人 / 後備軍人	hòu bèi jūn-ren

English	Pinyin	Simplified	Traditional
volunteer	zhì yùan bīng	志愿兵	志願兵
National Guard	guó mín bīng	国民兵	國民兵
infantry	bù bīng	步兵	步兵
artillery troops	pào bīng	炮兵	炮兵
ordnance	bīng gōng	兵工	兵工
engineering corps of troops	gōng bīng	工兵	工兵
armor troops	zhuāng jiǎ bīng	装甲兵	裝甲兵
transportation troops	shū sòng bīng	输送兵	輸送兵
signal corps	tōng xùn bīng	通讯兵	通訊兵
guard	wèi bīng	卫兵	衛兵
cordon	fàng shào	放哨	放哨
striker	qín-wu bīng	勤务兵	勤務兵
paratrooper	sǎn bīng	伞兵	傘兵
military police (M.P.)	xiàn bīng	宪兵	憲兵
frogman	wā rén	蛙人	蛙人
seaman	shuǐ bīng	水兵	水兵
sailor	hǎi yuán	海员	海員
crew	qǘan tǐ chuán yúan	全体船员	全體船員
deserter	táo bīng	逃兵	逃兵
deserted the post	kāi xiǎo chāir	开小差儿	開小差兒

English	Pinyin	Simplified	Traditional
absent without leave (AWOL)	shàn lí zhí shǒu	擅离职守	擅離職守
on furlough	fàng shì bīng jià	放士兵假	放士兵假
fall-in	pái duì	排队	排隊
close	kào lǒng	靠拢	靠攏
dismiss	jiě sàn	解散	解散
align	duì qí	对齐	對齊
at ease	shāo xí	稍息	稍息
attention	lì zhèng	立正	立正
dress	kàn qí	看齐	看齊
eyes right	xiàng yòu kàn	向右看	向右看
Dress right, dress!	xiàng yòu kàn qí	向右看齐	向右看齊
eyes left	xiàng zuǒ kàn	向左看	向左看
Dress left, dress!	xiàng zuǒ kàn qí	向左看齐	向左看齊
eyes front	xiàng qián kàn	向前看	向前看
count off	bào shù	报数	報數
roll call	diǎn míng	点名	點名
right turn	xiàng yòu zhuǎn	向右转	向右轉
left turn	xiàng zuó zhuǎn	向左转	向左轉
about turn	xiàng hòu zhuǎn	向后转	向後轉
forward march	qǐ bù zǒu	起步走	起步走

mark time march tà bù zǒu	踏步走 踏步走
march qí bù zǒu	齐步走 齊步走
march at ease biàn bù zǒu	便步走 便步走
goosestep zhèng bù zǒu	正步走 正步走
double time march pǎo bù zǒu	跑步走 跑步走
side step héng bù	横步 橫步
rear march xiàng hòu zhuán zǒu	向后转走 向後轉走
halt lì dìng	立定 立定
kneel guì xià	跪下 跪下
lie down pā xià	趴下 趴下
creeping pú fú qián jìn	匍匐前进 匍匐前進
officer in command zhǐ-hui guān	指挥官 指揮官
army commander jūn zhǎng	军长 軍長
divisional commander shī zhǎng	师长 師長
brigade commander lǔ zhǎng	旅长 旅長
brigade major fù lǔ zhǎng	副旅长 副旅長
regimental commander tuán zhǎng	团长 團長
battalion commander yíng zhǎng	营长 營長
company commander lián zhǎng	连长 連長
platoon leader pái zhǎng	排长 排長
platoon sergeant pái fù	排副 排副
leader bān zhǎng	班长 班長
military information dié bào	谍报 諜報
enemy dí-ren	敌人 敵人
curfew jiè yán; xiāo jìn	戒严；宵禁 戒嚴；宵禁
stand by dài mìng	待命 待命
cover yǎn-hu	掩护 掩護
counter attack fǎn gōng	反攻 反攻
trench zhàn háo	战壕 戰壕
germ warfare xì jùn zhàn	细菌战 細菌戰
war criminal zhàn fàn	战犯 戰犯
captive fú lǔ	俘虏 俘虜
disarmed jiǎo xiè	缴械 繳械
to swab rifles cā qiāng	擦枪 擦槍
brass polish cā tóng yóu	擦铜油 擦銅油
refugee camp nàn mín yíng	难民营 難民營
martyr liè shì	烈士 烈士
supplies bú jǐ	补给 補給
search light tàn zhào dēng	探照灯 探照燈
hedgehog jù mǎ	拒马 拒馬

Weapons 武器

weapon **wǔ-qi**	武器	武器
ammunition **jūn huǒ**	军火	軍火
helicopter **zhí shēng fēi jī**	直升飞机	直升飛機
bomber **hōng zhà jī**	轰炸机	轟炸機
fighter **zhàn dòu jī**	战斗机	戰鬥機
cargo plane **yùn shū jī**	运输机	運輸機
pursuit plane **qū zhú jī**	驱逐机	驅逐機
reconnaissance plane **zhēn chá jī**	侦察机	偵察機
jet plane **pēn shè jī**	喷射机	噴射機
trainer **jiào liàn jī**	教练机	教練機
patrol plane **xún luó jī**	巡逻机	巡邏機
supersonic plane **chāo yīn sù jī**	超音速机	超音速機
battleship **zhǔ lì jiàn**	主力舰	主力艦
supply ship **bú jǐ jiàn**	补给舰	補給艦
mine layer **bù léi jiàn**	布雷舰	佈雷艦
warship **jūn jiàn**	军舰	軍艦
aircraft carrier **háng kōng mǔ jiàn**	航空母舰	航空母艦
cruiser **xún yáng jiàn**	巡洋舰	巡洋艦
destroyer **qū zhú jiàn**	驱逐舰	驅逐艦
gun boat **pào jiàn**	炮舰	炮艦
mine-sweeper **sǎo léi jiàn**	扫雷舰	掃雷艦
submarine **qián shuí tǐng**	潜水艇	潛水艇
torpedo boat **yú léi tǐng**	鱼雷艇	魚雷艇
tank **tǎn kè chē**	坦克车	坦克車
armored car **zhuāng jiǎ chē**	装甲车	裝甲車
command car **zhǐ huī chē**	指挥车	指揮車
weapons carrier **jūn xiè yùn shū chē**	军械运输车	軍械運輸車
radar **léi dá**	雷达	雷達
missile **fēi dàn; dǎo dàn**	飞弹；导弹	飛彈；導彈
flying saucer **fēi dié**	飞碟	飛碟
bomb **zhà dàn**	炸弹	炸彈
shrapnel **liú xiàn dàn**	榴霰弹	榴霰彈

time bomb dìng shí zhà dàn	定时炸弹 定時炸彈	hand grenade shǒu liú dàn	手榴弹 手榴彈
dynamite zhà yào	炸药 炸藥	shell pào dàn	炮弹 炮彈
land mine dì léi	地雷 地雷	blank cartridge kōng bāo dàn	空包弹 空包彈
mine shuǐ léi	水雷 水雷	tear gas shell cuī lèi dàn	催泪弹 催淚彈
pistol shǒu qiāng	手枪 手鎗	star shell guāng dàn	光弹 光彈
revolver zuǒ lún shǒu qiāng	左轮手枪 左輪手鎗	illuminating shell zhào míng dàn	照明弹 照明彈
silencer xiāo yīn zhuāng zhì	消音装置 消音裝置	pyrotechnics bomb xìn hào dàn	信号弹 信號彈
rifle bù qiāng	步枪 步鎗	smoke bomb yān mù dàn	烟幕弹 煙幕彈
machine-gun jī guān qiāng	机关枪 機關鎗	hydrogen bomb qīng dàn	氢弹 氫彈
carbine kǎ bīn qiāng	卡宾枪 卡賓鎗	atomic bomb yuán zǐ dàn	原子弹 原子彈
bayonet cì dāo	刺刀 刺刀	ABC Weapons huà shēng fàng wǔ qì	化生放武器 化生放武器
submachine gun chōng fēng qiāng	冲锋枪 衝鋒鎗	atomic weapons jüán zǐ wǔ qì	原子武器 原子武器
anti-aircraft gun gāo shè pào	高　炮 高　炮	bacteriological weapons xì jùn wǔ qì	细菌武器 細菌武器
mortar pò jí pào	迫击炮 迫擊炮	chemical weapons huà xǔé wǔ qì	化学武器 化學武器
howitzer liú dàn pào	榴弹炮 榴彈炮	nuclear weapon hé zǐ wǔ qì	核子武器 核子武器
field gun yě pào	野炮 野炮	nuclear bomb hé zǐ zhà dàn	核子炸弹 核子炸彈
rocket huǒ jiàn	火箭 火箭	helmet gāng kuī	钢盔 鋼盔
bazooka huǒ jiàn pào	火箭炮 火箭炮	anti-gas clothes fáng dú yī	防毒衣 防毒衣
bullet zǐ dàn	子弹 子彈	gas mask fáng dú miàn jù	防毒面具 防毒面具
cartridge case dàn jiá	弹夹 彈夾	fire-proof unit fáng huǒ yī	防火衣 防火衣

Military Rank 军阶

military personnel **jūn-ren**	军人 軍人	
soldier **bīng; dāng bīng**	兵：当兵 兵：當兵	
forces **bù duì**	部队 部隊	
rank **jiē jí**	阶级 階級	
commissioned officer **gāo jiē jūn guān**	高阶军官 高階軍官	
noncommissioned officer **shì guān zhǎng**	士官长 士官長	
enlisted man **shì bīng**	士兵 士兵	
MP; military police **xiàn bīng**	宪兵 憲兵	
Chief Commander **zǒng sī lìng**	总司令 總司令	
Provost Marshal **xiàn bīng sī lìng**	宪兵司令 憲兵司令	
liaison officer **lián luò guān**	连络官 連絡官	
aide **fù-guan**	副官 副官	
advance to the rank of colonel **shēng wéi shàng xiào**	升为上校 陞為上校	

Army **lù jūn**	陆军 陸軍	

Army, Chief Commander **lù jūn zǒng sī lìng**	陆军总司令 陸軍總司令	
General of the Army (5★) **lù jūn wǔ xīng shàng jiàng**	陆军五星上将 陸軍五星上將	
General (4★) **lù jūn yī jí shàng jiàng**	陆军一级上将 陸軍一級上將	
Lt. General (3★) **lù jūn èr jí jiàng**	陆军二级上将 陸軍二級上將	
Major General (2★) **lù jūn zhōng jiàng**	陆军中将 陸軍中將	
Brigadier General (1★) **lù jūn shào jiàng**	陆军少将 陸軍少將	
Air Attaché **lù jūn wǔ guān**	陆军武官 陸軍武官	
Colonel (Col.) **lù jūn shàng xiào**	陆军上校 陸軍上校	
Lieutenant Colonel **lù jūn zhōng xiào**	陆军中校 陸軍中校	
Major **lù jūn shào xiào**	陆军少校 陸軍少校	
Captain (Capt.) **lù jūn shàng wèi**	陆军上尉 陸軍上尉	
First Lieutenant (1st.Lt) **lù jūn zhōng wèi**	陆军中尉 陸軍中尉	
Second Lieutenant (2nd. Lt) **lù jūn shào wèi**	陆军少尉 陸軍少尉	
Warrant Officer **lù jūn zhǔn wèi**	陆军准尉 陸軍準尉	
master sergeant **lù jūn shì guān zhǎng**	陆军士官长 陸軍士官長	
Sergeant **lù jūn shàng shì**	陆军上士 陸軍上士	

Staff Sergeant lù jūn zhōng shì	陆军中士 陸軍中士	Chief petty officer hǎi jūn shì guān zhǎng	海军士官长 海軍士官長
corporal lù jūn xià shì	陆军下士 陸軍下士	Petty officer 1st class hǎi jūn shàng shì	海军上士 海軍上士
Private First Class lù jūn yī děng bīng	陆军一等兵 陸軍一等兵	Petty officer 2nd class hǎi jūn zhōng shì	海军中士 海軍中士
Private lù jūn èr děng bīng	陆军二等兵 陸軍二等兵	Petty officer 3rd class hǎi jūn xià shì	海军下士 海軍下士

 **navy**

| | | Seaman 1st class
hǎi jūn yī děng bīng | 海军一等兵
海軍一等兵 |
| Navy
hǎi jūn | 海军
海軍 | Seaman 2nd class
hǎi jūn èr děng bīng | 海军二等兵
海軍二等兵 |

| Naval Chief of Operations
hǎi jūn zǒng sī ling | 海军总司令
海軍總司令 |

 **air-force**

Admiral of the Navy (5★) hǎi jūn wǔ xīng shàng jiàng	海军五星上将 海軍五星上將	Air Force kōng jūn	空军 空軍
Admiral (4★) hǎi jūn yī jí shàng jiàng	海军一级上将 海軍一級上將	Air Force, Chief Commander kōng jūn zǒng sī lìng	空军总司令 空軍總司令
Vice Admiral (3★) hǎi jūn èr jí shàng jiàng	海军二级上将 海軍二級上將	General of the Air Force (4★) kōng jūn yī jí shàng jiàng	空军一级上将 空軍一級上將
Lieutenant Admiral (2★) hǎi jūn zhōng jiàng	海军中将 海軍中將	Lieutenant General (3★) kōng jūn èr jí shàng jiàng	空军二级上将 空軍二級上將
Rear Admiral (1★) hǎi jūn shào jiàng	海军少将 海軍少將	Major General (2★) kōng jūn zhōng jiàng	空军中将 空軍中將
Captain hǎi jūn shàng xiào	海军上校 海軍上校	Brigadier General (1★) kōng jūn shào jiàng	空军少将 空軍少將
Commander hǎi jūn zhōng xiào	海军中校 海軍中校	Colonel kōng jūn shàng xiào	空军上校 空軍上校
Lt. Commander hǎi jūn shào xiào	海军少校 海軍少校	Lieutenant Colonel kōng jūn zhōng xiào	空军中校 空軍中校
Lieutenant hǎi jūn shàng wèi	海军上尉 海軍上尉	Major kōng jūn shào xiào	空军少校 空軍少校
Lt. Junior Grade hǎi jūn zhōng wèi	海军中尉 海軍中尉	Captain kōng jūn shàng wèi	空军上尉 空軍上尉
ensign hǎi jūn shào wèi	海军少尉 海軍少尉	First Lieutenant kōng jūn zhōng wèi	空军中尉 空軍中尉
Warrant Officer hǎi jūn zhǔn wèi	海军准尉 海軍準尉	Second Lieutenant kōng jūn shào wèi	空军少尉 空軍少尉

APPENDIX

Introduction To
The Sound Of
The Chinese Language
And
Its Unique
Pronunciation

■ **All Chinese Words Are
Monosyllabic.**
■ **Since Early 1950's
the PRC employed
the English Alphabet Letters
to Pronounce the Chinese Characters
Chinese has become
WORLD EASIEST LANGUAGE**

附加资料

漢語發音

- ■ 用汉语发音
- ■ 用英文字母拼、读汉语
- ■ 汉语只有 432 个音
- ■ 汉字的每一个音都有四个声
- ■ 汉语发音大全（依字母次序排列）

附加資料

THE SOUND OF CHINESE CHARACTERS
Table Of Contents

The Pronunciation Of Chinese Characters
漢字發音

The Phonetic System of Romanizing Hàn-yǔ Sounds

In China, although there has always been one common written language, there are numerous regional dialects of the spoken Chinese language. In fact, they can be so different that a person from Beijing may not understand a single word spoken by a person using the Cantonese dialect. To address this problem, the Chinese government mandated that a single dialect or pǔtōnghuà (Pǔ Tōng Huà 普通话) become the official standard for the entire country. The dialect chosen was hànyǔ (Hàn Yǔ 汉语) which is more commonly known as Mandarin outside of China. Not only are all the citizens of the People's Republic of China (PRC) required to learn Hàn Yǔ, it is also used in all the PRC's official business and other affairs of state.

Romanization of Chinese Language in this book is to Romanize this Hàn Yǔ (Hànyǔ)

In the early 1950's, the PRC established a Chinese language pronunciation system called Hàn Yǔ Pīn Yīn (Hànyǔpīnyīn 汉语拼音). This system employs letters in the Latin alphabet to indicate the sounds of Chinese characters, it is commonly known as the phonetic system of Romanizing Hàn Yǔ sounds. Romanization of the Chinese language, therefore, specifically refers to the process of expressing the sounds and tones of Chinese characters – as they sound in Hàn Yǔ or Mandarin – by the Latin (also known as Roman) alphabet used by most of the Western world today.

Although there are other systems available, such as the Wade System or the Inland Mission System, this book chooses to employ the Hàn Yǔ Pīn Yīn (HYPY) system throughout the book, because of its popularity for ease of use and its general acceptance as the global standard.

ONE
What is Hànyǔpīnyīn (HYPY)?

HYPY represents the basic method of using letters from Latin alphabet to express the sound of a Chinese character.

Prior to going into the details of HYPY, one must thoroughly understand the uniqueness of the Chinese Language:

1. In the Chinese language, each character is a word.
2. Each word is monosyllabic.
3. In the Mandarin dialect (Hàn Yǔ) every syllable has an associated characteristic "tone" or pitch.
4. There are four (4) "tones" for each syllable sound.

THE FOUR TONES

In the HYPY system, and throughout the book, the four tones are denoted by four marks as shown (‒ ⁄ ∨ ＼) respectively placed directly above the leading vowel of its phonic sounds. Please refer to the chart shown.

1) **The 1st tone's mark is (‒) :** The tone is level at a relatively high pitch.
2) **The 2nd tone's mark is (⁄) :** It starts in the middle register and rises.
3) **The 3rd tone's mark is (∨) :** The tone dips, starting from a mid-pitch, dropping low, then rises back to mid-pitch level.
4) **The 4th tone's mark is (＼) :** The tone falls sharply. It starts from a high pitch and drops right down to low.

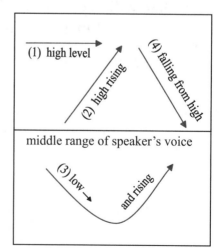

TWO

Illustration Of The Four Tones
易懂易學的四聲

By Professor William Liang (Inventor), Columbia University

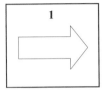 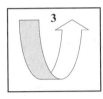 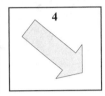

AFTER READING THE ABOVE ILLUSTRATIONS, READERS, ESPECIALLY BEGINNERS, MAY FIND IT DIFFICULT TO GRASP EXACTLY WHAT THE FOUR "TONES" SOUND LIKE WITHOUT ACTUALLY HEARING THEM. THE FOLLOWING EXERCISE HAS BEEN SPECIALLY DEVELOPED USING ENGLISH SYLLABLES TO SIMULATE THE "FOUR TONES" AND THEIR EXACT PITCHES.

The illustration goes like this:

Step **1** Read the following sentence first:

Lōndòn is Nót in Jǎpan

Step **2** Please note the four "Tone Marks" placed on top of the vowel of the four syllables selected and printed in blue.

1st (tone)	4th (tone)		2nd (tone)		3rd (tone)
Lōn	dòn	is	Nót	in	Jǎpan

NOTE: The four "marked syllables" represent the four tones
1st, 4th, 2nd and 3rd respectively.

Step **3** Read each of the marked syllables with the same tone and inflection as you read the whole word, but separately and individually as follows:

Lōn	dòn	Nó	Jǎ
1st tone	4th tone	2nd tone	3rd tone

AT this time, please practice reading these four syllables
"at each tone's pitch" a few times until
you can comprehend the difference between pitches.

Step **4** Now let's rearrange the (4) tones in order and practice:

Lōn	Nó	Jǎ	dòn
1st tone	2nd tone	3rd tone	4th tone

The reader should practice the four tones in this sequence a few
times until he/she has a feeling of the nature of the four tones.

Step **5** The reader should be aware that any syllable sound always has one of the "four tones". That is, the syllable "LŌN" of the word London is not limited to the 1st tone. It can have any of the other three tones as well.
To illustrate, let's keep the 1st syllable and its tone as is, but place the other three tone marks on this same syllable sound in the same sequence order. The resultant arrangement becomes:

1st tone	2nd tone	3rd tone	4th tone
lōn	lón	lǒn	lòn
dōn	dón	dǒn	dòn
nō	nó	nǒ	nò
jā	já	jǎ	jà

NOW the reader can practice the four tones in the same syllable sound.
Similarly, the reader may be able to practice a few syllable-tones on
their own.

TO EXPAND THE CONCEPT OF "THE FOUR TONES" FURTHER, WE LOOK AT THE SOUNDS OF SOME ENGLISH WORDS WHICH OFTEN HAVE DIFFERENT TONES UNDER DIFFERENT CIRCUMSTANCES. PLEASE REFER TO THE TABLE SHOWN:

1st. tone (−)	2nd.tone (✓)	3rd. tone (∨)	4th. tone (＼)
Dō it now!	I dón't understand.	Dǒ you know?	Of course I dò
Cān you or not?	I cán't tell you now.	Cǎn you do it?	Yes, you càn.
Yōu are right.	Was that yóu?	Yǒu love him?	Yes, It was yòu.

The purpose of this demonstration is to make it easier for English speaking readers to understand the concept of the "four tones" of a syllable, because they are not easily identified during speach.

C

BY NOW, THE READER SHOULD HAVE A FAIRLY GOOD IDEA OF WHAT THE "FOUR TONES" OF CHINESE CHARACTERS ARE. FOLLOWING THIS FORMAT, ONE CAN READ THE FOUR TONES OF ANY SINGLE SYLLABLE SOUND.

Try some now

1st tone	2nd tone	3rd tone	4th tone	1st tone	2nd tone	3rd tone	4th tone
nān,	nán,	nǎn,	nàn	bīng,	bíng,	bǐng,	bìng
mī,	mí,	mǐ,	mì	hōng,	hóng,	hǒng,	hòng
yīn,	yín,	yǐn,	yìn	wāng,	wáng,	wǎng,	wàng

Home work

Choose any syllable from each of the six given words to form a four-tone table in the 1st, 2nd, 3rd, & 4th tone order.

sailor   tango   dinner   longtime   before   garden

1st tone	2nd tone	3rd tone	4th tone	1st tone	2nd tone	3rd tone	4th tone

2 The Relationship Between HYPY & The English Alphabet

The following tables cover all necessary information concerning the use of English alphabet letters in expressing the Chinese Hàn-yǔ sounds.

Spoken Chinese Is Easy

18 Consonants • You Already Knew •

THE READERS SHOULD NOTE THAT THESE 18 CONSONANT PAIRS ARE PRONOUNCED THE SAME IN Hàn-yǔ AS IN THE ENGLISH ALPHABET.

Hàn yǔ Alphabet	m	n	p	b	k	d	f
English Sound	m	n	p	b	k	d	f
Hàn yǔ Alphabet	g	h	l	r	s	sh	z
English Sound	g	h	l	r	s	sh	z
Hàn yǔ Alphabet	ch	t	w	y			
English Sound	ch	t	w	y			

Ⓑ You Only Learn **5** Alphabet Letters

- These 5 letters involve the only sound transformation between Hàn-yǔ letters and Latin alphabet letters which the reader should memorize, because the pronunciation of these consonant letters are quite different from normal English sounds.

Hàn yǔ Alphabet	c	j	q	x	zh
English Sound	tsz	jyee	chyee	syee	jr

Tongue position for the "first four" sounds

The tip of your tongue must be positioned touching the back of the lower front teeth while maintaining a small opening between top teeth and tongue to permit air passage.

Tongue position for the "fifth" sounds

The tip of your tongue is raising high touching your hard palate like you say "Joe".

Remember: When one sees a **c** at the start of a HYPY., pronounce it **tsz** in the English way.
Similarly, when one sees a **j** pronounce it **jyee**, etc.

Once the reader becomes familiar with and then memorizes the interchange of each of the five pairs (Hàn-yǔ in blue and English Sound in black), he/she should be able to read any Chinese characters as long as it is denoted by HYPY since the rest of the Hàn-yǔ alphabet are pronounced the same as their English alphabet counterparts.

C
The Six Vowels in HYPY

IN addition to the 23 consonant sounds listed under *A* and *B*, vowels are treated with special care in this text. The reason is that Latin vowels can be expressed by different systems in English.

IN order to aid the reader in pronouncing Hàn-yǔ correctly by whichever English system he/she may choose, the author uses both **"K. K. Phonetic Alphabet"** (A pronunciation dictionary of American Language, by J.S. Kenyon & T.A. Knott) **and "Key to Pronunciation"** (Webster's New World Dictionary) **to symbolize the Hàn-yǔ vowel syllables in a broad and consistent manner so that speakers of every variety of American English can easily read their own pronunciation using the symbols used here.**

COMPARISON OF VOWELS IN Hàn-yǔ AND LATIN VOWELS

a

Hàn yǔ Syllables	a	ai	an	ang	ao
American K.K.	ɑ	aɪ	ɑn	ɑŋ	aU
Webster's	ä	ī	än	äŋ	ou
As in ⇨	god	high	on	ahng	now
Character Sound	阿	爱	安	昂	凹

e

Hàn yǔ Syllables	e	ei	en	eng	er
American K.K.	ʌ	e	ʌn	ʌŋ	ɝ
Webster's	u	ā	un	uŋ	ʉr
As in ⇨	cut	lay	bun	lung	early
Character Sound	饿	欸	恩	鞥	儿

i

Hàn yǔ Syllables	i	ia	ian	iang	iao	ie
American K.K.	i	ja	jan	jaŋ	jau	jɛ
Webster's	ē	yä	yän	yäŋ	you	ye
As in ⟹	bee	yacht	fiancé	eeahng	meow	yes
Character Sound	一	一阿	一安	一肮	一凹	耶

Hàn yǔ Syllables	in	ing	iu
American K.K.	in	iŋ	jo
Webster's	ēņ	ēŋ	yō
As in ⟹	bean	eeng	you
Character Sound	因	英	幽

o

Hàn yǔ Syllables	o	ong	ou
American K.K.	U	juŋ	o
Webster's	ᴑo	yōōŋ	ō
As in ⟹	book	oong	Coke
Character Sound	喔	瓮	欧

u and ü

Hàn yǔ Syllables	u	ua	uai	uan	uang	ui	un	uo
American K.K.	u	uɑ	uɑɪ	uɑn	uɑŋ	ue	un	uʌ
Webster's	ōō	ōōä	ōōī	ōōän	ōōäŋ	ōōā	ōōn	ōōu
As in ⇨	too	watt	why	one	wong	wait	when	waw
Character Sound	屋	挖	外	湾	汪	威	屋温	屋窝

Hàn yǔ Syllables	ü	üan	üe	ün
American K.K.	ü	üan	üɛ	ün
Webster's	yü	yüan	yüe	yün
As in ⇨ ✸				
Character Sound	淤	元	月	晕

✸ The Chinese sound "ü" cannot be recreated using the English alphabet. It has a unique pronunciation which may only be acquired through specific exercises.

To practice, position your tongue and lips as if you were going to whistle. While keeping lips in the "O" shape and the tip of your tongue touching the back of your lower front teeth lightly, practice and making prolonged "Y" sounds instead of blowing air .

D

The Tone Indicators

are always placed on one of the Six leading vowels
Example: **ní hǎo mā** (vowels in blue)
（**means: How are you?** 你好吗？）

Special Case

When **"i, u, ü"**

are followed by another vowel in one character syllable
i.e.: (sister 姐 **jie**); (money 钱 **qian**); (remove 脱 **tuo**); (learn 学 **xue**)
The tone indicators (stress) should be placed on the 2nd. vowel.
like: (ji**ě**) (qi**á**n) (tu**ó**) (xü**é**)..
Never On The 1st. Vowel.

In printing
"ü" can be substituted with "u".
"**Hàn yǔ Pīn Yīn**" can be substituted with "**Hanyupinyin**".
(The author uses HYPY)

Names, Countries,
Places, Business Firms and Special Events
are **Capitalized** by the first letter.
i.e.: 中國 Zhōng Guó

3 The Tones & Sounds Of Chinese Characters

EACH CHINESE CHARACTER HAS ONE AND ONLY ONE
SYLLABLE SOUND. THIS PARTICULAR SOUND ALWAYS
HAS ONLY "ONE OF THE FOUR" POSSIBLE TONES THAT
THE SYLLABLE MAY HAVE.

We Take the first 3 Lines of the "m" Table on Page 602
• FOR ILLUSTRATION •

Using "ma", the 1st sound in the "m" table as an Example

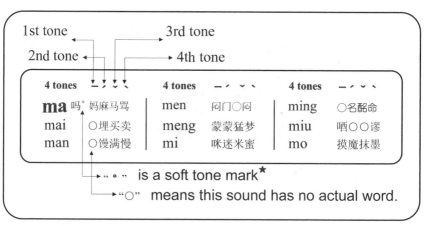

Please note that <u>NOT</u> all tones of a sound must have a character.
Throughout all the transcription tables of this text, wherever a "○"
is marked under a tone, it means that no character exists.

★ **Soft Tone** is a special feature of Chinese language. It is a necessary
end-tone of an end-character, thereby it ends the sentence. It carries no
meaning by itself, but the sentence is incompleted without it.

Four Tones Have Four Different Meanings

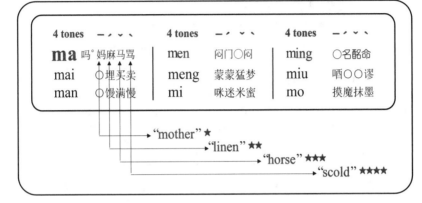

4 tones — ˊ ˇ ˋ		4 tones — ˊ ˇ ˋ		4 tones — ˊ ˇ ˋ	
ma	吗° 妈麻马骂	men	闷门〇闷	ming	〇名酩命
mai	〇埋买卖	meng	蒙蒙猛梦	miu	咻〇〇谬
man	〇馒满慢	mi	咪迷米蜜	mo	摸魔抹墨

→ "mother" ★
→ "linen" ★★
→ "horse" ★★★
→ "scold" ★★★★

Each Tone Has Many Characters

Each of the "Four Tones" of any sound may represent a number of different (words) characters that are all different in writings and meanings.

Just as English same sound words that have multiple meanings:

"eyes" "eye's" "ice" "I"s ...

The **Four Tones** of the sound **"ma"** creats four groups of different characters

★ The 1st tone (mā) represents: 媽嬤嬤贆妈妈嗎 ... **i.e.** 妈 is mother

★★ The 2nd tone (má) represents: 麻嘛蔴蟆摩仝痳 ... **i.e.** 麻 is linen

★★★ The 3rd tone (mǎ) represents: 馬螞瑪犸嗎鎷碼 ... **i.e.** 马 is horse

★★★★ The 4th tone (mà) represents: 罵禡傌榪犸閉螞 ... **i.e.** 骂 is scold

From the above TABLE, please note:

1 Each of these characters is actually a word which is different in writing and in meaning.

2 The sound "ma" is just one example. Any tone of any sound may also represent a number of different characters in writing and in meaning.

Chinese Characters Have Only 432 Han-yu Sounds

The author has grouped them into 26 tables

- Each alphabetical table gives a number of examples of Chinese characters accompanied by their HYPY letters respectively.
- Only one character example is given for each tone of a sound.
- Each character is denoted by its tone directly above it.
- Some places are marked by a "○" which means that there exists no word under that tone of that sound.

Only 5 Letters Pronounce Differently From English

j = jyee° (鸡°)
(tongue tip curles down, pushing the inside of the lower front teeth)

4 tones	ˉ ´ ˇ `	4 tones	ˉ ´ ˇ `	4 tones	ˉ ´ ˇ `
ji	雞级幾季	jie	接节姐借	jü	居局举句
jia	加夹假价	jin	今○紧近	jüan	捐○卷眷
jian	尖○剪见	jing	京○井敬	jüe	嗟绝蹶倔
jiang	江○讲降	jiu	纠○九旧	jün	君○○菌
jiao	交嚼脚叫	jong	坰○窘○		

q = chyee° (七°)
(tongue tip curles down, pushing the inside of the lower front teeth)

4 tones	ˉ ´ ˇ `	4 tones	ˉ ´ ˇ `	4 tones	ˉ ´ ˇ `
qi	七奇起氣	qie	切茄且妾	qü	区渠取去
qia	掐○卡恰	qin	亲琴寝撽	qüan	圈全犬劝
qian	千钱浅欠	qing	清情请庆	qüe	缺瘸○却
qiang	枪强抢呛	qiong	芎穷颍○	qün	竣群○○
qiao	敲桥巧翘	qiu	秋球糗○		

X = syee° (西°)
(tongue tip curls down, pushing the inside of the lower front teeth)

4 tones	— ´ ˇ `	4 tones	— ´ ˇ `	4 tones	— ´ ˇ `
xi	西习洗细	xie	些协写谢	xiu	休〇朽秀
xia	虾侠〇下	xin	心枕伈信	xü	需徐许序
xian	先咸险现	★**xing**	兴行醒幸	xüan	宣玄选炫
xiang	香祥想象	See Table "**h**" ★		xüe	薛学雪穴
xiao	消郁小笑	xiong	凶雄〇复	xün	熏巡〇训

C = tsz° (疵°) (position tongue as you would for "wants")

4 tones	— ´ ˇ `	4 tones	— ´ ˇ `	4 tones	— ´ ˇ `
ca	擦〇礤嚓	cen	參岑〇〇	cuan	汆攒〇篡
cai	猜财踩菜	ceng	噌层〇蹭	cui	摧〇璀脆
can	餐残惨灿	**ci**	疵辞此次	cun	村存忖寸
cang	苍藏〇〇	cong	聪从〇樅	·cuo	搓瘥瑳错
cao	操槽草夲	cou	〇〇〇凑		
ce	〇〇〇册	cu	粗殂〇醋		

zh = jr° (知°) (tongue position as you say "Joe")

4 tones	— ´ ˇ `	4 tones	— ´ ˇ `	4 tones	— ´ ˇ `
zha	渣炸眨诈	zhen	真〇枕震	zhuai	拽〇跩〇
zhai	摘宅窄债	zheng	蒸〇整正	zhuan	专〇转赚
zhan	詹〇展站	**zhi**	知姪纸至	zhuang	庄〇奘壮
zhang	张〇长涨	zhong	中〇种众	zhui	追〇〇缀
zhao	招着找照	zhou	周轴肘咒	zhuo	桌镯〇〇
zhe	着° 遮折者这	zhu	猪竹主住	zhun	谆〇准稕
zhei	〇〇〇这	zhua	抓〇爪〇		

Speak Chinese Fluently Before Learning the Characters

Consonants Are Not Complete Sounds
[O] is the *pronunciation* of the consonant
Significant sounds are only produced when
these consonants are combined with vowel sounds.

The Remaining 18 Consonants
(Pronounced as they are in English)

m = m°

4 tones — ˊ ˇ ˋ		4 tones — ˊ ˇ ˋ		4 tones — ˊ ˇ ˋ	
ma	吗°妈麻马骂	men	闷门○闷	ming	○名酩命
mai	○埋买卖	meng	蒙蒙猛梦	miu	哂○○谬
man	○馒满慢	mi	咪迷米密	mo	麽°摸魔抹墨
mang	○忙蟒○	mian	○棉免面	mou	哞谋某○
mao	猫毛卯帽	miao	喵苗秒庙	mu	○模母木
me	麽°○○○○	mie	咩○○灭		
mei	○眉美妹	min	○民敏○		

n = n°

4 tones — ˊ ˇ ˋ		4 tones — ˊ ˇ ˋ		4 tones — ˊ ˇ ˋ	
na	哪°那拿哪那	neng	○能○泞	niu	妞牛扭拗
nai	○○奶耐	ni	○泥你腻	nong	○农○弄
nan	囡男赧难	nian	蔫年碾念	nou	○○○耨
nang	囔囊曩齉	niang	○娘○酿	nu	○奴努怒
nao	猱挠脑闹	niao	○○鸟尿	nuan	○○暖○
ne	呢°○○○○	nie	捏茶○孽	nuo	○挪○糯
nei	○○馁那	nin	○您抷○	nü	○○女衄
nen	○○○嫩	ning	○宁拧佞	nüe	○○○虐

p = pº

4 tones	ー ́ ̌ ̀	4 tones	ー ́ ̌ ̀	4 tones	ー ́ ̌ ̀
pa	趴爬〇怕	pen	喷盆翸喷	pin	拼贫品聘
pai	拍牌排派	peng	烹朋捧碰	ping	乒平〇〇
pan	潘盘〇判	pi	批皮匹屁	po	坡婆颇破
pang	乓旁嗙胖	pian	偏胼諞片	pou	剖抔剖〇
pao	抛袍跑泡	piao	飘嫖漂票	pu	扑葡普铺
pei	呸陪培佩	pie	瞥〇撇		

b = bº

4 tones	ー ́ ̌ ̀	4 tones	ー ́ ̌ ̀	4 tones	ー ́ ̌ ̀
ba	吧º八拔把爸	ben	奔〇本笨	bin	宾〇〇殡
bai	掰白百拜	beng	崩甭绷蹦	bing	冰〇饼并
ban	般〇板半	bi	逼鼻比必	bo	卜玻伯跛薄
bang	邦〇榜棒	bian	边〇匾变	bu	晡不补布
bao	包薄保报	biao	标〇表鳔		
bei	杯〇北被	bie	鳖别瘪彆		

k = kº

4 tones	ー ́ ̌ ̀	4 tones	ー ́ ̌ ̀	4 tones	ー ́ ̌ ̀
ka	咖〇卡〇	ken	〇〇肯硍	kuai	喎〇蒯快
kai	开〇凯忾	keng	坑〇挳〇	kuan	宽〇款〇
kan	刊〇砍看	kong	空〇孔控	kuang	匡狂诓框
kang	康扛忼抗	kou	抠〇口扣	kui	虧葵傀溃
kao	尻〇考靠	ku	哭〇苦裤	kun	昆〇捆困
ke	科咳渴客	kua	誇〇垮跨	kuo	〇〇〇阔

d = d°

4 tones	— ´ ˇ `	4 tones	— ´ ˇ `	4 tones	— ´ ˇ `
da	搭答打大	deng	灯○等邓	dong	东○董洞
dai	呆○歹代	di	的° 低敌底弟	dou	兜○斗豆
dan	单○胆蛋	dian	颠○点电	du	督独赌度
dang	当○党荡	diao	雕○屌掉	duan	端○短段
dao	刀○倒到	die	爹碟○○	dui	堆○○对
de	得°○德○○	ding	钉○顶定	dun	敦○吨炖
dei	○○得○	diu	丢○○○	duo	多夺躲舵

f = f°

4 tones	— ´ ˇ `	4 tones	— ´ ˇ `	4 tones	— ´ ˇ `
fa	发罚发法	fei	飞肥匪费	fo	○佛○○
fan	翻烦反饭	fen	芬坟粉奋	fou	○罘否○
fang	方房访放	feng	风缝讽凤	fu	夫福腐父

g = g°

4 tones	— ´ ˇ `	4 tones	— ´ ˇ `	4 tones	— ´ ˇ `
ga	旮噶玍尬	gen	跟哏○艮	guan	官○管惯
gai	该○改盖	geng	耕○梗更	guang	光○广逛
gan	干○赶幹	gong	公○巩共	gui	规○鬼贵
gang	钢○港杠	gou	勾○狗购	gun	○○滚棍
gao	高○稿告	gu	姑骨古故	guo	锅国果过
ge	哥格葛各	gua	瓜○寡挂		
gei	○○给○	guai	乖○拐怪		

h = h°

4 tones	ー ′ ˇ `	4 tones	ー ′ ˇ `	4 tones	ー ′ ˇ `
ha	哈蛤○○	hen	○痕很恨	huan	欢环缓换
hai	咳孩海害	heng	亨恒○横	huang	慌黄谎晃
han	酣含喊汗	hong	轰红哄哄	hui	灰回毁会
★ hang	夯行○沆	hou	齁喉吼厚	hun	婚魂混浑
hao	蒿豪好号	hu	忽胡虎户	huo	劐活火货
he	喝河○贺	hua	花华○化		
hei	黑○黑○	huai	○怀○坏	See Table "**X**" ★	

Some characters have more than one pronunciation, and the meanings are usually totally different. Please look at the "hang" group characters in the "left column" of the "h" table: The "2nd tone" word "行" means "a company" or "a business firm", while the same "行" word pronounces "xing" in the "x" table (P.613) which means "walk".

It's just like the English words: "wind" (a watch) and "wind" (breeze) are different in pronunciation and meaning.

ch = ch° (吃°) (tongue position as you say "**Charch**")

4 tones	ー ′ ˇ `	4 tones	ー ′ ˇ `	4 tones	ー ′ ˇ `
cha	叉茶踏差	cheng	称成逞秤	chuan	穿船喘串
chai	拆柴○虿	chi	吃池尺赤	chuang	窗床闯创
chan	搀蝉产忏	chong	充虫宠衝	chui	吹垂○炊
chang	昌长厂唱	chou	抽酬丑臭	chun	春唇蠢○
chao	抄潮吵耖	chu	出厨楚处	chuo	戳○○绰
che	车○扯撤	chua	欻○○○		
chen	嗔晨碜趁	chuai	搋膗揣踹		

r = r° (日°)

(pronounce this sound as you do "r", **except** the tip of the tongue is raised up almost touching the hard palate with a light force)

4 tones	— ˊ ˇ ˋ	4 tones	— ˊ ˇ ˋ	4 tones	— ˊ ˇ ˋ
ran	○然染○	reng	扔仍扔○	ruan	○壖软○
rang	○攘壤让	ri	○○○日	rui	○蕤蕊瑞
rao	○饶扰绕	rong	○容冗○	run	○犉○润
re	○○惹热	rou	○揉糅肉	ruo	○挼○弱
ren	○人忍任	ru	○儒乳入		

S = s°

4 tones	— ˊ ˇ ˋ	4 tones	— ˊ ˇ ˋ	4 tones	— ˊ ˇ ˋ
sa	撒○洒萨	sei	塞○○○	su	苏俗○素
sai	鳃○○赛	sen	森○○○	suan	酸○○算
san	三○伞散	seng	僧○○○	sui	虽随髓岁
sang	桑○嗓丧	si	思○死四	sun	孙○损潠
sao	搔○扫臊	song	松○怂宋	suo	缩○锁逤
se	○○○色	sou	搜○叟嗽		

sh = sh° (師°)

4 tones	— ˊ ˇ ˋ	4 tones	— ˊ ˇ ˋ	4 tones	— ˊ ˇ ˋ
sha	沙啥傻煞	shen	深神沉慎	shuan	栓○○涮
shai	筛○骰晒	sheng	声绳省圣	shuang	双○爽灀
shan	山○闪扇	shi	失十使是	shui	○谁水睡
shang	伤○赏上	shou	收熟手受	shun	○○吮顺
shao	烧勺少绍	shu	书熟鼠树	shuo	说○○硕
she	奢蛇舍设	shua	刷○耍○		
shei	○谁○○	shuai	衰○甩帅		

Z = z° (資°)

4 tones	— ´ ˇ `	4 tones	— ´ ˇ `	4 tones	— ´ ˇ `
za	扎杂〇〇	zei	〇贼〇〇	zu	租足组〇
zai	灾〇宰在	zen	〇〇怎潛	zuan	躜〇缵钻
zan	簪咱攒赞	zeng	增〇〇赠	zui	〇〇嘴最
zang	脏〇驵葬	zi	资〇子字	zuo	〇昨左做
zao	糟凿早造	zong	宗〇总纵	zun	尊〇撙焞
ze	〇则怎仄	zou	邹〇走揍		

l = l° (醯°)

This symbol character 醯 does not exist in written Chinese. It represents the English "L" tongue-sound, which has no Chinese equivalent. The author has invented this character as an illustrated instruction for the Chinese speaker to produce this sound.   The left part of the character indicates the tongue to be positioned touching the roof of the mouth behind the top front teeth. The right part represents complete sound.

4 tones	— ´ ˇ `	4 tones	— ´ ˇ `	4 tones	— ´ ˇ `
la	啦°拉兎喇辣	lia	〇〇俩〇	lou	搂楼篓漏
lai	〇来〇赖	lian	〇连脸练	lu	噜炉鲁路
lan	〇兰览烂	liang	〇凉两亮	luan	〇峦卵乱
lang	啷狼朗浪	liao	撩聊了料	lun	抡轮稐论
lao	捞牢老烙	lie	咧〇咧猎	luo	啰罗裸洛
le	了°〇〇〇乐	lin	〇林凛吝	lü	〇驴吕绿
lei	勒雷磊累	ling	拎零领令	lüan	〇李娈〇
leng	〇楞冷愣	liu	溜刘柳六	lüe	〇〇〇略
li	哩离李立	long	〇龙拢挵	lün	〇淋〇〇

t = t °

4 tones	— ˊ ˇ ˋ	4 tones	— ˊ ˇ ˋ	4 tones	— ˊ ˇ ˋ
ta	他〇塔踏	teng	〇疼〇〇	tou	偷头娃透
tai	胎抬〇太	ti	踢提体替	tu	秃图土兔
tan	贪谈坦炭	tian	天甜舔瑱	tuan	湍团〇彖
tang	汤糖躺烫	tiao	挑调窕跳	tui	推颓腿退
tao	掏逃讨套	tie	贴〇铁帖	tun	吞屯吨褪
te	〇〇〇特	ting	听停挺听	tuo	脱驼妥拓
tei	忒〇〇〇	tong	通同统痛		

W = w °

4 tones	— ˊ ˇ ˋ	4 tones	— ˊ ˇ ˋ	4 tones	— ˊ ˇ ˋ
wa	挖娃瓦袜	wang	汪王往忘	weng	翁〇蓊甕
wai	歪〇舀外	wei	威为委位	wo	窝〇我握
wan	湾完晚万	wen	温文吻问	wu	屋无五勿

y = y °

4 tones	— ˊ ˇ ˋ	4 tones	— ˊ ˇ ˋ	4 tones	— ˊ ˇ ˋ
ya	呀°呀牙哑讶	yi	一宜以意	yü	瘀鱼雨玉
yai	〇崖〇〇	yin	因银引印	yüan	冤元远願
yan	烟言眼燕	ying	英营影硬	yüe	约〇〇月
yang	央羊养样	yo	唷〇〇〇	yün	晕云允运
yao	腰摇咬要	yong	庸嵱永用		
ye	耶爷也夜	you	优由有又		

The Six Vowel Sounds
3 Sounds Have No words

a = [a] in (fox)

4 tones	— ˊ ˇ ˋ	4 tones	— ˊ ˇ ˋ	4 tones	— ˊ ˇ ˋ
a	啊° 阿 嘎 啊 鋼	an	安 嘻 唵 案	ao	凹 敖 襖 澳
ai	哀 捱 矮 愛	ang	骯 昂 軮 盎		

e = [a] in (ago)

4 tones	— ˊ ˇ ˋ	4 tones	— ˊ ˇ ˋ	4 tones	— ˊ ˇ ˋ
e	婀 鵝 惡 餓	en	恩 ○○ 摁	er	儿 兒 耳 二
ei	欸 欸 欸 欸	eng	鞥 ○○○	-r	儿° ○○○○

o = [u] in (up)

4 tones	— ˊ ˇ ˋ	4 tones	— ˊ ˇ ˋ	4 tones	— ˊ ˇ ˋ
o	喔 哦 ○○	ong	○○○○	ou	欧 吽 藕 嘔

i = [i] in (fee)

No Chinese character under this vowel sound.

u = [u] in (too)   **ü** = [ü] in (yü)

No Chinese character under these 2 vowel sounds.

★ From Marco Liang, Getting Around in Chinese: (New York: Marco Liang & Company, 2005), pp. 47-70, quoted with permission of the publisher.

ONE OF THE KEY OBJECTIVES OF THIS BOOK IS
TO INTRUDUCE THE READERS TO CHINESE CHARACTERS
(WORDS), THEIR PRONUNCIATIONS AND THEIR MEANINGS.
THE METHOD OF USING THESE CHARACTERS
IN A LITERARY MANNER
IS GIVEN FROM TIME TO TIME IN THIS BOOK.

SOME PARTICULAR CASES

ONE

Two "3rd-tones" Never Meet.

e.g.:　❶ (总统 **zǒng tǒng**)　　the president
　　　❷ (顶好 **dǐng hǎo**)　　the best
　　　❸ (永远 **yǒng yüǎn**)　　forever
The "first" characters" must be changed to a "2nd tone".
It comes out like:　❶ (总统 **zóng tǒng**)
　　　　　　　　❷ (顶好 **díng hǎo**)
　　　　　　　　❸ (永远 **yóng yüǎn**).

TWO

Special cases of "3rd-tone characterss".

★ hǎo hāor-de dá-sao dá-sao (好好儿地打扫打扫) Clean it up thoroughly.
★ chuān-de nuǎn nuānr-de (穿得暖暖儿地)　　Wear your clothes warmly.
★ huà-ge xiǎo xiāor-de diǎn-zi (画个小小儿的点子) Draw a tiny little dot.
★ bù máng, màn mānr lái (不忙. 慢慢来)　　No hurry. Take your time.

THREE

Non-stressed Sounds

In order to avoid errors during Pīnyīn, the author has adopted the
following method to better indicate the non-stressed sound by using
a hyphenated smaller typeface size and with "no tone indicator" to
reflect the 2nd character less stressed.
　　For Example: husband　丈夫　"zhàng-fu"
　　　　　　　　　Son　　　儿子　"ér-zi"
　　　　　　　　　Brother　哥哥　"gē-ge"
　　　　　　　　　Fine!　　好吧！　"hǎo-ba! "

Chinese → English   English → Chinese
DICTIONARY

辭源
cí   yüán

INDEX

A

C

G

H

I

J

K

L

M

N

O

P

R

索引

INDEX

God's sake, I love you. It has nothing to do with duty. I want to be with you. I want to take care of you. We've wasted so much time, please don't let us squander what we have left. Marry me, Gina?'

Her heart felt as though it were bursting. She didn't deserve him, not after the way she'd treated him.

He cupped her chin in his hand, forcing her to look up into his face. 'Marry me?'

Slowly she nodded and then he kissed her gently on the lips.

'But I still don't feel as though I'm being fair.'

'All's fair in love and war, Gina, and as you and I are no longer at war, I'm the one who will decide if it's fair, and I've made up my mind that you will be Mrs Edward Vinetti.'

She smiled. 'But what will you do? The theatre is your life.'

'Not any more. I was leaving anyway, remember, and besides how could I go back to that? It would all seem so empty and useless.'

She was a little more composed now. Calmness and, in a strange way, relief and contentment filled her. 'What will you do?' she persisted. 'I don't want you to feel bound to play nursemaid.'

He leaned back against the cushions, drawing her head against his chest. 'I'd not thought. It's all happened so fast.' He fell silent and she lay in the crook of his arm, listening to the steady beat of his heart.

'What kind of a farmer do you think I'd make?' he asked.

A smile crossed her face. 'Are you serious?'

'Of course. I think I'd enjoy it and they say hard

labour is good for the soul. It could be my salvation.'

'Oh, Edward, you can't even ride a horse.' There wasn't a trace of mockery in her voice.

'I could learn.'

'You mean buy a farm of our own?'

'I was thinking more along the lines of throwing in my lot with Matty and Richard, if they'll have me. I could suggest that I buy my way into some sort of partnership.'

Edward was doing this for her sake, she knew, and she tightened her arms around his chest. 'I'm not the ideal person for a farmer's wife, am I? I could give the occasional performance. Sing in the choir or at a wedding or two.'

'You could, so long as it doesn't tire you, but there's no need.'

'I'd like to.'

'So, do you think they'd have me?'

'I think they'd be delighted. They'll be able to expand and buy more land and machinery. They'll hire more men and before you know where you are you'll be three "Gentleman Farmers" owning half the county. They may even have you out with the Tipperary Hunt.' She fought to keep her tone light.

'Then it's settled. I know it may sound insensitive of me to ask this right now, but what about the wedding?'

'It can't be right away, not with Ma . . .' The tears brimmed up again and the lump in her throat choked off her words.

'I know that, but I'm sure the priest will understand when we explain and arrange a dispensation or whatever is necessary.' He kissed the tip of her nose. 'And I'll have to go to confession for the first time in decades and hope they haven't excommunicated me by now. Oh, Gina O'Donnell, the tortures you're putting me through.' He wiped away the tears from her cheek with the tip of his finger and smiled in his old, half-cynical way.

She caught his hand and held it against her cheek. She was so lucky to have him. Despite the sorrow, she felt as though some of her old spirit had returned. 'I'm not giving in to it, Edward, I'm not going to become an invalid overnight!'

He laughed. 'That sounds more like you. I've a feeling that you are going to make a very unsatisfactory patient, but I'll let Doctor Byrne worry about that!'

Chapter Twenty-Eight

———•✦•———

EILEEN AND LESTER SINCLAIR had announced their
engagement and Bridget had put on a small family
party for them. She'd invited his parents and two sisters,
Archie and Bernie and two of the girls from Craig's that
Eileen was very friendly with.

The Sinclairs were nice people and everyone liked
Lester. Bridget was glad, for Eileen deserved a good man.
Bridget had promised to bear the full cost of a splendid
traditional wedding and had given the couple a good
deposit for a home of their own. So as not to injure
Archie's pride, she had agreed when he insisted on paying
for the drink, a far from small contribution since all of
Craig's and most of Dixon's Blazes appeared to have been
invited. They had all laughed when Bernie had said what
a pity it was that baby Louisa Bernadette Dalrymple
couldn't be bridesmaid, and she hoped that all Archie's
cronies would behave themselves, otherwise the whole
thing would end up a right stramash altogether, and she
wasn't having Eileen's day ruined, and Bridget's money
wasted, by a crowd of Scots-Irish drunks.

'Michael, will you see that Mr Sinclair has his glass refilled before you make your speech,' Bridget whispered, keeping an eagle-eye on her guests' comfort.

'Do I have to make a speech? It's really Archie's place, not mine. She's his sister.'

'Oh, you know Archie. He's grand on speeches about workers' rights, but when it comes to something like this he gets all embarrassed and tongue-tied. And anyway, you promised.'

'Oh, very well. You know you're getting to be a very domineering woman, Bridget O'Donnell,' he laughed.

'It's probably got something to do with my job,' she teased. They were so at ease with one another now, she thought. There was an understanding between them, although no words, no promises and no questions had been uttered. 'Is everyone here?'

'Everyone except Alizon from Craig's.'

Bridget's gaze swept the room. She nodded. 'She should be here any minute now. She's always late. Eileen says she will be late for her own funeral. We'll have to wait for her.'

'Not any longer,' he answered, as the doorbell rang.

'Don't you be thinking you're escaping! I'll go.'

Bridget pulled open the front door. 'Alizon MacLean, we're all waiting on you. Oh . . .' Her voice trailed off as she saw the boy on the bicycle.

'Miss O'Donnell?'

She nodded and he handed her the envelope. She went cold; telegrams were always such harbingers of bad news. She slipped into the morning room to open it.

She was still standing there, staring into space, her face white, when Michael came looking for her.

'Bridget?' He saw the piece of paper in her hand and took it from her. Then he took her in his arms.

'Why can't I cry, Michael? Why can't I cry?' she said in a strangled voice.

'It's the shock. The tears will come later.'

She looked up at him. Theirs was a love that had needed no words; words could be false and empty. Nor did they need constantly to reassure each other. There was no need to shout their feelings from the rooftops; they were kindred spirits. 'Will we go home, Michael?' was all she said.

He nodded slowly. He loved her deeply with a love that had matured and developed ever since that first night when they'd sat up and talked. That night she had set in motion the healing process that was gradually obliterating the deep scars of guilt. She'd offered him peace and stability and for the first time in years, happiness.

'Home for good, Bridget?'

'Yes.'

'What about all this? Your job – you've worked so hard?'

'None of that matters now, Michael. I've proved to myself that I could realize my dreams. I wish she could have come here, to have seen everything I've done. Oh, Michael, I do love you.' She leaned her cheek against his shoulder.

'Then we'll go home and we'll be married.' It was a statement made in a firm, quiet voice. It was time – time to put his feelings of trepidation aside, and time to think of Bridget and of building a new life together. For her he'd be prepared to face his fears. Fears that would probably always be with him. His love for her would help him. She was worth it.

Mary-Kate dropped her head in her hands. Oh, Ma! Why hadn't Matty said she was ill? Why hadn't he sent for her sooner? She'd planned to take Ellen and Jamie home this summer, but Sarah would never see her grandson now. The pain in her heart grew unbearable. Oh, there were so many things that had remained unsaid. Of them all, she had been closest to Sarah, but she had put off the visit and for what? Business, money, contracts. What were they beside the loss she now felt? Nothing. They didn't matter at all. They should never have mattered. Sarah had come to her when Lewis had died. She'd comforted her, but Mary-Kate hadn't been there to hold Sarah's hand at the end. Life had been good to her. God had been good to her, despite the loss of Lewis. But now the world was a bleak and bitter place and she had been left without the one person who understood her most. Left to cope with her grief, her loss and her guilt.

She felt a hand on her shoulder and lifted her head.

Ellen was standing beside her. 'Why are you crying, Ma?'

'It's my . . . your Grandma, Ellen. She died last night.'

Ellen stared directly at her. She had seen so much of death in her short life. Her mother, her baby brother, her Pa and now the grandmother she had grown to love and to whom she had written every week. Why was it that as

547

soon as you learned to love someone, God snatched them away from you? She reached out for Mary-Kate's hand. 'Will you be going home, Ma?'

Mary-Kate nodded. 'Yes, Ellen, we're all going home.'

There had been no traditional wake. Mary-Kate and Bridget had vehemently over-ruled Matty and Uncle Richard on that, because of Gina's condition. Bridget, nerves taut with grief, had stormed that she didn't care if everyone from here to Waterford talked about them, there would be no wake. So Sarah had been buried on the 21st February, on a damp, grey depressing morning. But the weather had not deterred half the town from turning out and the family had all been deeply touched by the gesture. The hard, frozen earth had been freshly dug. The grave-diggers had leaned on their shovels, caps respectfully in their hands, while Father Maguire had committed Sarah's body to the ground. On the white marble headstone that bore the names of their father and their elder brother, another name had already been added.

'Sarah Margaret O'Donnell
Wife of Patrick and
mother of Fergal
God Rest her Soul'

Mary-Kate, with Ellen at her side and her son in her arms, had watched with the calm composure that was so characteristic of her. Her time of weeping for Sarah was over, but the pain would always remain. Her mother's death had allowed her to come and find a brief period of happiness 'across the water' in Ireland. So near yet so far. But she had her son and Ellen and her memories, together with the promise she'd made, that for the rest of her life she would try to be as good a mother to them as Sarah had been to her. And Mary-Kate never broke a promise.

Gina's head had rested against Edward's shoulder, his arm firmly around her waist. It had taken her own illness and her mother's death to make her realize just what were the most precious things in life. Not fame or money. Not adulation or power. But there hadn't been time to tell Sarah that. Gina had accepted her fate now, thankful that she had been given the gifts of love and happiness – for a little while.

She had glanced at her younger sister. Bridget had got what she wanted from life, but she'd suffered and changed during the process and Gina's mind had gone back to that day – that April day so long ago – when they'd all stood here and Michael Feehey and his cronies had taunted them. He'd changed, too, she'd thought. His own parents were buried in that churchyard.

Edward had remembered that fine, sunny day when he'd first seen Clonmel. The few weeks he had spent here had been the happiest in his life, except for the bitter-sweet time that he and Gina had left. He grieved for Sarah but he knew she would have approved of their forthcoming marriage. Just how he would cope in the days that lay ahead he didn't know, but he'd make Gina happy and he'd pray for the courage to keep going. Silently he had thanked Sarah for the priceless legacy she'd left him.

Bridget had remembered her mother as she had been

the last time she'd seen her, at Mary-Kate's wedding, and she'd wished that she hadn't rushed straight back to Glasgow after Lewis Vannin had died, thereby missing seeing Sarah. She'd remembered how at the wedding she had been so ashamed of her shabby clothes and her poor job, and she wished that Sarah could have lived to see how she had put all that behind her and to have given her blessing to her marriage to Michael. Bridget had squeezed his hand, knowing that he, too, would be remembering.

He had, but not with a sorrow that was born only of love and loss. His sorrow was born of guilt and remorse. He hadn't even been there when they had buried his parents. He'd been hiding; skulking in the wild bog and bracken of the Comeraghs. He thought that time had healed those scars, but standing there in the churchyard had re-opened the wounds. The tightening of Bridget's hand in his reminded him that no amount of torturing himself would bring them back, or remove the fear of his former comrades' fanatical threats against him.

Matty's heart had been heavy. He hadn't been able to take it in that Sarah had gone. That she'd never again be waiting when he came in tired and cold from the fields, a hot meal on the table, a welcoming fire in the range and the unfailing admonition, 'Get those clumping great boots off my clean floor, Matty O'Donnell. This is my kitchen, not a shebeen.' Now it would be Gina's kitchen, but he was still struggling with the fact that his beautiful, talented sister would probably never see the red and gold leaves of the trees that bordered the churchyard flutter to the ground in autumn.

*

The following day could have been a day in April, so different was it from the day before. Winters in the south-east of Ireland were often damp and mild, with occasional days that were almost like spring. The sky was pale blue with not a cloud in sight and the sun was warm on their faces as they sat in a corner of the yard, where for the past four years Sarah had planted geraniums, marigolds and sweet, night-scented stock.

It was so mild that everyone had agreed it would benefit Gina to be out in the fresh air and she sat, with rugs tucked around her, between her two sisters. Of the men there was no sign. They had all gone off to look at some land that was up for sale out towards Ballyboe, after having stayed up half the night listening to Edward's proposal that he buy his way into a partnership with them and turn his hand to farming.

'So, Edward is to become a farmer then?' Mary-Kate sounded faintly amused.

'He's going to try,' Gina answered.

'Those two were quick enough to accept his offer, so they must have some faith in him or his money. But why Michael has gone as well I don't know.' Bridget sounded a little put out.

'Perhaps it was to give us some time alone, or maybe he feels a little unsure of himself and other people's attitude to him,' Mary-Kate suggested.

'You may be right but he shouldn't be unsure now. He never committed a crime, no matter what some people will think and besides, everyone is trying to forget. Trying to build a new life out of the ruins of the old.'

Mary-Kate sighed. 'There are some who will neither forgive nor forget.'

'I know, but Matty said they've nearly all gone – either fled or imprisoned – and we've nothing to fear from them now.' Bridget paused. 'I'm going to instruct Mr Prebble to sell all my stocks and shares and the house in Cartland Drive. Eileen is staying with Bernie until the wedding.'

'So, you've come home for good, too?' Mary-Kate sounded wistful.

'Yes, we talked about it on the journey. We're going to open a shop in Clonmel, a very small department store and we're going to be married.' She reached out and took Gina's hand. For Gina's sake, too, they had come home to stay. She wanted to spend all the time she could – all the time there was left – with Gina. And she wanted to make that time as happy as was humanly possible. 'But I won't steal your glory, Gina. You must be married first. I'll never forgive myself for walking out of your party. Never.'

'Oh, Bridget, don't be an eejit. It was a terrible party and I was acting disgracefully and besides, how were you to know that I was ill?'

At the mention of her condition, it was as though a small cloud had crossed the face of the sun, until Gina smiled again. 'There will be no more talk of "stealing anyone's glory". We'll be married on the same day at a double wedding – here at Kilsheelan, where Ma and Pa were married. It will be the first double wedding at St Mary's and I won't hear a single word of objection, not at all! Haven't we always been different from everyone else? Haven't we always done things in style? Haven't we all achieved what we set out to do? What was it I said to Michael?'

'Rich and famous or both,' Bridget reminded her laughingly.

'And between us all we managed it, one way or another,' Mary-Kate reflected.

'So it will be a double wedding,' Gina persisted.

'If that's what you want.'

'I do, so that's settled.'

'And when will it be?' Mary-Kate asked.

'Just as soon as we can get a dispensation and get things arranged. You will stay on, won't you?'

Mary-Kate smiled at Gina. 'Of course I will. The business will survive without me for a while and besides, I couldn't miss the event of the year now could I? Sure, they'll come from miles around, you see if they don't. The famous Miss Gina O'Donnell and the wealthy Miss Bridget O'Donnell. You'll be the talk of the place for months.'

Mary-Kate glanced out of the bedroom window. 'I don't think it's going to rain after all, there's a patch of bright sky over towards the river.'

The room was in complete disorder with clothes and boxes, small parcels and tissue paper on every available surface. Bridget and Gina were to be married at ten o'clock that morning and everyone, except Gina, had been up for hours. Mary-Kate turned around and surveyed the scene, shaking her head. It was just like the old days in Anne Street, before they had left Ireland. She herself was ready, dressed in a silver grey, long sleeved two-piece. The skirt was plain and almost straight as was the jacket, which ended just on the hipline. The top was fastened down the left side with black velvet frogging and the cuffs were trimmed with black. On the bed, grouped neatly together, were the silver-grey toque hat with its cluster of black feathers and her bag and gloves. Her expression softened as she watched Gina, seated before the dressing table, carefully applying just the slightest touch of rouge to her pale cheeks, while Bridget searched amongst the discarded boxes and tissue on the bed for her shoes.

She found one. 'Oh, just look at this mess. Where has the other one gone? I could have sworn I'd kept them in the box.'

'It's beside Gina's hat and you're right, this is a nice mess. The only consolation is that probably Matty's and Uncle Richard's rooms are in the same state.'

'Has Matty gone yet? He was supposed to be at Hearn's Hotel at a quarter past nine,' Gina said, hair brush halted in mid-stroke. As there was no one in Clonmel that Edward knew well enough, Matty was to be his best man. Uncle Richard was giving them both away.

'Stop fretting, he's gone.'

'Oh, I just hope Michael hasn't a hangover. Dinny MacGee isn't exactly a person who thinks in terms of moderation,' Bridget muttered.

'I hope none of them are feeling under the weather. I don't know what time it was when Matty and Uncle Richard got home last night, but they made enough noise trying to be quiet and Uncle Richard looked a bit sheepish early this morning,' Mary-Kate remarked.

All the male members of the wedding party had gone to Mulcahy's Bar the previous evening at the suggestion of Dinny MacGee, who was to be Michael's best man. He and Michael had quickly resumed their old friendship and Dinny was now a married man himself although, as Bridget remarked, Mary Kennedy didn't seem to have had much of a restraining influence on him.

'How do you feel?' Mary-Kate asked, taking the hair-brush from Gina and giving the shiny Titian waves a last brush, before placing the small, lilac cloche hat over them. As they were still in mourning, their choice of colours had been very limited. Bridget and Ellen had accompanied Mary-Kate to Dublin to buy all their outfits, including Gina's, and Mrs O'Leary had been most helpful with alterations and trimmings. Lilac suited Gina. She'd insisted that white would make her look ghastly, and she had been delighted with Bridget's idea of the cape.

Her dress was of crêpe de chine with a bias cut skirt and long sleeves. A small bunch of white artificial flowers – supplied by Mrs O'Leary – had been added at the high neckline. But the material was too flimsy to be worn in early March and so Bridget had bought yards of lilac wool crepon in the same shade and Mrs O'Leary had run up the cape to Bridget's design. Mary-Kate had unpicked the rows of pearl beading from one of Gina's evening gowns and had sewn this around the border. It had been a labour of love on her part and the loose, flowing garment that resembled an evening cloak, now lay on the bed.

'I feel nervous, that's how I feel. Not sickly nervous, just excitedly nervous,' Gina replied, smiling at Mary-Kate in the mirror. 'I haven't over done the rouge, have I?'

'No, you look beautiful. You both look beautiful.'

'I knew I should have let Celia Delaney trim my

hair, this hat just won't sit right!' Bridget was struggling with the small-brimmed white straw with its large white satin bow. 'Oh, I'm so nervous, I'm all fingers and thumbs.'

'Sit down and let me try.' Mary-Kate moved calmly from Gina to her youngest sister and began to smooth down the thick, auburn hair before placing the hat at just the right angle and securing it with a pearl-topped hat pin. 'You'll freeze in that dress, Bridget. Oh, I know you fell in love with it straight away and it's not needed to have a single alteration, but I did warn you that it was more suitable for summer. You're shivering already.'

'But not with cold.' Bridget smoothed down the white lace skirt. She'd chosen lace over heavy white satin, but the sleeves were unlined and her arms were covered only by the flimsy lace.

Ellen poked her head around the door. 'Ma, there's a woman downstairs asking to see Aunt Bridget.'

'Oh, not Mrs Butler-Power again! Ellen, tell her I can't see her, tell her anything,' Bridget cried.

Just as Mary-Kate had predicted, word of their weddings had soon got around and they had all been surprised by the gifts and tokens they had received. Mrs O'Leary – who was finally to become the second Mrs Ryan in May – had been most helpful, for Bridget and Michael were to buy her shop and the grocery next door. They were going to live above the premises, but until Mrs O'Leary had moved out they were renting a small house she had found for them down near the Quays. This arrangement had almost caused open warfare to break out between Mrs O'Leary and Mrs Butler-Power, who had no intention of being left out of the event which was becoming the talk of half the county. She had been 'dropping in' with increasing regularity in an attempt to become involved and therefore to gain first-hand information about what was going on. This was mainly to spite Mrs O'Leary, whom she considered to be a social upstart and quite unworthy of being the wife of a solicitor altogether.

'It's not her. I know *her* well enough by now,' Ellen replied.

'Who is it then?'

'She said to tell Aunt Bridget that she's Mrs Dalrymple's mother.'

Mary-Kate's eyebrows rose.

'Mrs O'Hagan? Bernie's Ma is downstairs?' Bridget sounded stunned.

Ellen nodded. 'Shall I tell her you're not dressed?'

'No. I'll come down.'

'Ellen, is Jamie all right?' Mary-Kate asked.

'Of course he is Ma and he's not even a little bit grubby.'

'I knew I could rely on you, dear, but just make sure you don't get any marks on your dress.'

Ellen raised her eyes to the ceiling and grinned, but secretly she was pleased. She was to be a bridesmaid and Mary-Kate was matron of honour. The plain russet taffeta dress with its dropped waist and softly pleated skirt was the first 'grown up' dress she'd had and, with her hair swept up and circled by a headband of matching material, she felt very much a young lady.

When Bridget entered the kitchen the small, thin woman in the drab dark brown coat looked as though she'd seen a vision. She bit her lip and nervously fiddled with the one button that held the coat fastened. 'Oh, don't you look just like an angel,' she stammered.

'Thank you, Mrs O'Hagan. It was nice of you to call.'

As Bridget extended her hand, she seemed to shrink further into the folds of the old, shabby garment. Awkwardly she rubbed her right hand on the side of the coat before giving Bridget a limp handshake. Then she looked around timorously. 'Sure, I don't think I should have come up here at all.'

'Why not?'

'Well, it's only folk like Mrs O'Leary, grand folk, who should come calling. But I wanted to thank you for my Bernie.' She bit her lip again. 'I wish I had something to give you . . . a Mass Card even, but . . .' She shuffled her feet. 'I just came to wish you good luck and God's Blessing on you. I'll be going now.' She turned away, her eyes fixed on the door as though she expected the Taoiseach himself to come through it at any minute.

'Mrs O'Hagan, don't go yet, please.'

She turned. 'Oh, I wouldn't want to be here when anyone else comes or to be holding up the "dressing up".'

Bridget smiled at this description of the morning's activities. 'We're all ready, and thank you for coming. I do mean that. Bernie is my closest friend and she was very good to me when I needed help.'

Some of the uneasiness left the older woman's face and her shoulders became less rounded. 'She's a fine, grand girl my Bernie, isn't she?' Before Bridget could reply, Mrs O'Hagan looked around and lowered her voice as though they were about to be overheard. 'She wants me to go to see her and stay with her. She said she'll send me the money. Father Maguire reads her letters to me.'

'So when are you going?'

'Oh, I'm not. Himself wouldn't stand for that. Not for me going off on my own all that way and leaving him with no one to see to him.'

Bridget nodded. What Mrs O'Hagan hadn't said was that her idle, useless husband would take any money Bernie sent and drink himself and his tinker friends under the table with it. 'Why don't I ask Bernie to have a photograph taken of herself and baby Louisa Bernadette in the nursery. She could send it to you.'

'Oh, would you do that? Would you really? Oh, isn't it a great thing altogether that a baby can have a room all to itself?'

Mrs O'Hagan was so proud that the expression on her face tugged at Bridget's heart. 'It is and she'll probably come home to see you all one day.'

Mary-Kate came into the room carrying her bag and gloves. 'Mrs O'Hagan, how good of you to call.'

'I just wanted to wish you all well. 'Tis little enough.' The timid, uncomfortable look was back and after waving her hands once in a gesture of nervous agitation she sidled towards the door. 'Well, I won't be keeping you now . . .'

Mary-Kate glanced at Bridget, then she smiled. 'Could you do me a great favour, Mrs O'Hagan?'

'Me? What can I be doing?'

'As Ellen is to be bridesmaid she won't be able to look after my son all the time. Would you look after him in church and see he doesn't start a riot?'

Mrs O'Hagan looked dumbfounded and Bridget looked at her sister as though she'd gone raving mad.

'Oh, I couldn't do that. Not me! Not with everyone from miles around there watchin'. I was just going to try to slip in at the back if there was room.'

'Of course you can do it. Haven't you a wealth of experience with small, unruly children?'

'But . . . but what will people say? We've never been . . . like you.'

'Haven't you the right to be up with the best of them? That house in Glasgow doesn't belong solely to Archie you know. It's half Bernie's too, Bridget tells me. Bernie's a woman of some standing now – a woman of property – and she's your daughter.'

A look of wonderment crept slowly over the pale, pinched face. 'She is that, too. I'd not thought of it like that.'

'Good, then Ellen will hand Jamie over to you. Usually he's not much trouble and then when we come out of church you can pass him back to me.'

'Right then. I'd best be getting down there, hadn't I?'

When she'd gone Bridget turned to Mary-Kate. 'Honestly, you'd find goodness in all the imps of Hell, Mary-Kate.'

'Lewis said something like that once, but God above, she's had such a desperate life, poor soul, that I felt sorry for her.'

'The tongues will be wagging all the way to Cahir and Mrs Butler-Power will be ready to commit murder!'

'Ah, let them talk. The only good thing Mrs O'Hagan has to cling to in her miserable life is the way her Bernie has turned out, and everyone should have something to be proud of. And I really did need someone to look after Jamie,' Mary-Kate added.

Ellen came back into the room. 'Uncle Richard is in the parlour having "a hair of the dog" and Aunt Gina's ready. She's on her way down. Where did you put the flowers, Ma?'

'They're out in the wash house. I hope they haven't wilted. Will you get them Ellen?'

Ellen disappeared and returned almost simultaneously with Gina. She handed the two bouquets of white Madonna lilies that Edward had had sent down from Dublin to Gina and Bridget. There was a spray of roses for Mary-Kate. Her own small posy she placed on the dresser.

'They're beautiful. It was so good of him and they must have cost a small fortune at this time of the year,' Mary-Kate said as Ellen helped her to pin the spray to her dress. 'I think Ma would have approved and she'd have been so proud of you both.'

Bridget swallowed hard. 'I thought it was very thoughtful of you to have chosen her favourite hymns. Sure, Gina can't sing at her own wedding and anyone else would have just murdered *Ave Maria*.' She tried to lift the air of sadness that had descended.

'Yes, everyone can join in with hymns they know well. Ma always said *Hail Queen of Heaven* reminded her of us and our wanderings and that *Sweet Saviour Bless Us* was guaranteed to give you hope and strength,' Mary-Kate said with a tender smile.

As she touched the soft petals of the lilies, Gina remembered the whole of the hymn whose few lines had filled her with fear and despair not so long ago. She sang them softly to herself.

> 'Sweet Saviour Bless us e're we go
> Thy love into our minds instil
> And make our lukewarm hearts to glow
> With thine own love and perfect peace
> Through life's long day
> And death's dark night
> O Gentle Jesus be our light'

Ellen broke the silent reverie by pouring four small glasses of sherry and suggesting that they all cheer up. Her smile crumpled as Mary-Kate pointed out that as they were all going to Holy Communion they couldn't break their fast.

'But Uncle Richard has!' Ellen was stricken.

'That's his affair! If he wants everyone to talk about him, it's on his own head,' Gina replied with some spirit.

Mary-Kate had been thinking of her own wedding day. Of her mother and Lewis and of the fact that Gina hadn't been there that day. But now at last the three of them were together. She smiled at Ellen while stroking the head of her son who was clinging to her skirt. Despite her smile and the love and joy in her heart for her sisters, she felt the tears prick her eyes. For Ellen and Jamie, Liverpool was home and for their sakes it would become home for her, too. And when her time came they would bury her body in Ford Cemetery with Lewis, but her heart and her spirit would always be here in Cluain Meala – the Honey Meadow.

Bridget picked up a glass. 'Never mind Ellen, it was a

lovely thought and we could still have a toast by just putting our glasses together.' She handed a glass to each of her sisters. 'To us all!'

With a laugh that reminded them of the healthy, vivacious girl who had enchanted the guests at the castle across the river with her pure, young voice, Gina touched her glass first to Mary-Kate's then to Bridget's.

'A toast then. To "The Sisters O'Donnell"!'

Author's Note

Many people have contributed and assisted me during the researching and writing of this book, but I would particularly like to express my gratitude to my friend, Mrs Brenda Whelan, for advice on the world of the Theatre Musical. For her wealth of knowledge and experience of both Glasgow and the Department Store, Copeland and Lye, which she so willingly and unstintingly shared with me, my friend and colleague, Mrs Kathleen Baird. And last but by no means least, all my friends at Marks & Spencer's Southport Store, for their unflagging interest and encouragement.

My Great-Grandmother, Mary O'Donnell, came to Liverpool from Clonmel, Co. Tipperary, in the latter part of the last century and this is, in part, her story. Therefore, I would like to dedicate this book to her memory. I never knew you but I owe you so much Mary-Kate.

Lyn Andrews

Every Mother's Son

Lyn Andrews

Molly Keegan and Bernie O'Sullivan have been friends forever. As young girls they left Ireland seeking exciting new beginnings in Liverpool. And now, as young women, they are marrying their sweethearts and looking forward to enjoying the lives they've worked so hard to build. But as the Liverpool Blitz begins, it seems as if their dreams are about to be destroyed.

Night after night, horrific bombing tears the city apart. Every day Molly and Bernie struggle to keep their families safe. As wives and mothers, both know that they could face great tragedy. But they also know that their friendship, and their love for their husbands and sons, will give them the strength to find the happiness they deserve . . .

Praise for Lyn Andrews' unforgettable novels

'Gutsy . . . a vivid picture of a hard-up, hard-working community . . . will keep the pages turning' *Daily Express*

'Lyn Andrews presents her readers with more than just another saga of romance and family strife. She has a realism that is almost tangible' *Liverpool Echo*

978 0 7553 0842 2

headline

From This Day Forth

Lyn Andrews

Next-door neighbours Celia and Lizzie are the best of friends. But their families, the Miltons and the Slatterys, are the worst of enemies, divided by religion and by their men's status at the Cammell Laird's shipyard. Lizzie and Celia must keep their friendship a secret – for if Celia's violent father Charlie ever found out about it the consequences would be appalling.

But one day the unthinkable happens. Joe Slattery, Lizzie's brother, does a good turn for the Milton family. From that day forth, Celia Milton just can't get the dark-eyed Joe out of her mind. And, despite himself, Joe Slattery finds that he is increasingly drawn to the girl next door and to a love that seems doomed to heart-break – unless they can find a way around the prejudice of generations and the terrifying bigotry of Charlie Milton.

Praise for Lyn Andrews' unforgettable novels

'A compelling read' *Woman's Own*

'Gutsy . . . A vivid picture of a hard-up, hard-working community . . . will keep the pages turning' *Daily Express*

'The Catherine Cookson of Liverpool' *Northern Echo*

978 0 7472 5177 4

headline

Friends Forever

Lyn Andrews

In 1928 Bernie O'Sullivan and Molly Keegan catch their first glimpse of the bustling city they're about to call home. Both seventeen, and best friends since childhood, the girls have left Ireland behind to seek work and an exciting new life in Liverpool.

The girls are dismayed to discover that the relatives they are to stay with have barely two pennies to rub together; the promised grand house is a run-down building in one of Liverpool's worst slum areas. Desperate to escape the filthy streets, Bernie secures a position as a domestic servant, while Molly is taken on as a shop assistant. Soon they have settled in new rooms and find themselves in love with local men. For both, though, love holds surprises and the danger of ruin in an unforgiving world.

Bernie and Molly have tough times to face but the bond of their lifelong friendship gives them the strength to rise to every challenge and to hold on to their dreams.

Praise for Lyn Andrews' unforgettable novels

'A compelling read' *Woman's Own*

'Gutsy . . . A vivid picture of a hard-up, hard-working community . . . will keep the pages turning' *Daily Express*

978 0 7553 0840 8

headline

Now you can buy any of these other bestselling books by **Lyn Andrews** from your bookshop or *direct from the publisher*.

FREE P&P AND UK DELIVERY
(Overseas and Ireland £3.50 per book)

Far From Home	£6.99
Every Mother's Son	£6.99
Friends Forever	£6.99
A Mother's Love	£6.99
Across a Summer Sea	£6.99
When Daylight Comes	£5.99
A Wing and a Prayer	£6.99
Love and a Promise	£6.99
The House on Lonely Street	£6.99
My Sister's Child	£6.99
Take These Broken Wings	£6.99
The Ties That Bind	£6.99
Angels of Mercy	£6.99
When Tomorrow Dawns	£6.99
From This Day Forth	£6.99
Where the Mersey Flows	£6.99
Liverpool Songbird	£6.99

TO ORDER SIMPLY CALL THIS NUMBER

01235 400 414

or visit our website: www.headline.co.uk

Prices and availability subject to change without notice.